Buffalo tours

D0497848

Inspirational Travel

Vietnam ❧ Cambodia ❧ Laos ❧ Thailand

Locally Based Specialists in Privately Guided, Fully Customised Holidays

email: info@buffalotours.com - **website:** www.buffalotours.com

Footprint story

It was 1921

Ireland had just been partitioned, the British miners were striking for more pay and the federation of British industry had an idea. Exports were booming in South America – how about a handbook for businessmen trading in that far away continent? The Anglo-South American Handbook was born that year, written by W Koebel, the most prolific writer on Latin America of his day.

1924

Two editions later the book was 'privatized' and in 1924, in the hands of Royal Mail, the steamship company for South America, it became The South American Handbook, subtitled 'South America in a nutshell'. This annual publication became the 'bible' for generations of travellers to South America and remains so to this day. In the early days travel was by sea and the Handbook gave all the details needed for the long voyage from Europe. What to wear for dinner; how to arrange a cricket match with the Cable & Wireless staff on the Cape Verde Islands and a full account of the journey from Liverpool up the Amazon to Manaus: 5898 miles without changing cabin!

1939

As the continent opened up, the South American Handbook reported the new Pan Am flying boat services, and the fortnightly airship service from Rio to Europe on the Graf Zeppelin. For reasons still unclear but with extraordinary determination, the annual editions continued through the Second World War.

1970s

Many more people discovered South America and the backpacking trail started to develop. All the while the Handbook was gathering fans, including literary vagabonds such as Paul Theroux and Graham Greene (who once sent some updates addressed to "The publishers of the best travel guide in the world, Bath, England").

1990s

During the 1990s the company set about developing a new travel guide series using this legendary title as the flagship. By 1997 there were over a dozen guides in the series and the Footprint imprint was launched.

2000s

The series grew quickly and there were soon Footprint travel guides covering more than 150 countries. In 2004, Footprint launched its first thematic guide: *Surfing Europe*, packed with colour photographs, maps and charts. This was followed by further thematic guides such as *Diving the World*, *Snowboarding the World*, *Body and Soul escapes*, *Travel with Kids* and *European City Breaks*.

2010

Today we continue the traditions of the last 89 years that have served legions of travellers so well. We believe that these help to make Footprint guides different. Our policy is to use authors who are genuine experts who write for independent travellers; people possessing a spirit of adventure, looking to get off the beaten track.

Vietnam Handbook

Claire Boobbyer

In modern-day Vietnam one thing in particular stands out. It is, quite simply, the remarkable speed at which the country is developing and the extraordinary ambitions its leaders are planning to achieve. Vietnam now hovers in an enigmatic and paradoxical time zone, somewhere between the late Industrial Revolution and the post-industrial age. School children in Ho Chi Minh City vie for the trendiest motorbikes, mobile phones and trainers, while those in the northern highlands are happy with a pair of sandals. Youngsters in the Mekong Delta have email accounts yet 10 years ago they didn't have a telephone. And while staff in call centres gossip about the latest fashions, their parents harvest rice by hand. Vietnam has experienced war and bloody revolution in the past 100 years. But the revolution it is now undergoing is peaceful and prosperous. Vast strides in economic development are apace, with the government hoping to be crowned a middle-income country by 2020. It is these changes that make Vietnam the absorbing and gripping place that it is.

War? Yes, Vietnam survived several, in fact, last century. The Vietnamese people have seen much water flow under the bridge since the last war ended but the government will not let it drop. Even now, 30 years on, new war memorials are being erected. It is as if the legitimacy of the government somehow depends on having won the war resulting in an odd mixture of war legacy in modern Vietnam. Heroic communist monuments and war memorabilia abound in museums but the Vietnamese people have set their sights firmly on the future. There is no looking back, no nostalgia for the past. And this explains the lack of fuss every time an old building is flattened. Forget yesterday, look to tomorrow.

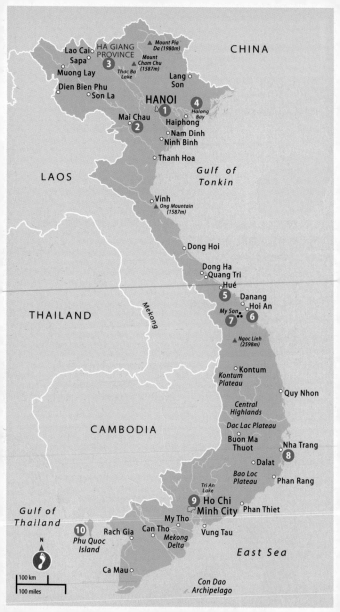

Highlights

See colour maps in centre of book

① Hanoi is a small city with a fascinating cultural legacy from the colonial to the communist eras. ▶▶ page 43.

⑥ Silk emporiums, glorious food and Chinese temples abound in the tranquil port of Hoi An. ▶▶ page 216.

② The Mai Chau Valley sits in stunning paddy field scenery with Thai ethnic minority villages. ▶▶ page 102.

⑦ My Son, the core seat of the Champa Empire, is immortalized in beautifully carved stone temples. ▶▶ page 222.

③ Ha Giang is a remote border region of ethnic markets, terraced rice paddies and karst mountain peaks. ▶▶ page 130.

⑧ The seaside town of Nha Trang is a popular hangout with plentiful bars, restaurants and cafés. ▶▶ page 266.

④ Limestone towers and jagged islands rise out of the waters of Halong Bay, a World Heritage Site. ▶▶ page 152.

⑨ Ho Chi Minh City is a manic, capitalist hothouse clogged with traffic and bursting with energy. ▶▶ page 310.

⑤ On the banks of the Perfume River, Hué is an imperial city with imperial tombs and an imperial setting. ▶▶ page 177.

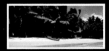

⑩ Phu Quoc, Vietnam's largest island, has few resorts and miles of white-sand beaches. ▶▶ page 395.

Clockwise from top
Phu Quoc.
My Son.
Nha Trang.
Hué.
Hoi An.

Clockwise from top
Ha Giang.
Mai Chau.
Ho Chi Minh City.
Hanoi.

Next page
Halong Bay.

Contents

↘11 Essentials
12 Planning your trip
20 Getting there
22 Getting around
26 Sleeping
28 Eating and drinking
31 Entertainment
32 Festivals and events
33 Shopping
34 Essentials A-Z

↘43 Hanoi
51 Sights
70 Listings

↘97 The North
100 Northwest
117 Sapa and around
129 Far North

136 Cao-Bac-Lang
146 Haiphong and around
152 Halong Bay
164 Ninh Binh and around

↘171 Central Vietnam
174 Thanh Hoa to Hué
177 Hué and around
207 Danang and around
216 Hoi An and around
232 Dalat and the
      Central Highlands
265 Nha Trang and around
284 Phan Thiet and Mui Ne
291 Vung Tau
298 Con Dao

↘303 Ho Chi Minh City
310 Sights
328 Listings

↘351 Mekong Delta
356 My Tho and around
370 Can Tho and around
380 Chau Doc and around
395 Phu Quoc Island

↘401 Background
402 History
434 Modern Vietnam
443 Economy
448 Culture
470 Religion
475 Land and environment
482 Books
486 Films

↘489 Footnotes
490 Useful words and phrases
495 Glossary
497 Index
503 Advertisers' index
504 Credits

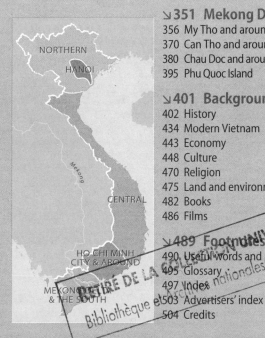

NORTHERN

HANOI

Mekong

CENTRAL

HO CHI MINH
CITY & AROUND

MEKONG DELTA
& THE SOUTH

Contents

12 Planning your trip
12 Where to go
16 When to go
16 What to do
19 Taking a tour
19 Local customs and laws

20 Getting there
20 Air
22 Rail
22 Road
22 Sea

22 Getting around
22 Air
23 Rail
23 River
23 Road

26 Sleeping

28 Eating and drinking
28 Food
30 Drink

31 Entertainment
31 Bars and clubs
31 Gambling
31 Music and theatre

32 Festivals and events

33 Shopping

34 Essentials A-Z

Footprint features

11 Packing for Vietnam
24 Open Tour Bus
    timetable example
25 Rules of the road
26 Vietnamese addresses
27 Sleeping price codes
29 Eating price codes
30 Bird's nest soup
32 Happy New Year

Essentials

Planning your trip

Where to go

If time is limited, by far the best option is to get an open-jaw flight where you fly into one city, say Hanoi, and out of Ho Chi Minh City (HCMC), although generally it is cheaper overall to fly into HCMC return and get an internal flight back to HCMC if needs be. Remember that distances are huge and one or two internal flights may be needed. **Vietnam Airlines** has an excellent domestic network and services are good. See also map, page 21. Hiring a self-drive car in Vietnam is not possible and trains (although a great way to travel) and public buses are very slow. Alternatives to the domestic air network include the tourist Open Tour Bus transport, taxis and tour operators for tours and transfers.

Particular highlights (from north to south) include Ha Giang province, a relatively unexplored border area (a permit is still required) of towering rice paddies, phallic limestone peaks and ethnic minority markets, the hill station of **Sapa** known for its stunning scenery and ethnic minority villages; **Hanoi**, which itself is historical, beautiful and cultured, lies at the heart of a vast range of architectural and scenic treasures (which can be visited on day trips out); and **Cat Ba Island** and **Halong Bay**, for their magical coastal scenery. Moving south there then follows a yawning gulf of mediocrity, so it is not until the imperial capital of **Hué** that the next stop should be made. Hué's palaces and mausoleums deserve at least two days. The wonderful coastal edge **train journey from Hué to Danang** should not be missed but Danang itself has little to commend it (apart from the Cham Museum), which is why most travellers head straight for nearby **Hoi An**, an enchanting 17th-century mercantile town, and a nearby beach right on the Eastern (South China) Sea. Between here and Ho Chi Minh City the seaside town of **Nha Trang** is the main attraction but the smaller resort of **Mui Ne** is a more tranquil alternative.

Energetic and exciting **Ho Chi Minh City**, although a city of more than seven million, is really a small town: not many will stray far from the historical core which, containing as it does all anyone could need in the way of hedonistic pleasures (and with scarcely any intellectual or cultural distractions), is the most popular destination in the country. The **Mekong Delta** has plenty of attractions, but to see it at its best it is necessary to get into the depths of the country beyond the main towns. The **Central Highlands** are slightly off the beaten track. The former hill station of **Dalat** is a cross between a French and a Home Counties town with old French villas, a central lake and a golf course. Further north, the real highlights once again are the villages around **Buon Ma Thuot**, **Pleiku** and **Kontum** and their fascinating cultures. For those with spare time, head to the islands: **Phu Quoc** for its golden sands and fishing culture; **Con Dao** for unspoilt wilderness, sea and war history.

Up to a week

In a short visit to Vietnam the two best destinations are Hanoi in the north and Ho Chi Minh City in the south. A seven-day stay in Hanoi will allow you to visit the plethora of museums, temples, pagodas and churches that are within the city limits and explore the boutique shops and wealth of restaurants. While here, a day trip to the World Heritage Site of Halong Bay is a must. A seven-day stay in Ho Chi Minh City should, apart from the architectural attractions and limited museums of the city itself, include day trips to the world famous **Cu Chi Tunnels**, the **Holy See of the Cao Dai religious sect** in Tay Ninh town.

Packing for Vietnam

Many travellers take too much. Clothes like shorts and T-shirts can be bought cheaply in Vietnam. Good-quality underwear and socks cannot, however. While not yet on a par with Bangkok there is far more available now in Vietnam than even a couple of years ago. Bottled water is widely available. There is no need to bring water filters unless trekking in remote areas. Good books are scarce, so bring plenty. A lot of travellers sensibly carry all their worldly goods in rucksacks and are referred to by the Vietnamese as *tay ba lo*, a term which has acquired derogatory overtones. Hotels, even the cheaper ones, usually provide mosquito nets so you shouldn't need to bring your own.

The following are also useful: passport photos (less important these days); small first-aid kit; torch (useful for viewing caves, dark pagodas and during power cuts); penknife; and photocopies of passport and visa (and entry permit, issued on arrival);

slide film is available in Ho Chi Minh City and Hanoi but rarely elsewhere (don't get slides processed in Vietnam as chemicals tend to be stale with disappointing results), print film is more widely sold; insect repellent; strong padlock for locking bags in hotel rooms and while travelling; money belt. For clothes, pack long-sleeved shirts for cool evenings, severely air-conditioned restaurants and to prevent sunburn. Long trousers and socks prevent mosquitoes from biting in the evening. Warm clothing is necessary for upland areas in winter. Women might consider wearing dresses rather than jeans when travelling, for easier access to squat toilets.

You don't need to pack: maps (cheap ones are sold in Ho Chi Minh City and Hanoi); dictionaries (available cheaply in most towns); foreign brands of cigarettes (smuggled ones are sold cheaply in Vietnam); waterproof/umbrella for the wet season (ubiquitous and cheap in Vietnam).

Up to two weeks

In an overwhelmingly rural country it is important to see not just the main historical and cultural highlights of the towns but to get out into the countryside and witness the way of life of the majority of the population. In a visit of less than two weeks it is possible to capture something of the essence of Vietnam.

Hanoi is an essential stop not only because Hanoi itself is teeming with temples and pagodas and ancient streets but also because it sits at the heart of a region similarly well endowed with monuments recording the nation's history. The scenery around Hanoi is some of the most attractive in the land. Excursions to the **Perfume Pagoda** and the temples and caves at **Tam Coc** are particularly worthwhile. The overnight train from Hanoi will get visitors to Sapa, the most scenic of all Vietnam's hill stations. This is the best chance to meet some of Vietnam's many ethnic minority people and to see Vietnam's most majestic and rugged scenery. Once in Sapa there is a good selection of excellent treks to undertake ranging from a gentle Sunday stroll to trekking up **Mount Fan Si Pan**, the highest mountain in continental Southeast Asia. Mountain-bike touring is another popular way of visiting Sapa and the surrounding areas although you need to be fit as the gradients are steep. Allow a minimum of three days to visit Sapa. The journey there and back is quickest by train. If a trip to Sapa does not fit, try Mai Chau, closer to Hanoi with its stunning paddyfield scenery. From Hanoi fly to Hué. Hué is an old capital, home to Vietnam's last imperial dynasty. There are numerous relics, tombs and palaces. The Citadel in Hué is one of the most impressive in Vietnam. From Hué, it is just 140 km to Hoi An. Hoi

An is an old mercantile port crammed with history and absolutely full of charm. It also has a pleasant, growing seaside area. A visit in the morning to the **Cham Museum** in Danang followed by a visit in the afternoon to the ancient Cham capital of My Son is a good day trip. Depending on time available, fly from Danang (the nearest airport to Hoi An) either to Nha Trang for a beach holiday, or straight to Ho Chi Minh City. Unfortunately it is not possible to fly to Dalat from Danang hence **Dalat** tends to get overlooked. It is not an essential stop but well worthwhile to get a flavour of upland Vietnam, particularly if you aren't visiting Sapa. Ho Chi Minh City is quite unlike the rest of Vietnam and has a dynamic atmosphere. There are some interesting relics and sites from the Vietnam War, such as the Cu Chi Tunnels and the old Presidential Palace. There is also some attractive French architecture (though not as much as in Hanoi). Ho Chi Minh City has restaurants and bars aplenty and it is impossible not to enjoy soaking up the feel of this vibrant city. Depending on time spent in earlier places there is probably only enough time left for a day trip to the Mekong Delta from Ho Chi Minh City.

Up to one month

In three to four weeks it is possible to take the two-week itinerary at a more leisurely pace and include some other interesting calls. From Hanoi, Halong Bay and Cat Ba can be visited. These are often done together as a chance to see one of Vietnam's most spectacular natural landscapes and one of the country's most accessible national parks. In a visit of a month it is easily possible to see more of the mountainous northwest than just Sapa. It may even be possible to fit in a circuit of the northwest, going via the delightful small settlements of **Mai Chau** and **Son La** to **Dien Bien Phu**, scene of the French defeat in 1954. From here complete the circuit to Sapa and back to Hanoi. You could be even more adventurous and take a motorbike trip to the very far north or northeast. You will get a completely different insight into Vietnam from that of most tourists. Alternatively, a visit to **Cat Ba Island** and other islands in Halong Bay or tranquil **Ba Be lake** would be worthwhile. It would be worth visiting Danang to see the Cham Museum. From Danang go to **My Son**, capital of the ancient civilization of Champa. There are Cham temples dating back 1000 years quietly overrun by vegetation. From Danang take a flight to **Play Ku**, which is in the Central Highlands, to experience highland life. A visit to nearby **Kontum** and its ethnic minority villages is fascinating. Drive from Play Ku to **Buon Ma Thuot**. The drive from Buon Ma Thuot to Dalat passes through stunning mountain scenery and through villages that modern life has passed by. Upon arrival in Dalat a stay of three days will allow you to visit the many sites and its environs. Nha Trang is definitely worth a visit as it has a fun seaside atmosphere, islands to explore and numerous excellent restaurants. Failing this, a stay in one of the resorts on **Mui Ne Beach** near Phan Thiet is highly recommended. Medium-stay visitors will have longer to get to know the people of Ho Chi Minh City and, equally important, to get into the Mekong Delta properly. Go at least as far as **Can Tho** (those going overland to Cambodia will go on to Chau Doc) and get out into the countryside either by motorbike or by boat to understand the truly vast scale of this productive agricultural region. Many towns such as **Soc Trang**, Sa Dec, Tra Vinh and Ben Tre are not on tourist routes at all and, for a flavour of real delta life, are worthwhile. Trips out of Chau Doc – to **Sam Mountain** and the fish farms – are interesting if you are in the area. **Phu Quoc Island**, with a small but rapidly growing tourist industry, has wonderful beaches and is a complete getaway. **Con Dao**, as yet untouched by rampant tourist development, is a true wilderness and wonderful for birdlife, walking, boat trips, diving and scenery.

When to go

Climatically the best time to see Vietnam is around December to March when it should be dry and not too hot. In the south it is warm but not too hot with lovely cool evenings. Admittedly the north and the highlands will be a bit chilly but they should be dry with clear blue skies. The tourist industry high season is normally November to May when hotel prices tend to rise and booking flights can be hard. Travel in the south and Mekong Delta can be difficult at the height of the monsoon (particularly September, October and November). The central regions and north sometimes suffer typhoons and tropical storms from May to November. Hué is at its wettest from September to January.

Despite its historic and cultural resonance Tet, or Vietnamese New Year, is not a good time to visit. This movable feast usually falls between late January and March and, with aftershocks, lasts for about a fortnight. It is the only holiday most people get in the year. Popular destinations are packed, roads are jammed and for a couple of days almost all restaurants are shut. All hotel prices increase, and car hire prices are increased by 50% or more. The best prices are from May to October.

During the school summer holidays some resorts get busy. At Cat Ba, Sapa, Phan Thiet, Long Hai and Phu Quoc, for example, prices rise, there is a severe squeeze on rooms and weekends are worse. The Central Highlands tend to fare much better with cool temperatures and a good availability of rooms.

What to do

Safety is always an issue when participating in adventurous sports: make sure you are fully covered by your travel insurance; check the credentials of operators offering adventure activities; and make sure that vehicles and safety equipment are in a good condition.
▶▶ *For tour operators, see page 39.*

Birdwatching

Vietnam may not seem like the first choice for a birdwatching holiday (indeed, many visitors comment that there are few birds around) but for those in the know it has become one of the top birding destinations of the region in recent years. The reason is that it has no less than 10 endemic species. This is the highest number of endemic bird species of any country in mainland Southeast Asia. Around 850 species have been recorded in Vietnam but in a 3-week birding trip it should be possible to tick off around 250-300 species. The best places for birdwatching are **Bach Ma National Park**, **Cuc Phuong National Park**, **Dalat Plateau**, **Nam Cat Tien National Park**. Other areas of particular interest are **Con Dao**, **Sapa**, **Tam Dao** and **Tam Nong Bird Sanctuary**.

Contact
Vietnam Birding, Vietnam Birding, www.vietnambirding.com. Contact Richard Craik for more information or advice on birding, or to organize birding tours throughout Vietnam.

Cookery classes

There are increasingly more of these available. Hotels and restaurants in major cities and resorts offer courses. Some operators offer tours that include half a day or 1 day of cooking for those who would like to see more than just the inside of a hotel kitchen. The variety is already quite broad. Check hotel flyers, the web or adverts in local magazines. Popular places for cookery classes include: **Can Tho, Hanoi, HCMC, Hoi An** and **Nha Trang**.

Cycling and mountain biking

Being flat over great distances, cycling is a popular activity in Vietnam. The main problem is the peril on roads due to traffic. It's recommended that any tour is planned off-road or on minor roads, not Highway 1. Many cyclists prefer to bring their own all-terrain or racing bikes but it's also possible to rent from tour organizers. Head for the Central Highlands, Hué or Ninh Binh.

Contact
Discover Adventure, Throope Down House, Blandford Rd, Coombe Bissett, Salisbury, SP5 4LN, Wiltshire, T01722-718444, www. discover adventure.com. Adventure specialist running group biking tours in Vietnam.
Spice Roads, 14/1-B Soi Promsi 2, Sukhumvit 39, Klongtan Nua, Wattana, Bangkok, T66 2-712 5305, www.spiceroads.com. A recommended biking company that operates throughout Asia.
Symbiosis, www.symbiosis-travel.com, has established an expertise in the organization of cycling challenges to Vietnam (from Bangkok) and around Vietnam.
Tien Bicycles, 12 Nguyen Thien Ke St, Hue, T54-382 3507, www.tienbicycles.com. Organises cross-country tours as well as those in and around Hué.

Climbing

Climbing is concentrated in Halong Bay. A few agencies organize the activity.

Contact
Asia Outdoors/Slo Pony Adventures, Cat Ba town, T91-376 0025, www.slopony.com.

Diving and snorkelling

Snorkelling in the seas of Vietnam is a limited activity. Much of the coast is muddy deltaic swamp. Away from the deltas the water is still quite turbid. In those places where snorkelling and diving is said to be good (such as Nha Trang's **Whale Island** or **Phu Quoc**) the best time of year to dive varies with location and is not necessarily dictated by the seasons. Seek professional advice.

Golf

Golf in Vietnam can be traced back to the 1930s when the emperor Bao Dai laid a course in Dalat. After a period of dormancy, golf in Vietnam has mushroomed over the past few years. Of course it remains chiefly an expat game and the first courses that were opened in the 1990s were able to command colossal fees. There are now more than 10 courses across the country with more under construction. Green fees are now more sensible. Although some will travel around the world to play golf, in Vietnam it is mainly Asians who come here on golf holidays. Head for **Dalat**, **HCMC**, **Phan Thiet** and **Montgomerie Links**.

Contact
Vietnamgolftours.com, www.vietnamgolftours.com.

Kayaking

Kayaking in Vietnam is virtually synonymous with **Halong Bay** and **Lan Ha Bay**. There are one or two canoes in places like Mui Ne, Lak Lake and Ba Be Lake but very few. The canoes at Ba Be are locally made and designed for a recreational potter rather than anything more serious. Therefore anyone wishing to kayak in Vietnam should head straight for Halong Bay. And given it is a World Heritage Site crammed with islands and grottoes it's actually a fantastic place to explore by kayak. A number of operators run (or can organize) special interest tours.

Motorbiking and Vespa tours

Touring northern Ha Giang province on a motorbike is one of the most exciting things you can do here. A permit and a sense of adventure is required. Other cross-country and cross-border tours are possible. Companies use a range of bikes including Minsk and Honda Baja. Vespa tours are available from **Ho Chi Minh City** to **Mui Ne** and **Nha Trang**.

Spas

There are a handful of devoted spa resorts in Vietnam including the **Ana Mandara** in Nha Trang and the **Evason Hideaway** in Ninh Van Bay. There are other good hotels such as **Life Wellness Resorts**, the **Sofitel Metropole Hanoi** and the **Victoria Hotels** that offer spa facilities. However, spas are not as well developed as they are in neighbouring Thailand. Previously most hotels offered massage. Now the canny ones offer a spa. So beware: new label on the door, everything else same same. Of course there are a number of honorable exceptions, see above, and given the attention that Vietnamese women bestow upon themselves, all types of beauty salon and body pampering services are available. In HCMC and Hanoi, central areas are full of hair salons, foot massage parlours and just about everything else. Generally good and quite good value for money. Some of course are sleazy but this you can tell from the outside.

Trekking

Trekking is an increasingly popular activity in Vietnam. The main focus for this activity is **Sapa**, in the north of the country, but some trekking is organized around **Dalat** and other Central Highland towns and other opportunities are opening up around **Ha Giang** and in the **Mai Chau** area. Around Sapa there are walks of varying durations demanding different fitness levels and degrees of stamina. Other popular areas for walking include **Cuc Phuong National Park, Nam Cat Tien National Park, Yok Don National Park, Ha Giang Province, Mai Chau**

and **Sapa**. For the fittest climbers visit **Mount Fan Si Pan**.

Many of the tour operators in Hanoi, listed on page 88, organize trekking tours as do those based in Sapa, see page 127. Some treks are straightforward and can be done without guides or support (ask your guesthouse for routes), whereas others need accommodation and a legal requirement to take a licensced guide. Unfortunately there are no accurate maps for walkers in Vietnam.

Windsurfing and kitesurfing

Kite and windsurfing is found largely in Mui Ne. Here **Jibe's Beach Club** is leading the way organizing international tournaments. Mui Ne offers near-perfect conditions all year; equipment can be rented or bought at many places in the sandy Mui Ne cove. Windsurfing is popular in Nha Trang where some diving schools have branched out into windsurfing. Good, but not quite the class of Mui Ne.

Contact
See www.windsurf-vietnam.com. Apart from conveying the colour and exhilaration of sport on offer at Mui Ne, the site also has useful records of wind data.

Vietnam War tours

All good travel agencies offer customized tours, so if a group belonged to an army battalion, agencies can arrange visits to the relevant sites. The most popular places include the **Central Highlands, Demilitarized Zone (DMZ)** and the **Cu Chi Tunnels**.

Contact
Vietnam Veterans Web ring, http://www.webring.org/hub?ring=vva, offers not just the chance of a virtual visit, with photos, maps and other interesting information, but also provides details on specialist veterans' tours to the country including visits to battle sites as well as reports and diaries from recent visitors.

Taking a tour

Many operators offer organized trips to Vietnam, ranging from a whistle-stop tour of the highlights to specialist trips that focus on a specific destination or activity. The advantage of travelling with a reputable operator is that your accommodation, transport and activities are all arranged for you in advance – particularly valuable if you only have limited time in the region. By travelling independently, however, you can be much more flexible and spontaneous about where you go and what you do although remember that self-drive car hire is not possible. You will be able to explore less-visited areas and you will save money, if you budget carefully. On arrival in Vietnam, many travellers contract tour operators to take them on day- and week-long trips. These tours cater for all budgets and you will benefit from an English-speaking guide and safe vehicles. Some of the most popular trips include week-long tours around the northwest or into the Mekong Delta. As well as being accompanied by knowledgeable guides these can often work out cheaper and are more time-efficient than trying to organize the trip yourselves. Specialist tour operators can be found on page 39.

Ecotourism

Since the early 1990s there has been a significant growth in ecotourism, which promotes and supports the conservation of natural environments and is also fair and equitable to local communities. While the authenticity of some ecotourism operators needs to be interpreted with some care, there is both a huge demand for this type of activity and also significant opportunities to support worthwhile conservation and social development initiatives.

The **International Eco-Tourism Society** (www.ecotourism.org), **Tourism Concern** (www.tourismconcern.org.uk) and **Planeta** (www.planeta.com) develop and promote ecotourism projects in destinations all over the world and their websites provide details for initiatives throughout Southeast Asia.

For a chance to participate directly in scientific research and development projects and in an environmentally responsible and ethical manner, consult www.responsibletravel.com.

Local customs and laws

Vietnam is remarkably relaxed and easy going with regard to conventions. The people, especially in small towns and rural areas, can be pretty old-fashioned, but it is difficult to cause offence unwittingly. The main complaint Vietnamese have of foreigners is their fondness for dirty and torn clothing. Backpackers come in for particularly severe criticism and the term *tay ba lo* (literally 'Western backpacker') is a contemptuous one reflecting the low priority many budget travellers seem to allocate to personal hygiene and the antiquity and inadequacy of their shorts and vests.

Shoes should be removed before entering temples and before going into people's houses. Modesty should be preserved and excessive displays of bare flesh are not considered good form. (Not that the Vietnamese are unduly prudish, they just like things to be kept in their proper place.) Shorts are fine for the beach and travellers' cafés but not for smart restaurants.

Kissing and canoodling in public are likely to draw attention, not much of it favourable. But walking hand in hand is now accepted as a Western habit. Hand shaking among men is a standard greeting and although Vietnamese women will consent to the process, it is often clear that they would prefer not to. The head is held by some to be sacred and people would rather you didn't pat them on it. The Vietnamese do not share the concern about having someone's feet higher than their head.

Terms of address

Vietnamese names are written with the surname first, followed by the first name. Thus Nguyen Minh is not called Nguyen as we would presume in the West but Minh. In addressing people who are the same age as you but who you don't know, you would call them *anh* (for a man) and *chi* (for a woman). When you know their first name you would say 'anh Minh', for example.

Someone your senior or of whose age you are unsure use *ông* for a man and *bà* for a woman. Those who are not able to grasp this it is acceptable to address someone as Mr Minh or Ms Hanh for example.

Religion

The Vietnamese are open to religious experiences of all kinds. Vietnam is predominantly a Buddhist country. Following Chinese tradition, ancestor worship is widely practiced and animism (the belief in and worship of spirits of inanimate objects such as venerable trees, the land, mountains and so on) is widespread. The government is hostile to proselytizing, particularly by Christians. But the Catholic Church is more vital than in many European countries and foreigners are perfectly free to attend services. In Ho Chi Minh City one or two services in the Notre Dame Cathedral are in French and in English. Protestant churches are found throughout the country to a lesser degree then the Roman Catholic Church but all services are in Vietnamese.

Getting there

Air

Vietnam is relatively isolated in comparison with Bangkok, Hong Kong and Singapore. Most major airlines have direct flights from Europe, North America and Australasia to these hubs. Ho Chi Minh City, and to a lesser extent Hanoi, is pretty well connected with other Southeast Asian countries which remain the source of most foreign visitors. Connections have also increased in the last few years with the rise of budget airlines. Prices vary according to high (November to April, July and August) and low season.

Flights from Europe

In Western Europe, there are direct flights to Vietnam from Paris and Frankfurt with **Vietnam Airlines/Air France**. These code-shared flights last 12 hours. **Vietnam Airlines** has an office in the UK or book flights online. There are also direct **Vietnam Airlines** flights from Moscow.

Flights from London and other European hubs go via Bangkok, Singapore, Kuala Lumpur, Hong Kong or UAE states. From London to Vietnam, flights take 16 to 18 hours, depending on the length of stopover. Airlines include **Air France**, **Cathay Pacific**, **Emirates**, **Gulf Air**, **Thai International**, **Singapore Airlines**, **Malaysia Airlines**, **Lufthansa**, and **Qatar**. It is possible to fly into Hanoi and depart from Ho Chi Minh City although this does seem to rack up the return fare. Check details with flight agents and tour operators (see pages 21 and 39).

Flights from the USA and Canada

By far the best option is to fly via **Bangkok**, **Taipei**, **Tokyo** or **Hong Kong** and from there to Vietnam. The approximate flight time from Los Angeles to **Bangkok** is 21 hours. **United** flies from LA and Chicago via Tokyo and from San Francisco via Seoul to Vietnam. **Thai**, **Delta**, **United** and **Air Canada** fly to Bangkok from a number of US and Canadian cities.

Flights from Australia and New Zealand

There are direct flights from Adelaide, Melbourne, Sydney, Perth, Auckland and Wellington with **Cathay Pacific**, **Malaysia Airlines**, **Singapore Airlines** and **Thai**. **Qantas** flies from Sydney, Adelaide and Melbourne to Ho Chi Minh City.

Budget airlines from Australia include **Jetstar** and **Tiger Airways**. From Sydney the flights to Vietnam are eight hours 45 minutes direct.

Flights from Asia

Thai flies from Bangkok to Ho Chi Minh City and Hanoi. **AirAsia** flies from Bangkok and Kuala Lumpur to Ho Chi Minh City and from Kuala Lumpur and Bangkok to Hanoi. **Vietnam Airlines** flies from Bangkok, Phnom Penh, Siem Reap, Vientiane, Luang Prabang, Beijing, Guangzhou, Kunming, Hong Kong, Kuala Lumpur, Singapore, Manila, Busan, Seoul, Japan and Taipei. **Laos Airlines** flies from Luang Prabang and Vientiane. **Malaysia Airlines** flies from Kuala Lumpur to Hanoi and Ho Chi Minh City. **Tiger Airways** flies from Singapore to Ho Chi Minh City and Hanoi. **Cathay Pacific** flies from Hong Kong. **China Airlines** flies from Taipei to Ho Chi Minh City. **Japan Airlines** flies from Tokyo to Ho Chi Minh City and Hanoi. **Korean Air** flies from Seoul to Ho Chi Minh City and Hanoi. **Philippine Airlines** flies from Manila to Ho Chi Minh City. **Singapore Airlines** flies to Hanoi and Ho Chi Minh City. **Thai International** flies from Bangkok to Ho Chi Minh City and from Sydney and Melbourne to Ho Chi Minh City and Hanoi.

Airport information

There are two main international airports in Vietnam: **Tan Son Nhat Airport** (SGN) in Ho Chi Minh City, see page 306, and **Noi Bai Airport** (HAN) in Hanoi, see page 48. **Danang** (DAD), see page 207, has a couple of international flights.

Discount flight agents

UK and Ireland

Expedia and **Ebooker** both offer competitive online fares to Vietnam.
STA Travel, www.statravel.co.uk. Branches across the UK. Specialists in student/youth flights and tours, student IDs and insurance.
Trailfinders, www.trailfinders.com.

North America

Air Brokers International, www.airbrokers.com. Consolidator and specialist on RTW and Circle Pacific tickets.
Discount Airfares Worldwide On-Line, http://www.etn.nl/discoun2.htm. A hub of consolidator and discount agent links.

STA Travel, www.sta-travel.com.
Travel CUTS, www.travelcuts.com. Specialist in student fares, IDs and other travel services. Branches in other Canadian cities.
Travelocity, www.travelocity.com. An online consolidator.

Australia and New Zealand

Flight Centres, www.flight centre.com.au. Branches in Australia and New Zealand.
STA Travel, www.statravel.com.au. Offices across New Zealand and Australia. Good deals on flights, insurance and hotels.
Travel.com.au, 80 Clarence St, Sydney, T02-9290 1500, www.travel.com.au.

Rail

Vietnam's only international rail connection is with China. There are connections with Beijing via Nanning to Hanoi crossing at Lang Son. The lines are slow and distances are great.

Road

From Cambodia

There is a road crossing at Moc Bai on Highway 1 connecting Phnom Penh in Cambodia with Ho Chi Minh City via Tay Ninh Province, see page 328. Further south, there is a second crossing to Phnom Penh via Chau Doc at Vinh Xuong in the Mekong Delta by boat. Further south still there is another road crossing into Cambodia at Tinh Bien, approximately 22 km south of Chau Doc. And, right at the very south of the country, you can cross at Xà Xía. For crossings at Chau Doc, Tinh Bien and Xà Xía, see page 383.

From China

There are three land crossings between China and Vietnam: at Lao Cai, Dong Dang and Mong Cai. There is no train across the border at Lao Cai at the moment, see page 123. The train from Hanoi does cross at Dong Dang, page 143. The Mong Cai crossing is by road, see page 158. If you enter Vietnam by land your visa must specify the exact road crossing.

From Laos

There is a popular road crossing open at Lao Bao, north of Hué, which enables travel through to Savannakhet in Laos, see page 176. In the north there is a crossing at Tay Trang near Dien Bien Phu, see page 106. Closer to Hanoi are the crossings at Nam Can (Nghe An Province) and Cau Treo (Ha Tinh Province) accessible from Vinh, see page 175. You can also cross close to Kontum at Bo-Y (Kontum Province), see page 252.

Sea

There are no normal sea crossings into Vietnam although an increasing number of cruise liners sail into Vietnamese waters. The only other international connection by boat is the Mekong River crossing from Phnom Penh to Chau Doc.

Getting around

Air

Vietnam Airlines is the national carrier and flies to multiple domestic destinations. **Vietnam Airlines** changes its schedule every six months so check before making any plans.

Refunds, rebookings and rerouting may not be allowed on certain ticket fares. Remember that during holiday periods flights get extremely busy.

Rail

Train travel is exciting and overnight journeys are a good way of covering long distances. The Vietnamese rail network extends from Hanoi to Ho Chi Minh City. **Vietnam Railways** (www.vr.com.vn) runs the 2600-km rail network down the coast. With overnight stays at hotels along the way to see the sights, a rail sightseeing tour from Hanoi to Ho Chi Minh City should take a minimum of 10 days but you would need to buy tickets for each separate section of the journey.

The difference in price between first and second class is small and it is worth paying the extra. There are three seating classes and four sleeping classes including hard and soft seats and hard and soft sleepers; some are air-conditioned, others are not. The prices vary according to the class of cabin and the berth chosen; the bottom berth is more expensive than the top berth. All sleepers should be booked three days in advance. The kitchen on the Hanoi to Ho Chi Minh City service serves soups and simple, but adequate, rice dishes (it is a good idea to take additional food and drink on long journeys). First-class long-distance tickets include the price of meals. The express trains (**Reunification Express**) take between an advertised 29½ to 34 hours; odd-numbered trains travel from Hanoi to Ho Chi Minh City, even-numbered trains vice versa.

Most ticket offices have some staff who speak English. Queues can be long and some offices keep unusual hours. If you are short of time and short on patience it may well pay to get a tour operator to book your ticket for a small commission or visit the Ho Chi Minh City railway office in Pham Ngu Lao or the Hanoi agency in the Old Quarter.

There are also rail routes from Hanoi to Haiphong, to Lang Son and to Lao Cai. The **Victoria** hotel chain (www.victoriahotels-asia.com) runs a luxury carriage on the latter route.

River

In the south, there are services from Chau Doc to Phnom Penh, see page 383. The **Victoria** hotel chain (www.victoriahotels-asia.com) runs a Mekong Delta service for its guests. Ferries operate between Ho Chi Minh City and Vung Tau; Rach Gia and Phu Quoc; Ha Tien and Phu Quoc; Haiphong and Cat Ba Island; and Halong City and Cat Ba and Mong Cai.

Road

Open Tour Buses, see below, are very useful and cheap for bridging important towns. Many travellers opt to take a tour to reach remote areas because of the lack of self-drive car hire and the dangers and slow speed of public transport.

Bus

Roads in Vietnam are notoriously dangerous. As American humourist PJ O'Rourke wrote: "In Japan people drive on the left. In China people drive on the right. In Vietnam it doesn't matter." Since Highway 1 is so dangerous and public transport buses are poor and slow, most travellers opt for the cheap and regular **Open Tour Bus** (private minibus or coach) that covers the length of the country. Almost every Vietnamese tour operator/ travellers' café listed in this guide will run a minibus service or act as an agent. The ticket is a flexible, one-way ticket from Ho Chi Minh City to Hanoi and vice versa, see box page 24. The buses run daily from their own offices and include the following stops: Ho Chi Minh City, Mui Ne, Nha Trang, Dalat, Hoi An, Hué, Ninh Binh and Hanoi. They will also

Open Tour Bus timetable example

Hanoi to HCMC	Distance (km)	Depart time	Arrival time
Hanoi–Ninh Binh–Hué	700	1830	0830
Hué–Hoi An	120	0800/1400	1200/1730
Hoi An–Nha Trang	530	1900	0600
Nha Trang–Dalat	214	0745	1330
Dalat–HCMC	308	0745	1600
Nha Trang–HCMC	450	0730/2030	1730/0600
Mui Ne–HCMC	220	0900/1300	1400/1800

HCMC to Hanoi			
HCMC–Dalat	308	0730	1430
HCMC–Mui Ne	220	0730/1500/2030	1230/2000/0130
Mui Ne–Nha Trang	225	1330/0100	1800/0600
HCMC–Nha Trang	450	0730/2030	1630/0530
Dalat–Nha Trang	214	0715	1330
Nha Trang–Hoi An	530	1930	0600
Hoi An–Hué	120	0800/1400	1200/1700
Hué–Hanoi	660	1700	0500

Trans-Vietnam Open Tour Bus ticket: 540,000-700,000d

Short distances:

Hanoi–Ninh Binh	95,000d	Hanoi–Hué	170,000d
Hué–Hoi An	60,000d	Hoi An–Nha Trang	180,000d
Nha Trang–Dalat	80,000d	Dalat–HCMC	100,000d
Nha Trang–HCMC	130,000d	Nha Trang–Mui Ne	90,000-160,000d
Mui Ne–HCMC	90,000d		

stop off at tourist destinations along the way such as Lang Co, Hai Van Pass, Marble Mountains and Po Klong Garai for quick visits. You may join at any leg of the journey, paying for one trip or several as you go. The Hanoi to Hué and vice versa is an overnight trip but although you might save on a night's accommodation you are unlikely to get much sleep.

If you do opt for **public buses** note that most bus stations are on the outskirts of town; in bigger centres there may be several stations. Long-distance buses invariably leave very early in the morning (0400-0500). Buses are the cheapest form of transport, although sometimes foreigners find they are being asked for two to three times the correct price. Prices are normally prominently displayed at bus stations. It helps if you can find out what the correct fare should be in advance. Less comfortable but quicker are the minibus services, which ply the more popular routes.

Car hire
Self-drive car hire is not available in Vietnam. It is, however, possible to hire cars with drivers and this is a good way of getting to more remote areas with a group of people. Cars

Rules of the road

The speed with which Vietnam has developed in the last decade means that people who, five years ago, were sitting on the back of trundling buffalo carts, are now driving 30-ton trucks down Highway 1. This has led to an enormous increase in road casualties.

Vietnam also has 21 million motorbikes, one of the highest densities of motorbikes in the world.

Debates in the press on road carnage concentrate almost exclusively on technical shortcomings – old cars, antique trucks, absence of road signs – and neatly sidestep the true cause: absence of respect for other road users. However, attention to road safety is now improving.

There are far more traffic lights and road dividers than before and more traffic police on the junctions ready to pounce on offenders. The Vietnamese are now more likely to heed the traffic lights and there is less of a tendency to carry on regardless of whether the lights are red or green.

Traffic police actively collect fines for supposed breaches of traffic law. If you are invited to make a contribution to the police widows and orphans fund, but clearly you have committed no offence, refuse point blank. Feign total ignorance of English. If this does not work and your motorbike keys have been confiscated, try to negotiate the size of your donation downwards.

with drivers can be hired for around US$60-110 per day. Longer trips would see a reduced cost. All cars are air-conditioned. Car hire prices increase by 50% or more during Tet.

Motorbike and bicycle hire

Most towns are small enough to get around by bicycle, and this can also be a pleasant way to explore the surrounding countryside. However, if covering large areas (touring around the Central Highlands, for example) then a motorbike will mean you can see more and get further off the beaten track.

Motorbikes and bicycles can be hired by the day in the cities, often from hotels and travellers' cafés. You do not need a driver's licence or proof of motorbike training to hire a motorbike in Vietnam, however, it became compulsory in 2007 to wear a helmet. Take time to familiarize yourself with road conditions and ride slowly. Motorbikes cost around US$6 per day including helmet; bicycles can be hired for US$1-2 including a lock. Always park your bicycle or motorbike in a gui xe (guarded parking place) and ask for a ticket. The small cost is worth every dong, even if you are just popping into the post office to post a letter.

Motorbike taxi and cyclo

Motorcycle taxis, known as *honda ôm* or *xe ôm* (*ôm* means to cuddle) are ubiquitous and cheap. You will find them on most street corners, outside hotels or in the street. With their baseball caps and dangling cigarette, *xe ôm* drivers are readily recognizable. If they see you before you see them, they will shout 'moto' to get your attention. In the north and upland areas the Honda is replaced with the Minsk. The shortest hop would be at least 10,000d. Always bargain though.

Cyclos are bicycle trishaws. Cyclo drivers charge double or more that of a *xe ôm*. A number of streets in the centres of Ho Chi Minh City and Hanoi are one-way or out of bounds to cyclos, necessitating lengthy detours which add to the time and cost. Do not take a cyclo after dark unless the driver is well known to you or you know the route. It is a

Vietnamese addresses

Unlike neighbouring countries, addresses in Vietnam generally follow quite a logical pattern. There are, however, a few points to note:

Odd numbers usually run consecutively on one side of the street, evens on the other; *bis* after a number – as in 16 bis Hai Ba Trung Street – means there are two houses with the same number, and *ter* after the number means there are three houses with the same number.

Large buildings with a single street number are usually subdivided 21A, 21B, etc; some buildings may be further subdivided 21B1, 21B2, etc.

An oblique (/ means *sec* or *tren* in Vietnamese) in a number, as in 23/16 Dinh Tien Hoang Street, means that the address is to be found in a small side street (*hem*) – in this case running off Dinh Tien Hoang Street by the side of No 23; the house in question will probably be signed 23/16 rather than just 16.

Usually, but by no means always, a *hem* will be quieter than the main street and it may be worth looking at a guesthouse with an oblique number for that reason (especially in the Pham Ngu Lao area of Ho Chi Minh City).

An address will sometimes contain the letter F followed by a number, as in F6; this is short for *phuong* (ward, a small administrative area); its inclusion as part of an address is a reflection of the tidy nature of the Vietnamese mind rather than an aid to locating one's destination.

The letter Q in an address stands for *quân* (district); this points you in the right general direction and will be important in locating your destination as a long street in Hanoi or Ho Chi Minh City may run through several *quan*. In suburban and rural areas districts are known as *huyên*, Huyên Nha Be, for instance.

Note that there are no postcodes or zip codes in Vietnam.

---

wonderful way to get around the Old Quarter of Hanoi, though, and for those with plenty of time on their hands it is not as hazardous in smaller towns.

Taxi

Taxis ply the streets of Hanoi and Ho Chi Minh City and other large towns and cities. They are cheap, around 12,000d per kilometre, and the drivers are better English speakers than cyclo drivers. Always keep a small selection of small denomination notes with you so that when the taxi stops you can round up the fare to the nearest small denomination. At night use the better known taxi companies rather than the unlicensed cars that often gather around popular nightspots.

Sleeping

Accommodation ranges from luxury suites in international five-star hotels and spa resorts to small, family hotels (mini hotels) and homestays with local people in the Mekong Delta and with the ethnic minorities in the Central Highlands and northern Vietnam. During peak seasons – especially December to March and particularly during busy holidays such as Tet, Christmas, New Year's Eve and around Easter – booking is essential. Expect staff to speak English in all top hotels. Do not expect it in cheaper hotels or in more remote places, although most places employ someone with a smattering of a foreign language.

Sleeping price codes

LL	over US$200	L	US$151-200	AL	US$101-150
A	US$66-100	B	US$46-65	C	US$31-45
D	US$21-30	E	US$12-20	F	US$7-11
G	US$6 and under				

Prices refer to the cost of a double room in high season, including taxes.

Private, mini hotels are worth seeking out as, being family-run, guests can expect good service. Mid-range and tourist hotels may provide a decent breakfast which is often included in the price. Many luxury and first-class hotels and some three-star hotels charge extra for breakfast and, on top of this, also charge 10% VAT and 5% service charge. When quoted a hotel price you should ask whether that includes these two taxes; it is marked as ++ (plus plus) on the bill.

There are some world-class beach resorts in Phu Quoc, Nha Trang, Mui Ne, Hoi An and Danang. In the northern uplands, in places like Sapa, Ha Giang province and Mai Chau, it is possible to stay in an ethnic minority house. Bathrooms are basic and will consist of a cold shower or warm shower and a natural or western toilet. To stay in a homestay, you must book through a tour operator or through the local tourist office; you cannot just turn up. Homestays are also possible on farms and in orchards in the Mekong Delta. Guests sleep on camp beds and share a Western bathroom. National parks offer everything from air-conditioned bungalows to shared dormitory rooms to campsites where, sometimes, it is possible to hire tents. Visitors may spend a romantic night on a boat in Halong Bay or on the Mekong Delta. Boats range from the fairly luxurious to the basic. Most people book through tour operators. In remote places where there is no competition, dour and surly service remain the order of the day. **The Vietnam Hostelling International Association** (www.hihostels.com) has been established, operating hostels in Hanoi, Hoi An and Sapa.

You will have to leave your passport at hotel reception desks for the duration of your hotel stay. It will be released to you temporarily for bank purposes or buying an air ticket. Credit cards are widely accepted but there is often a 2-4% fee for paying in this manner. Tipping is not expected in hotels in Vietnam.

Camping in Vietnam is limited mainly because the authorities insist on foreign visitors sleeping in registered accommodation. There are no campsites but visitors bringing tents may be able to use them around Sapa or on Cat Ba and surrounding islands. Some guesthouses in Mui Ne and other seaside places have tents.

If you wish to stay at the **house of a friend** this is normally permitted but your hosts will need to take your passport and arrival form to their local police station. Police and People's Committee regulations in some towns mean that a foreigner travelling with his Vietnamese wife must bring a marriage certificate in order to share a hotel room with her.

The age of consent in Vietnam is 18. There are rules relating to a Vietnamese person of the opposite sex being in your hotel room. It depends on the attitude of the hotel. If the Vietnamese person is your partner, as opposed to a one-night stand, hotels are more relaxed. However, Hoi An is the exception and you will have to rent a second room. This is also the policy in international hotels in big cities, not because international chains have moral qualms but because they get penalized by the police. Local hotels from which the police can collect bribes tend to be more 'accommodating'.

Travellers normally get their laundry done in hotels. In cheap hotels it's inexpensive. Cheaper hotels and laundries in the hotel districts charge by weight. The smarter places charge by the item and the bill can be a shock! Always check bills; overcharging is common.

Eating and drinking

Food

Food is a major attraction of Vietnam and it is one of the paradoxes of this enigmatic country that so much food should be so readily and deliciously available. Eating out is so cheap that practically every meal eaten by the visitor will be taken in a restaurant or café. Ho Chi Minh City and Hanoi offer a wide range of cuisines besides Vietnamese, so that only Congolese, Icelandic and English tourists will be deprived of home cooking.

Vietnam offers outstanding Vietnamese, French and international cuisine in restaurants that range from first class to humble foodstalls. The quality will be, in the main, exceptional. The accent is on local, seasonal and fresh produce and the rich pickings from the sea, along Vietnam's 2000-km coastline will always make it far inland too. You will find more hearty stews in the more remote north and more salad dishes along the coast. All restaurants offer a variety of cuisine from the regions and some specialize in certain types of food – Hué cuisine, Cha Ca Hanoi, etc. Pho (pronounced *fer*), a bowl of flat, white, noodle soup served with chicken or beef, is utterly delicious. The soup is made from stock flavoured with star anise, ginger and other spices and herbs but individual recipes often remain a closely guarded secret. Vietnamese usually eat *pho* in the morning, often in the evening but rarely at lunchtime, when they require a more filling meal accompanied by rice. On each table of a *pho* restaurant sits a plate of fresh green leaves: mint, cinnamon, basil and the spiky looking *ngo gai*, together with bean sprouts, chopped red chillies, barbecue sauce and sliced lemons, enabling patrons to produce their own variations on a theme.

Another local speciality which visitors often overlook is com tam or broken rice. *Com tam* stalls abound on the streets and do brisk trade at breakfast and lunch. They tend to be low-cost canteens, but in many cities they have appeal to the wealthier office market and have started to abandon tiny plastic stools in favour of proper tables and chairs and concentrate more on cleanliness and presentation. The steamed broken rice is eaten with fried chicken, fish, pork and vegetables and soup is normally included in the price.

There are many types of Vietnamese roll: the most common are deep-fried spring rolls (confusingly, *cha gio* in the south and *nem ranh* in the north) but if these appear on your table too frequently, look for the fresh or do-it-yourself types, such as bi cuon or bo bia. Essentially, these are salads with prawns or grilled meats wrapped in rice paper. Customers who roll their own cigarettes are at a distinct advantage while innocents abroad are liable to produce sagging Camberwell Carrots that collapse in the lap.

Vietnamese salads (*goi* in the south and *nom* in the north) are to die for. The best known is the green papaya salad with dried beef (*nom du du bo kho*); others include goi xoai (mango salad) and goi buoi (pomelo salad). They all involve a wonderful fusion of herbs and vegetables with sweet and spicy tastes rolled in.

Delicious seafood is a staple across the land. It would be invidious to isolate a particular seafood dish when there are so many to chose from. Prawns are prawns – the bigger and the less adulterated the better. But a marvellous dish that does deserve commendation

Eating price codes

🍴🍴🍴 over US$12   🍴🍴 US$6-12   🍴 under US$6

Prices refer to the cost of a two-course meal for one person, excluding drinks or service charge.

is crab in tamarind sauce. This glorious fusion of flavours, bitter tamarind, garlic, piquant spring onion and fresh crab is quite delicious. To the Vietnamese, part of the fun of eating crab is the fiddly process of extracting meat from the furthest recesses of its claws and legs. A willingness to crack, crunch, poke and suck is required to do it justice, not a task for the squeamish but great for those who aren't.

All Vietnamese food is dipped, whether in fish sauce, soy sauce, chilli sauce, peanut sauce or pungent prawn sauce (*mam tom* – avoid if possible) before eating. As each course is served so a new set of dips will accompany. Follow the guidance of your waiter or Vietnamese friends to get the right dip with the right dish.

When it comes to food, Vietnamese do not stand on ceremony and (perhaps rather like the French) regard peripherals such as furniture, service and ambience as mere distractions to the task of ploughing through plates, crocks, casseroles and tureens charged with piping hot meats, vegetables and soups. Do not expect good service, courses to arrive in the right order, or to eat at the same time as your companions, but do expect the freshest and tastiest food you will find anywhere.

While it is possible to eat very cheaply in Vietnam (especially outside Hanoi and Ho Chi Minh City) the higher class of restaurant, particularly those serving foreign cuisine, can prove quite expensive, especially with wine. But with judicious shopping around it is not hard to find excellent value for money, particularly in the small, **family restaurants**. In the listing sections we describe a range of diners which should satisfy every palate and every pocket and in the Hanoi chapter we provide information on street stalls. Some restaurants (mostly expensive ones) add 5% service charge and the government tax of 10% to the bill. See box, page 29 on restaurant classification.

For day trips, an early morning visit to the **markets** will produce a picnic fit for a king. Hard-boiled quails' eggs, thinly sliced garlic sausage and salami, pickled vegetables, beef tomatoes, cucumber, pâté, cheese, warm baguettes and fresh fruit. And, far from costing a king's ransom, it will feed four for around US$1 a head.

The thing that separates India from China is that in the former there are prohibitions governing the consumption of just about everything. In the latter anything and everything can be – and is – eaten. Vietnam of course falls under Chinese sway. Therefore anyone who self imposes restrictions on his eating habits is regarded as a bit of a crank. There are **vegetarian restaurants** in Vietnam but these usually sell different types of tofu dressed to look like meat. The vegetable section of most 'normal' restaurants has vegetables – but cooked with pork, with beef or with prawns, rarely pure vegetables. Nevertheless there are a few Vietnamese vegetarians and twice a month a great many people eat vegetarian so restaurants are aware of the concept. We have listed for most bigger towns some highly acclaimed vegetarian restaurants and places on the backpacker trail that are on the ball.

Given the large proportion of the population aged 16 and under no Vietnamese restaurant is put out by **children**. Indeed any restaurant frequented by Vietnamese families will have kids running around everywhere. So parents need have no fears about

Bird's nest soup

The tiny nests of the brown-rumped swift (*Collocalia esculenta*), also known as the edible-nest swiftlet or sea swallow, are collected for bird's nest soup, a Chinese delicacy, throughout Southeast Asia.

The semi-oval nests are made of silk-like strands of saliva secreted by the birds which, when cooked in broth, softens and becomes a little like noodles. Like so many Chinese delicacies, the nests are believed to have aphrodisiac qualities and the soup has even been suggested as a cure for HIV. The red nests are the most highly valued, and the Vietnamese Emperor Minh Mang (1820-

1840) is said to have owed his extraordinary vitality to his inordinate consumption of bird's nest soup. This may explain why restaurants serving it are sometimes associated with massage parlours.

Collecting the nests is a precarious but profitable business and in some areas mafias of concessionaires vigorously guard and protect their assets. The men who collect the nests on a piecework basis risk serious injury climbing rickety ladders to cave roofs in sometimes almost total darkness, save for a candle strapped to their heads.

their children's behaviour upsetting anyone. Obviously in smarter places unruly children may not be so popular so beware invitations to 'take a tour of the kitchen'.

Note that Vietnamese get up early and so lunch time starts at 1100 although restaurants catering for foreigners stay open until 1400, but don't leave lunch later than that as many places close the kitchen until the dinner trade at around 1700.

Drink

Locally produced fresh beer is called *bia hoi*. It is cold and refreshing, and weak and cheap enough to drink in quite large volumes. It is usually consumed in small pavement cafés where patrons sit on small plastic stools. Most *bia hoi* cafés serve simple and inexpensive food. Almost all customers are men and they can get a bit jolly. As the beer is fresh it has to be consumed within a short period of brewing hence most towns, even quite small ones, have their own brewery and impart to their beer a local flavour in a way that used to happen in England before the big brewers took over. Unfortunately bars and restaurants do not sell *bia hoi* as it's too cheap, at just 4000d per litre. Hence bar customers have a choice of Tiger, Heineken, Carlsberg, San Miguel, 333, Saigon Beer or Huda. All are brewed in Vietnam but many visitors try to stick to the local beers (333, Saigon and Huda) as they are cheaper and, to many, more distinctively flavoursome than the mass produced international brands. Unfortunately this is not always possible as many bars and restaurants stock only the more expensive beers of the big international brewers because they have higher mark-ups.

Rice and **fruit wines** are produced and consumed in large quantities in upland areas, particularly in the north of Vietnam. Rice wines are fairly easily found, however. There are two types of rice wine, *ruou nep* and *ruou de*. *Ruou nep* is a viscous wine made from sticky rice. It is purple and white due to the different types of rice used to make it. Among the ethnic minorities, who are recognized as masters of rice wine, *ruou nep* is drunk from a ceramic jar through a straw. This communal drinking is an integral part of their way of life and no doubt contributes substantially to strengthening the ties of the clan. It is possible to become very drunk drinking *ruou nep* without realizing it. *Ruou de* is a rice spirit and very strong.

The Chinese believe that **snake wines** increase their virility and are normally found in areas with a large Chinese population. It is called a wine despite being a spirit. Other wines include the body and parts of seahorses, gecko, silkworms and bees.

There is a fantastic range of different **fruit wines** but unless you make a real effort it can be quite hard to find them. Wines are made from just about all upland fruits: plum, strawberry, apple and, of course, grapes, although grape wine in Vietnam is generally disappointing. The others are fiery and warm, strong and, bought by the bottle, cheap.

Entertainment

Bars and clubs

Vietnamese nightlife divides into two categories: Vietnamese and Western. The edges are becoming more diffuse with time, particularly as some Vietnamese incline towards Western tastes. The average tourist will have a good meal and then visit a bar for a drink or two, preferably one with Western sounds. The Vietnamese will go for the meal and then either to a darkened café or nip into the karaoke (a huge hit in Vietnam).

Bars as we know them tend not to exist far from the tourist or expat populations. Cold beer, rock music and pool are easy to find in the main centres but are virtually non-existent elsewhere. Which is not to say the Vietnamese don't know how to enjoy themselves, it is just that they do things differently. A common type of Vietnamese bar is the *bia hoi*, see page 30. An integral part of Vietnamese social fabric, *bia ôm* are altogether different. In a Vietnamese *bia ôm*, women drink beer with the men. There may be a certain amount of touchy feely but nothing too overt and usually the women go home to their own beds. In seedier city quarters *bia ôm* bars are brothels.

Gambling

Gambling on the outcome of football matches is the most common form although people will have a flutter on anything. There is a popular state lottery. The money awarded is not much by Western standards (the top prize is slightly less than US$10,000) but it is a fortune in Vietnam. There is now a fair selection of casinos in the country (mainly in Ho Chi Minh City, Hanoi and Haiphong) although more are being developed. The casinos are only open to foreigners and Viet Kieu.

Music and theatre

Occasional performances can be enjoyed at the opera houses in Hanoi and Ho Chi Minh City. Hanoi also has a number of other performance stages. Royal music can be heard at the theatre in the citadel at Hué, on boat trips on the Perfume River and during buffets at the Hotel Saigon Morin, also in Hué. Water puppetry is best enjoyed at the Water Puppetry House in Hanoi, although there are also two water puppetry stages in Ho Chi Minh City. You can also hear Vietnamese traditional instruments played in Ho Chi Minh City.

Happy New Year

Tet is the traditional new year. The biggest celebration of the year, the word Tet is the shortened version of *tet nguyen dan* (first morning of the new period). Tet is the time to forgive and forget and to pay off debts. It is also everyone's birthday – the Vietnamese tend not to celebrate their birthdays; instead everyone adds a year to their age at Tet. Enormous quantities of food are consumed (this is not the time to worry about money), new clothes are bought, houses painted and repaired and firecrackers lit to welcome in the new year – at least they were until the government ban imposed in 1995. Cumquat trees are also bought and displayed. They are said to resemble coins and are a symbol of wealth and luck for the coming year. As a Vietnamese saying has it: 'Hungry all year but Tet three days full.' It is believed

that before Tet, the spirit of the hearth, Ong Tao, leaves on a journey to visit the palace of the Jade Emperor where he must report on family affairs. To ensure that Ong Tao sets off in good cheer, a ceremony is held before Tet, Le Tao Quan, and during his absence a shrine is constructed (Cay Neu) to keep evil spirits at bay until his return. On the afternoon before Tet, Tat Nien, a sacrifice is offered at the family altar to dead relatives who are invited back to join in the festivities. Great attention is paid to the preparations for Tet, because it is believed that the first week of the new year dictates the fortunes for the rest of the year. The first visitor to the house on New Year's morning should be an influential, lucky and happy person, so families take care to arrange a suitable caller.

Festivals and events

Vietnamese festivals are timed according to the Vietnamese lunar calendar. To help work out on which day these events fall, see the following website, which converts the Gregorian calendar to the lunar calendar: www.hko.gov.hk/gts/time/conversion1_text.htm.

Late Jan-Mar (movable, 1st-7th day of the new lunar year) **Tet**. See box, page 32.
Mar (movable, 6th day of 2nd lunar month) **Hai Ba Trung Day**. Celebrates the famous Trung sisters who led a revolt against the Chinese in AD 41 (see page 66).
Apr (5th or 6th, 3rd lunar month) **Thanh Minh** (New Year of the Dead or Feast of the Pure Light). People are supposed to walk outdoors to evoke the spirit of the dead and family shrines and tombs are traditionally cleaned and decorated.
May (15th day of the 4th lunar month) Celebration of the birth, death and enlightenment of the Buddha.
Aug (movable, 15th day of the 7th lunar month) **Trung Nguyen** (Wandering Souls

Day). One of the most important festivals. During this time, prayers can absolve the sins of the dead who leave hell and return, hungry and naked, to their relatives. The Wandering Souls are those with no homes to go to. There are celebrations in Buddhist temples and homes, food is placed out on tables and money is burned.
Sep (movable, 15th day of the 8th month) **Tet Trung Thu** (Mid-Autumn Festival) This festival is particularly celebrated by children. It is based on legend and there are various stories as to its history. One of the legends is about a Chinese king who went to the moon. When he returned, the king wished to share what he had seen with the people on earth.

In the evening families prepare food including sticky rice, fruit and chicken to be placed on the ancestral altars. Moon cakes (egg, green bean and lotus seed) are baked (with some variations on these ingredients offered by some of the smarter hotels such as chocolate), lanterns made and painted, and children parade through towns with music and lanterns. It is particularly popular in Hanoi and toy shops in the Old Quarter decorate stores with lanterns and masks. **Nov** (movable, 28th day of the 9th month) Confucius' Birthday.

Public holidays

1 Jan New Year's Day.
Late Jan-Mar (movable, 1st-7th day of the new lunar year) Tet.
3 Feb Founding anniversary of the Communist Party of Vietnam.
30 Apr Liberation Day of South Vietnam and HCMC.
1 May International Labour Day.
19 May Anniversary of the Birth of Ho Chi Minh (government holiday) The majority of state institutions will be shut on this day but businesses in the private sector remain open.
2 Sep National Day.
3 Sep President Ho Chi Minh's Anniversary.

Shopping

Vietnam is increasingly a good destination for shopping. A wide range of designer clothing, silk goods, high-quality handicrafts, ceramics and lacquerware are excellent value. The main shopping centres are Hanoi, Ho Chi Minh City and Hoi An. The latter is the best place to get clothes made. Sapa is also a good place to shop for ethnic minority wares. The majority of shops and markets in Vietnam are open daily from early in the morning to late at night and do not close for lunch. Shops and markets will accept US dollars and Vietnamese dong and most shops also accept credit cards.

Export of wood or antiques is banned and anything antique or antique-looking will be seized at customs. In order to avoid this happening you will need to get an export licence from the **Customs Department** ① *162 Nguyen Van Cu St, Hanoi, T4-3872 5260.* Do not buy marine turtle products.

Lacquerware is plentiful and cheap, but lacquer pictures are heavy to carry about. Small lacquer trinkets, such as boxes and trays, are more portable and make nice presents. **Ethnic products**, **fabrics**, **wickerware** and **jewellery** is best bought (and cheapest) in the uplands but plenty is available in the two main cities. Chám fabrics, for example, are available in Ho Chi Minh City while those of the Thai and Hmong minorities can be widely seen in Hanoi.

Beautiful and affordable women's **clothes** are now to be found in designer and boutique stores in Hanoi and Ho Chi Minh City in particular. There is a growing market in **homeware accessories** made of beautiful silks and woods. **Junk** collectors will have a field day in Ho Chi Minh City and Hanoi; many trinkets were left behind by French, Americans and Russians, including old cameras, watches, cigarette lighters (most Zippos are fake), 1960s Coca-Cola signs and 1930s Pernod ashtrays.

Manufacturers of **outdoor wear**, rucksacks, boots and trainers have factories in Vietnam. A considerable amount of genuine branded stock finds its way into the shops of Hanoi and Ho Chi Minh City at prices as little as 10% of European shop prices.

Essentials A-Z

Accident and emergency

Contact the relevant emergency service and your embassy. Make sure you obtain police/medical records in order to file insurance claims. If you need to report a crime, visit your local police station and take a local with you who speaks English.
Ambulance T115, **Fire** T114, **Police** T113.

Children

Vietnam is not particularly geared up for visiting children but there are activities that will appeal to both adults and children alike. Some attractions in Vietnam offer children's concessions. In terms of discounts, the railways allows children under 5 to travel free and charges 50% of the adult fare for those aged 5-10. The Open Tour Bus tickets and tours are likewise free for children under 2 but those aged 2-5 pay 75% of the adult price. Baby products are found in major supermarkets in the main cities, while nappies are available in supermarkets in the big towns. In remoter regions, such as the north and the Central Highlands and smaller towns, take everything with you.

Customs and duty free

Duty-free allowance is 400 cigarettes, 50 cigars or 100 g of tobacco, 1.5 litres of spirits, plus items for personal use. Export of wood products or antiques is banned, see page 33. You cannot import pornography, anti-government literature, photos or movies nor culturally unsuitable children's toys.

Disabled travellers

Considering the proportion of the country's population that is seriously disabled, foreigners might expect better facilities and allowances for the immobile. But there are very few. However, some of the more upmarket hotels do have a few designated rooms for the disabled. For those with walking difficulties many of the better hotels do have lifts. Wheelchair access is improving with more shopping centres, hotels and restaurants providing ramps for easy access. People sensitive to noise will find Vietnam, at times, almost intolerable.
RADAR, 12 City Forum, 250 City Rd, London, EC1V 8AF, T020-7250 3222, www.radar.org.uk.
SATH, 347 Fifth Av, Suite 605, New York City, NY 10016, T212-447 7284, www.sath.org.

Drugs

Drugs are common and cheap and the use of hard drugs by Vietnamese is a rapidly growing problem. Attitudes towards users are incredibly lax and the worst that will happen is that certain bars and nightclubs may be closed for a few weeks. In such an atmosphere of easy availability and tolerance, many visitors may be tempted to indulge, and to excess, but beware that the end result can be disastrous. Attitudes to traffickers are harsh, although the death penalty (now by lethal injection and not firing squad) is usually reserved for Vietnamese and other Asians whose governments are less likely to kick up a fuss.

Electricity

Voltage 110-240. Sockets are round 2-pin. Sometimes they are 2 flat pin. A number of top hotels now use UK 3 square-pin sockets.

Embassies and consulates

Australia, 6 Timbarra Cres, O'Malley Canberra, ACT 2606, T+61-2 6286 6059, www.vietnamembassy.org.au.
Cambodia, 436 Monivong, Phnom Penh, T+855 23-726274, www.vietnamembassy-cambodia.org.
Canada, 470 Wilbrod St, Ottawa, Ontario, K1N 6M8, T+1 613-236 0772, www.vietnamembassy-canada.ca.
China, 32 Guanghua R, Jiangou menwai, PO Box 00600, Beijing, T+86-10 6532 1155; 5/F, Great Smart Tower, 230 Van Chai Rd, Wan Chai, Hong Kong, T852-2591 4517, http://www.vnemb.org.cn/en.
France, 62 R Boileau-75016, Paris, T+33 144-146400, www.vietnamembassy-france.org/en.
Laos, 85 23 Singha Rd, Vientiane, T+856 21-413409, www.mofa.gov.vn/vnemb.la.
South Africa, 87 Brooks St, Brooklyn, Pretoria, T+27 12-362 8119, www.vietnamembassy-southafrica.org/en/.
Thailand, 83/1 Wireless Rd, Lumpini, Pathumwan, Bangkok 10330, T+66 2-251 5837, www.vietnamembassy-thailand.org/en.
UK, 12-14 Victoria Rd, London W8 5RD, T+44 (0)20-7937 1912, www.vietnamembassy.org.uk/consular.html.
USA, 1233, 20th St, NW Suite 400 Washington DC, 20036, T+1 202 861 0737, www.vietnamembassy-usa.org.

Gay and lesbian

The Vietnamese are tolerant of homosexuality. There are no legal restraints for 2 people of the same sex co-habitating in the same room be they Vietnamese or non-Vietnamese. There are several bars in central HCMC popular with gays. Cruising in dark streets is not advised. An Asian online resource for gays and lesbians that includes a list of scams and warnings in Vietnam as well as gay-friendly bars in Hanoi and HCMC is www.utopia-asia.com.

Health

See your doctor or travel clinic at least 6 weeks before your departure for general advice on travel risks, malaria and vaccinations (see also below). Make sure you have travel insurance, get a dental check-up (especially if you are going to be away for more than a month), know your own blood group and if you suffer a long-term condition such as diabetes or epilepsy make sure someone knows or that you have a **Medic Alert** bracelet/necklace with this information on it (www.medicalert.co.uk).

Health risks

Malaria exists in rural areas in Vietnam. However, there is no risk in the Red River Delta and the coastal plains north of Nha Trang. Neither is there a risk in Hanoi, HCMC, Danang and Nha Trang. The choice of malaria prophylaxis will need to be something other than chloroquine for most people, since there is such a high level of resistance to it. Always check with your doctor or travel clinic for the most up-to-date advice.

Malaria can cause death within 24 hrs. It can start as something just resembling an attack of flu. You may feel tired, lethargic, headachy, feverish; or more seriously, develop fits, followed by coma and then death. Have a low index of suspicion because it is very easy to write off vague symptoms, which may actually be malaria. If you have a temperature, go to a doctor as soon as you can and ask for a malaria test. On your return home if you suffer any of these symptoms, get tested as soon as possible, even if any previous test proved negative; the test could save your life.

The most serious viral disease is **dengue fever**, which is hard to protect against as the mosquitos bite throughout the day as well as at night. Bacterial diseases include **tuberculosis** (TB) and some causes of the more common traveller's **diarrhoea**. Lung fluke (**para-gonimiasis**) occurs in Vietnam.

A fluke is a sort of flattened worm. In the Sin Ho district the locals like to eat undercooked or raw crabs, but our advice is to leave them to it. The crabs contain a fluke which, when eaten, travels to the lungs. The lung fluke may cause a cough, coughing 'blood', fever, chest pain and changes on your X-ray which will puzzle a British radiologist. The cure is the same drug that cures schistosomiasis (another fluke which can be acquired in some parts of the Mekong delta).

Each year there is the possibility that **avian flu** or **SARS** may again rear their ugly heads. Check the news reports. If there is a problem in an area you are due to visit you may be advised to have an ordinary flu shot or to seek expert advice. Vietnam has had a number of fatalities from Avian influenza. Consult the WHO website, www.who.int, for further information and heed local advice on the ground. There are high rates of HIV in the region, especially among sex workers.

Medical services
Western hospitals staffed by foreign and Vietnamese medics exist in Hanoi and HCMC. See under medical services in each area for listings.

Useful websites
www.btha.org British Travel Health Association (UK). This is the official website of an organization of travel health professionals.
www.cdc.gov US government site that gives excellent advice on travel health and details of disease outbreaks.
www.fitfortravel.scot.nhs.uk A-Z of vaccine/health advice for each country.
www.who.int The WHO *Blue Book* lists the diseases of the world.

Vaccinations
The following vaccinations are advised: BCG, Hepatitis A, Japanese Encephalitis, Polio, Rabies, Tetanus, Typhoid and Yellow Fever.

Insurance

Always take out travel insurance before you set off and read the small print carefully. Check that the policy covers the activities you intend or may end up doing. Also check exactly what your medical cover includes, such as ambulance, helicopter rescue or emergency flights back home. Also check the payment protocol. You may have to pay up first before the insurance company reimburses you. Keep receipts for expensive personal effects, such as jewellery or cameras. Take photos of these items and note down all serial numbers. You are advised to shop around. **STA Travel** and other reputable student travel organizations offer good value policies. Companies like **BUPA** offer good and comprehensive cover. Young travellers from North America can try the **International Student Insurance Service** (ISIS), which is available through **STA Travel**, T1-800-781-4040, www.sta-travel. com. Other recommended companies in North America include: **Access America**, www.accessamerica.com; **Travel Insurance Services**, www.travelinsure.com; and **Travel Assistance International**, www.travel assistance.com. Older travellers should note that some companies will not cover people over 65 years old, or may charge higher premiums. The best policies for older travellers in the UK are offered by **Age UK**, www.ageuk.org.uk.

Internet

Although emailing is easy and Wi-Fi is widespread, access to the web is restricted as the authorities battle to firewall Vietnam-related topics. Facebook is restricted. Not all internet cafés have printing access.

Language

You are likely to find some English spoken wherever there are tourist services but outside tourist centres communication can be a problem for those who have no knowledge of Vietnamese. Furthermore, the Vietnamese language is not easy to learn. For example, pronunciation presents enormous difficulties as it is tonal: it has 6 tones, 12 vowels and 27 consonants. On the plus side, Vietnamese is written in a Roman alphabet making life much easier; place and street names are instantly recognizable. French is still spoken and often very well by the more elderly and educated Vietnamese.

In HCMC, language courses of several months' duration are offered by various organizations. In Hanoi, contact www. hiddenhanoi.com.vn.

Media

Unlike Western newspapers, Vietnamese papers are less interested in what has happened (that is to say, news), preferring instead to report on what will happen or what should happen, featuring stories such as 'Party vows to advance ethical lifestyles' and 'Output of fertilizer to grow 200%'. The English language daily *Viet Nam News* is widely available. Inside the back page is a 'What's on' section. *The Word* (www. wordhcmc.com and www.wordhanoi.com), a tourism and culture magazine, is available throughout the country and is the most useful. *The Guide*, a monthly magazine on leisure and tourism produced by the *Vietnam Economic Times*, can be found in tourist centres. *Asia Life* (www.asialifehcmc.com), *East&West* (www.east-westmag.com) and *Time Out* carry features as well as listings.

On the internet, check out the *New Hanoian* (http://newhanoian.xemzi.com) and *Grapevine* (http://hanoigrapevine. com) for news, views and events. Vietnam's official news agency is http://vietnamnews. vnagency.com.vn, and http://english. thesaigontimes.vn, offers news summaries with listings of what's on; www.saigontoday. net is a great round-up of local news.

There is news in English on the TV once in the evening, but if you have never lived in a communist country you will not know quite how tedious visits of Party members to tractor factories or presentations of medals to Heroic Mothers, meetings of People's Committee cadres around the table, etc can be. It makes the test card look exciting. The Vietnamese enjoy Chinese kung fu films which, like all foreign films, are dubbed over with a single monotone voice. VTV1 shows new politics and society programmes; VTV2, science and education; VTV3, sport and culture; VTV4 is for Viet Kieu and VTV5 is news and programmes for ethnic minorities in different languages. Good hotels will have cable TV that features a full range of cable options, such as CNN, Star Sport, BBC World, HBO, Cinemax and Star Movies.

Money

→ *US$1=19,500d, £1=35,950d, €1=26,900d.*
The unit of currency is the dong. Under law, shops should only accept dong but in practice this is not enforced and dollars are accepted almost everywhere. If possible, however, try to pay for everything in dong as prices are usually lower and in more remote areas people may be unaware of the exchange rate. Also, to ordinary Vietnamese, 18,000d is a lot of money, while US$1 means nothing.

ATMs are plentiful in HCMC and Hanoi and are now pretty ubiquitous in other major tourist centres, but it is a good idea to travel with US dollars cash as a back up. Try to avoid tatty notes. ATM withdrawals are limited to 2 million dong per transaction. Banks in the main centres will change other major currencies including UK sterling, Hong Kong dollars, Thai baht, Swiss francs, Euros, Australian dollars, Singapore dollars and Canadian dollars. **Credit cards** are increasingly accepted, particularly Visa, MasterCard, Amex and JCB. Large hotels, expensive restaurants and medical centres invariably take them but beware a surcharge of between 2.5% and 4.5%. Most hotels will not add a surcharge onto your bill if paying by credit card. Traveller's cheques are best denominated in US dollars and can only be cashed in banks in the major towns. Commission of 2-4% is payable if cashing into dollars but not if you are converting them direct to dong.

Cost of travelling

On a budget expect to pay around US$6-15 per night for accommodation and about US$6-12 for food. A good mid-range hotel will cost US$12-30. There are comfort and cost levels anywhere from here up to more than US$200 per night. For travelling, many use the Open Tour Buses as they are inexpensive and, by Vietnamese standards, 'safe'. Slightly more expensive are trains followed by planes.

Opening hours

Banks Mon-Fri 0800-1600. Many close 1100-1300 or 1130-1330.
Offices Mon-Fri 0730-1130, 1330-1630.
Restaurants, **cafés**, **bars** Daily from 0700 or 0800 although some open earlier. Bars are supposed to close at 2400 by law.
Shops Daily 0800-2000. Some stay open for another hour, especially in tourist centres.

Police and the law

If you are robbed in Vietnam, report the incident to the police (for your insurance claim). Otherwise, the police are of no use whatsoever. They will do little or nothing (apart from log the crime on an incident sheet that you will need for your claim). Vietnam is not the best place to come into conflict with the law. Avoid getting arrested. If you are arrested, however, ask for consular assistance and English-speaking staff.

Involvement in politics, possession of political material, business activities that have not been licensed by appropriate authorities, or non-sanctioned religious activities (including proselytizing) can result in detention. Sponsors of small, informal

religious gatherings such as bible-study groups in hotel rooms, as well as distributors of religious materials, have been detained, fined and expelled (source: US State Department). The army are extremely sensitive about all their military buildings and become exceptionally irate if you take a photo. Indeed there are signs to this effect outside all military installations.

Post

Postal services are pretty good. Post offices open daily 0700-2100; smaller ones close for lunch. Outgoing packages are opened and checked by the censor.

Safety

Travel advisories
The US State Department's travel advisory: Travel Warnings & Consular Information Sheets, www.travel.state.gov, and the UK Foreign and Commonwealth Office's travel warning section, www.fco.gov.uk, are useful. Do not take any valuables on to the streets of HCMC as bag and jewellery snatching is a common problem. Thieves work in teams, often with beggar women carrying babies as a decoy. Beware of people who obstruct your path (pushing a bicycle across the pavement is a common ruse); your pockets are being emptied from behind. Young men on fast motorbikes also cruise the central streets of HCMC waiting to pounce on victims. The situation in other cities is not so bad but take care in Nha Trang and Hanoi. Never go by cyclo in a strange part of town after dark.

Lone women travellers have fewer problems than in many other Asian countries. The most common form of harassment usually consists of comic and harmless displays of macho behaviour.

Unexploded ordnance is still a threat in some areas. It is best not to stray too far from the beaten track and don't unearth bits of suspicious metal.

Single Western men will be targeted by prostitutes on street corners, in tourist bars and those cruising on motorbikes.

Beware of the following scams: being overcharged on credit cards; the pretend tearing up of a credit card transaction and the issuing of a new one; massage parlours where your money is stolen when you're having a massage; newspapers being sold for 5 times their value; and motorbikes that go 'wrong' and need repairs costing the earth.

Student travellers

Discount travel is provided to those under 22 and over 60. Anyone in full-time education is entitled to an **International Student Identity Card** (www.isic.org). These are issued by student travel offices and travel agencies and offer special rates on all forms of transport and other concessions and services. They sometimes permit free admission to museums and sights, at other times a discount on the admission.

Telephone

Telephone numbers beginning with 091 or 090 are mobile phone numbers. Vietnam's IDD is 0084; directory enquiries: 1080; operator-assisted domestic long-distance calls 103; international directory enquiries 143; yellow pages 1081.

To make a domestic call dial 0 + area code + phone number. Note that all numbers in this guide include the area code. Most shops or cafés will let you call a local number for 2000d; look for the blue sign '*dien thoai cong cong*' (public telephone). All post offices provide international telephone services. The cost of calls has been greatly reduced but some post offices and hotels still insist on charging for a minimum of 3 mins. You start paying for an overseas call from the moment you ring even if the call is not answered. By dialling 171 or 178 followed by 0 or 00 to make an international call, it is around 30% cheaper.

Pay-as-you-go sim cards are available from a number of operators including **Mobiphone** and **Vinaphone**. A sim card costs around £10 and top-up cards are available. Calls are very cheap and it's the most convenient and cheapest way to keep in touch in country.

Time

Vietnam is 7 hrs ahead of GMT.

Tipping

Vietnamese do not normally tip if eating in small restaurants but may tip in expensive bars. Foreigners leave small change, which is appreciated. Big hotels and restaurants add 5-10% service charge and the government tax of 10% to the bill. Taxis are rounded up to the nearest 5000d, hotel porters 20,000d.

Tourist information

Contact details for tourist offices and other resources are given in the relevant Ins and outs sections throughout the text.

The national tourist office is **Vietnam National Administration of Tourism** (www.vietnamtourism.com), whose role is to promote Vietnam as a tourist destination rather than to provide tourist information. Visitors to its offices can get some information and maps but they are more likely to be offered tours. Good tourist information is available from tour operators in the main tourist centres.

Tour operators

For countrywide tour operators, see the Activities and tours sections throughout the guide. For details of specialist tours and activities, see pages 16-19.

In the UK
Adventure Company, Cross & Pillory House, Cross & Pillory Lane, Alton, Hampshire

GU34 1HL, T0845-450 5316,
www.adventurecompany.co.uk.
Audley Travel, New Mill, New Mill Lane,
Witney, Oxfordshire OX29 9SX, T01993-
838000, www.audleytravel.com.
Buffalo Tours UK, The Old Church, 89B
Quicks Rd, Wimbledon, London SW19 1EX,
T020 -8545 2830, www.buffalotours.com.
Exodus, Grange Mills, Weir Rd,
London SW12 0NE, T020-8772 3936,
www.exodus.co.uk
Explore, Nelson House, 55 Victoria Rd,
Farnborough, Hampshire GU14 7PA, T0845-
013 1537, www.explore.co.uk.
Guerba Adventure & Discovery Holidays,
Wessex House, 40 Station Rd, Westbury,
Wiltshire BA13 3JN, T01373-826611,
www.guerba.co.uk.
KE Adventure Travel, 32 Lake Rd, Keswick,
Cumbria CA12 5DQ, T01768-773966,
www.keadventure.com.
Silk Steps, Odyssey Lodge, Holywell Rd,
Edington, Bridgwater, Somerset TA7 9JH,
T01278-722460, www.silksteps.co.uk.
Steppes Travel, 51 Castle St, Cirencester,
Gloucestershire GL7 1QD, T01285-880980,
www.steppestravel.co.uk.
Symbiosis Expedition Planning,
1 Frenchies View, Denmead, Waterlooville,
Hampshire PO7 6SH, T0845-123 2844,
www.symbiosis-travel.com.
Trans Indus, 75 St Mary's Rd and the Old
Fire Station, Ealing, London W5 5RH, T020-
8566 3729, www.transindus.co.uk.
Travel Indochina Ltd, 2nd floor, Chester
House, George St, Oxford OX1 2AY, T01865-
268940, www.travelindochina.co.uk.
Tucan Travel, 316 Uxbridge Rd, London W3
9QP, T020-8896 1600, www.tucantravel.com.
Visit Asia 30-32 Fulham High St, London SW6
3LQ, T020-7736 4347, www.visitasia.co.uk.

In North America
Adventure Center, 1311 63rd St, Suite 200,
Emeryville, CA, T+1-800 228 8747,
www.adventurecenter.com.
Global Spectrum, 3907 Laro Court, Fairfax,
VA 22031, T+1-800 419 4446,

www.globalspectrumtravel.com.
Hidden Treasure Tours, 509 Lincoln
Boulevard, Long Beach, NY 11561, T877-761
7276 (USA toll free),
www.hiddentreasuretours.com.
Journeys, 107 April Drive, Suite 3, Ann Arbor,
MI 48103-1903, T734-665 4407,
www.journeys.travel/.
Myths & Mountains, 976 Tree Court, Incline
Village, Nevada 89451, T+1-800 670-MYTH,
www.mythsandmountains.com.

In Australia and New Zealand
Buffalo Tours, L9/69 Reservoir St, Surry Hills,
Sydney, Australia 2010, T61-2-8218 2198,
www.buffalotours.com.
Intrepid Travel, 360 Bourke St, Melbourne,
Victoria 3000, T+61-03-8602 0500, www.
intrepidtravel.com.au.
Travel Indochina, Level 10, HCF House, 403
George St, Sydney, NSW 2000, T1300-138755
(toll free), www.travelindochina.com.au.

In Vietnam
Asia Pacific Travel, 66 Hang Than St, Ba
Dinh District, Hanoi, T+84 4-3756 8868,
www.asiapacifictravel.vn.
Asiatica Travel, Suite A1203, Building
M3-M4, 91 Nguyen Chi Thanh St, Hanoi,
T+84 4-6266 2816, www.asiatica-travel.com.
Buffalo Tours, 94 Ma May St, Hanoi,
T+84 8-3828 0702. In HCMC, T8-3827 9170,
www.buffalotours.com.
Exotissimo, 80-82 Phan Xich Long St, Phu
Nhuan District, Ho Chi Minh City,
T+84 8-3995 9898, www.exotissimo.com.
Voyage Vietnam, MOTOTOURS ASIA, 1
Luong Ngoc Quyen and 20 Nguyen Huu
Huan, Hanoi, T+84 4-3926 2373/3926 2616,
www.voyagevietnam.net.

Visas and immigration

Tourist visa extensions need careful planning
as, although hotels will accept photocopies
of passports and visas, you cannot buy a
ticket or fly with Vietnam Airlines without
the original.

Valid passports with visas issued by a Vietnamese embassy are required by all visitors, irrespective of citizenship. Visas are normally valid only for arrival by air at Hanoi and HCMC. Those wishing to enter or leave Vietnam by land must specify the border crossing when applying. It is possible to alter the point of departure at immigration offices in Hanoi and HCMC. Contact the Vietnamese embassy in your country for specific application details. Visas on arrival at land crossings are not available and visas on arrival at airports are not exactly as they appear; they must be arranged in advance with licensed companies, paperwork signed before arriving and handed at desks at airports to get the visa. This may or may not work out cheaper than the embassy approach.

The standard tourist visa is valid for 1 month for 1 entry (*mot lan*) only. Tourist visas cost £44 and generally take 5 days to process. Express visas cost more and take 2 days. 2-month tourist visas are now available for £85. If you are planning on staying for a while or making a side trip to Laos or Cambodia with the intention of coming back to Vietnam then a 1-month multiple entry visa will make life much simpler. Business visas cost the same as multiple entry visas. Visa regulations are ever changing; usually it is possible to extend visas within Vietnam. Travel agencies and hotels will probably add their own mark-up but for many people it is worth paying to avoid the difficulty of making 1 or 2 journeys to an embassy. Visas can be extended for 1 month. Depending on where you are it will take between 1 day and a week. A visa valid for 1 month can only be extended for 1 month; a further 1 month extension is then possible. Citizens of Sweden, Norway, Denmark, and Finland may visit, visa free, for not more than 15 days.

Vietnam now operate a quasi 'visa on arrival' programme. An online application must be made through a company such as www.visa-vietnam.org. A pre-approved letter is granted and a service fee paid but payment for the actual visa is made on collection at the airport.

Working in Vietnam

Officially, anyone working in Vietnam should have a business visa and a work permit. Expats coming to work in Vietnam will, presumably, have all this taken care of by their firm. In practice there appears to be a relaxed attitude on the part of the authorities to foreigners working in Vietnam for short periods. Those with specific skills, notably IT and English-language teaching, will not find it hard to get work. In Hanoi and HCMC there are hundreds of language schools keen to engage native speakers and the best ones pay quite well – but only to those with relevant qualifications.

If you are planning on coming to work in Vietnam, contact your embassy or business group in Vietnam and they will be able to provide the most up-to-date information. The website www.business-in-asia.com provides excellent information about working and investing in Vietnam.

Voluntary work is available but best organized in advance through volunteer agencies such as **Voluntary Service Overseas** (www.vso.org.uk) and the **Australian Volunteers International** (www.osb.org.au). There are few NGOs in Vietnam compared with Thailand and Cambodia. In general, however, people with specific skills (speech therapists for instance) or with management expertise and those willing to make a commitment for 4 months or more will be of the greatest use. Charities in Vietnam are stretched responding to well-meaning but impractical offers of help from people who just happen to be passing through. The first port of call for further information should be the **NGO Resource Centre**, La Thanh Hotel, 218 Doi Can, Hanoi, T4-3832 8570, www.ngocentre.org.vn. **Buffalo Tours**, www.buffalotours.com, offers educational and volunteer travel in Vietnam. Recommended.

Contents

48 Ins and outs
49 History

51 **Sights**
51 Hoan Kiem Lake and
Central Hanoi
56 West of Hoan Kiem Lake
56 South of Hoan Kiem Lake
59 Ho Chi Minh's Mausoleum
complex and around
65 Outer Hanoi
67 Around Hanoi

70 **Listings**
70 Sleeping
73 Eating
81 Bars and clubs
82 Entertainment
83 Festivals and events
83 Shopping
87 Activities and tours
90 Transport
94 Directory

Footprint features

44 Don't miss…
54 Guild street name
meanings and their
current trades
55 Syndicated loans keep
the sharks away
61 The story of Quan Am
62 The examination of 1875
66 The Trung sisters
74 Bites but no bark in a
Vietnamese restaurant
86 Asian fusion fashion

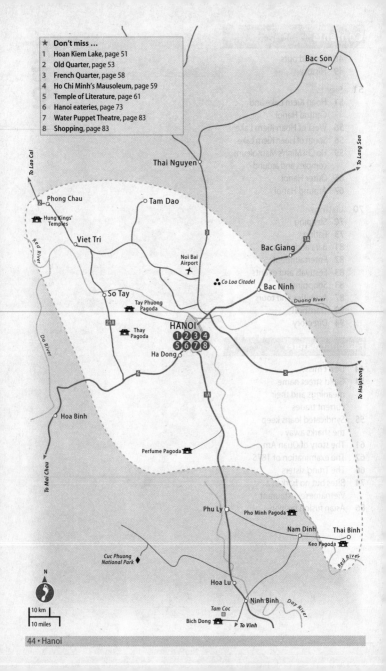

★ Don't miss …
1 Hoan Kiem Lake, page 51
2 Old Quarter, page 53
3 French Quarter, page 58
4 Ho Chi Minh's Mausoleum, page 59
5 Temple of Literature, page 61
6 Hanoi eateries, page 73
7 Water Puppet Theatre, page 83
8 Shopping, page 83

To Lao Cai

Phong Chau

Hung Kings' Temples

Red River

Viet Tri

Tam Dao

Thai Nguyen

To Lang Son

Bac Son

Bac Giang

Noi Bai Airport

Co Loa Citadel

Bac Ninh

So Tay

Tay Phuong Pagoda

Thay Pagoda

HANOI

Ha Dong

Duong River

Da River

Hoa Binh

Perfume Pagoda

To Mai Chau

To Haiphong

Phu Ly

Pho Minh Pagoda

Nam Dinh

Thai Binh

Keo Pagoda

Cuc Phuong National Park

Red River

N

Hoa Lu

Tam Coc

Ninh Binh

Day River

Bich Dong   To Vinh

10 km
10 miles

Hanoi is a small city of broad, tree-lined boulevards, lakes, parks, weathered colonial buildings, elegant squares and some of the newest office blocks and hotels in Southeast Asia. It lies nearly 100 km from the sea on a bend in the Red River and from this geographical feature the city derives its name – Hanoi means 'within a river bend'. The history of the city must be the most confusing of any oriental capital: established as a defensive citadel in the eighth century it has had at least seven names since then and has served a country of fluctuating borders.

It is the capital of the world's 14th most populous country, but, in an age of urban sprawl, the city remains small and compact, historic and charming. Hanoians may appear dour and xenophobic and their leaders austere but the large diplomatic community brings a cosmopolitan feel. And a younger generation has proved willing to engage with the outside world. Consequently the feel of Hanoi is very different – and pleasantly so – from what it was 15 years ago.

Hanoi has a wealth of historical sights lying as it does at the heart of a region rich in history and landscapes. It also has stylish shops and plentiful market stalls and increasingly diverse restaurants from French haute cuisine to Vietnamese street food.

"At Saigon one exists; at Hanoi one lives." This was the opinion of one 19th-century visitor (Joleaud-Barral) and it is a view increasingly echoed today.

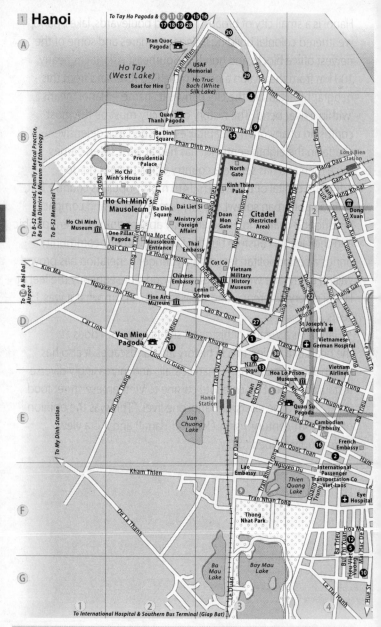

Hanoi

To Tay Ho Pagoda & ⑧ ⑪ ⑰ ⑦ ⑮ ⑯
⑰ ⑱ ⑲ ㉘

Tran Quoc Pagoda

USAF Memorial

Ho Tay (West Lake)

Boat for Hire

Ho Truc Bach (White Silk Lake)

Quan Thanh Pagoda

Ba Dinh Square

Quan Thanh

North Gate

Kinh Thien Palace

Presidential Palace

Ho Chi Minh's House

Citadel (Restricted Area)

Bac Son

Dai Liet Si

Ho Chi Minh's Mausoleum

Ba Dinh Square

Ministry of Foreign Affairs

Doan Mon Gate

Ho Chi Minh Museum

One Pillar Pagoda

Chua Mot Cot Mausoleum Entrance

Thai Embassy

Doi Can

Le Hong Phong

Cua Dong

Cot Co

Vietnam Military History Museum

Kim Ma

Tran Phu

Chinese Embassy

To ✈ & Noi Bai Airport

Nguyen Thai Hoc

Cat Linh

Fine Arts Museum

Lenin Statue

Cao Ba Quat

St Joseph's Cathedral

Vietnamese German Hospital

Van Mieu Pagoda

Nguyen Khuyen

Trang Thi

Quoc Tu Giam

Nam Ngu

Hoa Lo Prison Museum

Vietnam Airlines

Phan Boi Chau

Hai Ba Trung

Ton Duc Thang

Hanoi Station

Van Chuong Lake

Ly Thuong Kiet

Quan Su Pagoda

Tran Hung Dao

Cambodian Embassy

To My Dinh Station

Tran Quoc Toan

French Embassy

International Passenger Transportation Co Viet-Laos

Lao Embassy

Nguyen Du

Eye Hospital

Thien Quang Lake

Kham Thien

Tran Nhan Tong

De La Thanh

Thong Nhat Park

Ba Mau Lake

Bay Mau Lake

Le Dai Hanh

Hoa Ma

Bui Thi Xuan

Trieu Viet Vuong

Hue St

To International Hospital & Southern Bus Terminal (Giap Bat)

Long Bien Station

Hang Dau Station

Dong Xuan

46 • Hanoi

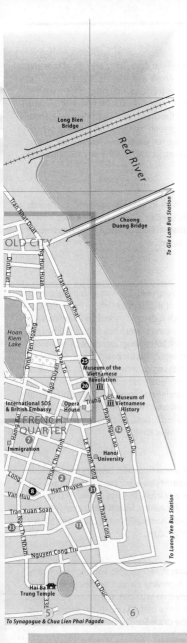

→ **Hanoi maps**
1 Hanoi, page 46
2 Hoan Kiem, page 52

N

400 metres
400 yards

Sleeping 🛏
Army **12** *E6*
Cay Xoai **1** *E3*
De Syloia & Cay
  Cau Restaurant **2** *F5*
Intercontinental Hanoi
  Westlake **8** *A2*
Galaxy **3** *B4*
Movenpick **5** *E3*
Hanoi Daewoo **14** *D1*
Hoa Binh **7** *E5*
Nikko Hanoi **9** *F3*
Sheraton **17** *A2*
Sofitel Plaza Hanoi **11** *A2*
Sunway **13** *F5*

Eating 🍴
252 Hang Bong **1** *D3*
Bobby Chinn **7** *A2*
Café 129 **10** *F4*
Café Puku **27** *D3*
Chien Beo **28** *A3*
Club de l'Oriental **26** *E5*
Com Chay Nang Tam **6** *E4*
Cong Café **5** *F4*
Daluva **17** *A3*

Don's Bistro **16** *A3*
Foodshop 45 **29** *A3*
Hanoi Cooking Centre **4** *B3*
Hanoi Gourmet **8** *F5*
La Badiane **10** *D3*
Le Co-operative **18** *A3*
Khazana **25** *D5*
Kitchen **19** *A3*
KOTO **11** *D2*
Mau House & Ceramic **20** *A3*
Pho Yen **9** *B3*
Quan An Ngon **13** *D3*
Seasons of Hanoi **14** *B3*
Shim Sáo **12** *F4*
Song Thu **16** *E4*
Verticale **2** *E4*
Vine Wine Boutique Bar
  & Café **15** *A3*

Bars & clubs 🍸
Finnegan's Irish Pub **22** *D4*
Hoa Vien **31** *F6*
House of Son Tinh **24** *A3*
R&R Tavern **30** *D3*
Tadioto **23** *F5*

Ins and outs → *Colour map 1, B4.*

Getting there

Noi Bai Airport is 35 km from the city, about a one-hour drive. There are official taxis and a minibus service that drops passengers at their hotels and thus receives commission. Hotels also have their own buses. There are regular flights to a number of international destinations as well as many domestic connections. The train station is central, about a five- to 10-minute taxi ride from the Old Quarter of the city north of Hoan Kiem Lake. There are regular trains from Ho Chi Minh City, and all points on the route south, as well as from Haiphong and Lao Cai (for Sapa) in the north. There is not just one bus terminal but several receiving buses from destinations in the north and major towns all the way south from Ho Chi Minh City. ▶▶ *See also Transport, page 90.*

Getting around

Hanoi is getting more frenetic by the minute. With its elegant, tree-lined boulevards walking and bicycling can be delightful. If you like the idea of being pedalled, then a cyclo is the answer – but be prepared for some concentrated haggling. There are also motorbike taxis (*xe ôm*) and self-drive motorbikes for hire as well as a fleet of metered taxis. Local buses are a last resort.

Orientation

Hanoi can be parcelled up into a number of districts each with its own feel and function. At the heart of the city is Hoan Kiem Lake. The majority of visitors make straight for the Old City (36 Streets and Guilds) area north of the lake, which is densely packed and bustling with commerce. The French Quarter, which still largely consists of French buildings, is south of the lake. Here you'll find the Opera House and the grandest hotels, shops and offices. A large block of the city west of Hoan Kiem Lake (Ba Dinh District) represents the heart of government and the civil and military administration of Vietnam. Imposing colonial architecture, the mark of authority of the French administration, now houses Vietnamese government ministries. All around this district colonial villas are occupied by foreign embassies. To the north of the city is the West Lake, Tay Ho District, fringed with the suburban homes of the new middle class and a new emerging expat quarter with bars and restaurants. Away to the southern and eastern edges of the city are the industrial and residential zones.

Best time to visit

For much of the year Hanoi's weather is decidedly non-tropical. It benefits from glorious European-like springs and autumns when temperatures are warm but not too hot and not too cold. From May until early November Hanoi is fearfully hot and steamy. You cannot take a step without breaking into a sweat. The winter months from November to February can be decidedly chilly and Hanoians wrap themselves up well in warm coats, woolly hats, gloves and scarves. Most museums are closed on Mondays.

Tourist information

The **Tourist Information Center** ① *7 Dinh Tien Hoang St, T4-3926 3366, www.ticvietnam.com, daily 0800-2200*, at the northern end of the lake, is proving useful. It provides information and maps and will book hotels and transport tickets at no extra cost; also currency exchange and ATM. The website www.hanoitourism.gov.vn is also useful. Good tourist information is available from the multitude of tour operators in the city. ▶▶ *See also Tour operators, page 87.*

Precolonial era

The original village on the site of the present city was located in a district with the local name of Long Do. The community seems to have existed as a small settlement as early as the third century AD, although the early history of the Red River Delta largely passed it by. At the beginning of the eighth century a general named Lu Yu became so enchanted with the scenery around the village of An Vien (close to Long Do), that he decided to move his headquarters there. Here he built a shrine to the Emperor Hsuan Tsung, erected an inscribed tablet, and dedicated a statue of the local earth spirit on which was inscribed a poem extolling the beauty of the spot.

The origins of Hanoi as a great city lie with a temple orphan, Ly Cong Uan. Ly rose through the ranks of the palace guards to become their commander and in 1010, four years after the death of the previous King Le Hoan, was enthroned, marking the beginning of the 200-year-long Ly Dynasty. On becoming king, Ly Cong Uan moved his capital from Hoa Lu to Dai La, which he renamed **Thang Long** (Soaring Dragon). Thang Long is present-day **Hanoi**. During the Ly Dynasty the heart of Thang Long was the king's sanctuary in the Forbidden City (Cam Thanh). Drawing both spiritual and physical protection, as well as economic well-being from their proximity to the king and his court, a city of commoners grew up around the walls of Cam Thanh. The Ly kings established a Buddhist monarchical tradition, which mirrored other courts in Southeast Asia. A number of pagodas were built at this time – most have since disappeared, although the One Pillar Pagoda and the Tran Vu Temple both date from this period (see below).

Thang Long, renamed **Tay Do** (Western Capital), was to remain the capital of Vietnam until 1400 when the Ho Dynasty (1400-1407) established a new capital at Thanh Hoa. But soon afterwards, the focus of power shifted back to Thang Long which, in turn, was renamed **Dong Kinh** (Eastern Capital). It is from Dong Kinh that the French name for North Vietnam – Tonkin – is derived. From 1786 to 1802 when Quang Trung established his capital in Hué the city was known as **Bac Thanh** (Northern Citadel). The present name of the city dates from 1831 when the Nguyen Emperor Tu Duc (1847-1883) made it the capital of the province of Hanoi. Hanoi celebrated its 1000th anniversary with a series of special events in October 2010.

Colonial era

During the period of French expansion into Indochina, the Red River was proposed as an alternative trade route to the Mekong. Indeed, the oldest name for Hanoi seems to have been Ke Cho, which means, 'a place where markets are'. Francis Garnier, a French naval officer, was dispatched to the area in 1873 to ascertain the possibilities of establishing such a route. Despite having only a modest force of men under arms, when negotiations with Emperor Tu Duc failed in 1882, Garnier attacked and captured the citadel of Hanoi under the dubious pretext that the Vietnamese were about to attack him. Recognizing that if a small expeditionary force could be so successful, then there would be little chance against a full-strength army, Tu Duc acceded to French demands. At the time that the French took control of Annam, Hanoi could still be characterized more as a collection of villages than a city. As late as the 1870s, the French scholar André Masson, for example, argued that Hanoi "was not a city but a composite agglomeration where an administrative capital, a commercial town and numerous villages were juxtaposed".

From 1882 onwards, Hanoi, along with the port city of Haiphong, became the focus of French activity in the north. Hanoi was made the capital of the new colony of Annam, and the French laid out a 2-sq-km residential and business district, constructing mansions, villas and public buildings incorporating both French and Asian architectural styles. Many of these buildings still stand to the south and east of the Old City and Hoan Kiem Lake – almost as if they were grafted onto the older Annamese city. In the 1920s and 1930s, with conditions in the countryside deteriorating, there was an influx of landless and dispossessed labourers into the city. In their struggle to feed their families, many were willing to take jobs at subsistence wages in the textile, cigarette and other industries that grew up under French patronage. Before long, a poor underclass, living in squalid, pathetic conditions, had formed. At the end of the Second World War, with the French battling to keep Ho Chi Minh and his forces at bay, Hanoi became little more than a service centre. By 1954 there were about 40,000 stallholders, shopkeepers, peddlars and hawkers operating in the city – which at that time had a population of perhaps 400,000. It has been calculated that half of all families relied on the informal sector for their livelihoods.

War damage

After the French withdrew in 1954, Ho Chi Minh concentrated on building up Vietnam and in particular Hanoi's industrial base. At that time the capital had only eight, small, privately owned factories. By 1965, more than 1000 enterprises had been added to this figure. However, as the US bombing of the north intensified with Operation Rolling Thunder in 1965, so the authorities began to evacuate non-essential civilians from Hanoi and to disperse industry into smaller, less vulnerable, units of operation. Between 500,000 and 750,000 people were evacuated between 1965 and 1973, representing 75% of the inner-city population. Nevertheless, the cessation of hostilities led to a spontaneous migration back into the capital. By 1984 the population of the city had reached 2.7 million, and today it is in excess of three million.

Urban renewal

Although Ho Chi Minh City has attracted the lion's share of Vietnam's foreign inward investment, Hanoi, as the capital, also receives a large amount. But whereas Ho Chi Minh City's investment tends to be in industry, Hanoi has received a great deal of attention from property developers, notably in the hotel and office sectors. Much of the development has been in prestigious and historical central Hanoi and has included the construction of a huge office complex on the site of the notorious 'Hanoi Hilton' prison, much to the mortification of Vietnamese war veterans, see page 58. Some commentators applauded the authorities for this attempt at putting the past behind them.

Although some architecturallly insensitive schemes have dominated the cityscape, in the past 15 years numerous old colonial villas have been tastefully restored as bars, restaurants and homes cater to the growing numbers of Western visitors, dipomats and businessmen with a very positive effect on Hanoi's architectural heritage.

Pollution levels in Hanoi have soared as a result of the construction boom: dust from demolition, piling, bricks and tiles and sand blown from the back of trucks add an estimated 150 cubic metres of pollutants to the urban atmosphere every day. But while asthmatics may wheeze, Hanoi's army of builders grows daily ever stronger. Hundreds of farmers join the urban job market each week and one can see bands of men standing around at strategic points waiting to be recruited; on Duong Thanh Street, for example, carpenters with their tool boxes wait patiently for the call to a day's work. But can Hanoi's economy keep pace with the rate of migration in from the countryside? Against the background of the Asian financial crisis of the late 1990s the situation looked ominous but the stage now seems set for a period of sustained growth. In addition, by means of a strict system of residential permits the Party is able to control the rate at which people settle in the capital. Without the proper papers stamped with a round red seal children cannot go to school. As education is one of the highest priorities for many Vietnamese parents it curbs their enthusiasm for moving to the city.

Hanoi is, in a great many ways, very different from Ho Chi Minh City. The Hanoians have an agreeable sense of history and appreciation for old buildings: indeed a great many of Hanoi's citizens also appear elderly. Whether practicing t'ai chi around one of the city's many lakes or squatting at a tiny pavement café the elderly are part of Hanoi's historical structure and charm. The old buildings, small scale and compact nature of Hanoi will make many Europeans feel very much at home and quickly develop a strong sense of attachment.

Sights

Much of the charm of Hanoi lies not so much in the official 'sights' but in the unofficial and informal: the traffic, small shops, stalls, the bustle of pedestrians, clothing, parents treating their children to an ice cream, an evening visit to Hoan Kiem Lake. Like China when it was 'opening up' to Western tourists in the late 1970s, the primary interest lies in the novelty of exploring a city which, until recently, has opted for a firmly socialist road to development and has been insulated from the West. Today, you'll find it enlivened by an entrepeneurial spirit manifest in new shops, bars, companies and building developments.

Hoan Kiem Lake and Central Hanoi

Hoan Kiem Lake
Hoan Kiem Lake or Ho Guom (the Lake of the Restored Sword) as it is more commonly referred to in Hanoi, is named after an incident that occurred during the 15th century. Emperor Le Thai To (1428-1433), following a momentous victory against an army of invading Ming Chinese, was sailing on the lake when a golden turtle appeared from the depths to take back the charmed sword which had secured the victory and restore it to the lake whence it came. Like the sword in the stone of British Arthurian legend, Le Thai To's sword assures Vietnamese of divine intervention in time of national crisis and the story is graphically portrayed in water puppet theatres across the country. There is a modest and rather dilapidated tower (the **Tortoise Tower**) commemorating the event on an islet in the southern part of the lake. In fact, the lake does contain large turtles; one captured in 1968 was reputed to have weighed 250 kg. The creatures that inhabit the lake are believed to be a variety of Asian softshell tortoise. It is thought that they were the species *Rafetus swinhoei* but a scientist reported that these species were in fact different from Ho Guom tortoises; the Ho Guom tortoise has now been named *Rafetus leloii*. In 2004 the water level fell quite dramatically and turtles were seen more often. The park that surrounds the lake is used by the residents of the city every morning for jogging and t'ai chi (Chinese shadow boxing) and is regarded by locals as one of the city's beauty spots. The light around the lake has a filmic quality, especially in the early morning. When the French arrived in Hanoi at the end of the 19th century, the lake was an unhealthy lagoon surrounded by so many huts that it was impossible to see the shore.

Ngoc Son Temple and Sunbeam Bridge
ⓘ 3000d.

The northeast corner of Hoan Kiem Lake is the place to have your photo taken, preferably with the **Ngoc Son Temple** in the background. The temple was built in the early 19th century on a small island on the foundations of the old Khanh Thuy Palace. The island is linked to the shore by the The Huc (Sunbeam) Bridge, constructed in 1875. The temple is dedicated to Van Xuong, the God of Literature, although the 13th-century hero Tran Hung Dao, the martial arts genius Quan Vu and the physician La To are also worshipped here. Shrouded by trees and surrounded by water, the pagoda's position is its strongest attribute. To the side of the temple is a room containing a preserved turtle and photographs of the creatures in the lake.

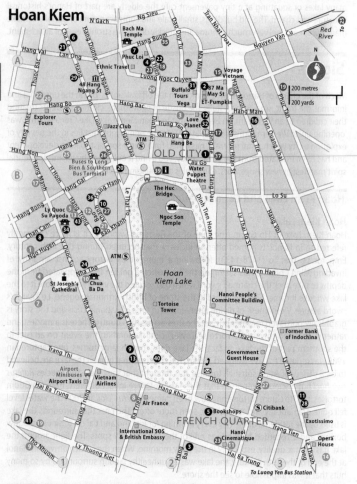

Hoan Kiem

Old City and 36 Streets

Stretching north from the lake is the Old City (36 Streets and Guilds or 36 Pho Phuong). Previously, it lay to the east of the citadel, where the emperor had his residence, and was squalid, dark, cramped and disease-ridden. This part of Hanoi has survived surprisingly intact, and today is the most beautiful area of the city. Narrow streets, each named after the produce that it sells or used to sell (**Basket Street**, **Paper Street**, **Silk Street**, etc), create an intricate web of activity and colour, see box, page 54.

By the 15th century there were 36 short lanes here, each specializing in a particular trade and representing one of the 36 guilds. Among them, for example, were the **Phuong Hang Dao (Dyers' Guild Street)**, and the **Phuong Hang Bac (Silversmiths' Street)**. In fact, Hang Bac (*hang* means merchandise) is the oldest street in Hanoi, dating from the 13th century. The 36 streets have interested European visitors since they first started coming to Hanoi. For example, in 1685 Samuel Bacon, noted how "all the diverse objects sold in this town have a specially assigned street", remarking how different this was from "companies and corporations in European cities". The streets in question not only sold different products, but were usually also populated by people from different areas of the country – even from single villages. They would live, work and worship together because each of the occupational guilds had its own temple and its own community support networks.

Some of this past is still in evidence: at the south end of Hang Dau Street, for example, is a mass of stalls selling nothing but shoes, while Tin Street is still home to a community of pot and pan menders (and sellers). Generally, however, the crafts and trades of the past have given way to new activities – karaoke bars and tourist shops – but it is remarkable the extent to which the streets still specialize in the production and sale of just one type of merchandise.

The dwellings in this area are known as *nha ong* (**tube houses**). The majority were built at the end of the 19th century and the beginning of the 20th; they are narrow, with shop fronts sometimes only 3 m wide, but can be up to 50 m long (such as the one at 51 Hang Dao). In the countryside the dimensions of houses were calculated on the basis of the owner's own physical dimensions; in urban areas the tube houses

➡ **Hanoi maps**
1 Hanoi, page 46
2 Hoan Kiem, page 52

Sleeping 🛏
Artist **11** *D3*
Church **10** *C1*
Cinnamon **4** *C1*
Eden Hanoi & Luna d'Autunno Restaurant **9** *D1*
Freedom **12** *B1*
Gold Spring **2** *A3*
Golden Lotus **5** *B1*
Hang Trong **13** *B1*
Hanoi Backpackers' Hostel **1** *C1*
Hilton Hanoi Opera **14** *D3*
Hoa Linh **15** *A1*
Hong Ngoc **17** *B1*
Hong Ngoc 3 **3** *B2*
Joseph's **7** *C1*
Mai Phuong **18** *B2*
Melia Hanoi **19** *D1*
My Lan **20** *A1*
Nam Phuong **21** *B1*
Ngoc Diep **22** *A1*
Real Darling Café **25** *B1*
Sofitel Legend Metropole Hanoi & Le Beaulieu Restaurant **27** *D3*
Thuy Nga **29** *A2*
Zephyr **8** *D2*

Eating 🍴
69 **2** *A2*
Al Fresco's **3** *D2*
Baan Thai **6** *A1*
Bit Tet **7** *A2*
Bon Mua **9** *C2*
Café des Arts & Stop Café **10** *B1*
Café Moca **24** *C1*
Café Puku **43** *B1*

Cha Ca La Vong **21** *A1*
Chica **4** *A2*
Club Opera **11** *D3*
Fanny Ice Cream **13** *C2*
Green Tangerine **1** *B2*
Hanoi Press Club **28** *D3*
Highlands Coffee **40** *C2*
Highway 4 **16** *B3*
Kangaroo Café **17** *B1*
Kem Trang Tien **5** *D2*
Lá **34** *B1*
Little Hanoi (Ta Hien St) **22** *A2*
Little Hanoi (Hang Gai St) **20** *B2*
Madame Hiem **8** *B1*
My Burger My **12** *B2*
Pepperonis **36** *B1*
Restaurant 22 **29** *A1*
San Ho **41** *D1*
Tamarind & Handspan Adventure Travel **31** *A2*
Tandoor **32** *B2*

Bars & clubs 🍸
Cheeky Quarter, Tet **33** *A2*
Dragonfly **35** *A2*
Funky Buddha **37** *B2*
Ho Guom Xanh **38** *C2*
Jo Jo's **30** *D2*
Half Man/Half Noodle **15** *A2*
Le Pub **17** *B2*
Mao's Red Lounge **18** *A2*
Legends **39** *B2*
Phuc Tan **19** *A3*
Polite Pub **27** *B1*
Roots **23** *A2*
Solace **25** *A3*
Rock Billy **26** *B2*

Guild street name meanings and their current trades

Bat Dan St – clay bowls
Bat Su – ceramic bowls
Hang Bac – silver, jewellery
Hang Bo – baskets, motorbike stickers, barbecue squid (late night)
Hang Bong – cotton
Hang Buom – sails, coffee, chocolate, booze
Hang But – calligraphy brushes
Hang Can – weighing scales
Hang Dao – silk (Pho Hang Dao means 'street where red-dyed fabrics are sold'), sewing things, feathers
Hang Dieu – smoking pipes, fake brand name handbags
Hang Duong – sugar
Hang Gai – hemp, silk, souvenirs, galleries, tailor shops
Hang Ma – votive paper, headstones
Hang Manh – bamboo screens/mats
Hang Non – conical hats
Hang Phen St – alum sulphate
Hang Quat – paper fans, religious artefacts
Hang Thiec – tinsmiths, tin ovens
Hang Tre – bamboo
Hang Trong – drums, boutiques, galleries
Lan Ong – traditional medicine
Hang Vai – cloth street
Ngo Gach – bricks
Thuoc Bac – medicine street
To Tich – undecorated mats, fruit cups
Yen Thai Alley – embroidery

evolved so that each house owner could have an, albeit very small, area of shop frontage facing onto the main street; the width was determined by the social class of the owner. The houses tend to be interspersed with courtyards or 'wells' to permit light into the house and allow some space for outside activities like washing and gardening. As geographers Brian Shaw and R Jones note in a paper on heritage conservation in Hanoi, the houses also had a natural air-conditioning system: the difference in ambient temperature between the inner courtyards and the outside street created air flow, and the longer the house the greater the velocity of the flow.

A common wall can sometimes still be seen between tube houses. Built in a step-like pattern, it not only marked land boundaries but also acted as a fire break. The position of the house frontages were not fixed until the early 20th century and consequently some streets have a delightfully irregular appearance. The structures were built of bricks 'cemented' together with sugar-cane juice.

The older houses tend to be lower; commoners were not permitted to build higher than the Emperor's own residence. Other regulations prohibited attic windows looking down on the street; this was to prevent assassination and to stop people from looking down on a passing king. As far as colour and decoration were concerned, purple and gold were strictly for royal use only, as was the decorative use of the dragon. By the early 20th century inhabitants were replacing their traditional tube houses with buildings inspired by French architecture. Many fine buildings from this era remain, however, and are best appreciated by standing back and looking upwards. Shutters, cornices, columns and wrought-iron balconies and balustrades are common decorative features. An ornate façade sometimes conceals the pitched roof behind. There are some good examples on **Nguyen Sieu Street**.

A fear among conservationists is that this unique area will be destroyed as residents who have made small fortunes with the freeing-up of the economy, redevelop their houses insensitively. The desire is understandable: the tube houses are cramped and squalid, and often without any facilities.

Syndicated loans keep the sharks away

Throughout Vietnam, and indeed across the world wherever there are large numbers of Vietnamese, one will find *hui* in operation. *Hui* (or *ho* as it is called in the north) is a credit circle of 10 to 20 people who meet every month; the scheme lasts as many months as there are participants. In a blind auction the highest bidder takes home that month's capital. Credit is expensive in Vietnam, partly because there are few banks to make personal loans, so in time of crisis the needy have to borrow from money-lenders at crippling rates of interest. Alternatively they can join a *hui* and borrow at more modest rates.

It works like this: the *hui* is established with members agreeing to put in a fixed amount, say 100,000d, each month. Each month the members bid according to their financial needs, entering a zero bid if they need no cash. If, in month one, Mr Nam's daughter gets married he will require money for the wedding festivities and, moreover, he has to have the money so he must bid high, maybe 25,000d. Assuming this is the highest bid he will receive 75,000d from each member (ie 100,000d less 25,000d). In future months Mr Nam cannot bid again but must pay 100,000d to whoever collects that month's pot. Towards the end of the cycle several participants (those whose buffalo have not died and those whose daughters remain unmarried) will have taken nothing out but will have paid in 100,000d (minus x) dong each month; they can enter a zero bid and get the full 100,000d from all participants and with it a tidy profit. There is, needless to say, strategy involved and this is where the Vietnamese love of gambling ("the besetting sin of the Vietnamese" according to Norman Lewis) colours the picture. One day, Mr Muoi wins one million dong on the Vinh Long lottery. He lets it be known that he intends to buy a Honda Dream, but to raise the necessary purchase price he must 'win' that month's *hui* and will be bidding aggressively. In the same month Thuy, Mrs Phuoc's baby daughter, celebrates her first birthday so Mrs Phuoc needs money to throw a lavish *thoi noi* party. She has heard of old Muoi's intentions but doesn't know if he is serious. In case he is, she will have to bid high. On the day, nice Mrs Phuoc enters a knock-out bid of 30,000d but wily old Muoi was bluffing all along and he and the others make a lot of interest that month.

48 Hang Ngang Street ⓘ *at the north end of Hang Dao St, before it becomes Hang Duong St, 0800-1130, 1330-1630, 10,000d*, is the spot where Ho Chi Minh drew up the **Vietnamese Declaration of Independence** in 1945, ironically modelled on the US Declaration of Independence. It now houses a **museum** with black and white photographs of Uncle Ho.

The house at **87 Ma May Street** ⓘ *daily 0800-1200, 1300-1700, 5000d, guide included*, is a wonderfully preserved example of an original shop house now open to the public. The house was built in the late 1800s as a home for a single family. The importance of the miniature interior courtyards providing light, fresh air and gardens can be appreciated. The wooden upstairs and pitched fish-scale-tiled roofs are typical of how most houses would have looked. From 1954 to 1999 five families shared the building as the urban population rose and living conditions declined. The **Bach Ma (White Horse) Temple** ⓘ *76 Hang Buom St*, dating from the ninth century, honours Long Do and is the oldest religious building in the Old Quarter. In 1010, King Ly Thai To honoured Long Do with the title of the capital. It is said that a horse revealed to King Ly Thai To where to build the walls of the citadel.

A walk through **Hang Be Market** (actually on Gai Ngu Street) reveals just how far Hanoi has developed over the past decade. There is a wonderful variety of food on sale – live, dead, cooked and raw. Quacking ducks, newly plucked chickens, saucers of warm blood, pigs' trotters, freshly picked vegetables as well as pickled ones; the quality of produce is remarkable and testimony to the rapid strides Vietnamese agriculture has made. In this market and surrounding streets beautiful cut flowers are on sale.

Venturing further north, is **Cua Quan Chuong**, the last remaining of Hanoi's 16 gates. In the 18th century a system of ramparts and walls was built around Hanoi. Quan Chuong Gate was built in 1749 and rebuilt in 1817.

Further north still, on Dong Xuan Street, is the large and varied **Dong Xuan Market**. This large covered market was destroyed in a disastrous fire in 1994. Stall holders lost an estimated US$4.5 million worth of stock and complained bitterly at the inadequacy of the fire services; one fire engine arrived with no water. The market has been rebuilt. It specializes mainly in clothes and household goods.

To the west, along Phung Hung Street is another live market of fish, dog, birds, vegetables and betel nut. It makes for a wonderful wander.

West of Hoan Kiem Lake

To the west of Hoan Kiem Lake in a little square stands the rather sombre, twin-towered neo-Gothic **Saint Joseph's Cathedral** ⓘ *open 0500-1130, 1400-1930 through a door at the back; Mass Mon-Fri 0530, 0815, Sat 0530, 1800, Sun 0500, 0700, 0900, 1100, 1600, 1800.* Built in 1886, the cathedral is important as one of the very first colonial-era buildings in Hanoi finished, as it was, soon after the Treaty of Tientsin which gave France control over the whole of Vietnam (see page 412). It was located at the centre of the Catholic Mission. Some fine stained-glass windows remain.

About 100 m in front of the cathedral on Nha Tho Street is a much older religious foundation, the **Stone Lady Pagoda (Chua Ba Da)**, down a narrow alley. It consists of an old pagoda and a Buddhist school. On either side of the pagoda are low buildings where the monks live. Although few of the standing buildings are of any antiquity it is an ancient site and a tranquil and timeless atmosphere prevails. Originally built in 1056 as Sung Khanh Pagoda, by the late 15th century it needed rebuilding. A stone statue of a woman was found in the foundations and was worshipped in the pagoda. By 1767 the walls needed rebuilding. Each time they were built they collapsed. The foundations were dug deeper and the stone statue was found again. Since then the walls have held fast. Although now a pagoda for the worship of Buddha it is clear that the site has had a mixed spiritual history.

North of the cathedral on Ly Quoc Su Street is the **Ly Quoc Su Pagoda**, once home to Minh Khong, a physician and the chief adviser to Ly Than Tong, the Ly dynasty emperor. He became famous in the 12th century after curing the emperor of a disease that other doctors had failed to treat. It was restored in 2010.

South of Hoan Kiem Lake

Opera House
ⓘ *Not open to the public except during public performances. See the billboards outside or visit the box office for details.*

To the south and east of Hoan Kiem Lake is the proud-looking French-era Opera House. It was built between 1901-1911 by François Lagisquet and is one of the finest French colonial buildings in Hanoi. Some 35,000 bamboo piles were sunk into the mud of the Red River to provide foundations for the lofty edifice. The exterior is a delightful mass of shutters, wrought-iron work, little balconies and a tiled frieze. The top balustrade is nicely capped with griffins. Inside, there are dozens of little boxes and fine decoration evocative of the French era. Having suffered years of neglect the Opera House was eventually lavishly restored, opening in time for the Francophone Summit held in 1997. Original drawings in Hanoi and Paris were consulted and teams of foreign experts were brought in to supervise local craftsmen. Slate was carried from Sin Ho to re-tile the roof, Italians oversaw the relaying of the mosaic floor in the lobby and French artists repainted the fine ornamental details of the auditorium. The restoration cost US$14 million, a colossal sum to spend on the reappointment of a colonial edifice. A Hanoi planning department architect explained that although the Opera House was French in style it was built by Vietnamese hands and represented an indelible part of Vietnamese history.

Sofitel Metropole
① *15 Ngo Quyen St.*
The Metropole, built in French-colonial style in 1901 is an icon of elegance in the French quarter of the city. It quickly became the focal point of colonial life for 50 years. In 1916, it screened the first movie shown in Indochina. In 1944, Japanese POWS were temporarily housed here. In the 1950s the Vietnamese government appropriated it, named it the **Thong Nhat Hotel**, and used it as a hotel for VIPs; during the Vietnam War years the press and diplomats used it as their headquarters. Many famous celebrities and diplomats have stayed here including Graham Greene (writing *The Quiet American*), Somerset Maugham, Noel Coward, Stephen Hawking, Oliver Stone, Charlie Chaplin, Sir Roger Moore, Jane Fonda, Mick Jagger, Catherine Deneuve, George Bush Senior, Fidel Castro, Robert McNamara, Jacques Chirac and Boutros Boutros Ghali.▸▸ *See also Sleeping, page 70.*

Museum of the Vietnamese Revolution
① *216 Tran Quang Khai St, T4-3825 4151, Tue-Sun 0800-1145, 1330-1615, 20,000d.*
The Museum of the Vietnamese Revolution (Bao Tang Cach Mang Vietnam), housed in an old French villa, traces the struggle of the Vietnamese people to establish their independence. Following the displays, it becomes clear that the American involvement in Vietnam has been just one episode in a centuries-long struggle against foreign aggressors. The 3000 exhibits are dryly presented across 29 rooms and in chronological order. They start with the cover the struggle for independence (1858-1945); the final rooms show the peace and prosperity of reunification: bountiful harvests, the opening of large civil engineering projects, and smiling peasants.

Museum of Vietnamese History
① *1 Trang Tien St, T4-325 3518, Tue-Sun 0800-1130, 1330-1630, 15,000d.*
A short distance south of the Museum of the Vietnamese Revolution is the History Museum (**Bao Tang Lich Su**). It is housed in a splendid building, completed in 1931. It was built as the home of the École Française d'Extrême-Orient, a distinguished archaeological, historical and ethnological research institute, by Ernest Hébrard. Hébrard, who was responsible for so many fine colonial-era buildings in Vietnam, here employed a distinctly Indochinese style appropriate to its original and, indeed, its current function. The museum remains a centre of cultural and historical research. The École Française d'Extrême-Orient played an important role in the preservation and restoration of

ancient Vietnamese structures and temples, many of which were destroyed or came under threat of demolition by the French to enable the growth of their colonial city. The museum remains a centre of cultural and historical research. The collection spans Vietnamese history from the neolithic to the 20th century of Ho Chi Minh and is arranged in chronological order. Galleries lead from the Neolithic (Bac Son) represented by stone tools and jewellery; the Bronze Age (Dong Son) with some fine bronze drums; Funan and the port of Oc-Eo; Champa is represented by some fine stone carvings of *apsaras*, mythical dancing girls. There are relics such as bronze temple bells and urns of successive royal dynasties from Le to Nguyen. An impressive giant turtle, symbol of longevity, supports a huge stela praising the achievements of Le Loi, founder of the Le Dynasty, who harnessed nationalist sentiment and forced the Chinese out of Vietnam. Unfortunately some of the pieces (including a number of the stelae) are reproductions.

Other French Quarter buildings

Other buildings of the 'French Concession' include the impressive **Government Guest House** ① *12 Ngo Quyen St*, diagonally opposite the Metropole. The bright ochre building was the former residence of the French Resident Superior of Tonkin.

The enormous **Post Office** ① *6 Dinh Le St*, facing Hoan Kiem lake, was designed by Henri Cerruti in 1942. Next door is the **Post and Telegraphic Office** ① *75 Dinh Tien Hoang St*, designed by Auguste-Henri Vildieu and completed in 1896. Further up Dinh Tieng Hoang is the **Hanoi People's Committee** building, formerly the town hall and built by Vildieu between 1897 and 1906. The main section at the front dates from the late 1980s and early 1990s demonstrating brutalist communist architecture. Vildieu also designed the **Supreme Court** ① *48 Ly Thuong Kiet*, between 1900 and 1906. It's a fine symmetrical building with a grey-tiled roof, two staircases and balustrades.

Ernest Hébrard, who worked at the Central Services of Urban Planning and Architecture, designed the **Indochina University**, now **Hanoi University** ① *19 Le Thanh Tong St*, which was completed in 1926. It bears a remarkable resemblance to the history museum, which he also designed. Furthermore, Hébrard designed the **Ministry of Foreign Affairs** (then the **Bureau des Finances**) ① *Dien Bien Phu St*, in 1931.

The architecturally remarkable former **Bank of Indochina** ① *49 Ly Thai To St*, was built in 1930 by architect Georges-André Trouvé. Its grey, heavy art deco appearance and isolated position evokes a bit of fear. One wonders what the bank vaults look like inside.

Around 1000 colonial villas are still scattered around Hanoi, especially west of the Old Quarter. Many of them have been superbly restored and are used by embassies.

Hoa Lo Prison

① *1 Hoa Lo, T4-3824 6358, Tue-Sun 0800-1130, 1330-1630, 10,000d.*

Hoa Lo Prison (Maison Centrale), better known as the **Hanoi Hilton**, is the prison where US POWs were incarcerated, some for six years, during the Vietnamese War. Up until 1969, prisoners were also tortured here. Two US Airforce officers, Charles Tanner and Ross Terry, rather than face torture, concocted a story about two other members of their squadron who had been court-martialled for refusing to fly missions against the north. Thrilled with this piece of propaganda, visiting Japanese communists were told the story and it filtered back to the US. Unfortunately for Tanner and Terry they had called their imaginary pilots Clark Kent and Ben Casey (both TV heroes). When the Vietnamese realized they had been made fools of, the two prisoners were again tortured. The final prisoners were not released until 1973, some having been held in the north since 1964.

At the end of 1992 a US mission was shown around the prison where 2000 inmates were housed in cramped and squalid conditions. Despite pleas from war veterans and party members, the site was sold to a Singapore-Vietnamese joint venture and is now a hotel and shopping complex, **Hanoi Towers**. As part of the deal the developers had to leave a portion of the prison for use as a museum, a lasting memorial to the horrors of war.

'Maison Centrale', reads the legend over the prison's main gate, which leads in to the museum. There are recreations of conditions under colonial rule when the barbarous French incarcerated patriotic Vietnamese from 1896: by 1953 they were holding 2000 prisoners in a space designed for 500. Many well-known Vietnamse were incarcerated here: Phan Boi Chau (founder of the Reformation Party; 1867-1940), Luong Van Can (Reformation Party leader and school founder; 1854-1927), Nguyen Quyen (founder along with Luong Van Can of the School for the Just Cause; 1870-1942) and five men who were later to become general secretaries of the Communist Party: Le Duan (served as general secretary 1976-1986), Nguyen Van Cu (served 1938-1940), Truong Chinh (served 1941-1956 and July-December 1986), Nguyen Van Linh (served 1986-1991) and Do Muoi (served 1991-1997). Less prominence is given to the role of the prison for holding American pilots, but Douglas 'Pete' Peterson, the first post-war American Ambassador to Vietnam (1997-2001), who was one such occupant (imprisoned 1966-1973) has his mug-shot on the wall, as does John McCain (imprisoned 1967-1973), now a US senator.

Ambassadors' Pagoda (Quan Su) and around
ⓘ73 Quan Su St.

In the 15th century there was a guesthouse on the site of the Ambassadors' Pagoda (Quan Su Pagoda) for visiting Buddhist ambassadors. The current structure was built between 1936 and 1942. Chinese in appearance from the exterior, the temple contains some fine stone sculptures of the past, present and future Buddhas. It is very popular and crowded with scholars, pilgrims, beggars and incense sellers. The pagoda is one of the centres of Buddhist learning in Vietnam (it is the headquarters of the Vietnam Central Buddhist Congregation): at the back is a school room which is in regular use, students often spill-over into the surrounding corridors to listen.

Nearby, on Le Duan Street just south of the railway station, stalls sell a remarkable array of US, Soviet and Vietnamese army-surplus kit.

Ho Chi Minh's Mausoleum complex and around

Ho Chi Minh's Mausoleum
ⓘSummer Tue-Thu, Sat and Sun 0730-1100. Winter Tue-Thu, Sat and Sun 0800-1100, closed 6 weeks from Sep for conservation. Before entering the mausoleum, visitors must leave cameras and possessions at the office (Ban To Chuc) on Huong Vuong, just south of and a few mins' walk from the Mausoleum. Visitors must be respectful: dress neatly, walk solemnly, do not talk and do not take anything in that could be construed as a weapon, for example a penknife.

The Vietnamese have made Ho Chi Minh's body a holy place of pilgrimage and visitors march in file to see Ho's embalmed corpse inside the mausoleum (Lang Chu Tich Ho Chi Minh).

The mausoleum, built between 1973 and 1975, is a massive, square, forbidding structure and must be among the best constructed, maintained and air-conditioned buildings in Vietnam. Opened in 1975, it is a fine example of the mausoleum genre and is modelled closely on Lenin's Mausoleum in Moscow. Ho lies, with a guard at each corner of his bier. The embalming of his body was undertaken by the chief Soviet embalmer Dr Sergei

Debrov who also pickled such communist luminaries as Klement Gottwald (President of Czechoslovakia), Georgi Dimitrov (Prime Minister of Bulgaria) and Forbes Burnham (President of Guyana). Debrov was flown to Hanoi from Moscow as Ho lay dying, bringing with him two transport planes packed with air conditioners (to keep the corpse cool) and other equipment. To escape US bombing, the team moved Ho to a cave, taking a full year to complete the embalming process. Russian scientists still check-up on their handiwork, servicing Ho's body regularly. Their embalming methods and the fluids they use are still a closely guarded secret, and in a recent interview, Debrov noted with pleasure the poor state of China's Chairman Mao's body, which was embalmed without Soviet help.

The embalming and eternal display of Ho Chi Minh's body was however contrary to Ho's own wishes: he wanted to be cremated and his ashes placed in three urns to be positioned atop three unmarked hills in the north, centre and south of the country. He once wrote that "cremation is not only good from the point of view of hygiene, but it also saves farmland".

Ba Dinh Square

In front of Ho Chi Minh's Mausoleum is Ba Dinh Square where Ho read out the Vietnamese Declaration of Independence on 2 September 1945. Following Ho's declaration, 2 September became Vietnam's National Day. Coincidentally 2 September was also the date on which Ho died in 1969, although his death was not officially announced until 3 September.

In front of the mausoleum on Bac Son Street is the **Dai Liet Si**, a memorial to the heroes and martyrs who died fighting for their country's independence. It appears to be modelled as a secular form of stupa and inside is a large bronze urn.

Ho Chi Minh's house and the Presidential Palace

ⓘ *Ho Chi Minh's house, 1 Bach Thao St, T4-3804 4529; Summer Tue-Thu, Sat and Sun, 0730-1100, 1400-1600, Fri 0730-1100; winter Tue-Thu, Sat and Sun 0800-1100, 1330-1600, Fri 0800-1100; 15,000d; the Presidential Palace is not open to the public.*

From the mausoleum, visitors are directed to Ho Chi Minh's house built in the compound of the former Presidential Palace. The palace, now a Party guesthouse, was the residence of the Governors-General of French Indochina and was built between 1900 and 1908 by Auguste-Henri Vildieu. In 1954, when North Vietnam's struggle for independence was finally achieved, Ho Chi Minh declined to live in the palace, saying that it belonged to the people. Instead, he stayed in what is said to have been an electrician's house in the same compound. Here he lived from 1954 to 1958, before moving to a new stilt house built on the other side of the small lake (Ho Chi Minh's 'Fish Farm', swarming with massive and well-fed carp). The house was designed by Ho and an architect, Nguyen Van Ninh. This modest house made of rare hardwoods is airy and personal and immaculately kept. Ho conducted meetings under the house, which is raised up on wooden pillars, and slept and worked above (his books, slippers and telephones are still here) from May 1958 to August 1969. Built by the army, the house mirrors the one he lived in while fighting the French from his haven near the Chinese border. Behind the house is Ho's bomb shelter, and behind that, the hut where he actually died in 1969.

One Pillar Pagoda

Close by is the One Pillar Pagoda (Chua Mot Cot), one of the few structures remaining from the original foundation of the city. It was built in 1049 by Emperor Ly Thai Tong, although the shrine has since been rebuilt on several occasions, most recently in 1955 after the

The story of Quan Am

Quan Am was turned onto the streets by her husband for some unspecified wrong-doing and, dressed as a monk, took refuge in a monastery. There, a woman accused her of fathering, and then abandoning, her child. Accepting the blame (why, no one knows), she was again turned out onto the streets, only to return to the monastery much later when she was on the point of death –

to confess her true identity. When the Emperor of China heard the tale, he made Quan Am the Guardian Spirit of Mother and Child, and couples without a son now pray to her.

Quan Am's husband is sometimes depicted as a parakeet, with the Goddess usually holding her adopted son in one arm and standing on a lotus leaf (the symbol of purity).

French destroyed it before withdrawing from the country. The emperor built the pagoda in a fit of religious passion after he dreamt that he saw the goddess Quan Am (Vietnam's equivalent of the Chinese goddess Kuan-yin) sitting on a lotus and holding a young boy, whom she handed to the emperor. On the advice of counsellors who interpreted the dream, the Emperor built this little lotus-shaped temple in the centre of a water-lily pond and shortly afterwards his queen gave birth to a son. As the name suggests, it is supported on a single (concrete) pillar with a brick and stone staircase running up one side. The pagoda symbolizes the 'pure' lotus sprouting from the sea of sorrow. Original in design, with dragons running along the apex of the elegantly curved tiled roof, the temple is one of the most revered monuments in Vietnam. But the ungainly concrete pillar and the pond of green slime in which it is embedded detract considerably from the enchantment of the little pagoda. Adjacent is the inhabited Dien Huu Pagoda; a sign says they don't like people in shorts, but they are quite friendly and it has a nice courtyard.

Ho Chi Minh Museum
ⓘ*19 Ngoc Ha St, T4-3846 3752, Tue-Thu and Sat 0800-1130, 1400-1600, Fri 0800-1130, 10,000d, 40,000d for a guide.*
Overshadowing the One Pillar Pagoda is the Ho Chi Minh Museum – opened in 1990 in celebration of the centenary of Ho's birth. Contained in a large and impressive modern building, likened to a white lotus, it is the best-arranged and most innovative museum in Vietnam. The displays trace Ho's life and work from his early wanderings around the world to his death and final victory over the south.

Temple of Literature (Van Mieu Pagoda)
ⓘ*The entrance is on Quoc Tu Giam St, T4-3845 2917, open daily summer 0730-1730, winter 0730-1700, 5000d, 45-min tour in French or English 50,000d, 3000d for brochure. ATM inside.*
The Temple of Literature (Van Mieu Pagoda) is the largest, and probably the most important, temple complex in Hanoi. It was founded in 1070 by Emperor Ly Thanh Tong, dedicated to Confucius who had a substantial following in Vietnam, and modelled, so it is said, on a temple in Shantung, China, the birthplace of the sage. Some researchers, while acknowledging the date of foundation, challenge the view that it was built as a Confucian institution pointing to the ascendancy of Buddhism during the Ly Dynasty. Confucian principles and teaching rapidly replaced Buddhism, however, and Van Mieu subsequently became the intellectual and spiritual centre of the kingdom as a cult of

The examination of 1875

The examinations held at the Temple of Literature and which enabled, in theory, even the most lowly peasant to rise to the exalted position of a Mandarin, were long and difficult and conducted with great formality.

André Masson quotes Monsieur de Kergaradec, the French Consul's, account of the examination of 1875.

"On the morning of the big day, from the third watch on, that is around one o'clock in the morning, the big drum which invites each one to present himself began to be beaten and soon students, intermingled with ordinary spectators, approached the Compound in front of the cordon formed around the outer wall by soldiers holding lances. In the middle of

the fifth watch, towards four or five o'clock in the morning, the examiners in full dress came and installed themselves with their escorts at the different gates. Then began the roll call of the candidates, who were thoroughly searched at the entrance, and who carried with them a small tent of canvas, and mats, cakes, rice, prepared tea, black ink, one or two brushes and a lamp. Everyone once inside, the gates were closed, and the examiners met in the central pavilion of the candidates' enclosure in order to post the subject of the composition. During the afternoon, the candidates who had finished withdrew a few at a time through the central gate, the last ones did not leave the Compound until midnight."

Going to the examination camp with apparatus (bamboo bed, writing box, bamboo tube for examination papers). From an illustration by H Oger in 1905.

Doctor Laureate on his wayhome. From an illustration by H Oger in 1905.

literature and education spread among the court, the mandarins and then among the common people. At one time there were said to be 20,000 schools teaching the Confucian classics in northern Vietnam alone.

The temple and its compound are arranged north-south, and visitors enter at the southern end from Quoc Tu Giam Street. On the pavement two pavilions house stelae bearing the inscription *ha ma* (climb down from your horse), a nice reminder that even the most elevated dignitaries had to proceed on foot. The main **Van Mieu Gate** (Cong Van Mieu Mon) is adorned with 15th-century dragons. Traditionally, the large central gate was opened only on ceremonial occasions. The path leads through the Cong Dai Trung to a second courtyard and the **Van Khue Gac Pavilion** which was built in 1805 and dedicated to the Constellation of Literature. The roof is tiled according to the yin-yang principle.

Beyond lies the **Courtyard of the Stelae** at the centre of which is the rectangular pond or Cieng Thien Quang (Well of Heavenly Clarity). More important are the stelae themselves, 82 in all, on which are recorded the names of 1306 successful examination scholars (*tien si*). Of the 82 that survive (30 are missing) the oldest dates back to 1442 and the most recent to 1779. Each stela is carried on the back of a tortoise, symbol of strength and longevity but they are arranged in no order; three chronological categories, however, can be identified. Fourteen date from the 15th and 16th centuries; they are the smallest and are embellished with floral motifs and yin-yang symbols but not dragons (a royal emblem). Twenty-five stelae are from the 17th century and are ornamented with dragons (by then permitted), pairs of phoenix and other creatures mythical or real. The remaining 43 stelae are of 18th-century origin; they are the largest and are decorated with two stylized dragons, some merging with flame clouds.

Passing the examination was not easy: in 1733, out of some 3000 entrants only eight passed the doctoral examination (*Thai Hoc Sinh*) and became Mandarins – a task that took 35 days. This tradition was begun in 1484 on the instruction of Emperor Le Thanh Tong, and continued through to 1878, during which time 116 examinations were held. The Temple of Literature was not used only for examinations, however: food was also distributed to the poor and infirm, 500 g of rice at a time. In 1880, the French Consul Monsieur de Kergaradec recorded that 22,000 impoverished people came to receive this meagre handout.

Continuing north, the **Dai Thanh Mon** (Great Success Gate) leads on to a courtyard flanked by two buildings which date from 1954, the originals having been destroyed in 1947. These buildings were reserved for 72 disciples of Confucius. Facing is the **Dai Bai Duong** (Great House of Ceremonies), which was built in the 19th century but in the earlier style of the Le Dynasty. The carved wooden friezes with their dragons, phoenix, lotus flowers, fruits, clouds and yin-yang discs are all symbolically charged, depicting the order of the universe and by implication reflecting the god-given hierarchical nature of human society, each in his place. It is not surprising that the communist government has hitherto had reservations about preserving a temple extolling such heretical doctrine. Inside is an altar on which sit statues of Confucius and his closest disciples. Adjoining is the **Dai Thanh Sanctuary** (Great Success Sanctuary), which also contains a statue of Confucius.

To the north once stood the first university in Vietnam, Quoc Tu Giam, which from the 11th to 18th centuries educated first the heir to the throne and later sons of mandarins. It was replaced with a temple dedicated to Confucius' parents and followers, which was itself destroyed in 1947.

Fine Arts Museum

ⓘ *66 Nguyen Thai Hoc St, T4-3733 2131, www.vnfineartsmuseum.org.vn, Tue-Sun 0830-1700, Wed and Sat 0800-2100, 7000d. Free tours in English or French, register in advance, no photography. Restaurant in museum grounds.*

Not far from the northern walls of the Van Mieu Pagoda is the Fine Arts Museum (Bao Tang My Thuat), contained in a large colonial building. The oriental roof was added later when the building was converted to a museum. The ground-floor galleries display pre-20th-century art – from Dongsonian bronze drums to Nguyen Dynasty paintings and sculpture, although many works of this later period are on display in the Museum of Royal Fine Arts in Hué. There are some particularly fine stone Buddhas. The first floor is given over to folk art. There are some lovely works from the Central Highlands and engaging Dong Ho woodblock prints – one block for each colour – and Hang Trong woodblock prints, a single black ink print which is coloured in by hand. There are also some fine lacquer paintings. The top floor contains 20th-century work including some excellent water colours and oil paintings. Contemporary Vietnamese artists are building a significant reputation for their work (see box, Modern Vietnamese Art, page 465). There is a large collection of overtly political work, posters and propaganda (of great interest to historians and specialist collectors), and a collection of ethnic minority clothes is exhibited in the annex.

Vietnam Military History Museum and Citadel

ⓘ *28 Dien Bien Phu St, T4-3733 6453, www.btlsqsvn.org.vn, Tue-Thu, Sat and Sun 0800-1130, 1300-1630, 20,000d, camera use, 5000d, ATM and Highlands Coffee Café on site.*

A five-minute walk east from the Fine Arts Museum, is the Military History Museum (Bao Tang Quan Doi). Tanks, planes and artillery fill the courtyard. Symbolically, an untouched Mig-21 stands at the museum entrance while wreckage of B-52s, F1-11s and Q2Cs is piled up at the back. The museum illustrates battles and episodes in Vietnam's fight for independence from the struggles with China (there is a good display of the Battle of Bach Dang River of AD 938) through to the resistance to the French and the Battle of Dien Bien Phu (illustrated by a good model). Inevitably, of course, there are lots of photographs and exhibits of the American War and although much is self-evident, unfortunately a lot of the explanations are in Vietnamese only.

In the precincts of the museum is the Cot Co, a flag tower, raised up on three platforms. Built in 1812, it is the only substantial part of the original citadel still standing. There are good views over Hanoi from the top. The walls of the **citadel** were destroyed by the French in 1894 to 1897, presumably as they symbolized the power of the Vietnamese emperors. The French were highly conscious of the projection of might, power and authority through large structures, which helps explain their own remarkable architectural legacy. Other remaining parts of the citadel are in the hands of the Vietnamese army and out of bounds to visitors. Across the road from the museum's front entrance is a **statue of Lenin**.

The North Gate of the Citadel is on Phan Dinh Phung St and can be visited, 10,000d. The new Kinh Thien Palace is due to open on Hoang Dieu St. Further south on Hoang Dieu is the Doan Mon Gate (free, 0800-1130, 1400-1630) where you can nose at the previously off-limits citadel exploration and get a new view of Cot Co and the citadel complex from the roof. The citadel was named a UNESCO World Heritage Site in August 2010.

North of the Old City

North of the Old City is **Ho Truc Bach (White Silk Lake)**. Truc Bach Lake was created in the 17th century by building a causeway across the southeast corner of Ho Tay. This was the site of the 11th-century **Royal Palace** which had, so it is said, 'a hundred roofs'. All that is left is the terrace of Kinh Thien with its dragon staircase, and a number of stupas, bridges, gates and small pagodas.

At the southwest corner of the lake, on the intersection of Hung Vuong, Quan Thanh and Thanh Nien streets is the **Quan Thanh Pagoda** ①*2000d*, originally built in the early 11th century in honour of Huyen Thien Tran Vo (a genie) but since much remodelled. Despite renovation, it is still very beautiful. The large bronze bell was cast in 1677.

To the east of here the Long Bien and Chuong Duong bridges cross the Red River. The former of these two bridges was built as a road and rail bridge by Daydé & Pillé of Paris and named **Paul Doumer Bridge** after the Governor General of the time. Construction was begun in 1899 and it was opened by Emperor Thanh Thai on 28 February 1902. Today it is used by trains, bicycles, motorbikes and pedestrians. Over 1.5 km in length, it was the only river crossing in existence during the Vietnam War and suffered repeated attacks from US planes, only to be quickly repaired. The Chuong Duong Bridge was completed at the beginning of the 1980s.

The much larger **Ho Tay (West Lake)** was originally a meander in the Red River. The **Tran Quoc Pagoda**, an attractive brick-red building, can be found on an islet on the east shores of the lake, linked to the causeway by a walkway. It was originally built on the banks of the Red River before being transferred to its present site by way of an intermediate location. The pagoda contains a stela dated 1639 recounting its unsettled history. Just south, on a white boat is a **Highlands Coffee** café. Pedaloes are available for hire (US$2.50 per hour; motorboat US$16 per 20 minutes). Opposite, facing Truc Bach Lake, is a monument recording the shooting down of USAF's John (now US Senator) McCain on 26 October 1967. It reveals the pilot falling out of the sky, knees bent.

A few kilometres north, on the tip of a promontory, stands **Tay Ho Pagoda**, notable chiefly for its setting. It is reached along a narrow lane lined with stalls selling fruit, roses and paper votives and a dozen restaurants serving giant snails with *bun oc* (noodles) and fried shrimp cakes. Dominating it is an enormous bronze bell held by a giant dragon hook supported by concrete dragons and two elephants; notice the realistic glass eyes of the elephants.

However, West Lake is fast losing its unique charm as development spreads northwards. The nouveau riche of Hanoi are rapidly turning the area into a middle-class suburb and new restaurants and bars have clustered around Xuan Dieu Street. New houses go up in an unplanned and uncoordinated sprawl. Nguyen Ngoc Khoi, director of the Urban Planning Institute in Hanoi, estimates that the area of the lake has shrunk by 20%, from 500 ha to 400 ha, as residents and hotel and office developers have reclaimed land. The lake is also suffering encroachment by water hyacinths, which are fed by organic pollutants from factories (especially a tannery) and untreated sewage. The view from Nghi Tam Road, which runs along the Red River dyke, presents a contrasting spectacle of sprawling houses interspersed with the remaining plots of land which are intensively and attractively cultivated market gardens supplying the city with flowers and vegetables.

The Trung sisters

Vietnamese history honours a number of heroines, of whom the Trung sisters are among the most revered. At the beginning of the Christian era, the Lac Lords of Vietnam began to agitate against Chinese control over their lands. Trung Trac, married to the Lac Lord Thi Sach, was apparently of a 'brave and fearless disposition' and encouraged her husband and the other lords to rise up against the Chinese in AD 40. The two sisters often fought while pregnant, apparently putting on gold-plated armour over their enlarged bellies. Although an independent kingdom was created for a short time, ultimately the uprising proved fruitless; a large Chinese army defeated the rebels in AD 43, and eventually captured Trung Trac and her sister Trung Nhi, executing them and sending their heads to the Han court at Lo-yang. An alternative story of their death has it that the sisters threw themselves into the Hat Giang River to avoid being captured, and turned into stone statues. These were washed ashore and placed in Hanoi's Hai Ba Trung Temple for worship.

Museum of Ethnology and B-52 memorials

ⓘ*Some distance west of the city centre in Cau Giay District (Nguyen Van Huyen Rd), T4-3756 2193, www.vme.org.vn, Tue-Sun 0830-1730, 25,000d, photography 50,000d, tour guide, 50,000d. Catch the No 14 minibus from Dinh Tien Hoang St, north of Hoan Kiem Lake, to the Nghia Tan stop; turn right and walk down Hoang Quoc Viet St for 1 block, before turning right at the Petrolimex station down Nguyen Van Huyen; the museum is down this street, on the left. Alternatively take a taxi. Branch of Baguette & Chocolat bakery on site.*

The museum opened in November 1997 in a modern, purpose-built structure. The collection here of some 25,000 artefacts, 15,000 photographs and documentaries of practices and rituals is excellent and, more to the point, is attractively and informatively presented with labels in Vietnamese, English and French. It displays the material culture (textiles, musical instruments, jewellery, tools, baskets and the like) of the majority Kinh people as well as Vietnam's 53 other designated minority peoples. While much is historical, the museum is also attempting to build up its contemporary collection. There is a shop attached to the museum and in the grounds of the museum, ethnic minorities' homes have been recreated.

On the routes out to the Ethnology Museum are two B-52 memorials. The remains of downed B-52s have been hawked around Hanoi over many years but seem to have found a final resting place at the **Bao Tang Chien Tang B-52 (B-52 Museum)** ⓘ *157 Doi Can St, free*. This curious place is not really a museum but a military hardware graveyard, but this doesn't matter because what everyone wants to do is walk over the wings and tail of a shattered B-52, and the B-52 in question lies scattered around the yard. As visitors to Vietnamese museums have by now come to expect, any enemy objects are literally heaped up as junk while the 'heroic' Vietnamese pieces are painted, tended for and carefully signed with the names of whichever heroic unit fought in them. Here we have anti-aircraft guns, the devastating SAMs that wreaked so much havoc on the USAF and a MIG21. Curiously the signs omit to mention the fact that all this hardware was made in Russia. The size and strength of the B-52 is simply incredible and needs to be seen to be believed.

On Hoang Hoa Tham Street, between Nos 55 and 57, a sign points 100 m down an alley to the wreckage of a B-52 bomber sticking up out of the pond-like Huu Tiep Lake. There's a plaque on the wall stating that at 2305 on 27 December 1972, Battalion 72 of Regiment 285 shot down the plane. At the time Huu Tiep was a flower village and the lake a lot bigger.

South of Hanoi

Down Hué Street is the hub of motorcycle sales, parts and repairs. Off this street, for example along Hoa Ma, Tran Nhan Tong and Thinh Yen, are numerous stalls and shops, each specializing in a single type of product – TVs, electric fans, bicycle parts and so on. It is a fascinating area to explore. At the intersection of Thinh Yen and Pho 332, people congregate to sell new and second-hand bicycles, as well as bicycle parts.

Not far away is the venerable **Den Hai Ba Trung** (**Hai Ba Trung Temple**) ① *open 1st and 15th of each lunar month, 0600-1800, free*, the temple of the two Trung Sisters – overlooking a lake. The temple was built in 1142, but like others, has been restored on a number of occasions. It contains crude statues of the Trung sisters, Trung Trac and Trung Nhi (see box, page 66), which are carried in procession once a year during February.

Further south still from the Hai Ba Trung, is another pagoda – **Chua Lien Phai**. This quiet pagoda, which can be found just off Bach Mai Street, was built in 1732, although it has since been restored.

Around Hanoi

Compared with Ho Chi Minh City and the south, Hanoi and its surrounds are rich in places of interest. Not only is the landscape more varied and attractive, but the 1000-year-old history of Hanoi has generated dozens of sights of architectural appeal, many of which can be visited on a day trip.

Co Loa Citadel

① *16 km north of Hanoi. Drive north up Highway 3, Co Loa is signposted to the east.*

In the third-century BC Co Loa Citadel was the region's capital, built by King An Duong with walls in three concentric rings; the outer ring is 8 km in circumference. It is an important Bronze Age site and thousands of arrow heads and three bronze ploughshares have been excavated here. Today there is little to see as electricity sub-stations and farms have obliterated much of archaeological interest.

Hung Kings' Temples

① *South of Yen Bai and approximately 100 km northwest of Hanoi near the industrial town of Viet Tri in Vinh Phu Province; turn off Highway 2 about 12 km north of Viet Tri; it's a morning or afternoon excursion by car from Hanoi.*

The Hung Kings' Temples (Phong Chau) are popular with Vietnamese visitors especially during the **Hung Kings' Festival**. In purely topographical terms the site is striking, an almost perfectly circular hill rising unexpectedly out of the monotonous Red River floodplain with two lakes at the bottom. Given its peculiar physical setting it is easy to understand how the site acquired its mythical reputation as the birthplace of the Viet people and why the Hung Vuong kings chose it as the capital of their kingdom.

In this place, myth and historical fact have become intertwined. Legend has it that the Viet people are the product of the union of King Lac Long Quan, a dragon, and his fairy wife Au Co. Au Co gave birth to a pouch containing 100 eggs that hatched 50 boys and 50 girls. Husband and wife decided to separate in order to populate the land and propagate the race, so half the children followed their mother to the highlands and half remained with their father on the plains, giving rise to the Montagnards and lowland peoples of Vietnam. Historically easier to verify is the story of the Hung kings (Hung Vuong) who built a temple in order to commemorate the legendary progenitors of the Vietnamese people.

A new **Hung Kings' Museum** ⓘ *0800-1130, 1300-1600*, was opened in mid-2010 and displays interesting items excavated from the province. Exhibits include pottery, jewellery, fish hooks, arrow heads and axe heads (dated 1000-1300 BC), but of particular interest are the bronze drums dating from the Dongsonian period. The Dongsonian was a transitional period between the neolithic and bronze ages and the drums are thought to originate from around the fifth to the third centuries BC. Photographs show excavation in the 1960s when these items were uncovered.

Ascending the hill, a track leads to a **memorial to Ho Chi Minh**. Ho said he hoped that people would come from all over Vietnam to see this historic site. Nearby is the **Low Temple** dedicated to Au Co, mother of the country and supposedly the site where the 100 eggs were produced. At the back of the temple is a statue of the Buddha of a thousand arms and a thousand eyes. Continuing up the hill is the **Middle Temple** where Prince Lang Lieu was crowned seventh Hung king and where the kings would play chess and discuss pressing affairs of state. Prince Lang Lieu was (like the English King Alfred) something of a dab hand in the kitchen and his most enduring creation is a pair of cakes, *banh trung* and *banh day*, which to this day remain popular, eaten at Tet. This temple has three altars and attractive murals.

Further on, towards the top of the hill is the **oath stone** on which the 18th Hung king, Thuc Phan, swore to defend the country from its enemies. Adjacent is the **Top Temple** dating from the 15th century. The roof is adorned with dragons and gaudily painted mural warriors stand guard outside. A not particularly ancient drum hangs from the ceiling but smoke rising from burning incense on the three altars helps add to the antiquity of the setting. Here it was that the kings would supplicate God for peace and prosperity.

Steps lead from the back right-hand side of this temple down the hill to the mausoleum of the sixth Hung king. These steps then continue down the far side of the hill to the **Well**

Hung King's Temples

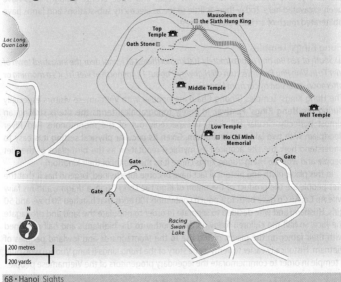

Temple built in memory of the last princess of the Hung Dynasty. Inside is a well in the reflection of which this girl used to comb her hair. Today worshippers throw money in and, it is said, they even drink the water. Turn right to get back to the car park.

Perfume Pagoda
ⓘ *30,000d entrance plus 210,000d for the boat (maximum 4 people). Taking a tour is the best way to get here.*

The Perfume Pagoda (Chua Huong or Chua Huong Tich) is 60 km southwest of Hanoi. A sampan takes visitors along the Yen River, a diverting 4-km ride through a flooded landscape to the Mountain of the Perfume Traces. From here it is a 3-km hike up the mountain to the cool, dark cave wherein lies the Perfume Pagoda. Dedicated to Quan Am (see page 61), it is one of a number of shrines and towers built among limestone caves and is regarded as one of the most beautiful spots in Vietnam. The stone statue of Quan Am in the principal pagoda was carved in 1793 after Tay Son rebels had stolen and melted down its bronze predecessor to make cannon balls. Emperor Le Thanh Tong (1460-1497) described it as "Nam Thien de nhat dong" ("foremost cave under the Vietnamese sky"). It is a popular pilgrimage spot, particularly during the festival months of March and April.

Pagodas around Hanoi
Tay Phuong Pagoda is about 6 km from the Thay Pagoda in the village of Thac Xa. It may date back to the eighth century, although the present structure was rebuilt in 1794. Constructed of ironwood, it is sited at the summit of a hill and is approached by means of a long stairway. The pagoda is best known for its collection – all 74 of them – of 18th-century *arhat* statues (statues of former monks). They are thought to be among the best examples of the woodcarver's art from the period.

   Thay Pagoda (Master's Pagoda), also known as Thien Phuc Tu Pagoda, lies 40 km southwest of Hanoi in the village of Sai Son, in Ha Son Binh Province. Built in the 11th century, the pagoda honours a herbalist, Dao Hanh, who lived in Sai Son village. It is said that he was reborn as the son of Emperor Le Thanh Tong after he and his wife had come to pray here. The pagoda complex is divided into three sections. The outer section is used for ceremonies, the middle is a Buddhist temple, while the inner part is dedicated to the herbalist. The temple has some fine statues of Buddhas, as well as an array of demons. Water puppet shows are performed during holidays and festivals on a stage built in the middle of the pond at the front of the pagoda (see page 83). Dao Hanh, who was a water puppet enthusiast, is said to have created the pond. It is spanned by two bridges built at the beginning of the 17th century. There are good views from the nearby Sai Son Hill – a path leads up from the pagoda.

Handicraft villages
Many tour operators arrange excursions to villages just outside of Hanoi including Van Phuc, where silk is produced, Bat Trang, where ceramics and bricks are made, and Le Mat, a snake village; here visitors can try eating snake meat.

Further afield
Cuc Phuong National Park (see page 167 for details) is about 160 km south of Hanoi and can be visited as a day trip or over-nighter from Hanoi or as an excursion from Ninh Binh. Other possible day trips are excursions to **Hoa Binh** (see page 101) and **Mai Chau** (see page 102) **Haiphong** (see page 146) **Ninh Binh** (see page 164), **Hoa Lu** (see page 165), **Tam Coc** (see page 166) and **Phat Diem Cathedral** (see page 166).

Hotel prices
LL over US$200 L US$151-200 AL US$101-150
A US$66-100 B US$46-65 C US$31-45
D US$21-30 E US$12-20 F US$7-11
G US$6 and under

Restaurant prices
††† over US$12 †† US$6-12 † under US$6
See pages 26-31 for further information.

⊙ Sleeping

There has been a spate of hotel building and renovation in recent years. There's still a lack of good, attractive 3- to 4-star hotels in Hanoi. The more expensive hotels offer a full range of services. Cheaper hotels tend to be found in the Old Quarter. Old Quarter buildings are tightly packed and rooms small, sometimes without windows. Hotels in this area offer the best value for money, most budget travellers head straight for this area. Many hotels now offer Wi-Fi, if not in the room, in the lobby. Watch out for scams. Tourists are often told by taxi drivers that their hotel is full or has closed and are taken to another hotel where they will receive commission. Have a booking in advance and be insistent. Readers may read reviews of the Green Mango. We cannot recommend it. We were shown one room with a dirty bathroom and duvet; the second room's bathroom featured a sink overflowing with green candle wax. Breakfast service was slow and other customers complained at the service continuously. We have received other reports of unsatisfactory service too.

Hoan Kiem Lake and Central Hanoi
p51, maps p46 and p52
LL-L Sofitel Legend Metropole Hanoi, 15 Ngo Quyen St, T4-3826 6919, www. accorhotelsasia.com. The only hotel in its class in central Hanoi. The French-colonial-style cream building with green shutters is beautifully and lusciously furnished

and exudes style. The historic **Metropole** wing contains the original more classically stylish rooms while the new wing is named the **Opera** with rooms exhibiting a modern flair. It boasts a diversity of bars and restaurants including the new Italian Angelina restaurant. **Le Beaulieu** is one of the finest restaurants in Hanoi; a pianist plays nightly at Le Club bar. The new **Le Spa du Metropole** is seriously chic. There's also a business centre, cluster of luxury shops and smart deli, and a small pool with attractive poolside **Bamboo Bar**. The hotel has retained most of its business despite competition from newer business hotels away from the city centre and remains a hub of activity and the classiest hotel address in the country. The Graham Greene suite is sumptuous Indochine chic.
A Cinnamon Hotel, 26 Au Trieu St, T4-3993 8430, http://cinnamonhotel.net. This is a cute, stylish hotel with lovely, comfortable rooms. However, the regular bong of the cathedral bell is disturbing so you may wish to avoid the cute balconied rooms overlooking the cathedral square and opt for a back room with a lesser view. Breakfast service is slow and watch for overcharging on laundry. Little English is spoken.
A Golden Lotus Hotel, 32 Hang Trong St, T4-3928 8583, www.goldenlotushotel.com. vn. On Hang Trong street, home to many galleries, the **Golden Lotus** has a series of smart, attractive rooms from standard single to deluxe. Balcony rooms afford a better view but anything facing the street is bound to be noisier.
A-B Galaxy, 1 Phan Dinh Phung St, T4-3828 2888, www.tctgroup.com.vn. Well-run 3-star business hotel (built in 1918) with 50 carpeted rooms and full accessories including the all-important bedside reading lights, which too many expensive hotels forget.
B Church Hotel, 9 Nha Tho St, T4-3928 8118, www.churchhotel.com.vn. Markets

itself as a boutique hotel, which it isn't. It has 16 small rooms with wooden floors and attractive bed linen with nice en suite bathrooms. Ask for a room away from the street to avoid the noise.

B Hong Ngoc, 30-34 Hang Manh St, T4-3828 5053, www.hongngochotel.com. This is a real find. A small, family-run hotel with comfortable rooms and huge bathrooms with bathtubs. It's spotlessly clean throughout and run by cheerful and helpful staff. Breakfast is included. This Hong Ngoc has put its prices up but there are 2 other cheaper Hong Ngocs in the Old Quarter.

B Joseph's Hotel, 5 Au Trieu St, T4-3938 1048, www.josephshotel.com. Right near St Joseph's Cathedral, on Au Trieu St – a cosy street filled with good cafés, salons and souvenir shops – Joseph's Hotel is small, with just 10 rooms. However small can equal cosy, and it does here. This mid-range hotel has Wi-Fi in all rooms, as well as standards such as a/c, cable and mini-bar. Breakfast is included in the price.

C Gold Spring Hotel, 22 Nguyen Huu Huan St, T4-3926 3057, www.goldspringhotel.com.vn. On the edge of the Old Quarter. 22 fine rooms that are attractively decorated. Breakfast and free internet included.

D Freedom, 57 Hang Trong St, T4-3826 7119. freedomhotel@hn.vnn.vn. Not far from Hoan Kiem lake and the cathedral. 11 spacious rooms with desks. Some have bathtubs; those without have small bathrooms. Friendly family. Breakfast not included on the cheaper rate.

D Hang Trong, 56 Hang Trong St, T4-3825 +1346, thiencotravelvn@yahoo.com. A/c and hot water (showers only), a few unusual and quite decent rooms set back from the road, either on a corridor or in a courtyard. The ones that don't overlook the courtyard are dark and airless. Very convenient position for every part of town. Internet and booking office for Sinh Tourist tours. Staff are very helpful.

D Hong Ngoc 3, 39 Hang Bac St, T4-3926 0322, www.hongngochotel.com. Some staff

here are exceptionally helpful, others are not. A real mixed bag. Rooms are clean and comfortable with TVs, a/c and bathtubs in the bathrooms and it's in a great central location and surprisingly quiet. You may want to pass on the breakfast.

D-E Hoa Linh, 35 Hang Bo St, T4-3824 3887, hoalinhhotel@hn.vnn.vn. Right in the centre of the 36 Streets area, attractive lobby and willing staff. 17 rooms, price includes breakfast.

D-F Hanoi Backpackers' Hostel, 48 Ngo Huyen St, T4-3828 5372 (last-minute reservations T1800 1552 toll free), www.hanoibackpackershostel.com. Dorm rooms (with bedside lights, lockers and a/c) and double suites in a house that belonged to a Brazilian ambassador. This is a friendly and busy place to stay with plenty of opportunities to meet other travellers and gather advice. Breakfast, internet, tea and coffee and luggage store is included. Don't miss the BBQs on the roof terrace and the Sunday sessions. There is also a busy bar. Many kinds of tours, including more off-the-beaten-track options such as island stays near Ha Long Bay, can be arranged.

E Mai Phuong, 32 Hang Be St, T4-3092 63269, www.maiphuonghotel.com. Fan and a/c rooms that are slightly cramped, but the place is friendly and clean.

E Nam Phuong, 16 Bao Khanh St, T4-3825 8030. Pleasant position near Hoan Kiem Lake, 9 a/c rooms with soundproofing. Rooms at the back are cheaper. Breakfast and free internet included.

E Thuy Nga, 24C Ta Hien St, T4-3826 6053, thuyngahotel@hotmail.com. Just 6 rooms. A/c, hot water, cramped, but friendly with good English and good value. Wi-Fi included.

E-G Real Darling Café, 33 Hang Quat St, T4-3826 9386, darling_cafe@hotmail.com. Travellers' café which has 16 rooms, though only 10 have a/c. Food is available, excellent English is spoken and visas for both overseas and extensions for within Vietnam can be organized. Wi-Fi.

F My Lan, 70 Hang Bo St, T4-3824 5510, hotelmylan@yahoo.com. Go through the dentist's surgery where an elderly French-speaking dentist has 10 rooms to rent, a/c or fans. Rather tightly packed but light and breezy; nice apartment with kitchen and terrace, US$400 a month. Super-friendly family. Recommended.

F Ngoc Diep, 83 Thuoc Bac St, through the Chinese pharmacy, T4-3825 0020, thugiangguesthouse@yahoo.com. Cheaper rooms have fan; more expensive rooms a/c. All rooms have hot water and TV, and free internet; breakfast can be included. Bus station and railway station pick-up, popular and friendly. Long-stay discounts available.

South of Hoan Kiem Lake *p56, maps p46 and p52*

LL Hilton Hanoi Opera, 1 Le Thanh Tong St, T4-3933 0500, www1.hilton.com. Opened in 1999 and built adjacent to, and architecturally sympathetically with, the Opera House. It is a splendid building and provides the highest levels of service and hospitality. But whereas the **Metropole** is normally busy the **Hanoi Opera** is often quieter.

LL-AL Movenpick, 83A Ly Thuong Kiet St, T4-3822 2800, www.moevenpick-hotels.com. Formerly the **Guoman** this Swiss-run hotel chain is housed in an attractive building on Ly Thuong Kiet street, in the middle of Hanoi's business district. Rooms are smart and stylish.

L Sunway Hotel, 19 Pham Dinh Ho St, T4-3971 3888, www.sunway-hotel.com. This extremely comfortable, quiet and friendly hotel is located just south of the lake and close to **Hanoi Gourmet**, which is an attraction in itself, see Eating, below. The breakfast is good and varied and the fact that you can control all the room's lighting from a panel by your bed is a huge plus. There are 145 rooms in this business hotel.

L-AL Melia Hanoi, 44B Ly Thuong Kiet St, T4-3934 3343, www.meliahanoi.com. A huge tower block in Central Hanoi. Well-appointed rooms but not a welcoming feel and a small swimming pool. There's an ATM and **Thai Airways** office on site. Popular

venue for international conferences and national days held by many embassies, usually with excellent food.

AL Zephyr, 4 Ba Trieu St, T4-3934 1256, www.zephyrhotel.com.vn. Popular among business travellers, **Zephyr** is under a minute's walk to the lake and sits at the end of Ba Trieu street, which heads south to the city's interesting Hai Ba Trung district, home to Hanoi's only international-standard cinema. There is a café and restaurant downstairs. Special deals are offered in the low season.

AL-A De Syloia, 17A Tran Hung Dao St, T4-3824 5346, www.desyloia.com. Very attractive and friendly small boutique, business hotel with 33 rooms and suites, a business centre and gym in a good central location. The popular **Cay Cau** restaurant specializes in Vietnamese dishes and the daily set-lunch is excellent value.

AL-A Hoa Binh, 27 Ly Thuong Kiet St, T4-3825 3315, www.hoabinhhotel.com. Old but renovated hotel with quite large rooms. **Le Splendide** French restaurant attached.

A-B Army Hotel, 33C Pham Ngu Lao St, T4-3825 2896, armyhotel@fpt.vn. Owned and run by the Army this is a surprisingly pleasant and attractive hotel. Set around a decent-sized swimming pool, which some people worry about swimming in, it is quiet and comfortable. The hotel has a total of 78 a/c rooms and a restaurant. Reception could be more welcoming though.

B-C Eden Hanoi, 78 Tho Nhuom St, T4-3942 3273, www.edenhanoihotel.com. Good location but small rooms; worth paying more for the suites. Nevertheless popular and handy for **Luna d'Autunno** restaurant.

E Artist Hotel, 22A Hai Ba Trung St, T4-3824 4433, artist_hotel@yahoo.com.This small hotel is set above the pleasant and quiet courtyard of the **Hanoi Cinematique**. Some of the rooms, all with a/c, are a little dark but the price is great for such a central and unusual location. Although there is no breakfast you can always snack at the **Cinemateque** instead.

E Cay Xoai (Mango), formerly the Railway Hotel, 118 Le Duan St, T4-3942 3704. Adjacent to the station, *bia hoi* and *pho* stalls in the compound. Expensive for what it is. Busy, noisy area but quite friendly with 35 rooms. Reception can be indifferent.

Outer Hanoi *p65, map p46*

Hanoi's relatively small central district means that some new office complexes and hotels have tended to open a short distance out of the centre.

LL InterContinental Hanoi Westlake, 1A Nghi Tam, Tay Ho District, T4-3829 3939, www.intercontinental.com. One of the newer 5-stars in the city, the InterContinental sits on West Lake, almost beside the Sheraton. Rooms are large and decorated using traditional Vietnamese elements. The bar and pool areas facing the lake are lovely, especially in early evening when *den choi* (fire-powered paper balloons) drift across the sky above the water. Cocktails are good but prices are international standard.

LL Nikko Hanoi, 84 Tran Nhan Tong St, T4-3822 3535, www.hotelnikkohanoi.com. Rather a forbidding appearance from the outside but a tranquil marble lobby. Somewhat impersonal but a nice pool and good Japanese restaurant. Particularly popular with Japanese businessmen.

LL Sheraton Hotel, K5 Nghi Tam, 11 Xuan Dieu, Tay Ho District, T4-3719 9000, www.sheraton.com/hanoi. Opened in early 2004, the Sheraton is many miles out of town on a scenic spot overlooking the West Lake. Its position will attract some but probably prove awkward for many visitors. It is opulent and luxurious and rooms are fully equipped. The swimming pool backs onto a lawn that leads down to the lakeshore.

LL-L Hanoi Daewoo, 360 Kim Ma St, Ba Dinh District, T4-3831 5000, www.hanoi-daewoo.com. Giant hotel with 411 rooms and suites opened in 1996. Adjoining apartment complex and office tower. The hotel is one of Vietnam's most luxurious

with a large pool, shops and 4 restaurants; Chinese, Japanese, Italian and international. The hotel has also accumulated a large collection of Vietnamese modern art. Popular with large busloads of well-heeled Koreans and surrounded by Korean restaurants, many not very good.

LL-AL Sofitel Plaza Hanoi, 1 Thanh Nien St, T4-3823 8888, www.sofitel.com. The 2nd Sofitel in town, it lacks the cache of the **Metropole** but is in an equally good location, by Truc Bach Lake. Restaurants, galleries, wine cellars and rice wine restaurants are all within walking distance. The rooftop has one of the best views in town, but the prices, music and garish carpet do leave something to be desired. The 322-room hotel offers Italian and Chinese restaurants, excellent business facilities and a large all-weather swimming pool with retractable roof.

❶ Eating

Hanoi has Western-style coffee bars, restaurants and watering holes. It also has a good number of excellent Vietnamese restaurants catering both to local people and visitors from overseas. Korean and Japanese food is found everywhere thanks to huge expat populations, see box page 74.

In short, there is a super-abundance of food in Hanoi: shortage of time means most people will only sample a few of the places recommended below.

A few words of caution: dog (*thit chó* or *thit cay*) is a delicacy in the north – "who can resist a steaming bowl of broth with a pair of dogs paws?" demands one restaurateur – but dog is usually served only in specialist outlets – usually shacks on the edge of town – so is unlikely to be ordered inadvertently.

Eating on the street is one of the joys of a trip to Hanoi.

Bites but no bark in a Vietnamese restaurant

Quang Vinh's restaurant was the ideal place for the ordeal to come. The palm-thatched house near the West Lake, on the outskirts of the Vietnamese capital Hanoi, was far from the accusing eyes of fellow Englishmen.

It was dark outside. At one table, a Vietnamese couple were contentedly finishing their meal. At another, a man smoked a bamboo pipe. A television at the end of the room showed mildly pornographic Chinese videos.

But then came the moment of truth: could an Englishman eat a dog? Could he do so without his stomach rebelling, without his thoughts turning to labradors snoozing by Kentish fireplaces, Staffordshire bull terriers collecting sticks for children, and Pekinese perched on the laps of grandmothers?

One Englishman could: I ate roast dog, dog liver, barbecued dog with herbs and a deliciously spicy dog sausage, for it is the custom to dine on a selection of dog dishes when visiting a dog restaurant. The meat tastes faintly gamey. It is eaten with noodles, crispy rice-flour pancakes, fresh ginger, spring onions, apricot leaves and, for cowardly Englishmen, plenty of beer.

I had been inspired to undergo this traumatic experience – most un-British unless one is stranded with huskies on a polar ice cap – by a conversation earlier in the week with Do Duc Dinh, a Vietnamese economist, and Nguyen Thanh Tam, my official interpreter and guide.

They were much more anxious to tell me about the seven different ways of cooking a dog, and how unlucky it was to eat dog on the first five days of the month, than they were to explain Vietnam's economic reforms. "My favourite," began Tam, "is minced intestines roasted in the fire with green beans and onions." He remembered proudly how anti-Vietnamese protesters in Thailand in the 1980s had carried placards saying "Dog-eaters go home!"

During the Vietnam War, he said, a famous Vietnamese professor had discovered that wounded soldiers recovered much more quickly when their doctors prescribed half a kilogram of dog meat a day. Dinh insisted I should eat dog in Hanoi rather than Saigon. "I went to the south and ate dog, but they don't know how to cook it like we do in the north," he said. I asked where the dogs came from. "People breed it, then it becomes the family pet." And then they eat it? "Yes," he said with a laugh. I told myself that the urban British, notorious animal lovers that they are, recoil particularly at the idea of eating dogs only because most of them never see the living versions of the pigs, cows, sheep and chickens that they eat in meat-form every day. And the French, after all, eat horses. Resolutely unsentimental, we put aside our dog dinner and went to Vinh's kitchen. Two wire cages were on the floor; there was one large dog in the first and four small dogs in the second. Two feet away, a cauldron of dog stew steamed and bubbled. Vinh told us about his flourishing business. The dogs are transported from villages in a nearby province. A 10 kg dog costs him about 120,000d, or just over US$10. At the end of the month – peak dog-eating time – his restaurant gets through about 30 dogs a day. The restaurant, he said, was popular with Vietnamese, Koreans and Japanese. Squeamish Westerners were sometimes tricked into eating dog by the Vietnamese friends, who would entertain them at the restaurant and tell them afterwards what it was they had so heartily consumed.

Source: Extracted from an article by Victor Mallet, *The Financial Times*.

Hoan Kiem Lake and Central Hanoi
p51, maps p46 and p52

Club de l'Oriental, 22 Tong Dan St, T4-3826 8801. From the same people who run **Emperor**, this newer iteration serves traditional Vietnamese in a very high-end manner: don't expect to escape without a lighter wallet. Though the setting is gorgeous, and the downstairs wine cellar and dining area cosy, you may ask, at some stage, why you are paying several times as much for competently rendered, high-end versions of quite usual Vietnamese cuisine.

Hanoi Press Club, 59A Ly Thai To St, T4-3934 0888, www.hanoi-pressclub.com. This is an odd building with some style inside directly behind the **Sofitel Metropole Hotel**. **The Restaurant** has remained one of the most popular dining experiences in Hanoi. The dining room is luxuriously furnished with polished, dark wood floors and print-lined walls. The food is superb and there's a fine wine list. Service has slipped though. **The Terrace**, a large outdoor space, hosts live music events and at the time of writing is still holding big parties popular with every hard-networking local and expat in town the 1st Fri of each month. The **Library Bar** stocks a good range of cigars and whiskies.

Lá, 25 Ly Quoc Su St, T4-3928 8933. This attractive green and cream building houses a restaurant serving up marvellous Vietnamese and international food. Behind the modest exterior is one of the best-loved restaurants in the city. Chef Wayne Sjothun's menu offers traditional Vietnamese as well as a range of unpretentious fusion meals and daily specials. The bistro atmosphere is comfortable and the wine list excellent. The small bar is, on close inspection, surprisingly well stocked.

Le Beaulieu, 15 Ngo Quyen St (in the **Metropole Hotel**), T4-3826 6919. A good French and international restaurant open for breakfast, lunch and dinner; last orders 2200. Its Sun brunch buffet is regarded as

Wine & Dine

Hanoi's Hot Spot

Hanoi's favorite dining and social venue offers

- **Free WIFI throughout the Club**
- **Formal Dining**
  Fantastic wine list
  Superb steak menu
  Seasonal dishes
- **Casual Dining & Bar Lounge**
  Hearty deli menu
  Lunch buffet & daily specials
  Happy Hour everyday
- **Thirsty Thursdays**
  2 for 1 drinks
  Free appetizers
  Live Music
- **Friday Nights on the Terrace**
  1st Friday of the month
  Free entrance for all
  Live band & DJ party

There's always something happening at the Press Club!

Corner of 59A Ly Thai To & 12 Ly Dao Thanh, Hanoi
Tel: (84-4) 3934 0888 - Fax: (84-4) 3934 0899
www.hanoi-pressclub.com

PRESS
Club

one of the best in Asia. A great selection of French seafood, oysters, prawns, cold and roast meats and cheese. The buffet is good enough that even *Forbes* magazine waxed ecstatic over it. Famous chef Didier Corlou has left to open his own restaurants (see **Verticale**, page 78) and **Madame Hien**, below, but remains a culinary consultant.

♕♕-♕♕ Club Opera, 59 Ly Thai To St, T4-3824 6950, clubopera@fpt.vn. 1100-1400, 1730-2230. Good restaurant with extensive Vietnamese menu in the attractive setting of a restored French villa. The menu is varied, the tables are beautifully laid and the food is appealingly presented.

♕♕-♕ Green Tangerine, 48 Hang Be St, T4-3825 1286, greentangerine@vnn.vn. This is a gorgeous French restaurant with a lovely spiral staircase, wafting fans, tasselled curtain cords and abundant glassware. It's a Hanoi stalwart in a lovely 1928 house in the centre of the Old Quarter serving fusion and Vietnamese food. Recommended dining areas are the courtyard and downstairs; upstairs can lack atmosphere. Many have decried the drop in quality but it remains popular with the tourist crowd. However, the set lunch is still excellent and good value. The cheese platter is intriguing and delicious.

♕♕♕-♕ Madame Hien, 15 Chan Cam St, T4-3938 1588, madame.hien@didiercorlou. com. 1100-2200. Closed during Tet. An addition to the Didier Corlou empire, this charming restaurant is in the former Spanish embassy building and named after Corlou's wife's grandmother. Its small proportions encourage intimate dining. Tasty and intricate Vietnamese fare. You won't go hungry. Exceptional service.

♕♕ Baan Thai, 3B Cha Ca St, T4-3828 8588. 1030-1400, 1630-2200. Longstanding Thai restaurant. Food is good, service decent to indifferent, and the atmosphere sometimes like a shut-down shopping mall before the zombies attack.

♕♕♕ Khazana, 1C Tong Dan St, T4-3934 5657. A longstanding Indian restaurant once famous for its amiable and helpful owner. It has

since changed hands but the large menu of south and north Indian dishes remains top notch. All curries come served in traditional copper bowls, and breads arrive at the table soft and piping hot. Hugely popular with the often unseen Indian expatriate crowd.

♕♕ Pepperonis, 31 Bao Khanh St, T4-3928 7030. Mon-Sat 1130-1330. A popular pizza and pasta chain, marketed to Vietnamese more than foreigners, right in the heart of a busy bar/restaurant area. Cheap and cheerful. Known for its buffet lunch.

♕♕-♕ 69 Restaurant Bar, 69 Ma May St, T4-3926 1720. 0700-2300. Set in a nicely restored 19th-century house in the Old Quarter, this is an atmospheric experience. Try and get 1 of the 2 tables squeezed onto the tiny balcony. The restaurant is up a steep flight of wooden stairs. There's a good menu with plenty of Vietnamese and seafood dishes and some with a Chinese influence – the Hong Kong duck is good, as is the sunburnt beef (beef strips deep-fried in 5-spice butter). There's a bar downstairs serving mulled wine on chilly nights and other traditional rice wines.

♕♕-♕ Highway 4, 3 Hang Tre St, T4-3926 4200. 0900-0200. Therea are other branches too. The original restaurant has moved next door. It specializes in ethnic minority dishes from North Vietnam (Highway 4 is the most northerly road in Vietnam running along the Chinese border and favoured by owners of Minsk motorbikes) but now includes a full menu of dishes from other provinces. The fruit and rice wines – available in many flavours – are the highlight of this place. For those unable to make up their minds sampler shots are available, but after a couple of these they all taste good. Upstairs, guests sit cross-legged on cushions; downstairs there's conventional dining. There's plenty to eat and it's a great fun and memorable experience.

♕♕-♕ Restaurant Number Five, 5 Hang Be St, T4-3926 3761. The smart, classy interior and large windows are inviting. The menu is eclectic but offering something a little different in the old quarter such as Lebanese lamb pizza and spinach, ricotta and walnut ravioli. The profiteroles stuffed with peanut butter ice cream and served with chocolate sauce are a treat!

Tandoor, 24 Hang Be St, T4-3824 5359. 1100-1430, 1800-2230. A smallish but long-standing restaurant serving excellent Indian food freshly prepared. Authentic curries, tandooris and breads. Don't miss the branch in HCMC.

Bit Tet (Beefsteak), 51 Hang Buom St, T4-3825 1211. 1700-2100. If asked to name the most authentic Vietnamese diner in town it would be hard not to include this on the list. The soups and steak frites are simply superb: it's rough and ready and you'll share your table as, at around US$2-3 per head, it is understandably crowded. (Walk to the end of the alley and turn right for the dining room.)

Café des Arts and **Stop Café**, 11b Ngo Bao Khanh St, T4-3828 7207, www.cafedesarts. com. Housed in 1 building and owned by the same people: upstairs is home to a fine dining French restaurant, **Café des Arts**, and downstairs, **Stop Café**, a more pared-back bistro with cheap steaks and excellent pizza. **Stop Café** also delivers. Popular among the French community.

Café Moca, 14-16 Nha Tho, T4-3825 6334. 0700-2400. From cinnamon-flavoured cappuccino to smoked salmon, and from dry martinis to Bengali specials, this is a good place to come and snack. It's a longstanding tourist favourite though these days less beloved than the days when foreign dining options were scant. The high ceilings and marble floors still make it a comfortable spot for a coffee and it's a favourite for people-watching.

Cha Ca La Vong, 14 Cha Ca St, T4-3825 3929. 1100-2100. Serves 1 dish only, the eponymous *cha ca Hanoi*, fried fish fillets in mild spice and herbs served with noodles. It's utterly delicious and popular with visitors and locals, although expensive at 1,300,000d for the meal and the service is

now complacent, slap dash and verging on the rude. They've definitely had too much of a good thing and treat the customers now with disdain rather than a warm welcome.

Little Hanoi, 9 and 14 Ta Hien St, T4-3926 0168. Reputedly the original **Little Hanoi**, these small restaurants offer inexpensively priced traditional Vietnamese food and are incredibly popular. Try the steamed tuna in beer with rice. Watch out for the staircase if you're heading upstairs.

Little Hanoi, 21 Hang Gai St, T4-3828 8333. 0730-2300. An excellent little place. An all-day restaurant/café serving outstanding sandwiches. The cappuccinos, home-made yoghurt with honey and the apple pie are also top class.

My Burger My, 5 Hang Bac St, T4-7309 0777. Though portions are small, American **Burger My** serves US-style burgers with many toppings, on grilled buns in a small but comfortable shop in the Old Quarter. Those preferring gut-busters are advised to look elsewhere but for a snack it's worth the stop. Also has a Mexican menu. Delivery available.

Restaurant 22, 22 Hang Can St, T4-3826 7160. 1200-2100. Good menu, popular and tasty Vietnamese food, succulent duck. At just a couple of dollars per main course it represents excellent value for money.

Tamarind, 80 Ma May St, T4-3926 0580, tamarind_café@yahoo.com. A vegetarian restaurant that goes beyond traditional 'veggie' fare. There is a comfortable café at the front and a smart restaurant behind in the **Handspan Adventure Travel** office. There's a lengthy vegetarian selection, delicious juices and the recommended Thai glass noodle salad.

Cafés

Bon Mua, 38-40 Le Thai To St, T4-3825 6923. 0700-2300. Popular ice cream shop on the west bank of Hoan Kiem Lake.

Cafe Puku, 16/18 Tong Duy Tan St, T4-3928 5244. An old favourite recently relocated to a new location in a large colonial villa.

Puku has kept everything that made it good and still managed improvements, such as cheaper beer and an astonishing 24-hr licence. Set on famous Food Street now, it still even smells the same: like your university café, all friendly garlic and fresh brewed coffee.

Fanny Ice Cream, 48 Le Thai To St, T4-3828 5656, www.fanny.com.vn. Refreshing ice cream and sorbet with an ice cream buffet at 95,000d.

Highlands Coffee, southwest corner of Hoan Kiem Lake. Lovely spot under the trees overlooking the lake. Great place for a coffee or cold drink. This home-grown chain is often referred to by people as equally lacking in taste and imagination as 'Vietnam's Starbucks'. It is more than that, and better. While an iced coffee is twice or more what you'd pay in a smaller café, quality is assured and ambience relaxing. Food is reasonable and desserts are more of a draw for most than mains.

Kem Trang Tien, 35 Trang Tien St. This is probably the most popular ice cream parlour in the city and it's a drive-in and park your moto affair. It's also a flirt joint for Hanoian young things. Flavours are cheap and change as to what's available.

South of Hoan Kiem Lake p56, maps p46 and p52

ȚȚȚ-ȚȚ Chica, 27 Hang Be St. Inside the **Hoa Binh Hotel**, floor 9, T4-2243 4370. One of the city's more hidden gems, Chica is an 8-floor ride at the top of the **Hoa Binh Hotel**. Known best for its steaks, Chica has a small but loyal following. Desserts come recommended too.

ȚȚȚ-ȚȚ La Badiane, 10 Nam Ngu St, T4-3942 4509. A relative newcomer to Hanoi, from a couple of Hanoi old hands, **La Badiane's** French aesthetic stops at the food. Fusion, and of more than Vietnamese and French, is what this restaurant is about and while its intricately decorated plates of seasonal meals won't appeal to everyone there are many who swear this is the best restaurant in town. Service is good, if over-attentive at

times. Portions have increased but order a starter too if you're hungry. The converted colonial villa is delightful. The set lunch menu, a bargain US$10.

ȚȚȚ-ȚȚ San Ho, 58 Ly Thuong Kiet St, T4-3934 9184, ando@hn.vnn.vn. 1100-1400, 1700-2200. This is Hanoi's most popular seafood restaurant. Located in a colonial villa in Hoan Kiem district, it's a better bet than some of the seafood barns closer to the river. Set menus, fish tanks, and local seafood.

ȚȚȚ-ȚȚ Verticale, 19 Ngo Van So St, T4-3944 6317, verticale@didiercorlou.com. 0900-1400, 1700-2400. Didier Corlou, former chef at the **Sofitel Metropole**, opened this new restaurant in a small street in the French quarter. The tall, multi-storey building includes a spice shop, restaurant, private rooms and a terrace bar. The food and presentation are an adventurous culinary journey of gustatory delight; this is certainly one of the best dining experiences in the city. Highly recommended.

ȚȚ Al Fresco's, 23L Hai Ba Trung St, T4-3826 7782. Part of a chain, **Al Fresco's** is a popular Australian-run grill bar serving ribs, steak, pasta, pizza and fantastic salads. Portions are large, hugely so, and it's a very child-friendly place, with paper table cloths and crayons on every table. Recommended.

ȚȚ Luna d'Autonno, 78 Tho Nhuom St, T4-3823 7338. Regarded as one of the city's best Italian restaurants, **Luna** has a large menu of pizza, pasta and mains. Though it has recently moved to a far less prepossessing setting, the food, if not ambience, remains good.

ȚȚ Song Thu, 28A Ha Hoi St (off Tran Hung Dao St), T4-3942 4448, www.hoasuaschool. com. 0700-2200. French training restaurant for disadvantaged youngsters where visitors can eat excellently prepared French and Vietnamese cuisine in an attractive and secluded courtyard setting. Reasonably cheap and popular. Cooking classes now available, see Activities and tours, page 87.

¶¶-¶ Cay Cau, 17A Tran Hung Dao St, T4-3933 1010. In the **De Syloia Hotel**. Good Vietnamese fare at reasonable prices in this popular place. Daily set lunch at 130,000d is good value.

¶¶-¶ Chim Sáo, 65 Ngo Hue St, T4-3976 0633, www.chimsao.com. Set in an atmospheric old colonial villa, **Chim Sao** is famous for its Northern Vietnamese food, cooked by a French chef. Seating is on the floor upstairs.

¶ Café 129, 129 Mai Hac De St. Does excellent breakfast fry-ups and cheap but filling Mexican meals in what is still one of Hanoi's most basic settings. Despite serving a mostly Western menu, **Café 129** has never moved past its pho shop vibe of low tables and plastic stools. And its long-standing fan club wouldn't have it any other way.

¶ Com Chay Nang Tam, 79A Tran Hung Dao St, T4-3942 4140. 1100-1400, 1700-2200. This popular little a/c vegetarian restaurant is down an alley off Tran Hung Dao St and serves excellent and inexpensive 'Buddhist' dishes in a small, family-style dining room. There are numerous options and jugs full of freshly squeezed juices.

¶ Hanoi Gourmet, 1B Ham Long, T4-3943 1009, www.hanoigourmet.com. 0830-2100. Not a restaurant but a delicatessen with a couple of tables at the back. For lovers of fine wine, cheese and cold cuts, **Hanoi Gourmet** is a great discovery. Find a free afternoon, go short on breakfast, then go for a long leisurely lunch. Freshly restocked from France every few weeks.

¶ Quan An Ngon, 18 Phan Boi Chau St, T4-3942 8162, ngonhanoi@vnn.vn. Daily 0700-2130. This place is insanely popular at lunch and dinner time. In a massive open-air courtyard setting with enormous umbrellas shading wooden tables you can wander around looking at all the street stalls with signage in Vietnamese. The menu is in English and you order from a waitress. All the food is delicious and you'll be keen to return again to sample the huge array on display.

Cafés

252 Hang Bong, actually in what is now Cua Nam St. Pastries, yoghurt and crème caramel, very popular for breakfast.

Cong Café, 152D Trieu Viet Vuong St. A communist parody in a city which, in the main, doesn't view such a sense of humour favourably. Music here is generally excellent and coffee a cut above the rest. Trieu Viet Vuong St is the café quarter of Hanoi.

Ho Chi Minh's Mausoleum complex and around *p59, map p46*

¶¶-¶ Seasons of Hanoi, 95B Quan Thanh St, T4-3843 5444, seasonsofhanoi@fpt.vn. 1100-1400, 1800-2200. Bookings recommended. This admirable restaurant has, inevitably, become very well known and is one of the most agreeable dining experiences in Hanoi. The building is a finely restored and authentically furnished colonial villa, the Vietnamese food is fresh and delicious and service attentive.

¶ KOTO, 59 Van Mieu St, T4-3747 0337, www.koto.com.au. Mon 0730-1800, Tue-Sun 0730-2230. A training restaurant for underprivileged young people. Next to the **Temple of Literature**, in new premises, pop in for a good lunch after a morning's sightseeing. The food is international, filling and delicious but avoid the fatty pork. Upstairs is the **Temple Bar** with Wi-Fi. Recommended.

North of the Old City *p65, map p46*

¶¶¶-¶¶ Bobby Chinn, 77 Xuan Dieu, T4-3719 2640, www.bobbychinn.com. Bobby has been in Vietnam for many years having ventured out on his culinary career in HCMC. The restaurant is arguably one of Hanoi's most famous restaurants thanks to its TV star chef. Though now moved from its central Hoan Kiem Lake location, the food and decor remain the same: rich reds, comfortable tables and the same intricate fusion that made Bobby famous.

₩₩-₩ Daluva, 33 To Ngoc Van St, T4-3718 5831. A wine bar with tapas and some main meals, Daluva is located in Hanoi's posher Tay Ho district. Though with prices beginning at 100,000d per glass it might seem expensive, keep in mind that all wine is exorbitantly priced in Vietnam.

₩₩-₩ Vine Wine Boutique Bar & Café, 1A Xuan Dieu, T4-3719 8000, www.vine-group.com. 0800-2330. One of the most extensive cellars in town, housed in one of the more expensive restaurant's in Hanoi. Vine has been a fixture for years. It's fine dining with excellent food and service and many Western and Vietnamese dishes. Surrounds and service alone justifies the tab. Drinks selection is excellent. Make sure to stop in at Vine Cellar Door a few doors down as well.

₩ Don's Bistro, 16/27 Xuan Dieu, T4-3719 2828, www.donviet.vn. A new venture from one of the founding chefs of both the Press Club and Vine, Don's is a multi-level restaurant, café and cocktail bar on the shores of West Lake. Though expensive, it has a lovely view and the pizzas are some of the best in the city. Cocktails are also excellent though the spirits list tends towards overpriced. Snatch the day-bed on top-floor cocktail bar for the best view.

₩ Hanoi Cooking Centre, 44 Chau Long St, T4-3715 0088, http://hanoicookingcentre.com. A restaurant, café and cooking centre housed in a restored colonial villa near Truc Bach Lake, it has quickly become popular with expats and tourists. Past the excellent cooking classes, which provide a useful overview of street food dishes and others, the cooking centre serves things rarely seen in Hanoi, such as a seasonal Sunday Roast.

₩₩-₩ Chien Beo, 192 Nghi Tam St, T4-3716 1461. A Vietnamese steakhouse serving huge platters of beef cooked in various ways and sometimes stuffed with cheese. It's rumoured the chef trained in some of the city's 5-star hotel kitchens before opening his own joint. The setting may be basic but it's worth it. Don't expect to linger, it's all about fast turnaround.

₩ Pho Yen, 66 Cua Bac St, T4-3715 0269. This down-at-heel tables and chair joint does tasty *pho cuon*. Popular with locals.

₩ Foodshop 45, 59 Truc Bach St. A Vietnamese-run Indian restaurant facing Truc Bach Lake. Offers the city's cheapest Indian meals. The menu is compact but good and vegetarian dishes begin at a bit over US$1.75. Also very popular for delivery. Traditional Vietnamese rice wines are also on the menu.

₩ Kitchen, Lane 40, 7A Xuan Dieu, T4-3719 2679. 0700-2130. Down an alley with a small courtyard, a cheap and cheerful very popular hang-out serving great Mexican, sandwiches and salads and healthy juices. Greg's chicken shawarma pita is hugely filling.

₩ Le Cooperative, 46 An Duong St, T4-3716 6401. A French-run restaurant and bar from the same people behind famous Vietnamese restaurant Chim Sao. Le Cooperative has a compact but good French menu of classics and the best-value steak in the city. The cold cuts are recommended. The Vietnamese menu is large but receives mixed reviews. Upstairs is done up like an ethnic minority stilt house and there's also a selection of rice wines; some are even drinkable.

Cafés

Duy Tri, 43A Yen Phu St, T4-3829 1386. Considered the best coffee in Hanoi. This tiny tube café is full on atmosphere and the smell of beans. The coffee with yoghurt (*ca phe sua chua*) is the signature drink.

Mau House & Ceramic, 17a Truc Bach, T4-3829 3744. A cute balcony café amid a clutter of interesting sculptures and handicrafts for sale overlooking the lake.

Outer Hanoi *p65, map p46*

₩ Edo, Daewoo Hotel, 360 Kim Ma St, T4-3831 5000. Japanese restaurant in a Korean hotel, considered some of the finest Japanese food in town.

🍸 Bars and clubs

Hanoi's main bar street is Ta Hien, heading towards Hang Buom after it has cut across the famous Bia Hoi Corner (at Luong Ngoc Quyen). There are some 5 bars on this small strip and several around the corner. Though officially all bars are supposed to close at midnight, it's a rule sporadically enforced and one that often leads to a convivial, speakeasy atmosphere – as long as you know which closed roller door to knock on.

The Cheeky Quarter, 1A Ta Hien St, T9 0403 2829 (mob). Owned by the same family as **Tet bar**, and spitting distance away, **Cheeky** packs a lot into what space it has. A fussball table, bar stools, and an upstairs area with airplane-esque toilet are all part of the charm – as is the dodgy flock wallpaper and Old Master's style paintings of friends of the bar. Late night food here is arguably better.

Dragonfly, 15 Hang Buon St, T4-3926 2177. An all-red, 2-storey Hanoi bar popular for drinks specials and its Arabian Nights shisha pipe room, with many flavours of tobacco. Apple is the most popular but you can also opt for chocolate or cappuccino.

Finnegan's Irish Pub, 16A Duong Thanh St, T4-3828 9065. Longstanding Irish pub that manages to be far less tacky than the average. Food, especially stews, is good and the range of whisky reasonable. Despite the backpacker scrawl all over the walls of the back, with the inevitable shonkily drawn phalluses, it's popular with expats too.

Funky Buddha, 2 Ta Hien St, T4-3926 7615. A lounge/club bar that is something of an anomaly in Hanoi: equally popular with foreigners and Vietnam's rapidly growing middle class. Though it looks plenty glitzy, spirit prices are only a shade above anything else on the street and staff are extremely competent. Bottle service is on offer.

Golden Cock, 5A Bao Khanh St, T4-3825 0499. A popular 'gay friendly' bar a few doors away from **Polite Pub**, the **Golden Cock** has been around a long time and is still crowded years on.

Half Man/Half Noodle, 64 Dao Duy Tu St, T4-3926 1943. This oddly named bar is basic, but comfortable. Think beer, bamboo and a play list you can choose yourself. Of late they've begun doing late night food, including heartier meals such as schnitzels and chips. Planning a big night out? Ask for the alcoholic coconuts, which are exactly as they sound.

Hoa Vien, 1 Tang Bat Ho St, T4-3972 5088. Possibly the biggest and best-known of Hanoi's European-style beer halls, **Hoa Vien** is a multi-level behemoth serving beer in glasses ranging from standard to 1 litre steins. Pilsner and dark beer are both on offer as well as heart-clogging wonders such as fried cheese and pork cutlets.

Ho Guom Xanh, 32 Le Thai To St, T4-3828 8806. Few people passing by just yards away outside could imagine the colour and operatic spectacle of the stage shows this nightclub puts on. Performers, often dressed like something out of Miami Vice, arrive on stage via a pneumatic pole. It's loud, packed and popular with a mainly local crowd but a real visual treat. Drinks are fairly expensive, which is par for the course in most nightclubs aimed at rich Vietnamese.

The House of Son Tinh, 31 Xuan Dieu, T4-3718 6377, www.houseofsontinh.com. Tapas dining and a liquor lounge for multiple rice wine tastings. This new kid on the block is already a hit in this expat quarter.

JoJo's, 23C Hai Ba Trung St, T4-3824 1028. Owned by the same company as **Al Fresco's**, **Jaspa's** and **Pepperoni's**, this dark, sleek and shiny wine bar has a good cocktail list and menu. Bottles and wines by the glass don't come cheap but it's a good list and weekend specials, such as Sun brunches, make up for it.

Legends, 1-5 Dinh Tien Hoang St, T4-3936 0345, www.legendsbeer.com.vn. Daily 0800-2300. Another of Hanoi's popular microbreweries. The German *helles bier* (light) and the *dunkels bier* (dark) are strong and tasty. This café bar has views over Hoan Kiem Lake. An extensive food menu too and good for snacks and ice cream.

Le Pub, 25 Hang Be St, T4-3926 2104, www. lepub.org. One of Hanoi's best pubs, now with a 2nd location on the shores of West Lake. Popular with tourists and expats, prices remain reasonable, beer is some of the coldest in the city and nightly drinks specials keep the wallet intact. Food is reasonably priced and competent but, excepting the breakfasts and Vietnamese, largely uninspiring. Le Pub has outdoor seating on one of the Old Quarter's busiest streets.

Library Bar, Press Club, 59A Ly Thai To St. Tranquil setting in which to tipple a few malts while smoking a fine Havana.

Mao's Red Lounge, 7 Ta Hien St, T4-3926 3104. A hugely popular hole-in-the-wall bar mostly frequented by young English teachers. Music is good though dependent on whomever of the publican's friends has control of the iPod. Some of the cheapest beers in town with famously honest staff.

Phuc Tan Bar, 51 Phuc Tan St. An out and out dive bar, and proud of it. Come the weekend there are precious few places open late at night where you can both drink and dance. Though basic, and with nightmare toilets, **Phuc Tan Bar** has a gorgeous view over the Red River, large outdoor seating area and often stays open late. Be very wary of catching any cabs from outside the bar on your way home. Ask staff to phone for one instead.

Polite Pub, 5 Bao Khanh St, T4-3825 0959. Good bar snacks and cocktails and a pool table at this popular expat haunt, which despite being supplanted by more popular bars on the other side of the Old Quarter has retained its high standards.

R & R Tavern, 10 Tho Nhuom St, T4-6295 8215. One of Hanoi's oldest bars, this new location outside the Old Quarter has everything its predecessor had, right down to the crowd. A mostly American bar, with reasonably priced Tex-Mex meals and one of Vietnam's best beers – the hard-to-find Huda.

Rock Billy, corner of Luong Van Can and Hang Gai streets. Climb up to the tiny balcony and look out on the adjacent shops

and road junction for one of the best bird's eye views of the Old Quarter.

Roots, 2 Luong Ngoc Quyen St. A French-run reggae bar serving rums from the Francophile Caribbean and local rums infused with fruits and spices. **Roots** gets busy on weekends but tends to be quiet until mid-week. The bamboo and rattan add to the atmosphere but be prepared: the drinks pack a punch.

Solace, end of Chung Duong Do St. Expats might try their hand at word play and call this bar on a boat 'soul less' but you can bet come the weekend they'll wash up on the dance floor. A place to keep your hand on your dong, to be sure, but one of the few viable late-night clubs around and interesting for the most diverse clientele in the whole city, from foreign executives to overworked chefs to stumbling English teachers to loaded expat brats to backpackers to the local gay mafia.

Tadioto, 113 Trieu Viet Vuong St, T4-2218 7200, www.tadioto.com. Tadioto has no precedent in the city or other neighbours in the area. An art gallery-cum-bar, it's one of the few places to host poetry readings, play Tom Waits albums or play local to the local art community. Far from the centre of town it might be, but it's always worth the trip.

Tet bar, 2A Ta Hien St, T4-3926 3050. One of the city's late night mainstays and formerly known as 'Le Marquis', **Tet** closes when the last customers go home, pretty much. For some reason better known to fate, the toasted sandwiches here – a Croque Monsieur – are considered the best after hours snack in the city.

⊙ Entertainment

Cinema
See Vietnam News, the New Hanoian (http://newhanoian.xemzi.com) and *Hanoi Grapevine* (http://hanoigrapevine.com) for current listings.

Hanoi Cinematique, 22A Hai Ba Trung St, T4-3936 2648, info2@hanoicinema.org.

This small club shows films in the original version. Membership is 100,000d; a 1-off visit costs 50,000d. Plenty of more unusual films, film festivals and a nice courtyard to enjoy a drink in.

Megastar Cineplex, Vincom City Towers, 191 Ba Trieu St, T4-3974 3333, www. megastarmedia.met. Western films with Vietnamese subtitles 50,000d; Wed is cheaper. Popcorn, snacks and beer available.

Dance and theatre

Opera House, T4-3933 0113, nthavinh@ hn.vn, box office 0800-1700. A French-era building at the east end of Trang Tien St (see page 56) staging a variety of Vietnamese and Western concerts, operas and plays. Check *Vietnam News* or at the box office.

Water Puppet Theatre, 57b Dinh Tien Hoang St, at the northeast corner of Hoan Kiem Lake, T4-3936 4335, www. thanglongwaterpuppet.org. In recent years the troupe has performed in Japan, Australia and Europe. Entrance 60,000d (1st class), 40,000d (2nd class). Children half price on Sun 0930. Fabulous performances with exciting live music and beautiful comedy daily at 1530, 1700, 1830 and 2000 and 2130; an additional matinee on Sun at 0930. This is not to be missed. Very popular so advanced booking is required at the box office.

Music

Jazz Club (CLB Jazz), 31 Luong Van Can St, T4-3828 7890. Vietnamese jazz saxophonist, Quyen Van Minh, plays here. Open 1000-2400; live jazz every night 2100-2400.

⊛ Festivals and events

Jan/Feb Dong Da Hill festival (5th day of Tet). Celebrates the battle of Dong Da in which Nguyen Hue routed 200,000 Chinese troops. Processions of dancers carry a flaming dragon of straw.

Perfume Pagoda Festival, 6th day of the 1st lunar month-end of the 3rd lunar month. This focuses on the worship of Quan Am.

There are dragon dances and a royal barge sails on the river.

Hai Ba Trung Festival, 3rd-6th day of the 2nd lunar month. The festival commemorates the Trung sisters, see page 66. On the 3rd day the temple is opened; on the 4th, a funeral ceremony begins; on the 5th the sisters' statues are bathed in a ceremony; on the 6th day a ritual ceremony is held.

Hung Kings' festival, 10th day of the 3rd lunar month. A 2-week celebration when the temple site comes alive as visitors from all over Vietnam descend on the area, as Ho Chi Minh encouraged them to. The place seethes with vendors, food stalls and fairground activities spring up. There are racing swan boats on one of the lakes.

2 Sep National Day, featuring parades in Ba Dinh Sq and boat races on Hoan Kiem Lake.

○ Shopping

The city is a shopper's paradise with cheap silk and good tailors, handicrafts and antiques and some good designer shops. **Hang Gai St** is well geared to souvenir hunters and stocks an excellent range of clothes, fabrics and lacquerware. It's rather like the small-time Silk Road of Hanoi. Hats of all descriptions abound. You will not be disappointed.

Antiques

Along **Hang Khay** and **Trang Tien** streets, south edge of Hoan Kiem Lake. Shops sell silver ornaments, porcelain, jewellery and carvings – much is not antique, not all is silver; bargain hard.

Art galleries

Hanoi has always been known as the 'artistic' city compared to Saigon's powerhouse economy. Though many galleries do the typical Beautiful Hanoi paintings, more galleries stocking the work of serious artists are popping up. If you decide to get a painting commissioned, treat it much like an experience at the tailors': give it plenty of time and don't always expect perfection first time round. Galleries abound near Hoan Kiem Lake, especially **Trang Tien St** and on **Dinh Tien Hoang St** at northeast corner.

Apricot Gallery, 40B Hang Bong St, T4-3828 8965, www.apricot-artvietnam.com. High prices but spectacular exhibits.

Art Vietnam Gallery, 7 Nguyen Khac Nhu St, T4-3927 2349, www.artvietnamgallery.com. Mon-Sat 1000-1800. Art director Suzanne Lecht has created a cool interior in a chic space to display delectable works of art by Vietnamese and Vietnam-based artists. This is Hanoi's premier art space.

Dien Dam Gallery, 4b Dinh Liet St, T4-3825 9881, www.diendam-gallery.com. Beautiful photographic images in black and white and colour.

Hanoi Gallery, 17 Nha Chung St, T4-3928 7943, propaganda_175@yahoo. com. Sells propaganda posters. Original posters cost US$200 upwards; US$8 for a rice paper copy. Some of the reproductions aren't faithful to the colours of the originals; choose carefully.

Propaganda Art, 8 Nha Chung St, T4-3928 6588. More propaganda posters and other propaganda items like mugs and keyrings.

Bicycles

At the second-hand bike market at the intersection of Thinh Yen St and Pho 332, south of the city centre and on Ba Trieu St south of junction with Nguyen Du St.

Books and maps

Private booksellers operate on Trang Tien St and have pavement stalls in the evening; be sure to bargain (maps also available here and outside the post office. On Sun book stalls appear on Dinh Le St, parallel with Trang Tien St. Many travel cafés operate book exchanges. Some travel companies, such as Love Planet on Hang Bac St also sell books. Expect the typical travel fare interspersed with a few gems. Make sure to bargain.

Bookworm, 4b Yen The St, Ba Dinh District, T4-3747 8778, bookworm@fpt.vn. Tue-Sun 1000-1900. A couple of thousand books in stock. Unlike other bookshops in town imports new releases and harder-to-find things, though these aren't cheap. Also specializes in books about Vietnam and Southeast Asia. Stocks translations of famous Vietnamese stories. *Dumb Luck*, written about the rising Vietnamese petit bourgeousie in 1930s Hanoi, is worth buying.

Ethnic Travel, 35 Hang Giay St, T4-3928 3186. Books sold, exchanged (2 for 1).

Foreign Language Bookshop, 61 Trang Tien St. Also the alley by the side of this bookshop sells copies of books otherwise out of stock.

Xunhasaba, 32 Hai Ba Trung St. The state book distributor's shop. Many books in English, including books about Vietnam.

Camera shops

Processing and film is available all around Hoan Kiem Lake. Several shops also have download and printing services for digital cameras. Ma May street has a number and also do cheap passport photos. Quality may not be perfect.

Clothes, fashions, silk and accessories

Vietnam has produced some exciting fashion designers in the past couple of years (see box, page 86) and there is a growing number of stylish boutiques in the fashionable cathedral shopping cluster and a new 'designer' outlet in southern Hai Ba Trung district stocking labels like Mango and FCUK. Few can walk past the glittering displays of jackets, dresses, handbags, scarves and shoes without feeling some temptation to go in and buy. This is all the more remarkable considering how dowdy the dress sense of most Hanoians was just a few short years ago and how relatively uninviting the shop displays were. The greatest concentration is in the Hoan Kiem Lake area particularly on Nha Tho, Nha Chung, Hang Trong and Hang Gai streets.

Outer suburbs arteries are home to endless shops selling cheap, Chinese-made t-shirts and outfits.

Bo Sua, beside skate shop Boo on Ta Hien St. Owned by the same people as **Boo**, **Bo Sua** is revolutionary for a Hanoian label. Plastic bags have been banned, t-shirts carry environmental awareness cartoons, and designs are mainly done by young Hanoians. If you want a sartorial souvenir that goes beyond the standard Captain Vietnam shirt – the Vietnamese flag shirt – shop here. Day-to-day objects, such as coal briquettes, plastic sandals or foamy glasses of *bia hoi* have been turned into stylish t-shirt icons.

Co, 18 Nha Tho St, T4-328 9925, conhatho@ yahoo.com. 0830-1900. This tiny clothes tailor shop has a very narrow entrance on this popular street. It has some unusual prints and the craftsmanship is recommended.

Grace, 5 Nha Tho St and 72 Hang Trong St, T4-3928 7456, grace.vn@vn.vn. Jewellery and lovely flouncy dresses.

Ipa Nima, 34 Han Thuyen St, T4-3933 4000, www.ipa-nima.com. Enter the glittering and sparkling world of **Ipa Nima**. Shiny shoes, bags, clothes and jewellery boxes. Hong Kong Chinese Christina Yu is the creative force behind the designer label. Not cheap, but well made, unlike her legion of copycats.

Kien Boutique, 1B To Tich St, T4-3928 6835, kiensilk40@yahoo.com. Recommended tailors for good-quality clothes.

Song, 27 Nha Tho St, T4-3928 8733, www. asiasongdesign.com, 0900-2000. Its sister shop is in HCMC. Here the **Song** shop is on the fashionable Nha Tho and run by friendly staff. Clothes and gorgeous homeware. The French designer is well known in Vietnam and her clothes are designed for the heat: natural fibres and airy looseness.

Things of Substance, 5 Nha Tho St, T4-3828 6965, contrabanddesign@hn.vnn.vn. 0900-2000. Selling swimwear, silk jewellery bags and attractive jewellery, this small shop, with excellent service in the shadow of the cathedral, offers something a bit different.

An Australian designer is in charge and everything is made with the motto 'Western sizes at Asian prices' in mind. Popular enough that you're likely to run into someone else sporting your outfit, at some stage.

Tina Sparkle, 17 Nha Tho St, T4-3928 7616. 0900-2000. Funky boutique that sells mostly bags in a glittering array of colours – from tropical prints to big sequinned flower bags. Also stocks items by Spanish design team Chula. A good option if you want an Ipa Nima bag without a taxi ride to the next district.

Vincom City Towers, 191 Na Trieu St. Large mall in the city's south. Though the range of things stocked isn't amazing, the newly built 'high-end' addition behind, connected by a walkway, is home to plenty of well-known brands. Mango is marketed, and priced, as a high-end not high-street brand here.

Handicrafts and homeware

There has been a great upsurge in handicrafts on sale as the tourist industry develops. Many are also made for export. A wide range of interesting pieces is on sale all around the popular cathedral shopping cluster of Nha Tho, Ly Quoc Su and Nha Chung streets. Further shops can be found on Hang Khay St, on the southern shores of Hoan Kiem Lake, and Hai Gai St. A range of hand-woven fabrics and ethnographia from the hill tribes is also available.

Aloo Store, 37 Hang Manh St, T4-3928 9131, aloo181@yahoo.com. An abundance of well-priced ethnic goods from the north.

Chi Vang, 63 Hang Gai St, T4-3936 0601, chivang@fpt.vn. Chi Vang has moved to the centre of the Old Quarter – the Silk Road – and sells exquisitely embroidered cloths, baby's bed linen and clothing, cushion covers, table cloths and unusual-shaped cushions artfully arranged. All the goods displayed are embroidered by hand.

Craft Link, 43 Van Mieu St, T4-3843 7710, www.craftlink-vietnam.com. Traditional handicrafts from a not-for-profit organization. Many are made by ethnic minorities.

Asian fusion fashion

The new entrepreneurial streak in Vietnam has proved a catalyst for fabulous design and ingenuity in the fashion world. Although known for the beautiful *ao dai*, the classic-cut trouser tunic of local women, Vietnam was not known for its haute-couture. Nowadays, fashionistas flock for the latest in desirable clothes, bags, shoes and other accessories from the country's designers who have come so far in just a few short years. From the inception of ideas to fabrication to the clothes rails, this has been fashion development on speed. Just 15 years ago, dour communist wear was the nation's lot but since economic liberalization national and international designers have gained fame at home and abroad with some selling to halls of sartorial fame such as **Harrods** and **Harvey Nichols** in London, and **Henri Bendel** in New York. Hollywood actress Cate Blanchett, Shakira Caine, wife of Oscar-winner Sir Michael, and US Senator Hillary Rodham Clinton are all followers of one such designer working under the **Ipa-Nima** label. Christina Yu, a Hong-Kong lawyer, now based in Vietnam, set up glitzy label **Ipa-Nima**. Her bags, clothes and shoes now decorate two shops in Hanoi. Valerie Gregori-McKenzie, a native Frenchwoman who lives in Vietnam, releases beautiful, ethereal clothes, embroidered cushions and bags under the label **Song**. She has two shops gracing Hanoi and Ho Chi Minh City. Sylvie Tran Ha, who is Viet Kieu, set up **SXS** in Ho Chi Minh City, which uses suede, among other materials. Many of these women have combined local materials with ideas, methods and motifs from the ethnic minority clothing of Vietnam. **Mai Lam Mai**, a Viet Kieu from Australia, has a boutique – Mai's – underneath the Continental Hotel. She sells cutting-edge fashions including a wonderful modern brightly coloured take and twist on the *ao-dai*.

Most of the fashion designers using Vietnam as their creative hub are women. The exception to this rule is the elegantly dressed Hoang Khai of the ubiquitous **Khaisilk** empire. **Khaisilk** began as a workshop in Hanoi in 1980. Since then the empire has expanded with shops in Hanoi, Ho Chi Minh City and Hoi An. Now entrepreneurial owner Mr Khai has combined silk with food to create a series of stylish restaurants that are some of the most chic and glamorous in Vietnam. In the hotel domain, he has established the Hoi An Riverside Resort, a peaceful haven just outside Hoi An where attention to detail combined with the setting has produced one of the most exquisite hotels in the country. Mr Khai, who always dresses in black, wins award after award for his silk output and **Khaisilk**, with a winning marketing thrust, has ensured its place as the number one boutique shop in the country.

La Casa, 12 Nha Tho St, T4-3828 9616, www.lacasavietnam.com. Lovely individual homeware items.
Mosaique, 22 Nha Tho St, T4-3928 6181, mosaique@fpt.vn. 0830-2000. An Aladdin's cave of embroidered table runners, lamps and stands, silk flowers for accessorizing, silk curtains, silk cushions, ball lamps, pillow cushions and lotus flower-shaped lamps.

Nagu, 20 Nha Tho St, T4-3928 8020, www.zantoc.com. Japanese designed and catering to that market. Things have a more minimalist tinge but conform to Japanese sizing: small. The teddy bears are popular.
Ngoc Oanh, 34 Hang Da Market, T4-3928 5479. Does a lovely line in all the Bat Trang village ceramics. Hang Da Market is lined with ceramic stalls.

Phuc Loi, 2b Ta Hien St. A little shop run by a husband and wife making and selling hand-carved wooden chopsticks or stamps. They come in a variety of oriental signs of the zodiac, etc. Cheap, fun and make excellent lightweight gifts.

Musical instruments
For unusual souvenirs visit the shop at 76 Hang Bong St, where they make wooden percussion instruments.

Shoes
Walking boots, trainers, flip flops and sandals, many in Western sizes, are sold in the shops around the northeast corner of Hoan Kiem Lake. Most are genuine brand name items and, having 'fallen off the back of a lorry', are remarkably inexpensive – but do bargain.

Supermarkets
Hapromart, 35 Hang Bong St. 0800-1200, 1230-2200. Stocks Western items.
Fivimart, 27a Ly Thai To St. Large-ish supermarket stocking all the necessities.

▲Activities and tours

Cookery classes
Hanoi Cooking Centre, 44 Chau Long St, T4-3715 0088, http://hanoicookingcentre. com. A large kitchen in a spacious building. Cooking classes for kids and adults. Western and Vietnamese.
Hidden Hanoi, 137 Nghi Tam, Tay Ho, T91-225 4045 (mob), www.hiddenhanoi.com.vn. A recommended outfit offering insightful Vietnamese cultural and culinary tours. Walking tours of the Old Quarter, French Quarter, excellent and fascinating street food tours and walking tours US$20 min 2 people; cooking classes from US$40 per person and language classes from US$20.
Highway 4, 7 Truc Bach, T4-3715 0577. Visit the markets then head to the kitchen to learn how to cook some of the restaurant's best-loved signature items as well as simpler fare, such as fried rice.

Sofitel Metropole Hotel, 15 Ngo Quyen St, T4-3826 6919 ext 8110, concierge@ sofitelhanoi.vnn.vn. Offers 3 programmes. You visit the market to buy ingredients, return to the **Metropole** kitchens for a cooking demonstration and then eat at the **Spices Restaurant** in the hotel.

Health clubs
All the big hotels provide fitness facilities, pool and gyms. Open usually free of charge to residents and to non-residents for a fee or subscription. **Sofitel Metropole** and the **Daewoo** boast the best facilities (see Sleeping, above). **Van Phuc Diplomatic Compound** (1 Pho Kim Ma, Ba Dinh District) and **Trung Tu Diplomatic Compound** (Dang Van Ngu, Dong Da District) give priority to diplomats but their facilities are available to the public.

Therapies
A Top Spot, 52 Au Trieu, T4-3828 8344. The top spot for pampering, hair and superior pedi and manicures.
Le Spa du Metropole, Sofitel Metropole, 15 Ngo Quyen St. A truly luscious and deliciously designed spa in the grounds of the hotel. Themed rooms provide the ambience for the ultimate spa rituals. Expensive but worth it.

Walking tours
Douglas Jardine, dougjardine76@gmail. com. Adjunct Professor, History and Humanity Studies at Hanoi University. Runs excellent, insightful and informative tours covering various subjects in the city.

Tour operators
The most popular option for travellers are the budget cafés that offer reasonably priced tours and an opportunity to meet fellow travellers. While an excellent way to make friends, these tours do tend to isolate visitors from local people. Operators match their rival's prices and itineraries closely and indeed many operate

a clearing system to consolidate passenger numbers to more profitable levels.

Make sure to use only recommended tour operators. Also keep in mind that you get what you pay for and if something is too cheap to be true, it probably is. Many trips to Ha Long, for example, may seem cheap but once aboard the boat, you'll discover beer is expensive. Examples of tour prices include: **Perfume Pagoda**, US$18; **Hoa Lu and Tam Coc**, US$16; **Hanoi city tour**, US$16; 1 night on **Halong Bay** from US$29; **Halong Bay and Cat Ba Island** from US$70; **Cuc Phuong National Park**, US$30; overnight in **Mai Chau** from US$32.

Asian Trails, 24 Hang Than St, Ba Dinh District, T4-3716 2736, www.asiantrails.travel. Offers various package tours across Asia.

Asia Pacific Travel, 66 Hang Than St, Ba Dinh District, T4-3836 4212, www.asiapacifictravel. vn. Affordable small-group adventure travel and a wide selection of tours.

Asiatica Travel, A1203, building M3-M4, 91 Nguyen Chi Thanh St, T4-6266 2816 ext 114, www.asiatica-travel.com. Ask for Pham Duc Quynh as your guide; he is very knowledge-able and speaks fluent English and French.

Blue Star Hotel, 21 Bat Dan St, T4-3923 1585, www.bluestar-hotels.com. Recommended for its budget Halong Bay excursions which are good value.

Buffalo Tours, 94 Ma May St, Hoan Kiem, T4-3828 0702, www.buffalotours.com. Well-established and well-regarded organization. It has its own boat for Halong Bay trips and offers tours around the north as well as day trips around Hanoi. Cross-country and cross-border tours and tailor-made trips too. Staff are friendly and the guides are informative and knowledgeable.

Discovery Indochina, 63A Cua Bac St, T4-3716 4132, www.discoveryindochina. com. Organizes private and customized tours throughout Vietnam, Cambodia and Laos.

Ethnic Travel, 35 Hang Giay St, T4-3926 1951, www.ethnictravel.com.vn. Owner, Mr Khanh, runs individual tours to Bai Tu Long Bay – next to Halong Bay – and to Ninh Binh, the Red River Delta and trekking in the Black River area around Mai Chau. Always offers homestays and always, in a non-gimicky way, tries to ensure that travellers see the 'real' Vietnam. Book exchange inside.

ET-Pumpkin, 89 Ma May St, T4-3926 0739, www.et-pumpkin.com. Very professional in attitude, offering a good selection of travel services, particularly for visitors to the northwest. Now also offering motorbike tours of the north. Good and reasonably priced place for jeep hire and visa extensions too. Also has its own very comfortable train carriage which goes to Sapa. Footprint received reports that it has not been as helpful as it used to be.

Exotissimo, 26 Tran Nhat Duat St, T4-3828 2150, www.exotissimo.com. Specializes in more upmarket tours, good nationwide service.

Explorer Tours, 85 Hang Bo St, T4-3923 0713, www.explorer.com.vn. Useful for both individual travel needs and small groups.

Green Bamboo, 97/19 Van Cao St, Ba Dinh district, T4-3761 8638, www.greenbambootravel.com. Another well-established leader in the budget market, organizes tours of Halong Bay and Sapa.

Halong Travel, 10 Hang Be St, T4-3926 3606, www.halongtravel.com. A countrywide operator with friendly staff.

Handspan Adventure Travel, 80 Ma May St, T4-3926 2828, www.handspan.com. A reputable and well-organized business. Specializes in adventure tours, trekking in the north and kayaking in Halong Bay. It has its own junk in Halong Bay and kayaks. Booking office in Sapa also.

Hanoi Toserco, 8 To Hien Thanh St, T4-3976 0066, www.tosercohanoi.com. It runs an efficient Open Tour service.

Kangaroo Café, 18 Pho Bao Khanh, Quan Hoan Kiem, T4-3828 9931, www.kangaroocafe.com. Specializes in small group and tailor-made tours.

Love Planet, 25 Hang Bac St, T4-3828 4864, www.loveplanettravel.com. Individual and

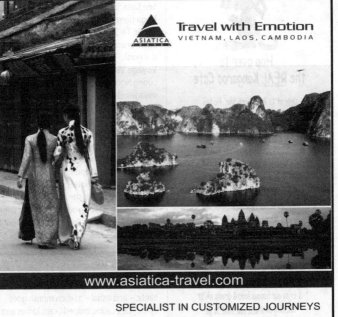

small group tours; also organizes visas. Very helpful and patient service; good book exchange too.

Luxury Travel, 5 Nguyen Truong To St, Ba Dinh District, T4-3927 4120, www. luxurytravelvietnam.com. A newer tour operator offering countrywide tours and alternative excursions.

Real Darling Café, 33 Hang Quat St, T4-3826 9386, darling_café@hotmail.com. Long-established and efficient, this café concentrates on tours of the north and has a visa service. Motorbike hire US$5 per day; car hire US$50 minimum per day.

Sinh Tourist (formerly Sinh Cafe), 40 Luong Ngoc Quyen St, T4-3926 1568. This is the one and only official branch of **Sinh** in Hanoi. It is only listed here so that you know it is the official office. However, it is not recommended. There are dozens of far superior, switched on and efficient tour operators in the city far more deserving of your patronage. It is, however, good in other parts of the country.

Topas, 52 To Ngoc Van St, Tay Ho, T4-3715 1005, www.topasvietnam.com. Good, well-run tour operator offering cross-country tours as well as those in the north. Also has an office in Sapa using local guides. It also organizes treks to Pu Luong Nature Reserve. Draw card is its eco-lodge in Sapa, with 3-star villas overlooking spectacular scenery. See Sapa Sleeping, page 124.

Vega (formerly Fansipan Tours), 24A Hang Bac St, T4-3926 2092, www.vega-travel.com. Small operator organizing tours of Sapa and the north.

Voyage Vietnam Co, Mototours Asia, 1-2 Luong Ngoc Quyen St, T4-3926 2616, www. voyagevietnam.net. Well-organized, reliable and great fun motorbiking, trekking and kayaking tours, especially of the north. The super-friendly and knowledgeable Tuan will take professional bikers to China, Laos, and the Golden Triangle. Trips include all protective gear and nights are spent in homestays and hotels. 4WD car hire also available. This is the only company permitted to import your bike into Vietnam and to organize trips from Vietnam through to China and Tibet.

Hop over to the REAL Kangaroo Cafe

Only at 18 Bao Khanh Str., Ha Noi.
(just around the corner from the ANZ bank)

Since 1994 Griswalds Vietnamese Vacations & our Kangaroo Café have been the leaders in affordable, GENUINE small group tours. We're listed in all the leading guide books & have received great reviews in The New York Times, The Sydney Morning Herald & The Boston Globe to name a few.

Unfortunately we're always being copied by any number of unscrupulous & arrogant dills. HOP over to the REAL Kangaroo Café & enjoy our famous food & drinks whilst deciding on where you want to go!

18 Bao Khanh Str., Ha Noi
Tel: +844 3 828 9931 or you can visit our website at: www.kangaroocafe.com

☺ Transport

The traffic in Hanoi is becoming more frantic – and lethal – as each month goes by. Bicycles, cyclos, mopeds, cars, lorries and buses fight for space with little apparent sense of order, let alone a highway code. At night, with few street lamps and some vehicles without lights, it can seem positively dangerous. Pedestrians should watch out.

Air

Airport information

There are an increasing number of direct international air connections with Hanoi's **Noi Bai Airport**, north of the city. (Cat Bi Airport, at Haiphong, has been identified as a replacement international airport for Noi Bai in the future.) See page 20.

The airport has the **Aero Café**, post office, exchange facilities and **Pacific Travel** (www.pacifhotelsgroup-travel.com) has a tour desk offering hotel reservations. Lost and found, T4-3884 0008/3866 5013.

The official **Noi Bai Taxi**, 2A Quang Trung St, T4-3873 3333, charges a price of US$12-15 to and from the airport. Journey time is approximately 45-60 mins. When leaving the airport go out to the official taxi line and pay at the kiosk/with the seller there.

If you get any other kind of cab do set the price before leaving. Taxi scams have become problems in both Ho Chi Minh City and Hanoi and agreeing a price beforehand is very important.

You can also catch a minibus from the airport to various locations around the city, where you will likely be beset by more cab drivers and *xe ôms*; 30,000d. **Jet Star** passengers get their bus free.

Minibuses leave for the airport from opposite the **Vietnam Airlines** office, 2A Quang Trung St, US$2, running a service at regular intervals from 0500-1800, 50 mins.

There's also an a/c **city bus** that leaves the airport every 20 mins, 5000d.

Chartering a taxi from a hotel to the airport should cost no more than around US$10. Meter taxis may cost over US$20 and will charge an additional road toll of 10,000d.

Airline offices

Air Asia, 30 Le Thai To St, www.airasia.com. **Air France**, 1 Ba Trieu St, T4-3825 3484, www.airfrance.com. **American Airlines**, 99 Ba Trieu St, T4-3933 0330, www.aa.com. **Asiana Airlines**, 604, 4 Da Tuong St, Hoan Kiem District, T4-3822 2671. **Cathay Pacific**, 49 Hai Ba Trung St, T4-3826 7298, www.cathaypacific.com/vn. **China Airlines**, 6B Trang Tien St, T4-3936 6364, www.china-airlines.com. **China Southern Airlines**, 27 Ly Thai To St, T4-3826 9233, www.cs-air.com. **Japan Airlines**, 5th floor, 63 Ly Thai To St, T4-3826 6693, www.vn.jal.com. **Jetstar**, 204 Tran Quang Khai St, Hoan Kiem District, www.jetstar.com/vn. **Korean Air**, 330 Ba Trieu St, Hai Ba Trung District, T4-3974 0240, www.koreanair.com. **Lao Airlines**, 46 Tho Nhuom St, Hoan Kiem District, T4-3822 9951, www.laoairlines.com. **Malaysia Airlines**, 49 Hai Ba Trung St, T4-3826 8820, www.malaysiaairlines.com. **Singapore Airlines**, 17 Ngo Quyen St, T4-3826 8888, www.singaporeair.com. **Thai**, 44B Ly Thuong Kiet St, T4-3826 7921, www.thaiair.com. **Tiger Airways**, T120-60114, www.tigerairways.com. **Vietnam Airlines**, 1 Quang Trung St, T4-3832 0320, www.vietnamairlines.com. Mon-Fri 0700-1830, Sat and Sun 0800-

1130, 1330-1700 for both domestic and international bookings. Telephone sales are Mon-Fri 0700-1900, Sat and Sun 0730-1700. Branch offices: 25 Trang Thi St, T4-3832 0320; 221B Tran Ding Ninh St, T4-73930 0507; 231 Nguyen Trai St, T4-3558 7341; Noi Bai International Airport, T4-3884 3389.

Bicycle
This is the most popular form of local mass transport and it is an excellent way to get around the city. Bikes can be hired from the little shops at 29-33 Ta Hien St and from most tourist cafés and hotels; expect to pay about US$2 per day. For those staying longer, it might be worth buying a bicycle (see Shopping, page 83).

Bus
Local
The Hanoi city bus service, www.hanoibus. com.vn, is still lacking in some ways – routes may be re-routed and drivers continue to drive colourfully. Though to be fair the system is weighted against them – any late returns incur fines so they tend to speed at breakneck pace and sometimes don't stop for passengers.

Buses go all over but you'll want to catch them from around Hoan Kiem Lake, the new bus station on the dyke road at the top of the Old Quarter. Further afield is the Cau Giay bus station, also a relatively new transport hub in the west. Most journeys are 3000-5000d.

Long distance
Hanoi has a number of bus stations. The Kim Ma bus station is closed.

The **Southern bus terminal** (Giap Bat, T4-3864 1467) is out of town, but linking buses run from the northern shore of Hoan Kiem Lake. The terminal serves destinations south of Hanoi: **HCMC, Buon Ma Thuot, Vinh, Danang, Thanh Hoa, Nha Trang, Dalat, Qui Nhon, Ninh Binh, Nam Dinh** and **Nho Quan** for **Cuc Phuong National Park**.

Express buses usually leave at 0500; advance booking is recommended.

Luong Yen bus station, 1 Nguyen Khoai St. The **Hoang Long** bus company, T4-3928 2828, https://hoanglongasia.com, runs deluxe buses to **HCMC** with comfortable beds, 690,000d one way, including all meals and drinks, 36 hrs, 12 a day 0500-2300. **Hoang Long**, also leaves for **Haiphong** from here; 7 daily from 0415-1645 and on to **Cat Ba Island** by ferry. Hoang Long also runs to other desinations. Other bus companies run to, **Haiphong** 0450-1920, 42 daily.

Other buses leave for **Haiphong** and **Halong** from the Gia Lam bus station, Nguyen Van Cu, Gia Lam District, T4-3827 1529, over Chuong Duong Bridge.

From **Ha Dong bus station** Tran Phu Rd, Ha Tay Province, T4-3825 209, buses leave for **Mai Chau, Hoa Binh, Son La** and **Dien Bien Phu**. Take a local bus or xe ôm to the bus station.

From **My Dinh station**, T4-3768 5549, there are buses to **Halong**, every 20 mins, 3 hrs 15 mins, US$2.80. Other destinations in the north are also served from here such as **Thai Nguyen, Tuyen Quang** and **Ha Giang**.

International
To **Vientiane** via Cau Treo. Several travellers have contacted Footprint to complain of this journey. Complaints usually centre around the fact that there always appears to be a delay at or just before the border meaning a 20-hr journey takes nearly 24 hrs. The lesson is be prepared for this to happen, or take alternative transport. For visa info, see page 40 and under Embassies and consulates, page 94. Tickets can be booked through tour operators for straight through services or those where you change buses or direct with one of the bus companies that runs a straight through service such as the **International Passenger Transportation Co Viet-Laos**, 3A Nguyen Gia Thieu St, T4-3942 0554, phongvelao@ yahoo.com.vn, daily 0700-1900. This agency runs a direct bus service to **Vientiane** (Laos), daily 1900, 20 hrs, US$17-22. Book ahead. It dissuades passengers from buying Lao

visas at the border as it alleges the bus won't wait. This is a ploy to get you to buy the visa through them at US$40 for 1 month.

Cyclo

Hanoi's cyclo drivers have obviously heard through the cyclo grapevine that foreigners pay more than locals, but have taken this to extremes; prices quoted are usually 500% more than they should be. Drivers also tend to forget the agreed fare and ask for more: be firm; some ask that the price be written down. A trip from the railway station to Hoan Kiem Lake should not cost more than 30,000d. The same trip on a *xe ôm* would be 15,000d.

Motorbike

Hiring a motorbike is a good way of getting to some of the more remote places. Tourist cafés and hotels rent a variety of machines for US$5-40 per day. Honda scooter 100/110, US$5 per day; Minsk Russian 125, US$7 per day; Honda scooter 125cc, US$10 per day; off-road bike Honda Baja 250 (old), US$25 per day and US$40 per day for a new one. **Voyage Vietnam**, see Tour operators, above, will rent you a Minsk including riding pans, jacket, helmet and saddle-bags, or an off-road Yamaha XT 250 including riding pans, jacket, helmet and saddle-bags and 3rd-party insurance. Note that hire shops insist on keeping the renter's passport.

Taxi and private car

Watch out for taxi scams in Hanoi. There are rogue taxis waiting for the early morning train arrivals; drivers have been known to almost triple the fare to the Old Quarter. Some rogue drivers have been known to lock customers in the car during a fare dispute. Be careful. Make enquiries at hotels about reasonable fares. Small cabs, not saloon cars, can be dodgy. Also be careful catching cabs at night from bars. Agree on a fare first in these situations. It is unlikely you will be hurt but it has happened.

The following are recommended:
Noi Bai Taxi, T4-3873 3333; **Mai Linh Taxi**, T4-3822 2666.

Private cars can be chartered from most hotels and from many tour operators, see page 87.

Train

The **central station (Ga Hanoi)** is at 120 Le Duan St, at the end of Tran Hung Dao St (a 10-min taxi ride from the centre of town), T4-3747 0666. There's an information desk at the entrance, T4-3942 3697, 0700-2300 but minimal English is spoken, and luggage lockers at the end of the ticket hall. The **Thong Nhat** (north-south train) booking office is on the left; northern trains office, on the right. Train times and prices can be found at www.vr.com.vn. The train station remains old-fashioned but fast-food joints – such as the Korean-owned Lotteria – have opened up near the premises if you need a last minute snack before boarding. There's a **VNR** ticket agency at 41 Ma May St, T4-3210 9775, daily 0900-2100. There's a US$1 commission and the ticket can be brought to your hotel.

For trains to **HCMC** and the south, enter the station from Le Duan St. For trains to **Haiphong** and **Lao Cai,** enter the station from Tran Quy Cap St, T4-3747 0308 (take care arriving here at night). It is possible to walk through corridors to get to these platforms from the main entrance if you go to the wrong part.

5 daily connections with **HCMC**, approx 30-40 mins. Advance booking is required. There are daily trains to **Haiphong**, 1 from the the central station, 3 from Long Bien station, T4-3747 0308. There are 3 trains daily to **Ninh Binh**. **Long Bien Station** is at the western end of Long Bien Bridge near the Red River. Get there by taxi or *xe ôm*.

Trains to **Lao Cai** (Sapa). For the full timetable, see page 128. **ET-Pumpkin**, www.et-pumpkin.com and **Ratraco**, www.ratraco.com.vn, run standard comfortable a/c 4-berth cabins in its carriages with complimentary water, bedside lights and space for luggage. For luxury, the **Victoria Hotel** carriages (http://www.victoriahotels-asia.com/eng/hotels-in-vietnam/sapa-resort-spa/victoria-express-train) run Sun-Fri at 2150 to **Sapa** arriving 0630. The dining carriage is only available Mon, Wed and Fri. Places are only available to **Victoria Sapa** hotel guests. The a/c carriages, wood-panelled and with comfortable mattresses and reading lights are very attractive and comfortable; the train caters for 52 people in 2-4 berth cabins. All carriages have a loo and washbasin at one end. The dining carriage is a real treat with big cushions to pad the seats and everything from plum wine to snacks to meals served.

For details of the train from Hanoi to **Beijing** see Dong Dang and the Chinese border, page 143.

ⓘ Directory

Banks

Commission is charged on cashing TCs into US dollars but not if cashing directly into dong. It is better to withdraw dong from the bank and pay for everything in dong. Most hotels will change dollars, often at quite fair rates. ATMs are increasingly common and most Vietnamese banks these days are linked into the large international networks such as Visa and Maestro. You will be charged a fee but it's generally not exorbitant. These days banks aren't as free with the US dollar so if you need some head to Hang Bac or Ha Trung streets. Both black-market changers will give you more favourable rates on your US dollar-dong exchanges. **ANZ Bank**, 14 Le Thai To St, T4-3825 8190, Mon-Fri 0830-1600. Provides full banking services including cash advances on credit cards, 2% commission on TCs, 24-hr ATMs. **Citibank**, 17 Ngo Quyen St, T4-3825 1950. Only cashes TCs into dong. **Vietinbank**, 37 Hang Bo St, T4-3825 4276. Dollar TCs can be changed here. Deals with Amex, Visa, MasterCard and Citicorp. **Foreign Exchange Centre**, 2 Le Lai St. **National Bank**, 10 Le Lai

St, T4-3824 9042, 0800-1100 and 1300-1600. **Sacombank**, 87 Hang Bac St, has a 24-hr Visa and MasterCard ATM. **VID Public Bank**, 2 Ngo Quyen St, T4-3826 6953. Charges 1.5% on TCs. **Vietcombank**, 198 Tran Quang Khai St, T4-3824 3108.

Embassies and consulates

Australia, 8 Dao Tan St, T4-3831 7755. **Belgium**, 49 Hai Ba Trung St, T4-3934 6179. **Burma**, 289 Kim Ma St, T4-3845 3369. **Cambodia**, 71A Tran Hung Dao St, T4-3942 7646. **Canada**, 31 Hung Vuong St, T4-3734 5000. **China**, 46 Hoang Dieu St, T4-3845 3736. For Chinese visa information, see page 122. **Denmark**, 19 Dien Bien Phu St, T4-3823 1888. **France**, 57 Tran Hung Dao St, T4-3944 5700. **Germany**, 29 Tran Phu St, T4-3845 3836. **Israel**, 68 Nguyen Thai Hoc St, T4-3843 3140. **Italy**, 9 Le Phung Hieu St, T4-3825 6256. **Japan**, 27 Lieu Giai St, T4-3846 3000. **Laos**, 22 Tran Binh Trong St, T4-3942 4576. A 1-month Lao visa costs US$32-40; visas are available at all international crossings from Vietnam. **Malaysia**, 43-45 Dien Bien Phu St, T4-3734 3836. **Netherlands**, 360 Kim Ma, T4-3831 5650. **New Zealand**, 5th floor, 63 Ly Thai To St, T4-3824 1481.**Russia**, 191 de La Thanh St, T4-3833 6991. **Singapore**, 41-43 Tran Phu St, T4--3944 5700. **Sweden**, 2 Nui Truc St, T4-3726 0400. **Switzerland**, 44B Ly Thuong Kiet St, T4-3934 6589. **Thailand**, 63-65 Hoang Dieu St, T4-3823 5092. **UK**, Central Building, 31 Hai Ba Trung St, T4-3936 0500. **USA**, 7 Lang Ha St T4-772 1500; Consulate: 1st floor, Rose Garden Tower, 170 Ngoc Khanh St, T4-3850 5000.

Hospitals

Eye Hospital, 85 Ba Trieu St, T4-3826 3966. **Family Medical Practice Hanoi**, Building A1, Van Phuc Compound, 298 Kim Ma Rd, Ba Dinh, T4-3843 0748, www.vietnammedicalpractice.com. 24-hr medical service, including intensive care, also dental care. **Hospital Bach Mai**, Giai Phong St, T4-3869 3731. English-speaking doctors. Also dental service. **International Hospital**, Giai Phong St, T4-3574 0740. **International SOS**, Central Building, 31 Hai Ba Trung St, T4-3934 0555, www.internationalsos.com. 24-hr, emergencies and medical evacuation. Dental service too. **L'Hôpital Français de Hanoi**, 1 Phuong Mai St, Dong Da, T4-3577 1100, www.hfh.com.vn. **Vietnamese-German Hospital**, 40 Trang Thi St, T4-3825 5934. Dental treatment also available.

Pharmacies are as common as *pho* stands in Hanoi and basic drugs, such as painkillers, are generally reliable. Most pharmacy proprietors aren't trained and some of the drugs are fake and/or expired. The **Nha Thuoc Pharmacy** is at 47 Hang Bo St.

Immigration
Immigration Department, 40A Hang Bai St, T4-3826 6200.

Internet
Internet access and emailing is cheap and easy in Hanoi. Many hotels now have free internet use. Failing that, all the travel cafés have internet services. Wi-Fi is everywhere and even outer suburban cafés with no sit-down toilet will have Wi-Fi.

Post office, courier and telephone
GPO, 75 Dinh Tien Hoang St. **DHL** at the GPO. **Express Mail Service** at the GPO and at 778 Duong Lang St, T4-3775 0144 and 49 Nguyen Thai Hoc St, T4-3733 2086. International telephone, telex and fax services also available at the PO at 66-68 Trang Tien St and at 66 Luong Van Can St and at the PO on Le Duan next to the railway station. **TNT** International Express, 25D-25E Lang Ha St, T4-3514 2575. **UPS**, 4C Dinh Le St, T4-3824 6483.

Contents

100 Northwest
  100 Hanoi to Sapa via Dien Bien Phu
  102 Mai Chau
  104 Son La
  105 Around Son La
  106 Dien Bien Phu
  110 Dien Bien Phu to Muong Lay
  111 Muong Lay (formerly Lai Chau)
  113 Around Muong Lay
  114 Listings

117 Sapa and around
  117 Sapa
  120 Treks around Sapa
  122 Lao Cai
  123 Bac Ha
  124 Listings

129 Far North
  130 Ha Giang
  131 Dong Van-Meo Vac Region
  133 East from Ha Giang
  134 Listings

136 Cao-Bac-Lang
  136 North from Hanoi
  137 Cao Bang and around
  139 Pac Bo
  141 Northeast Frontier
  142 Lang Son and around
  144 Bac Son
  144 Listings

146 Haiphong and around
  147 Sights
  150 Listings

152 Halong Bay
  152 Karsts and caves in Halong Bay
  153 Halong City and around
  155 Cat Ba Island
  158 Bai Tu Long and towards the Chinese border
  158 Listings

164 Ninh Binh and around
  169 Listings

Footprint features

  98 Don't miss…
  101 People of the North
  108 Battle of Dien Bien Phu
  132 Hmong Kings of Sa Phin

The North

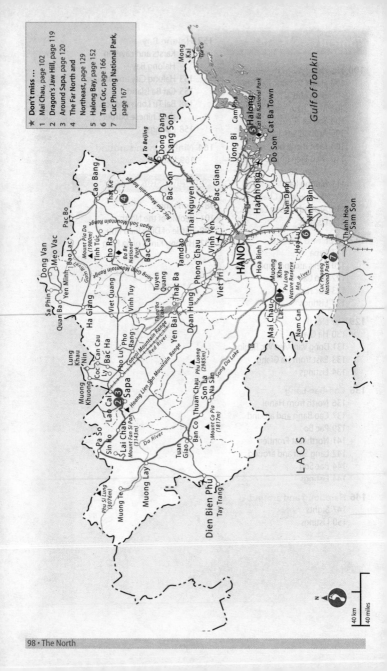

★ Don't miss ...
1 Mai Chau, page 102
2 Dragon's Jaw Hill, page 119
3 Around Sapa, page 120
4 The Far North and
  Northeast, page 129
5 Halong Bay, page 152
6 Tam Coc, page 166
7 Cuc Phuong National Park,
  page 167

Gulf of Tonkin

LAOS

N

40 km
40 miles

To many the Northwest and Far North represents the finest Vietnam has to offer. In terms of scenery, colour, human interest and for the thrill of discovering the unknown, it is unrivalled. The region has wider significance too: the course of world history was altered at Dien Bien Phu in 1954. It is, in short, that myth of travellers' folklore: unspoilt Vietnam. There are good reasons for this. The distance, rugged environment and primitive infrastructure have all contributed to placing the Northwest at the edge of Vietnamese space. Pockets of the north have already been discovered – Sapa, for example, is no longer a secret. But for those who wish to avoid the backpacker trail and are prepared to put up with a little discomfort, the rewards are great.

The fertile river valleys dividing the mountain ranges of North Vietnam have long been inhabited by people of the Austro-Asiatic language family, including forebears of the modern Vietnamese and their upland cousins the Muong. They are thought to have migrated from southern China during the latter half of the first millennium BC; there they joined other groups including the ancestors of the Mon-Khmer-speaking peoples.

Rugged, but lacking the lofty grandeur of Northwest Vietnam, the scenery of the Northeast consists of limestone hills dissected by fast-flowing streams – tributaries of the Gam and Red rivers – hurrying south with their burden of silt. Localized landscapes draw admiration but extensive tracts are unremarkable. Hilltribe minorities, particularly the Dao, Nung and Tay, are much in evidence. Despite its sparse population, Northeast Vietnam features prominently in the annals of nationalist and revolutionary history: decisive victories over invading Chinese, armed resistance against the French and momentous events in the founding of the Vietnamese Communist Party took place here.

Northwest

→ *Colour map 1.*

The geology of much of Northwest Vietnam is limestone; the effect on this soft rock of the humid tropical climate and the resulting numerous streams and rivers is remarkable. Large cones and towers (hence tower karst), sometimes with vertical walls and overhangs, rise dramatically from the flat alluvial plains. Dotted with bamboo thickets, this landscape is one of the most evocative in Vietnam; its hazy images seem to linger deep in the collective Vietnamese psyche and perhaps symbolize a sort of primeval Garden of Eden, an irretrievable age when life was simpler and more innocent.

Interwoven into this landscape are the houses of the ethnic minorities, beautiful tiled houses in the main. Passing through you will see people tending paddies in traditional clothing and boys on the backs of buffalo. In the far-flung northwest corner is Dien Bien Phu, the site of the overwhelming defeat of the French in Vietnam in 1954 and now home to the largest monument in Vietnam, erected in 2004 to commemorate the 50th anniversary of the Vietnamese victory. ▶▶ *For listings, see pages 114-116.*

Ins and outs

Getting there and around There are three points of entry for the Northwest circuit: the south around Hoa Binh (reached by road); the north around Lao Cai/Sapa (reached by road or by train) and in the middle Dien Bien Phu reached by plane or road. Which option you pick will depend upon how much time you have available and how much flexibility you require. It is possible to hire a jeep in Hanoi to do the clockwise circuit via Hoa Binh and Dien Bien Phu and pay off your driver at Sapa leaving you free to return by train. Most people arrive by train or by luxury bus, the cheapest option, to Sapa.

Another option for those so inclined is to do the whole thing by motorbike. The rugged terrain and relatively quiet roads make this quite a popular choice for many people. It has the particular advantage of enabling you to to make countless side trips and get to remote and untouched tribal areas. It is not advisable to attempt the whole circuit using public transport as this would involve fairly intolerable levels of discomfort and a frustrating lack of flexibility and would be very time-consuming. ▶▶ *For further details, see Transport, page 116, and Hanoi tour operators, page 87.*

Best time to visit The region is wet from May to September, making travel quite unpleasant at this time. Owing to the altitude of much of the area winter can be quite cool, especially around Sapa, so make sure you go well prepared.

Tourist information The Northwest is not a single administrative area so see the province and town tourist authorities for local information. Otherwise tour operators in Hanoi are the best source of information, see page 87.

Hanoi to Sapa via Dien Bien Phu → *For listings, see pages 114-116.*

The road from Hanoi to Dien Bien Phu winds its way for 420 km into the Annamite Mountains that mark the frontier with the Lao People's Democratic Republic. The round trip from Hanoi and back via Dien Bien Phu and Sapa is about 1200 km and offers some of the most spectacular scenery anywhere in Vietnam. There are, of course, opportunities

People of the north

Ethnic groups belonging to the Sino-Tibetan language family such as the Hmong and Dao, or the Ha Nhi and Phula of the Tibeto-Burman language group are relatively recent arrivals. Migrating south from China only within the past 250-300 years, these people have lived almost exclusively on the upper mountain slopes, practising slash-and-burn agriculture and posing little threat to their more numerous lowland-dwelling neighbours, notably the Thai.

Thus was established the pattern of human and political settlement that would persist in North Vietnam right up until the colonial period – a centralized Viet state based in the Red River Delta area, with powerful Thai vassal lordships dominating the Northwest. Occupying lands located in some cases almost equidistant from Hanoi, Luang Prabang and Kunming, the Thai, Lao, Lu and Tay lords were obliged during the pre-colonial period to pay tribute to the royal courts of Nam Viet, Lang Xang (Laos) and China, though in times of upheaval they could – and frequently did – play one power off against the other for their own political gain. Considerable effort was thus required by successive Viet kings in

Thang Long (Hanoi) and later in Hué to ensure that their writ and their writ alone ruled in the far north. To this end there was ultimately no substitute for the occasional display of military force, but the enormous cost of mounting a campaign into the northern mountains obliged most Viet kings simply to endorse the prevailing balance of power there by investing the most powerful local lords as their local government mandarins, resorting to arms only when separatist tendencies became too strong. Such was the political situation inherited by the French colonial government following its conquest of Indochina in the latter half of the 19th century. Its subsequent policy towards the ethnic minority chieftains of North Vietnam was to mirror that of the Vietnamese monarchy whose authority it assumed; throughout the colonial period responsibility for colonial administration at both local and provincial level was placed in the hands of seigneurial families of the dominant local ethnicity, a policy which culminated during the 1940s in the establishment of a series of ethnic minority 'autonomous zones' ruled over by the most powerful seigneurial families.

to meet some of Vietnam's ethnic minorities and learn something about their lives and customs (see page 19). The loop can be taken in a clockwise or anti-clockwise direction; the advantage of following the clock is that you'll have the opportunity to recover from the rigours of the journey in Sapa.

Highway 6, which has been thoroughly rebuilt along almost the entire route from Hanoi to Son La, leads southwest out of Hanoi to Hoa Binh. Setting off in the early morning the important arterial function of this road is evident. Ducks, chickens, pigs, bamboo and charcoal (the energy and building materials of the capital) all pour in to Hanoi – a remarkable volume of it transported by bicycle. Beyond the city limit the fields are highly productive, with bounteous market gardens and intensive rice production.

Hoa Binh

Hoa Binh, on the banks of the Da (Black) River, marks the southern limit of the interior highlands. It is 75 km from Hanoi, a journey of about 2½ hours. Major excavation sites of the Hoabinhian prehistoric civilization (10,000 BC) were found in the province, which is its main claim to international fame. In 1979, with Russian technical and financial assistance, work began on the **Hoa Binh Dam** and hydroelectric power station; it was complete 15 years later. The reservoir has a volume of nine billion cubic metres: it provides two functions, to prevent flooding on the lower reaches of the Red River (that is Hanoi) and to generate power. Architecture buffs may want to swing by to see the Russian-influenced industrial architecture. Vietnam is so dependent on Hoa Binh for its electricity that when water levels fall below critical thresholds in the dry season large areas of the country are blacked out. More than 4000 households had to be moved from the valley floor to rugged, infertile hillsides where ironically they are too poor to afford electricity.

The **Hoa Binh Province Museum** ① *0800-1030, 1400-1700, 10,000d*, contains items of archaeological, historical and ethnographical importance. Relics of the First Indochina War, including a French amphibious landing craft, remain from the bitterly fought campaign of 1951-1952 that saw Viet Minh forces successfully dislodge the French.

Muong and **Dao minority villages** are accessible from Hoa Binh. **Xom Mo** is around 8 km from Hoa Binh and is a village of the Muong minority. There are around 10 stilt houses, where overnight stays are possible through **Hoa Binh Tourism** ① *next to the Hoa Binh 1 Hotel, T18-385 4374, www.hoabinhtourism.com*, and there are nearby caves to visit. **Duong** and **Phu** are villages of the **Dao Tien** (Money Dao), located 25 km upriver. A permit is required for an overnight stay. Permits and boat hire are available from **Hoa Binh Tourism**, which can also organize homestays and trekking tours to Thanh Hoa and Mai Chau. So many foreign travellers are bypassing Hoa Binh for the stunning Mai Chau Valley that a homestay may be a more authentic and less touristy experience.

Mai Chau → *For listings, see pages 114-116. Colour map 1, B3.*

After leaving Hoa Binh, Highway 6 heads in a south-southwest direction as far as the Chu River. Thereafter it climbs through some spectacular mountain scenery before descending into the beautiful Mai Chau Valley. During the first half of this journey, the turtle-shaped roofs of the Muong houses predominate, but after passing Man Duc the road enters the territory of the Thai, northwest Vietnam's most prolific minority group, heralding a subtle change in the style of stilted-house architecture. While members of the Thai will be encountered frequently on this circuit, it is their Black Thai sub-ethnic group which will be seen most often. What makes the Mai Chau area interesting is that it is one of the few places en route where travellers can encounter their White Thai cousins.

An isolated farming community until 1993, Mai Chau has undergone significant change in just a few short years. Its tranquil valley setting, engaging White Thai inhabitants and superb rice wine make Mai Chau a very worthwhile stop.

Background

The growing number of foreign and domestic tourists visiting the area in recent years has had a significant impact on the economy of Mai Chau and the lifestyles of its inhabitants. Some foreign visitors complain that the valley has already gone a long way down the same road as Chiang Mai in northern Thailand, offering a manicured hill-tribe village experience to the less adventurous tourist who wants to sample the quaint lifestyle of the ethnic people without too much discomfort. There may be some truth in this allegation, but there is another side to the coin. Since the region first opened its doors to foreign tourists in 1993, the Mai Chau People's Committee has attempted to control the impact of tourism in the valley. **Lac** is the official tourist village to which tour groups are led (there are some 108 guesthouses), and although it is possible to visit and even stay in the others, by 'sacrificing' one village to tourism it is hoped the impact will be limited. Income generated from tourism by the villagers of Lac has brought about a significant enhancement of lifestyles, not just in Lac but also throughout the entire valley, enabling many villagers to tile their roofs and purchase consumer products such as television sets, refrigerators and motorbikes. Of course, for some foreign visitors the sight of a television aerial or a T-shirt is enough to prove that an ethnic village has already lost its traditional culture, but in Lac they are wily enough to conceal their aerials in the roof space.

Lac (White Thai village)

ⓘ *Lac is easily accessible from the main road. From the direction of Hoa Binh take the track to the right, immediately before the ostentatious, red-roofed People's Committee Guesthouse. This leads directly into the village of Lac.*

This village is popular with day-trippers and overnight visitors from Hanoi. Turning into the village one's heart may sink: minibuses are drawn up and stilt houses in the centre of the village all sport stickers of Hanoi tour operators. But before you turn and flee take a stroll around the village, find a non-stickered house and by means of gestures, signs, broken English and the odd word of Vietnamese ask whether you can spend the night.

Rent a bicycle from your hosts and wobble across narrow bunds to the neighbouring hamlets, enjoying the ducks, buffaloes, children and lush rice fields as you go. It is a most delightful experience. If you are lucky you will be offered a particularly refreshing tea made from the bark of a tree.

Grottoes

About 5 km south of Mai Chau on Route 15A is the Naon River on which, in the dry season, a boat can be taken to visit a number of large and impressive grottoes. Others can be reached on foot. Ask your hosts for details.

Around Mai Chau

A number of interesting and picturesque walks and treks can be made in the countryside surrounding Mai Chau. These cover a wide range of itineraries and durations, from short circular walks around Mai Chau, to longer treks to minority villages in the mountains beyond. One such challenging trek covers the 20 km to the village of **Xa Linh**, just off Highway 6. This usually takes between two and three days, with accommodation provided in small villages along the way. Genial host Mr Gia in the Hmong village of **Hung Kia** will warmly welcome you for a couple of dollars per night, copious amounts of rice wine included. Be forewarned that this route can become dangerously slippery in the wet and a guide is required; ask at the People's Committee Guesthouse or in Lac. Expect to pay US$15-20 for two days and arrange for transport to collect you in Xa Linh.

Pu Luong Nature Reserve

ⓘ *Ba Thuoc Project Office, Trang Village, Lam Xa Commune, Ba Thuoc District, Thanh Hoa, T37-388 0494/671, ffiplcpbto@hn.vnn.vn.*

Pu Luong Nature Reserve is a newly protected area of limestone forest southeast of Mai Chau that harbours the endangered Delacour's langur, clouded leopard, Owston's civet and bear. Bird watching is best from October to March. From Ban Sai, 22 km south of Mai Chau, trekkers can visit caves and local Thai and Muong communities. From the south, near the reserve headquarters close to Canh Nang, there is the Le Han ferry crossing. From here visitors can see the traditional water wheels at Ban Cong, trek deep east to Ban Son and then, after overnighting, trek up north back to Highway 6. Also from Le Han, trekkers can overnight in Kim Giao forest in the west of the reserve before visiting an old French airbase, Pu Luong mountain (1700 m) and trekking north back to the Mai Chau area. Biking and boat in and around the reserve is also possible. Contact the reserve office or Hanoi tour operators, see page 87, for details.

Moc Chau and Chieng Yen

North of Mai Chau on the road to Son La is Chieng Yen. Home to 14 villages of Thai, Dao, Muong and Kinh, there are new homestay options with trekking and biking opportunities as well as tea farm visits at Moc Chau. A highlight is the weekly Tuesday market.

Son La → For listings, see pages 114-116. Colour map 1, B2.

The road to Son La is characterized by wonderful scenery and superb Black Thai and Muong villages. The road passes close to several attractive villages each with a suspension footbridge and fascinating hydraulic works. Mini hydroelectric generators on the river supply houses with enough power to run a light or television and water power is also used to husk and mill rice. The succession of little villages located just across the river to the left-hand side of the road between 85 km and 78 km from Son La, affords an excellent opportunity to view Black Thai stilt-house architecture. **Cuc Dua** village at the 84-km mark is photogenic. Typically there is a suspension bridge over the incised river in which you can see fish traps and swimming children as clouds of butterflies flutter by on the breeze.

History

It was not until the 18th century, under the patronage of the Black Thai seigneurial family of Ha, that Son La began to develop as a town. During the late 1870s the region was invaded by renegade Chinese Yellow Flag bands taking refuge after the failed Taiping Uprising. Allying himself to Lin Yung-fu, commander of the pursuing Black Flag forces, Deo Van Tri, Black Thai chieftain, led a substantial army against the Yellow Flags in 1880, decisively defeating and expelling them from the country. Thus Tri established hegemony over all the Black and White Thai lords in the Son La area, enabling him to rely on their military support in his subsequent struggle against the French – indeed, the chieftains of Son La were to take an active role in the resistance effort between 1880 and 1888.

As the French moved their forces up the Da River valley during the campaign of 1888, the chieftains of the area were one by one obliged to surrender. A French garrison was quickly established at Son La. As elsewhere in the Northwest, the French chose to reward the chieftains of Son La district for their new-found loyalty by reconfirming their authority as local government mandarins, now on behalf of a colonial rather than a royal master.

While large-scale resistance to French rule in the Northwest effectively ceased after 1890, sporadic uprisings continued to create problems for the colonial administration. The French responded by establishing detention centres throughout the area, known to the Thai as *huon mut* (dark houses). The culmination of this policy came in 1908 with the construction of a large penitentiary designed to incarcerate resistance leaders from the Northwest and other regions of Vietnam. Just one year after the opening of the new Son La Penitentiary, prisoners staged a mass breakout, causing substantial damage to the prison itself before fleeing across the border into Laos.

During the final days of colonial rule Son La became an important French military outpost, and accordingly an air base was built at Na San, 20 km from the town. Both Na San air base and the colonial government headquarters in Son La town were abandoned to the Viet Minh in November 1953, on the eve of the Battle of Dien Bien Phu.

Sights

There is little to see other than the **Son La Provincial Museum** ① *on Youth Hill, just off Highway 6 and near the centre of town, daily 0700-1100, 1330-1730, 10,000d*. The museum building is in fact the town's old French Penitentiary, constructed in 1908, damaged in 1909, bombed in 1952 and now partially rebuilt for tourists. The original 3-m-deep dungeon and tiny cells complete with food-serving hatches and leg-irons, can be seen together with an exhibition illustrating the history of the place and the key individuals who were incarcerated here.

Around Son La

To reach **Tham Coong** (Coong Caves), walk or drive to the north end of town (Hoa Ban Street); after a few hundred metres (roughly opposite a petrol station) are the tanks of the Son La Water Company; turn left off the road and follow the track gently uphill towards a small group of houses, turning left again just before it forks. Follow the stream or take the path and yomp across the bunds of the rice fields. There are two caves, the wet cave is now fenced off but a scramble up the limestone face brings you to a **dry cave** ① *5000d*, from which the views are lovely. As you have probably come to expect by now in Vietnam, the caves are rather unremarkable, the walk a never-ending joy – with wet feet. The fields, ponds and streams below the caves are a miracle of inventiveness and beauty: stilt houses, gardens, hibiscus hedgerows, poinsettia plants and a range of colours and smells that are particularly appealing in the late-afternoon sunlight. Fish are bred in the ponds covered with watercress (*salad soong*) and what looks like a red algal bloom, but it actually a small floating weed (*beo hoa dau*) fed to ducks and pigs.

Ban Co is a Black Thai village and a visit here can be combined with a trip to Tham Coong. Returning from the caves, rejoin the road then turn left and take a track across the fields and over a small bridge to the village of Co. The village is a largish and fairly ordinary Black Thai settlement but a diverting twilight hour can be spent watching its inhabitants returning from the fields with a fish or duck for the pot and a basket of greens, washing away the day's grime in the stream and settling down to a relaxing evening routine that has changed little in the last few hundred years.

West to Dien Bien Phu or north to Muong Lay from Son La

The scenery on leaving Son La is breathtaking. Reds and greens predominate – the red of the soil, the costumes and the newly tiled roofs, and the green of the trees, the swaying fronds of bamboo and the wet-season rice. Early morning light brings out the colours in their finest and freshest hues, and as the sun rises colours transmute from orange to pink to ochre.

Around every bend in the road is a new visual treat. Most stunning are the valley floors, blessed with water throughout the year. Here generations of ceaseless human activity have engineered a land to man's design. Using nothing more than bamboo technology and human muscle, terraces have been sculpted from the hills: little channels feed water from field to field illustrating a high level of social order and common purpose. Water powers devices of great ingenuity: water wheels for raising water from river level to field level, rice mills and huskers and mini electrical turbines. And, in addition, these people, who for centuries have been isolated from outside perceptions of beauty, have produced a fusion of natural and human landscape that cannot fail to please the eye. Shape, form, scale and colour blend and contrast in a pattern of sympathy and understanding wholly lost to the modern world. Then the road climbs away from the river to a village dependent on rain for its water: the grey and red dust and the meagre little houses indicate great poverty and make one realize the importance of a constant water supply.

There is a small and colourful market village 25 km from Son La and 10 km further on is **Thuan Chau**, another little market town where, in the early morning, people of different minorities in traditional dress can be seen bartering and trading. Thuan Chau is a good spot for breakfast and for buying headscarves. The settlements along this route nicely illustrate the law that describes the inverse relationship between the size of a place and the proportion of the population traditionally garbed. The road is remarkably good with crash barriers, mirrors positioned strategically on hair-pin bends and warning signs, which, considering the precipitous nature of the terrain from Thuan Chau to Tuan Giao, and that visibility is often obscured by cloud and fog, is just as well.

Tuan Giao is 75 km and approximately three hours from Son La (accommodation is available). From Tuan Giao travellers have the choice of either going north across the mountains direct to Muong Lay (formerly Lai Chau), or taking the longer route via Dien Bien Phu.

Highway 6 from Tuan Giao heads north across the Hoang Lien Son Range direct to Muong Lay. From Tuan Giao, the road climbs up through some spectacular scenery reaching altitudes of around 1800-1900 m. Red and White Hmong villages are passed en route.

The journey from Tuan Giao to Dien Bien Phu on Highway 279 is 80 km (about four hours) and tends to be chosen by those with a strong sense of Vietnamese history.

Dien Bien Phu → For listings, see pages 114-116. Colour map 1, B1.

Situated in a region where even today ethnic Vietnamese still represent less than one-third of the total population, Dien Bien Phu lies in the Muong Thanh valley, a heart-shaped basin 19 km long and 13 km wide, crossed by the Nam Yum River.

For such a remote and apparently insignificant little town to have earned itself such an important place in the history books is a considerable achievement. And yet the Battle of Dien Bien Phu in 1954 was a turning point in colonial history (see box, page 108). It marked the end of French involvement in Indochina and heralded the collapse of its North African empire. Had the Americans, who shunned French appeals for help, taken more careful note of what happened at Dien Bien Phu they might have avoided their own calamitous involvement just a decade later.

Ins and outs

Getting there Dien Bien Phu is deep in the highlands of Northwest Vietnam, close to the border with Laos and 420 km from Hanoi (although it feels much further). The airport is 2 km north of town. Buses snake their way up from Hanoi via Hoa Binh and Son La, and there are also connections onward with Muong Lay, Sapa and Lao Cai. Expect overland journeys to be slow and sometimes arduous in this mountainous region but the discomfort is compensated for by the sheer majesty of the landscapes. It is also possible to reach the town via the border with Laos at Tay Trang (Sop Hun border gate in Phongsaly Province).

Getting around The town of Dien Bien Phu with its neat streets is quite easy to negotiate on foot. The battlefield sites, most of which lie to the west of the Nam Yum River, are, however, a bit spread out and best visited by car or by motorbike. Since the majority of visitors arrive in Dien Bien Phu using their own transport, this is not normally a problem.

History

Modern Dien Bien Phu is a growing town. This reflects the decision to make it the provincial capital of the newly created Dien Bien Phu Province and attempts to develop it as a tourist destination.

Settled from an early date, Muong Thanh valley has been an important trading post on the caravan route between China and Burma for 2000 years. Over the years numerous fortifications were constructed in and around Muong Thanh, the best known being the fabled Citadel of the Thirty Thousand (Thanh Tam Van) built by the Lu during the 15th century. Remnants of this citadel can still be seen today, near Xam Mun.

The early years of the 18th century were a period of acute political instability throughout Vietnam. During this time the Northwest was overrun by armies of the Phe from China's southern Yunnan Province who committed unspeakable acts of barbarism against the inhabitants of the area. In 1751, however, a Vietnamese peasant leader from the Red River Delta named Hoang Cong Chat, whose army had retreated into the region to escape from royal troops, rallied local Lu, Lao and Thai chieftains to his cause and expelled the Phe back across the border to China. Building a new fortress at Ban Phu, Chat set himself up as lord of a large area including most of modern Son La and Lai Chau provinces, winning the hearts of the local people by carrying out important land and taxation reforms.

The town of Dien Bien Phu itself only came into existence in 1841 when, in response to continued Lao, Siamese and Chinese banditry in the area, the Nguyen dynasty ordered the establishment of a royal district governed from a fortified settlement at Muong Thanh.

Occupied by French forces during the course of their major Northwest campaign of 1888-1889, Dien Bien Phu was subsequently maintained as a garrison town. The town

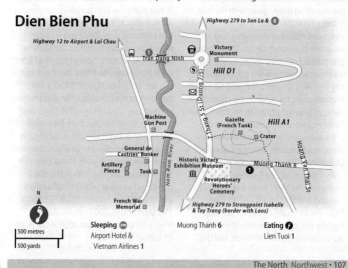

Dien Bien Phu

Highway 279 to Son La & 6

Highway 12 to Airport & Lai Chau

Tran Dang Ninh

Victory Monument

Hill D1

Machine Gun Post

Gazelle (French Tank)

Hill A1

Crater

General de Castries' Bunker

Artillery Pieces

Tank

Historic Victory Exhibition Museum

Muong Thanh 8

Revolutionary Heroes' Cemetery

Highway 279 to Strongpoint Isabelle & Tay Trang (border with Laos)

French War Memorial

Nam Rom River

Thang 5 St (Duong 7/5)

Hoang Van Thai St

N

500 metres
500 yards

Sleeping
Airport Hotel &
Vietnam Airlines 1

Muong Thanh 6

Eating
Lien Tuoi 1

Battle of Dien Bien Phu

On 20 November 1953, after a series of French successes, Colonel Christian de Castries and six battalions of French and French-colonial troops were parachuted into Dien Bien Phu. The location, in a narrow valley surrounded by steep, wooded peaks, was chosen specifically because it was thought by the French strategists to be impregnable. From there, they believed, their forces could begin to harry the Viet Minh close to their bases as well as protect Laos from Viet Minh incursions. At the centre of the valley was the all-important airstrip – Colonel de Castries' only link with the outside world.

In his history of Vietnam, Stanley Karnow describes de Castries thus: "Irresistible to women and ridden with gambling debts, he had been a champion horseman, dare-devil pilot and courageous commando, his body scarred by three wounds earned during the Second World War and earlier in Indochina."

In response, the famous Vietnamese General Giap moved his forces, some 55,000 men, into the surrounding area, manhandling heavy guns (with the help, it is said, of 200,000 porters) up the impossibly steep mountainsides until they had a view over the French forces. The French commander still believed, however, that his forces would have the upper hand in any set-piece confrontation and set about strengthening his position. He created a series of heavily fortified strongholds, giving them women's names (said to be those of his numerous mistresses): Anne-Marie, Françoise, Huguette, Béatrice, Gabrielle, Dominique, Claudine, Isabelle and Eliane.

As it turned out, de Castries was not luring the Viet Minh into a trap, but creating one for himself and his men. From the surrounding highlands, Giap had the French at his mercy. The shelling started in the middle of March, and the strongholds fell one by one; Béatrice first and then Gabrielle and Anne-Marie by mid-March until de Castries' forces were concentrated around the airstrip. Poor weather, which prevented the French from using their air power, and human-wave attacks gradually wore the French troops down. By this time, de Castries had withdrawn to his bunker and command had effectively been taken over by his junior officers. A furious bombardment by the heavy guns of the Viet Minh from 1 May led to the final massed assault five days later. On the final night, the Viet Minh taunted the French defenders by playing the *Song of the Partisans*, the theme of the French Resistance, over the garrison's radio frequencies. The colonel's HQ fell on 7 May at 1730 when 9500 French and French-colonial troops surrendered. A small force of paratroopers at the isolated southern position, Isabelle, continued to resist for a further 24 hours. The humiliation at Dien Bien Phu led the French to sue for peace at a conference in Geneva. On 20 July 1954 it was agreed that Vietnam should be divided in two along the 17th parallel: a communist north and a capitalist south. In total, 20,000 Viet Minh and over 3000 French troops were killed at Dien Bien Phu. The Geneva agreement set terms so that the dead from both sides would be honoured in a massive ossuary. But when Ngo Dinh Diem, the President of the Republic of South Vietnam, symbolically urinated over Viet Minh dead in the South rather than bury them with honour, Giap and Ho Chi Minh decided to leave the French dead to lie where they had fallen. Over the nine years of war between the Viet Minh and the French, the dead numbered between a quarter of a million and one million civilians, 200,000-300,000 Viet Minh and 95,000 French-colonial troops. Who was to guess another 20 years of warfare lay ahead.

fell briefly to Thai insurgents during the latter stages of the 1908 Son La Penitentiary uprising (prompting the suicide of Dien Bien Phu's French commander) and again during the course of the 1914-1916 uprising of Son La chieftains, but perhaps the most serious threat to French rule in the region came in 1918 when the Hmong rebelled against the harsh fiscal policies of the new Governor General Paul Doumer, by refusing to pay taxes in silver coins or to supply opium to the French and taking up arms against the garrison. The insurrection quickly spread east to Son La and south across the Lao border into Samneua, and although the French responded ruthlessly by devastating rebel areas, destroying food crops to provoke famine and setting a high price on the heads of prominent rebels, the revolt persisted until March 1921.

In Vietnam, as elsewhere in Asia, the defeat of the European Allies during the early years of the Second World War utterly shattered the image of Western colonial supremacy, fuelling the forces of incipient nationalism. French attempts to resume their authority in the region in 1945 thus encountered stiff resistance from Viet Minh forces, and in the nine years of fighting which followed, the Northwest became a cradle of national resistance against French colonialism.

Following the French defeat at Hoa Binh in 1952 the Vietnamese Army went on the offensive all over the Northwest, forcing the French to regroup at their two remaining strongholds of Na San (Son La) and Lai Chau. Early the following year, acting in conjunction with Pathet Lao forces, the Viet Minh overran Samneua in upper Laos and proceeded to sweep north, threatening the Lao capital of Luang Prabang. By November 1953 the French colonial government headquarters at Lai Chau (now Muong Lay), just 110 km north of Dien Bien Phu, had also come under siege.

Dien Bien Phu was the site of the last calamitous battle between the French and the forces of Ho Chi Minh's Viet Minh, and was waged from March to May 1954. The French, who under Vichy rule had accepted the authority of the Japanese during the Second World War, attempted to regain control after the Japanese had surrendered. Ho, following his Declaration of Independence on 2 September 1945, thought otherwise, heralding nearly a decade of war before the French finally gave up the fight after their catastrophic defeat here. The lessons of the battle were numerous, but most of all it was a victory of determination over technology. In the aftermath, the French people, much like the Americans two decades later, had no stomach left for a war in a distant, tropical and alien land.

Sights

On the sight of the battlefield **General de Castries' bunker** ① *daily 0700-1100, 1330-1700, 5000d*, has been rebuilt and eight of the 10 French tanks (known as bisons) are scattered over the valley, along with numerous US-made artillery pieces.

On **Hill A1** (known as Eliane 2 to the French) ① *daily 0700-1800*, scene of the fiercest fighting, is a bunker, the bison named Gazelle, a war memorial dedicated to the Vietnamese who died on the hill and around at the back is the entrance to a tunnel dug by coal miners from Hon Gai. Their tunnel ran several hundred metres to beneath French positions and was filled with 1000 kg of high explosives. It was detonated at 2300 on 6 May 1954 as a signal for the final assault. The huge crater is still there. The hill is a peaceful spot and a good place from which to watch the sun setting on the historic valley. After dark there are fireflies. Hill A1 was extensively renovated in readiness for Dien Bien Phu's 50th anniversary of the French defeat in 2004.

The **Historic Victory Exhibition Museum** (Nha Trung Bay Thang Lich Su Dien Bien Phu) ① *daily 0700-1100, 1330-1800, 5000d*, has a good collection of assorted Chinese, American and French weapons and artillery in its grounds. It has been renovated and there are photographs and other memorabilia together with a large illuminated model of the valley illustrating the course of the campaign and an accompanying video. It's interesting to note that, while every last piece of Vietnamese junk is carefully catalogued, displayed and described, French relics are heaped into tangled piles.

The **Revolutionary Heroes' Cemetery** ⓘ *opposite the Exhibition Museum adjacent to Hill A1, 0700-1100, 1330-1800*, contains the graves of some 15,000 Vietnamese soldiers killed during the course of the Dien Bien Phu campaign.

Located close to the sight of de Castries' command bunker is the **French War Memorial** (Nghia Trang Phap). It consists of a white obelisk surrounded by a grey concrete wall and black iron gates sitting on a bluff overlooking the Nam Yum River.

Dien Bien Phu's newest sight towers over the town. Erected on Hill D1 at a cost of US$2.27 million, the **Victory Monument** (Tuong Dai Chien Dien Bien Phu) ⓘ *entrance next to the TV station on 6 Pho Muong Thanh (look for the tower and large, gated pond)*, is an enormous, 120-tonne bronze sculpture and is, as such, the largest monument in Vietnam. It was sculpted by former soldier Nguyen Hai and depicts three Vietnamese soldiers standing on top of de Castries' bunker. Engraved on the flag is the motto *Quyet Chien, Quyet Thang* (Determined to Fight, Determined to Win). One of the soldiers is carrying a Thai child. It was commissioned to mark the 50th anniversary of the Vietnamese defeat over the French in 1954.

Dien Bien Phu to Muong Lay

It is 104 km on Highway 12 from Dien Bien Phu to Muong Lay (formerly Lai Chau). The road was originally built by an energetic French district governor, Auguste Pavie, and was used by soldiers fleeing the French garrison at Lai Chau to the supposed safety of the garrison at Dien Bien Phu in 1953. Viet Minh ambushes along the Pavie Track meant that the French were forced to hack their way through the jungle and those few who made it to Dien Bien Phu found themselves almost immediately under siege again.

The five-hour journey is scenically interesting and there are a few minority villages – Kho-mú and Thai on the valley floors and Hmong higher up on the way.

The scenery is different from any you will have encountered so far. What is amazing around Son La is the exquisite human landscape. From Dien Bien Phu to Muong Lay what impresses is the scenery in its natural state. It is unfriendly but spectacular. The agents at work here are rivers, rain, heat and gravity, and the raw materials are rock and trees. There are no rice terraces but forested hills in which slash-and-burn farming takes place. This is the land of rockslide and flood. It is geologically young and dangerous; the steep slopes of thinly bedded shales collapse after heavy rain, in contrast to the more solid limestone bands of Son La. The density of population is low and evidence abounds that the living here is harsh. A less romantic side to minority-village life is evident: tiny four-year-old children stagger along with a baby strapped to their back, there is no colourful dress or elaborate costume, just ragged kids in filthy T-shirts.

Pu Ka village, 46 km from Muong Lay, is a White Hmong settlement newly established by the authorities to transplant the Hmong away from their opium fields.

Muong Lay (formerly Lai Chau) → *For listings, see pages 114-116. Colour map 1, B1.*

If Son La is notable for the colour of its minorities (Red, Black and White Thai) and Dien Bien Phu for its history, then Muong Lay, should be noted for the splendour of its trees. The town occupies a majestic setting in a deep and wide valley which is cloaked in dense tiers of forest. For various reasons the trees have not been felled and the beauty they confer on Muong Lay presumably extended over a much wider reach of country in an age gone by.

Background

Much of the present town of Muong Lay dates from 1969-1972, when it was expanded to accommodate the large numbers of Chinese engineers posted here to upgrade the road from Dien Bien Phu to the Chinese border (the Friendship Road). In 1993 the status of capital of Lai Chau Province was transferred from Lai Chau town to Dien Bien Phu, partly in recognition of the latter's growing importance as a hub of economic and tourist activity and partly in deference to the side effects of the massive **Son La hydroelectric power scheme** being planned for the Da River valley in which Muong Lay rests. (Dien Bien Phu later became capital of its own eponymous province when this was created in 2004). The dam and reservoir will be three times bigger than the Hoa Binh complex, currently the biggest in Southeast Asia, and as many as 100,000 people could be displaced. For a rather paltry sum of money and a promise of a plot of land the government appears to have bought grudging acquiescence – at least from the people interviewed by *Vietnam News*. The damming of the Da River will drive the final nail into the coffin of this unhappy but lovely town. In 1996 floods killed 29, making 4000 homeless. Some 20,000 will have lost their homes as residents continue to be moved north to Tam Dung in preparation for the Son La project's anticipated completion date; it is expected to be fully operational by 2012.

History

The history of Lai Chau (present-day Muong Lay) is inextricably entwined with that of the Black Thai seigneurial family of Deo who had achieved ascendancy over the former White Thai lords of Muong Lay by the first half of the 15th century. In 1451 the Vietnamese King Le Thai To is recorded as having led a campaign against the Deo family of Muong Lay (then a village 13 km south of the town) for its disloyalty to the crown.

The Deo family in fact comprised a number of separate Black Thai lineages dotted around what is now Northwest Vietnam and the Yunnan Province of China, but it was the marriage during the 1850s of Deo Van Xeng, a wealthy merchant from Yunnan, to the daughter of a Muong Lay Deo chieftain, which established the most notorious line of the Deo family. When his father-in-law died, Xeng seized control of the Muong Lay dominions and, with the support of the royal court in Luang Prabang and the mandarinate of Yunnan, quickly established himself as one of the most powerful lords in the Northwest.

Deo Van Xeng's eldest son, the energetic Deo Van Tri, continued his father's expansionist policies. Allying himself with Chinese Black Flag commander Lin Yung-fu, Tri succeeded in expelling a Chinese Yellow Flag occupation force from Son La, instantly winning the respect and allegiance of the Black and White Thai chieftains of that area. Apart from a small number who stayed and were subsequently integrated into the Thai community, the Black Flags also left the country shortly after this, enabling Tri to assume suzerainty over a large area of Northwest Vietnam.

When French forces launched their campaign to pacify the Northwest, Tri initially took an active part in the resistance, leading a joint Black and White Thai force against the colonial army at the battle of Cau Giay in 1883. Consequently, king-in-exile Ham Nghi appointed Tri military governor of 16 districts. But the garrisoning of French troops at Lai Chau during the campaign of 1888-1889 marked a turning point in the war of resistance and Tri was ultimately obliged to surrender to the French at Lai Chau in 1890.

As elsewhere in the north, the French moved quickly to graft their colonial administrative systems onto those already established by the Nguyen court, and they ensured Deo Van Tri's future co-operation by awarding him the hereditary post of Supreme Thai Chieftain.

After his death in 1915, Tri was succeeded as Governor of Lai Chau by his son Deo Van Long who later took office as mandarin of the colonial government in 1940. However, as the Viet Minh war of resistance got under way in 1945, the colonial government sought to ensure the continued allegiance of ethnic minority leaders by offering them a measure of self-government. Accordingly, in 1947 Muong, Thai, Tay, Hmong and Nung Autonomous Regions were set up throughout the Northwest and, in Lai Chau, Deo Van Long was duly installed as king of the Thai.

King Deo Van Long is remembered with loathing by most older inhabitants of the Lai Chau area. By all accounts he was a tyrant who exercised absolute authority, striking fear into the hearts of the local people by occasionally having transgressors executed on the spot. The overgrown ruins of Long's mansion lie just across the river from Doi Cao (High Hill) and may be visited either by boat or by road (see below).

During the latter days of French rule, as the security situation began to deteriorate throughout the Northwest, Lai Chau became an important French military base; older citizens of the town remember clearly the large numbers of Moroccans, Algerians and Tunisians who were posted here between 1946 and 1953. The French were finally forced to abandon Lai Chau during the winter of 1953 on the eve of the momentous battle of Dien Bien Phu. Bereft of his colonial masters, a discredited Deo Van Long fled to Laos and then to Thailand, whence he is believed to have emigrated to France. A few remaining relatives still live in the area, but have wisely changed their family name to Dieu.

Sights

Former French Colonial Government Headquarters are used as offices and house the local hospital. To get there walk up High Hill past the hospital and fork left up a track leading to the crest of the hill, 500 m further along. Also, on a terrace above the river, is a former airfield (Sang Bay Phap). A very pleasant couple of hours can be whiled away pottering around the largely overgrown and derelict French remains. In trying to identify French areas any budding Indiana Jones can put botanical archaeology to good use. The French were fond of ornamental trees and planted many exotic types: straight rows of huge century-old trees (*muong*) fringe what may have been a former parade ground or playing field; the vivid colours of the flame trees (*phuong*) flag the nascent archaeologist up flights of decaying steps and balustrades towards what looks to have been the sanitorium.

The ruins of **Deo Van Long's House**, originally a plush colonial mansion, lie on Road 127 to Muong Te on the opposite bank of the Da River from High Hill (Doi Cao). The remains are wonderfully overgrown with creeper and strangling figs. Older inhabitants of the six or seven remaining houses recall that for many years Deo Van Long and his family lived in great luxury with a large retinue of servants. Some say that before fleeing the country in 1953, Long had all his servants poisoned so they could not inform the advancing Viet Minh forces of his whereabouts. Beware of piles of loose masonry and deep vaults (dungeons or wine cellars, who can be sure?) covered with only a matting of creeper. You can get to the house by boat from below High Hill (not when river levels are too high or too low); otherwise, it's a circuitous 8-km road trip, crossing one especially rickety suspension bridge

Around Muong Lay → *For listings, see pages 114-116.*

Phi Hay (White Hmong village)
① *Take Highway 6 in the direction of Tuan Giao until just beyond the 10 km way marker from Muong Lay. Stop next to a group of small shops as the road begins to level out, and walk either steeply down left from the road between two shops, or up the path also to the left of the road, but in the direction of a small school building. Continue for a further 2 km.*

This makes an interesting morning's excursion for those who made the detour via Dien Bien Phu. It offers a snapshot of the stunning scenery along the more direct Muong Lay-Tuan Giao mountain route. Phi Hay village is very old and comprises some 50 houses spread out over a considerable area.

Sin Ho
Driving to Sin Ho is hazardous as you need to negotiate the hairpin bends and precipitous drops that characterize the road. If the weather is clear you would be strongly advised to walk some stretches to appreciate the full majesty of the scenery. It will also give you a chance to absorb the delicious cool air, the forest sounds and smells and the wayside flowers. You will also have the opportunity to witness the extraordinary perpendicular fields and to wonder how it is that local farmers can actually harvest slopes on which most people could not even stand.

The first 20 km towards Sin Ho off the main highway is possibly the most spectacular and terrifying drive in Vietnam. After 20 km the road levels off and meanders over the Sin Ho plateau passing hamlets of Red, White and Flower Hmong and Dao minorities. Sin Ho provides little that won't have been seen already, although the Sunday morning market is worthy of note. As with other markets in the region, the Sunday market is an important social occasion.

Lai Chau (formerly Tam Duong)
There are some interesting walks to **Na Bo**, a Pu Na (Giay sub-group) minority village, **Giang** (Nhang minority) and **Hon** minority villages. Pu Na and Nhang people are similar in culture and clothes. Na Bo is 7 km from Lai Chau from which Giang is a further 1.5 km and Hon a further 5 km still. Alternatively a motorbike and driver can be hired.

About 35 km southeast of Lai Chau, Highway 4D swings sharply to the northeast and the altitude climbs abruptly into the Hoang Lien Son range. Here is harsh mountain scenery on a scale previously unencountered on this circuit of Northwest Vietnam. The geology is hard and crystalline as is the skyline, with sharp jagged peaks punching upwards into the sky. Vertical cliffs drop below and soar above; friendly rolling scenery has been replaced by 3000-m-high mountains. There are buses from Lai Chau to Sapa.

For Sleeping and Eating price codes and other relevant information, see Essentials pages 26-31.

⊜ Sleeping

Hoa Binh *p101*

D Hoa Binh 1, 54 Phuong Lam, T18-385 2051. On Highway 6, 1 km out of Hoa Binh towards Mai Chau. Clean rooms with a/c and TV; some rooms built in ethnic style. There's also an 'ethnic dining experience' complete with rice drunk through bamboo straws. The gift shop stocks local produce.

Mai Chau *p102*

AL-A Mai Chau Lodge, a short walking distance southwest of Lac village, T18-386 8959, www.maichaulodge.com. Owned and operated by Buffalo Tours and staffed by locals, there are 16 warmly furnished rooms with modern facilities. The attractive lodge has 2 restaurants, a bar, swimming pool, sauna and jacuzzi. Bicycling, kayaking and trekking tours are offered. Room prices include round-trip transfer from Hanoi.

E Ethnic Houses, Lac village. Visitors can spend the night in a White Thai house on stilts. Mat, pillow, duvet, mosquito net, communal washing facilities (some hot showers) and sometimes fan provided. This is particularly recommended as the hospitality and easy manner of the people is a highlight of many visitors' stay in Vietnam. Food and local rice wine provided. Avoid the large houses in the centre if possible. **Guesthouse No 6**, T18-386 7168, is popular with plentiful food and rice wine. Minimal English is spoken.

Moc Chau and Chieng Yen *p104*

G Homestays with meals are possible. Contact **Son La Province**, T22-385 5714 or tour operator **Handspan** in Hanoi. Breakfasts are 12,000-15,000d; lunch and dinner 40,000-50,000d each.

Son La *p104*

E Hoa Ban 2, Hoa Ban St, T22-385 2395. All rooms have a/c and hot water; it's clean and fairly comfortable.

E Nha Khach Cong Doan (Trade Union Guesthouse), Chieng Le St, T22-385 2804. A short distance off the main road, located behind a large, white exhibition building, beyond the red façade sports department. A/c, fan rooms, basic, some English spoken. Breakfast included in more expensive rooms.

E Nha Khach Uy Ban Nhan Dan (People's Committee Guesthouse), Highway 6, T22-385 2080. Signed Nha Khach just off Highway 6. This hotel has upgraded and expanded to 40 rooms with a/c and fans. It's in a lovely setting overlooking hillsides and villages; breakfast included.

E Phong Lan 1, Chu Van Thinh St, T22-385 3515. Opposite Central Market. A/c, clean and ordinary.

Dien Bien Phu *p106, map p107*

D Muong Thanh Hotel, 25 Him Lam, T230-381 0043. Breakfast included with the more expensive rooms. 62 rooms with TV, a/c, minibar and fan. Internet service, swimming pool (open to non-guests), karaoke, Thai massage and airport transfer free for guests. Souvenir shop and bikes for rent.

F Airport, Tran Dang Ninh, near the bus station, T230-382 5052. Fairly basic, 20 rooms, a/c, hot water.

Muong Lay (formerly Lai Chau) *p111*

C-E Lan Anh Hotel, 9 Phuong Song Da, T23-385 2682, www.lananhhotel.com. Clean fan and a/c rooms in the main part of town with restaurant, not far from the treacherous Da River; a new block has been built on stilts. The hotel organizes transport and tours, hotel, bus and airline reservations. It has also opened a hotel in Pa So. Tours to the weekend markets. Ring in advance as this place will no longer be open once the Son La hydropower scheme is fully operational.

Sin Ho p113

F-G People's Committee Guesthouse, on the right as you enter the town, T23-387 0168. The long, low building is very basic.

Lai Chau (formerly Tam Duong) p113
D Phuong Thanh, T23-387 5235, phuongthanhotel@yahoo.com. 21 fan rooms, hot water, clean, comfortable, lovely views.

🍴 Eating

Hoa Binh p101

The **Hoa Binh hotel** (see Sleeping, above) is open for breakfast, lunch and dinner.
† Thanh Toi, 22a Cu Chinh Lan St, T18-385 3951. Local specialities, wild boar and stir-fried aubergine.

Mai Chau p102

Most people will eat with their hosts. Mai Chau town itself has a couple of simple *com pho* places near the market. The rice wine in Mai Chau is excellent, particularly when mixed with local honey. The **Mai Chau Lodge**, see Sleeping, has 2 restaurants.

Son La p104

† Hai Phi, 189 Dien Bien St, just down from the turning for the Provincial Museum, T22-385 2394. Goat specialities.

Dien Bien Phu p106, map p107

† Lien Tuoi, 27 Muong Thanh 8 St, next to the Vietnamese cemetery and Hill A1, T230-382 4919. Daily 0700-2200. Delicious local fare in a family-run restaurant.
† Muong Thanh Hotel Restaurant, 25 Him Lam, T230-381 0043. Daily 0600-2200. Breakfasts, plenty of Vietnamese dishes, a few spaghettis and pastas. Also duck, boar, pork, frog, curry and some tofu dishes and quite a bit of seafood.

Muong Lay (formerly Lai Chau) p111

† Lan Anh Hotel (see Sleeping, above).

Sin Ho p113

Eat early at one of the cafés around the market. They may only have instant noodles at night and eggs for breakfast. But, washed down with the local rice wine, it tastes like a feast. Wine costs less than US$0.50 a bottle.

🎭 Entertainment

Hoa Binh p101

Hoa Binh Ethnic Minority Culture Troupe, 1-hr shows featuring dance and music of the Muong, Thai, Hmong and Dao in the **Hoa Binh 1** hotel.

Mai Chau p102

Mai Chau Ethnic Minority Dance Troupe, Thai dancing culminating in the communal drinking of sweet, sticky rice wine through straws from a large pot. This troupe performs most nights in Lac in one of the large stilt houses; admission is included as part of the package for people on tours; otherwise you'll need to make a small contribution.

🛍 Shopping

Mai Chau p102

Villagers offer a range of woven goods and fabrics on which they are becoming dependent for a living. There are also local paintings and well-made wicker baskets, pots, traps and pouches.

⛰ Activities and tours

Hoa Binh p101

Hoa Binh Tourism, next to the Hoa Binh 1 hotel, T18-385 4374, www.hoabinhtourism.com. Daily 0730-1100, 1330-1700. Can arrange boat hire as well as visits to minority villages, trekking and transport.

Mai Chau p102

Hanoi tour operators, see page 87, run overnight tours to the area.

☺ Transport

Hoa Binh p100
Bus
Bus station on Tran Hung Dao St. Morning departures to **Hanoi**, 2 hrs.

Mai Chau p102
Bus
Connections with **Hoa Binh**, 2 hrs, **Hanoi**, 4 hrs, and onward buses northwest to **Son La**. While it is easy and cheap to get here by bus most people visit on an organized tour.

Son La p104
Bus
Connections with **Hanoi**, 8 hrs, 5 services daily between 0400 and 0900. En route to Hanoi, services also to **Mai Chau** and **Hoa Binh**. Onward services to **Dien Bien Phu**, 5½ hrs.

Dien Bien Phu p106, map p107
Air
The airport (T230-382 4416) is 2 km north of town, off Highway 12; there are daily flights to **Hanoi**.

   Airline offices Vietnam Airlines, Nguyen Huu Tho Rd, T230-382 4948.

Bus
Note that public transport in the mountains can be time-consuming and arduous. The bus station is close to the centre of town, on Highway 12. It's an easy walk to the hotels. There are daily direct bus connections with **Hanoi**, 13 hrs; daily connections to **Son La**, 5½ hrs; to **Muong Lay**, 3 hrs and some buses to **Sapa**. It is also possible to reach **Mai Chau** via Thai Binh and to **Hoa Binh** en route to Hanoi. There's a bus to the Laos border crossing at Tay Trang to **Muang Khua** (Laos) every other day leaving at 0500. A Laos visa is available at the border; Vietnamese visas are not available at land borders.

Car
The main roads in the Northwest have been improved in the last few years, but a 4WD is

still recommended. The price of hiring a jeep has come down, and many tour operators in Hanoi (see page 87) rent them out for the 5- or 6-day round trip (1200 km via Sapa). A cheaper option is to leave the jeep in Sapa and catch the train to Hanoi from Lao Cai.

Muong Lay (formerly Lai Chau) p111
Bus
Connections south with **Dien Bien Phu**, 4 hrs (and from there to **Hanoi** via **Son La**) and north and east with **Sapa**, 7 hrs. The bus station is south of town, on the road to Dien Bien Phu; try to get dropped off by the bridge in the centre.

Sin Ho p113
Bus
Sin Ho is a 40-km detour off Highway 12. Connections with **Dien Bien Phu** via **Muong Lay**, daily from the market.

Lai Chau (formerly Tam Duong) p113
From Muong Lay, Highway 12 heads almost due north following the Na river valley towards the Chinese border. At Pa So, 10 km from China (border crossing closed), take Highway 4D, southeast. Lai Chau is in fact a collection of 3 settlements, all new.

Bus
Connections with **Hanoi** via **Sapa**; connections with **Lao Cai** also via **Sapa**, and south with **Dien Bien Phu** via **Muong Lay**.

☺ Directory

Hoa Binh p101
Post office Tran Hung Dao St.

Son La p104
Bank Vietcombank, 57 To Hieu St.
Post office 43 To Hieu St.

Dien Bien Phu p106, map p107
Banks Vietcombank and Agribank.
Internet Muong Thanh Hotel, 25 Him Lam St.

Sapa and around

Despite the countless thousands of tourists who have poured in every year for the past decade Sapa retains great charm. Its beauty derives from the impressive natural setting high on a valley side with Fan Si Pan, Vietnam's tallest mountain, either clearly visible or brooding in the mist.

Sapa's access point is Lao Cai, which is also the Chinese border crossing. The markets of the region are popular one-day or overnight trips for visitors. One such local market is Bac Ha.
▸▸ *For listings, see pages 124-128.*

Sapa → *For listings, see pages 124-128. Colour map 1, A2.*

The beauty of the town is a little compromised by the new hotels sprouting up everywhere. Certainly none of the new ones can compare with the lovely old French buildings – pitched roofs, window shutters and chimneys each with their own neat little garden of temperate flora, foxgloves, roses, apricot and plum trees, carefully nurtured by generations of gardeners. Weekends are peak tourist time but during the week the few visitors who remain will have the town to themselves.

Ins and outs

Getting there You get to Sapa either by road as part of the Northwest loop or by overnight train from Hanoi, via Lao Cai. A fleet of minibuses ferries passengers from Lao Cai railway station to Sapa. There are numerous classes of seat or berth on the trains and some hotels have their own private carriages (see Sleeping, page 124, for details). It is quite easy to make the travel arrangements yourself, but booking with an operator removes the hassle. A railway office in Sapa also sells tickets for the journey back to Hanoi. Tour operators in Hanoi sell tours and packages that include treks of various lengths. New comfortable buses now also run the Hanoi–Sapa route. ▸▸ *See Transport, page 127, and Hanoi tour operators, page 87.*

Getting around Sapa is small enough to walk around easily. From Sapa there are a great many walks and treks and the tracks and paths are fun to explore on a Minsk.

Best time to visit At 1650 m Sapa enjoys warm days and cool evenings in the summer but gets very cold in winter. Snow falls on average every couple of years and settles on the surrounding peaks of the Hoang Lien Son Mountains. Rain and cloud can occur at any time of year but the wettest months are May to September with nearly 1000 mm of rain in July and August alone, the busiest months for Vietnamese tourists. December and January can be pretty miserable with mist, low cloud and low temperatures. Spring blossom is lovely but even in March and April a fire or heater may be necessary in the evening.

Tourist information **Sapa Tourist Information Center** ① *2 Phan Si Pang St, T20-387 1975, www.sapa-tourism.com, daily 0800-1130, 1330-1730.* Free tourist information, tours with local guides offered including Fan Si Pan, markets and homestays in local villages; tickets booked; border questions helpfully answered.

Background

Originally a Black Hmong settlement, Sapa was first discovered by Europeans when a Jesuit missionary visited the area in 1918. By 1932 news of the quasi-European climate and beautiful scenery of the Tonkinese Alps had spread throughout French Indochina. Like Dalat in the south it served as a retreat for French administrators when the heat of the plains became unbearable. By the 1940s an estimated 300 French buildings, including a sizeable prison and the summer residence of the Governor of French Indochina, had sprung up. Until 1947 there were more French than Vietnamese in the town, which became renowned for its many parks and flower gardens. However, as the security situation began to worsen during the latter days of French rule, the expatriate community steadily dwindled, and by 1953 virtually all had gone. Immediately following the French defeat at Dien Bien Phu in 1954, victorious Vietnamese forces razed a large number of Sapa's French buildings to the ground.

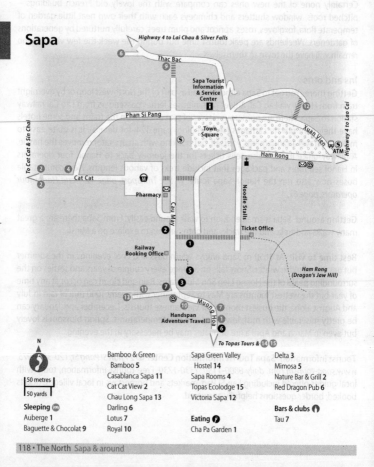

Sapa

Sleeping
Auberge 1
Baguette & Chocolat 9
Bamboo & Green Bamboo 5
Casablanca Sapa 11
Cat Cat View 2
Chau Long Sapa 13
Darling 6
Lotus 7
Royal 10
Sapa Green Valley Hostel 14
Sapa Rooms 4
Topas Ecolodge 15
Victoria Sapa 12

Eating
Cha Pa Garden 1
Delta 3
Mimosa 5
Nature Bar & Grill 2
Red Dragon Pub 6

Bars & clubs
Tau 7

Sapa was also one of the places to be invaded by the Chinese in the 1979 border skirmish. Chinese soldiers found and destroyed the holiday retreat of the Vietnamese Communist Party Secretary-General, Le Duan, no doubt infuriated by such uncomradely display of bourgeois tendencies.

The huge scale of the Fan Si Pan range gives Sapa an Alpine feel and this impression is reinforced by *haute savoie* vernacular architecture with steep-pitched roofs, window shutters and chimneys. But, with an alluring blend of European and Vietnamese vegetation, the gardeners of Sapa cultivate their foxgloves and apricot trees alongside thickets of bamboo and delicate orchids, just yards above the paddy fields.

People

Distinctly oriental but un-Vietnamese in manner and appearance are the Hmong, Dao and other minorities who come to Sapa to trade. Interestingly, the Hmong (normally so reticent) have been the first to seize the commercial opportunities presented by tourism; they are engaging but very persistent vendors of hand-loomed indigo shirts, trousers and skull caps and other handicrafts. Of the craftwork, the little brass and bamboo Jew's-harp is particularly notable. The Dao women, their hands stained purple by the dye, sell clothing on street corners, stitching while they wait for a customer. The girls roam in groups, bracelets, earrings and necklaces jingling as they walk. "*Jolie, jolie*" they say as they push bracelets into your hand and it is hard to disagree. '*Mua mot cai di, mua mot cai di*' (buy one, buy one), the little ones sing, and most people do.

Saturday night is always a big occasion for Black Hmong and Red Dao teenagers in the Sapa area, as youngsters from miles around come to the so-called Love Market to find a partner. The market proved so popular with tourists that the teenagers now arrange their trysts and liaisons in private. The regular market is at its busiest and best on Sunday morning when most tourists scoot off to Bac Ha.

Sights

Sapa is a pleasant place to relax in and unwind, particularly after the arduous journey from Dien Bien Phu. Being comparatively new it has no important sights but several French buildings in and around are worth visiting.

The small church, built in 1930, dominates the centre of Sapa. Recently rebuilt, the church was wrecked in 1952 by French artillerymen shelling the adjacent building in which Viet Minh troops were billeted. In the churchyard are the tombs of two former priests, including that of Father Jean Thinh, who was brutally murdered. In the autumn of 1948, Father Thinh confronted a monk named Giao Linh who had been discovered having an affair with a nun at the Ta Phin seminary. Giao Linh obviously took great exception to the priest's interference, for shortly after this, when Father Thinh's congregation arrived at Sapa church for mass one foggy November morning, they discovered his decapitated body lying next to the altar.

Ham Rong (Dragon's Jaw Hill) ① *0600-1800, 30,000d, free for children under 5*, on which the district's TV transmitter is stuck, is located immediately above Sapa town centre. Apart from offering excellent views of the town, the path winds its way through a number of interesting limestone outcrops and miniature grottoes as it nears the summit. Traditional dance performances take place on the mountain, see Entertainment, page 127.

The derelict French seminary is near the village of Ta Phin. The names of the bishop who consecrated it and the presiding Governor of Indochina can be seen engraved on stones at the west end. Built in 1942 under the ecclesiastical jurisdiction of the Parish of Sapa, the building was destroyed 10 years later by militant Vietnamese hostile to the intentions of the order.

To get there from Sapa, take the road 8 km east towards Lao Cai then follow a track left up towards Ta Phin; it's 3 km to the monastery and a further 4 km to Ta Phin.

Beyond the seminary, the path descends into a valley of beautifully sculpted rice terraces and past Black Hmong settlements toTa Phin.

Note – You should never just turn up in a village for homestay opportunities; book with a tour operator.

Mount Fan Si Pan

At a height of 3143 m, Vietnam's highest mountain is a three-day trek from Sapa. It lies on a bearing of 240 degrees from Sapa; as the crow flies it is 9 km but by track it is 14 km and involves dropping to 1200 m and crossing a rickety bamboo bridge before ascending. The climb involves some steep scrambles which are quite nasty in wet conditions. Only the very fit will make it to the summit. A three-day expedition is recommended. There are few suitable spots for camping other than at the altitudes suggested here: **Day 1**: depart Sapa (1650 m) 0800. Lunch at 1400 m, 1200. Camp at 2285 m; **Day 2**: reach summit late afternoon. Return to camp at 2800 m; **Day 3**: descend to Sapa. A good tour operator, either in Sapa or Hanoi, will provide camping equipment and porters.

Lau Chai (Black Hmong) village and Ta Van (Giáy) village

This is a round trip of 20 km taking in minority villages and beautiful scenery. Heading southeast out of Sapa (see map, page 121), past the **Auberge** guesthouse, Lao Chai is 6 km away on the far valley side. Follow the track leading from the right-hand side of the road down to the valley floor, cross the river by the footbridge (*cau may*) and then walk up through the rice fields into Lao Chai village. You will find Ta Van 2 km further on.

A leisurely stroll through these villages could well be the highlight of a trip to Vietnam. It is a chance to observe rural life led in reasonable prosperity. Wet rice forms the staple income; weaving for the tourist market puts a bit of meat on the table. Here nature is kind, there is rich soil and no shortage of water. Again it's possible to see how the landscape has been engineered to suit human needs. The terracing is on an awesome scale (in places more than 100 steps), the result of centuries of labour to convert steep slopes into level fields which can be flooded to grow rice. Technologically, and in no sense pejoratively, the villages might be described as belonging to a bamboo age. Bamboo trunks carry water huge distances from spring to village; water flows across barriers and tracks in bamboo aqueducts; mechanical rice huskers made of bamboo are driven by water requiring no human effort; houses are held up with bamboo; bottoms are parked on bamboo chairs; and tobacco and other substances are inhaled through bamboo pipes. Any path chosen will lead to some hamlet or other; the Hmong in villages further from Sapa tend to be more reserved and suspicious; their fields and houses are often securely fenced off.

Cross back to the north side of the river by the suspension bridge. A dip in the deep pools of the Muong Hoa river is refreshingly invigorating. Engraved stones are a further 2 km southeast (away from Sapa, that is) by the side of road; they are believed to be inscribed in ancient Hmong. The return walk to Sapa from the inscribed stones is a steady 10-km uphill climb. It's exhausting work but, stimulated by the views and the air and fuelled by hard-boiled eggs and warm Lao Cai beer from roadside shacks, and the prospect of cold beer at home, it is a pleasure, not an ordeal. In the late afternoon sun the rice glows with more shades of green than you would have thought possible and the lengthening shadows cast the entire landscape into vivid three-dimensional relief – even through a camera lens.

Cat Cat and Sin Chai villages
ⓘ 15,000d fee for taking the track.

The track heading west from Sapa through the market area offers either a short 5-km round-trip walk to Cat Cat Black Hmong village or a longer 10-km round-trip walk to Sin Chai Black Hmong village; both options take in some beautiful scenery. The path to Cat Cat leads off to the left of the Sin Chai track after about 1 km, following the line of pylons

Around Sapa

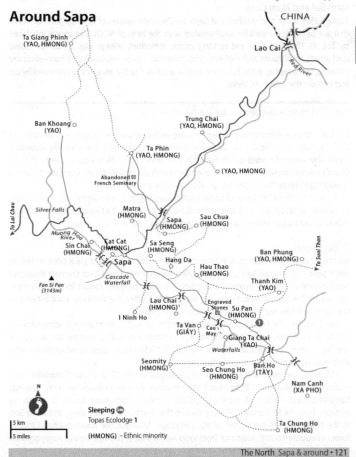

Ta Giang Phinh
(YAO, HMONG)

CHINA

Lao Cai

Red River

Ban Khoang
(YAO)

Trung Chai
(YAO, HMONG)

Ta Phin
(YAO, HMONG)

(YAO, HMONG)

Abandoned
French Seminary

Silver Falls

Matra
(HMONG)

Sapa
(HMONG)

Sau Chua
(HMONG)

Muong Hoa River

Sin Chai
(HMONG)

Cat Cat
(HMONG)

Sapa

Sa Seng
(HMONG)

Hang Da
(HMONG)

Hau Thao
(HMONG)

Ban Phung
(YAO, HMONG)

To Lai Chau

Fan Si Pan
(3143m)

Cascade
Waterfall

Lau Chai
(HMONG)

Engraved
Stones

Su Pan
(HMONG)

Thanh Kim
(YAO)

To Suoi Than

I Ninh Ho

Ta Van
(GIÁY)

Cau
May

Giang Ta Chai
(YAO)

Waterfalls

Seomity
(HMONG)

Seo Chung Ho
(HMONG)

Ban Ho
(TAY)

Nam Canh
(XA PHO)

N

5 km

5 miles

Sleeping 🛌
Topas Ecolodge 1

(HMONG) - Ethnic minority

Ta Chung Ho
(HMONG)

down through the rice paddies to Cat Cat village; beyond the village over the river bridge you can visit the **Cascade Waterfall** (from which the village takes its name) and an old French hydroelectric power station that still produces electricity. Sin Chai village is 4 km northwest of here.

The **Silver Falls** are 12 km west of Sapa on the Muong Lay road and are spectacular following rain. They are hardly worth a special visit but if passing it's quite nice to stop for a paddle in the cold pools.

Other market villages
In the region it's possible to visit Can Cau (Saturday market), Muong Hum (Sunday market), Muong Khuong (Sunday market), Coc Ly (Tuesday market), Lung Khau Nhin (Thursday market), Tam Duong (Thursday market).

Nam Sai and Nam Cam
Some 40 km south and southeast of Sapa are the communities of Nam Sai and Nam Cam that are being developed for local tourism with the help of NGOs. The area is inhabited by Tay, Xa Pho, Red Dao and Hmong ethnic minorities. Village way of life (including cardamom, mushroom and soybean crop growing) can be explored and homestays are possible; see Sleeping, page 125. Treks can be arranged to the area or you can travel by car and explore the area from there.

Lao Cai → *For listings, see pages 124-128. Colour map 1, A2.*

Lao Cai is the most important border crossing with China. A two-way flow of people and trade cross through the city each day. But whereas the balance of human traffic is roughly equal, the value of traded goods is highly one-sided: an endless flow of products from China's modern factories wreaks havoc on Vietnam's own hapless state-owned enterprises struggling to fill quotas of shoddy goods that no one wants to buy.

If you travel from Lao Cai back to Hanoi, the road begins in a beautiful valley where rice, cinnamon (in places the air is scented) and tea are grown. By Viet Tri it has become a drab industrial landscape and remains so all the way back.

Background
An important north-south transit stop for traders with caravans of pack oxen or horses since time immemorial, Lao Cai has changed hands many times over the past thousand years as rival Chinese, Vietnamese and ethnic minority chieftains fought for ascendancy in the region. The town itself dates back at least to 1463, when the Viet kings established it as the capital of their northernmost province of Hung Hoa.

Lao Cai fell to the French in 1889 and thereafter served as an important administrative centre and garrison town. The direct rail link to Hanoi was built during the first decade of the last century, a project notable for the 25,000 Vietnamese conscripted labourers who died during its seven-year construction period.

Following the Vietnamese invasion of Cambodia in late 1978, China, Cambodia's ally, responded in February 1979 by launching a massive invasion of North Vietnam, 'to teach the Vietnamese a lesson'. More than 600,000 Chinese troops were deployed occupying territory from Pa So (formerly Phong Tho) in the Northwest to Cao Bang and Lang Son in the Northeast. From the start of the campaign, however, the poorly trained Chinese forces encountered stiff resistance from local militia and, as the Vietnamese Army got into gear, the Chinese invasion force ground to a halt. After two weeks Chinese troops had penetrated no further than 30 km into Vietnamese territory and, with an estimated 20,000 casualties already incurred by the People's Army, the Chinese government withdrew its troops, declaring the operation "a great success".

Trade with China, much of it illegal, has turned this former small town into a rich community of (dong if not dollar) millionaires and Lao Cai is experiencing something of a construction boom. Huge boulevards flanked by some enormous local government buildings are sprouting up in the main part of town, west of the Red River. In 2006 Lao Cai became a city; by 2020 it looks set to get an airport. Other than for border-crossers Lao Cai holds little appeal.

There is a branch of **Sapa Tourism Center** ① *306 Khanh Yen St, T20-362 52506, www. sapa-tourism.com*, very close to the train station.

International border crossing

The border is open to pedestrians (0700-2200) with the correct exit and entry visas for both countries. Travellers must report to the International Border Gate Administration Center south of the bridge and near the level crossing for passport stamping and customs clearance. Visas into Vietnam must be obtained in Hong Kong or Beijing and must specify the Lao Cai crossing; they normally take a week to process and are not obtainable at the border. Visas for China must be obtained in Hanoi and must also specify the Lao Cai crossing. The Chinese visa costs US$30 but US citizens need to pay US$100; the visa takes four days to be issued. An express 24-hour service costs a further US$20; a two-hour service, a further US$30. **Binh Minh Travel** ① *39 Nguyen Hue, T20-383 6666, www. binhminhtravel.com.vn*, can arrange visas and foreign currency. It costs 10,000d from the train station to the border on a *xe ôm*.➤➤ *See Transport, page 127.*

➤➤ *See Transport, page 127.*

Bac Ha → *For listings, see pages 124-128. Colour map 1, A2.*

① *If you have your own transport, arrive early. If you don't, nearly all the hotels and all the tour operators in Sapa organize trips.*

Bac Ha is really only notable for one thing and that is its Sunday market. That 'one thing', however, is very special. Hundreds of local minority people flock in from the surrounding districts to shop and socialize, while tourists from all corners of the earth pour in to watch them do it. Otherwise there is very little of interest and neither the appeal nor comforts of Sapa.

Bac Ha now has a branch of **Sapa Tourism Center** ① *Hoang A Tuong's Palace, T20-378 0662, www.sapa-tourism.com*.

Around 18 km before Bac Ha the scenery is wonderful; huge expanses of mountains, pine trees and terracing engraved by the winding road as it climbs skywards towards Bac Ha.

The **Sunday market** ① *0600-1400*, draws in the Flower Hmong, Phula, Dao Tuyen, La Chi and Tay – the Tay being Vietnam's largest ethnic minority. It is a riot of colour and fun: the Flower Hmong wear pink and green headscarves; children wear hats with snail motifs and tassles. While the women trade and gossip, the men consume quantities of rice wine and cook dog and other animal innards in small cauldrons. By late morning they can no longer walk so are heaved onto donkeys by their wives and led home.

There are a number of walks to outlying villages. **Pho** village of the Flower Hmong is around 4 km north; **Thai Giang Pho** village of the Tay is 4 km east; and **Na Hoi** and **Na Ang** villages, also of the Tay, are 2 km and 4 km west respectively.

◉ Sapa and around listings

For Sleeping and Eating price codes and other relevant information, see Essentials pages 26-31.

◉ Sleeping

Sapa *p117, map p118*

Prices tend to rise at weekends and Jun-Oct to coincide with northern hemisphere university vacations. Hoteliers are accustomed to bargaining; healthy competition ensures fare rates in Sapa.

AL Victoria Sapa, T20-387 1522, www. victoriahotels-asia.com. Opened in 1998, the hotel has 77 rooms with heating, fans and TVs and comfortable furnishings. It has a nice position above the town and a pleasant aspect: this hotel is easily the best in town and is a lovely place in which to relax and enjoy the peace. In winter there are lovely open fires in the bar and dining rooms. The food is excellent and the set buffets are superb value. The health centre offers everything from traditional massage to reflexology. The centre, pool, tennis courts and sauna are open to non-guests. Packages are available. The hotel has private sleeper carriages on the train from Hanoi to Lao Cai.

AL-B Chau Long Sapa Hotel, 24 Dong Loi St, T20-387 1245, www.chaulonghotel. com. 2 buildings – the old wing and new wing (opposite each other) – in faux castle style make up this hotel with a restaurant boasting great views of the valley. However, the prices in the new wing are unjustified. The old wing represents excellent value although it is looking a little unloved. There's a health centre and indoor pool on site.

A-E Bamboo and Green Bamboo, Cay Mau St, T20-387 1075, www.sapatravel.com. A lovely valley-side location. All 26 rooms in this nice old building have wonderful views and have electric heaters in winter. Breakfast is included in the price. However, rooms are damp and shabby compared with those in the new hotel next door, where the 20 nice rooms have good views and bathtubs.

B-C Sapa Rooms, 18 Phan Xi Pang St, T20-387 2130, www.saparooms.com. Brand new and popular hotel in town with smart rooms and heaps of facilities including recommended restaurant, see Eating. Supports the local ethnic minority community.

B-D Cat Cat View, 46 Phan Xi Pang St, on the Cat Cat side of town through the market. T20-387 1946, www.catcathotel.com. The guesthouse has expanded up the hillside, with new terraces and small bungalows with balconies all with views down the valley. A friendly and popular place, its 40 rooms span the price range but all represent good value for money. Some of its rooms enjoy the best views in Sapa. The hotel has a good restaurant and, like most others, arranges tours and provides useful information. More expensive rooms come with breakfast.

D Casablanca Sapa Hotel, 26 Dong Loi St, T20-387 2667, http://casablancasapahotel. com. This is a new popular spot so book in advance. Rooms are standard but attractively furnished.

D Darling, Thac Bac St, T20-387 1349, www. tulico-sapa.com.vn. It's a short walk from town to this secluded building but for those seeking peace it's worth every step of the way: simple and clean with a warm welcome, stunning views and a colourful garden. There are 45 rooms, most with fabulous views. The top terrace bedroom has the best view in all of Sapa. Swimming pool, gym and pool table.

D-E Auberge, Muong Ha St, T20-387 1243, www.sapanowadays.com. Mr Dang Trung, the French-speaking owner, shows guests his wonderful informal garden with pride: sweet peas, honeysuckle, snapdragons, foxgloves, roses and irises – all familiar to visitors from temperate climes – grow alongside sub-Alpine flora and a fantastic collection of orchids. The rooms are simply furnished but clean and boast bathtubs, and log fires in winter. Restaurant on a lovely terrace. Tours also offered. More expensive rooms enjoy views and a breakfast included in the price.

D-E Royal, Cay Mau St, T20-387 1313, royalhotel_sapa@hotmail.com. A not particularly attractive and quite large (28-room) hotel that spoils some views, although it is friendly enough and quite popular. Cheaper rooms overlook the town, more expensive rooms are rewarded with magnificent views of the valley. The hotel has a special train carriage for the Hanoi to Lao Cai route. Changes money and TCs; cash withdrawn on credit cards attracts a 6% fee.

E Baguette & Chocolat, Thac Bac St, T20-387 1766, www.hoasuaschool.com. From the same company that brought you Hoa Sua training restaurant in Hanoi, this tastefully decorated training hotel offers year-long placements in Hanoi for local ethnic minority girls. With only 4 rooms it is small, well run and extremely clean and comfortable. The downstairs comprises a stylish restaurant and café, with small boulangerie attached. Highly recommended.

E Lotus, Muong Ha St, next to Auberge, T20-387 1308. A small guesthouse with a nice terrace. Rooms have open fire and TV, etc. Those with a view cost more.

F-G Sapa Green Valley Hostel, 45 Muong Hoa Rd, T20-387 1449, www.hihostels.com. A very friendly place on the road out of Sapa, a 10-min walk from the centre. There are 14 private rooms and 1 dorm of 4 beds (US$3 per person in dorm) with mosquito nets and an en suite bathroom. One private room has its own terrace. Breakfast is included if you book through the internet. Free internet.

Treks around Sapa *p120, map p121*
A Topas Ecolodge, 18 km southeast from Sapa, www.topasecolodge.com (Sapa office: 24 Muong Hoa St, T20-387 1331). 25 bungalows with balconies built from white granite are built around a hill overlooking Ban Ho village in the stunning valley. Bungalows are simply furnished and powered by solar energy. The food is good and abundant. Butterflies, flowers and fire

flies abound. Treks organized from the lodge can take you to less touristy Red Dao areas. Unfortunately a hydroelectric power station is being built in the valley, near Seo Trung Ho, spoiling the view. However, for peace and quiet in a natural setting this eco-lodge is unique in Vietnam.

F Nha San Dan Toc (Ethnic Houses). It is possible to spend the night in one of the ethnic houses in the Sapa district. Those of the Black Hmong are probably the best bet, though facilities are more basic than in the Muong and Thai stilted houses of Hoa Binh, Mai Chau and Son La. This can only be arranged through tour operators.

Nam Sai and Nam Cam *p122*
G Homestays. Contact Sapa-based operators, **Sapa Tourism Center** or the tourism department of Lao Cao province, T30-384 6586, svhttdllaocai@gmail.com, for homestays in this newly opened up area.

Lao Cai *p122*
A Lao Cai International Hotel, 88 Thuy Hoa St, T20-382 6668. This grand-looking hotel faces the border gate across the river and has 34 rooms with all facilities. There's a restaurant, health centre and staff can help with obtaining visas if necessary.

E-F Binh Minh, 39 Nguyen Hue St, T20-383 0085. A/c, hot water, fridge and TV in top-end rooms.

F Hoa Lan, 82 Nguyen Hue St, T20-383 0126. One of the more clean and comfortable of the hotels listed. 12 rooms, all with a/c, fridge and TV. No English spoken but nevertheless friendly and helpful.

Bac Ha *p123*
C-D Sao Mai, a short walk north of the centre, T20-388 0288, saomaibh@vnn. vn. Quiet, clean and with a restaurant and free internet. The new building has 25 rooms with a/c and TV; the old wooden building incorporates 15 rooms with fan. The hotel also offers trekking, motorbike hire, jeep tours and can book train tickets

for you. There's an ethnic song and dance performance every Sat night.

E Dang Khoa, northwest of the market, T20-388 0290. Hotel with 20 clean rooms with TV, but overpriced.

F Anh Duong, opposite the original market site, T20-388 0329. A family-run place. 12 rooms with toilet, shower, fan and TV. Nice courtyard in which to sit. No English spoken.

❶ Eating

Sapa *p117, map p118*

There are rice and noodle stalls in the market and along the path by the church.

♈♈♈ Ta Van, in Victoria Sapa, see Sleeping, above, T20-387 1522. The food served in this large restaurant is 1st class and the service is exceptional. Choose from à la carte or buffet dinners; the latter are excellent value. The soups are particularly tasty; you'll want to eat here at least twice to savour the full range of haute cuisine. The large dining room is dominated by an open fire that is hugely warming during those chilly days and nights.

♈♈ Delta, Cay Mau St, T20-387 1799. Open 0730-2200. Sapa's Italian restaurant serves good portions of pasta and pizzas as well as tasty seafood. It's great for people-watching from its big windows as it's on the main bend on the main road. There's a good wine list too.

♈♈-♈ Cha Pa Garden, 23b Cau May St, T20-387 2907, www.chapagarden.com. A peaceful little oasis where you can hide from the street vendors during a romantic meal. Try to ignore the bizarre lounge area with flatscreen TV right off the main dining room while you watch the staff prepare roasted red peppers in a wood fire beside you for a tasty sandwich. The staff are kind and the wine selection is extensive.

♈♈-♈ Sapa Rooms, 18 Phan Xi Pang St, T20-387 2130, www.saparooms.com. If you can't manage to snag a room at its boutique hotel, stop in for a meal at its delightful restaurant. An Aussie owner and an Hanoian artist have worked together to decorate this establishment with whimsical, hilltribe-

inspired works, while the KOTO-trained chefs (see page 79) whip up delicious meals, though the portions are on the smaller side. Try the home-made cookie and ice-cream dessert. Across the street, check out Sapa Rooms' small gallery and cooking school.

♈ Auberge, see Sleeping, above. Popular terrace with partial views of the valley and overlooking the town; it's a lovely breakfast setting. The full menu includes vegetarian food and several types of rice wine.

♈ Baguette & Chocolat, see Sleeping, above, T20-387 1766. Open 0700-2100. The ground floor of the guesthouse comprises a stylish restaurant and café, with small boulangerie attached; lovely home-made cakes for exhausted trekkers go down a treat.

♈ Mimosa, up a small path off Cau May St, T20-387 1377. Open 0700-2300. This small family-run restaurant is in an old house. Sit cosy indoors or in the fresh air on a small terrace. Long menu of good Western and Asian dishes and a reasonably good vegetarian menu.

♈ Nature Bar & Grill, Cau May St, T20-387 2091. This place is great for cosy evenings with an open fire in a cauldron close to the bar. It has nice comfy seats by the window overlooking the main street. There's a decent selection of soups and juices, meat and fish.

♈ Red Dragon Pub, 21 Muong Hoa St, T20-387 2085, reddragonpub@hn.vnn.vn. Open 0800-2230. Done out like an English tearoom with mock Tudor beams and red and white checked table cloths with nosh to match – teas, cornflakes and a mean shepherd's pie. There is a pub upstairs with a tiny balcony that is great for people-watching. Run by a British expat and his Vietnamese wife.

Lao Cai *p122*

♈ Hiep Van, 342 Nguyen Hue St, opposite the station, T20-383 5470. This place with tables spilling out onto the street serves up reasonable Vietnamese and Western food at slightly inflated prices. Its real attraction lies in the fact that you can store luggage and take a shower for 20,000d (towel, soap and shampoo lent) while you wait the odd hour or 2 for the train back to Hanoi.

Bac Ha *p123*

¶ **Cong Phu**, on the right-hand side of the road walking towards the traditional market site, T20-388 0254. Caters for the tourist trade with pancakes and Vietnamese dishes and a large range of drinks.

¶ **Ngan Nga**, just north of **Dang Khoa Hotel**, T20-388 0251. This restaurant, used by tour groups, serves up abundant and reasonable fare. The set lunch menu is very good value. There's good service and a clean WC despite the numbers passing through.

🍷 Bars and clubs

Sapa *p117, map p118*

Red Dragon Pub, see Eating, above.
Tau Bar, 42 Cau May St, T912-927756. Open 1500-late. Beneath the **Tau Hotel**. It must have the longest bar made of a single tree trunk in the world and worth a beer just to see it. There's a darts board and pool table and a large range of beers and spirits.

🎭 Entertainment

Sapa *p117, map p118*

Ethnic minority dancing, Dragon's Jaw Hill, daily at 0930 and 1500, 10,000d. Also at the **Bamboo Hotel**, 2030-2200; free as long as you support the bar and at the **Victoria Sapa** every Sat at 2030.

🛍 Shopping

Sapa *p117, map p118*

Sapa is the place for buying ethnic clothes. Nowhere in Vietnam has the range of shirts, baggy trousers, caps, bags and other garments of Sapa. Sold by vendors or in shops, a lot is second-hand but all the more authentic for that. Note that it is not possible to buy walking shoes or decent climbing equipment in Sapa. Quite a good range is available in Hanoi. Temperate fruit, plums

and apricots and delicious baby pineapples are sold in the market.

⛰ Activities and tours

Sapa *p117, map p118*

Therapies
Victoria Sapa, see Sleeping, above. Massage and other treatments are available. The hotel also has an indoor swimming pool.

Tour operators
Handspan, 7 Cau May St, T20-387 1214, www.handspan.com. Tours in the vicinity of Sapa, including treks, mountain bike excursions, homestays and jeep expeditions. This is a booking office for the **Handspan Adventure Travel** group with offices in Hanoi.
Topas, 24 Muong Hoa St, T20-387 1331, http://topastravel.vn. A combined Danish and Vietnamese operator offering numerous treks varying from fairly leisurely 1-day walks to an arduous 4-day assault on Mount Fan Si Pan. It also organizes bicycling tours and family tours. Well-run operation employing hundreds of local people and providing equipment where necessary. It has an office in Hanoi.

🚌 Transport

Sapa *p117, map p118*

Roads to Sapa have been improved but heavy rain and trucks can destroy a good surface very quickly. For train information, see Transport, Lao Cai, below.

Bus
Frequent connections from the bus station, T20-387 1006, with **Lao Cai**, US$2, 1½ hrs; minibuses also congregate on the corner next to the church. To **Hanoi** on more comfortable buses, several departures daily, 150,000-160,000d, T167-412 6412, or contact them at Lao Cai Railway station. Bus to **Kunming**, China, passing through Lao Cai, US$25, 10 hrs.

Lao Cai p122

Bus

Minibuses to **Sapa** from the train station, US$2 or some hotels have their own pickup.

Town bus station on Hong Ha St. Bus to **Dien Bien Phu**, 0730, 250,000d, 12 hrs. To **Hanoi**, 3 a day 0300-0500, 10 hrs, 100,000d. To **Bac Ha**, 0530, 0730, 30,000d.

Train

The station is about 2 km south of the hotel area. Trains run to and from **Hanoi** daily. See below for timetable. Tickets from Lao Cai can be booked for a small charge at the railway booking office in Sapa.

Tour operators in Hanoi (see page 87) can also book your ticket for you for a small fee from the top of the class – the Victoria Sapa carriage – downwards. It is often less hassle than organizing it yourself and, if you are in a hurry, it's a great time saver.

The train service into China is suspended. Enquire locally before travel.

To take a motorbike on the train you need a ticket, luggage ticket, registration papers, and the petrol tank must be empty. You must be on the platform at least 30 mins before departure and pay an uploading fee of 20,000d-25,000d. If the machine is larger than 150 cc, you will require a special permit.

Hanoi – Lao Cai

Train	Depart	Arrive
LC3	0610	1540
SP1	2115	0615
LC5	2040	0435
SP3	2155	0600
LC1	2005	0710
SP5	0820	1705

Lao Cai – Hanoi

Train	Depart	Arrive
LC4	0915	2015
LC2	1845	0400
SP2	2015	0430
LC6	1930	0415
LC8	1930	0415
SP4	2100	0505

The **Victoria carriages** (www.victoriahotels-asia.com/eng/hotels-in-vietnam/sapa-resort-spa/victoria-express-train) run Sun-Fri at 2045 to **Hanoi** and 2150 from Hanoi. See Hanoi, page 93, for further information.

Bac Ha p123

The drive from Sapa to Hanoi is very long. Those wanting a detour to Bac Ha on the way home face a gruelling day; **Sapa** to Bac Ha is 3 hrs, Bac Ha to **Hanoi** around 10 hrs.

Bus

Bus to **Lao Cai** departs 0500; 2 buses daily to **Pho Lu**, 0900 and 1100, 15,000-20,000d.

Train

From Lao Cai or Hanoi (10 hrs) to **Pho Lu**, then bus up to Bac Ha.

Directory

Sapa p117, map p118

Banks Agribank, 1 Pho Cau May St, T20-387 1206, Mon-Fri and Sat morning, will change US dollars, euro, Australian dollar, Chinese yuan and Canadian dollar cash, as will most hotels but at poor rates. It will also change US dollar and euro TCs. **BIDV**, Ngu Chi Son St, T20-387 2569, has a Visa ATM and will change cash and TCs. Convert before you travel.

Internet There are now a dozen internet places in town. **Post office** 2 in Sapa from where international calls can be made. The main post office offers internet.

Lao Cai p122

Banks Agribank, Nguyen Hue St, T20-383 0013, has a Visa and MasterCard ATM. Techombank, 19 Nguyen Hue St, T20-383 0655, accepts Visa, MasterCard and Amex. **Internet** Lao Cai Internet opposite the shopping centre. **Post office** Opposite railway station and just south of border at 13 Nguyen Hue St.

Bac Ha p123

Internet Opposite the Ngan Nga restaurant.

Far North

The Far North of Vietnam is a beautiful, mainly mountainous region that skirts the Chinese border. Its steep slopes have been carved into curved rice terracing with paddies shimmering in the strong sun; further north where the steepness increases, majestic limestone mountain peaks will enthrall. The sparse populations that live here are predominantly indigenous groups and, thankfully, they have not yet been corrupted by commercialization to the same extent as their cousins in the Northwest. The way of life in the traditional villages remains just that, traditional; it is not a show put on for the entertainment of tourists. The far north is still one of the least-visited areas of the country and, as such, it offers the chance to see Vietnamese life as it really is. ▶▶ For listings, see pages 134-135.

Ins and outs

Getting there and around Unlike Northwest Vietnam, which has so conveniently aligned its attractions along one road circuit, the far north is somewhat fragmented although through road links have improved. For much of the area a **permit** is required to visit. Dutch NGO **SNV** is trying to encourage tourism in this area as the Northern Highlands Trail and is seeking to ease restrictions in the area ▶▶ *See Ha Giang Ins and outs, page 130, and Transport, page 135.*

Best time to visit The best time to visit this area is from October until March. Although this is winter and spring, the weather is milder than if you were to visit later in the year.

The road to Ha Giang

For much of its length the well-maintained Highway 2 follows the Lo River northwards from Hanoi through some delightful scenery. During the early stages of the journey as the road passes the eastern shores of the **Thac Ba Lake**, tea plantations may be seen everywhere, but northwards from Ham Yen, 41 km beyond Tuyen Quang, it is orange groves which carpet the hillsides. At Thac Ba it's possible to stay in White Trouser Dao communities and take boats out onto the lake.

Tuyen Quang Province has a large ethnic minority population and, not long after leaving the provincial capital, travellers will begin to see people from the two main groups of this province, the Tay and the Dao. The delightful little town of **Vinh Tuy**, near the banks of the Lo River, is a possible lunch stop. Boats can be seen on the river most days, dredging the bed for gold.

Detouring to **Xin Man** in the far east of Ha Giang province is worth the hike. This ethnic minority town mostly draws Hmong, Nung, Tay and Dao minorities, and Sunday market time is busy and hectic.

From Xin Man, a road twists and turns towards Hoang Su Phi passing Heaven's Gate II and the Hoang Su Phi Pass.

Tan Quang is a sizeable market town located some 60 km before Ha Giang at the junction with Highway 279, the mountain road west to Bao Yen in Lao Cai Province.

The provincial capital of Ha Giang lies on the banks of the Lo River just south of its confluence with the River Mien, perched picturesquely between the beautiful Cam and Mo Neo mountains. Like Cao Bang and Lang Son, Ha Giang was badly damaged during the border war with China in 1979 and has since undergone extensive reconstruction.

Ins and outs

Getting there and around From Hanoi Highway 2 goes directly to Ha Giang. The journey should take between six and seven hours. Ha Giang can be reached comfortably in a day from Sapa. Within the town, there are a few taxis and also the ubiqitous *xe ôm*.

Best time to visit There are four distinct seasons in the north (spring, summer, autumn and winter). The best time to visit would be either during autumn or spring.

Tourist information Ha Giang Tourist company ⓘ *5 Nguyen Trai St, T219-387 5288/ T219-386 7054, dulichhagiang@gmail.com, Mon-Fri 0800-1130, 1330-1700.* To visit the surrounding area you will need a special **permit** which the company can obtain for you; 250,000d for up to a group of five and you must hire a local guide.

History

Archaeological evidence unearthed at Doi Thong (Pine Hill) in Ha Giang town indicates there was human settlement in the region at least 30,000 years ago. It was during the Bronze Age, however, that the most important flowering of early culture took place under the Tay Vu. This was one of the most significant tribes of the Hung kingdom of Van Lang, whose centre of power was in the Ha Giang region. Some of the most beautiful Dong Son bronze drums were found in Ha Giang Province, most notably in the Meo Vac region, where the tradition of making bronze drums for ceremonial purposes continues even to this day among the Lolo and Pu Peo communities.

The original settlement in Ha Giang lay on the east bank of the Lo River and it was here that the French established themselves following the conquest of the area in 1886. The town subsequently became an important military base, a development confirmed in 1905 when Ha Giang was formally established as one of four North Vietnamese military territories of French Indochina.

The Ha Giang area saw a number of important ethnic rebellions against the French during the early years of the colonial period, the most important being that of the Dao who rose up in 1901 under the leadership of Trieu Tien Kien and Trieu Tai Loc. The revolt was quickly put down and Trieu Tien Kien was killed during the fighting, but in 1913 Trieu Tai Loc rose up again, this time supported by another family member known as Trieu Tien Tien, marching under the slogans: "No corvées, no taxes for the French; Drive out the French to recover our country; Liberty for the Dao".

Carrying white flags embroidered with the four ideograms *To Quoc Bach Ky* (White Flag of the Fatherland) and wearing white conical hats (hence the French name 'The White Hat Revolt'), the rebels launched attacks against Tuyen Quang, Lao Cai and Yen Bai and managed to keep French troops at bay until 1915 when the revolt was savagely repressed. Hundreds of the insurgents were subsequently deported and 67 were condemned to death by the colonial courts.

Sights

The **Ha Giang Museum** ① *next to Yen Bien Bridge in the centre of town, daily 0800-1130, 1330-1700, free,* contains important archaeological, historical and ethnological artefacts from in and around the region, including a very helpful display of ethnic costumes.

Located close to the east bank of the River Lo in the old quarter of the town, Ha Giang Market is a daily affair although it is busiest on Sunday. Tay, Nung and Red Dao people are always in evidence here, as are members of northern Ha Giang Province's prolific White Hmong.

Doi Thong (Pine Hill) lies just behind the main Ha Giang Market. The pine trees are newly planted but the hill itself is an area of ancient human settlement believed to date back some 30,000 years to the Son Vi period. Many ancient axe-heads and other primitive weapons were discovered on the hill during land clearance; these are now in the local museum and in the History Museum in Hanoi.

Dong Van-Meo Vac Region → *For listings, see pages 134-135. Colour map 1, A4.*

This is the northernmost tip of Vietnam, close to the Chinese border and just 30 km south of the Tropic of Cancer. It's an impressive natural setting high on a valley side with Fan Si Pan, Vietnam's tallest mountain, either clearly visible or brooding in the mist.

Ins and outs

Getting there All foreign visitors are required to obtain a special permit and take a licensed guide before proceeding beyond Ha Giang into the remote Dong Van-Meo Vac area on the Chinese border including the districts of Quan Ba and Yen Minh. This can be obtained either directly from the local police or alternatively through the **Ha Giang Tourist Company** (see page 135). One possible advantage of booking a tour in Hanoi is that they do it for you, although the permit arrangement must be completed in the Ha Giang tourist office.

Getting around Local bus services are infrequent and slow. The roads north of Ha Giang have now been sealed and are in good condition but the roads are narrow and windy with high mountain slopes. A 4WD vehicle or sturdy motorbike is highly advisable. Ha Giang to Dong Van via Yen Minh is 148 km, five hours; Dong Van to Meo Vac, 22 km, one hour. Returning from Meo Vac to Ha Giang head straight to Yen Minh via Highways 176 and 180 bypassing Dong Van and cutting off 22 km. It is a straight small and windy 50-km road in good condition but the most superb scenery is the Dong Van-Meo Vac road. Note that since both Dong Van and Meo Vac are located very close to the Chinese border, hill-walking by foreigners around both towns is forbidden, making the number of things to do in Dong Van and Meo Vac somewhat limited although Hanoi tour operators (see page 87) can organize four- to seven-day trekking tours in the area.

Quan Ba

Quan Ba is 45 km from Ha Giang. The road climbs up the Quan Ba Pass to 'Heaven's Gate' – identifiable by the TV transmitter mast to the left of the summit – from where there are wonderful views of the Quan Ba Valley with its extraordinary row of uniformly shaped hills. Quan Ba has a Sunday market, one of the largest in the region, which attracts not only White Hmong, Red Dao, Dao Ao Dai and Tay people but also members of the Bo Y ethnic minority who live in the mountains around the town.

Hmong Kings of Sa Phin

While it is clear that Hmong people have lived in the Dong Van-Meo Vac border region for many centuries, the ascendancy of White Hmong in the area is believed to date from the late 18th century, when the powerful Vuong family established its seat of government near Dong Van. In subsequent years the Vuong lords were endorsed as local government mandarins of Dong Van and Meo Vac by the Nguyen kings in Hué and later, following the French conquest of Indochina, by their colonial masters.

Keen to ensure the security of this key border region, the French authorities moved to further bolster the power of the Vuong family. Accordingly, in 1900 Vuong Chi Duc was recognized as king of the Hmong, and Chinese architects were brought in to design a residence befitting his newly elevated status. A site was chosen at Sa Phin, 16 km west of Dong Van; construction commenced in 1902 and was completed during the following year.

During the early years of his reign, Vuong Chi Duc remained loyal to his French patrons, participating in numerous campaigns to quell uprisings against the colonial government. In 1927 he was made a general in the French army; a photograph of him in full military uniform may be seen on the family altar in the innermost room of the house. But, as the struggle for Vietnamese independence got underway during the 1930s, Duc adopted an increasingly neutral stance. Following his death in 1944, Duc was succeeded as king of the Hmong by his son, Vuong Chi Sinh, who the following year met and pledged his support for President Ho Chi Minh.

Built between 1902 and 1903, the house of the former Hmong king faces south in accordance with the geomantic principles which traditionally govern the construction of Northeast Asian royal residences, comprising four, two-storey sections linked by three open courtyards. The building is surrounded by a moat, and various ornately carved tombs of members of the Vuong family lie outside the main gate. Both the outer and cross-sectional walls of the building are made of brick, but within that basic structure everything else is made of wood. The architecture, a development of late 19th-century Southern Chinese town-house style, features *mui luyen* or *yin-yang* roof tiles.

Yen Minh and Pho Bang

Yen Minh is located 98 km northwest of Ha Giang and is a convenient place to stop for lunch on the way to Dong Van and Meo Vac – a possible overnight stop for those planning to spend longer in the region. It has a Sunday market where, in addition to the groups mentioned above, you'll see Giay, Pu Peo, Co lao, Lolo and the local branch of Red Dao.

Northwest of Yen Minh right on the Chinese border lies the town of Pho Bang. Time seems to have stood still here with mud construction homes with a second galley floor to house firewood. This is remote but worth the hike for the ambience in the town.

Sa Phin

Crossing the old border into the former demesne of the White Hmong kings the very distinctive architecture of the White Hmong houses of the area becomes apparent; it is quite unlike the small wooden huts characteristic of Hmong settlements elsewhere in North Vietnam. These are big, two-storey buildings, constructed using large bricks fashioned from the characteristic yellow earth of the region and invariably roofed in Chinese style. But it is not only the Hmong who construct their houses in this way – the dwellings of other people of the area such as the Co lao and the Pu Péo are of similar design, no doubt a result of their having lived for generations within the borders of the former Hmong kingdom.

The remote Sa Phin valley is just 2 km from the Chinese border. Below the road surrounded by conical peaks lies the village of Sa Phin, a small White Hmong settlement of no more than 20 buildings from which loom the twin, white towers of the Hmong royal house, at one time the seat of government in the Dong Van-Meo Vac region, see box, left. The **Sa Phin tourist office** ① *T219-288290*, just below the house, provides a guide with a little English, 5000d. A visit to the royal house is fascinating. The Sa Phin market is a treat and is held every 12 days. Duck into the food market and drink beer with the locals from bowls.

Lung Cu
Lung Cu is the most northern point in Vietnam. It is marked by a hillock, flag pole and observation tower. From the top of the hill low mounds and China can be spied. There's an army post there so you'll need to register in the small town before walking up the steep steps.

Dong Van
This remote market town is itself nothing special (situated 16 km from Sa Phin) but is set in an attractive valley populated mainly by Tay people. However, it does have a street of ancient houses that is very attractive. One has been converted into a café. Dong Van has a Sunday market, but is very quiet at other times of the week. Since the town is only 3 km from the Chinese border, foreigners are not permitted to walk in the surrounding hills or visit villages in the vicinity. (Interestingly no two maps of this part of Vietnam tell the same story.)

Meo Vac
Passing through the **Ma Pi Leng Pass** around 1500 m above the Nho Que River, the scenery is simply awesome. Like Dong Van, Meo Vac is a restricted border area, and foreigners are not permitted to walk in the surrounding hills or visit villages outside the town. Phallic-shaped mountainous peaks and chasms of running rivers make up the scenery. A small market is held every day in the town square, frequented mainly by White Hmong, Tay and Lolo people. Meo Vac is also the site of the famous Khau Vai 'Love Market' held once every year on the 27th day of the third month of the lunar calendar, which sees young people from all of the main ethnic groups of the region descending on the town to look for a partner. The Lolo people, with their highly colourful clothes, make up a large proportion of the town's population. A Lolo village is nearby, up the hill from the town centre.

If you are lucky to pass Lung Phin, 15 km after Meo Vac on the way back to Yen Minh on market day you will see the wildest market on the village hillside. It is the most colourful of the markets in the Ha Giang region. This market is held every six days.

East from Ha Giang → *For listings, see pages 134-135.*

Beyond Meo Vac the road used to be impassable to motorized vehicles but new bridges mean direct access to Bac Me, Bao Lac, and Tinh Túc and onward to Cao Bang and Lang Son. **Bao Lac** is a small town but visitors can be put up for the night at the People's Committee Guesthouse. There is a busy morning market but this is far from anywhere and food is limited. **Tinh Túc** is a tin mining town in a pretty valley. It has a simple but adequate hotel next to the post office; there's also a canteen-type diner with very cold beer. Tinh Túc to **Cho Ra** (for Ba Be Lake) is a scenic and rewarding trip.

For Sleeping and Eating price codes and other relevant information, see Essentials pages 26-31.

☻ Sleeping

The road to Ha Giang *p129*

● **E-F Gia Long Hotel**, Xin Man, T219-383 6479, gialonghotel.2001@gmail.com. It's the only thing going in Xin Man with rooms with kitsch decor down to dorms.

F-G Lavie Vu Linh Resort, a sustainable tourism project in Ngoi Tu village, Vu Linh commune, Yen Bai province, www.lavievulinh. com. Sleep in a longhouse on the floor or a private room with en suite. The shared bathroom has the most fabulous bathtub. Hot water is available. Trekking, rafting, fishing, boating, biking and badminton is possible. Dinner is with a local family and costs 110,000d. This is billed as a sustainable tourism project. It has a great lookout across the lake but there is some criticism of the project in the community. It may be better to stay with a local family in the nearby village.

G Ethnic minority homestay at Thac Ba Lake. Mr Thuong and Miss Nhat offer homestay in the village of Ngoi Tu, Vu Linh, Yen Bai province, T9-7284 5982 (English not spoken). Dinner is US$4.50 and breakfast is US$1.20.

Ha Giang *p130*

D-F Huy Hoan Hotel, 10 Nguyen Trai St, T219-386 1288. Follow the main road coming into the town centre and on the left-hand side, just 20 m after the junction of Yen Bien 2 bridge is the hotel. The best hotel in Ha Giang with 41 very comfortable a/c rooms with private bathroom. Very little English is spoken but they are fluent in Chinese. Wi-Fi available.

E Pan Hou Village, T219-383 3565, www. panhouvillage.hebergratuit.com, is some distance south of Ha Giang off the main road. You would need to have your own transport to get to this lodge in the

mountains. It would be a good place from where to trek which is organized.

F Hotel Hoang Anh, 5 Nguyen Trai St, T219-386 3559. 39 rooms in this town centre spot. Drawcard is the bathtubs.

F Phuong Dong Hotel, 5 Nguyen Trai St, T219-386 7979. A total of 17 a/c rooms all with en suite facilities. Helpful staff.

G Thon Tha Hamlet (Lam Phuong cooperative), T219-386 0647, T123-852 2447 (mob). Mr Nguyen Van Quyen is in charge of the homestay rota at this picturesque Tay ethnic minority village amid paddy fields, 5 km west of Ha Giang.

The **Yen Bien**, 517 Nguyen Trai St, T219-386 8229. The biggest hotel in town was being rebuilt at the time of going to press.

Yen Minh and Pho Bang *p132*

F Nha Nghi Noa Hong, T219-859557. There is 1 hotel in Pho Bang in a small courtyard. Rooms are spacious with comfortable beds and mosquito nets but bathrooms are tiny and running cold water may not even be available. Dinner is what's available.

F People's Committee Guesthouse, Yen Minh Tinh Ha Giang, T219-385 2297. 12 rooms all equipped with a/c and hot water. The staff are friendly but speak no English.

Dong Van *p133*

E Cao Nguyen Da (Rocky Plateau Hotel), T219-385 6868. Service is appalling but you've got to dig the orange suede and white retro furniture in the lobby and the clay pot sculpture in the stairwell. 14 overdecorated rooms with small bathrooms. Prices rise at weekends. Breakfast not included.

F Khai Hoan Hotel, T219-385 6147. A 25-roomed hotel with large rooms; fan only. It's the biggest and cleanest hotel in town. Breakfast not included.

Meo Vac *p133*

E Hoa Cuong Hotel, T219-387 1888. This new 26-roomed hotel is luxurious for these parts. Hot gushing showers and firm beds with crisp linens are most welcome up here.
F Nho Que Guesthouse, T219-387 2322. A good guesthouse with 12 a/c rooms and hot water showers.

❶ Eating

The road to Ha Giang *p129*
¶ **Nhat Thuy Com Binh Dan** (Common Rice Restaurant), Xin Man, T219-383 6117. A basic restaurant serving tasty pork dishes, sardines, soups and fried spring rolls.

Ha Giang *p130*
¶ **Com Pho Bo**, 200 m from the **Huy Hoan Hotel** on Nguyen Trai St serving simple dishes.
¶ **Com Vietnam**, 1 Quang Trung St, T219-386 8034. Open daily. The menu's not in English but there's chicken, duck, beef, water buffalo, fish and spring rolls.
¶ **Tourist Company Quan Com Pho**, 160 Tran Hung Dao St, corner of Nguyen Trai St. The most traveller-friendly place to eat in Ha Giang. Another restaurant next door. There are numerous other small places to eat down side streets off Tran Hung Dao and on the other side of town near the main market. The **Pho Da** café is nearby.

Yen Minh and Pho Bang *p132*
There are plenty of rice restaurants along Thi Tran Yen Minh St in Yen Minh.
¶ **Minh Hai**, by the market, is a good place for food.

Dong Van *p133*
¶ **Pho Co Cafe**. A charming café with an interior courtyard and wooden balustrading in an old building. Just drinks on offer.
¶ **Tien Nhi Restaurant**, main road, Dong Van, T219-385 6217. Get yourself a slice of superb roasted pig from here. Failing that a coffee from this friendly restaurant.

❷ Shopping

Tea is the speciality produce of the region, which grows many different varieties including green, yellow, black and flower-scented. Best known is Shan Tuyet tea, a flavoursome variety which is exported but will not be to everyone's taste.

Ha Giang *p130*
Minisupermarket, 143 Nguyen Trai St.

⛰ Activities and tours

Ha Giang *p130*
Ha Giang Tourist Company, see page 130. Permits for Dong Van-Meo Vac region are obtainable here, 250,000d for up to a group of 5; takes 1 hr.

❸ Transport

Ha Giang *p130*
Bus
The bus station is at 13 Nguyen Trai St. Departures to **Hanoi**'s Gia Lam terminal, 6 hrs. 4WD vehicle recommended in the far north, whatever the season.

East from Ha Giang *p133*
Bus
Buses from Ha Giang to **Bao Lam** via Bac Me on Route 34. Direct to **Bac Me** also. From **Bao Lam** to **Bao Lac**, **Tinh Túc**, **Nguyen Binh** and **Cao Bang** daily; 7-8 hrs to **Cao Bang**.

❹ Directory

Ha Giang *p130*
Banks Agribank, Tran Hung Dao St. BIDV with ATM, 159 Nguyen Trai St. **Post office** Nguyen Trai St.

Cao-Bac-Lang

The three provinces of Cao Bang, Bac Can and Lang Son – the famous Cao-Bac-Lang resistance zone of the 1947-1950 Frontier Campaign – form the heartland of the Viet Bac (literally North Vietnam). This a mountainous region, heavily populated by Tay and Nung people, became the cradle of the revolution during the twilight years of the French colonial period. ▶▶ *For listings, see pages 144-146.*

Ins and outs

Getting there and around Tours are available from the plethora of tour operators in Hanoi. It is possible to tour this beautiful area by way of a circuit which leads north along Highway 3 from Thai Nguyen to Bac Can, making a small diversion to Ba Be National Park before continuing north to Cao Bang and the historic border district of Pac Bo. From here, Highway 4, scene of some of the most bitter fighting during the First Indochina War, leads south to the important frontier town of Lang Son. The return journey from Lang Son to Hanoi may then be made either directly along Highway 1A or across the mountains along Highway 1B. Although it is possible to reach the larger centres by bus from Hanoi, the going is tough and detours are not possible. A 4WD vehicle is recommended.
▶▶ *See Transport, page 145.*

North from Hanoi → *For listings, see pages 144-146.*

Heading north from Hanoi you'll pass through the indutrial town of Thai Nguyen; the only reason to stop would be to visit the **Thai Nguyen Museum of Ethnology** ① *Tue-Sun 0800-1630, 20,000d*. This notable museum houses a collection of artefacts relating to all of Vietnam's 54 ethnic groups. It includes clothes, agricultural and handicraft tools and textiles.

Bac Can

The market town and eponymous capital of Bac Can Province lies on the River Cau. Bac Can acquired enormous strategic significance during the First Indochina War as the westernmost stronghold of the Cao-Bac-Lang battle zone. The town was captured by the Viet Minh in 1944 and its recovery was considered crucial to the success of the 1947 French offensive against the Viet Bac resistance base. Although colonial troops did succeed in retaking Bac Can, and built military outposts along Highway 3 in the autumn of 1947, guerilla attacks on the town's garrison subsequently became so frequent that the French were forced to abandon the town two years later.

Bac Can's daily market is frequented by all the main ethnic groups of the region, which include not only Tay but also local branches of the White Hmong and Red Dao, in addition to Coin Dao (*Dao Tien*) and Tight-Trousered Dao (*Dao Quan Chet*).

Ba Be National Park → *Colour map 1, A4.*

① *44 km west of Na Phac on Highway 279, 1 hr from Cho Ra town, T281-389 4026, 10,000d plus 1000d insurance per person and 10,000d per car.* The park centre is located on the eastern shore of Ba Be Lake. It runs many different tours led by English-speaking guides with an expert knowledge of the area and its wildlife. These tours range from 2-hr boat trips to 2-day mountain treks staying overnight in Tay or Dao villages and visiting caves, waterfalls and other local beauty spots.

Ba Be National Park (Vuon Quoc Gia Ba Be) was established in 1992. It is Vietnam's eighth national park and comprises 23,340 ha of protected area plus an additional 8079 ha of buffer zone. It is centred on the very beautiful Ba Be Lake (*ba be* means 'three basins'), 200 m above sea level. The lake is surrounded by limestone hills carpeted in tropical evergreen forest. The park itself contains a very high diversity of flora and fauna, including an estimated 417 species of plant, 100 species of butterfly, 23 species of amphibian and reptile, 110 species of bird and 50 species of mammal. Among the latter are 10 seriously endangered species, including the Tonkinese snub-nosed langur (*Rhinopitecus avunculus*) and the black gibbon (*Hylobates concolor*). Within the park there are a number of villages inhabited by people of the Tay, Red Dao, Coin Dao and White Hmong minorities.

Cao Bang and around → For listings, see pages 144-146. Colour map 1, A5.

Cao Bang stands in a valley on a narrow peninsula between the Bang Giang and Hien rivers, which join just to the northwest of the town. Cao Bang was badly damaged during the 1979 border war with China and has since been extensively rebuilt. The market here is one of the largest in the country.

Ins and outs
Getting there and around Cao Bang is located on Highway 3 and is 270 km from Hanoi. Na Phac to Cao Bang is 83 km, 1½ hours along a well-metalled road. The Cao Bac Pass runs between 39 km and 29 km before Cao Bang, with stunning scenery all the way and breathtaking views at its summit. Arriving in Cao Bang, fork left over a bridge and keep going until the **Bang Giang Hotel** appears straight in front of you. Once in the town, there are plenty of taxis and *xe ôm*. Walking is an option as many of the sights in Cao Bang itself are easy reach. ▶ *See Transport, page 145.*

Best time to visit As Cao Bang is only 300 m above sea level, the climate is temperate all year round.

Tourist information **Cao Bang Tourist** ① *1 Nguyen Du St, T26-385 2245*. As provincial travel agencies go, it is good and offers a selection of tours at reasonable prices. The staff are friendly and helpful.

History
Tay-Thai settlement in the area began at a very early date, leading to the emergence of the powerful Tay Au kingdom here during the Bronze Age. The Tay Au kings moved their capital south to Co Loa in the Red River Delta where, over the ensuing centuries, they gradually succumbed to the dominant Viet culture.

In the mid-10th century the Viet kings set about establishing fortifications in and around Cao Bang owing to its strategic position near the Chinese border, but the region continued to pose a significant security problem throughout the feudal era, as indicated by the revolts of Tay lords, Be Khac Thieu and Nung Dac Thai, against the Le Dynasty during the 1430s.

During the late 16th and early 17th centuries Cao Bang became a hotbed of revolt against royal authority. The essential background to the events of that period was the usurpation of the Le throne in 1527 by the Mac; although the Le kings were reinstated in 1592, members of the Mac family subsequently seized Cao Bang and proceeded to rule the region as an independent kingdom for a further 75 years. The ruins of a temple which once functioned as the palace of the Mac kings may still be seen today near the small market town of Cao Binh, 12 km northwest of Cao Bang town.

Before the arrival of the French, the market town of Cao Binh served as the administrative headquarters of Cao Bang Province. However, the Cao Bang Peninsula had also been settled from an early date and, following the French conquest of the area in 1884, the colonial authorities decided to transfer the provincial capital to the current site. A substantial fortress was subsequently constructed on the hill overlooking the town centre – the outer walls of this fortress still stand today, although what's left of the fortress itself currently serves as a base for the People's Army and is therefore off-limits to visitors.

From the late 1920s onwards Cao Bang became a cradle of the revolutionary movement in the north. The following years saw the establishment of many party cells through which a substantial programme of subversive activity against the colonial regime was organized. It was thus no accident that in 1940, when he returned to Vietnam after his long sojourn overseas, Ho Chi Minh chose to make remote Cao Bang Province his revolutionary headquarters during the crucial period from 1940 to 1945.

Sights

There is not a lot to see in the town. A few late-19th-century **French buildings** have survived the ravages of war and redevelopment in the old quarter of town which stretches down the hill from the fortress to the Hien River Bridge, making that area worth exploring on foot.

Cao Bang Exhibition Centre ① *Hoang Nhu St, T26-385 2616, Wed and Sat 0800-1100, 1300-1700, free,* records the history of the revolutionary struggle in Cao Bang Province, with particular reference to the years leading up to the establishment of the Democratic Republic of Vietnam when Ho Chi Minh's headquarters were based at Pac Bo, 56 km north of Cao Bang. Pride of place in the exhibition hall is given to Ho's old staff car, registration number 'BAC 808'. Unfortunately all information is in Vietnamese only.

Ky Sam Temple

① *18 km north of Cao Bang town on Highway 203 to Pac Bo. It is located in the Nung village of Ngan, 200 m east of Highway 203.*
This temple honours the memory of Nung Tri Cao, Nung lord of Quang Uyen, who led one of the most important ethnic minority revolts against the Vietnamese monarchy during the 11th century.

The story of Nung Tri Cao began in 1039 when Nung Tri Cao's father Nung Ton Phuc and his elder brother Nung Tri Thong rose in rebellion against Le Thai Tong. An expeditionary force was swiftly assembled by the Viets and the rebels were caught and summarily executed. However, two years later Nung Tri Cao himself gathered an army, seizing neighbouring territories and declaring himself ruler of a Nung kingdom which he called Dai Lich. He too was quickly captured by Viet troops, but having put his father and elder brother to death two years earlier, King Le Thai Tong took pity on Nung Tri Cao and let him return to Quang Uyen. For the next seven years peace returned to the area, but in 1048, Nung Tri Cao rose up in revolt yet again, this time declaring himself 'Emperor of Dai Nam' and seizing territories in southern China. For the next five years he managed to play the Viet and Chinese kings off against each other until Le Thai Tong finally captured and executed him in 1053.

There has been a temple in the village of Ngan for many centuries, but the one standing today dates from the 19th century. It comprises two buildings, the outer building housing an altar dedicated to one of Nung Tri Cao's generals, the inner sanctum originally containing statues of the king, his wife and his mother; unfortunately these statues were stolen many years ago. The poem etched onto the walls in the outer building talks of Nung Tri Cao's campaigns and declares that his spirit is ever ready to come to the aid of his country in times of need.

Ruins of Cao Binh Church
ⓘ *5 km north of Ky Sam Temple along Highway 203 to Pac Bo, fork left at a junction; the ruins are 500 m from the junction.*
Constructed in 1906, Cao Binh Church was one of three churches administered from Cao Bang during the French period, the others being those of Cao Bang and That Khe. There used to be many French houses in the vicinity of the church, but the majority of those that survived the French war were destroyed in 1979. However, the former vicar's house still stands relatively intact, adjacent to the ruins of the church. The family which currently occupies it runs one of the Cao Bang region's most famous apiaries.

Mac Kings' Temple
ⓘ *1.5 km beyond Lang Den (Temple village), located on the west bank of the Dau Genh River, opposite Cao Binh. Accessible either on foot or by 4WD capable of fording the river.*
Cao Binh is situated on the east bank of the Dau Genh River, a tributary of the Bang Giang River. On the opposite bank lies Lang Den (Temple village), which takes its name from the ruined 16th-century palace of the Mac Dynasty located on a hill just above the village.

This structure is believed to have been built during the early 1520s by Mac Dang Dung, a general of the Le army who in 1521-1522 seized control of the kingdom, forcing the 11-year-old King Le Chieu Tong into exile and setting up his younger brother Le Thung as king. Two years later Mac Dang Dung forced Le Thung to abdicate, declaring himself king of Dai Viet.

The Mac Dynasty retained control of Dai Viet for 65 years, during which period representatives of the deposed Le Dynasty mounted numerous military campaigns against the usurpers. The Le kings were finally restored to power in 1592 by the powerful Trinh family, but in that year a nephew of Mac Mau Hop, the last Mac king, seized Cao Bang and set up a small kingdom there. Over the next 75 years three successive generations of the Mac family managed to keep the royal armies at bay, even managing to launch two successful attacks on Thang Long (Hanoi) before Cao Bang was finally recaptured by Trinh armies in 1667.

It is apparent that this building was originally constructed as a small royal residence; the original cannon placements may still be seen on the hill in front of the main entrance.

Pac Bo

The road from Cao Bang to Pac Bo passes through 56 km of stunning scenery, 1½ hours. Despite its proximity to China, no special permit is needed, but walking outside the area is not permitted.

On 28 January 1941 Ho Chi Minh crossed the Sino-Vietnamese border, returning home to take charge of the resistance movement after 30 years overseas. In the days which followed, he and his colleagues set up their revolutionary headquarters in a cave in the Pac Bo valley. Of interest primarily to scholars of the fledgling Vietnamese Socialist Party, Pac Bo is the sort of pilgrimage spot that model carpet-weavers or revolutionary railwaymen might be brought to as a reward.

History

Taking advantage of the surrender of the French administration to the Japanese, Ho Chi Minh returned to Vietnam setting up his headquarters at Pac Bo, an area populated mainly by the Nung people. It was from here that Ho Chi Minh – dressed in the traditional Nung costume – guided the growing revolutionary movement, organizing training programmes for cadres, translating *The History of the Communist Party in the USSR* into Vietnamese and editing the revolutionary newspaper *Independent Vietnam*.

The eighth Congress of the Communist Party Central Committee, convened by Ho Chi Minh at Pac Bo from 10-19 March 1941, was an event of great historic importance which saw the establishment of the Vietnam Independence League (*Vietnam Doc Lap Dong Minh Hoi*), better known as the Viet Minh. This Congress also assisted preparations for the future armed uprising, establishing guerilla bases throughout the Viet Bac.

The years from 1941 to 1945 were a period of severe hardship for the Vietnamese people, as the colonial government colluded with Japanese demands to exploit the country's natural resources to the full in order to support the Japanese war effort. But, by 1945, the Vichy Government in France had fallen and the French colonial administration belatedly drew up plans to resist the Japanese. However, on 9 March 1945, their plans were foiled by the Japanese who set up a new government with King Bao Dai as head of state.

At this juncture, Viet Minh guerilla activity was intensified all over the country with the result that by June 1945, almost all of the six provinces north of the Red River Delta were under Communist control. On 13 August Japan surrendered to the Allied forces; three days later Ho Chi Minh headed south from Pac Bo to Tan Trao near Tuyen Quang to preside over a People's Congress which declared a general insurrection and established the Democratic Republic of Vietnam. The August Revolution that followed swept all in its wake; within a matter of weeks the three major cities of Hanoi, Hué and Saigon had fallen to the Viet Minh and King Bao Dai had abdicated. On 2 September 1945 President Ho Chi Minh made a historic address to the people in Hanoi's Ba Dinh Square, proclaiming the nation's independence.

Sights

The **Pac Bo Vestiges Area Exhibition Center** ① *T26-385 2425, daily 0800-1700*, houses artefacts concerning the revolution and Ho Chi Minh's part in it. The centre is 2 km from the vestiges themselves and comprises two buildings: the **Ho Chi Minh House of Remembrance** contains an altar dedicated to Ho Chi Minh, while the **museum** has background information on the Pac Bo area and its historical role in the revolutionary struggle. It also contains information about Ho Chi Minh's long journey back to Vietnam between 1938 and 1941, culminating in his arrival at Pac Bo on 28 January 1941. There is a series of artefacts associated with the various periods between 1941 and 1945 during which Ho Chi Minh lived and worked at Pac Bo, including many of his private possessions. Then there are further exhibits surrounding the events leading up to Ho's journey south from Pac Bo to Tan Trao near Tuyen Quang, where a decision was taken in August 1945 to launch a general insurrection to seize power and found the Democratic Republic of Vietnam.

A further 2 km by road is a parking area located next to the Lenin Stream under the shade of Karl Marx Mountains; both names chosen by Ho Chi Minh (the place is festooned with commemorative plaques). From here, visitors can do two walks: one to **Coc Bo Cave** (500 m), where Ho lived and worked after his return from overseas, and the other to Khuoi Nam Jungle Hut (800 m).

Ban Doc (Ban Zop), Vietnam's most recently discovered waterfall, and apparently the highest, is about 80 km due north of Cao Bang. Views of the waterfall are incredible.

Northeast frontier

From Cao Bang to Lang Son along Highway 4 is a journey of 135 km; the road is in relatively poor condition and the going can be quite hard, taking 3½ hours, but it is not without its rewards. About 10 km south of Dong Khe, Highway 4 climbs up to the infamous **Lung Phay Pass**. From here to the village of Bong Lau the wonderful mountain scenery makes it difficult to imagine the carnage that took place between 1947 and 1950, when convoy after convoy of French supply trucks ran into carefully planned Viet Minh ambushes. The **War Heroes' Cemetery** at Bong Lau is sited on a hill where a French military outpost once stood and marks the border between Cao Bang and Lang Son provinces.

About 30 km south of That Khe the road passes through more towering limestone outcrops before commencing its climb up through another of the Frontier Campaign's infamous battle zones, the beautiful **Bo Cung Pass**.

The Frontier Campaign of 1947-1950

The government established by Ho Chi Minh in September 1945 soon found itself in a cleft stick. The terms of the Potsdam Conference had provided for the surrender of Japanese forces to be accepted south of the 16th parallel by British-Indian forces and north of that line by the Chinese Kuomintang (Nationalist Party) troops of Chiang Kai-shek. In the south, General Gracey promptly freed thousands of French troops detained in the wake of the Japanese coup.

Unable to confront both the French and the Chinese, Ho Chi Minh decided to negotiate with the French, concluding, as we have already seen, that they were the lesser of the two evils. In February 1946 the French signed a treaty with the Chinese Nationalists which secured their withdrawal from Vietnamese territory. The following month a Franco-Vietnamese agreement confirmed the status of Vietnam as a free state within the French Union and the Indochinese Federation.

After consolidating their positions in the Red River Delta, the French resolved to launch a major offensive against the Viet Bac in October 1947 with the objective of destroying the resistance leadership. Their plan involved a pincer movement of two armed columns – one under Colonel Communal moving by water up the Red and Lo rivers to attack and occupy Tuyen Quang and Chiem Hoa, the other under Colonel Beaufre travelling to Lang Son and then north along Highway 4 to That Khe, Dong Khe and Cao Bang before heading southwards to Bac Can. The offensive was intended to take the Viet Minh by surprise but, just six days after the attack had begun, an aircraft carrying the French chief of staff was shot down near Cao Bang, allowing the plans to fall into the hands of the Viet Minh High Command.

Sailing up the Lo River, Communal's column fell into a Viet Minh ambush suffering a humiliating defeat and losing some 38 gunboats before being forced to retreat to Tuyen Quang. Meanwhile, Beaufre's forces suffered repeated ambushes at the hands of Viet Minh before finally managing to recapture the fortresses of Cao Bang and Bac Can in late October 1947. Having failed to achieve the objective of their offensive, the French were now obliged to dig-in for a long and costly war.

The position of the French became steadily more and more precarious. Supply convoys travelling from Lang Son to Cao Bang and Bac Can were ambushed repeatedly, particularly along Highway 4. Thousands of colonial troops lost their lives en route, on what French press dubbed the 'Road of Death', the most dangerous stretches of which were the Lung Phay Pass 10 km south of Dong Khe and the Bo Cung Pass 30 km south of That Khe.

Despite massive subsidy from the United States under the emerging Truman doctrine of containing Communism, the cost of air-dropping supplies into the region was becoming an intolerable burden. The French High Command finally concluded that their position in the Viet Bac was no longer tenable and began to draw up plans for the abandonment of Cao Bang. Before these plans could be implemented, however, the Viet Minh launched a surprise attack on Dong Khe, capturing the post. Taken aback by this bold move and desperate to secure the speedy and safe retreat of its Cao Bang garrison, the French High Command ordered the post's commander, Colonel Charton, to withdraw to Lang Son.

Leaving Cao Bang on 3 October 1950, Charton's column made it no further than Nam Nang, 17 km south of the town, before running into a Viet Minh ambush. Travelling northwards from That Khe to rendezvous with Charton, Lepage's forces were also intercepted in the vicinity of Dong Khe. The subsequent battle in the hills to the west of Highway 4 resulted in a resounding Viet Minh victory, in the aftermath of which, on 8 October, some 8000 French troops had been either killed or taken prisoner. Within days the French had abandoned all their remaining posts on Highway 4.

The Viet Minh victory on Highway 4 was a major turning point in the war, which threw the colonial forces throughout the north into complete disarray. During the following two weeks the French were obliged to withdraw all their forces from Lang Son, Thai Nguyen and Tuyen Quang, while in the northwest, the French garrisons at Hoa Binh and Lao Cai were also driven out. Thus was the scene set for the final stage of the First Indochina War, which would culminate four years later in the momentous battle at Dien Bien Phu (see page 108).

Lang Son and around → *For listings, see pages 144-146. Colour map 1, B5.*

The town of Lang Son lies on the Ky Lung River in a small alluvial plain surrounded by 1000-m-high mountains. Like Cao Bang, Lang Son was badly damaged during the border war of 1979 and has since been substantially rebuilt. But, the old quarter of the town, south of the Ky Cung River still contains a number of interesting historic buildings as well as the town's markets.

Ins and outs

Getting there and around Lang Son is 155 km northwest of Hanoi on Highway 1. The direct route from Hanoi is along Highway 1A via Chi Lang and Bac Giang, 154 km, 3½ hours. (Chi Lang Pass is the site of Le Loi's historic victory over 100,000 Ming invaders in 1427, effectively bringing to an end 1000 years of Chinese hegemony.) The longer, more scenic route is along Highway 1B via Bac Son and Thai Nguyen, 237 km, seven hours. The road passes through some delightful highland countryside settled by Tay, Nung and Dao. There are early morning bus departures from Hanoi. One train runs daily from Hanoi and back – at 1830, arriving 2240, returning 0350, arriving 0810 – to Dong Dang (Border Gate) and to Lang Son at 0540 arriving 1100. There are plenty of taxis and *xe ôm* in Lang Son. ► *See Transport, page 145.*

Best time to visit It is fairly temperate all year round. The best time is spring or autumn.

Tourist information **Lang Son Tourism and Export company** ① *9 Tran Hung Dao St, T25-381 4848.* It arranges a good selection of tours within the vicinity. Staff have a good command of English. Friendly and helpful.

History

Lang Son rose to prominence as early as the Bronze Age, when emergent trade routes between India and China turned it into an important transit stop on the main road from the Red River Delta through Nanning to Guangzhou.

Between 1527 and 1592 the Mac devoted considerable attention to the task of fortifying the strategically important Lang Son border region. Vestiges of a number of Mac Dynasty fortifications may still be seen today in Lang Son Province, the best preserved of which is the citadel, which lies on a limestone outcrop to the west of the present town.

By the time of its seizure by French troops in 1885 Lang Son had developed into a sizeable and prosperous market town. In subsequent years it became a French military base second in importance only to Cao Bang.

Sights

The rebuilt **Dong Kinh Market** is chock-full of Chinese consumer goods brought through Dong Dang. Although rebuilt many times and finally sidelined by the gleaming new structure at Dong Kinh, **Ky Lua Market** is the oldest in Lang Son and still sees a trickle of trading activity every day. Members of the Tay and Nung are regular visitors here. **Lang Son Citadel** comprises a large section of the ancient city walls, dating back to the 18th century. The former **Lang Son monastery**, which once stood on the other side of the city walls, is south down Nguyen Thai Hoc Street from the old quarter to My Son junction.

The east- and west-facing walls of the imposing 16th-century **Mac Dynasty Citadel** are located on a limestone outcrop west of Lang Son. To get there, head out of town past the six-way junction on the Tam Thanh Road.

At the **Tam Thanh Cave** ① *on the road to the Mac Dynasty Citadel, 10,000d,* there are three chambers; the outer one functions as a pagoda with two shrines and the second one contains a fresh water pool. A poem by Ngo Thi Sy (1726-1780), military commander of the Lang Son garrison who first discovered this and other caves in the area, is carved on the wall near the entrance.

Nhi Thanh (10,000d) perhaps the best known of Lang Son's caves, is located south of Tam Thanh Cave (from the six-way junction take the Nhi Thanh road). There are in fact two separate caves here – the one on the right contains the Tam Giao Pagoda, established in 1777 by Ngo Thi Sy, in which are six shrines, while the one on the left follows the Ngoc Tuyen stream deep into the mountain: the latter is particularly dramatic. More of Ngo Thi Sy's poetry adorns the walls here. The ladies who sit in front of the pagoda are very friendly and will offer visitors tea and bananas.

Dong Dang and the Chinese border

Some 18 km north of Lang Son is the border with China at Dong Dang. The Chinese border town is Ping Xiang. It is possible to cross by road and by train. The road crossing is at Cua Khau Huu Nghi Dong Dang (the Friendship Pass). It is a couple of kilometres between the two international border posts. You will need to obtain a Chinese visa at the embassy in Hanoi and specify the Dong Dang crossing. For Chinese visa costs see page 123. Entering Vietnam, you will have needed to obtain a Vietnamese visa in Beijing or Hong Kong as these are not available at the border.

Settled mainly by members of the Tay and Nung ethnicity, this small market town has two important reasons to claim significance in the history of the Vietnamese nation. The first derives from the very large number of prehistoric artefacts unearthed here by archaeologists. The so-called Bac Son period (5000-3000 BC) was characterized by the development of pottery and the widespread use of refined stone implements, including distinctive axes with polished edges known as Bacsonian axes.

The second is the Bac Son Uprising. In September 1940, revolutionaries detained in Lang Son prison, seized the opportunity afforded by the Japanese attack on the town to escape, heading northwest across the mountains to Bac Son. With the support of the local Communist Party organization they fomented a general insurrection in the town, disarming the fleeing French troops and taking over the district centre to set up the first revolutionary power base in the Viet Bac.

The following year French forces responded by launching a campaign of terror in the Viet Bac, forcing the leaders of the uprising to retreat into the mountains. The Bac Son uprising did, however, prove to be an important milestone in the revolutionary struggle and, in the years which followed, the tide turned steadily against the French throughout the region.

On the way into the town the road passes an unmarked white building on stilts with a Vietnamese flag fluttering on its roof – this is the **Museum of the Bac Son Rebellion** ① *0700-1600, free*, which contains a collection of prehistoric axe-heads and other tools dating from the Bac Son period plus a large display of artefacts relating to the Bac Son Uprising. These include the weapons and personal effects of those involved in the uprising, plus letters and other documents written by Ho Chi Minh and revolutionaries such as Hoang Van Thu.

◉ Cao-Bac-Lang listings

For Sleeping and Eating price codes and other relevant information, see Essentials pages 26-31.

● Sleeping

Bac Can *p136*
E Huong Son, T281-387 0375. Better rooms have a/c and adjoining shower/toilet; cheaper rooms have fan and shared outside facilities.

Ba Be National Park *p136*
D-E Ba Be Hotel, Nguyen Cong Quynh St, Cho Ra, T281-387 6115, about 15 km east of Ba Be National Park. Twin, fan rooms with hot water, shower/toilet. The hotel manager can arrange a whole-day trip including 2 hrs on the river to the lake passing a small ethnic community homestead where you will be fed and filled with rice wine. Opposite the hotel is a 5-day market for Dao

and Tay people, some of whom will have walked through the night to get there.
E Ba Be National Park Guesthouse, T281-389 4026. 62 nice and comfortable a/c rooms with adjoining bathrooms with hot water. Meals available in the park office.
E Hoanh Tu Homestay, T281-389 4071, T1688-472446 (mob). A lovely homestay with balcony overlooking the lake. Bathrooms are not next to the living quarters.

Cao Bang *p137*
E Bang Giang Hotel, Kim Dong St, T26-385 3431. New 70-room building, 1st floor a/c, 2nd floor fan, all with adjoining bathroom.
E Giao Te Hotel, Hoang Nhu St, T26-385 1023. 28 rooms a/c and fan.
E Phong Lan, K83 Kim Dong St, T26-385 2260. 50 rooms, better ones a/c, cheaper fan and shared facility.

Lang Son p142

D Bac Son, 41 Le Loi St, T25-387 1849.
22 rooms, all with adjoining bathroom;
pricier rooms have a/c.

D Kim Son, 3 Nguyen Minh Khai St, T25-387
0378. Chinese joint-venture hotel, 29 rooms
all a/c, adjoining bathroom. Quang Chau
Chinese restaurant on the premises.

E Dong Kinh, 25 Nguyen Du St, T25-387
0166. Near market, better rooms with own
bathroom, a/c, fridge, etc, cheapest rooms
shared facilities, basic but comfortable
accommodation, restaurant.

E-F Hoa Binh, 127 Tran Dang Ninh St, T25-
387 0807. Comfortable accommodation,
15 rooms all a/c, adjoining bathroom.

● Eating

Bac Can p136
▌**Lac Lon restaurant**. Simple fare.
▌**Thin Vien Restaurant**, in the the Huong
Son hotel (see Sleeping, above), T281-387
0375. Serves simple local fare. Shuts early.

Cao Bang p137
▌**Bac Lam**, K025 Hoang Nhu St, T26-385
2697. Local dishes, open 1000-2000.
▌**Huong Sen restaurant**. Good place to try
the local speciality of roast duck.
▌**Thanh Truc**, 133 Xuan Truong St, T26-385
2798. Serves basic fare from 0800 until 2000.

Lang Son p142
▌**Cua Hang An Uong**, corner of Le Loi
and the market street, looks like a 1970s
English clubhouse, but serves fantastic *lau*
(steamboat) at good prices.

● Transport

Bac Can p136
Bus
The bus station is on Duc Xuan St. There are
buses to **Ha Giang**, **Cao Bang** and **Hanoi**.
Hanoi is about 288 km away, 9-10 hrs.

Cao Bang p137
Bus
The bus station is on Kim Dong St. Buses
to **Hanoi**, 10 hrs; to **Thai Nguyen**, 7 hrs.
To **Nguyen Binh**, **Tinh Túc**, **Bao Lac**, **Bao
Lam** on Route 34, 1 bus leaves between
0530-0700, another at 1400 and the last
leaves at 1500.

Lang Son p142
Bus
The bus station is at 28A Ngo Quyen St,
T25-371 5975. A main highway links Lang
Son with **Hanoi** and public buses travel
along this route, 5 hrs. **Hoang Long Co**
operates frequently.

Car and motorbike
It is possible to return (on a Minsk) via
Halong Bay and the coast; the road to **Tien
Yen** is a shocker and carry lunch and spare
fuel with you as there are no supplies en
route. From Tien Yen the road improves.

Train
To **Hanoi** on the Dong Dang line.

Dong Dang and the Chinese border p143
Minibuses and *xe ôms* travel from Lang
Son to the Friendship Pass for the Chinese
border, 30 mins. The train to **Nanning** and
Beijing runs through Dong Dang from
Hanoi. You change trains at Dong Dang.
Some travellers say it is cheaper to get a
ticket from Hanoi to Ping Xiang, just inside
the Chinese border and then change trains.
The Hanoi train departs at 1830 Tue and Fri,
arriving in Ping Xiang at 0141, in Nanning at
0700, and in Beijing at 1209. The train leaves
Dong Dang for Hanoi at 0350 on Tue and Sat
arriving 0810.

   In China From Ping Xiang, catch a
minibus near the main bus station to the
border. Tell the driver you want to go to
YuteLarm GorGwarn (Cantonese for Vietnam
border). At the drop-off point you will be
greeted by a crowd of willing motorbike
drivers one of whom can take you to the

border, a 5- to 10-min drive. He will take you to the policed border-gate leaving you to walk the 500 m or so down an almost deserted road before reaching the Chinese Immigration Building. After paying ¥10 for the privilege of leaving China and other obligatory stages of red tape, you have to continue, unescorted, down the same road for another 5 mins with the occasional truck going past, but little else. The silence is quite eerie and out-of-place for a border point.

Bac Son *p144*
Bus
Connections with **Hanoi** and **Lang Son**. The best method is to return to Lang Son and get a bus from there.

ⓘ Directory

Bac Can *p136*
Banks Agriank, Phung Chi Kien St. **Internet** Minh Khai St. **Post office** Phung Chi Kien St.

Cao Bang *p137*
Bank Agriank, Kim Dong St. **Post office** on Be Van Dan St.

Lang Son *p142*
Banks Agriank, 1 Tran Hung Dao St. Vietcombank, 1 Quang Trung St. **Post office** 49 Le Loi St.

Haiphong and around

→ *Colour map 1, B5.*
Haiphong is still the Vietnam of yesteryear. There are beautiful old French buildings, a peaceful but busy city life where men still pedal ancient cyclos, and sidecars are in generous abundance. There is little to attract the tourist other than an authentic glimpse into life without tourism.

The port of Haiphong was established in 1888 on the Cua Cam River, a major distributory of the Red River. It is the largest port and the second largest city in the north. Over and above its natural attributes Haiphong is blessed with a go-ahead and entrepreneurial People's Committee (no surprises that the district sports Vietnam's first casino) and this attitude is reflected in the bustle in the streets and the industry and vitality of the population. Haiphong's prosperity looks set to redouble with heavy investment in port and communications infrastructure and major investment from overseas in manufacturing plants. Despite this (from the tourists' viewpoint) seemingly inauspicious framework, central Haiphong remains remarkably attractive and its people open and warm. ▶▶ *For listings, see pages 150-151.*

Ins and outs

Getting there As the north's second city after Hanoi, and the region's premier port, Haiphong is well connected. Cat Bi, Haiphong's airport, is 7 km from the city and there are flights from Ho Chi Minh City. The road from Hanoi is now excellent (for Vietnam) and there are frequent bus and minibus connections. Choose a big bus in the interests of comfort and safety. There are trains each day in either direction between the two cities. Haiphong is the departure point for Cat Ba Island and from there with Halong Bay. The 100 km road from Hanoi to Haiphong, the north's principal port, passes through the flood-prone riceland of the Red River Delta. In places the land lies below sea-level and a system of dykes and bunds has been built up over the centuries to keep the river in place. ▶▶ *See Transport, page 151.*

Getting around Central Haiphong is sufficiently compact for most sights to be visited on foot. But a journey from, for example, the railway station to the port, or a trip to the outer temples, merits a taxi, cyclo or *xe ôm*. Because Haiphong does not receive many Western tourists it is not normally possible to rent a motorbike for independent exploring. From Haiphong it is a one-hour hydrofoil ride to Cat Ba Island, one of Vietnam's more accessible national parks, see page 155.

Tourist information Vietnamtourism ⓘ *57 Dien Bien Phu St, T31-384 2989, www. hptourism.com.vn, Mon-Sat 0800-1100, 1400-1700*. Your hotel should be able to provide you with information too.

History
Haiphong witnessed the initial arrival of the French in 1872 (they occupied Hanoi a year later) and, appropriately, their final departure from the north at 1500 in the afternoon of 15 May 1955. As the major port of the north, it was subjected to sustained bombing during the war. To prevent petrol and diesel fuel reaching the Viet Cong, nearly 80% of all above-ground tanks were obliterated by US bombing in 1966. The US did not realize that the North Vietnamese, anticipating such action, had dispersed much of their supplies to underground and concealed tanks. This did not prevent the city from receiving a battering, although Haiphong's air defence units are said to have retaliated by shooting down 317 US planes.

Sights

Much of outer Haiphong is an ugly industrial sprawl that will win no environmental beauty contests. But, considering the bombing the city sustained, there is still a surprising amount of attractive **colonial-style architecture** in the city centre. Central Haiphong is pleasantly green with tree-lined streets.

Right in the heart of town is the **Great Theatre** ⓘ *corner of Tran Hung Dao St and Quang Trung St*, built in 1904 using imported French materials, with a colonnaded front, and facing a wide tree-lined boulevard. In November 1946, 40 Viet Minh fighters died here in a pitched battle with the French, triggered by the French government's decision to open a customs house in Haiphong. A plaque outside commemorates the battle. The streets around the theatre support the greatest concentration of foodstalls and shops.

Other colonial architecture includes the **People's Court** ⓘ *31 Tran Phu St*, a fine French building with shutters; the **post office** ⓘ *5 Nguyen Tri Phuong St*, in an attractive building, and the **bank (Vietcombank)** ⓘ *11 Hoang Dieu St*, a handsome yellow and cream building.

Haiphong Museum (Bao Tang Thanh Pho Hai Phong) ⓘ *66 Dien Bien Phu St, Tue and Thu 0800-1030, Wed and Sun 1930-2130, 2000d*, is an impressive colonial edifice in a wash of desert-sand red, and contains records of the city's turbulent past (some labels are in English).

There are a number of **street markets** and **flower stalls** off Cau Dat Street, which runs south from the theatre, along Tran Nhat Duat and Luong Khanh Thien streets. **Sat Market** is to be found in the west quarter of town, at the end of Phan Boi Chau Street. A market has stood on this site since 1876. The present building is a huge six-storey concrete edifice that has never quite taken off.

Near the centre of town on Me Linh Street is the **Nghe Pagoda** built at the beginning of the 20th century. The pagoda is dedicated to the memory of heroine General Le Chan who fought with the Trung sisters against the Chinese. A festival is held on the eighth day of the second lunar month to commemorate her birthday and offerings of crab and noodles, her favourite foods, are made. There is also an enormous statue of her in front of a cultural building diagonally opposite the Great Theatre.

Du Hang Pagoda ⓘ *1 km south of the city centre on Chua Hang St (take a* xe ôm*)*, was originally built in 1672 by wealthy mandarin-turned-monk Nguyen Dinh Sach. It has been renovated and remodelled several times since. Arranged around a courtyard, this small temple has some fine traditional woodcarving.

Haiphong

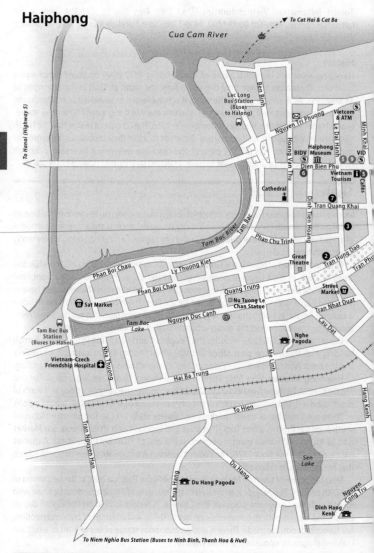

Dinh Hang Kenh (Hang Kenh communal house or *dinh*) ① *2 km south of the centre at 51 Nguyen Cong Tru St*, dates back to 1856. Although built as a communal house, its chief function today is as a temple. The main building is supported by 32 columns of ironwood and the wood carvings in the window grilles are noteworthy. From the outside, the roof

N

200 metres
200 yards

Sleeping
Bach Dang **1**
Harbour View **11**
Hoa Binh **6**
Hotel du Commerce
& Vietnam Airlines **5**
Huu Nghi **9**

Eating
Chie **7**
Hoa Bien **2**
Hoa Dai **3**

Bars & clubs
Corner Café &
Sound Club **6**
Maxim's **5**

is the most dramatic feature, tiled in the fishscale style, and ornamented with a number of dragons. The corners of the roof turn up and it appears that the sheer weight is too much, as the roof is now propped up on bricks. There are a number of *dinh* in and around Haiphong, reflecting the traditional importance of Chinese in this area. Today Taiwanese businessmen are counted among the major investors in Haiphong.

◉ Haiphong and around listings

For Sleeping and Eating price codes and other relevant information, see Essentials pages 26-31.

⬤ Sleeping

Haiphong *p146, map p148*
Haiphong offers plenty of accommodation to meet the demands of industrialists and expats rather than travellers; standards tend to be fairly good but prices a little high.
L-AL Harbour View, 4 Tran Phu St, T31-382 7827, www.harbourviewvietnam. com. Haiphong's most luxurious hotel. Near the river, this under-utilized 127-room hotel has 2 restaurants and a bar. It is well managed and comfortable but watch out for overcharging in the bar. Daily buffet lunch.
A-B Huu Nghi, 60 Dien Bien Phu St, T31-382 3244. Central and, with 11 storeys and 162 rooms, one of Haiphong's largest. It's efficient enough although overpriced. Rooms are fully equipped and quiet. Staff are helpful. Gym, pool and tennis court on site. Popular with Chinese tour groups; breakfast included. From the top storey the view of the port and French colonial buildings is incredible.
C-E Bach Dang, 40-42 Dien Bien Phu St, T31-384 2444. Newly renovated with 35 comfortable rooms at a range of prices in a central location, restaurant. Steam baths.
E Hoa Binh, 104 Luong Khanh Thien St, T31-385 9029. Conveniently opposite the station with 31 standard a/c rooms.
E Hotel du Commerce, 62 Dien Bien Phu St, T31-384 2706. Attractive colonial style, renovated but still atmospheric, large rooms, restaurant.

⑦ Eating

Haiphong *p146, map p148*
Foreign business influence is reflected in the form of Japanese, Chinese and Taiwanese restaurants. See also under Bars and clubs, below, for eating premises.
₸₸₸-₸ Chie, 18 Tran Quang Khai St, T31-382 1018. Open 1100-1400, 1630-2200. This small Japanese restaurant seems out of place in Haiphong but in fact it's a must. Totally delicious sushi and sashimi are served up by staff in maroon and white kimonos. The sushi platter with 14 dishes is very good value; the spaghetti bolognese is incongruous.
₸ Hoa Bien, 24 Tran Hung Dao St, T31-374 5633. Excellent Vietnamese fare with Chinese influence in a street-side setting. All dishes served fresh and piping hot.
₸ Hoa Dai, 39 Le Dai Hanh St, T31-382 2098. Popular with well-off locals. Good Vietnamese food, particularly busy at lunchtime, and welcoming staff.

⑥ Bars and clubs

Haiphong *p146, map p148*
Corner Café and Sound Club, 107 Dien Bien Phu St, T31-374 6970. Open 0700-1300. The former **Saigon Café** is a bar, café and restaurant with good ice cream and drinks.
Maxim's, 51B Dien Bien Phu St, T31-382 2934. Bar/café with live music in the evening. Also serves Asian and European food; drinks prices rise after 1830.

⊙ Shopping

Haiphong *p146, map p148*
The large **Minh Khai** supermarket, Minh Khai St, will supply all your needs.

⊖ Transport

Haiphong *p146, map p148*
Air
Cat Bi, Haiphong's airport, lies 7 km southeast of town; the only air connections are with HCMC.
Airline offices Vietnam Airlines, 166 Haong Van Thu St, T31-381 0890.

Boat
Check all ferry information before setting out as timetables are liable to change. Connections with **Cat Ba** from the wharf on Ben Binh St where there are a number of ticket offices. Services may take motorbikes depending on ferry size. **Transtour Co** runs the Haiphong-Cat Ba ferry, T31-384 1099, www.transtourco.com.vn. To **Cat Ba** at 0700, 0900, 1100, 1330 (a/c express boat), 45 mins, 100,000d, children 50,000d; slow boat at 0630 and 1230, 80,000d, 2 hrs 10 mins. Should you miss the boats or want another route, **Hoang Long Co**, 5 Pham Ngu Lao St, T31-392 0920, www.hoanglongasia.com, runs buses from Hanoi (Luong Yen bus station, T4-3987 7225) and Haiphong to the **Dinh Vu** ferry terminal (30 mins) and a boat from here to Cat Ba (1 hr 30 mins), 100,000d. Buses leave at 0800, 1000, 1400 and 1600. There is also a ferry to **Cat Hai** from **Ben Binh wharf** at 0650, 40,000d.

If it is not running late the 0600 train from Hanoi will get you to Haiphong just in time to *xe ôm* across town to catch the morning boat.

It's worth weighing up the pros and cons of taking a tour or making your own way to Cat Ba. While the do-it-yourself method is easy and cheap, by the time you add in all the little incidental costs and the cost of a boat excursion from Cat Ba it may be just as cheap to take a tour.

Bus
Highway 5 is a fast motorway connecting capital with coast. There are regular bus departures to **Hanoi** leaving from Tam Bac bus station in front of Sat Market. **Hoang Long bus company** leaves Tam Bac station 42 times a day from 0455-1925.

Buses to **Halong** leave from the Lac Long bus station every 15 mins. Buses to **Ninh Binh**, **Thanh Hoa** and **Hué** leave from the Niem Nghia bus station.

Taxi
Mai Linh Taxi, T31-383 3833.

Train
5 departures daily in either direction between **Hanoi** and Haiphong, T31-392 0026. Trains depart from Long Bien station on Gam Cau St, Hanoi, or from the Central Station.

ⓘ Directory

Haiphong *p146, map p148*
Banks BIDV, 68-70 Dien Bien Phu St. Cash major currencies but no TCs. Visa ATM. **VID Bank**, 56 Dien Bien Phu St. Changes US and Singapore dollars and Malaysian ringit, TCs and cash. **Vietcombank**, 11 Hoang Dieu St. Cashes TCs, has an ATM. **Hospitals** Vietnam-Czech Friendship Hospital, 1 Nha Thuong St, T31-384 6236.
Internet On Tuyen Sinh Tin Hoc St and at 8 Tran Quang Khai St. **Post office** 5 Nguyen Tri Phuong St.

Halong Bay

→ *Colour map 1, B6.*

Halong means 'descending dragon', and an enormous beast is said to have careered into the sea at this point, cutting the fantastic bay from the rocks as it thrashed its way into the depths. Vietnamese poets (including the 'Poet King' Le Thanh Tong) have traditionally extolled the beauty of this romantic area with its rugged islands that protrude from a sea dotted with sailing junks. Artists have been just as quick to draw inspiration from the crooked islands seeing the forms of monks and gods in the rock faces, and dragon's lairs and fairy lakes in the depths of the caves. Another myth says that the islands are dragons sent by the gods to impede the progress of an invasion flotilla. Historically more believable, if substantially embellished, the area was the location of two famous sea battles, in the 10th and 13th centuries (see box, page 108). The bay is now a UNESCO World Heritage Site. ▸▸ *For listings, see pages 158-164.*

Ins and outs

Getting there There are two bases from which to explore Halong Bay: Halong City or Cat Ba. Traditionally, visitors went direct to Halong City from Hanoi and took a boat from there. This is still a valid option, especially for those who are short of time. But Cat Ba is becoming increasingly popular as a springboard to Halong Bay, largely because Cat Ba itself is interesting. Many people, however, take an all-inclusive tour from Hanoi, and if you are short of time, this is your best option.

Getting around Boat tours of the bay can be booked at the Bai Chay Tourist Wharf in Halong City and Cat Ba Town. To see the bay properly allow four to five hours but an overnight trip is enjoyable and preferable. One option is to buy a day ticket for a boat trip and get off at Cat Ba town when it docks thus allowing you a few hours in the bay too. Tour operators in Hanoi, see page 87, also offer tours of the bay of varying duration. ▸▸ *For boat tours and transport details, see pages 161-163.*

Best time to visit It can be stormy in June, July and August. July and August are also the wettest months. Winter is cool and dry. The bay is no fun in the rain or fog so get a weather forecast if you can. If there are warnings of cyclones, stay away. Several tourists died in 2009 when boats took risks in this dangerous weather.

Tourist information **Quang Ninh Tourism Information Promotion Centre** ① *C29 Royal Park Area opposite the Halong 1 Hotel and near the Novotel, T33-362 8862, www.halongtourism. com.vn, Mon-Fri 0730-1630,* is super helpful and can provide a whole heap of advice about boats and hotels. It advises only to book boat trips through its tourist office, the Bai Chay Tourist Wharf and the larger hotels and tourist companies. It advises against staying at and booking tours with the Phuong Vi guesthouse at 25 Vuon Dao St and advises paying at least US$50 for a boat trip or US$15 for a day trip. For rescue services contact the **Halong Bay Management Department** ① *166 Le Thanh Tong St, on T33-362 2761/091-326 3474 (mob).*

Karsts and caves in Halong Bay

① *Grotto of Wonders, Customs House Cave and Surprise Grotto all charge 30,000d (the Ti Tov cave is 10,000d) and are open 0730-1700. Fees for cave visits and boats to enter caves will not be included in the price of your boat tour. Many are a disappointment with harrying vendors, mounds of litter and disfiguring graffiti. Many are lit but some are not so bring a torch. Rocks can be treacherously slippery, so sensible footwear is advised.*

Geologically the tower-karst scenery of Halong Bay is the product of millions of years of chemical action and river erosion working on the limestone to produce a pitted landscape. At the end of the last ice age, when glaciers melted, the sea level rose and inundated the area turning hills into islands. The islands of the bay are divided by a broad channel: to the east are the smaller outcrops of Bai Tu Long, see page 158, while to the west are the larger islands with caves and secluded beaches.

Among the more spectacular caves are **Hang Hanh**, which extends for 2 km. Tour guides will point out fantastic stalagmites and stalactites that, with imagination, become heroes, demons and animals. **Hang Luon** is another flooded cave that leads to the hollow core in a doughnut-shaped island. It can be swum or navigated by coracle/canoe. **Hang Dau Go** is the cave wherein Tran Hung Dao stored his wooden stakes prior to studding them in the bed of the Bach Dang River in 1288 to destroy the boats of invading Mongol hordes. **Hang Thien Cung** (Heavenly Palace) is a hanging cave, a short 50-m haul above sea level, with dripping stalactites, stumpy stalagmites and solid rock pillars. A truly enormous cave and one of those most visited is **Sung Sot Cave** (Surprise Cave).

Halong City and around → *For listings, see pages 158-164. Colour map 1, B6.*

The route from Hanoi passes newly industrializing satellite towns whose factories, petrol stations and houses spill onto what were recently paddy fields. After Uong Bi, the scenery improves with the limestone hills which rise out of the alluvial plain giving a foretaste of the better things to come. Following the admission of Halong Bay to UNESCO's hallowed roll of World Heritage Sites, the two small towns of Bai Chay and Hon Gai were, in 1994, collectively elevated in status by the government and dubbed Halong City, a moniker largely ignored by locals. Halong City is an unattractive place with little to recommend it. What appeal it does have is strung along the seafront, which is being spruced up. For reasons unknown, the **Novotel** has opened and the **Sheraton Four Points** is to open.

Ins and outs

Getting there There are regular bus connections from Hanoi's My Dinh terminal to Bai Chay, across the water from Hon Gai, four to five hours. The Bai Chay station has moved from the waterfront to 5 km west of the city. ▶▶ *See Transport, page 163.*

Getting around Given the paucity of sites in the town, pretty much anywhere of relevance can be reached on foot. For venturing further afield, the town has the usual gangs of *xe ôm* drivers.

History

It was at Halong that, arguably, Vietnam's fate under the French was sealed. In late 1882 Captain Henri Rivière led two companies of troops to Hon Gai to seize the coal mines for France. Shortly afterwards he was ambushed and killed and his head paraded on a stake from village to village. His death persuaded the French parliament to fund a full-scale expedition to make all of Vietnam a protectorate of France. As the politician Jules Delafosse remarked at the time: "Let us, gentlemen, call things by their name. It is not a protectorate you want, but a possession."

Sights

The twin towns, Bai Chay to the west and Hon Gai to the east, separated by a river estuary and now linked by a huge new 903-m-long bridge (10,000d toll), could not be more different. Few visitors made the short ferry crossing to Hon Gai which, with its port and adjacent coal mines, could fairly be described as the industrial end of town.

Bai Chay has made great efforts and not a little progress towards turning itself into a destination rather than merely a dormitory for those visiting Halong Bay. At huge expense a narrow beach has been constructed in front of the hotels; casuarina, palm and flame trees have been planted along the prom, old hotels renovated and new ones built. There is no denying the effect of the plans to create the feel of a seaside town. But the charm is not likely to work its magic with travellers from abroad in the same way that it does with Vietnamese who are drawn in huge numbers, rapidly swamping the little beach every weekend. And, in any case, UNESCO officials have instructed the Vietnamese to stop building new resorts in the area before the unlimited developments threaten the protected bay area. Several large and attractive modern hotels have been built, including the **Halong Plaza**, one of the most luxurious in the country. But quite who is going to occupy all these junior and executive suites is a problem the marketing men appear to have overlooked.

Hon Gai, connected to its neighbour by a US$134 million bridge since December 2006, is, as mining areas go, quite a nice one, but it does not live up to the 'natural wonderland' image Quang Ninh Tourism is trying to promote. The port of Hon Gai is busy with plenty of

Cat Ba Island & Halong Bay

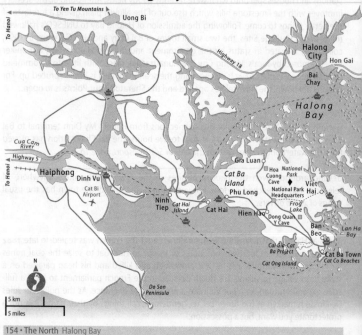

little bamboo and resin coracles (*thung chai*) which are used by the fishermen as tenders to get out to their boats and to bring ashore the catch.

There is a thriving market and near the ferry dock is the 106-m-high **Poem Mountain** (Nui Bao Tho), so named following a visit in 1486 by King Le Thanh Tong who was so taken by the beauty of Halong Bay that he composed a poem celebrating the scenery and carved his verse into the rock. It is quite a scramble up the hill and finding the right path may require some help. At the foot of the mountain nestles the little **Long Tien Pagoda** which dates from the early 20th century. Twenty minutes' walk north up from Hon Gai is a **ruined colonial church** damaged by a bomb in 1972 but the site affords lovely views.

Yen Tu Mountains

The Yen Tu Mountains are 14 km northwest of Uong Bi and climb to a maximum elevation of 1068 m. Peppered with pagodas from the 13th to 16th centuries, much has been lost to the ravages of war and climate but stupas and temples of more recent foundation survive. The site has attracted pilgrims since the 13th century when King Tran Nhan Tong abandoned the throne in favour of a spiritual life. He washed the secular dust from his body in the Tam stream and entered the Cam Thuc (Abstinence) Pagoda. His 100 concubines traced him here and tried to persuade him of the folly of his ways but despite their undoubted allure he resisted all appeals and clung to his ascetic existence. Distraught by their failure, the poor women drowned themselves. Tran Nhan Tong later built a temple to their memory.

Climbing the hills, visiting the temples and admiring the views can take a full day.

To Cam Pha & Mong Cai

Highway 18

To Bai Tu Long National Park & Quan Lan Island

Monkey Island

Cat Ba Island → *For listings, see pages 158-164. Colour map 1, B6.*

Cat Ba occupies a stunning setting in the south of Halong Bay. Much of the island and the seas around are designated a national park and, while perhaps not quite teeming with wildlife (already eaten), it is pleasantly wild and green. Cat Ba's remoteness has been steadily eroded (it only plugged into mains electricity in 1999) and it now represents a handy weekend break for many Hanoians. Despite the growth in numbers of karaoke-loving weekenders, Cat Ba remains an attractive place (minus a few of the uglier buildings) but best of all it is a great springboard into the surrounding waters of Halong Bay and an increasingly popular alternative to Halong City. The chief advantage is that there is a lot to see on the island including the stunning scenery of the interior. Cat Ba, however, will come under intense tourism and ecological pressure with the proposed building of a bridge from Dinh Vu on the mainland to Cat Hai Island (improving the links between the island and the mainland) and the building of the US$600 million 72-ha Cai Gia-Cat Ba urban project for people from Cat Hai Island along with villas, hotels, shopping centres, a marina and entertainment attractions.

Ins and outs

Getting there There are direct hydrofoils from Haiphong or via the Dinh Vu ferry from Haiphong. Boats also leave Bai Chay and Tuan Chau 'Island' in Halong City for Gia Luan in the north of Cat Ba Island where a bus transports you to Cat Ba Town in the south. It is also possible to get a one-way ride with a tour leaving from the tourist wharf at Bai Chay (Halong City) direct to Cat Ba Town where tourist boats dock. Alternatively, organize a tour from Hanoi. ➤ See Transport, page 163, and Haiphong Transport, page 151.

Getting around Either by tour organized by a local hotel or tour operator in Hanoi, or by *xe ôm* or hire a motorbike. There is a bus service between Cat Ba town and Phu Long where the Haiphong ferry docks along the new road and to Gia Luan where the Bai Chay and Tuan Chau 'Island' boats dock. Tourist boats use the new Cat Ba pier in the middle of town but when strong westerly winds are blowing they use the old harbour. From the old harbour (Ban Beo) it is a 10-minute *xe ôm* ride to the hotels.

Best time to visit Cat Ba is at its wettest from July to August, and driest and coolest (15°C) from November to January. The busiest and most expensive time is during school summer holidays from May to September, when hotel rates double.

Tourist information The **Cat Hai District People's Committee Tourism Information Centre** ⓘ *along the seafront, T31-368 8215, www.catba.com.vn*, offers free travel information as well as tours. Most of the hotels also offer information and tours.

Exploring the island

Cat Ba is the largest island in a coastal archipelago that includes more than 350 limestone outcrops. It is adjacent to and geologically similar to the islands and peaks of Halong Bay but separated by a broad channel as the map illustrates. The islands around Cat Ba are larger than the outcrops of Halong Bay and generally more dramatic. Cat Ba is the ideal place from which to explore the whole coastal area: besides the quality of its scenery it is a more agreeable town in which to stay, although the countless new hotels springing up are slowly eroding the difference. The island is rugged and sparsely inhabited. Outside Cat Ba town there are only a few small villages. Perhaps the greatest pleasure is to hire a motorbike and explore, a simple enough process given the island's limited road network. Half of the island forms part of a national park, see below.

For an island of its size Cat Ba has remarkably few **beaches** – only three within easy access, creatively named **Cat Co 1**, **Cat Co 2** and **Cat Co 3**. It's a 1-km walk to the first and a further 1-km to the second which is quieter, cleaner and more secluded; Cat Co 2 is accessible by a walkway from Cat Co 1 or by boat. Cat Co 1 and 2 feature the **Cat Tien Tourism Complex**: there's food, sun loungers for hire, showers, toilets, lockers, campground and bungalows for hire on Cat Co 2, see Sleeping, page 160. The **Catba Island Resort & Spa** on Cat Co 1 is also open to non-guests to use the pool and water slides, US$10; see under Sleeping. There's also a restaurant and drinks here on the beach. Cat Co 3 (home of the Sunrise Resort) is also accessible by walkway from Cat Co 1 and by road and then stairs also.

These lie just to the east of town behind a steep hill in the southern fringes of the national park. They are popular with locals and visitors, especially in the late afternoon and at weekends but are also tending to attract tourist paraphernalia and litter, national park status notwithstanding.

On the way to the national park is the Dong Quan Y cave built between 1960 and 1965 and used by the Americans as a hospital. It has 17 rooms and three floors; 20,000d. Near **Gia Luan** village is **Hoa Cuong Cave**, 100 m from the road. From the park headquarters to Gia Luan the scenery is increasingly dramatic with soaring peaks rising out of the flat valley floor. It is so outstandingly beautiful it is almost other-worldly. Gia Luan harbour is used by Halong boats; there's plenty of mangrove, karst scenery, a fishing village (black oysters and snails) and no services. Heading west, passing pine trees, you will arrive at **Hien Hao**, a village of 400 people where water is collected from wells. There's a small temple on the village outskirts; homestay is possible, see Sleeping, page 160.

Behind the town winds a road, right, up to a peak from where the views of Cat Co 2 and Lan Ha Bay are utterly spectacular. You could walk but the heat may see you on the back of a moto.

Offshore **Monkey Island** can be visited. It is close to Cat Ba and can be combined within a day-long cruise of Halong Bay or shorter four-hour excursion in a small boat. Accommodation is available here.

Cat Ba National Park → Colour map 1, B5.

ⓘ *Park office, T31-388 8741, open 0700-1700; 3 km trek, 15,000d (with guide, 65,000d); 15 km trek 35,000d (with guide 135,000d); park accommodation, 50,000d; 15,000d per meal. Town to park gate, 15 km, is 30 mins on a motorbike.*

The national park (**Vuon Quoc Gia Cat Ba**), established in 1986, covers roughly half the island and is some 252 km sq. Of this area, a third consists of coast and inland waters. Home to 109 bird and animal species, and of particular importance is the world's last remaining troupe of **white-headed langur** (around 59 animals). Their numbers dropped from around 2500 in the 1960s to 53 in 2000; the primate is critically endangered and on the World Conservation Union 2006 Red List (www.catbalangur.org). These elusive creatures (*Trachypithecus poliocephalus poliocephalus*) are rarely spotted and then only from the sea as they inhabit wild and remote cliff habitats. There are also several types of rare **macaque** (rhesus, pig-tailed and red-faced) and **moose deer**. Vegetation ranges from mangrove swamps in sheltered bays and densely wooded hollows, to high, rugged limestone crags sprouting caps of hardy willows. The marine section of the park is no less bounteous: perhaps less fortunate is the high economic value of its fish and crustacea populations, which keeps the local fishing fleet hard at work and prosperous. In common with other coastal areas in the region the potential for snorkelling here is zero.

Visitors are free to roam through the forest but advised not to wander too far from the path. Many hotels arrange treks from the park gate through the forest to **Ao Ech** (Frog Lake) on to the village of **Viet Hai** for a light lunch then down to the coast for a boat ride home. This takes the best part of a day (six to 10 hours) and costs around US$10. It is a good way to see the park but those preferring solitude can go their own way or go with a park guide. A short trek leads to the **Ngu Lam Peak** behind the park headquarters. July to October is the wet season when leeches are a problem and mosquitoes are at their worst. Bring leech socks if you have them and plenty of insect repellent. Collar, long sleeves and long trousers advisable.

Bai Tu Long and towards the Chinese border

→ *For listings, see pages 158-164. Colour map 1, B6.*

Bai Tu Long is east of Halong Bay in the Gulf of Tonkin stretching towards the Chinese border. The group of islands makes up the Bai Tu Long National Park, covering 15,783 ha. **Quan Lan Island**, a remote island just south of Bai Tu Long is home to a very small community, some guesthouse accommodation, small restaurants, beaches and wild, untamed land. Bicycles can be hired at guesthouses as well as small boats.

Mong Cai

Mong Cai is located on the Gulf of Tonkin and is next to Dong Xing, China. The main point of interest in Mong Cai is the plethora of cheaply made Chinese goods available. It would also be the sensible place to cross if you are planning to go to Hainan Island. Apart from that there is not a lot to do or see. The border crossing is open from 0730 to 1630. The Chinese entry visa must be issued by the embassy in Hanoi and specify the Mong Cai crossing. For costs, see page 123.

The only tourist attraction is **Tra Co Beach** which is 7 km from Mong Cai itself. It is a delightful sandy peninsula and, as it is 17 km long, you are bound to find a quiet spot. The best time to vist would be anytime except May to August; also avoid the Vietnamese holidays if possible as it will be crowded.

⊙ Halong Bay listings

For Sleeping and Eating price codes and other relevant information, see Essentials pages 26-31.

⊙ Sleeping

Halong City *p153*
The past few years have seen an explosion in the number of hotels and guesthouses in Bai Chay and Hon Gai; this reflects the popularity of Halong Bay as a destination for both Vietnamese and foreign visitors. Many of the newer hotels are badly built and, apart from the fact that some of the taller ones look structurally unsound, are quite frequently damp and musty; check the room first.

There are few hotels in **Hon Gai** but they tend to be more competitively priced than those in Bai Chay. In **Bai Chay** there are 2 main groups of hotels, 2 km apart. Most are to be found at the west end on the way in to town, set back a little from the seafront, and include Vuon Dao St composed entirely of 5- to 8-room mini hotels. 2 km further on, nearer the bridge, is a smaller group, some of which

have good views. Their main advantage used to be that they were close to the bus station but as this has moved they are rather isolated from the bulk of restaurants, tourist office, post office and night market.

L-AL Halong Dream, 10 Halong Rd, T33-384 9009, www.halongdreamhotel.com. A huge, characterless place but it's quiet and close to all the local services. It's also got a pool and spa and the breakfast is reasonable.

L-AL Halong Plaza, 8 Halong Rd, Bai Chay, T33-384 5810, www.halongplaza.com. A Thai joint venture with 200 rooms and suites and fantastic views over the sea, especially from upper floors, luxuriously finished, huge bathrooms, every comfort and extravagance, pool, restaurants and engaging staff; a lovely hotel by any standards. The evening dinner buffet at US$22 and half price for children aged 12 and under represents good value.

A-B Saigon Halong, Halong Rd, Bai Chay, T33-384 5845, www.saigonhalonghotel. com. Run by **Saigontourist** with 23 rooms in 'villas' and 205 rooms; comfortable, all mod cons, set back from the road on the way into town; relaxed and attractive surroundings.

C Viethouse Lodge, Tuan Chau Island, T33-384 2233, www.viethouselodge.com. With rooms scattered around a hillside this can be a more pleasant alternative to staying in the city. There's a restaurant, bar, games and transport to hire. The island is now connected to the mainland by a bridge.

D Ha Long 1, Halong Rd, Bai Chay, T33-384 6321. A converted French villa with stacks of charm set among frangipani and raised up on a hill overlooking the sea. Some of the 23 rooms have sea outlook, huge bathrooms, bathtubs, bidets, etc but in now in need of a bit of a spruce up. The exterior and wooden shutters have recently been renovated.

D-E Bach Dang, 2 Halong Rd, Bai Chay, T33-384 6330, www.bachdanghotelqn.com. Next to the Halong Plaza, an older but well-kept establishment, a/c, sea views and restaurant.

F Halong Guesthouse, 80-82 Le Thanh Tong, Hon Gai, T33-382 6509. 16 a/c rooms with hot water and private bathroom; clean and good value. Fairly close to the bridge near cafés and small restaurants. Several other guesthouses on Le Thanh Tong St.

F Minh Tuan, Ho Xuan Huong St, Bai Chay, T33-384 6200. Up a quiet lane off the main road in a low-key Vietnamese neighbourhood. 14 a/c rooms with bathroom, clean, well managed but bargain hard as the rooms are looking a little neglected. No longer convenient for the bus station but recommended for its position in a quiet local street with a small market nearby.

F Peace Hotel, 39 Vuon Dao St, T33-384 6009. A mini-hotel offering reasonable rooms. 1 hr free internet for guests.

Cat Ba Beach *p155, map p154*

While in summer prices may be slightly higher than those listed, as far as possible the price ranges below give a fair indication of seasonal variations. It may still be possible to negotiate discounts in quieter periods. There are no addresses, and to confuse matters further, many hotels claim the same name.

L-A Cat Ba Island Resort & Spa, Cat Co 1, T31-368 8686, www.catbaislandresort-spa.com. There are 109 pleasant rooms decorated with white rattan furniture across 3 buildings facing the bay with a lovely out-look and fronting right on to the beach. The obtrusive water slides cannot be seen from the 2nd and 3rd building. 3 restaurants provide Western and Asian food and there are 2 pools, water slides, jacuzzi, massage, billiards and a tennis court. Trekking and Halong Bay tours are offered. Eagles, for some reason, find it an attractive spot.

AL Sunrise Resort, Cat Co 3, T31-388 7360, www.catbasunriseresort.com. An attractive low-keyish resort on a beach linked by road to the town and by footpath to Cat Co 1. It has beach loungers and thatched umbrellas, a pool, jacuzzi, massage, 3 restaurants and travel services. Note that you cannot drive to the door of the hotel. You must walk around 50 m up and down stairs to reach the reception and beach.

A-B Holiday View Hotel, T31-388 7200, www.holidayviewhotel-catba.com. A hotel this size should never have been allowed to be built; it dominates the Cat Ba seafront. Rooms are furnished with all mod-cons.

B Princes, T31-388 8899, www.princeshotel-catba.com. The rooms are nice and light and airy and, unlike all the vertical shoebox hotels, this one has made an effort to look decent and has an open courtyard at the back. Well-furnished rooms and friendly reception. It is quite large, 80 rooms, takes credit card and breakfast is included in the price. It also rents motorbikes, bikes and kayaks.

C Ocean Beach Resort, Cat Ong Island, 3.5 km southeast of Cat Ba town, T4-3210 2727, www.oceanbeachresort.com.vn. 7 bungalows with fans and mosquito nets situated on 2 beaches on this island getaway.

D Family (Quang Duc), just west of the pier, T31-388 8231. The original 'Family' hotel, a/c, hot water, 7 spotlessly clean rooms, views from most, a very well-run little hotel, owners are knowledgeable on local matters and helpful, newly renovated and now offers a range of watersports. Recommended.

D Gieng Ngoc, east of the pier, Cat Ba town, T31-388 8286. Among the best of the budget hotels. Quiet, front rooms overlook sea. There are 59 rooms that are basic, clean and come with a/c.

D Sun and Sea, past the post office on the right, T31-388 8315. One of the plushest in town, 32 rooms, all mod cons including satellite TV, tall; seaview from some rooms.

D-E Cat Tien Tourism Complex, Cat Co 1 and 2, T31-388 7988, giathanh@ flamingovietnam.com. Cat Co 2 is more beautiful but Cat Co 1 is more accessible from town. There are 7 fan-cooled small bungalows and 2 large ones on Cat Co 2; camping (**F**) with your own tents is possible.

E Noble House, T31-388 8363. Overlooking the pier with 5 comfortable and well-appointed rooms. A/c and fridge, good views, more expensive rooms include breakfast. Popular bar and restaurant serving reasonably priced Vietnamese and Western dishes. Tours are offered.

F Monkey Island. The My Ngoc hotel, see below, will rent tents and arrange boat transfer. There are no washing facilities.

F My Ngoc, quite central, not far from the ferry pier, T31-388 8199. 23 rooms, a/c, hot water. Restaurant and tours arranged.

G Homestay, Hien Hao Village, on the west coast of the island. Hien Hao People's Committee office, T31-888 732/90-8693 4099 (mob). Hien Hao is 12 km from Phu Long, 20 km from Cat Ba town and 4 km from the National Park HQ. If you get the Hoang Long bus, it can drop you there on its way to and from Phu Long. Meals provided on request.

Cat Ba National Park *p157, map p154*
D Park guesthouse, Viet Hai Village, Viet Hai Community Based Tourism Association, T31-388 8836. Homestays have beds with mosquito nets. A mattress and bed sheets can also be provided.

Bai Tu Long and towards the Chinese border *p158*
There are a couple of hotels and guesthouses on Quan Lan Island. Go direct from Hon Gai or Bai Dai (see Transport) or arrange through **My Ngoc** hotel.

E Quan Lan Resort, Son Hao Beach, T33-387 7316. Wooden huts with en suite showers. A restaurant is available.

Mong Cai *p158*
E Nha Nghi Hai Van, 2 Thang Loi St, T33-388 6479. A relatively new hotel. The rooms are well equipped but more importantly the staff are friendly and helpful. It is centrally located and 3 mins' walk to the market.

Eating

Halong City *p153*
Seafood is fresh and abundant and fairly priced. Le Qui Don St in Hon Gai has good seafood restaurants. Other than the hotels (see **Halong Plaza** especially), Halong Rd, near the junction with Vuon Dao St, Bai Chay, is lined for several hundred metres with restaurants all of which are pretty good.

₮₮₮-₮₮ Co Ngu, Halong Rd, beyond the Post Office, T33-351 1363, www.halongcongu. com. A new restaurant in a building over 3 floors. Everything from fried chicken and salmon dishes to sautéed bladder.

₮₮ Emeraude Café, Co/Royal Park, T33-384 9266. Open 0900-2100. An oasis of comfort food close to the main hotels and restaurants. Free internet and Wi-Fi. Expensive shuttle bus arranged to Hanoi.

₮ Lavender, 99 Halong Rd, Bai Chay, near the junction, T33-384 6185, does a good squid with chilli and lemongrass.

Cat Ba Island *p155, map p154*
After dark there is a charged atmosphere along the front as tanned Westerners crowd into small restaurants to quaff bottles of chilled beer, consume fresh seafood and strike up lively conversations. Some hotels listed above have restaurants.

Green Mango, T31-388 7151. This is an outstanding addition to Cat Ba cuisine. The sesame-encrusted *ahi* tuna on a bed of cellophane noodles is worth the ferry trip to Cat Ba alone. Other culinary delights include home-smoked duck with vindaloo rice, green mustard and pomegranate jus and warm chocolate pudding, raspberry purée and cream. Indoor and outdoor seating is available. Highly recommended.

Truc Lam or **Bamboo Forest**, T31-388 8654, truclamrestaurant@yahoo.com. Mr Dau, the owner, is a relative newcomer to Cat Ba, but knowledgeable and can arrange tours; he also rents rooms (**E-F**). His restaurant serves usual seafood and also vegetarian dishes as well as rice wines.

♪ Bars and clubs

Cat Ba Island *p155, map p154*
Flightless Bird, on the seafront, T31-388 8517. Run by Graeme Moore, a New Zealander, the only real pub in town. See also **Noble House**, Sleeping, above.

▲ Activities and tours

Halong City *p153*
Boat tours
Boat tours can be booked from hotels in Halong and in Hanoi, see below, although it may be cheaper to organize the trip independently; to do so go to the Bai Chay Tourist Wharf and visit the ticket office only, not the 'tourist office' in the compound. Prices displayed on a board start from 180,000d. Children under 5 are free; those aged 5-10 are half price. On Sat, Sun and holidays, prices are reduced by 20%. Foreign-language speaking guides can also be hired here. The wharf has snack places, an ATM and internet. There's a taxi stand and bus stop right outside. Or, go direct to the **Quang Ninh Tourism Information Promotion Center**, which regulates the boats, see Tourist information, page 152. Because it takes about 1 hr to get into the

bay proper, 1 long trip represents better value than 2 short ones. A tour of the bay including a cave or 2 and a swim needs 4-5 hrs. A number of day trips are on offer: **Route 1** goes to Thien Cung Grotto, Dau Go Cave, Dinh Huong islet and Ga Choi islet (4 hrs); **Route 2** follows the same route plus Sung Sot Grotto and Ti Tov Beach (6 hrs); **Route 3** follows the same route as Route 2 but is longer (7-8 hrs); **Route 4** sails to Me Cung Cave and the floating villages of Cua Van and **Route 5** goes to Bai Tu Long: Ngoc Vung Island, Quan Lan Island and Minh Chau Island (2 days). Trips leave between 0730-0900. Tickets for visits to the cave can be bought at the tourist wharf or at the caves. It's also possible to charter a boat if you are a large group.

Buffalo Tours, 94 Ma May St, Hanoi, T4-3828 0702, www.buffalotours.com. Operates the luxury *Jewel of the Bay* boat. This comfortably furnished boat with capacity for 10 includes children's toys, a deck for sunbathing and star-watching; enormous quantities of superb food are served and the staff are welcoming. Kayaks can be used to explore from the boat.

Cruise Halong Co, Suite 328, 33B Pham Ngu Lao St, Hanoi, T4-3933 5561, www.cruisehalong.com. The *Halong Ginger* is a luxury junk cruising the waters and is a beautiful sight on the bay with its proud orange sails. It has 10 cabins, restaurant, lounge, 2 bars, shop and a library. Kayaking, snorkelling and cooking classes are available.

Emeraude Classic Cruises, 46 Le Thai To St, Hanoi, T4-3935 1888, www.emeraude-cruises.com. Also at Royal Park, Halong Rd, Bai Chay, T33-849 266. The best way to see Halong Bay in style is on the reconstructed French paddle steamer, the *Emeraude*. There are 39 cabins with extremely comfortable beds and nice touches (gift-wrapped biscuits) and old-style fans although the bathrooms are on the tiny side. There's a sumptuous buffet lunch and more delicious food than you can eat for dinner. Entertainment includes a Vietnamese spring roll demo, swimming off the boat, squid fishing, t'ai chi exercise on the sun deck at dawn and a massage service. There's a sundeck and bar. **Emeraude** is also now offering day trips: 1130-1700 for US$100 per person (for 2 people); cheaper if there are more people. Shuttle service arranged from Hanoi. Worth pitching up at the Halong City office for last-minute options.

Life Heritage Resort Halong Bay, www. life-resorts.com. 22 private deluxe boats with a living area, sun deck, DVD player and TV and their own captain and staff. Therapy treatments are available on board.

The **Huong Hai Junk Halong Company** (www.halongdiscovery.com) also operates in the bay.

Cat Ba Island *p155, map p154*
Boat tours
Halong Bay is the most famous excursion from Cat Ba. Almost all hotels in Cat Ba offer tours as do the touts along the seafront.

It is better to use a service provided by a reputable hotel (as listed in Sleeping, above), as you are less likely to be left stranded or charged extra for lunch.

Kayaking
Kayaking in Halong Bay and Lan Ha Bay are now regular features, especially in the summer months. It is best to go via one of the established tour operators in Hanoi, such as **Handspan** and **Buffalo Tours** but **Family Hotel** and **My Ngoc Hotel** in Cat Ba also have kayaks. These are best taken out on a larger boat and paddled from the open sea. **Family Hotel** is the place to ask about watersports.

Rock climbing
Climbing the rock karst limestone faces and towers on Cat Ba and Halong Bay is now possible with experienced, licensed and enthusiastic climbers, see Tour operators below. At least 140 climbing routes have been established.

Tour operators

The Cat Hai District People's Committee Tourism Information Centre, along the seafront, T31-368 8215. Daily 0700-2200, runs guided tours to the national park and Halong Bay; organizes xe ôm to park HQ; 1-hr boat trip to Lan Ha Bay; boat charter; car hire; motorbike hire; bicycle hire.

Slo Pony Adventures/Asia Outdoors, 222 1/4 St, Group 19, Ward 4, T31-368 8450, www.slopony.com. Rock climbing, kayaking, trekking, environmentally conscious boat cruises and other adventures. Slo Pony works directly with the local community on Cat Ba Island, employs both domestic and international staff and assists the national park with efforts to protect the endangered langur as well as with the park's conservation efforts.

⊖ Transport

Halong City p153
Bus

Halong City bus station is now 5 km west of Halong city, near Halong train station. Local bus No 3 runs to and from the centre of town, 5000d. There is a bus stop right outside the Bai Chay Tourist Wharf. There are regular connections from Bai Chay bus station to **Hanoi** from 0700, last bus departs 1600. Buses are slow, crowded, uncomfortable and full of pickpockets. Regular connections with **Haiphong**'s Lac Long bus station 0900-1500. There are also buses to **Mong Cai** every 15 mins and to **Bai Dai** (for ferries to **Quan Lan**), every 15 mins, 13,000d.

Boat

To Cat Ba Jump on a tourist boat for a 1-way (4-hr) ride for 200,000d from the **Bai Chay Tourist Wharf** (Halong Rd, T33-384 6592) open daily 0730-1700; get there early as last group departures (ie cheaper leave around 1230) and get off at the port of Gia Luan which is in the north of Cat Ba. A bus runs from Gia Luan to Cat Ba Town, 10,000d. Ferries also run from Tuan Chau 'Island' to

Gia Luan in the summer at 0730, 0930, 1100, 1330, 1600, and in the winter at 0800 and 1400, 30,000d.

From Hon Gai (Halong City) boat station (98 Ben Tau Road near Long Tien pagoda) to **Quan Lan Island** at 1000, 140,000d, 2½ hrs. There is an 0700 boat service to **Mong Cai**, 300,000d, 3 hrs.

Cat Ba Island p155, map p154
Boat

It would be wise to check all ferry information before setting out as timetables change.
To Haiphong Transtour Co runs the Cat Ba–Haiphong ferry, T31-388 8314, office on the seafront. Express boat to Haiphong, 0700, 1445, 120,000d, children 60,000d; slow boats at 0545 and 1230. Hoang Long Co, T31-388 7244 (Cat Ba), with an office on the seafront, runs a bus to **Phu Long** on Cat Ba and then boat to the **Dinh Vu ferry terminal** (1½ hrs), and then bus (30 mins) to Haiphong. Several buses a day. You can also continue the journey to **Hanoi**'s Luong Yen bus station.
To Tuan Chau 'Island' (Halong City) From Gia Luan at 0900, 1100, 1330, 1500 and 1700 in summer, 30,000d. In winter at 0900, 1500. A bus runs from Cat Ba Town to Gia Luan, 10,000d.

Bai Tu Long and towards the Chinese border p158
Boat

Daily boat service from Mong Cai to **Hon Gai** (Halong City) at 1330, 300,000d, 3 hrs From Quan Lan Island to Hon Gai at 1500, 140,000d, 2½ hrs. From Bai Dai (northeast of Halong City) to **Quan Lan Island**, 0900 returning 1500 in summer, 0815 in winter, returning 1415, 80,000d. 1½ hrs. This Bai Dai ferry also goes on to **Minh Chau Island**.

Bus

Mong Cai is 360 km from **Hanoi**. There are 5 departures between 0530-0730, 10 hrs. There are many buses between Mong Cai and **Halong City** from 0500-1700, 6 hrs. There is also a 5-hr journey to **Lang Son** but this •

schedule is erratic. The buses will only leave if there are sufficient people on board.

◑ Directory

Halong City p153
Banks Vietcombank, Halong St, Bai Chay, with ATM. Agribank, 2 Vuon Dao St, Bai Chay, also with ATM. **Hospitals** Bai Chay Hospital, T33-384 6557. **Internet** Many hotels and cafés provide email services at reasonable prices. **Post office** In Bai Chay at junction of Halong Rd and Vuon Dao St. Internet service also.

Cat Ba Island p155, map p154
Banks Agribank, T31-388 8227, on the back road will change dollars. ATM on seafront. Hotels will exchange US$ cash at poor rates. Alternatively there are a couple of gold shops at the west end of the town. Vu Binh, T31-388 8641, will give cash on Amex, Visa and MasterCard. **Internet** A couple of hotels have email as does the tourist information place. **Post office** In town centre, opposite pier.

Mong Cai p158
Bank Vietcombank change TCs and there's an ATM. **Internet** Lots of internet cafés along Hung Vuong St. **Post office** Corner of Tran Phu and Hung Vuong St.

Ninh Binh and around

→ *Colour map 1, C4.*

Ninh Binh is capital of the densely populated province of Ninh Binh. It marks the most southerly point of the northern region. The town itself has little to commend to the tourist but it is a useful and accessible hub from which to visit some of the most interesting and attractive sights in the north. Within a short drive lie the ancient capital of Hoa Lu with its temples dedicated to two of Vietnam's great kings; the exquisite watery landscape of Tam Coc, an 'inland Halong Bay', where sampans carry visitors up a meandering river, through inundated grottoes and past verdant fields of rice; the Roman Catholic landscape around Phat Diem Cathedral, spires and towers, bells and smells; and the lovely Cuc Phuong National Park, with its glorious butterflies, flowers and trees. The town of Nam Dinh is a centre for visiting several pagodas in the area.
▸▸ *For listings, see pages 169-170.*

Ins and outs

Getting there It is a three-hour journey from Hanoi by bus or by train. From Hanoi, the route south runs through expanding industrial towns which, in the last few years, have been convulsed with change: road widenings, demolition of old buildings to make way for industrial zones and factories gobbling up 'ricefield' sites. Communities which for centuries were divided by nothing more than a dirt track now find themselves rent asunder by four-lane highways, but ancient ties of kith and kin and tradition have yet to adjust. Beyond Phu Ly the limestone karsts start to rise dramatically out of the flat plain.
▸▸ *For further details, see Transport, page 170.*

Getting around Visitors can get to the places around Ninh Binh as a day trip from Hanoi through tour agencies or by taking tours or hiring transport from the hotels in Ninh Binh.

Tourist information **Ninh Binh Tourism** ⓘ www.ninhbinhtourism.com.vn. The hotels all have good information.

Hoa Lu

ⓘ US$1.

Hoa Lu lies about 13 km from Ninh Binh near the village of **Truong Yen**; it is a couple of kilometres signposted off the main road and can be reached by bicycle or *xe ôm* (6 km north of Ninh Binh and 6 km west of Highway 1, follow signs to Truong Yen).

It was the capital of Vietnam from AD 968 to AD 1010, during the Dinh and Early Le dynasties. Prior to the establishment of Hoa Lu as the centre of the new kingdom, there was nothing here. But the location was a good one in the valley of the Hong River – on the 'dragon's belly', as the Vietnamese say. The passes leading to the citadel could be defended with a small force, and defenders could keep watch over the plains to the north and guard against the Chinese. The kings of Hoa Lu were, in essence, rustics. This is reflected in the art and architecture of the temples of the ancient city: primitive in form, massive in conception. Animals were the dominant motifs, carved in stone.

A large part of this former capital, which covered over 200 ha, has been destroyed, although archaeological excavations have revealed much of historical and artistic interest. The two principal temples are those of Dinh Bo Linh, who assumed the title King Dinh Tien Hoang on ascending the throne (reigned AD 968-980), and Le Hoan, who assumed the title King Le Dai Hanh on ascending the throne (reigned AD 980-1009).

The **Temple of Dinh Tien Hoang** was originally constructed in the 11th century but was reconstructed in 1696. It is arranged as a series of courtyards, gates and buildings. The inscription on a pillar in the temple, in ancient Vietnamese, reads 'Dai Co Viet', from which the name 'Vietnam' is derived. The back room of the temple is dedicated to Dinh Tien Hoang, whose statue occupies the central position, surrounded by those of his sons, Dinh Lien (to the left), Dinh Hang Lang and Dinh Toan (to the right). In the 960s, Dinh Tien Hoang managed to pacify much of the Red River plain, undermining the position of a competing ruling family, the Ngos, who accepted Dinh Tien Hoang's supremacy. However, this was not done willingly, and banditry and insubordination continued to afflict Hoang's kingdom. He responded by placing a kettle and a tiger in a cage in the courtyard of his palace and decreed: 'those who violate the law will be boiled and gnawed'. An uneasy calm descended on Dinh Tien Hoang's kingdom, and he could concern himself with promoting Buddhism and geomancy, arranging marriages, and implementing reforms. But, by making his infant son Hang Lang heir apparent, rather than Lien (his only adult son), he sealed his fate. History records that the announcement was followed by earthquakes and hailstorms, a sign of dissension in the court, and in AD 979 Lien sent an assassin to kill his younger brother Hang Lang. A few months later in the same year, an official named Do Thich killed both Dinh Tien Hoang and Lien as they lay drunk and asleep in the palace courtyard. When Do Thich was apprehended, it is said that he was executed and his flesh fed to the people of the city.

The **Temple of King Le Dai Hanh** is dedicated to the founder of the Le Dynasty who seized power after the regicide of Dinh Tien Hoang. In fact Le Dai Hanh took not only Hoang's throne but also his wife, Duong Van Nga. Representations of her, Le Dai Hanh and Le Ngoa Trieu (also known as Le Long Dinh), his fifth son, each sit on their own altar in the rear temple. Near this temple the foundations of King Dinh's (10th century) royal palaces were found by Vietnamese archaeologists in 1998.

A short walk beyond Le Dai Hanh's temple is **Nhat Tru Pagoda**, a 'working' temple. In front of it stands a pillar engraved with excerpts from the Buddhist bible (*Kinh Phat*). Opposite Dinh Tien Hoang's temple is a hill, Nui Ma Yen, at the top of which is **Dinh Tien Hoang's tomb**. Locals will tell you it is 260 steps to the top. There are boat trips on the river to **Xuyen Thuy cave** ⓘ *15,000d*, less spectacular than Tam Coc (see below).

Tam Coc and Bich Dong

ⓘ *Daily 0700-1700, 60,000d (1-2 people) for the boat, 30,000d for the grottoes including Bich Dong (a tip and purchase will be requested on the boat). The turning to Tam Coc and Bich Dong is 4 km south of Ninh Binh on Highway 1. A small road leads 2-3 km west to Tam Coc. Tam Coc can easily be reached by bicycle or xe ôm from Ninh Binh or by car from Hanoi (on a day trip). It's possible to go from Bich Dong to Xuyen Thuy cave by boat, 20,000d. There are a couple of hotels and restaurants.*

Tam Coc means literally 'three caves'. The highlight of this excursion is an enchanting boat ride up the little Ngo Dong River through the eponymous three caves. Those who have seen the film *Indochine*, some of which was shot here, will be familiar with the nature of the beehive-type scenery created by limestone towers, similar to those of Halong Bay. The exact form varies from wet to dry season; when flooded the channel disappears and one or two of the caves may be under water. In the dry season the shallow river meanders between fields of golden rice. You can spot mountain goat precariously clinging to the rocks and locals collecting snails in the water. Women row and punt pitch-and-resin tubs that look like elongated coracles through the tunnels. It is a most leisurely experience and a chance to observe at close quarters the extraordinary method of rowing with the feet. Take plenty of sun cream and a hat. The villagers have a rota for rowing and supplement their fee by trying to sell visitors embroidered table cloths and napkins. On a busy day the scene from above is like a two-way, nose-to-tail procession of waterboats; to enjoy Tam Coc at its best make it your first port of call in the morning.

A short drive to the south is Bich Dong. This is much harder work, so not surprisingly it is a lot quieter than Tam Coc. Bich Dong consists of a series of temples and caves built into, and carved out of, a limestone mountain. The temples date from the reign of Le Thai To in the early 15th century. It is typical of many Vietnamese cave temples but with more than the average number of legends attached to it, while the number of interpretations of its rock formations defies belief. The lower temple is built into the cliff face. Next to the temple is a pivoted and carved rock that resonates beautifully when tapped with a stone. Next see Buddha's footprints embedded in the rock (size 12, for the curious) and the tombs of the two founding monks.

Leading upwards is the middle temple, an 18th-century bell, a memorial stone into which are carved the names of benefactors and a cave festooned with rock forms. Here, clear as can be, are the likenesses of Uncle Ho, a turtle and an elephant. More resonant rock pillars follow and a rock which enables pregnant women to choose the sex of their baby: touch the top for a boy and the middle for a girl. But best of all scramble right to the pinnacle of the peak for a glorious view over the whole area. Unfortunately, the view has been marred by a horrible new orange and sickly green concrete building.

Phat Diem Cathedral

ⓘ *24 km southeast of Ninh Binh in the village of Kim Son, daily 0800-1700, English and French guidebook; 15,000d; there are several services daily. The journey takes in a number of more conventional churches, waterways and paddy fields. Take a motorbike from Ninh Binh or hire a car from Hanoi. Hoa Lu, Tam Coc and Phat Diem can all be comfortably covered in 1 day; there are souvenir shops selling nuoc mam (fish sauce) and Virgin figures side by side.*

Phat Diem Cathedral is the most spectacular of the church buildings in the area, partly for its scale but also for its remarkable Oriental style with European stylistic influences. Completed in 1899, it boasts a bell tower in the form of a pagoda behind which stretches for 74 m the nave of the cathedral held up by 52 ironwood pillars. The cathedral was built under the leadership of parish priest Father Tran Luc between 1875 and 1899. He is buried in a tomb between the bell tower and the cathedral proper. Surrounding the cathedral are several chapels: St Joseph's, St Peter's, the Immaculate Heart's, the Sacred Heart's and St Roch's.

In 1953 French action in the area saw artillery shells damage the eastern wing of the cathedral causing part of the roof to collapse.

The cathedral was bombed in 1972 by Americans who despatched eight missiles. St Peter's Church was flattened, St Joseph's blown to an angle, the cathedral forced to a tilt, the roof tiles hurled to the floor, and 52 of the 54 cathedral doors were damaged. Restoration of different parts of the complex is ongoing.

The approach to the cathedral is impressive: you drive down a narrow valley to be confronted with a statue of Christ the King in the middle of a huge square pond; behind are the cathedral buildings.

The Red River Delta was the first part of the country to be influenced by Western missionaries: Portuguese priests were proselytizing here as early as 1627. Christian influence is still strong despite the mass exodus of Roman Catholics to the south in 1954 and decades of Communist rule. Villages (which are built of red brick, often walled and densely populated) in these coastal provinces may have more than half-a-dozen churches, all with packed congregations, not only on Sundays. The churches, the shrines, the holy grottoes, the photographs of the parish priest on bedroom walls and the holy relics clearly assume huge significance in people's lives.

Cuc Phuong National Park → *Colour map 1, C4.*

ⓘ *Nho Quan district, T30-384 8006, www.cucphuongtourism.com, daily 0500-2100, 40,000d, children 20,000d; botanic garden 5000d. 1- to 6-day treks can be arranged with a guide; short treks of a couple of hours are also available (trail to silver cloudy peak and ancient tree; trail to Muong village; wildlife experience tour; night spotting; bicycle tours can also be arranged as well as a tour to Van Long Nature Reserve, see page 168). Mr Hai who is head of the tour guide section is very helpful and has worked at the park for more than 10 years. A visit to the park can be done as a day trip from Ninh Binh or from Hanoi. Direct access by car only. An organized tour from Hanoi may be a sensible option for lone travellers or pairs, otherwise charter a car or hire a motorbike. See also Transport, page 170, for independent travel.*

The park, which is around 120 km south of Hanoi and 45 km west of Ninh Binh, is probably the second most accessible of Vietnam's national parks, and for nature lovers not intending to visit Cat Ba Island, it is worthy of consideration. It is also Vietnam's oldest park, established in 1962. Located in an area of deeply cut limestone and reaching elevations of up to 800 m, the park is covered by 22,000 ha of humid tropical montagne forest. It is home to an estimated 2000 species of flora including the giant parashorea, cinamomum and sandoricum trees. Wildlife has been much depleted by hunting; only 117 mammal and 307 bird species and 110 reptile and amphibian species are thought to remain. The government has resettled a number of the park's 30,000 Muong minority people, although Muong villages do remain and can be visited. April and May see fat grubs and pupae metamorphosing into swarms of butterflies that mantle the forest in fantastic shades of greens and yellows.

The **Endangered Primate Rescue Center** ⓘ *www.primatecenter.org, 0900-1100, 1330-1600, limited entrance every 30 mins, 10,000d,* is a big draw in the park. There are more than 30 cages, four houses and two semi-wild enclosures for the 130 animals in breeding programmes; there are some 15 different species and sub-species. The centre is repsonsible for discovering a new species in Vietnam, the grey-shanked douc langur (*Pygathrix cinereus*), in 1997. The centre's work is extremely interesting and it is well worth a visit.

There's also the **Turtle Conservation Center**. Visitors can arrange tours to visit the 16 species kept there. Cuc Phuong also has a botanical garden that is excellent for birdwatching in the early morning as well as listening to the nearby primates' dawn chorus!

Visitors can take a number of trekking tours in the park and also spend the night at homestays with the Muong. Night spotting could enable you to see black giant squirrel, Indian flying squirrel, samba deer and Loris. Birdwatchers could see the rare feathers of the silver pheasant, red-collared woodpecker, brown hornbill and bar-bellied pitta. Two lucky tourists and their guide saw an Asiatic black bear in early 2007.

Facilities at the park headquarters include accommodation, a restaurant, visitor centre and guides' headquarters; a museum is planned. From here you can trek 15 km (two to three days) to the Muong village or trek for 25 km camping, accompanied by a guide From headquarters to the park centre is 20 km. The drive will take you past Mac Lake, the path for the walk to the 45-m-high Ancient Tree (*Tetrameles nudiflora*), and Cave of Prehistoric man. At the park centre you can walk the 7-km paved hike through forest to the 1000-year-old tree (45 m high and 5 m wide) and a 1000-m-long liana (*Entada tonkinensis*) and palace cave. The centre area has accommodation and a restaurant. ▸▸ *See Sleeping, page 169.*

Van Long Nature Reserve and around

① *The Van Long-Ninh Binh Tourist Ecological Area ticket office, T30-386 8798, is just beyond the Van Long hotel; boat and entrance ticket, 35,000d; daily 0700-1700.*

The 3000-ha Van Long Nature Reserve is 17 km north of Ninh Binh and 8 km from Highway 1 towards Cuc Phuong (take a right down the road on the corner of which is a restaurant). It is the home to the endangered Delacour's langur (*Trachypithecus delacouri*), one of the 25 most endangered primates in the world. The species is endemic to Vietnam. Less than 320 are said to be living in northern Vietnam with just 40 at Van Long. The best time to spot the primates known as Vooc Mong Trang in Vietnamese, is early morning or just before sunset. Several caves can also be visited. Boat tours last around two hours. The **Van Long Restaurant**, Gia Van, Gia Vien, T30-364 1248, on the main road, organizes buffalo rides in the area.

Kenh Ga floating village is 21 km north of Ninh Binh on the Hoang Long River and 3 km from the main road. Visitors can paddle 3 km to Kenh Ga past the yellow Roman Catholic church and watch village life go by amid limestone towers. The boat operation (0600-1600, 40,000d) is run by **Ninh Binh Tourism Joint Stock Co** ① *T30-386 8560*, and it takes you to a cave and other villages.

Nam Dinh

Nam Dinh is a large and diverse industrial centre, with a reputation for its textiles. The Nam Dinh Textile Mill was built by the French in 1899, and is still operating.

Thien Truong and **Pho Minh pagodas** – both highly regarded – are to be found in the village of Tuc Mac (My Loc district), 3 km north of Nam Dinh. Also here are the few remains of the Tran Dynasty. Thien Truong was built in 1238 and dedicated to the kings of the Tran family; Pho Minh was built rather later, in 1305, and contains an impressive 13-storey tower. You can get to the pagodas either by *xe ôm* from Nam Dinh or as part of a day trip by car from Hanoi or Ninh Binh.

Doi Son and **Doi Diep Pagodas** are situated on two neighbouring mountains (Nui Doi Son and Nui Doi Diep). The former was originally built at some point during the early Ly Dynasty (AD 544-602). When the Emperor Le Dai Hanh (AD 980-1005) planted rice at the foot of the mountain, legend has it that he uncovered two vessels, one filled with gold and the other with silver. From that season on, the harvests were always bountiful.

North of the main channel of the Red River, 10 km southwest of Thai Binh, is the site of the 11th-century **Keo Pagoda**, which was destroyed in a flood. The present building dates back to the 17th century but has been remodelled several times. Its chief architectural attraction is a wooden, three-storey campanile containing two bronze bells.

⦿ Ninh Binh and around listings

For Sleeping and Eating price codes and other relevant information, see Essentials pages 26-31.

⦿ Sleeping

Ninh Binh *p164*

C-D Thuy Anh, 55A Truong Han Sieu St, T30-387 1602, www.thuyanhhotel.com. 37 rooms, with fridge, etc in this spotless hotel in the town centre; the deluxe rooms come with a view. Breakfast included. Will arrange tours and are a useful source of information. The restaurant is good and there is the **Lighthouse Café** and rooftop garden.
C-E Thanh Thuy's Guesthouse, 128 Le Hong Phong St, T30-387 1811, www. hotelthanhthuy.com. A friendly place with cheap rooms and newer, more expensive rooms; most bathrooms have bathtubs.
D Hoa Lu, Tran Hung Dao St, T30-387 1217, hoaluhotel@hn.vnn.vn. On Highway 1 towards Hanoi. 84 rooms at a range of prices for a range of standards. Cars and motorbikes for rent and tours arranged. English not spoken at reception.
E Hoang Hai Hotel, 36 Truong Han Sieu St, T30-3871 5177, www.ninhbinhhotel.com.vn. The 11 rooms are divided into 3 types; the bigger rooms are more expensive.
E-G Queen, Hoang Hoa Tham St, T30-387 1874, luongvn2001@yahoo.com. Near the station. Simpler rooms; the more expensive ones are larger, have a/c and bathtubs. There's also a dorm with TV, fan and shared bathroom. Transport, tours and internet offered. Restaurant.

Hoa Lu *p165*

B-C Van Xuan, just off Highway 1 towards Hoa Lu and on the right, T30-362 2617. This hotel has a/c, hot water and a restaurant.

Cuc Phuong National Park *p167*

Four different areas with accommodation: at the park HQ; 1 km from the main gate, at Mac Lake; 2 km from the park HQ, at the park centre (20 km from the main gate); and at the Muong village, 15 km from the park HQ.
D Park centre concrete bungalows with en suite and a/c but more expensive than at HQ. The 4 bungalows, are set around a lawn. Electricity only available 1800-2200.
D-F Headquarters concrete bungalows with en suite facilities, TV and a/c and fan. These are lined up across the road from the restaurant and are clean and comfortable.
E Headquarters detached bungalow. One bungalow with en suite facilities, hot water and a/c and fan.
E Mac Lake Bungalow. 4 bungalows with a/c and private bathroom.
E Park centre stilt houses. These are near the start of the 1000-year-old walk. They have shared bathroom facilities and no hot water. **G** per person.
G Headquarters stilt house. These rooms have fan and shared bathrooms with hot water. **G** per person.
G Homestay with ethnic minorities in the park. Price per person.

Van Long Nature Reserve *p168*

C-E Van Long Resort, Gia Van, Gia Vien, Ninh Binh (coming from Hanoi, turn right off Highway 1 at the Gian Khau crossroads towards Cuc Phuong. After 5 km turn right to Van Long and drive for 2 km), T30-364 1290, www.resortvanlong.vn. The 47 rooms are spacious and there's a pool and tennis courts. It is next door to the ticket office at the entrance to the Van Long Reserve. The **Van Long Restaurant**, Gia Van, Gia Vien, T30-364 1248, on the main road, 1.5 km away.

Nam Dinh *p168*
C-D Vi Hoang, 153 Nguyen Du St, T350-384 9290. Somewhat uncared for, restaurant.

🍽 Eating

Ninh Binh *p164*
Y Hoang Hai Hotel, 36 Truong Han Sieu St, T30-3871 5177. Open 0800-2200. This centrally located restaurant has zero atmosphere but service is prompt. Breakfast, lunch and dinner served.
Y Thanh Thuy's Guesthouse (see Sleeping, above). The portions are plentiful.
Y Thuy Anh (see Sleeping, above). A choice of Vietnamese fare across a range of prices.

Cuc Phuong National Park *p167*
Y There are 2 restaurants in the national park, one at the main gate, the other 1 km further in. Both serve a limited, and sometimes unavailable, range of food. Drinks available.

🏔 Activities and tours

Ninh Binh and around *p164*
Queen, see Sleeping, above, runs tours to the local attractions.
Thanh Thuy's Guesthouse, see Sleeping, above, organizes a recommended 3-day trip to the Pu Luong Nature Reserve near Mai Chau. Also trips to the local attractions.
Thuy Anh, see Sleeping, above, runs tours to Tam Coc, Bich Dong, Hoa Lu, Kenh Ga, Van Long reserve, Phat Diem and Cuc Phuong. Can also arrange trips to Haiphong, Cat Ba and Halong and trekking.
Vic Travel, 17 Pham Ngu Lao St, T30-388 3438/91-230 1640 (mob), http://victravel. net. Recommended.

See also Hanoi tour operators, page 87.

🚌 Transport

Ninh Binh *p164*
Bus
From Ninh Binh's bus station at 207 Le Dai Hanh St to **Hanoi**'s southern terminal,

Giap Bat, hourly, 3 hrs, 30,000d and also to **Haiphong**, 4 a day, 40,000d; minibuses to Hanoi, 2 hrs. To **Phat Diem**, 1 hr; to **Kenh Ga** at 1000, 30 mins; then get a motorbike at the turn-off for the final 2 km. Take the same bus for **Van Long** and take a moto at the turn-off to the reserve. Some Open Tour Buses stop here on their way to Hanoi and Hué.

Car, motorbike and bicycle
Hoang Hai Hotel (see Sleeping, above) rents cars, motorbikes and bicycles. **Queen** rents too and Thuy Anh rents all these services at slightly cheaper prices and offers English- or French-speaking guides. **Thanh Thuy's Guesthouse** also rents bikes and motorbikes at similar prices. To get to **Cuc Phuong National Park** independently of a tour, take a *xe ôm* or hire a car for the day.

Cuc Phuong National Park *p167*
Bus
For independent travel: buses depart Giap Bat terminal in Hanoi for **Nho Quan** at 0800, 0900, 1200, 1300, 1500, 1600 and return at 0700, 0800, 1100, 1200, 1300 and 1400. From Nho Quan take a *xe ôm*. There's also 1 daily return bus direct from Hanoi to Cuc Phuong.

Nam Dinh *p168*
Bus
Regular connections with **Hanoi**'s Southern terminal, 3 hrs, and with **Haiphong** on Highway 10, 4 hrs.

Taxi
Ninh Binh taxi, T30-387 6876.

ℹ Directory

Ninh Binh *p164*
Bank Vietcombank, Tran Hung Dao St. Cashes TCs, ATM. **Internet** Thuy Anh Hotel. **Post office** Tran Hung Dao St.

Nam Dinh *p168*
Post office 4 Ha Huy ap St.

Contents

174 Thanh Hoa to Hué
175 Dong Hoi and around
176 Listings

177 Hué and around
180 Hué
185 Along the Perfume River
and the Imperial tombs
193 North of Hué
196 West of Hué
196 South of Hué
199 Listings

207 Danang and around
208 Danang
210 Around Danang
212 Listings

216 Hoi An and around
217 Hoi An
221 Around Hoi An
224 Listings

**232 Dalat and the
Central Highlands**
235 Dalat
242 Dalat to Ho Chi Minh City
242 Dalat to Buon Ma Thuot
242 Buon Ma Thuot
245 Around Buon Ma Thuot
247 Play Ku (Pleiku)
249 Kontum
252 Listings

265 Nha Trang and around
266 Nha Trang
269 Around Nha Trang
274 Phan Rang and around
277 Listings

284 Phan Thiet and Mui Ne
286 Listings

291 Vung Tau
292 Sights and beaches
295 Towards Phan Thiet,
Ke Ga and Tien Thanh
295 Listings

298 Con Dao
302 Listings

Footprint features

170 Don't miss…
182 Nguyen Dynasty Emperors
(1802-1945)
183 Eunuch Power
188 Death and burial of Emperor
Gia Long (1820)
191 Tu Duc's lament
194 The funeral of Khai Dinh
196 Battle at Khe Sanh (1968)
197 Ho Chi Minh Trail
206 By train from Hué to Danang
222 Silk worms
233 Central Highlands
269 Alexandre Yersin
272 Tay Son Rebellion (1771-1788)
273 Son My (My Lai) massacre
274 My Lai – rewriting history
294 Superior God of the
Southern Sea
300 Vo Thi Sau
301 Turtles

Central Vietnam

★ **Don't miss ...**
1 Tomb of Emperor Minh Mang, page 190
2 Hué to Danang train, page 206
3 An Bang Beach, page 221
4 Hoi An tailor shops, page 230
5 Hoi An river trip, page 231
6 Kontum, page 249
7 Nha Trang, page 266
8 Mui Ne, page 285

The Central Region extends more than 1000 km north to south. It includes the mountains of the Annamite chain which form a natural frontier with Laos to the west and in places extend almost all the way to the sea in the east. Many of Vietnam's ethnic minorities are concentrated in these mountains. The narrow, coastal strip, sometimes only a few kilometres wide, supported the former artistically accomplished Kingdom of Champa.

The narrow central region is traversed by Highway 1 which runs all the way from Hanoi to Ho Chi Minh City. Along much of its route, the road runs close to the coast, passing through a succession of interesting, though rather unattractive, towns. These northern provinces – such as Nghe An – are among the poorest in the country but their inhabitants are among the friendliest. Villagers here grow barely enough to feed themselves.

The middle part of the Central Region is home to no less than four World Heritage Sites: Phong Nha Cave, one of the longest cave systems in the world; the old Imperial City at Hué, a former capital of Vietnam; My Son, one-time capital of the Cham Kingdom; and Hoi An, an old mercantile port town which retains traditional architecture. The southern part of this diverse region has stunning coast and beaches and Nha Trang and Mui Ne are ideal spots for a few days by the sea. Vast swathes of wild, beautiful and untamed coastline has piqued the curiosity of developers who are moving in by the truckload backed by millions of dollars of foreign investment.

Thanh Hoa to Hué

→ *Colour map 2, A2-3, A4.*

Let us not beat about the bush: this is one of the least interesting and least visited areas of Vietnam. The two main sites are largely of specialist interest. Phong Nha Cave, at the heart of an 85,000-ha nature reserve, has been partially explored by British speleologists. Explorations suggest that this is one of the most extensive underground systems in the world, with several species of wildlife unique to the area. UNESCO has granted the caves World Heritage status. North of Hué in Dong Ha is the so-called Demilitarized Zone (DMZ), which was the scene of heavy fighting in the American War. Relics of this era can still be seen.

▶ *For listings, see pages 176-177.*

Thanh Hoa

The **Citadel of Ho** was built in 1397 when Thanh Hoa was the capital of Vietnam. Much of this great city has been destroyed, although the massive city gates are preserved. Art historians believe that they rival the finest Chinese buildings, and the site is in the process of being excavated. This town and province mark the most northerly point of the central region. For tourist information, there's **Thanh Hoa Province Tourism** ① *34 Le Loi St, T37-385 4140*.

The 160-m-long **Ham Rong Bridge** or 'Dragon's Jaw' which crosses the Ma River north of Thanh Hoa was a significant spot during the Vietnam War. The bridge, a crucial transport link with the south, was heavily fortified and the US lost 70 planes in successive abortive raids from 1965. Eventually, in 1972, they succeeded by using laser-guided 'smart' bombs, at which point the Vietnamese promptly built a replacement pontoon bridge.

About 15 km east of Thanh Hoa lies the coastal resort of **Sam Son**. This is truly a bizarre place catering mainly for the holidaying Vietnamese. The place is teeming with karaoke cafés and commercial sex workers. The beach is long and crowded with deckchairs. If you walk south along the beach and over the hill you can find a deserted cove (walk past the temple). This beach is full of tiny crabs.

Vinh and around

Vinh is a diversified industrial centre and the capital of Nghe An Province. It was damaged by the French before 1954, and then suffered sustained bombing by US and ARVN (Army of the Republic of Vietnam) aircraft from 1964 through to 1972. In the process it was virtually razed. Vinh lies at the important point where the coastal plain narrows, forcing roads and railways to squeeze down a slender coastal strip of land. The town has since been rebuilt with assistance from the former East Germany, in startlingly unimaginative style. The dirty-brown apartment blocks make Vinh one of the most uninspired cities in Vietnam. The province of Nghe An also happens to be one of the poorest, and the mini-famine of 1989 struck hard. For tourist information go to **Nghe An Tourist Office** ① *13 Quang Trung St, T38-384 4298*.

There is nothing of historical interest here, unless socialist architecture can be thought of as such. The **Central Market**, at the south end of Gao Thang Street (the continuation of Quang Trung Street), is a bustle of colour and activity.

Kim Lien village, 14 km west of Vinh, is the place where Ho Chi Minh was born in 1890. There is a reconstruction of the house he was born in together with a memorial altar.

Sen, another village close to Kim Lien, is where Ho lived with his father from the age of six. Although the community and surrounding area were hardly wealthy, Ho was fortunate to be born into a family of modest means and his father was highly educated. The house where he lived (in fact a replica built in 1955) may be thatched and crude, but it was a great deal better than the squalor that most of his countrymen had to endure (see page 414, for an account of Ho's life). There is a small museum. The province of Nghe Tinh has a reputation for producing charismatic revolutionary leaders: Phan Boi Chau – another fervent anti-colonialist – was also born here (see box, page 406).

Cua Lo, 20 km north of Vinh, boasts 8 km of white sandy beach and is a very popular (if slightly downmarket) holiday spot with the locals. There are a number of hotels but finding a room during the holiday period (June to August) can be tricky and the prices are double what they are at other times.

From Vinh, buses leave for Nam Can on the border with Laos (Nam Khan on the Laos side) and Cau Treo (Nam Phao in Laos), also on the Laos border. It is possible to buy Laos visas at the border. ➧ *See also Transport, page 177.*

Ngang Pass or Porte d'Annam

Running between the Central Highlands and the coast is a small range of mountains, the Hoanh Son, which neatly divides the north from Central Vietnam. In French times the range marked the southern limit of Tonkin and northern limit of Annam. The mountains, which reach up to 1000 m, have a marked effect on climate, blocking cold northerly winds in winter and receiving up to 3000 mm of rain. During the reign of Minh Mang a gate was built, the Hoanh Son Quan. Subsequently, Emperor Thieu Tri on a visit north composed a poem which is inscribed on a nearby rock.

Dong Hoi and around → *For listings, see pages 176-177.*

Travelling between Vinh and Hué, there is little to entice the traveller to stop. Along this stretch of coastal plain, which crosses from the province of Nghe An to Ha Tinh to Quang Binh then to Quang Tri and on to Thua Thien Hué, the inhabitants have been struggling against floods and encroaching sand dunes for years. During the Vietnam War, the area was pounded by bombs and shells, and sprayed with defoliants. Unexploded bombs still regularly maim farmers (1,000,000 bombs have been unearthed since the end of hostilities), and it is claimed that the enduring effects of Agent Orange can be seen in the high rates of physical deformity in both animals and humans.

The town of **Dong Hoi** can be used as a stopping-off point on the way north or south. It was virtually annihilated during the war as it lies just north of the **17th parallel**, marking the border between North and South Vietnam. Just south of the town is the **Hien Luong Bridge** which spans the Ben Hai River – the river forming the border between the two halves of former North and South Vietnam.

Phong Nha-Ke Bang National Park

ⓘ *www.phongnhakebang.vn, 30,000d plus 150,000d for the boat ride. North on Highway 1 for 20 km, 30 km west to the Son River landing stage. Take a motorbike or a tour from Dong Hoi.*
Phong Nha Cave is about 50 km from Dong Hoi. It is a true speleological wonder. Visitors are taken only 600 m into the cave by boat and are dropped off to explore. The brick foundations of a Cham temple remain in one of the chambers. There are stalagmites and stalactites and those with a powerful torch can pick out the form of every manner of ghoul and god in the rocks. A team of British divers explored 9 km of the main cave system in 1990 but less than 1 km is accessible to visitors.

Dong Ha and the border with Laos

The **Demilitarized Zone (DMZ)**, **Khe Sanh** and the **Ho Chi Minh Trail** lie to the south of Dong Hoi. These war-time sights are normally visited on a tour from Hué and are described in detail on page 193. About 94 km south, at Dong Ha, Highway 9 branches off the main coastal Highway 1 and proceeds to the border with Laos at **Lao Bao** (Dansavanh in Laos). Dong Ha sits on the junction of Highways 1 and 9 and is prospering from the growth of trade with Laos. Dong Ha is a convenient overnight stop for those crossing into or coming from Laos. Buses now travel regularly to the border from Hué. Travellers have also reported successfully hitching lifts with trucks bound for Laos. Along this route is Khe Sanh (now called Huong Hoa) – one of the most evocative names associated with American involvement in Vietnam (see page 195).

Close to Khe Sanh are parts of the famous **Ho Chi Minh Trail** (see box, page 197) along which supplies were ferried from the north to the south. Highway 9 has been extensively improved in recent years to provide land-locked Laos with an alternative access route to the sea. This **Lao Bao** crossing (2 km beyond Lao Bao village) to Savannakhet provides Laos visas on arrival.

⊙ Thanh Hoa to Hué listings

For Sleeping and Eating price codes and other relevant information, see Essentials pages 26-31.

⊖ Sleeping

Thanh Hoa *p174*
E-F Thanh Hoa, 25A Quang Trung St, T37-385 2517. Everything from a/c and satellite TV to sauna and massage in 93 rooms.

Vinh *p174*
Because so few visitors stay in Vinh, hotel rates can be bargained down considerably.
AL-C Saigon Kimlien, 25 Quang Trung St, T38-383 8899, www.saigonkimlien.com. vn. Perhaps the best in town with a/c, restaurant, bar and sauna.
C Hong Ngoc, 86B Le Loi St, T38-384 1314. Comfortable accommo-dation with a/c. Prices can be bargained to reasonable levels.
E-F Thai Binh Duong, 92 Binh Minh St, Cua Lo, T38-382 4301. All with a/c and hot water. Restaurant and breakfast included.
F Nha Nghi Son Mai, Cua Lo. Friendly family offering nice rooms in a small place.

Dong Hoi *p175*
E Hotel Hanoi, 36 Phan Chu Trin, T52-382 9888. Friendly, hotel with restaurant.

Dong Ha and the border with Laos *p176*
E Mekong Hotel, 66 Le Duan St, T53-385 2292, mekongtouristqtri@gmail.com. Rock hard mattresses but nicer than Melody. Vietinbank ATM on site.
F Melody Hotel, 62 Le Duan St, T53-355 4664, www.melodyhotel.net. 25 rooms that are in quite good shape. Not much English spoken.

⊙ Eating

Dong Ha and the border with Laos *p176*
Ψ Dong Que Restaurant, 109 Le Duan St. Typical Vietnamese fare catering for passing tourist trade.

⊖ Transport

Thanh Hoa *p174*
Bus
Station on Ba Trieu St has regular connections with **Hanoi**'s Ha Dong bus station, 4 hrs, **Ninh Binh**, **Vinh** and other towns on Highway 1.

Train
Express trains between **Hanoi** and **HCMC** stop here, 4¼ hrs to Hanoi.

Air
Vietnam Airlines, 2 Le Hong Phong St,
T31-381 0890.

Bus
The bus station is at 2 Le Loi St. Express
buses leave for **Hanoi**, **HCMC** and **Danang**.
For the border of Laos at **Nam Can** there are
several buses a day. There are several buses a
week to **Phonsavan**, Laos. For **Cau Treo** you
need to catch an early morning bus to Trung
Tam and a moto or minibus to the Laos
border, 25 km away. Take any bus going
north to **Cua Lo**. Get a *xe ôm* for the last
8 km, 20,000d. To **Dong Hoi**, 4½ hrs.

Car
Car hire available from **Vinh Tourist**, 83 Tran
Phu St, T38-384 2226, and from most hotels.

Train
The station is in the west quarter of town,
3 km from the central market, T38-353 0666.
Connections with **Hanoi** and all points
south to **HCMC**. Express trains stop here.

Dong Hoi *p175*
Bus
The bus station is on Tran Hung Dao St.
Buses travelling up Highway 1 linking
HCMC with **Hanoi** pass through Dong Hoi.

Train
Regular connections with **Hanoi** and **HCMC**.

Dong Ha and the border with Laos *p176*
Bus
Sepon Travel, 189 Le Duan St, T53-385 5289,
www.sepontour.com, runs buses to Laos. The
new bus station is at 425 Le Duan St, 1.5 km
from the old one, T53-385 1488. Bus to **Vinh**,
12 hrs. Dong Ha is 74 km from **Hué**, buses
every 30 mins 0630-1800 and 80 km from the
Lao Bao border crossing; to **Huong Hoa** (Khe
Sanh) every 30 mins, 0500-1800; to **Lao Bao**
every 30 mins. To **Hanoi**, 1800.

❶ Directory

Thanh Hoa *p174*
Banks Agriank, 11 Phan Chu Trinh St.
Post office 33 Tran Phu St.

Vinh *p174*
Banks Vietcombank, 9 Nguyen Si Sach St
with ATM. **Post office** 2 Nguyen Thi Minh
Khai St.

Dong Hoi *p175*
Banks Agribank, 2 Me Sut St. **Post
office** 2 Tran Hung Dao St.

Dong Ha and the border with Laos *p176*
Banks Vietcombank, 189 Le Duan St.
Post office 20 Tran Hung Dao St.

Hué and around

→ *Colour map 3, A.*
*Hué, an imperial city that housed generations of the country's most powerful emperors was
built on the banks of the Huong Giang, or 'Perfume River', 100 km south of the 17th parallel.
The river is named after a scented shrub which is supposed to grow at its source.*

*Hué does, in many respects, epitomize the best of Vietnam and in a country that is rapidly
disappearing under concrete, Hué represents a link with the past where the people live in old
buildings and don't lock their doors. Whether it is the royal heritage or the city's Buddhist
tradition, the people of Hué are the gentlest and the least aggressive in the country. They speak
good English and drive their motorbikes more carefully than anyone else.*

*Just south of the city are the last resting places of many Vietnamese emperors (see page
185). A number of war relics in the Demilitarized Zone (DMZ) can be easily visited from Hué.*

Also in the region are the nearby Thuan An Beach, the charming Thanh Hoan Covered Bridge, the misty heights of Bach Ma National Park, the Lang Co Peninsula and the stunning Hai Van Pass which should be travelled by train. ▶▶ *For listings, see pages 199-207.*

Ins and outs

Getting there Hué's Phu Bai airport is a 25-minute drive from the city. **Vietnam Airlines** runs a bus service in to town or you can take a taxi. The two bus stations and one railway station are more central and there are connections to Hanoi and Ho Chi Minh City – and all points between. The trains fill up, so advance booking is recommended, especially for sleepers.

Getting around For the city itself, walking is an option – interspersed, perhaps, with the odd cyclo journey. However, most guesthouses hire out bicycles and this is a very pleasant and slightly more flexible way of exploring Hué and some of the surrounding countryside. A motorbike provides even more flexibility: it makes it possible to fit so much more into a day and this, in Hué, is very important. Boats are available for hire on the river (a pleasant way of getting to the tombs) and there is also the usual array of *xe ôm* motorbike taxis.

Getting to and around the **Imperial Tombs** is easiest by motorbike or car as they are spread over a large area. Most hotels and tour operators organize tours either by minibus, bike or by boat. Set out early if bicycling; all the tombs are accessible by bicycle. It is also possible to go on the back of a motorcycle taxi (*Honda ôm*). Finally, boats can be chartered to sail up the Perfume River – the most peaceful way to travel, but only a few of the tombs can be reached in this way (see Activities and tours, page 204). ▶▶ *For details see also under each individual tomb and see Transport, page 205.*

Best time to visit Hué has a reputation for its bad weather. The rainy season runs from September to January and rainfall is particularly heavy between September and November; the best time to visit is therefore between February and August. However, even in the 'dry' season an umbrella is handy. Rainfall of 2770 mm has been recorded in a single month. Humidity levels can be gauged from the trees along Le Loi Street by the Perfume River which sprout mossy ferns from their trunks and branches. Temperatures in Hué can also be pretty cool in winter, compared with Danang, Nha Trang and other places to the south, as cold air tends to get bottled here, trapped by mountains to the south. For several months each year, though, neither fans nor air-conditioning are required.

Tourist information   The many tour operators in the city will provide plenty of information and advice.

History

Hué was the capital of Vietnam during the Nguyen Dynasty and is one of the cultural cores of the country. The Nguyen Dynasty ruled Vietnam between 1802 and 1945, and for the first time in Vietnamese history a single court controlled the land from Yunnan (southern China) southwards to the Gulf of Siam. To link the north and south – more than 1500 km – the Nguyen emperors built and maintained the Mandarin Road (Quan Lo), interspersed with relay stations. Even in 1802, when it was not yet complete, it took couriers just 13 days to travel between Hué and Saigon, and five days between Hué and Hanoi. If they arrived more than two days late, the punishment was a flogging. There cannot have been a better road in Southeast Asia or a more effective incentive system. The city of Hué was equally impressive. George Finlayson, a British visitor in 1821-1822 wrote that its "style of neatness, magnitude, and perfection" made other Asian cities look "like the works of children". Although the Confucian bureaucracy and some of the dynasty's technical achievements may have been remarkable, there was continual discontent and uprisings against the Nguyen emperors. The court was packed with scheming mandarins, princesses, eunuchs (see box, page 183) and scholars writing wicked poetry. The female writer Ho Xuan Huong, wrote of the court and its eunuchs: "Why do the twelve midwives who cared for you hate each other? Where have they thrown away your youthful sexual passions? Damned be you if you should care about the twitterings of mice-like lovers, or about a bee-like male gallant caressing his adored one ... At least, a thousand years from now you will be more able to avoid the posthumous slander that you indulged in mulberry-grove intrigues."

In 1883 a French fleet assembled at the mouth of the Perfume River, not far from Hué, and opened fire. After taking heavy casualties, Emperor Hiep Hoa sued for peace, and signed a treaty making Vietnam a protectorate of France. As French influence over Vietnam increased, the power and influence of the Nguyen waned. The undermining effect of the French presence was compounded by significant schisms in Vietnamese society. In particular, the spread of Christianity was undermining traditional hierarchies. Despite the impressive imperial tombs and palace, many scholars maintain that the Nguyen Dynasty was simply too short-lived to have ever had a 'golden age'. Emperor Tu Duc may have reigned for 36 years (1847-1883), but by then the imperial family had grown so large that he had to contend with a series of damaging attempted coups d'état as family members vied for the throne. Although the French, and then the Japanese during the Second World War, found it to their advantage to maintain the framework of Vietnamese imperial rule, the system became hollow and, eventually, irrelevant. The last Nguyen Emperor, Bao Dai, abdicated on 30 August 1945.

Unfortunately for art lovers, the relative peace which descended upon Hué at the end of the Second World War was not to last. During the 1968 Tet offensive, Viet Cong soldiers holed up in the Citadel for 25 days. The bombardment which ensued, as US troops attempted to root them out, caused extensive damage to the Thai Hoa Palace and other monuments. During their occupation of Hué, the North Vietnamese Army forces settled old scores, shooting, beheading and even burning alive 3000 people, including civil servants, police officers and anyone connected with, or suspected of being sympathetic to the government in Saigon. This action lent support to the notion that, should the north ever achieve victory over the south, it would result in mass killings.

Imperial City

ⓘ *Entrance to the Imperial City through the Ngo Mon Gate, 23 Thang 8 St, 0700-1730, 55,000d. 100,000d for a guide for 1½ hrs. English, French, Russian, Mandarin and Japanese spoken. Guiding can last until 1900 after the ticket desk closes.*

The Citadel was built to a design of Vauban (France's 17th-century fortifications designer) and covers 520 sq ha. Its walls are 6.6 m high, 21 m thick and 10,000 m in circumference with 10 entrances topped by watch towers. Inside the Citadel, the Great Enclosure contains the Imperial City and Forbidden City.

The Imperial City is built on the same principles as the Forbidden Palace in Beijing. It is enclosed by 7- to 10-m-thick outer walls, the **Kinh Thanh**, along with moats, canals and towers. Emperor Gia Long commenced construction in 1804 after geomancers had decreed a suitable location and orientation for the palace. The site enclosed the land of

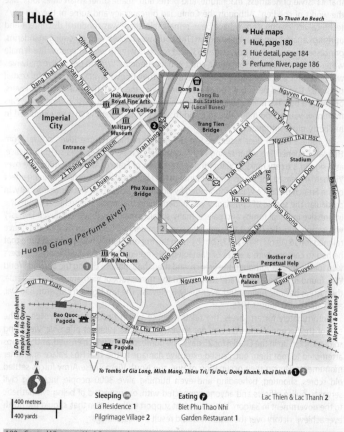

① Hué

→ **Hué maps**
1 Hué, page 180
2 Hué detail, page 184
3 Perfume River, page 186

To Thuan An Beach

Chi Lang

Dinh Tien Hoang
Dang Thai Than
Don Thi Dien

Imperial City

Hué Museum of Royal Fine Arts
Royal College

Military Museum

Entrance

Le Duan
23 Thang 8
Ong Ich Khiem
Le Duan
Tran Hung Dao

Dong Ba
Dong Ba Bus Station (Local Buses)

Nguyen Cong Tru
Chu Van An

Trang Tien Bridge
Le Loi
Nguyen Thai Hoc

Stadium

Phu Xuan Bridge

Tran Cao Van
Ng Tri Phuong
Ben Nghe
Le Quy Don
Ba Trieu

Ha Noi
Hung Vuong

Huong Giang (Perfume River)

Le Loi
Ngo Quyen
Ly Thuong Kiet
Dong Da

Ho Chi Minh Museum

Nguyen Hue
An Dinh Palace

Mother of Perpetual Help

Nguyen Khuyen

To Phia Nam Bus Station, Airport & Danang

Bui Thi Xuan

To Den Voi Re (Elephant Temple & Ho Quyen) (Amphitheatre)

Bao Quoc Pagoda
Dien Bien Phu
Phan Chu Trinh

Tu Dam Pagoda

N

To Tombs of Gia Long, Minh Mang, Thieu Tri, Tu Duc, Dong Khanh & ❶ ❷

400 metres
400 yards

Sleeping 🛏
La Residence **1**
Pilgrimage Village **2**

Eating 🍴
Biet Phu Thao Nhi
Garden Restaurant **1**

Lac Thien & Lac Thanh **2**

eight villages (for which the inhabitants received compensation), and covers 6 sq km; sufficient area to house the emperor and all his family, courtiers, bodyguards and servants. It took 20,000 men to construct the walls alone. Not only has the city been damaged by war and incessant conflict, but also by natural disasters such as floods which, in the mid-19th century, inundated the city to a depth of several metres.

Chinese custom decreed that the 'front' of the palace should face south (like the emperor) and this is the direction from which visitors approach the site. Over the outer moat, a pair of gates pierce the outer walls: the **Hien Nhon** and **Chuong Duc** gates. Just inside are two groups of massive cannon; four through the Hien Nhon Gate and five through the Chuong Duc Gate. These are the **Nine Holy Cannon** (**Cuu Vi Than Cong**), cast in 1803 on the orders of Gia Long from bronzeware seized from the Tay Son revolutionaries. The cannon are named after the four seasons and the five elements, and on each is carved its name, rank, firing instructions and how the bronze of which they are made was acquired. They are 5 m in

Hué Imperial City

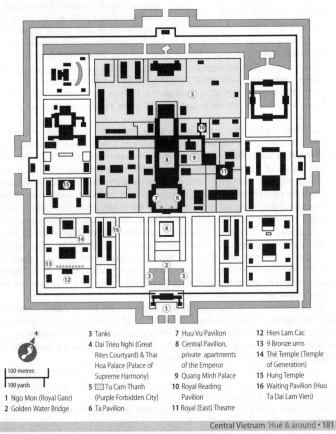

100 metres
100 yards

1 Ngo Mon (Royal Gate)
2 Golden Water Bridge
3 Tanks
4 Dai Trieu Nghi (Great Rites Courtyard) & Thai Hoa Palace (Palace of Supreme Harmony)
5 Tu Cam Thanh (Purple Forbidden City)
6 Ta Pavilion
7 Huu Vu Pavilion
8 Central Pavilion, private apartments of the Emperor
9 Quang Minh Palace
10 Royal Reading Pavilion
11 Royal (East) Theatre
12 Hien Lam Cac
13 9 Bronze urns
14 Thé Temple (Temple of Generation)
15 Hung Temple
16 Waiting Pavilion (Huu Ta Dai Lam Vien)

length, but have never been fired. Like the giant urns outside the Hien Lam Cac (see page 183), they are meant to symbolize the permanence of the empire. Between the two gates is a massive **flag tower**. The flag of the National Liberation Front flew here for 24 days during the Tet Offensive in 1968 – a picture of the event is displayed in Hué's Ho Chi Minh Museum.

Northwards from the cannon, and over one of three bridges which span a second moat, is the **Ngo Mon (Royal Gate) (1)**, built in 1833 during the reign of Emperor Minh Mang. The ticket office is just to the right. The gate, remodelled on a number of occasions since its original construction, is surmounted by a pavilion from where the emperor would view palace ceremonies. Of the five entrances, the central one – the Ngo Mon – was only opened for the emperor to pass through. The other four were for procession participants, elephants and horses. UNESCO has thrown itself into the restoration of Ngo Mon with vigour and the newly finished pavilion, supported by 100 columns, atop the gate now gleams and glints in the sun; those who consider it garish can console themselves with the thought that this is how it might have appeared in Minh Mang's time.

North from the Ngo Mon, is the **Golden Water Bridge (2)** – again reserved solely for the emperor's use – between two **tanks (3)**, lined with laterite blocks. This leads to the **Dai Trieu Nghi (Great Rites Courtyard) (4)**, on the north side of which is the **Thai Hoa Palace (Palace of Supreme Harmony) (4)**, constructed by Gia Long in 1805 and used for his coronation in 1806. From here, sitting on his golden throne raised up on a dais, the emperor would receive ministers, foreign emissaries, mandarins and military officers during formal ceremonial occasions. In front of the palace are 18 stone stelae, which stipulate the arrangement of the nine mandarinate ranks on the Great Rites Courtyard: the upper level was for ministers, mandarins and officers of the upper grade; the lower for those of lower grades. Civil servants would stand on the left, and the military on the right. Only royal princes were allowed to stand in the palace itself, which is perhaps the best-preserved building in the Imperial City complex. Its red and gold ironwood columns decorated with dragon motifs, symbol of the emperors' power, the tiled floor and fine ceiling have all been restored.

North of the Palace of Supreme Harmony is the **Tu Cam Thanh (Purple Forbidden City) (5)**. This would have been reserved for the use of the emperor and his family, and was surrounded by 1-m-thick walls: a city within a city. Tragically, the Forbidden City was virtually destroyed during the 1968 Tet offensive. The two **Mandarin Palaces** and the **Royal Reading Pavilion** (see below) are all that survive.

At the far side of the Thai Hoa Palace, are two enormous **bronze urns (Vac Dong)** decorated with birds, plants and wild animals, and weighing about 1500 kg each. To either side of the urns are the **Ta (6)** and **Huu Vu (7)** pavilions – one converted into a souvenir art shop, the other a mock throne room in which tourists can pay to dress up and play the part

Eunuch power

Eunuchs were key members of the Nguyen Dynasty court in Hué. They were the only men allowed inside the Purple Forbidden City serving the Son of Heaven, the emperor, alongside his wives and concubines. Eunuchs became quite powerful and would play off the concubines against one another. The castrated men, who wore green and red floral gowns with flat, oval hats, arranged the emperor's night time activities and would be bribed by the concubines who wanted to be chosen for that night's sexual adventure. In 1836 Emperor Minh Mang limited their powers so they would not rise to the position of mandarin or become too powerful. He also graded their services. The premier eunuch (clerks) were paid 6 yuans and 0.8 quintals of rice (39.16 kg); the lowliest were the errand boys who earnt one yuan and 0.2 of a quintal of rice (9.8 kg). Some saw this edict as a reaction to the courtier Le Van Duyet, who was himself a eunuch. The employment of eunuchs was abolished in 1914 by Emperor Duy Tan, who reigned between 1907 and 1916.

of the emperor for five minutes. The **Royal Reading Pavilion** (10) has been renovated but, needless to say, has no books. On the far side of the palace are the outer northern walls of the citadel and the north gate.

Most of the surviving buildings of interest are to be found on the west side of the palace, running between the outer walls and the walls of the Forbidden City. At the southwest corner is the well-preserved and beautiful **Hien Lam Cac** (12), a pavilion built in 1821, in front of which stand nine massive **bronze urns** (13) cast between 1835 and 1837 on the orders of Emperor Minh Mang. It is estimated that they weigh between 1500 kg and 2600 kg, and each has 17 decorative figures, animals, rivers, flowers and landscapes representing between them the wealth, beauty and unity of the country. The central, largest urn is dedicated to the founder of the empire, Emperor Gia Long. Next to the urns walking northwards is **Thé Temple (Temple of Generations)** (14). Built in 1821, it contains altars honouring 10 of the emperors of the Nguyen Dynasty behind which are meant to be kept a selection of their personal belongings. It was only in 1954, however, that the stelae depicting the three Revolutionary emperors Ham Nghi, Thanh Thai, and Duy Tan were brought into the temple. The French, perhaps fearing that they would become a focus of discontent, prevented the Vietnamese from erecting altars in their memory. North of the Thé Temple is **Hung Temple** (15) built in 1804 for the worship of Gia Long's father, Nguyen Phuc Luan, the father of the founder of the Nguyen Dynasty. The temple was renovated in 1951.

UNESCO began the arduous process of renovating the complex in 1983: Vietnam at that time was a pariah state due to its invasion of Cambodia in 1978-1979 and the appeal for funds and assistance fell on deaf ears. It was, therefore, fitting testimony to Vietnam's rehabilitation in the eyes of the world when, in 1993, UNESCO declared Hué a World Heritage Site. Although it is the battle of 1968 which is normally blamed for the destruction, the city has in fact been gradually destroyed over 50 years. The French shelled it, fervent revolutionaries burnt down its buildings, typhoons and rains have battered it, thieves have ransacked its contents and termites have eaten away at its foundations. In some respects it is surprising that as many as a third of the monuments have survived relatively intact.

City centre

Just east of the Imperial City is the **Hué Museum of Royal Fine Arts** ① *3 Le Truc St, Tue-Sun 0700-1700, summer (14 Apr-14 Oct) until 1730, 35,000d, no cameras or video cameras, overshoes must be worn and are provided, information in English. Undergoing refurbishment in 2010, the collection still may be temporarily housed at An Dinh Palace, 97 Phan Dinh Phung St and also with an entrance at 150 Nguyen Hue St.* Housed in the Long An Palace, the museum contains a reasonable collection of ceramics, furniture, screens and bronzeware and some stunning, embroidered imperial clothes. In the front courtyard are stone mandarins, cannon, gongs and giant bells. The building itself is worthy of note for its elegant construction with its stunning interior of 128 ironwood columns. It was built by Emperor Thieu Tri in 1845 it was dismantled and erected on the present site in 1909 as the National University Library before being renamed in 1958.

Directly opposite the Royal Fine Arts museum is the **Royal College** ① *2 Le Truc St, daily 0700-1700, free,* established in 1803 and moved to this site in 1908. It is lamentably short of exhibits. Immediately in front is the **Military Museum** ① *23 Thang 8 St (between Dinh Tien Hoang and Doan Thi Diem Sts), T54-352 2397, Tue-Sun 0730-1100, 1330-1700, free.* Missiles, tanks and armoured personnel carriers fill the courtyard.

② Hué detail

Hué maps
1 Hué, page 180
2 Hué detail, page 184
3 Perfume River, page 186

Sleeping 🛏
Canh Tien Guesthouse **1** A3
Century Riverside **4** A2
Dong Loi, & La Carambole Restaurant **6** B2
Duy Tan **7** C2
Hoang Huong **9** A2
Hué Backpackers Hostel **14** A2
Hung Vuong Inn & La Huong Giang **10** A2
Imperial **13** B2
Mercure Hue Gerbera **2** B2
Mimosa **12** B2
Saigon Morin **15** B1
Thanh Thuy **16** A2
Villa Hué **17** B3

Eating 🍴
An Phu **1** B3
Club Garden **3** B3
La Boulangerie Française **7** C2
Little Italy **1** B3
Mandarin **6** C2
Mediterraneo D2 Hue **5** B2
Ong Tao **9** A3
Stop & Go **10** B2
Tropical Garden **12** A3

Bars & clubs 🍸
DMZ **4** A2
Why Not **12** B2

Further east still, but still on the north bank of the river, next to the Dong Ba bus station, is the covered **Dong Ba Market** ① *Tran Hung Dao St*.

The Perfume River is spanned by two bridges; downstream is the ill-fated **Trang Tien Bridge**, named after the royal mint that once stood at its northern end. It was built in 1896 and destroyed soon after by a typhoon; after having been rebuilt it was then razed once more in 1968 during the Tet Offensive. Upstream is **Phu Xuan Bridge**, built by the US Army in 1970. This carries Highway 1, in other words the main north-south highway, but a new bypass with a huge new river crossing 10 km upriver has seen traffic levels fall.

On the south side of the river is the requisite **Ho Chi Minh Museum** ① *7 Le Loi St, T54-382 2152, Tue-Sun 0730-1100, 1330-1630, 10,000d*, which displays pictures of Ho's life plus a few models and personal possessions. The 'tour' begins at the end of the corridor on the second floor. Some interesting photographs (for example of Ho as a cook's assistant at the Carlton Hotel in London), but does not compare with the Ho Chi Minh Museum in Hanoi.

Further south, the **Bao Quoc Pagoda** ① *just off Dien Bien Phu St to the right, over the railway line*, is said to have been built in the early 18th century by a Buddhist monk named Giac Phong. Note the 'stupa' that is behind and to the left of the central pagoda and the fine doors inscribed with Chinese and Sanskrit characters. Further along Dien Bien Phu Street, at the intersection with Tu Dam Street, is the **Tu Dam Pagoda**. According to the Hué Buddhist Association this was originally founded in 1690-1695 but has been rebuilt many times. The present-day pagoda was built shortly before the Second World War. In August 1963, the Diem government sent its forces to suppress the monks here who were alleged to be fomenting discontent among the people. The specially selected forces – they were Catholic – clubbed and shot to death about 30 monks and their student followers, and smashed the great Buddha image here.

The skyline of modern Hué is adorned by the striking pagoda-like tower of the **Church of Mother of Perpetual Help**. This three-storey, octagonal steel tower is 53 m high and an attractive blend of Asian and European styles. The church was completed in 1962 and marble from the Marble Mountain in Danang was used for the altar. The church lies at the junction of Nguyen Hue and Nguyen Khuyen streets.

Along the Perfume River and the Imperial tombs

As the geographical and spiritual centre of the Nguyen Dynasty, Hué and the surrounding area is the site of numerous pagodas and seven imperial tombs, along with the tombs of numerous other royal personages and countless courtiers and successful mandarins.

Each of the tombs follows the same stylistic formula, although at the same time they reflect the tastes and predilections of the emperor in question. The tombs were built during the lifetime of each emperor, who took a great interest in the design and construction – after all they were meant to ensure his comfort in the next life. Each mausoleum, variously arranged, has five design elements: a courtyard with statues of elephants, horses and military and civil mandarins (originally, usually approached through a park of rare trees); a stela pavilion (with an engraved eulogy composed by the emperor's son and heir); a Temple of the Soul's Tablets; a pleasure pavilion; and a grave. Geomancers decreed that they should also have a stream and a mountainous screen in front. The tombs faithfully copy Chinese prototypes, although most art historians claim that they fall short in terms of execution.

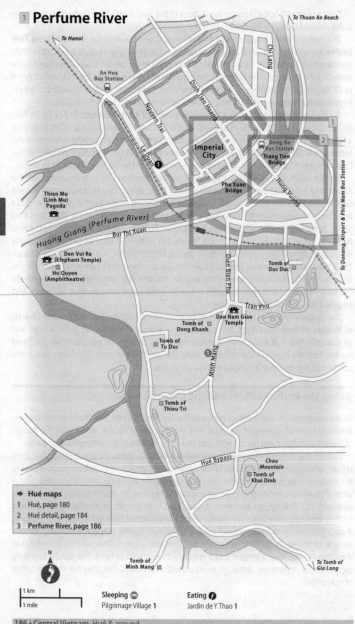

Perfume River

To Thuan An Beach

To Hanoi

An Hoa Bus Station

Chi Lang

Dinh Tien Hoang

Nguyen Trai

Le Duan

Imperial City

Dong Ba Bus Station

Trang Tien Bridge

Phu Xuan Bridge

Hung Vuong

Thien Mu (Linh Mu) Pagoda

Huong Giang (Perfume River)

Bui Thi Xuan

Den Voi Re (Elephant Temple)

Ho Quyen (Amphitheatre)

Dien Bien Phu

Tomb of Duc Duc

To Danang, Airport & Phia Nam Bus Station

Tran Phu

Dan Nam Giao Temple

Tomb of Dong Khanh

Tomb of Tu Duc

Minh Mang

Tomb of Thieu Tri

Hué Bypass

Chau Mountain

Tomb of Khai Dinh

➡ **Hué maps**
1 Hué, page 180
2 Hué detail, page 184
3 Perfume River, page 186

Tomb of Minh Mang

To Tomb of Gia Long

| 1 km |
| 1 mile |

N

Sleeping 🛏
Pilgrimage Village **1**

Eating 🍴
Jardin de Y Thao **1**

Thien Mu Pagoda

ⓘ *It is an easy 4-km bicycle (or cyclo) ride from the city, following the north bank of the river upstream (west).*

Thien Mu Pagoda (the Elderly Goddess Pagoda), also known as the Thien Mau Tu Pagoda, and locally as the **Linh Mu Pagoda** (the name used on most local maps), is the finest in Hué. It is beautifully sited on the north bank of the Perfume River, about 4 km upstream from the city. It was built in 1601 by Nguyen Hoang, the governor of Hué, after an old woman appeared to him and said that the site had supernatural significance and should be marked by the construction of a pagoda. The monastery is the oldest in Hué, and the seven-storey **Phuoc Duyen** (Happiness and Grace Tower), built by Emperor Thieu Tri in 1844, is 21 m high, with each storey containing an altar to a different Buddha. The summit of the tower is crowned with a water pitcher to catch the rain, water representing the source of happiness.

Arranged around the tower are four smaller buildings one of which contains the **Great Bell** cast in 1710 under the orders of the Nguyen Lord, Nguyen Phuc Chu, and weighing 2200 kg. Beneath another of these surrounding pavilions is a monstrous **marble turtle** on which is a 2.6-m-high stela recounting the development of Buddhism in Hué, carved in 1715. Beyond the tower, the entrance to the pagoda is through a triple gateway patrolled by six carved and vividly painted guardians – two on each gate. The roof of the sanctuary itself is decorated with *jataka* stories. At the front of the sanctuary is a brass, laughing Buddha. Behind that are an assortment of gilded Buddhas and a crescent-shaped gong cast in 1677 by Jean de la Croix. The first monk to commit suicide through self immolation, Thich Quang Duc, came from this pagoda (see box, page 318) and the grey Austin in which he made the journey to his death in Saigon is still kept here in a garage in the temple garden.

In May 1993, a Vietnamese – this time not a monk – immolated himself at Thien Mu. Why is not clear: some maintain it was linked to the persecution of Buddhists; others that it was because of the man's frustrated love life.

Tomb of Emperor Gia Long

ⓘ *Daily 0630-1730, 55,000d for the upkeep of the tomb. Get there by bike or motorbike.*

The Tomb of Emperor Gia Long is the most distant and the most rarely visited but is well worth the effort of getting there (see below). The tomb is overgrown with venerable mango trees, the only sound is bird call and, occasionally, the wind in the trees: otherwise a blessed silence. Devoid of tourists, touts and ticket sellers it is the most atmospheric of all the tombs, and as the political regime in Vietnam is not a fan of Gia Long it is likely to remain this way. However, given the historical changes that were to be wrought by the dynasty Gia Long founded, it is arguably the most significant

Tomb of Emperor Gia Long

To River Crossing
Vinh Mau Tomb
Hoang Co Tomb
Thoai Thanh Tomb
Quang Hung Tomb
Thoai Thanh Temple
Gia Thanh Temple
Tomb of Gia Long's second wife
Truong Phong Tomb
Minh Thanh Temple
Gia Long's Tomb
Stela House
N
Obelisks
Not to scale

Death and burial of Emperor Gia Long (1820)

When the Emperor Gia Long died on 3 February 1820, the thread on the ancestors' altar (representing his soul) was tied. The following day the corpse was bathed and clothed in rich garments, and precious stones and pearls were placed in his mouth. Then a ritual offering of food, drink and incense was made before the body was placed in a coffin made of catalpa wood (*Bignonia catalpa*) – a wood impervious to insect attack.

At this time, the crown prince announced the period of mourning that was to be observed – a minimum of three years. Relatives of the dead emperor, mandarins and their wives each had different forms and periods of mourning to observe, depending upon their position.

Three days after Gia Long's death, a messenger was sent to the Hoang Nhon Pagoda to inform the empress, who was already dead, of the demise of her husband. Meanwhile, the new Emperor Minh Mang had the former ruler's deeds recorded and engraved on golden sheets which were bound together as a book. Then astrologers selected an auspicious date for the funeral, picking 27 May after

some argument (11 May also had its supporters). On 17 May, court officials told the heaven, the earth and the dynastic ancestors, of the details for the funeral and at the same time opened the imperial tomb. On 20 May, the corpse was informed of the ceremony. Four days later the coffin left the palace for the three-day journey to its final resting place. Then, at the appointed time, the coffin was lowered into the sepulchre – its orientation correct – shrouded in silk cloth, protected by a second outer coffin, covered in resin, and finally bricked in. Next to Gia Long, a second grave was dug into which were placed an assortment of objects useful in his next life. The following morning, Emperor Minh Mang, in full mourning robes, stood outside the tomb facing east, while a mandarin facing in the opposite direction inscribed ritual titles on the tomb. The silk thread on the ancestors' altar – the symbol of the soul – was untied, animals slaughtered, and the thread then buried in the vicinity of the tomb.

(This account is adapted from James Dumarçay's *The palaces of South-East Asia*, 1991.)

tomb in Hué. It was built between 1814 and 1820 (see box, above, for an account of the emperor's burial). Being the first of the dynasty, Gia Long's mausoleum set the formula for the later tombs. There is a surrounding lotus pond and steps lead up to a courtyard with the Minh Thanh ancestral temple, rather splendid in its red and gold. To the right of this is a double, walled and locked burial chamber where Gia Long and his wife are interred (the Emperor's tomb is fractionally taller). The tomb is perfectly lined up with the two huge obelisks on the far side of the lake. Beyond this is a courtyard with five now headless mandarins, horses and elephants on each side; steps lead up to the stela eulogizing the Emperor's reign, composed, presumably, by his eldest son, Minh Mang, as was the custom. This grey monolith engraved in ancient Chinese characters remained miraculously undisturbed during two turbulent centuries.

Gia Long's geomancers did a great job finding this site: with the mountainous screen in front it is a textbook example of a final resting place. Interestingly, despite their getting first choice of all the possible sites, it is also the furthest tomb from the palace; clearly they took their task seriously.

Nguyen Anh, or Gia Long as he was crowned in 1802, came to power with French support. Back in 1787, Gia Long's son, the young Prince Canh, had caused a sensation in French salon life when, along with soldier/missionary Georges Pigneau de Béhaine, he had sought military support against the Tay Son from Louis XVI. In return for Tourane (Danang) and Poulo Condore (Con Dao), the French offered men and weapons – an offer that was subsequently withdrawn. Pigneau then raised military support from French merchants in India and in 1799 Prince Canh's French-trained army defeated the Tay Son at Quy Nhon.

Gia Long's reign was despotic – to his European advisers who pointed out that encouragement of industry would lead to the betterment of the poor, he replied that he preferred them poor. The poor were virtual slaves – the price for one healthy young buffalo was one healthy young girl. Flogging was the norm – it has been described as the 'bamboo's golden age'. One study by a Vietnamese scholar estimated that there were 105 peasant uprisings between 1802 and 1820 alone. For this, and the fact that he gave the French a foothold in Vietnam, the Vietnamese have never forgiven Gia Long. Of him they still say "*cong ran can ga nha*" (he carried home the snake that killed the chicken).

To get to the Tomb of Emperor Gia Long take Dien Bien Phu Street out of town past the railway station. After a couple of kilometres turn right at the T-junction facing pine-shrouded Dan Nam Giao Temple (where Vietnamese emperors once prayed for good weather) and take first left onto Minh Mang. Continue on, passing the sign marking your departure from Hué and taking the right-hand branch of the fork in the road. After a short distance the road joins the river bank and heads for some 2 km towards the river crossing (the new Hué bypass – Highway 1). Follow the riverbank directly underneath this bridge and continue straight on as the road begins to deteriorate. A few metres beyond the Ben Do 1-km milestone is a red sign reading Gia Long Tomb. Down a steep path a sampan is waiting to ferry passengers across this tributary of the Perfume River (bargain); on the far

Tomb of Emperor Minh Mang

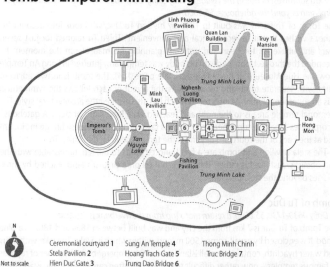

N

Not to scale

Ceremonial courtyard **1**
Stela Pavilion **2**
Hien Duc Gate **3**

Sung An Temple **4**
Hoang Trach Gate **5**
Trung Dao Bridge **6**

Thong Minh Chinh
Truc Bridge **7**

side follow the track upstream for about 1 km. By a café with two billiard tables turn right and then almost immediately turn left. Keep on this path (ask for directions along the way).

Tomb of Emperor Minh Mang

ⓘ *Daily 0630-1730, 55,000d. Get there by bicycle or motorbike. To get there follow the instructions for Gia Long's tomb, but cross the Perfume River using the new road bridge; on the far side of the bridge turn immediately left.*

The Tomb of Emperor Minh Mang is possibly the finest of all the imperial tombs. Built between 1840 and 1843, it is sited among peaceful ponds, about 12 km from the city of Hué. In terms of architectural poise, balance and richness of decoration, it has no peer in the area. The tomb's layout, along a single central and sacred axis (*Shendao*), is unusual in its symmetry; no other tomb, with the possible exception of Khai Dinh (see page 192), achieves the same unity of constituent parts, nor draws the eye onwards so easily and pleasantly from one visual element to the next. The tomb was traditionally approached through the **Dai Hong Mon**, a gate which leads into the ceremonial courtyard containing an array of statuary; today visitors pass through a side gate. Next is the stela pavilion in which there is a carved eulogy to the dead emperor composed by his son, Thieu Tri. Continuing downwards through a series of courtyards there is, in turn, the **Sung An Temple** dedicated to Minh Mang and his empress, a small garden with flower beds that once formed the Chinese character for 'longevity', and two sets of stone bridges. The first consists of three spans, the central one of which (**Trung Dao Bridge**) was for the sole use of the emperor. The second, single bridge leads to a short flight of stairs with naga balustrades, at the end of which is a locked bronze door (no access). The door leads to the tomb itself which is surrounded by a circular wall.

Tomb of Thieu Tri

ⓘ *7 km southwest of Hué in the village of Thuy Bang, daily 0630-1730, ticket required only for admission beyond the gatehouse, 55,000d.*

The Tomb of Thieu Tri was built in 1848 by his son Tu Duc, who took into account his father's wishes that it be 'economical and convenient'. Thieu Tri reigned for just seven years and unlike his forebears did not start planning his mausoleum the moment he ascended the throne. Upon his death his body was temporarily interred in Long An Temple (now the Hué Museum of Royal Fine Arts, see page 184). The tomb is in two adjacent parts, with separate tomb and temple areas; the layout of each follows the symmetrical axis arrangement of Minh Mang's tomb which has also inspired the architectural style. The memorial temple area is to the right and reached via a long flight of steps. A gatehouse incorporates Japanese triple-beamed columns (as seen in the Japanese Bridge in Hoi An) and at the back of the courtyard beyond is the temple dedicated to Thieu Tri.

The stela pavilion and tomb are a few hundred yards to the left, unmissable with the two obelisks. Just like his father, Thieu Tri is buried on a circular island reached by three bridges beyond the stela pavilion.

Tomb of Tu Duc

ⓘ *Daily 0630-1730, 55,000d; a return moto trip from the riverbank is 30,000d.*

The Tomb of Tu Duc is 7 km from the city and was built between 1864 and 1867 in a pine wood. It is enclosed by a wall, some 1500 m long, within which is a lake. The lake, with lotus and water hyacinth, contains a small island where the emperor built a number of replicas of famous temples – now rather difficult to discern. He often came here to relax, and from

"Never has an era seen such sadness, never a year more anguish. Above me, I fear the edicts of heaven. Below, the tribulations of the people trouble my days and nights. Deep in my heart I tremble and blush, finding neither words or actions to help my subjects.

Alone, I am speechless. My pulse is feeble, my body pale and thin, my beard and hair white. Though not yet 40, I have already reached old age, so that I lack the strength to pay homage to my ancestors every morning and evening. Evil must be suppressed and goodness sought. The wise must offer their counsel, the strong their force, the rich their wealth, and all those with skills should devote them to the needs of the army and the kingdom. Let us together mend our errors and rebuild.

Alas! The centuries are fraught with pain, and man is burdened by fear and woe. Thus we express our feelings that they may be known to the world."

(Taken from *Vietnam*, S Karnow.)

the pavilions that reach out over the lake, composed poetry and listened to music. The **Xung Khiem Pavilion**, built in 1865, has recently been restored with UNESCO help and is the most attractive building here. The tomb complex follows the formula described above: ceremonial square, mourning yard with pavilion and then the tomb itself. To the northeast of Tu Duc's tomb are the tombs of his empress, Le Thien Anh and adopted son, Kien Phuc.

Tomb of Tu Duc

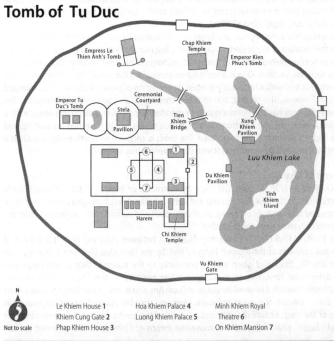

Le Khiem House **1**
Khiem Cung Gate **2**
Phap Khiem House **3**
Hoa Khiem Palace **4**
Luong Khiem Palace **5**
Minh Khiem Royal
Theatre **6**
On Khiem Mansion **7**

Not to scale

Many of the pavilions are crumbling and ramshackle – lending the tomb a rather tragic air. This is appropriate: although he had 104 wives, Tu Duc fathered no sons. He was therefore forced to write his own eulogy, a fact which he took as a bad omen. The eulogy itself recounts the sadness in Tu Duc's life. A flavour of its sentiment can be gleaned from a confession he wrote in 1867 following French seizure of territory. It was shortly after Tu Duc's reign that France gained full control of Vietnam.

Tomb of Duc Duc
① *11 Tan Lang St, 2 km south of the city centre, daily 0630-1730, 55,000d.*
Despite ruling for just three days and then dying in prison, Emperor Duc Duc (1852-1883) has a tomb, built in 1899 by his son, Thanh Thai, on the spot where, it is said, the body had been dumped by gaolers. (Duc Duc was dethroned by the court for his pro-French sympathies). Emperors **Thanh Thai** and his son **Duy Tan** are buried in the same complex. Unlike Duc Duc, though, both were strongly anti-French and were, for a period, exiled in Réunion Island, Africa. Although Thanh Thai later returned to Vietnam and died in Vung Tau in 1953, his son Duy Tan was killed in an air crash in central Africa in 1945. It was not until 1987 that Duy Tan's body was repatriated and interred alongside his father Thanh Thai. The tomb is in three parts: the Long An Temple; Duc Duc's tomb to the south; and Thanh Thai and Duy Tan's tombs adjacent to each other.

Tomb of Dong Khanh
① *The Tomb of Dong Khanh is 500 m from Tu Duc's tomb (walk up the path on the other side of the road from the main entrance to Tu Duc's tomb – the path is partly hidden in amongst the stalls), daily 0630-1730, 55,000d.*
Dong Khanh was the nephew and foster son of Emperor Tu Duc. His tomb was built in 1889, it is the smallest of the imperial mausoleums, but nonetheless one of the most individual; it was not completed until 1923 under the authority of his son Khai Dinh. Unusually, it has two separate sections. One is a walled area containing the usual series of pavilions and courtyards and with a historically interesting collection of personal objects that belonged to the Emperor. The second, 100 m away, consists of an open series of platforms. The lower platform has the honour guard of mandarins, horses and elephants along with a stela pavilion; the third platform is a tiled area which would have had an awning; and the highest platform is the tomb itself. The tomb is enclosed within three open walls, the entrance protected by a dragon screen (to prevent spirits entering).

Tomb of Khai Dinh
① *Daily 0630-1730, 55,000d. Get there by motorbike or bicycle. As for Gia Long's tomb, continue under the new river crossing, but turn immediately left, through a collection of small shops and head straight on, over a small crossroads and parallel to the main road. From the riverbank a return moto trip is 30,000d.*
The Tomb of Khai Dinh is 10 km from Hué. Built between 1920 and 1931, it is the last of the mausoleums of the Nguyen Dynasty and, by the time Khai Dinh was contemplating the afterlife, brick had given way in popularity to the concrete that is now beginning to deteriorate. Nevertheless, it occupies a fine position on the Chau Mountain facing southwest towards a large white statue of Quan Am, also built by Khai Dinh. The valley, used for the cultivation of cassava and sugar cane, and the pine-covered mountains, make this one of the most beautifully sited and peaceful of the tombs. Indeed, before construction could begin, Khai Dinh had to remove the tombs of Chinese nobles who had already

selected the site for its beauty and auspicious orientation. A total of 127 steep steps lead up to the Honour Courtyard with statuary of mandarins, elephants and horses. An octagonal Stela Pavilion in the centre of the mourning yard contains a stone stela engraved with a eulogy to the emperor. At the top of some more stairs are the tomb and shrine of Khai Dinh, containing a bronze statue of the Emperor sitting on his throne and holding a jade sceptre. The body is interred 9 m below ground level (see box, page 194, for a description of Khai Dinh's interment). The interior is richly decorated with ornate and colourful murals (the artist incurred the wrath of the emperor and only just escaped execution), floor tiles and decorations built up with fragments of porcelain. It is the most elaborate of all the tombs and took 11 years to build. Such was the cost of construction that Khai Dinh had to levy additional taxes to fund the project. The tomb shows distinct European stylistic influences; Khai Dinh himself toured France in 1922, three years before he died.

Amphitheatre and Elephant Temple
① *Free. Get there by bicycle or motorbike.To get there, head about 3 km west of Hué railway station on Bui Thi Xuan St; turn left up a paved track opposite 203 Bui Thi Xuan St; the track for the Elephant Temple runs in front of the amphitheatre (off to the right).*

Ho Quyen (Amphitheatre) lies about 4 km upstream of Hué on the south bank of the Perfume River. The amphitheatre was built in 1830 by Emperor Minh Mang as a venue for the popular duels between elephants and tigers. Elephants were symbolic of emperors and strength whereas tigers were seen as anti-imperial beasts and had their claws removed before the fight. This royal sport was in earlier centuries staged on an island in the Perfume River or on the river banks, but by 1830 it was considered desirable for the royal party to be able to observe the duels without placing themselves at risk from escaping tigers. The amphitheatre is said to have been last used in 1904 when, as was usual, the elephant emerged victorious: "The elephant rushed ahead and pressed the tiger to the wall with all the force he could gain. Then he raised his head, threw the enemy to the ground and smashed him to death," wrote Crosbie Garstin in *The Voyage from London to Indochina*. The walls of the amphitheatre are 5 m high and the arena is 44 m in diameter. At the south side, beneath the royal box, is one large gateway (for the elephant) and, to the north, five smaller entrances for the tigers. The walls are in good condition and the centre is filled either with grass or immaculately tended rows of vegetables, depending on the season.

Den Voi Re, the Temple of the Elephant Trumpet, dedicated to the call of the fighting elephant, is a few hundred metres away. It is a modest little place and fairly run down with a large pond in front and contains two small elephant statues. Presumably this is where elephants were blessed before battle or perhaps where the unsuccessful ones were mourned.

North of Hué → For listings, see pages 199-207.

The Demilitarized Zone (DMZ)
Getting there and around Most visitors visit the sights of the DMZ, including Khe Sanh and the Ho Chi Minh Trail, on a tour. But buses do leave for the town of Huong Hoa (Khe Sanh) from the An Hoa bus station; the former site of the US base is 3 km from Huong Hoa bus station. From here it is possible to arrange transport to the Ho Chi Minh Trail and to other sights. A one-day tour of all the DMZ sights can be booked from any of Hué's tour operators. The cost is from US$10; departs 0600 and returns 1800-2000.

As nearly all war paraphernalia has been stripped from the DMZ the visit is more of a 'pilgrimage' than anything else.

The funeral of Khai Dinh

On 6 November 1925, Dai-Hanh- Hoang-Khai-Dinh, King of Annam, 'mounted the dragon's back,' or, in other words, died. Seven diamonds were put in the mouth of the corpse, which was washed, embalmed, dressed in state robes, placed in a huge red and gold lacquer coffin and covered over with young tea leaves. Ten days later official mourning was inaugurated with the sacrifice of a bullock, a goat and a pig. A portrait of the late monarch, painted on silk, was placed on the throne. Paper invocations were burnt, massed lamentations rent the air four times daily for 60 days.

All Annam was in Hué, dressed in its best and brightest. Packed sampans swarmed about the bridge. Gay shrines lined the way, hung with flowers and paper streamers. Bunting, citron and scarlet, fluttered in the breeze. Route-keepers in green and red held the crowds in check, chasing small boys out of the way, whacking them over their mushroom hats. At the head of the column were two elephants, hung with tassels and embroidered cloths and topped with crimson *howdahs* and yellow umbrellas. Never have I seen animals so unutterably bored. They lolled against each other, eyes closed – and slumbered. But for an occasional twitch of an ear or tail they might have been dead. Their boredom was understandable when you came to think of it. An elephant is a long-lived beast. These two were full-grown; elderly, even. It is possible that they featured at the obsequies of Thieu-Tri, and there have been innumerable royal funerals since. At one period kings weren't stopping on the throne of Annam long enough to get the cushions warm. What was a very novel and splendid exhibition to me was stale stuff to these beasts. "All very fine for you, mister", they might have said. "First

time and all that. Can drop out and buy yourself a drink any time you like. All very well for you, Henry, in a featherweight gent's suiting; but what about us, tight-laced front and back with about a ton of passengers, brollies, flags and furniture up top?" An old bearded mandarin in a coat of royal blue struck with a wooden hammer on a silver gong. The procession began to shuffle forward – somebody in front had found means to rouse the elephants, apparently.

Some 160 trained porters, clad in black and white, crouched under the red lacquer poles of the giant bier – slips of bamboo had been placed between their teeth to stop them from chattering. Slowly, steadily, keeping the prescribed horizontal, the huge thing rose. Six tons it weighed and special bridges had to be built to accommodate it. Slowly, steadily it moved towards us, preceded by solemn-stepping heralds in white; flagbearers in sea-green carrying dragon banners of crimson and emerald, blue and gold. The second day was spent in getting the coffin from Nam-Gio to the mausoleum and was a mere repetition of the first. The actual interment took place on the morning of the third day. In a few minutes the mourners were out in the daylight again and the vault doors were being sealed. The spirit of Khai-Dinh was on its way to the Ten Judgement Halls of the Infernal Regions, to pass before the Mirror of the Past wherein he would see all his deeds reflected, together with their consequences; to drink the Water of Forgetfulness, and pass on through transmigration to transmigration till he attained the Pure Land and a state of blessed nothingness. And Bao-Dai – weeping bitterly, poor little chap – reigned in his stead.

(Adapted from *The Voyage from London to Indochina*, Crosbie Garstin.)

The incongruously named Demilitarized Zone (DMZ), scene of some of the fiercest fighting of the Vietnam War, lies along the **Ben Hai River** and the better-known **17th Parallel**. The DMZ was the creation of the **1954 Geneva Peace Accord**, which divided the country into two spheres of influence prior to elections that were never held. Like its counterpart in Germany the boundary evolved into a national border separating communist (the northern Democratic Republic of Vietnam) from capitalist (South Vietnam), but unlike its European equivalent it was the triumph of communism that saw its demise.

Khe Sanh is the site of one of the most famous battles of the war (see box, page 196). The battleground lies along Highway 9 which runs west towards Laos, to the north of Hué, and south of Dong Hoi and is 3 km from the village of the same name. There a small **museum** ① 25,000d, at the remains of the Tacon military base, surrounded by military hardware.

The **Ho Chi Minh Trail** is another popular but inevitably disappointing sight, given that its whole purpose was to be as inconspicuous as possible. Anything you see was designed to be invisible – from the air at least; rather an artificial 'sight' but a worthy pilgrimage considering the sacrifice of millions of Vietnamese porters and the role it played in the American defeat (see box, page 196). The trail runs close to Khe Sanh.

The **tunnels of Vinh Moc** ① 20,000d, served a function similar to that of the better-known Cu Chi tunnels (see page 330). They evolved as families in the heavily bombed village dug themselves shelters beneath their houses and then joined up with their neighbours. Later the tunnels developed a more offensive role when Viet Cong soldiers fought from them. Some visitors regard these tunnels as more 'authentic' than the 'touristy' tunnels of Cu Chi. To get to the tunnels head 6 km north of Ben Hai River and turn right in Ho Xa village; Vinh Moc is 13 km off Highway 1.

Offshore is **Con Co Island**, an important supply depot and anti-aircraft stronghold in the war. Life for ordinary peasants in the battle zone just north of the DMZ was terrifying; some idea of conditions (for revolutionary peasants at least) can be gained from the 1970 North Vietnamese film *Vinh Linh Steel Ramparts*.

The **Rock Pile** is a 230-m-high limestone outcrop just south of the DMZ. It served as a US observation post. An apparently unassailable position, troops, ammunition, Budweiser and prostitutes all had to be helicoptered in. The sheer walls of the Rock Pile were eventually scaled by the Viet Cong. Jon Swain, the war correspondent, describes in his memoirs, *River of Time*, how his helicopter got lost around the Rock Pile and nearly came to disaster in this severely contested zone. The **Hien Luong Bridge** crossing the Ben Hai river on the 17th parallel which marked the boundary between north and south (see page 175) is included in most tours. There's a striking national monument, police post, and meeting hall equipped with mannequins in meeting pose next to the bridge.

Private tours can also visit Doc Mieu Fire Base, Con Thien Fire Base and the Truong Son National Cemetery where there are more than 10,000 graves.

Thuan An Beach

Thuan An town and beach is 13 km to the northeast of Hué. Six kilometres in length, it offers swimming in both a protected lagoon and in the East Sea. The beach is nothing special, however. Local buses leave for Thuan An from the Dong Ba bus station; boats can be chartered from the dock behind the Dong Ba Market (one hour). Alternatively it's a 30-minute motorbike ride or car ride. At the main gate to the beach there is a bicycle park.

Battle at Khe Sanh (1968)

Khe Sanh (already the site of a bloody confrontation in April and May 1967) is the place where the North Vietnamese Army (NVA) tried to achieve another Dien Bien Phu (see page 106); in other words, an American humiliation.

One of the NVA divisions, the 304th, even had Dien Bien Phu emblazoned on its battle streamers. General Westmoreland would have nothing of it, and prepared for massive confrontation. He hoped to bury Ho Chi Minh's troops under tonnes of high explosive and achieve a Dien Bien Phu in reverse. But the American high command had some warning of the attack: a North Vietnamese regimental commander was killed while he was surveying the base on 2 January and that was interpreted as meaning the NVA were planning a major assault. Special forces long-range patrols were dropped into the area around the base and photo reconnaissance increased. It became clear that 20,000-40,000 NVA troops were converging on Khe Sanh. With the US Marines effectively surrounded in a place which the assistant commander of the 3rd Marine Division referred to as "not really anywhere", there was a heavy exchange of fire in January 1968. The Marine artillery fired 159,000 shells, B-52s carpet-bombed the surrounding area, obliterating each 'box' with 162 tonnes of bombs. But, despite the haggard faces of the Marines, the attack on Khe Sanh was merely a cover for the Tet offensive – the commanders of the NVA realized there was no chance of repeating their success at Dien Bien Phu against the US military. The Tet offensive proved to be a remarkable psychological victory for the NVA – even if their 77-day seige of Khe Sanh cost many thousands (one estimate is 10,000-15,000) of NVA lives, while only 248 Americans were killed (43 of those in a C-123 transporter crash). Again, a problem for the US military was one of presentation. Even Walter Cronkite, the doyen of TV reporters, informed his audience that the parallels between Khe Sanh and Dien Bien Phu were "there for all to see".

West of Hué

Thanh Toan Covered Bridge

① *Take a bicycle or motorbike as the route to the bridge, 8 km west of Hué, passes through beautiful countryside where ducks waddle along roads and paddy fields line the route. Best done in the glow of the late afternoon sun.*

Than Toan Covered Bridge was built in the reign of King Le Hien Tong (1740-1786) by Tran Thi Dao, a childless woman as an act of charity hoping that God would bless her with a baby. The bridge, with its shelter for the tired and homeless, attracted the interest of several kings who granted the village immunity from a number of taxes. The original yin-yang tiles have been replaced with ugly green enamelled tube tiles, unfortunately, but the structure is still in good condition.

South of Hué → *For listings, see pages 199-207.*

Between Hué and Danang a finger of the Truong Son Mountains juts eastwards, extending all the way to the sea: almost as though God were somewhat roguishly trying to divide the country into two equal halves. This barrier to north–south communication has resulted

Ho Chi Minh Trail

The Ho Chi Minh trail was used by the North Vietnamese Army to ferry equipment from the North to the South via Laos. The road, or more accurately roads (there were between eight and 10 to reduce 'choke points') were camouflaged in places, allowing the NVA to get supplies to their comrades in the South through the heaviest bombing by US planes. Even the use of defoliants such as Agent Orange only marginally stemmed the flow.

The road was built and kept operational by 300,000 full-time workers and by another 200,000 part-time North Vietnamese peasant workers. Neil Sheehan, in his book *A Bright Shining Lie*, estimates that at no time were more than one-third of trucks destroyed and by marching through the most dangerous sections, the forces themselves suffered a loss rate of only 10-20%.

Initially, supplies were transported along the trail by bicycle; later, as supplies of trucks from China and the Soviet Union became more plentiful, they were carried by motorized transport. By the end of the conflict the Ho Chi Minh trail comprised 15,360 km of all-weather and secondary roads. One Hero of the People's Army is said, during the course of the war, to have carried and pushed 55 tonnes of supplies a distance of 41,025 km – roughly the circumference of the world.

The Ho Chi Minh Trail represents perhaps the best example of how, through revolutionary fervour, ingenuity and weight of people (not of arms), the Viet Cong were able to vanquish the might of the USA.

But American pilots did exact a terrible toll through the years. Again, Sheehan writes: "Driving a truck year in year out with 20-25 to perhaps 30% odds of mortality was not a military occupation conducive to retirement on pension."

The cemetery for those who died on the trail at Truong Son, Quang Tri Province, covers 16 ha and contains 10,306 named headstones; many more died unnamed and unrecovered.

in some spectacular engineering solutions: the **railway line** closely follows the coastline (fortunately it is single track and narrow gauge) sometimes almost hanging over the sea – while Highway 1 winds its way equally precariously over the **Hai Van Pass**. The coastline is stunning. You catch sight of silky sheets of deep blue water, random glimpses of crescent yellow sands, slabs of rock thrusting out into the sea, and layers of lush vegetation leaning over their roots peering into the water. All around people are working in the paddies, their conical hats bobbing up and down. The road used to be littered with broken-down trucks and buses for whom the long haul up to the summit was just too much; drivers seemed to spend more time on their backs under their vehicles than they did behind the steering wheel. However, very few vehicles now use the pass following the opening of the 6-km **Hai Van Tunnel**.

The difficult terrain means that much remains wooded, partly because the trees are too inaccessible to cut down and partly because of government edicts preventing the clearance of steep slopes. The hilly woodlands of Bach Ma National Park stretch from the Lao border right down to the coast and although little is virgin forest quite a lot of bird and animal life flourishes within its leafy branches (see below).

Bach Ma National Park and Hill Station

Ins and outs www.bachma.vnn.vn, national park entry 20,000d. Using your own transport go south down Highway 1 from Hué and turn off at the small town of Cau Hai. From here it is about 3 km to the park entrance and the national park office. Visitors must report here. Cars and minibuses are available from here. Accommodation is available.

Climatically it is at least 7°C colder than the coastal plain and annual rainfall of 8000 mm falls mainly between September and January, which is when the leeches are most active. It is busiest on summer weekends; March and April are particularly worthwhile for the rhododendron blossom.

Sights The French established a great many hill stations in Vietnam. Dalat was the only one to really develop as a town. Others, like Sapa, were rejuvenated a few years ago and yet others, like Bach Ma, had been forgotten about until very recently. Only now are the ruins of villas being uncovered, flights of steps unearthed and old gardens and ponds cleared. Bach Ma was established as a hill station in 1932 when the construction of a road made it accessible. By the outbreak of the Second World War there were 139 villas and a hotel. Recognizing its natural beauty and biological diversity the French gave it protected status. In 1991 the Vietnamese government classified it as a national park with 22,031 ha at its core and a further buffer zone of 21,300 ha. The area is rugged granite overlain in places by sandstone rising to an altitude of 1448 m at the summit of Bach Ma. There are a number of trails past cascades, through rhododendron woods and up the summit trail overlooking the remains of colonial villas.

The mammal species of the park have yet to be comprehensively surveyed and so far only 48 species of mammal have been confirmed. Included in this figure, however, are some species of special interest such as the **red-shanked douc langur** and the buff-cheeked or **white-cheeked gibbon**.

Birdlife here is particularly interesting. Four restricted range species are the **Annam partridge**, **crested argus**, **short-tailed scimitar babbler** and the **grey-faced tit babbler**. The most characteristic feature of Bach Ma's birdlife is the large number of pheasants. Of the twelve species of pheasant recorded in Vietnam, seven have been seen in the park. A subspecies of the silver pheasant lives here and Edwards' pheasant, believed extinct until it was rediscovered in 1996, was seen just outside the park buffer zone in 1998. There are many other species of interest including the red-collared woodpecker, Blyth's kingfisher and the coral-billed ground cuckoo.

Lang Co

The road from Hué to Lang Co passes through many pretty, red-tiled villages, compact and surrounded by clumps of bamboo and fruit trees which provide shade, shelter and sustenance. And, for colour, there's the bougainvillea – which through grafting produces pink and white leaves on the same branch. Just north of Hai Van Pass lies the once idyllic fishing village of Lang Co (about 65 km south of Hué) on a spit of land, which has a number of cheap and good seafood restaurants along the road. Shortly after crossing the Lang Co lagoon, dotted with coracles and fish traps, the road begins the long haul up to Hai Van Pass but the majority of traffic now diverts through the tunnel.

Apparently, in the first year of his reign, Emperor Khai Dinh visited Lang Co and was so impressed that he ordered the construction of a summer palace. This, it seems, was never carried out, not even by his son Bao Dai who was so fond of building palaces. There are several guesthouses and tourist resorts on Lang Co, some of the resorts with the poorest standards of rooms in the entire country. But, new standards are to be introduced with the arrival of the Banyan Tree Group that has also been given the go-ahead to build the **Laguna Vietnam**, a US$276 million resort of hotels, restaurants, a spa, shops and a golf course on a 200-ha site at Lang Co. Pilgrimage Village is also building a resort in the area.

Hai Van Pass

Hai Van Pass (Deo Hai Van, 'Pass of the Ocean Clouds' or, to the French, Col des Nuages) lies 497 m above the dancing white waves that can be seen at its foot. In historic times the pass marked the border between the kingdoms of Vietnam and Champa. The mountains also act as an important climatic barrier trapping the cooler, damper air-masses to the north and bottling it up over Hué, which accounts for Hué's shocking weather. They also mark an abrupt linguistic divide, with the Hué dialect (the language of the royal court) to the north, the source of bemusement to many southerners.

The pass is peppered with abandoned pillboxes and crowned with an old fort, originally built by the dynasty from Hué and used as a relay station for the pony express on the old Mandarin Road. Subsequently used by the French, today it is a pretty shabby affair collecting wind-blown litter and sometimes used by the Army for a quiet brew-up and a smoke. Looking back to the north, stretching into the haze is the littoral and lagoon of Lang Co. To the south is Danang Bay and Monkey Mountain, and at your feet lies a patch of green paddies which belong to the leper colony, accessible only by boat.

Highway 1 passes through the village of **Nam O**, once famous for firework manufacture. Pages of old school books were once dyed pink, laid out in the sun to dry, rolled up and filled with gunpowder. But, alas, no more. Like other pyrotechnical villages, Nam O has suffered from the government's ban on firecrackers. Just south of Nam O is **Xuan Thieu Beach**, dubbed 'Red Beach II' by US Marines who landed here in March 1965, marking the beginning of direct intervention by the USA in the Second Indochina War. The tarmac and concrete foundations of the military base still remain.

⊚ Hué and around listings

For Sleeping and Eating price codes and other relevant information, see Essentials pages 26-31.

⊜ Sleeping

Hué *p180, maps p180, p184 and p186*
Most hotels lie to the south of the Perfume River. Hué still suffers from a a dearth of quality accommodation but this has improved in recent years and more properties are planned.
LL-AL La Residence Hotel & Spa, 5 Le Loi St, T54-383 7475, www.la-residence-hue. com. Anyone who knew this hotel before will be stunned at its fabulous makeover. For lovers of art deco, it is an essential place to stay and to visit. Home of the French governor of Annam in the 1920s, it has been

beautifully and decadently restored with 122 rooms, restaurant, lobby bar, spa and swimming pool close to the Perfume River. The citadel can be seen from the hotel. The rooms in the original governor's residence are the most stylish, with 4-poster beds and lovely dark wood furnishings; other rooms are extremely comfortable too, with all mod-cons. The breakfasts are very filling; guests also enjoy free internet. The hotel has a fascinating collection of old colonial-era photographs that are hung along the corridors. Highly recommended.
LL-A Huong Giang (**Perfume River Hotel**), 51 Le Loi St, T54-382 2122, www. huonggianghotel.com.vn. Gorgeous position on the river with comfortable rooms despite the heavy wooden, lacquered

'royal' furniture many Hué hotels insist on using. Only the pricier rooms overlook the river. A new wing has pushed the number of rooms to 164 and a white paint job has improved the aesthetics. Service is efficient.

LL-A Imperial Hotel, 8 Hung Vuong St, T54-388 2222, www.imperial-hotel.com.vn. If you can stop cringing at the utterly ostentatious lobby, heavily over decorated beyond belief, then the rooms here are tastefully decorated. In a great central location the hotel boasts excellent facilities including a rooftop pool and spa. Breakfast is not included.

LL-B Saigon Morin, 30 Le Loi St, T54-382 3526, www.morinhotels.com.vn. Recognizable as the fine hotel originally built by the Morin brothers in the 1880s. Arranged around a courtyard with a small pool, the rooms are large and comfortable. All come with a/c, satellite TV and hot water. The courtyard, lit with candles, is a delightful place to sit in the evening and enjoy a quiet drink. Service is friendly and the overall effect most agreeable. Recommended.

L-A Century Riverside, 49 Le Loi St, T54-382 3390, www.centuryriversidehue.com. Fabulous river views and comfortable, rooms in this imposing building. Note that not all rooms have been renovated, so enquire before booking. Vietnamese and Western food is served at the restaurants. There's a pool and tennis courts and massage service. The hotel is used by many tour operators.

AL Pilgrimage Village boutique resort and spa, 130 Minh Mang Rd, T54-388 5461, www.pilgrimagevillage.com. Tastefully designed rooms in a village setting ranging from honeymoon and pool suites to superior rooms. The rooms in small houses with private pools are gorgeous and recommended. There are 2 restaurants (see Eating), a number of bars, a beautiful and atmospheric spa (the Vietnamese aromatherapy massage is outstanding), open to outside guests also, and 2 inviting pools. Cooking and t'ai chi classes are available. There's a complimentary shuttle service to and from town.

AL-B Mercure Hue Gerbera, 38 Le Loi St, T54-393 6688, www.mercure.com. This brings a new class of hotel to Hué with 110 rooms, a pool and restaurant that serves an excellent buffet breakfast. The vast lobby is rather characterless but service is excellent. The hotel location is downtown and rooms are super comfortable.

A-B Villa Hué, 4 Tran Quang Khai St, T54-383 1628, www.villahue.com. Villa Hué, in an attractive building, is a 12-room hotel used by the Hué Tourism School to train up future hotel managers in conjunction with the Luxembourg Development Cooperation. All rooms are spacious and comfortable and have TV, a/c, and tea- and coffee-making facilities and come with attractive soft-furnishings appeal. Vietnamese and Western food is served at the restaurant. There's a lobby bar and an outdoor seating area in the courtyard. Cooking classes are offered. Recommended.

A-D Duy Tan, 12 Hung Vuong St, T54-382 5001, www.duytanhotel.com.vn. Large building in a bustling part of town, with comfortable superior rooms. The standard rooms are spartan but fully equipped.

E Dong Loi, 19 Pham Ngu Lao St, T54-382 2296, www.hoteldongloi.com. Well situated and surrounded by internet cafés, shops and restaurants, this is a bright, breezy, airy and comfortable hotel. All rooms come with a/c and hot water and all except the cheapest rooms have a bathtub. Family run, friendly and helpful service. The excellent La Carambole restaurant (see Eating, below) adjoins the hotel.

E Hung Vuong Inn, 20 Hung Vuong St, T54-382 1068, hung.vuong.inn@gmail. com. No longer above La Boulangerie and a little sadder for it (although they still serve pastries). There are 9 double and twin rooms above the shop that are all spotlessly clean. Rooms have a TV and mini-bar and bathtubs; some have a balcony. It is quieter on the back side of the building.

E-G Hué Backpackers' Hostel, 10 Pham Ngu Lao St, T54-382 6567, www. vietnambackpackershostels.com. A fabulous new travellers' hostel with a bar downstairs and ultra clean rooms and dorms upstairs with a lovely balcony over the street for chilling. Tours offered too. Prices include breakfast. Happy hour 2000-2100.

Guesthouses
The little *hem* (alley) opposite the Century Riverside has some really nice rooms in comfortable and cheerful guesthouses in what is easily the best value accommodation in Hué. Particularly recommended are:

E-F Canh Tien Guesthouse, 9/66 Le Loi St, T54-382 2772, http://canhtienhotel.chez. tiscali.fr. 12 rooms that come with fan or a/c. Cheaper rooms have fans; the most expensive have a balcony. Wi-Fi.

E-G Thanh Thuy, 66/6 (6 Kiet 66) Le Loi St, T54-382 4585, thanhthuy66@dng.vnn.vn. Another small, peaceful, clean and friendly

family-run guesthouse, with 6 rooms, a/c and hot water. Can arrange car hire at good rates (around US$25 per day). Super helpful. Offers an excellent tour to the elephant springs, Lang Co, Hai Van Pass, Cham Museum and Marble Mountains for US$30. Rents motos and car with driver.

F Mimosa, 66/10 (10 Kiet 66) Le Loi St, T54-382 8068. French is spoken when the owner is here. 8 rooms with a/c, hot water and bathtub that are quiet, simple and clean. Rooms with fan are cheaper. Wi-Fi available.

F-G Hoang Huong, 66/2 (2 Kiet 66) Le Loi St, T54-382 8509. Some a/c; cheaper room with fan; a friendly and helpful family guesthouse. Cheap dormitories too and bicycles and motos rented.

Thuan An Beach *p195*
E Dong Hai Hotel, near the bridge, T54-386 6115. About 1 km from the beach.

Bach Ma National Park and Hill Station *p198*
There are 6 guesthouses, 2 near the park gate with 10 rooms (**F-G**) and the other 4 near the summit (**F**) with 26 rooms. There's a dorm with shared bathrooms (**G**) and camping is possible (**G**). Near the gate there is some a/c, near the summit it tends to be fireplaces. T54-387 1330, www.bachma.vnn. vn. There is also the **C Morin-Bach Ma Hotel**, T54-387 1199, www.huonggiangtourist. com with 12 rooms in the national park.

Lang Co *p198*
LL Vedana Lagoon Resort and Spa, Zone 1, Phu Loc town, T54-381 9397, www.vedanaresorts.com. A new resort of bungalows sited in the lagoon and run by the same folk as the **Pilgrimage Village**, 1 hr south of Hué city centre.

AL-C Lang Co Beach Resort, T54-387 3555, www.langcobeachresort.com. A large, full-service resort with pool, restaurant and bar. All rooms have a/c. There are some cheap budget rooms, otherwise go for an oceanfront villa with veranda, which is much larger with a better outlook than a garden-view villa. Although in much better shape than the **Lang Co Hotel**, these rooms are not quite as luxurious as they should be for the high prices. There are well-tended gardens here and a nice pool. This is the best of the current crop on Lang Co.

D Thanh Tam Seaside Resort, T54-387 4456, www.thanhtam-langcoresort.com.vn. Friendly staff make this a welcome place but again, wear and tear in rooms at these prices is just unacceptable. You'll therefore want to opt for the 2nd-floor (overpriced) VIP rooms. The standalone bungalows are sweet but decoration is much needed in these and the standard rooms. A swimming pool is due to be built.

D-F Lang Co Hotel Resort, T54-387 4426, codolangco@dng.vnn.vn. Has a few rooms at the top of the dunes looking down to the sea, with a/c and hot water. You'll want to pay more for a VIP room (overpriced) as the standard garden view and seaview rooms are shockingly under repaired. Peeling paint and general wear and tear are not attended to. Also some furniture needs replacing. You would not see this kind of disrepair in a mini-hotel for half the price. There are cheaper fan rooms too. The beach here is wide, clean and usually deserted, but somewhat spoilt by the high-voltage power lines which run its length.

❼ Eating

The influence of the royal court on Hué cuisine is evident in a number of ways: there are a large number of dishes served – it tends to be 'nibble' food – each dish being relatively light. Hué food is delicately flavoured and requires painstaking preparation in the kitchen: in short, it's a veritable culinary harem in which even the most pampered and surfeited emperor could find something to tickle his palate. Other Hué dishes are more robust, notably the famed *bun bo Hué*, round white noodles in soup with slices of beef and laced with chilli oil of exquisite

piquancy. Restaurants for local people usually close early; it's best to get there before 2000. Traveller cafés and restaurants tend to keep serving food until about 2200.

Hué *p180, maps p180, p184 and p186*

♔♔-♔ Junrei, Pilgrimage Village, 130 Minh Mang Rd, T54-388 5461. Open 0600-2200. Lovely Hué-lite stylized restaurant building serving Vietnamese *bun bo Hué* and passionfruit mousse among other delights. Western menu too. Attentive service.

♔ La Carambole, 19 Pham Ngu Lao St, see **Dong Loi**, page 201, T54-381 0491, la_carambole@hotmail.com. 0700-2300. One of the most popular restaurants in town and deservedly so. The ceiling is decorated with beautiful kites shot through with sticks capped by feathers. It is incredibly busy, especially for dinner where the imperial-style (ie multi-course) dinner is recommended. Telephone reservations may not be honoured and so come early or be prepared to wait.

♔ Little Italy, 2A Vo Thi Sau, T54-382 6928, www.littleitalyhue.com. Good filling pizzas and pastas at this very popular restaurant. Service is efficient despite it being very busy.

♔ Ong Tao, 31 Chu Van An St, T54-823031. A not particularly atmospheric restaurant located in the eating quarter, but serves excellent Vietnamese dishes at very fair prices and service is prompt.

♔ Saigon Morin, see Sleeping, above. Excellent buffets for US$19 in a lovely garden setting with a range of speciality Hué cuisine. While you dine, be entertained by Royal Music performers. These are held irregularly so call in advance to get the weekly schedule, which now seems dependent on large tour groups.

♔♔-♔ Biet Phu Thao Nhi Garden Restaurant, Hamlet Cu Chanh 1, Thuy Bang, Huong Thuy (Provincial Rd 13 to Khai Dinh Tomb), T54-3855 5037, www.bietphuthaonhi.com. A large restaurant, popular with Vietnamese serving up multiple options, in a lovely garden setting.

¶¶-¶ Club Garden, 8 Vo Thi Sau St, T54-382 6327, clubgarden@vnn.vn. A relaxed and attractive setting with a Vietnamese and fairly ambitious Western menu.

¶¶-¶ Mediterraneo D2 Hué, 7 Ben Nghe St, T54-381 9849. The softest, doughiest pizza in Vietnam. Highly recommended. Ice cream served too in the double courtyard set up.

¶¶-¶ The Tropical Garden Restaurant, 27 Chu Van An St, T54-384 7143, tropicalgarden@vnn.vn. Dine al fresco in a small leafy garden or inside, and eat good Vietnamese food while being served by attentive staff.

¶ An Phu 1, 48 Chu Van An St, T54-382 6090. Slightly more polished and therefore favoured by cautious tour leaders. Decent enough food, Western and local, but lots of kids selling postcards.

¶ Jardin de Y Thao, 3 Thach Han St, T54-352 3018, ythaogarden@gmail.com. Eating here is an extraordinary experience. The set menu of 8 courses is a culinary adventure with some amazing animals-from-food sculpture. The old house in a pretty garden is delightful. Recommended.

¶ La Boulangerie Française, 48 Nguyen Tri Phuong St, T54-383 7437, www. laboulangeriefrancaise.org. 0700-2030. There's a large range of Western and Vietnamese food served up by the very friendly staff. Proceeds from the bakery go to help Vietnamese orphans via a French charity (AEVN-France).

¶ Lac Thien, 6 Dinh Tien Hoang St, T54-352 7348, and **¶ Lac Thanh**, 6A Dinh Tien Hoang St, T54-352 4674. Arguably Hué's most famous restaurants, which have been trading since 1965. Run by schismatic branches of the same deaf-mute family in adjacent buildings. You go to one or the other; under no circumstances should clients patronize both establishments. Many years ago providence took us to Lac Thien, which serves excellent dishes from a diverse and inexpensive menu, its Huda beers are long and cold, the family is riotous and entertaining and we have never looked back. However, service has been known to be slack. (One of the daughters set up the **Lac Thien Restaurant** in HCMC.) Similar reports have been heard about **Lac Thanh** next door but we can't believe it's as good.

¶ Mandarin, 24 Tran Cao Van St, T54-382 1281, www.mrcumandarin.com. Recently moved again to larger premises but still with the trademark lovely photos adorning the walls. Serves a variety of cheap food. Travel services and bike rental. Mr Cu is one of the most helpful café owners in the whole of Vietnam and is helped by his staff.

¶ Omar Khayyam's or Nha Hang An Do, 22 Pham Ngu Lao St, T54-381 0310 and 34 Nguyen Tri Phuong St, T54-382 1616. Hué's Indian restaurant. Pretty authentic tandoori dishes and curries and decent portions.

¶ Stop and Go, 3 Huong Vuong St, T54-382 7051, stopandgocafe@yahoo.com. Travel café run by the relatives of the silver-haired Mr Do. His specialities include rice pancakes and the Hué version of spring rolls which are excellent and cheap.

Bars and clubs

Hué p180, maps p180, p184 and p186
DMZ Bar, 60 Le Loi St, T54-382 3414, www. dmzbar.com.vn. 0900-0200. Hué's 1st bar: cold beer and spirits at affordable prices and budget travellers around a pool table and a new outdoor terrace facing the traffic on the corner. Good place to meet people and pick up tourist information.

King's Panorama Bar, Imperial Hotel, 8 Hung Vuong Blvd. Make your way through the ostentatiously decorated foyer to take the lift to the top floor. The tallest building in Hué has superb views of the surrounding city and Perfume River. The bar is a little lacking in atmosphere though.

Why Not?, 21 Vo Thi Sau St. Slightly arty café bar, with a decent selection of food and drink and a pool table. Popular with Vietnamese and Westerners.

🎭 Entertainment

Hué p180, maps p180, p184 and p186
Rent a **dragon boat** and sail up the Perfume
River with your own private singers and
musicians. Tour offices and major hotels will
arrange groups.

See a **Royal Court performance** in the
Imperial City's theatre or listen to performers
during the **Saigon Morin's** occasional
evening buffet.

🛍 Shopping

Hué p180, maps p180, p184 and p186
There is a much wider range of goods
on sale in Hué now than was the case in
the past, no longer just the *Non bai tho* or
poem hats. These are a form of the standard
conical hat, *Non Lá*, which are peculiar to
Hué. Made from bamboo and palm leaves,
love poetry, songs, proverbs or simply a
design are stencilled on to them, which are
only visible if the hat is held up to the light
and viewed from the inside. Shops around
the **Huong Giang Hotel**, for example **Le Loi**
and **Pham Ngu Lao** streets, sell ceramics, silk
and clothes. There are a number of new art
galleries. Perfectly decent stuff but not the
range of Hoi An, where visitors are advised
to shop.

No Vietnamese visitor would shake the
dust of Hué off his feet without having
previously stocked up on *me xung*, a sugary,
peanut and toffee confection coated in
sesame seeds: quite a pleasant energy
booster to carry while cycling around the
tombs, and with the significant advantage
over Mars bars, that while it may pull your
teeth out it won't melt in your pocket.
Healing the Wounded Heart Shop,
23 Vo Thi Sau St, T54-383 3694, www.
spiralfoundation.org. Recycled products
such as water bottles and electricity wires
are fashioned into bags and homeware by
disabled people. Profits fund heart surgery
for poor children and support the livelihoods
of Hué's disabled craftsmen.

⛰ Activities and tours

Hué p180, maps p180, p184 and p186
Many hotels organize bus and boat tours
to the **Imperial Tombs**. It is also possible
to charter boats to the tombs (the most
romantic way to visit them) and to **Thuan
An Beach** (see page 195). Local tour
operators charge around US$5-6 per person
(excluding tomb entrance fees) to visit
Thien Mu Pagoda, Hon Chien Temple, Tu
Duc, Minh Mang and Khai Dinh's Tombs,
departing at 0800-0830, returning 1530-
1630. Boats are available on the stretch of
river bank between the **Huong Giang Hotel**
and the Trang Tien Bridge and also from the
dock behind the Dong Ba Market.

From Hué, there are also tours organized
to some of the **sights of the Vietnam War**.
Tour operators (see below) charge from
US$8-75 for a day's programme depending
on group size and mode of transport, taking
in sights including Vinh Moc tunnels and
museum, the Ho Chi Minh Trail and Khe
Sanh. Those wishing to travel overland to
Laos can arrange to be dropped off in Khe
Sanh and pay less.

SNV, a Dutch NGO, in conjunction with
local tour operators have developed new
Hué region tours to promote tourism
in disadvantaged communities. These
include a handicrafts village tour; a trip to
the ancient village of Phuoc Tic with its
preserved old Hué-style houses; visiting a
fishing village at Tam Giang Lagoon with a
homestay option; a visit to the Katu ethnic
minority area of Nam Dong with homestay
option and visit to A Luoi district home of Ta
Oi ethnic minorities, also with a homestay
option, One operator includes **Asia Travel
Land**, 42 Nguyen Tri Phuong St, T54-384
0888, www.asiatravelland.com.

Swimming
The Dong Tam hotel, 66/7 Le Loi St, T54-
382 8403, www.hueimpressionhotel.com,
has a pool for US$3 use for outside guests.

Tour operators

Almost every travellers' café acts as an agent for a tour operator and will take bookings but they do not run the tours themselves.

DMZ Cafe Open Tour, T9-8519 7538, dmzdodienat@gmail.com. Mr Do Dien was a translator for the US Army. This means it's an opportunity to speak to and be guided with someone who can speak English. Mr Dien is knowledgable and can take you to the principal spots but you will need patience as his English is now not clearly understood. However, a private tour with him beats a large minibus tour any day.

Café on Thu Wheels, 3/34 Nguyen Tri Phuong St, T54-383 2241, minhthuhue@yahoo.com. Run by Minh Toan Thu. Good-value US$10 motorbike tours. The formidable Thu allows you to tailor your own tour taking in the best pagodas and sites around Hué, with well-informed English-speaking guides. DMZ tours are US$13.

Mandarin Café, 24 Tran Cao Van St, T54-382 1281, www.mrcumandarin.com. This café offers many services and its staff are also helpful. Open Tour Buses arranged. All-day trip to the tombs, US$5; to Bach Ma National Park, US$60; DMZ tour, US$14. Sunset boat trip US$10. Free internet available.

Sinh Tourist (formerly Sinh Café), 60 Nguyen Tri Phuong St,12 Hung Vuong St, T54-382 6867, www.thesinhtourist.vn. Offers a number of competitively priced tours and money-changing facilities.

Stop and Go Cafe, 3 Huong Vuong St, T54-382 7051, T090-512 6767 (mob), stopandgocafe@yahoo.com. Known for its tours of the DMZ (all-day tour, US$35 on a motorbike, US$75 in a car) which are led by ARVN veterans, which brings the landscape to life and an insight you won't get on a much cheaper tour. Run by the helpful Thien and his sister. City tours, a trip to Bach Ma National Park and public transport arranged.

Tien Bicycles, 12 Nguyen Thien Ke St, T54-382 3507, www.tienbicycles.com. Mr Tien runs recommended bicycling tours around the country, including one to the DMZ, including bike, support car, guide, accommodation and entrance fees.

Transport

Hué *p180, maps p180, p184 and p186*

Air

Phu Bai Airport is a 25-min drive south of Hué. There is an airport bus, 30 mins, 40,000d run by **Vietnam Airlines** from 20 Ha Noi St that leaves 1 hr 40 mins before the flight. Returns also after flights.

Airline offices Vietnam Airlines, 23 Nguyen Van Cu St, T54-382 4709, open 0715-1115, 1330-1630.

Bicycles

Bicycles can be hired from most hotels, guesthouses and cafés; bicycles are about 20-25,000d a day. **Nam Thanh**, 48 Le Loi St, T54-382 8951, has a good solid selection.

Boat hire

Boats can be hired through tour agents and from any berth on the south bank of the river, east of Trang Tien Bridge or through travel cafés. Good for either a gentle cruise, with singers in the evening, or an attractive way of getting to some of the temples and mausoleums, around US$5-10 depends on time and if singers are employed. Note that if you travel by boat to the tombs you will often have to pay a moto driver to take you to the tomb as they are often a kilometre or so from the riverbank.

Bus and Open Tour Bus

The **Ben Xe Phia Nam**, 97 An Duong Vuong St, T54-382 5070, serves destinations mostly south of Hué: **Saigon** and **Dalat** and **Danang** but also services to **Savannakhet** Tue-Fri, Sun, 0830, 200,000d. Buses to **Vientiane** leave at 1930 Wed and Sun, 350,000d. To **Pakse** at 0830. Book with tour operators, see above. The Hoang Long Co, departs for **Hanoi** from here, 9 a day, 210,000d.

The **Ben Xe Phia Bac** station, An Hoa Ward, T54-358 0562, is up at the northwest

By train from Hué to Danang

The train journey from Hué to Danang is regarded as not just one of the most scenic in Vietnam, but in the world.

Paul Theroux in his book *The Great Railway Bazaar* recounts his impressions as the train reached the narrow coastal strip, south of Hué and approaching Danang.

"The drizzle, so interminable in the former Royal Capital, gave way to bright sunshine and warmth; 'I had no idea,' I said. Of all the places the railway had taken me since London, this was the loveliest. We were at the fringes of a bay that was green and sparkling in bright sunlight. Beyond the leaping jade plates of the sea was an overhang of cliffs and the sight of a valley so large it contained sun, smoke, rain, and cloud – all at once – independent quantities of colour. I had been unprepared for this beauty; it surprised and humbled me ... Who has mentioned the simple fact that the heights of Vietnam are places of unimaginable grandeur? Though we can hardly blame a frightened draftee for not noticing this magnificence, we should have known all along that the French would not have colonized it, nor would the Americans have fought so long, if such ripeness did not invite the eye to take it." (Penguin, London, 1977)

As the mist descends, or the sea slips out of sight the interior view comes sharply into focus. Used ragged flannels dangle from the overhead racks, litter is chucked on the floor and the smell of of squid and pepper pervades the carriage. Train staff walk through the train, not stopping to shut the doors of the a/c carriage, drawing tuts all round. They are followed by locals pushing trolleys of coffee in coke bottles that are topped up with the syrupy dollop of condensed milk poured from cans. People with shoes off and legs outstretched onto the armrest of the chair in front listen to the odd bit of piped Vietnamese classical music amid the chatter. A woman dressed in purple eats a purple ice cream.

corner of the citadel and serves destinations north of Hué: **Dong Hoi**, 50,000d, **Dong Ha**, 24,000d, 20 services daily to **Hanoi**. To **Khe Sanh** 5 buses 1100-1620. Also buses to **Lao Bao**, for Laos, at 0630, 0700, 0730, 0800, 0830, 0900, 50,000d.

The Dong Ba station serves villages and **Thuan An Beach**. Open Tour Buses can be booked to major destinations from hotels or tour agencies. Tourist buses to **Savannakhet**, Laos, via Lao Bao, leave at 0600 on odd days arriving 1600, US$16-19. Returns 0800 on even days, arriving 1730. Sepon Travel are good. There is a bus change at the border.

Cyclos

Cyclos are available everywhere. They are pleasant for visiting the more central attractions. Cyclo drivers in Hué win the country's Oscar for persistence.

Motorbikes

Bikes can be hired from most hotels and guesthouses for around US$6 per day with a driver or US$3 without. *Xe ôm* are available everywhere. They are the speedier way to see the temples as the terrain south of town is quite hilly.

Huynh Van Tu (Mr Teo) is a reliable and very safe driver who will charge US$6 for a day's excursions/use with him as the driver, T54-383 0501/091-447 8429 (mob).

Taxi

Mai Linh Taxi, T54-389 8989.

Train

The station is at the west end of Le Loi St, T54-382 2175, and serves all stations south to **HCMC** and north to **Hanoi**. Advance booking, especially for sleepers, is essential.

The 4-hr journey to **Danang** is especially recommended for its scenic views. See box, page 206. Booking office open 0700-2200.

ⓘ Directory

Hué p180, maps p180, p184 and p186
Banks Vietinbank, 2A Le Quy Don St, 0700-1130, 1330-1700. Has a Visa and MasterCard ATM **Agribank**, 10 Hoang Hoa Tham St with a Visa and MasterCard ATM and **Western Union**. Vietcombank, 2A Hung Vuong St, 0800-1100, 1345-1600. A number of ATMs in town. **Hospitals** Hué General Hospital, 16 Le Loi St, T54-382 2325. **Internet** Most hotels and guesthouses listed here offer internet services. **Post office and telephone** 8 Hoang Hoa Tham St and 91 Tran Hung Dao St, 0630-2130.

Danang and around

→ *Colour map 3, A2.*

Danang is Vietnam's third largest port and a commercial and trading centre of growing importance. The city has a frenetic buzz but no real charm and no sense of permanence. Only a few French buildings survive, near the river. Few cities in the world, however, have such spectacular beaches on their doorstep let alone three UNESCO World Heritage Sites (Hué, Hoi An and My Son) within a short drive.

Originally Danang was known as Cua Han (Mouth of the Han River). When the French took control they renamed it Tourane, a rough transliteration of Cua Han. Then it acquired the title Thai Phien, and finally Danang. The city is sited on a peninsula at the point where the Han River flows into the East Sea. An important port from French times, Danang gained world renown when two US Marine battalions landed here in March 1965 to secure the airfield. They were the first of a great many more who would land on the beaches and airfields of South Vietnam.
▶▶ *For listings, see pages 212-216.*

Ins and outs

Getting there The airport is on the edge of the city. Danang is extremely well connected. A taxi into town is US$3-5 and takes five to 10 minutes. A taxi from Hoi An along the new coastal road is US$10-15. Danang is on the north-south railway line linking Hanoi and Ho Chi Minh City and there are also regular bus and minibus connections with all major cities in the south as far as Ho Chi Minh City, and in the north as far as Hanoi from the new bus station, 7 km north of the city at Hoa Minh. Open Tour Buses stop in the town centre. The border with Laos at Lao Bao is open to foreign travellers and daily buses leave Danang for the Lao town of Savannakhet, on the Mekong; 30-day visas are available at the border or from the Lao consulate in Danang. ▶▶ *See Transport, page 215.*

Getting around Danang is a sizeable town, rather too large to explore on foot, but there is abundant public transport including cyclos, taxis and *Honda ôm*. Bicycles and motorbikes are available for hire from most hotels and guesthouses.

Tourist information Sinh Tourist ⓘ *154 Bach Dang St, T511-384 3259*, www.thesinh tourist.vn, is helpful and can book buses as well as help with information as can other tour operators, see page 215. The website www.indanang.com is worth consulting for news and events.

History

Danang lies in a region of great historical significance. Fairly close to the city – but often not particularly easy to reach – lies **My Son** – the ruins of the powerful kingdom of Champa, one of the most glorious in ancient Southeast Asia. The Cham were probably of Indonesian descent, and Chinese texts give the date AD 192 as the year when a group of tribes formed a union known as Lin-Yi, later to become Champa. The polytheistic religion of Champa was a fusion of Buddhism, Sivaism and local elements – and later Islam – producing an abundance of religious (and secular) sculptures and monuments. Siva is represented as a *linga* (see Glossary, page 495). The kingdom reached its apogee in the 10th and 11th centuries but, unlike the Khmers, Champa never had the opportunity to create a capital city matching the magnificence of Angkor. For long periods the Cham were compelled to pay tribute to the Chinese, and after that they were dominated in turn by the Javanese, Annamese (the Vietnamese) and then the Khmers. The Cham state was finally eradicated in 1471, although there are still an estimated 90,000 Cham living in central Vietnam (mostly Brahmanists and Muslims). Given this turbulent history, it is perhaps surprising that the Cham found any opportunity for artistic endeavours. It should perhaps be added that since the demise of the kingdom, the number of Cham sculptures has grown enormously as forgers have carved more of these beautiful images. (See Background, page 458, for more information on Hindu deities.)

Danang today has a population of 800,000, making it the fourth largest city in Vietnam. Its position, roughly equidistant between Hanoi and Ho Chi Minh City, gives Danang strategic significance. Danang Bay is a marvellous natural harbour and the port is the third busiest in the country after Ho Chi Minh City and Haiphong. Danang represents modern Vietnam and is a pointer to the way many of Vietnam's towns will look in not so many years to come. Its transformation in the past 20 years has been quite remarkable. It has undergone a whirlwind-like period of growth and continues to expand at a phenomenal rate. The city is ringed by huge dual carriageways and new roads have been driven out into the empty spaces beyond. Within months of the new roads' arrival they are fleshed out with factories, shops and houses. The new River Han Bridge has opened up the Son Tra Peninsula for commercial development (there are several resorts including the **Son Tra Resort** and the future **InterContinental**), which has added a major new dimension to Danang's expansion. China Beach (see page 210) stretching from Danang to Hoi An is rapidly disappearing under concrete as hotel expansion advances at a very rapid rate. The Han River is large enough to take passenger cruise liners which are arriving in greater numbers. Danang and its region need sensitive development from a far-sighted and disciplined authority if both its commercial and tourist potential is to be realized. Currently commercial interests are dominant and risk swamping irreplaceable tourist attractions.

Danang → *For listings, see pages 212-216.*

Danang Museum of Cham Sculpture

① *At the intersection of Trung Nu Vuong and Bach Dang Sts, daily 0700-1730, 30,000d. The museum booklet (US$9) has been written as an art history, not as a guide to the collection, and is of little help. However, there are now books to Champa art which extensively catalogue the exhibits, US$8. Labels are in English. Guided tours are held 0800-1030 and 1400-1630, 5 people minimum, T511-357 2414.*

The museum was established by academics of the École Française d'Extrême Orient and contains the largest display of Cham art anywhere in the world. The museum buildings alone are worth the visit: constructed in 1916 in a beautiful setting, the complex is open-plan in design, providing an environment in which the pieces can be exhibited to their best advantage. There are a number of rooms each dedicated to work from a different part of Champa: **Tra Kieu**, **My Son** and **Dong Duong** and a new extension. Because different parts of Champa flowered artistically at different times from the fourth to the 14th centuries, the

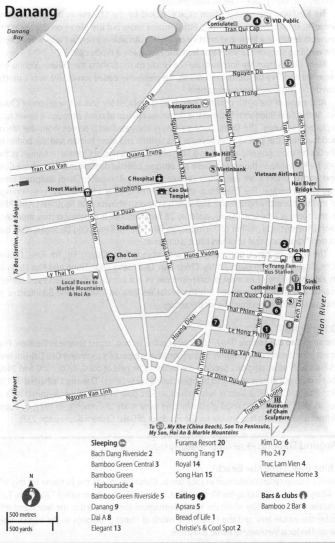

Danang

Danang Bay

Lao Consulate ⑨ ④ Ⓢ VID Public
Tran Qui Cap
Ly Thuong Kiet
Nguyen Du ⑬
Ly Tu Trong ③
Dong Da
Immigration (Pol)
Nguyen Chi Thanh
Tran Phu
Bach Dang
Quang Trung ⑭
Ba Na Hill
Tran Cao Van
Vietinbank Ⓢ
Street Market Ⓜ
Haiphong
C Hospital ✚
Cao Dai Temple
Le Loi
Vietnam Airlines
Han River Bridge
Ong Ich Khiem
Le Duan
Stadium
Ngo Gia Tu
Hung Vuong ②
Cho Han
Cho Con Ⓜ
To Trung Tam Bus Station
Ly Thai To
Local Buses to Marble Mountains & Hoi An
Cathedral ⛪ ④ ⑰ Ⓢ Sinh Tourist
Tran Quoc Toan
Hoang Dieu
Thai Phien ⑧ @ Ⓢ ⑥
⑦ Yen Bai
Le Hong Phong ① ⑧
Hoang Van Thu ⑤
③ Phan Chu Trinh
Le Dinh Duong
Han River
To Airport
Nguyen Van Linh
Trung Nu Vuong
Museum of Cham Sculpture 🏛
To ⑳, My Khe (China Beach), Son Tra Peninsula, My Son, Hoi An & Marble Mountains

N

500 metres
500 yards

Sleeping 🛏	Furama Resort 20	Kim Do 6
Bach Dang Riverside 2	Phuong Trang 17	Pho 24 7
Bamboo Green Central 3	Royal 14	Truc Lam Vien 4
Bamboo Green	Song Han 15	Vietnamese Home 3
Harbourside 4		
Bamboo Green Riverside 5	Eating 🍴	Bars & clubs 🍸
Danang 9	Apsara 5	Bamboo 2 Bar 8
Dai A 8	Bread of Life 1	
Elegant 13	Christie's & Cool Spot 2	

rooms show the evolution of Cham art and prevailing outside influences from Cambodia to Java. One problem with the display is the lack of any background information. The pieces are wonderful, but the visitor may leave the museum rather befuddled by the display.

Principal periods are: My Son E1 (early eighth century); Hoa Lai (early ninth century); Dong Duong (late ninth century); Late Tra Kieu (late 10th century); Thap Mam (12th to 13th century); Po Klong Garai (13th to 16th century).

Tra Kieu was the earliest Cham capital sacked by the Chinese in the fifth century. Some 40 km southwest of Danang, little remains today but the pieces on display at the museum testify to a lively and creative civilization. An altar is inscribed with scenes from the wedding story of Sita and Rama from the Ramayana, a Hindu epic.

Many pieces from My Son illustrate the Hindu trinity: Brahma the Creator, Vishnu the Preserver and Siva the Destroyer. Ganesh, the elephant-headed son of Siva, was a much-loved god and is well represented here.

At the end of the ninth century Dong Duong replaced My Son as the centre of Cham art. At this time Buddhism became the dominant religion of court although it never fully replaced Hinduism. The Dong Duong room is illustrated with scenes from the life of Buddha. From this period faces become less stylistic and more human and the bodies of the figures more graceful and flowing. The subsequent period of Cham art is known as the late Tra Kieu style. In this section there are *apsaras*, celestial dancing maidens whose fluid and animated forms are exquisitely captured in stone. Thereafter Cham sculpture went into artistic decline. The Thap Mam style (late 11th to early 14th century) sees a range of mythical beasts whose range and style is unknown elsewhere in Southeast Asia. Also in this room is a pedestal surrounded by 28 breast motifs. It is believed they represent Uroha, the mythical mother of the Indrapura (My Son, Tra Kieu, Dong Duong) nation, but its significance and that of others like it is unknown.

The museum has a new collection with objects from Quang Tri, Tra Kieu, Quang Nam, Thap Mam-Binh Dinh, An My, Chien Dan, Qua Giang-Khue Trung and Phu Hung in its extension. One of its most outstanding pieces is a bronze with golden eyes, perfect breasts and stretched earlobes. It is the Avalokites Vara, an image of the Bodhisattva of compassion and dates from the ninth century.

Other sights

Danang's **Cao Dai Temple** ① *63 Haiphong St*, is the second largest temple in Vietnam. The priest here is particularly friendly and informative – especially regarding Cao Dai-ism and its links with other religions. Services are meant to be held at 0600, 1200, 1800 and 2400 (but it does not always appear to be open during these times). **Danang Cathedral** ① *156 Tran Phu St, 0500-1700, Mass is held 6 times on Sun*, built in 1923, is single-spired with a sugary-pink wash. The stained-glass windows were made in Grenoble, in 1927, by Louis Balmet who was also responsible for the windows of Dalat Cathedral (see page 237).

Around Danang → *For listings, see pages 212-216.*

China Beach (My Khe Beach)

Once a fabled resort celebrated in rock songs, China Beach was the GI name for this US military R&R retreat during the Vietnam War. Since 1975 it has been called T20 Beach. T20 was the military code by which the North Vietnamese Army referred to the beach and still today the whole area and the hotels (like much of Danang) belongs to the Vietnamese Army. The local Vietnamese name is My Khe.

Until recently, My Khe was a real 'undiscovered' asset, despite being only 20 minutes from the centre of Danang. However, investors have now recognized that it has the potential to transform Danang into the Rio de Janeiro of Asia. This once-abandoned, wild stretch of beach is now nearly all sectioned off for massive hotel development and resonates to the sound of construction clatter. Miles and miles of fine white sand, clean water and a glorious setting (the hills of Monkey Mountain to the north and the Marble Mountains clearly visible to the south) have attracted a new breed of hotels, such as the Nam Hai, Sandy Beach Resort and the Furama, see Sleeping , page 213. Some 39 new hotel complexes are also under construction including the Park Hyatt and Raffles Resort. The latter is a massive US$65 million project with 150 rooms by Kingdom Hotels Investments Company, managed by the Crown Prince of Saudi Arabia.

Only several kilometres of a 30-km stretch between Danang and Hoi An remains untainted. For those who knew it just five years ago, it is quite incredible. In the undeveloped section, there is a merciful absence of vendors and no litter. Of course, it retains the white sand and surf that brought it such popularity with American soldiers. At times too, there is a strong and dangerous cross-current and undertow.

Bac My An Beach
Two kilometres south of China Beach and 8 km from the centre of Danang is Bac My An Beach, next to the **Furama Resort**. There is no longer public beach here as the Life Resort has built next door to Furama and Furama has acquired a kilometre stretch of beach for further construction.

Marble Mountains (Nui Non Nuoc)
ⓘ *12 km from Danang and 20 km from Hoi An. Many visitors stop off at Marble Mountain en route to Hoi An, daily 0600-1700, 15,000đ.*

The Marble Mountains overlook the city of Danang and its airfield, about 12 km to the west. The name was given to these five peaks by the Nguyen Emperor Minh Mang on his visit in 1825 – although they are in fact limestone crags with marble outcrops. They are also known as the mountains of the five elements (fire, water, soil, wood and metal). An important religious spot for the Cham, the peaks became havens for communist guerrillas during the war owing to their commanding view over Danang airbase. From here, a force with sufficient firepower could control much of what went on below, and the guerrillas harried the Americans incessantly. The views from the mountain sides, overlooking Danang Bay, are impressive although they will be less impressive once every chain resort on the planet has made its stake on the beach. On the Marble Mountains are a number of important sights, often associated with caves and grottoes formed by chemical action on the limestone rock.

At the foot of the mountains is a village with a large number of shops selling marble carvings. Touts try to inveigle tourists into 'their' shop; do not follow them, it is not their shop but they get paid commission. Go into whichever shop you fancy.

Of the mountains, the most visited is **Thuy Son**. There are several grottoes and cave pagodas in the mountain which are marked by steps cut into the rock. The **Tam Thai Pagoda**, reached by a staircase cut into the mountain, is on the site of a much older Cham place of worship. Constructed in 1825 by Minh Mang, and subsequently rebuilt, the central statue is of the Buddha Sakyamuni (the historic Buddha) flanked by the Bodhisattva Quan Am (a future Buddha and the Goddess of Mercy), and a statue of Van Thu (symbolizing wisdom). At the rear of the grotto is another cave, the **Huyen Khong Cave**. Originally a place of animist worship, it later became a site for Buddhist pilgrimage. The entrance is protected by four door guardians. The high ceiling of the cave is pierced by five holes through which the sun filters and, in the hour before midday, illuminates the central statue of the Buddha Sakyamuni. In the cave are various natural rock formations which, if you have picked up one of the young cave guides along the way, will be pointed out as being stork-like birds, elephants, an arm, a fish and a face.

A few hundred metres to the south on the right is a track leading to **Chua Quan The Am**, which has its own grotto complete with stalactites, stalgmites and pillars. Local children will point out formations resembling the Buddha and an elephant.

Non Nuoc Beach
A 1-km walk from Marble Mountain, this huge, white sandy beach was developed as a beach resort for Russians after 1975. This perhaps explained the ugliness of the concrete **Non Nuoc Beach Resort**, which has been demolished and replaced by the **Sandy Beach Resort**. There's also the popular backpacker joint, Hoa's Place. See page 214 and restaurants on the beach. Heading further south is the new Montgomerie Links golf course (www.montgomerielinks.com).

Bana Hill Station
ⓘ *Head south through Danang towards Highway 1 then take road 604 to Hoa Nhon, Hoa Phong and Hoa Phu. It's easily accessible by motorbike from Danang, or else you can take a tour (see Tour operators, page 215).*

Bana is a recently rehabilitated hill station. It is 38 km west of Danang on Chua Mountain (Nui Chua). The mountain rises to a height of 1467 m, while Bana itself is tucked in to the hillside at an altitude of 1200 m. The view in all directions is spectacular, the air is fresh and cool and encompassed into each day are four seasons: morning is spring, noon the summer, afternoon is autumn and night the winter. Bana was founded in 1902 by the French, who brought their febrile and palsied here to convalesce in a more benevolent clime. Flora and fauna are diverse and interesting, and villas have been fashioned from the foundations of former French fabrications, some of which accept guests. A new cable car leads up to the mountain and the hotels. Packages can be arranged.

ⓞ Danang and around listings

For Sleeping and Eating price codes and other relevant information, see Essentials pages 26-31.

ⓢ Sleeping

Danang *p208, map p209*

A-C Bamboo Green, there are 3 hotels in this chain: Bamboo Green Central, 158 Phan Chu Trinh St, T511-382 2996, www.bamboogreenhotel.com.vn; Bamboo Green Harbourside (a somewhat tenuous claim), 177 Tran Phu St, T511-382 2722; and Bamboo Green Riverside, 68 Bach Dang St, T511-383 2591. All are well-run, well-

equipped, comfortable, business-type hotels with efficient staff and in central locations offering excellent value for money. Riverside has a particularly attractive outlook opposite the cathedral and is currently being rebuilt in a more fashionable boutique style.

B-C Bach Dang Riverside Hotel, 50 Bach Dang St, T511-382 3649, bdhotel@dng.vnn. vn. Large and centrally located hotel. Rooms rather cramped for the price; some with river views; cheaper rooms also. All rooms have satellite TV and bathtubs. There's a good restaurant on site, a pool and tennis court.

B-E Danang, 1-3 Dong Da St, T511-382 1986, danang hotel@dng.vnn.vn. Hotel with 160 rooms, some around a courtyard at the back with balconies. Restaurant and tour services merged with the old **Marble Mountain** hotel next door. Breakfast included.

C Elegant Hotel, 22A Bach Dang St, T511-389 2893, elegant@dng.vnn.vn. It's fairly elegant and in a nice position overlooking the river. 32 standard rooms including breakfast and Wi-Fi.

C Royal, 17 Quang Trung St, T511-382 3295, www.royaldananghotel.com.vn. With its discounted rates (breakfast included) this 60-room hotel offers quite good value. There's a restaurant and nightclub too. Staff are helpful. Breakfast and Wi-Fi included.

C-E Dai A, 51 Yen Bai St, T511-382 7532, www.daiahotel.com.vn. In the centre of town, close to the cathedral; there's a variety of rooms. The cheapest rooms don't have windows. Breakfast and Wi-Fi included.

E Phuong Trang (formerly Tan Minh), 142 Bach Dang St, T511-389 9900. On the riverfront, a small, well-kept hotel with Wi-Fi; friendly staff speak good English.

Son Tra Peninsula

D-E Tien Sa Beach Resort, T511-392 1502, tiensaresort@dng.vnn.vn. There are 35 rooms; chalets are sweet if a wee bit pokey. Breakfast not included.

China Beach (My Khe Beach) *p210*

An explosion of hotel growth has led to most of China Beach and Bac My An Beach being concreted over. As well as those listed below, new huge hotels on the block include and will include **Furama Villas**, **Fusion Maia, Ocalani, Silver Shores, Crowne Casino, Hyatt** and **Raffles**.

A-C Tourane, T511-393 2666, www.touranehotel.com.vn. A resort-type hotel with accommodation in villa-type blocks surrounding a pool. 69 rooms all with a/c and hot water; breakfast included. This is one of the more attractive resorts at this northern end of the beach. Tennis court too.

B-D My Khe Beach, 241 Nguyen Van Thoai St, T511-383 6125, mykhehotel@yahoo.com. vn. This hotel group has 3 sets of buildings. The nicest is **My Khe Beach 1** with 54 rooms. **My Khe 2** is a little bigger and **My Khe 3** is half the size. Accommodation at **My Khe 1** is in plain blocks set among the sea pines. All the hotels face an undeveloped stretch of beach with thatched umbrellas, fishing boats and lifeguard kiosks. All a/c and hot water and price includes breakfast.

D-E Jimmy Hotel, F18 An Cu 3, An Hai Bac, Son Tra, T511-394 5888, www. jimmyhoteldanang.com.vn One very large block back from the sea not too far from the **Tourane** and **My Khe** hotel grouping and a line of seafood restaurants including the **My Hanh** facing the beach. Rooms are clean with mucky windows. The VIP has a bathtub and showers have the all over body power shower units.

Bac My An Beach *p211*

LL Life Resort, T511-395 8888, www.life-resorts.com. This new resort of 187 rooms and 11 villas has copied the Nam Hai design but it lacks any kind of warmth whatsoever. The public areas are overwhelmingly large and impersonal but the rooms themselves are super stylish and comfortable. Staff are very friendly.

LL-AL Furama Resort, 68 Ho Xuan Huong St, T511-384 7888, www.furamavietnam. com. 198 rooms and suites beautifully designed and furnished. One of the most attractive aspects is its fabulously opulent foyer with smart seating and warm lighting. It has 2 pools, 1 of which is an infinity pool overlooking the beach. All facilities are 1st class. Watersports facilities, diving, mountain biking, tennis and a health centre offering a number of massages and treatments. Operates a free and very useful shuttle to and from the town, Marble Mountains and Hoi An. Surprisingly the price does not include breakfast.

Non Nuoc Beach *p212*

F Hoa's Place, 215/14 Huyen Tran Cong Chua St, T511-396 9216, hoasplace@hotmail.com. A laid-back but quite busy hangout that is popular with those who want to kick back for a while in simple surrounds. The small rooms, across 3 buildings, have fans, a/c (costs extra) and private bathrooms. Call beforehand as rumours are that **Hoa** will be evicted to make way for yet another large upmarket resort. US$5 to rent a surfboard. Taxi from the new bus station, US$7, *xe ôm*, US$2. There are 2 restaurants on the beach near **Hoa's Place**.

Bana Hill Station *p212*

A-C Morin Hotel, An Son Hamlet, T511-379 1999, www.vietnamhotels.biz/banaresort/index.htm. Access to the resort is by cable car. The 4-star hotel features 51 rooms. Price includes breakfast. 2-star accommodation is also available.

❷ Eating

Danang *p208, map p209*

Seafood is good here and Danang has its own beers, Da Nang 'Export' and Song Han. There are a number of cafés and restaurants along **Bach Dang St**, overlooking the river. Bread in Danang is particularly good, which makes *banh mi ôp la* (fried eggs and bread) a great start to the day.

♥♥-♥ Apsara, 222 Tran Phu St, T511-356 1409, www.apsara-danang.com. Open 1000-1400, 1700-2100. The most elegant dining option in town with crisp white linens on the table, attentive staff and icy a/c. There's a good spread on the menu.

♥♥-♥ Christie's and **Cool Spot**, 112 Tran Phu St, T511-382 4040, ccdng@dng.vnn.vn. Open 1000-2300. The old premises were demolished in the construction of the River Han Bridge, the new location is 1 block in from the river and has merged forces with the **Cool Spot** bar. Frequented by expats from Danang and outlying provinces. Small bar downstairs and a restaurant upstairs.

Cold beer, Western and Japanese food and tasty home-made pizzas.

♥♥-♥ Kim Do, 180 and 205 Tran Phu St, T511-382 1846, www.kimdocom.vn. Now a huge Chinese restaurant on the site of the popular old restaurant. Typical Chinese menu, reasonable food at fair prices. Popular with tour groups.

♥♥-♥ Pho 24, 90 Tran Quoc Toan St. Part of the ubiquitous **Pho** chain.

♥♥-♥ Truc Lam Vien, 8 Tran Quy Cap St, T511-258 2428. A delightful courtyard restaurant approached by wandering over a bridge crossing a pretty pond. Dine under umbrellas amid the greenery. A large menu of predominantly seafood. Very friendly staff.

♥ Bread of Life, 12 Le Hong Phong St, T511-356 5185, www.breadoflifedanang.com. Closed Sun. This is a restaurant that provides training and jobs to deaf people. It's a worthwhile cause to support and the pizzas are very tasty. Baked goods and other comfort food too. Motorbike rental also.

♥ Vietnamese Home, 34 Bach Dang St, T511-388 9575. A very popular place – both with Vietnamese and Westerners – in an interior courtyard setting with fountain and bamboo chairs. The menu is full of fish, frog, eel and pork as well as those catering to the western palate.

❸ Bars and clubs

Danang *p208, map p209*

Christies and **Cool Spot**, see Eating. Popular with expats and a friendly place with a ground-floor bar and 1st-floor restaurant.
Bamboo 2 Bar, 230 Bach Dang St. Travel services as well as a popular bar overlooking a promenade of sculptures on the river bank.

❹ Shopping

Danang *p208, map p209*
Marble carvings
Available from shops in town, but particularly from the stalls around the foot of Marble Mountains (see page 211).

Markets

The city has a fair array of markets. There is a covered **general market** (Cho Han) in a building at the intersection of Tran Phu and Hung Vuong streets. Another market, **Cho Con**, is at the intersection of Hung Vuong and Ong Ich Khiem streets. The stalls close by sell basketwork and other handicrafts. On Haiphong St, running east from the railway station, there is a **street market** selling fresh produce.

▲▲ Activities and tours

Danang *p208, map p209*
Tour operators
Asia Pacific Travel, 79 Thang St, Hai Chau District, T511-628 6088, www.asiapacifictravel.vn. Small-group adventure travel.
Asian Trails, 262 Tran Phu St, T511-325 1664, www.asiantrails.travel. Package tours across Asia.
Ba Na Hill, 72 Nguyen Chi Thanh St, T511-374 9888, www.banahills.com.vn. Day trips, 520,000d, including transfers from Danang, cable car, lunch and tour guide.
Sinh Tourist, 154 Bach Dang St, T511-843259, www.thesinhtourist.vn. Open Tour Buses stop at 1030 and 1600 to go to Hoi An, 1 hr, 50,000d and 60,000d respectively. To Hué at 0915 and 1400, 50,000d. Every even day to Lao Bao for Savannakhet, Laos, at 0600, arriving 1400 with a change of bus at the border, 60,000d.

☉ Transport

Danang *p208, map p209*
Air
There are connections with **Bangkok**, **Phnom Penh**, **Siem Reap**, **Singapore**, **Hong Kong**, **Paris**, **Tokyo**, **Vientiane**, **Nha Trang**, **Hanoi**, **HCMC** and **Play Ku**, **Buon Ma Thuot**, **Quy Nhon** , **Kuala Lumpur**, **Luang Prabang**, and **Sydney**. The airport at Danang is probably the easiest airport in Vietnam to negotiate and has a particularly

good restaurant – Song Ham – facing the main terminal. The airport is 2.5 km southwest of the city.
   Airline offices Vietnam Airlines, 58 Bach Dang St, T511-381 1111.

Bicycle and motorbike
Bicycles are available from many hotels. Some cafés and hotels also rent motorbikes for US$5-7 per day. **Mr Tung**, T090-576 1042, is a reliable moto driver with reasonable English. Bargain very hard on prices though.

Bus
Buses to **Hoi An** run from the station at the west end of Hung Vuong St, opposite Con Market, 10,000d. The new bus station, **Ben Xe Trung Tam Danang**, at Hoa Minh is 7 km north of Danang and 15 km south of the Hai Van Tunnel, on the corner of Nam Tram and Ton Duc Thang streets, T511-366 1402. *Xe ôm* to town is 50,000d. Connecting buses to and from Han market to **Hoa Minh**, 5000d. Buses to **Hanoi**, **Dong Hoi**, **Hué**, **HCMC**, **Buon Ma Thuot**, **Kontum** and **Pakse**. Mai Linh, T511-224 6246, offers a reliable service as do Dien Thoai, T511-376 7678.
   International connections It is possible to get a visa for Laos in Danang from the Lao consulate (see page 216) here (US$41 for a 1-month tourist visa returned in one day; US$35 for a 3-day wait). However, 30-day visas are available at the border on arrival. There are daily departures for the Lao town of **Savannakhet**, on the Mekong River from the Hoa Minh station. The road runs west from Dong Ha into the Annamite mountains and crosses the border at Lao Bao, not far from the former battlefield of Khe Sanh, see page 196.

Taxi
Airport Taxi, T511-327 2727.

Train
The train station is on Haiphong St, 2 km west of town, T511-375 0666, and there are express trains to and from **Hanoi**, **HCMC** and **Hué**. See also box, page 206.

Danang *p208, map p209*
Banks Eximbank, 205 Phan Chu Trinh
St. ATM. **Vietinbank**, 5 Tran Quoc Toan St.
ATM. **Embassies and consulates** Lao
Consulate, 12 Tran Quy Cap St, T511-382
1208, ketkeomanivong@yahoo.com, 0800-
1130, 1330-1630. **Hospitals** C Hospital, 74
Haiphong St, T511-382 1480. **Family Medical
Practice**, 50-52 Nguyen Van Linh St, Nam

Duong ward, Hai Chau district, T511-358
2699, www.vietnammedicalpractice.com.
Internet Danang is one of only 3 cities
in Vietnam to have its own internet portal
with the outside world. There are numerous
internet cafés all over town including at
172 Tran Phu St. Most hotels listed also
offer internet services and Wi-Fi to their
customers. **Post office** 64 Bach Dang
St, corner of Bach Dang St and Le Duan St.
Internet and telephone facilities. 0630-2100.

Hoi An and around

→ *Colour map 3, A2.*

The ancient town of Hoi An (formerly Faifo) lies on the banks of the Thu Bon River. During its heyday 200 years ago, when trade with China and Japan flourished, Hoi An became a prosperous little port. Much of the merchants' wealth was spent on family chapels and Chinese clan houses which remain little altered today. Today Hoi An is seeing a late but much-deserved revival: the river may be too shallow for shipping but it is perfect for tourist boats; the silk merchants may not export any produce but that's because all they can make leaves town on the back of satisfied customers.

Hoi An's tranquil riverside setting, its diminutive scale (you can touch the roof of many houses), friendly and welcoming people and its wide array of shops and galleries have made it one of the most popular destinations for foreign travellers. There is plenty to see of historical interest, there is a nearby beach and, as if that were not enough, it has superb and inexpensive restaurants.▶▶ *For listings, see pages 224-232.*

Ins and outs

Getting there There are direct minibus connections with Ho Chi Minh City, Hanoi, Hué and Nha Trang. The quickest way of getting from Hanoi or Ho Chi Minh City is by flying to Danang and then getting a taxi from the airport direct to Hoi An, US$12-15, 40 minutes.
▶▶ *See also Transport, page 232.*

Getting around Hoi An is compact and quite busy and is best explored on foot. Guesthouses hire out bicycles. Motos are banned from the old town centre on Monday, Wednesday, Friday and Saturday and every evening; when they are not, the mix of traffic and tourist pedestrians is an uncomfortable experience.

Best time to visit The Full Moon Festival is held on the 14th day of the lunar month. The town converts itself into a Chinese lantern fest and locals dress in traditional costume. The old town is pedestrianized for the night, lighting is reduced and poetry is recited and music played in the streets. Candles are lit and floated in plastic lotus flowers along the river; it is an exceptionally pretty sight.

Tourist information Entrance to most historic buildings is by sightseeing ticket, 90,000d for three days, on sale at **Hoi An Tourist Offices** ⓘ *see map for locations, T510-386 1327, www.hoianworldheritage.org.vn, open 0700-1730*, which have English-speaking staff, car and minibus hire and guides to Hoi An (70,000d for two hours). Sights in Hoi An are open for the same hours or a bit longer. The sightseeing ticket is segregated into five categories of different sights, allowing visitors admission to one of each. It is valid for three days. If you want to see additional sites and have used up your tokens you must buy additional tickets. The tourist kiosks provide a good map. At least a full day is needed to see the town properly.

History

Hoi An is divided into five quarters, or 'bangs', each of which would traditionally have had its own pagoda and supported one Chinese clan group. The Chinese, along with some Japanese, settled here in the 16th century and controlled trade between the islands of Southeast Asia, East Asia (China and Japan) and India. Portuguese and Dutch vessels also docked at the port. During the Tay Son rebellion (1771-1788) the town was almost totally destroyed, although this is not apparent to the visitor. By the end of the 19th century the Thu Bon River had started to silt up and Hoi An was gradually eclipsed by Danang as the most important port of the area. Hoi An has emerged as one of the most popular tourist destinations in Vietnam and there has been no diminution in its status, in fact quite the reverse: walking along Tran Phu Street you'll see more Western than Vietnamese faces.

Hoi An's historic character is being submerged by the rising tide of tourism. Although remaining physically intact, virtually every one of its fine historic buildings either markets some aspect of its own heritage or touts in some other way for the tourist dollar; increasingly it is coming to resemble the 'Vietnam' pavilion in a Disney theme park. Nevertheless, visitors to Hoi An are charmed by the gentleness of the people and the sedate pace of life. The tempo has picked up in recent years, however, and although the police are vigilant in guarding Hoi An's morals (try getting even a foot massage in the historic core), every boat and café owner by the river will attempt to press passers-by into using their services.

Hoi An → For listings, see pages 224-232.

Most of Hoi An's more attractive buildings and assembly halls (*hoi quan*) are found either on, or just off, Tran Phu Street. Tran Phu stretches west to east from the Japanese Covered Bridge to the market, running parallel to the river. People are friendly and will generally not mind inquisitive, but polite, foreigners.

The **Japanese Covered Bridge (Cau Nhat Ban)** ⓘ *Tran Phu St, 1 token; keep your ticket to get back*, also known as the Pagoda Bridge, the Faraway People's Bridge and, popularly, as the Japanese Covered Bridge, is Hoi An's most famous landmark. The bridge was built in the 16th century. On its north side there is a pagoda, Japanese in style, for the protection of sailors. At the west end of the bridge are statues of two dogs, and at the east end, of two monkeys – it is said that the bridge was begun in the year of the monkey and finished in the year of the dog. Some scholars have pointed out that this would mean a two-year period of construction, an inordinately long time for such a small bridge; they maintain that the two animals represent points of the compass, WSW (monkey) and NW (dog). Father Benigne Vachet, a missionary who lived in Hoi An between 1673 and 1683, notes in his memoirs that the bridge was the haunt of beggars and fortune tellers hoping to benefit from the stream of people crossing over it. Its popular name reflects a long-standing belief that it was built by the Japanese, although no documentary evidence exists to support this. One of its other names, the Faraway People's Bridge, is said to have been coined because vessels from far away would moor close to the bridge.

Just east of the Covered Bridge is the **Museum of Sa Huynh Culture** ① *149 Tran Phu St, 1 'museum' token, daily 0700-2100.* Housed in an attractive colonial-era building the museum contains a modest collection of mostly pottery unearthed at Sa Huynh, 120 km south of Hoi An. The artefacts, dating from around 200 BC, are significant because they have called into question the previous understanding that the only cultures native to Central Vietnam have been the Cham and the Viet.

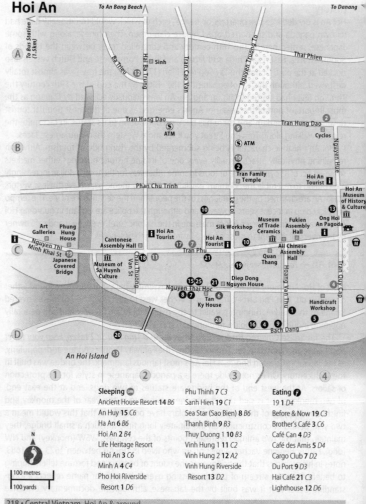

Hoi An

Sleeping 🛏
Ancient House Resort **14** *B6*
An Huy **15** *C6*
Ha An **6** *B6*
Hoi An **2** *B4*
Life Heritage Resort
  Hoi An **3** *C6*
Minh A **4** *C4*
Pho Hoi Riverside
  Resort **1** *D6*

Phu Thinh **7** *C3*
Sanh Hien **19** *C1*
Sea Star (Sao Bien) **8** *B6*
Thanh Binh **9** *B3*
Thuy Duong **1 10** *B3*
Vinh Hung **1 11** *C2*
Vinh Hung **2 12** *A2*
Vinh Hung Riverside
  Resort **13** *D2*

Eating 🍴
19 **1** *D4*
Before & Now **19** *C3*
Brother's Café **3** *C6*
Café Can **4** *D3*
Café des Amis **5** *D4*
Cargo Club **7** *D2*
Du Port **9** *D3*
Hai Café **21** *C3*
Lighthouse **12** *D6*

Just south of the Covered Bridge is **Bach Dang Street** which runs along the bank of the Thu Bon River. Here there are boats, activity and often a cooling breeze. The road loops round to the Hoi An Market (see below). The small but interesting **French quarter** around Phan Boi Chau Street is worth taking time over. At No 25 you can visit an 1887 building that has belonged to the same family for four generations, US$2. The French-speaking owner is happy to talk. The colonnaded fronts are particularly attractive. As everywhere in historical quarters in Vietnam visitors should raise their gaze above street level to appreciate the architectural detail of upper floors, which is more likely to have survived, and less likely to be covered up.

Heading east along Tran Phu Street, the **Museum of Trade Ceramics** ① *80 Tran Phu St, 1 'museum' token, daily 0700-2100*, was opened with financial and technical support from Japan. It contains a range of ancient wares, some of them from shipwrecks in surrounding waters. There are also architectural drawings of houses in Hoi An. Upstairs, from the front balcony, there is a fascinating roofscape.

At the east end of Tran Phu Street, at No 24, close to the intersection with Nguyen Hué Street, is the **Ong Hoi An Pagoda** ① *one token*. This temple is in fact two interlinked pagodas built back-to-back: **Chua Quan Cong**, and behind that **Chua Quan Am**. Their date of construction is not known, although both certainly existed in 1653. In 1824 Emperor Minh Mang made a donation of 300 luong (1 luong being equivalent to 1½ oz of silver) for the support of the pagodas. They are dedicated to Quan Cong and Quan Am, respectively.

Adjacent to Ong Hoi An Pagoda is **Hoi An Museum of History and Culture** ① *13 Nguyen Hué St, 1 'museum' token, 0700-2100*, housed in a former pagoda. The museum sets the history of the town in its trading context with sections on all the main cultural influences.

Virtually opposite the Ong Hoi An Pagoda, is the **Hoi An Market (Cho Hoi An)**. The market extends down to the river and then along the river road (Bach Dang Street). At the Tran Phu Street end is a market selling mostly dry goods. Numerous cloth merchants and seamstresses will produce made-to-measure shirts in a few

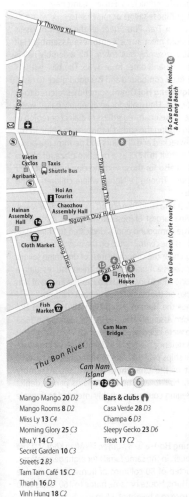

Mango Mango **20** *D2*
Mango Rooms **8** *D2*
Miss Ly **13** *C4*
Morning Glory **25** *C3*
Nhu Y **14** *C5*
Secret Garden **10** *C3*
Streets **2** *B3*
Tam Tam Café **15** *C2*
Thanh **16** *D3*
Vinh Hung **18** *C2*

Bars & clubs ◐
Casa Verde **28** *D3*
Champa **6** *D3*
Sleepy Gecko **23** *D6*
Treat **17** *C2*

hours. The riverside of the market is the fish market which comes alive at 0500-0600 as boats arrive with the night's catch.

Assembly Halls (Hoi Quan)

Chinese traders in Hoi An (like elsewhere in Southeast Asia) established self-governing dialect associations or clan houses which owned their own schools, cemeteries, hospitals and temples. The clan houses (*hoi quan*) may be dedicated to a god or an illustrious individual and may contain a temple but are not themselves temples. There are five *hoi quan* in Hoi An, four for use by people of specific ethnicities: Fukien, Cantonese, Hainan, Chaozhou and the fifth for use by any visiting Chinese sailors or merchants.

Strolling east from the Covered Bridge down Tran Phu Street all the assembly halls can be seen. Merchants from Guangdong would meet at the **Cantonese Assembly Hall (Quang Dong Hoi Quan)** ① *176 Tran Phu St, 1 'assembly hall' token*. This assembly hall is dedicated to Quan Cong, a Han Chinese general and dates from 1786. The hall, with its fine embroidered hangings, is in a cool, tree-filled compound and is a good place to rest.

Next is the **All Chinese Assembly Hall (Ngu Bang Hoi Quan)**, sometimes referred to as **Chua Ba (Goddess Temple)** ① *64 Tran Phu St, free*. Unusually for an assembly hall, it was a mutual aid society open to any Chinese trader or seaman, regardless of dialect or region of origin. Chinese vessels tended to visit Hoi An during the spring, returning to China in the summer. The assembly hall would help ship-wrecked and ill sailors and perform the burial rites of merchants with no relatives in Hoi An. Built in 1773 as a meeting place for all five groups (the four listed above plus Hakka) and also for those with no clan house of their own, today it accommodates a Chinese School, Truong Le Nghia, where children of the diaspora learn the language of their forebears.

The **Fukien Assembly Hall (Phuc Kien Hoi Quan)** ① *46 Tran Phu St, 1 'assembly hall' token*, was founded around 1690 and served Hoi An's largest Chinese ethnic group, those from Fukien. It is an intimate building within a large compound and is dedicated to Thien Hau, goddess of the sea and protector of sailors. She is the central figure on the main altar, clothed in robes, who, together with her assistants, can hear the cries of distress of drowning sailors. Immediately on the right on entering the temple is a mural depicting Thien Hau rescuing a sinking vessel. Behind the main altar is a second sanctuary, which houses the image of Van Thien whose blessings pregnant women invoke on the lives of their unborn children.

With a rather more colourful history comes the **Hainan Assembly Hall (Hai Nam Hoi Quan)** ① *10 Tran Phu St, 100 m east of the Fukien Assembly Hall, free*. It was founded in 1883 in memory of the sailors and passengers who were killed when three ships were plundered by an admiral in Emperor Tu Duc's navy. In his defence the admiral claimed the victims were pirates and some sources maintain he had the ships painted black to strengthen his case.

Exquisite wood carving is the highlight of the **Chaozhou (Trieu Chau Assembly Hall)** ① *362 Nguyen Duy Hieu St, 1 'assembly hall' token*. The altar and its panels depict images from the sea and women from the Beijing court, presumably intended to console homesick traders.

Merchants' houses

Just west of the Japanese Bridge is **Phung Hung House** ① *4 Nguyen Thi Minh Khai St, 1 'old house' token*. Built over 200 years ago it has been in the same family for eight generations. The house, which can be visited, is constructed of 80 columns of ironwood on marble pedestals. During the floods of 1964, Phung Hung House became home to 160 locals who camped upstairs for three days as the water rose to a height of 2.5 m.

Tan Ky House ① *101 Nguyen Thai Hoc St, 1 'old house' token*, dates from the late 18th century. Built by later generations of the Tan Ky family (they originally arrived in Hoi An from China 200 years earlier), it reflects not only the prosperity the family had acquired but also the architecture of their Japanese and Vietnamese neighbours, whose styles had presumably worked their influence on the aesthetic taste and appreciation of the younger family members.

Diep Dong Nguyen House ① *80 Nguyen Thai Hoc St*, with two Chinese lanterns hanging outside, was once a Chinese dispensary. The owner is friendly, hospitable and not commercially minded. He takes visitors into his house and shows everything with pride and smiles.

Quan Thang ① *77 Tran Phu St, 1 'old house' token*, is another old merchant's house, reputed to be 300 years old.

Tran Family Temple ① *on the junction of Le Loi and Phan Chu Trinh streets, 1 'old house' token*, has survived for 15 generations; the current generation has no son which means the lineage has been broken. The building exemplifies well Hoi An's construction methods and the harmonious fusion of Chinese and Japanese styles. It is roofed with heavy *yin* and *yang* tiling which requires strong roof beams; these are held up by a triple-beamed support in the Japanese style (seen in the roof of the covered bridge). Some beams have Chinese-inspired ornately carved dragons. The outer doors are Japanese, the inner are Chinese. On a central altar rest small wooden boxes which contain the photograph or likeness of the deceased together with biographical details; beyond, at the back of the house, is a small, raised Chinese herb, spice and flower garden with a row of bonsai trees. As with all Hoi An's family houses guests are received warmly and courteously and served lotus tea and dried coconut.

Around Hoi An → *For listings, see pages 224-232.*

Cua Dai Beach and around
① *You must leave your bicycle (5000d) or moto (10000d) just before Cua Dai Beach in a parking lot unless you are staying at one of the beach resorts. The first shop kiosk on the beach at the end of the road offer lockers for 20,000d.*

A white-sand beach with few facilities, Cua Dai Beach is 4 km from Hoi An, east down Tran Hung Dao Street, and is a pleasant 25-minute bicycle ride or one-hour walk from Hoi An. Alternatively, a quieter route is to set off down Nguyen Duy Hieu Street. This peters out into a footpath which can be cycled. It is a lovely path past paddy fields and ponds. Nothing is signed but those with a good sense of direction will make their way back to the main road a kilometre or so before Cua Dai. Those with a poor sense of direction can come to no harm. North up the coast, development has started on the beautiful expanse of China Beach between Hoi An and Danang. Much of the development is nearer the Danang end. At the Hoi An end, on Ha My Beach is the opulent **Nam Hai** (see Sleeping, page 226, and Therapies, page 231) and 1 km closer to Hoi An is the new **Le Belhamy Hoi An Resort and Spa**. A new dual carriageway has been built from Cua Dai to Danang and development has already started with the **Palm Garden Resort** and **Boutique Hoi An Resort**, between Cua Dai and An Bang. South of the Victoria Hoi An, more development is taking place in the shape of the **Novotel Imperial Hoi An**. Four kilometres north of Hoi An, off the dual carriageway, is **An Bang Beach** where a collection of popular beach bars has gathered. It can be more pleasantly reached by cycling 2.5 km north past paddies on Hai Ba Trung St (15 minutes). A Cua Dai-An Bang-Hoi An loop is a pleasant couple of hours' cycle ride.

Silk worms

Sericulture was introduced to Vietnam from China more than 1000 years ago, where the process had remained secret for years. Today Vietnam cultivates 20,000 ha of mulberry bushes which yield 1500-1800 tons of silk, around 1.8% of world output.

More recently, silk-making was developed in North Vietnam during Chinese rule and in 1975, on reunification, it was brought to Dalat. Silkworm larvae are fed mulberry leaves for about a month. They are then ready to construct their cocoons when they start rejecting food. For three days they secrete a sticky substance that binds a 750-m-long fibre into a cocoon. On completion the cocoon is plunged into boiling water to soften the thread and kill the caterpillars. Single threads are too weak and so the thread of 10 cocoons is spun into one yarn used to weave the silk. The caterpillars are then fried and eaten as a delicacy.

The **Cham Islands** are 15 km from Cua Dai Beach and clearly visible offshore. There are seven islands in the group – Lao (pear), Dai (long), La (leaf), Kho (dry), Tai (ear), Mo (tomb) and Nom (east wind). Bird's nests are collected here. You can visit the fishing villages and snorkel and camp overnight (see **Cham Island Diving Center**, page 231). At the moment they are undeveloped but a Four Seasons hotel may be open by the time you read this.

My Son → *Colour map 3, A2.*
ⓘ *Daily 0630-1630, 60,000d. Cham performance Tue-Sun 0930 and 1030. It is not clear how thoroughly the area has been de-mined so it is advisable not to stray too far from the road and path. Take a hat, sun cream and water as it is hot and dry.*

To get to My Son from Danang, drive south on Highway 1 and turn right towards Tra Kieu after 34 km (some 2 km after crossing the Thu Bon River). Drive through Tra Kieu to the village of Kiem Lam. Turn left; the path to My Son is about 6 km further along this road. At this point is the ticket office, a short bamboo bridge crossing and a 2-km jeep ride (included in the ticket price) with a 500-m walk at the end to My Son where there are toilets, refreshments and the Cham performance. My Son can be reached just as easily from Hoi An (45 km); take Phan Dinh Phung out of town. Turn left onto the main road (heading away from Danang) at Vinh Dien, the first sizeable settlement some 8 km from Hoi An, and follow this busy road for 18 km to the market town of Nam Phuoc where a large signpost points the way right to My Son. The road is well signposted from here. Alternatively, it's a 1½-hour trip each way by *Honda ôm*, as a half-day coach tour, or a full-day boat excursion.
▶▶ *Tour operators in Danang and Hoi An offer tours to My Son, see pages 215 and 231.*

Declared a World Heritage Site by UNESCO in 1999, My Son is one of Vietnam's most ancient monuments. Weather, jungle and years of strife have wrought their worst on My Son. But arguably the jungle under which My Son remained hidden to the outside world provided it with its best protection, for more has been destroyed in the past 40 years than the previous 400. Today, far from anywhere, My Son is a tranquil archaeological treasure with some beautiful buildings and details to look at. Not many visitors have time to make an excursion to see it which makes it all the more appealing to those that do. The thin red bricks of which the towers and temples were built have been carved and the craftsmanship of many centuries remains obvious today. The trees and creepers have been pushed back but My Son remains cloaked in green; shoots sprout up and one senses that were its custodians to turn their backs for even a short time My Son would be reclaimed by the forces of nature.

Tra Kieu, My Son and Dong Duong are the three most important centres of the former Cham Kingdom (see page 409). My Son is located about 60 km south of Danang (28 km west of Tra Kieu) and consists of more than 70 monuments spread over a large area. The characteristic Cham architectural structure is the tower, built to reflect the divinity of the king: tall and rectangular, with four porticoes, each of which is 'blind' except for that on the west face. Because Cham kings were far less wealthy and powerful than the *deva-rajas* (god kings) of Angkor, the monuments are correspondingly smaller and more personal. Originally built of wood (not surprisingly, none remains), they were later made of brick, of which the earliest (seventh century) are located at My Son. These are so-called Mi-Son E1 – the unromantic identifying sequence of letters and numbers being given, uncharacteristically, by the French archaeologists who rediscovered and initially investigated the monuments in 1898. Although little of these early examples remains, the temples seem to show similarities with post-Gupta Indian forms, while also embodying Chen-La stylistic influences. Bricks are exactly laid and held together with a form of vegetable cement probably the resin of the day tree. It is thought that on completion, each tower was surrounded by wood and fired over several days in what amounted to a vast outdoor kiln.

It is important to see My Son in the broader context of the Indianization of Southeast Asia. Not just architecture but spiritual and political influences are echoed around the region. Falling as it did so strongly under Chinese influence it is all the more remarkable to find such compelling evidence of Indian culture and iconography in Vietnam. Indeed this was one of the criteria cited by UNESCO as justification for its listing. Nevertheless one of the great joys of Cham sculpture and building is its unique feel, its graceful lines and unmistakable form. Angkor in Cambodia is the most famous example but Bagan in Burma, Borobudur in Java and Ayutthaya in Thailand, with all of which My Son is broadly contemporaneous, are temple complexes founded by Hindu or Sivaist god kings. In all these places Buddhism appeared in the seventh century and by the 11th century was in the ascendent with the result that, My Son excepted, these are all widely regarded as Buddhist holy sites. The process whereby new ideas and beliefs are absorbed into a pre-existing culture is known as syncretism. The Hindu cult of *deva-raja* was developed by the kings of Angkor and later employed by Cham kings to bolster their authority. The king was the earthly representative of the god Siva. Sivaist influence at My Son is unmissable. Siva is one of the Hindu holy trinity, destroyer of the universe. Siva's dance of destruction is the very rhythm of existence and hence also of rebirth. Siva is often represented, as at My Son and other Cham relics throughout Vietnam, by the lingam, the phallus. My Son was obviously a settled city whose population is unknown but it seems to have had a holy or spiritual function rather than being the seat of power and it was, very probably, a burial place of its god kings.

Much that is known of My Son was discovered by French archaeologists of the École Française d'Extrême-Orient. Their rediscovery and excavation of My Son revealed a site that had been settled from the early eighth to the 15th centuries, the longest uninterrupted period of development of any monument in Southeast Asia. My Son architecture is notable for its use of red brick which has worn amazingly well. Sandstone plinths are sometimes used, as are sandstone lintels, the Cham seemingly – like the Khmer of Angkor – never having learnt the art of arch building, one of the few architectural techniques in which Europe was centuries ahead of Asia. Linga and yoni, the female receptacle into which the carved phallus was normally inserted, are also usually made of sandstone. Overwhelmingly, however, brick is the medium of construction and the raw material from which Hindu, Sivaist and Buddhist images and ornaments are so intricately carved.

Unfortunately, My Son was a Viet Cong field headquarters and therefore located within one of the US 'free fire' zones and was extensively damaged – in particular, the finest sanctuary in the complex was demolished by US sappers. Of the temple groupings, Groups A, E and H were badly damaged in the war. Groups B and C have largely retained their temples but many statues, altars and linga have been removed to the Cham Museum in Danang. Currently Group C is being restored by UNESCO; the F building is covered in cobwebs and propped up by scaffolding.

Dong Duong and Tra Kieu

Dong Duong, 20 km from My Son, supplanted My Son as the centre of Cham art and culture when King Indravarman II built a large Buddhist monastery there at the end of the ninth century. Artistically, little changed – the decoration of the towers simply became more ornate and involved, and the reliefs more deeply cut. There is a room in the Cham Museum in Danang devoted to sculptures from Dong Duong, including carved Buddha images. Cham Buddhism saw its finest artistic flowering in the 10th century. In the early 10th century, the focus of Cham art returned to My Son once again under the patronage of Indravarman III (so-called Mi-Son A1 style). Here, a new and far more elegant architecture, evolved. The towers became taller and more balanced, and the decoration purer and less crude.

Tra Kieu, which today is a nondescript little place en route to My Son was, in fact, the first Cham capital in the fourth century. That it supported a flourishing artistic and religious life can be gleaned from the exhibits in the Cham Museum in Danang. Tra Kieu was sacked by the Chinese in the fifth century but appears to have flourished again in the late 10th century. Today, alas, there is little to see.

◉ Hoi An and around listings

For Sleeping and Eating price codes and other relevant information, see Essentials pages 26-31.

● Sleeping

There has been a dramatic increase in the number of hotel rooms available in Hoi An but it is still advisable to book in advance as during peak times, rooms are scarce. There are no ultra-cheap places to stay in Hoi An.

Hoi An *p216, map p218*
LL-AL Life Heritage Resort Hoi An,
1 Pham Hong Thai St, T510-391 4555, www.
life-resorts.com. This small, quiet resort is in an excellent location right on the river next to the town. The spacious and extremely comfortable rooms are decorated beautifully in Japanese style and some feature sunken baths and rain showers. The lovely granite pool plus baby pool is centrally focused with

the Life Wellness Spa. The buffet breakfast is filling and varied. There's a restaurant, café and bar on site. The passion fruit mojito – an exciting twist on a cocktail classic – is drink of the year; it's absolutely unmissable.
AL-A Ancient House Resort, 377 Cua Dai St, T510-392 3377, www.ancienthouseresort. com. This is a beautiful, small hotel set around a small garden with a series of landscaped ponds and potted frangipani. All the 42 rooms are decorated in virginal white. There is a pool, shop, billiards, free shuttle to town and beach, free bicycle service and a restaurant. Behind the hotel is a traditional **Ancient House**. Below ground art work and an unusual linga sculpture are displayed.
AL-A Hoi An, 10 Tran Hung Dao St, T510-386 1445, www.hoiantourist.com. Attractive colonial building set well back from the road in spacious grounds with attractively furnished, comfortable rooms with all mod-

cons and en suite bathrooms with bathtubs. The pool is especially inviting and the hotel has a new Zen spa and beauty salon. Discounts are offered in Hoi An's summer low season. Staff are welcoming and there are a host of activities from Chinese lantern making to trips to local villages.

AL-A Vinh Hung Riverside Resort, 111 Ngo Quyen St, An Hoi Islet, T510-391 0393, www.vinhhungresort.com. This hotel is focused around a multi-form pool with a swim-up bar. The pool here is a lot nicer than the pools at Vinh Hung Nos 2 and 3. There are 82 spacious rooms with full amenities. Some may like its seclusion away from the bustle of the centre of Hoi An.

A Vinh Hung 1, 143 Tran Phu St, T510-386 1621, www.vinhhunghotels.com.vn. An attractive old building with a splendid and ornate reception room decorated with dark wood in Chinese style. It halved its room capacity and upgraded the 6 remaining rooms to some very lovely stylish retreats; these are now some of the most appealing rooms in the old city. Recommended.

A-B Ha An Hotel, T510-386 3126, 6-8 Phan Boi Chau St, http://haanhotel.com. This is a lovely hotel with a flourishing courtyard garden. Rooms are decorated with ethnic minority accents but are on the small side but the overall ambience is delightful and relaxing in the garden is a bonus in a city with no outdoor green space.

A-C Pho Hoi Riverside Resort, T1, Cam Nam Island, T510-386 2628, www.phohoiresort.com. Strung along the riverbank with 38 pleasant, reasonably priced cabins. Swimming pool and restaurant on site. A 30-room hotel, also now part of the complex, is less attractive.

B-C Van Loi Hotel, Cam Nam Island, T510-393 6205, www.vanloihotelhoian.com. Although on quieter Cam Nam Island, this is heavily used by tour groups and is not quiet at all. If you fancy a lie-in opt for a room not on the 4th floor otherwise you'll hear the breakfast patter for hours on the 5th floor. Pool.

B-C Vinh Hung 2, Ba Trieu St, T510-386 3717, www.vinhhungresort.com. A sister hotel with 40 rooms, a short walk away, built in traditional style, with a pool and all mod cons but lacking the atmosphere of the original.

C-D An Huy Hotel, 30 Phan Boi Chau St, T510-386 2116, www.anhuyhotel.com. A sweet little hotel, opposite **Brother's Café**, with courtyards that create a breeze and shutters that keep the noise out. The 14 spacious rooms are beautifully decorated in Japanese style and the staff are very friendly. Breakfast and free internet is included.

E Pho Hoi 1, 7/2 Tran Phu St, T510-386 1633, www.phohoiresort.com. Near the market. All a/c rooms.

E Thanh Binh, 1 Le Loi St, T510-386 1740, www.thanhbinhhotel.com.vn. A hotel with 14 rooms, which follows the common (and good value) Hoi An standard of price and quality with rooms with TV, fridge, mosquito nets and bathtub.

E Thuy Duong 1, 11 Le Loi St, T510-386 1574. 10 rooms, some a/c, friendly.

E-F Minh A, 2 Nguyen Thai Hoc St, T510-386 1368. This is a very special little place. An old family house with just 5 guest rooms that are all different. Guests are made to feel part of the family. Communal bathrooms have hot water and fan. Right next to the market in a busy part of town. Very welcoming.

E-F Phu Thinh, 144 Tran Phu St, T510-386 1297, www.phuthinhhotels.com. Behind an attractive Chinese-looking façade stands a very ordinary 1970s hotel. Except for a couple of rooms upstairs all rooms are on a long internal corridor. Rooms with a/c cost more; rooms have bathtubs. Rather dark and airless but efficient staff.

E-F Sea Star (**Sao Bien**), 489 Cua Dai St, on the road to the beach, T510-386 1589, saobien_hotel@yahoo.com. A privately run hotel with all rooms coming with a/c and hot water. Travel services, bicycle, motorbike and car hire on offer. Efficient and popular.

F Sanh Hien, 7 Nguyen Thi Minh Khai St, T510-386 3631. Another family home; not as characterful as the Minh A but an 'old house' nonetheless with 3 rooms and in a quieter part of town.

Cua Dai Beach and around p221

LL The Nam Hai, Hamlet 1, Dien Duong Village, 11 km north of Hoi An, 30 km south of Danang on Ha My Beach, T510-394 0000, www.ghmhotels.com. The **Nam Hai** is a stunning creation of 100 beachside villas overlooking the East Sea. Raised platforms inside the villas create a special sleeping and living space enveloped with white silk drapes; egg-shell lacquered baths in a black marble surround are incorporated into the platform. At the back behind delicately carved screens are his and hers sinks made from lacquered egg shell on marble bases and an indoor and outdoor shower. Facing the sitting area are doors on to an outdoor terrace on the beach. 40 of the villas have private granite pools. There are 2 restaurants flanking the vast infinity pool. 3 pools, a gym, tennis, badminton and basketball courts will keep you toned. For relaxing there's a lovely library, spa (see Therapies, page 231) and boutique. **The Restaurant**, 0700-2300, is behind the main pool.

LL-L Swiss-Belhotel Golden Sand Resort, www.goldensandvn.com. A modern and Vietnamese-style resort set in 6 ha of landscaped garden with a massive swimming pool. It's family friendly with a kids' pool, play area and kids' club. There are plenty of watersports too.

LL-AL Palm Garden Resort, Lac Long Quan St, Cua Dai Beach, T510-392 7927, www.palmgardenresort.com.vn. The **Palm Garden Resort** offers its guests plenty of watersports activities, a massive pool and a **Qi Shiseido Salon and Spa**. Rooms are in bungalows or 3-storey villas.

LL-AL Victoria Hoi An Beach Resort & Spa, T510-392 7040, www.victoriahotels-asia.com. A charming and attractive **Victoria** hotel, this resort is right on the beach and laid out like a small fisherman's village. It has 105 beautifully furnished rooms facing the sea or the river either in Vietnamese, French or Japanese style. There is a large pool, the **L'Annam Restaurant** (which serves very tasty but expensive dishes), a couple of bars, a kids' club, BBQ beach parties, live music and dancing, a host of watersports and all with charming service. Free shuttle bus runs between the hotel and the town. See Therapies, page 231, for the **Tamarind Spa** and Activities and tours, page 230 for its sporting facilities.

L-AL Hoi An Riverside Resort, 175 Cua Dai Rd, T510-386 4800, www.hoianriverresort.com. This really lovely hotel is in a slightly strange place neither on the beach nor in town. A short 5-min cycle ride from the beach and a 15-min pedal from town, the resort is right on the road, admittedly not a busy one but slightly exposed to passing traffic. The accommodation is comfortable and belonging as it does to Mr Khai (of Khai Silk fame) everything is nicely designed. The views overlooking the river are lovely. There is a dark, slate-lined pool.

AL Hoi An Beach Resort, 1 Cua Dai Beach Rd, T510-392 7011, www.hoiantourist.com. A tastefully designed peacefully quiet hotel that benefits from being just across the road from the beach and lining the river bank at the same time. Rooms are comfortable, the pools are perfect and the food is good. Free shuttle bus into town; baby sitting and many other services.

A Le Domaine de Tam Hai, 45 km south of Hoi An on Tam Hai Island, T510-354 5105, www.domainedetamhai.com. 12 cottages on a tropical island with all mod cons, outdoor bathrooms and private gardens. There's a spa, pool and watersports activities. Access can be via Chu Lai Airport, 20 mins away.

❶ Eating

Hoi An p216, map p218
A Hoi An speciality is *cao lau* – a special noodle soup with slices of pork and croutons and traditionally made with water from one particular well. Fresh seafood is

also readily available. The quality of food in Hoi An, especially the fish, is outstanding and the value for money is not matched by any other town in Vietnam. Bach Dang St is particularly pleasant in the evening when tables and chairs are set up almost the whole way along the river. Restaurants in Hoi An are virtually all geared to the tourist trade so are open for lunch and stay open until about 2200 but it's best to order before 2100. There's now a line of restaurants on the opposite riverbank that have the advantage of facing all the attractive buildings on the other side.

¶¶-¶¶ Brother's Café, 27 Phan Boi Chau St, T510-391 4150, www.brothercafehoian. com.vn. These little cloistered French houses have been renovated in exquisite taste. The house and garden leading down to the river are beautifully restored. The menu is strong on Vietnamese specialities, especially seafood, and the daily set menu offers good value in such charming surroundings. Highly recommended, although a tad overpriced; you are paying for the setting. The Japanese Slipper cocktail is highly palatable.

¶¶-¶ Secret Garden, 132/2 Tran Phu St, off Le Loi St, T510-391 1112, www. secretgardehoian.com. An oasis amid the shopping malestrom of downtown Hoi An. Superior and attentive service in a delightful courtyard garden with delicious dishes. Try the sublime thin slices of beef with garlic and pepper, lemon juice, soya sauce, and sesame oil or the star fruit soup. Live music is played nightly and there's a cooking school.

¶¶ Nhu Y (aka **Mermaid**), 2 Tran Phu St, T510-386 1527, www.hoianhospitality.com. Miss Vy turns out all the local specialities as well as some of her own. The 5-course set dinner is particularly recommended.

¶¶ Tam Tam Café, 110 Nguyen Thai Hoc St, T510-386 2212, www.tamtamcafe-hoian. com. This is a great little café in a renovated tea house. Cocktails, draft beer, music, book exchange, plus attached restaurant serving French and Italian cuisine. A relaxing place for a drink, expresso or meal.

¶¶ Thanh, 76 Bach Dang St, T510-386 1366. A charming old house overlooking the river which is recognizable by its Chinese style and being draped in *Hoa cat dang*, a fetching flowering creeper; the shrimp is excellent.

¶¶ Vinh Hung, 147B Tran Phu St, T510-386 2203. Belongs to the hotel of the same name. Another attractive building finely decked with Chinese lanterns and traditional furniture. An excellent range of seafood dishes and Vietnamese specials at fair prices.

¶¶-¶ Café des Amis, 52 Bach Dang St, near the river, T510-386 1616. The set menu of fish/seafood or vegetarian changes daily and is widely acclaimed and excellent value. The owner, Mr Nguyen Manh Kim, spends several months a year cooking in Europe. Highly recommended.

¶¶-¶ Mango Mango, 45 Nguyen Phuc Chu St, T510-391 1863, www.themangomango. com. Sister to the original **Mango Rooms**, this restaurant across the river has a nicer view. The red and white theme is stylish; staff are friendly and the cuisine is creative, imaginatively put together and consistently delicous. Try the large prawns seasoned and grilled in a delectable white wine and passion fruit butter-garlic sauce with a touch of bitter chocolate and finish with the espresso-ristretto over NZ vanilla bean ice cream.

¶¶-¶ Mango Rooms, 111 Nguyen Thai Hoc St, T510-391 0839, www.mangorooms.com. With its bright, bold colours, superlative food and comfy seating out back overlooking the river, the **Mango Rooms** is a very welcome addition to Hoi An. The superior cooking makes a repeat visit a must. Enjoy slices of baguette layered with shrimp mousse served with a 'delectable' mango coconut curry or the delicious ginger and garlic-marinated shrimps wrapped in tender slices of beef and pan-fried with wild spicy butter and soy-garlic sauce; the seared tuna steak with mango salsa is outstanding. Complimentary tapas-style offerings such as tapioca crisps are a welcome touch. The lovely daiquiris slip down a treat or opt for the BYO bottle option. A little more ventilation would really help the dining experience. Highly recommended.

19, 19 Hoang Van Thu St, T510-391 0409. Serves locally brewed beer at just 4000d per glass and simple inexpensive dishes.

Before & Now, 51 Le Loi St, T510-391 0599, www.beforennow.com. 0900-2200; happy hour 1700-2100. Pool, darts and table football pull the punters in. The menu is full of sandwiches, pasta and risotto, Vietnamese and Australian beef, and beef, chicken and fish pizza. There's also a great Vietnamese menu: *bo nuong me*: grilled beef with sesame, lemongrass, onion and garlic. The Vietnamese food here is tastier than the Italian pizzas.

Café Can, 74 Bach Dang St, T510-386 1525. Good Vietnamese and Western menu and seafood specialities in an attractive setting by the river.

Cargo Club, 107 Nguyen Thai Hoc, T510-910489. This extremely popular venue serves up filling Vietnamese and Western fodder including club sandwiches, Vietnamese salads and overpriced fajitas. The service is quicker downstairs than up on the balcony overlooking the river. The patisserie, groaning with cakes and chocolate, is the best thing about this place. Avoid the awful *café sua da*.

Du Port, 70 Bach Dang St, T510-386 1786. Success has bred a complacent attitude in service but the fish is outstanding.

Hai Café, 111 Tran Phu St/98 Nguyen Thai Hoc St, T510-386 3210, www.visithoian.com. The central area of this café offers good food in a relaxing courtyard or attractive café setting. Cookery courses can be arranged.

Lighthouse Restaurant, T510-224 1503, www.lighthousecafehoian.com. Wed-Mon 1200-2200. Reservations after 1900. The food is tasty, the views are enticing and the set menus are good value. Shame about the appalling service.

Miss Ly, 22 Nguyen Hué St. T510-386 1603, lycafe22@hotmail.com. Cheap, cheerful and very popular.

Morning Glory, 106 Nguyen Thai Hoc St, T510-324 1555. In an attractive building with a balcony serving up Vietnamese street food such as crispy mackerel and mango salsa, caramel fish in clay pot and spicy prawn curry. The restaurant is run by Miss Vy of Mermaid fame.

Red Bridge Cooking School, Thon 4, Cam Thanh, T510-393 3222, www.visithoian.com. This lovely restaurant in a river setting, 2 km from Hoi An, with a pool is a great place to pass an afternoon after lunch.

Streets, 17 Le Loi St, www.streets international.org. A professional training restaurant for disadvantaged youngsters that serves up very tasty Vietnamese and Western cuisine in a lovely old property. Trainee chefs complete an 18-month programme at the restaurant.

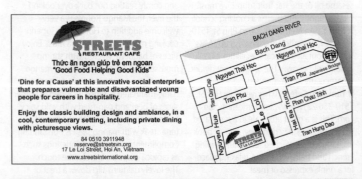

♪ Bars and clubs

Hoi An *p216, map p218*
Casa Verde, 99 Bach Dang St, T510-391
1594. With its tables overlooking the river,
it's a good spot to sample the wine list.
Champa, 75 Nguyen Thai Hoc St, T510-386
1159. This is a rambling place with pool
tables and an upstairs cultural show in the
evenings. Downstairs, hits from the 1960s
and 1970s predominate.
Sleepy Gecko, first major right (signposted)
on Cam Nam Island, past **Randy's
BookXchange**. A lovely little haven of jollity
with beers, breakfasts and Saturday BBQs
from 1600. Friendly and genuinely helpful
with advice. Ask about **Steve's Byke** tours
(T90-842 6349, sleepygecko@gmail.com).
Movies to view too.
Tam Tam Café, 110 Nguyen Thai Hoc St.
Mainly a café/restaurant but also has a good
bar and pool table. An attractive place to sit.
Treat, 158 Tran Phu St, T510-386 1125. Open
till late. One of Hoi An's few bars and a very
well run one. 2 pool tables, airy, attractive
style: popular happy hour and attractive
balcony. Also at 69 and 93 Tran Hung Dao St,
which are very popular at night.

Cua Dai Beach and around *p221*
La Plage Beach Club, An Bang Beach,
T510-392 8244, www.laplagehoian.com.
Drinks and food on candy-pink sun loungers
on this lovely stretch of beach. There's also
movies, yoga and weekend BBQs.
Phattie's, An Bang Beach. A popular
hangout for backpackers and expats with a
genial atmosphere and pool table.
Zero Seamile Beach Club, aka **Hoi An
Beach Club**, Cua Dai Beach, T510-391 1911,
www.hoianbeachclub.vn. A club with a pool,
chairs, pool table, table football, TV screen,
dancing and a happy hour (1800-2100).
There's also **La Biniou Creperie** and a host of
friendly Vietnamese shacks serving up fresh
fish at **An Bang**.

⊕ Entertainment

Hoi An *p216, map p218*
Hoi An Handicraft Workshop, 9 Nguyen
Thai Hoc St, T510-391 0216, www.
hoianhandicraft.com. Traditional music
performances at 1015, 1515 and 1930 with
the Vietnamese monochord and dancers
(part of the ticket programme). At the back
there is a potter's wheel, straw mat making
with loom, embroiderers, conical hat makers,
wood carvers and iron ornament makers.

⊙ Shopping

Hoi An *p216, map p218*
Hoi An is a shopper's paradise – **Tran Phu**
and **Le Loi** streets being the main shopping
areas. Two items stand out: paintings
and clothes. Hoi An is also the place to
buy handbags and purses and attractive
Chinese silk lanterns, indeed anything that
can be made from silk, including scarves
and shoes. There is also a lot of quite nice
chinaware available, mostly modern, some
reproduction and a few antiques. There
is blue and white and celadon green, the
ancient Chinese pale green glaze, here
often reproduced with fine cracks. Note,
however, that it is illegal to take items more
than 200 years old out of the country and
the customs officials are likely to confiscate
anything that takes their fancy.

Countless galleries sell original works of
art. Vietnamese artists have been inspired by
Hoi An's old buildings and a Hoi An school
of art has developed. Hoi An buildings are
instantly recognizable even distorted into
a variety of shapes and colours on canvas
or silk. Galleries are everywhere but in
particular the more serious galleries are to
be found in a cluster on **Nguyen Thi Minh
Khai St** west of the Japanese Bridge.

Books
Randy's BookXchange, Cam Nam Island,
T93-608 9483, randy@randysbookxchange.
com. Randy's got a proper book store here

with a range of genres including travel guides. It's a welcoming place to browse.

Handicrafts and jewellery
Memory, 96A Bach Dang St and 62 Le Loi St. Wonderful, imaginative designs using a range of materials. T510-391 1483.
Reaching Out Handicrafts, 103 Nguyen Thai Hoc St, T510-391 0168, www. reachingoutvietnam.com. Arts and crafts, cards and notebooks, lovely jewellery, textiles and silk sleeping bags all made by disabled artisans living in Hoi An. The shop is a fair trade one and profits support the disabled community. There is usually someone at work in the shop so you can see what they are getting up to.

Tailors and fashion
Hoi An's tailors are famed – there are now reckoned to be more than 150 – and will knock up silk or cotton clothing in 24 hrs. The quality of the stitching varies from shop to shop, so see some samples first. The range of fabrics is limited so many people bring their own. Note that Thai silk will cost more than Vietnamese silk. Hoi An silk is quite coarse. A suit can cost anywhere from US$55-395 depending on the fabric and quality of workmanship. Visitors talk of the rapid speed at which shops can produce goods. Apart from the workers staying up all night if every visitor to Hoi An wants something done within 12-24 hrs, this creates enormous strain on staff and quality could suffer. Therefore if you are in Hoi An for a few days, do your clothes shopping on the 1st day. Tailors themselves recommend a minimum 36-hr period. This will give you time to accommodate extra fittings.
41 Le Loi Street, T510-386 2164, quanghiep@dng.vnn.vn. Open 0745-2200. A silk workshop where the whole process from silkworm to woven fabric can be seen and fabrics purchased.
Kimmy Tailor, 70 Tran Hung Dao St, T510-386 2063, http://kimmytailor.com. Has been recommended.

Lan Ha, 1A Hai Ba Trung St, T510-391 0706, leco50@hotmail.com. 0900-2200. This shop unit is recommended because of the speed of service, the quality of the goods, the excellent prices and the fact that compared to many other tailors in town that have been used, 2nd, 3rd or even 4th fittings were not required.
Song, 76 Nguyen Thai Hoc St. Lovely outlet for the clothes of a French designer with shops also in Hanoi and Saigon.
Yaly, 47 Nguyen Thai Hoc St, T510-391 0474, yalyshop@dng.vnn.vn. Open 0700-2030. Professional staff, very good, quality results across a range of clothing including shoes in a lovely old building. Ladies' blouses are around US$20 and dresses from US$30. There are now 4 branches of **Yaly** but this is the original.

▲▲ Activities and tours

Hoi An *p216, map p218*
The **Hotel Hoi An** (see page 224) runs several activities including how to be a farmer, fisherman, make Chinese lanterns and visits to carpentry and pottery villages.

Cookery classes
Morning Glory Cooking School, 106 Nguyen Thai Hoc St, T510-324 1555, morningglory@hoianhospitality.com. Cooking classes run by Miss Vy of **Mermaid** fame and her assistants. Courses include daily Vietnamese food cooking demonstration and meal; a hands-on class and meal; cooking for special occasions; and taught by Ms Vy only, intensive hands-on cooking for culinary specialists.
Red Bridge Cooking School, run out of the Hai Café, 98 Nguyen Thai Hoc St, T510-386 3210. Visit the market to be shown local produce, then take a 20-min boat ride to the cooking school where you're shown the herb garden. Next you watch a demonstration by chefs on how to make a number of dishes such as warm squid salad served in half a pineapple, and grilled eggplant

stuffed with veg. Move inside and you get to make your own fresh spring rolls and learn Vietnamese food carving – which is a lot harder than it looks. US$24. (**Red Bridge Cooking School**, Thon 4, Cam Thanh, T510-393 3222, www.visithoian.com. Boat rides Boat rides are available on the Thu Bon River. Local boatwomen charge a dollar or so per hr, a tranquil and relaxed way of spending the early evening.

Diving and snorkelling
Cham Island Diving Center, 88 Nguyen Thai Hoc St, T5103-910782, www.chamislanddiving.om. A PADI dive centre where 2 dives cost US$75. Its Cham Island excursion is recommended for snorkellers as it gives time to explore the village on Cham Island, US$40, led by Italians who lived on the island for a year. For double the amount you can camp on the beach in tents (food included). Helpful, good advice given.
Rainbow Divers, 39B Tran Hung Dao St, T510-391 1914. A well-regarded Western-run national operation.

Motorbiking
Hoi An Motorbike Adventures, 54A Phan Chau Trinh St, T91-823 0653, www.motorbiketours-hoian.com runs good half-day to 5-day tours in the area.
Victoria Hoi An Beach Resort & Spa, T510-392 7040, www.victoriahotels-asia.com. The hotel offers a variety of services priced by the hour including boating, kayaking, fishing, windsurfing, hobie-cat sailing, tennis court use, and a trip in a restored sidecar; you can also take an adventurous 5-day sidecar trip to the Laos border.

Therapies
The Spa at the Nam Hai, Hamlet 1, Dien Duong Village, Dien Ban District, 7 km from Cua Dai Beach, T510-394 0000 ext 7700, www.ghmhotels.com. Open 0900-2100. This is one of the most gorgeous spas in southeast Asia. Centred around a lotus pond with stilted buildings in the water, succumb

to the delicious treatments on offer including massage, body polishes, facials and spa rituals. The spa's ritual treatment – 2 hrs of pampering – means submitting to an aromatherapy foot polish, aromatherapy massage, silk body scrub, honey and milk body masque and a rose and petal milk bath to complete the experience.
Spa & Beauty, Victoria Hoi An Beach Resort & Spa, Cua Dai Beach, T510-927040, www.victoriahotels-asia.com. 0900-2100. A lovely, friendly spa centre covering a wide range of treatments from body wraps to facials. The reflexology treatment is especially good.

Tour operators
Hoi An Travel, Hotel Hoi An, 10 Tran Hung Dao St, and at Hoi An Beach Resort, T510-391 0911, www.hoiantravel.com. Open 0800-2000. Offers a variety of tours including some unusual ones: a visit to a vegetable village, fishing at Thanh Nam, lantern making, visiting Kim Bong carpentry village, Thanh Ha pottery village, and visiting the Cham Islands. You can also arrange trips from Savannakhet and Pakse, Laos and from Bangkok to Hoi An, Danang and Hué and returning to Laos and Thailand.
Phattireventures, 619 Hai Ba Trung St, T510-391 7839, www.ptv-vietnam.com. Trekking, biking, rockclimbing around Hoi An from Phattireventures of Dalat fame.
Seventeen's, 17 Tran Hung Dao St, T510-386 1947, www.seventeenstravel.com. Offers tours to My Son, from US$4; My Lai, US$55 in car; motorbike hire, US$5; snorkelling at Cham Islands, US$25; river tour US$20; canoeing, US$25; diving US$65 and organizes transport to the Central Highlands. Taxi to Danang, US$10.
Sinh Tourist (formerly Sinh Café), 587 Hai Ba Trung St, T510-386 3948, www.thesinhtourist.vn. Open 0630-2200. Branch of the ubiquitous chain offering tours and transport My Son tour, 96,000d; with return boat trip via Kim Bong carpentry village; 115,000d.

Θ Transport

Hoi An *p216, map p218*

Air

Hoi An does not have an airport. A taxi from Danang airport to Hoi An will cost about US$10-15 (bargain hard), 40 mins. Taxi from Hoi An to Danang is around US$10. Transport to Hoi An can also be arranged through operators.

Vietnam Airlines and Jetstar sales agent, 10 Tran Hung Dao St, T510-391 0912.

Bicycle and motorbike

Hotels and tour operators have 2WD and 4WD vehicles for hire. Bicycle hire is 20,000d per day, motorbike US$4-6 per day.

Bus and Open Tour Bus

The bus station is about 1 km west of the centre of town on Ly Thuong Kiet St. Motos into town 15,000d; to the beach, 20,000d. There are regular connections from Danang's local bus station, 1 hr, from 0530 until 1800, 20,000d. Open Tour Buses go

north to **Hanoi** and south to **HCMC**. Book through local tour operators (see above). Seventeen's organizes travel to **Kontum**, 0500, US$25, 8½ hrs and on to **Play Ku** (10 hrs) and **Buon Ma Thuot** (11½ hrs).

Taxi

Mai Linh, T510-391 4914.

ℹ Directory

Hoi An *p216, map p218*

Banks Vietinbank, 4 Hoang Dieu St, T510-386 1340. Accepts most major currencies, US dollar withdrawal from credit/debit card, no commission for cashing American Express TCs, ATM. Agribank, 6 Hoang Dieu St. Has foreign exchange and ATM. **Hospitals** 4 Tran Hung Dao St, T510-386 4750, 0700-2200. There's a line of pharmacies next to the hospital. Immigration, 88 Phan Chu Trinh St, T510-910093. Only available Mon, Wed and Fri. **Internet** Widely available in cafés and hotels, as is Wi-Fi. **Post office** 4 Tran Hung Dao St, T510-861480, next to Hoi An Hotel.

Dalat and the Central Highlands

Dalat is an attractive town situated on a plateau in the Central Highlands at an altitude of almost 1500m. The town itself, a former French hill station, is centred on a lake – Xuan Huong – amid rolling countryside and is dotted with more than 2000 French villas. To the north are five volcanic peaks of the Lang Biang mountains, rising to 2400 m. In the area are forests, waterfalls, and an abundance of orchids, roses and other temperate flora.

The Central Highlands consist of the Truong Son Mountain Range and its immediate environs. It is commonly referred to as the backbone of Vietnam. It borders Laos and Cambodia to the west and the East Sea to the east. It is primarily an agrarian area; it is the main source of flowers and vegetables to the southern lowlands and also has many tea and coffee plantations that supply the whole world (Vietnam is the world's second largest producer of coffee). Tourism is an additional source of revenue for many of the inhabitants. This is due to its elevation and also to the fact that most of the inhabitants are from Vietnam's indigenous groups (26 of whom live here). Outside the main towns of Dalat, Buon Ma Thuot, Play Ku (Pleiku) and Kontum the way of life remains unchanged. ›› *For listings, see pages 252-264.*

Ins and outs

Getting there   Dalat is on Highway 20. There are daily flights from Ho Chi Minh City and Hanoi. Many buses go to Play Ku, Kontum, Ho Chi Minh City, Nha Trang, Buon Ma Thuot, Phan Thiet, and Phan Rang. Open Tour Buses go to Nha Trang, Mui Ne and Ho Chi Minh City.

Central Highlands

The Central Highlands have long been associated with Vietnam's hill tribes. French missionaries were active among the minorities of the Central Highlands (the colonial administration deterred ethnic Vietnamese from settling here) although with uneven success. Bishop Cuenot dispatched two missionaries from Quy Nhon to Buon Ma Thuot where they received a hostile reception from the Mnong, so travelled north to Kontum where among the Ba-na they found more receptive souls for their evangelizing. Today, many of the ethnic minorities in the Central Highlands are Roman Catholic, although some are Protestant (Ede around Buon Ma Thuot, for instance).

At the same time French businesses were hard at work establishing plantations to supply the home market. Rubber and coffee were the staple crops. The greatest difficulty they faced was recruiting sufficient labour. Men and women of the ethnic minorities preferred to cultivate their own small plots rather than accept the hard labour and slave wages of the plantation owners. Norman Lewis travelled in the Central Highlands and describes the situation in his book, *A Dragon Apparent.*

Since 1984 there has been a bit of a free-for-all and a scramble for land. Ethnic Vietnamese have encroached on minority land and planted it with coffee, pepper and fruit trees. From the air one sees neat rows of crops and carefully tended plots, interrupted only by large areas of scrub that are too dry to cultivate. The scene is reinforced at ground level where the occasional tall tree is the only reminder of the formerly extensive forest cover. The way of life of the minorities is disappearing with the forests – there are no trees to build their stilt houses from or shady forests in which to live and hunt.

The Mnong, Coho, Sedang and Bahnar people speak a language that stems from the Mon Khmer language. The language of the Ede, Giarai, Cham and Raglai originates from the Malayo-Polynesian language.

Getting around Dalat is rather a large town and there are a number of hills. A plentiful selection of taxis is available as are the ubiquitous *Honda ôm* drivers, including those from Easy Riders. ▸▸ *See also Transport, page 262.*

Best time to visit The best time to visit is from November to May when there is less rainfall and pleasant temperatures. At the weekends the centre is closed to traffic between 1900 and 2200 allowing for stalls to set up on Nguyen Thi Minh Khai Street. As different indigenous groups live in the Central Highlands, there are festivals all year round. Buffalo sacrifice ceremonies take place in Mnong, Sedang and Cotu communities after the spring harvest.

Tourist information **Dalat Travel Bureau** ①*www.dalattourist.com.vn*, is the state-run travel company for Lam Dong Province. There are also a number of tour operators that offer good information and tours. ▸▸ *See Activities and tours, page 260.*

History

Dr Alexandre Yersin, a protégé of Louis Pasteur, founded Dalat in 1893. He stumbled across Dalat as he was trying to find somewhere cool to escape from the sweltering summer heat of the coast and lowlands. The lush alpinesque scenery of Dalat impressed the French and it soon became the secondary main city in the south after Saigon. (In the summer months the government moved lock, stock and barrel to Dalat where it was cooler). There are plenty of original French-style villas, many of which have been converted into hotels while some remain in private ownership; others are government offices. The last emperor of Vietnam, Bao Dai, lived here and it is possible to see his former imperial residence.

Dalat soon took on the appearance of Paris in the mountains. A golf course was made and a luxurious hotel was built. In both the Second World War and the American War high-ranking officials of the opposing armies would while away a pleasant couple of days playing golf against each other before having to return to the battlefields.

Of all the highland cities Dalat was the least affected by the American War. The main reason being that at the time the only entrance into Dalat was up the Prenn Pass. There was a small heliport at Cam Ly (part of Dalat) and also a radio listening station on Langbian Mountain but nothing else of note.

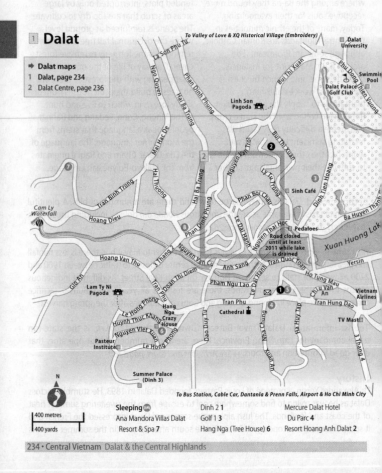

1 Dalat

➡ **Dalat maps**
1 Dalat, page 234
2 Dalat Centre, page 236

Sleeping ●
Ana Mandora Villas Dalat Resort & Spa **7**

Dinh 2 **1**
Golf 1 **3**
Hang Nga (Tree House) **6**

Mercure Dalat Hotel Du Parc **4**
Resort Hoang Anh Dalat **2**

The town is currently undergoing a huge renovation programme. New roads are being built and existing roads are being upgraded. Dalat airport is being modernized and having its runway elongated in order to make it an international airport and there is talk of a full rail link between Dalat and Nha Trang in the future. A large new Phuong Trang bus station has been constructed near the cable car station. Dalat is the honeymoon capital of southern Vietnam. There is a quaint belief – not widely held – that unless you go on honeymoon to Dalat then you are not really married.

Xuan Huong Lake

Originally the Grand Lake, Xuan Huong Lake was renamed in 1954. It was created in 1919 after a small dam was constructed on the Cam Ly River. It is the attractive centrepiece of the town and a popular exercise area for the local inhabitants of whom many will, first thing in the morning, walk around the lake stopping every so often to perform t'ai chi exercises.

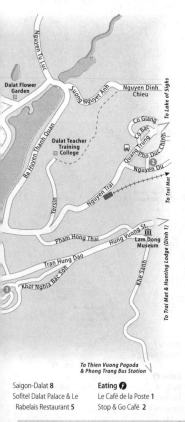

Power-walking at dusk is also popular. The lake was drained in 2010 so as to remove accumulated silt and construct a new road across the center. It should be refilled by the time you read this.

Dalat Flower Garden

ⓘ *Vuon Hoa Dalat, 2 Phu Dong Thien Vuong St, daily 0700-1800, 10,000d.*

At the northeast end of the lake is the Dalat Flower Garden. It supports a range of plants including orchids, roses, lilies and hydrangeas. Signs are not in English, only Latin and Vietnamese; the one English sign directs visitors to the orchidarium. There are kiosks selling drinks and ice creams and there's a lake with pedaloes.

Colonial villas

Many of the large colonial villas – almost universally washed in pastel yellow – are 1930s and 1940s vintage. Some have curved walls, railings and are almost nautical in inspiration; others are reminiscent of houses in Provence. Many of the larger villas can be found along **Tran Hung Dao Street** and a number of these are now being converted into villa hotels. Sadly many of the villas have fallen into a very sorry state and are looking decidedly unloved. Given their architectural significance this is a great pity. Perhaps the largest and most impressive house on Tran Hung Dao is the former residence of

Saigon-Dalat **8**
Sofitel Dalat Palace & Le Rabelais Restaurant **5**

Eating 🍴
Le Café de la Poste **1**
Stop & Go Café **2**

the Governor General at 12 Tran Hung Dao Street – now the **Hotel Dinh 2** (see Sleeping, page 254). The villa is 1930s in style, with large airy rooms and furniture and occupies a magnificent position set among mountain pines and overlooking the town and lake. The house is a popular place for domestic tourists to have their photographs taken. It is possible to stay here although it is often booked up and is popular with members of Lam Dong People's Committee.

Dalat centre

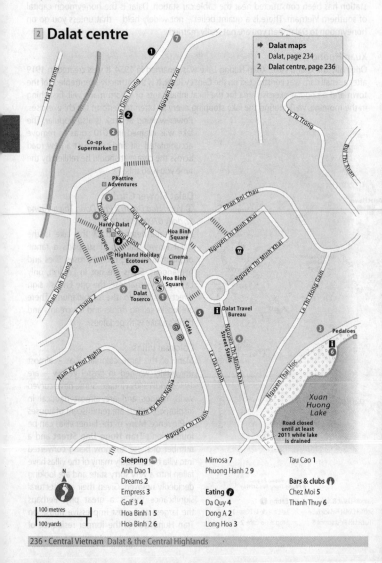

→ **Dalat maps**
1 Dalat, page 234
2 Dalat centre, page 236

Sleeping
Anh Dao 1
Dreams 2
Empress 3
Golf 3 4
Hoa Binh 1 5
Hoa Binh 2 6

Mimosa 7
Phuong Hanh 2 9

Eating
Da Quy 4
Dong A 2
Long Hoa 3

Tau Cao 1

Bars & clubs
Chez Moi 5
Thanh Thuy 6

Dalat Cathedral

ⓘ *Tran Phu St. Mass is held twice a day Mon-Sat 0515 and 1715 and on Sun at 0515, 0700, 0830, 1600 and 1800. The recently painted tan and cream-coloured cathedral has a good choir and attracts a large and enthusiastic congregation.*

The single-tiered cathedral is visible from the lake and 100 m from the Novotel hotel. At the top of the turret is a chicken-shaped wind dial. It is referred to locally as the 'Chicken Cathedral'. Construction began in 1931, although the building was not completed until the Japanese 'occupation' in 1942. The stained-glass windows, with their vivid colours and use of pure, clean lines, were crafted in France by Louis Balmet, the same man who made the windows in Nha Trang and Danang cathedrals, between 1934 and 1940. Sadly, most have not survived the ravages of time. Lining the nave are blocks of woodcarvings of Christ and the crucifixion.

Summer Palace (Dinh 3) and Dinh 1

ⓘ *Le Hong Phong St, T63-382 6858, 0730-1100 and 1330-1600, 10000d. Visitors have to wear covers over their shoes to protect the wooden floors. You can dress up in emperors' clothing and have your picture taken, 30,000d. Café, ice creams available.*

Vietnam's last emperor, Bao Dai, had a Summer Palace on Le Hong Phong Street, about 2 km from the town centre and now known as Dinh 3. Built on a hill with views on every side, it is art deco in style both inside and out, and rather modest for a palace. The palace was built between 1933 and 1938. The stark interior contains little to indicate that this was the home of an emperor – almost all of Bao Dai's personal belongings have been removed. The impressive dining room contains an etched-glass map of Vietnam, while the study has Bao Dai's desk, a few personal ornaments and photographs, noticeably of the family who, in 1954, were exiled to France where they lived. One of the family photos shows Bao Dai's son, the prince Bao Long, in full military dress uniform. He died in July 2007 in France aged 71. Emperor Bao Dai's daughters are still alive and were, in a spirit of reconciliation, invited back to visit Vietnam in the mid-1990s. They politely declined (one of the reasons given was that as they were both in their 70s it would have been too much effort), although the grandchildren may one day return. The emperor's bedroom and bathroom are open to public scrutiny as is the little terrace from his bedroom where, apparently, on a clear night he would gaze at the stars. The family drawing room is open together with a little commentary on which chair was used by whom. The palace is very popular with rowdy Vietnamese tourists who have their photographs taken wherever they can. The gardens are colourful and well maintained, though have a carnival atmosphere. From the moon balcony you can see the garden has been arranged into the shape of the Bao Dai stamp.

Pasteur Institute

ⓘ *Le Hong Phong, not open to the public.*

The yellow-wash institute was opened in 1935 and was built to produce vaccines for keeping the colonial population healthy. Although small and modest it is quite an attractive building fashioned in a series of cubes.

Lam Ty Ni Pagoda

ⓘ *Down a track off Le Hong Phong St.*

Lam Ty Ni Pagoda is unremarkable save for a charming monk, Vien Thuc, who lives here. Vien Thuc arrived in 1968 and in 1987 he finished the gateway that leads up through a garden to the figure of Quan Am. Vien Thuc originally named his garden – which is almost Japanese in inspiration – An Lac Vien, or Peace Garden, but has now decided that Divine Calmness Bamboo Garden has a better ring to it. Vien Thuc is a scholar, poet, artist, philosopher, mystic, divine and entrepreneur but is best known for his paintings of which, by his own reckoning, there are more than 100,000. And, wandering through the maze of rustic huts and shacks tacked on to the back of the temple one can easily believe this: the walls are lined deep with hanging sheets which bear his simple but distinctive calligraphy and philosophy: "Living in the present how beautiful this very moment is", "Zen painting destroys millennium sorrows", "The mystique, silence and melody universal of love" and so on. Vien Thuc shows visitors around with a mixture of pride "I work very hard" and self-deprecating modesty, chuckling to himself as if to say, "I must be mad". His work is widely known: he has exhibited in Paris, New York and Holland as well as on the web. His paintings and books of poetry are for sale at prices that are creeping up to levels high enough for you to wish you could buy shares in him.

The main sanctuary of the pagoda was built in 1961 and contains an image of the Buddha with an electric halo. Nowadays, the gates are often locked; he is unwelcoming to Vietnamese and has been known to turn certain nationalities away.

Hang Nga Crazy House
ⓘ *3 Huynh Thuc Khang, T63-382 2070, daily 0700-1800, 8000d.*

The slightly wacky theme is maintained at the nearby Tree House leading many to wonder what they put in the water for this corner of Dalat to nurture so many creative eccentrics. Doctor Dang Viet Nga has, over a period of many years, built up her hotel in organic fashion. The rooms and gardens resemble scenes taken from the pages of a fairy storybook. Guests sleep inside mushrooms, trees and giraffes and sip tea under giant cobwebs. There is a honeymoon room, an ant room and plenty more. It is not a particularly comfortable place to stay and the number of visitors limits privacy. (Dr Dang Viet Nga also built the Children's Centre at 38 Tran Phu Street.)

Dalat Market
ⓘ *At the end of Nguyen Thi Minh Khai St.*

Dalat Market (Cho Dalat) sells a dazzling array of exotic fruits and vegetables grown in the temperate climate of the area – plums, strawberries, carrots, potatoes, loganberries, artichokes, apples, onions and avocados. The forbidding appearance of the market is masked by the riot of colour of the flowers on sale, including gladioli, irises, roses, gerbera, chrysanthemums and marigolds. Sampling the immense variety of candied fruit here is the highlight of any visit to Dalat.

Linh Son Pagoda
ⓘ *120 Nguyen Van Troi St just up from the intersection with Phan Dinh Phung St.*

The Linh Son Pagoda, built in 1942, is kept in immaculate condition. Perched on a small hillock, two dragon balustrades front the sanctuary, themselves flanked by two ponds with miniature mountain scenes. To the right is a small, Dutch-looking pagoda tower. Behind is a school of Buddhist studies attended by dozens of young, grey-clad men and women.

Dalat University
ⓘ *1 Phu Dong Thien Vuong St.*

Out near the golf course, Dalat University was founded as a Roman Catholic University in 1957 and taken over by the government in 1975. It provides for thousands of students from central and southern Vietnam and sits in grounds with cherry trees. It is strong on English teaching and science and has links with the Nuclear Research Institute. Symbolic of the change in political fortunes, a huge red communist star atop the grey obelisk in the University's grounds actually conceals a crucifix.

Dalat Teacher Training College
① *Yersin St.*

Some of the finest buildings in town are educational. One of these is the Dalat Teacher Training College, the old Lycée Yersin. The long curved wall of the school can be seen from the outside. It ends in a blind tower the top of which can be seen from miles away. Sadly the college has neglected its architectural heritage and many of the buildings are abandoned and overgrown. Foreigners cannot walk into the grounds. The track that skirts around the side of the college has an interesting row of modest houses, perhaps originally for teachers.

Dalat Railway Station
① *20 m off Quang Trung St, T63-383 4409.*

Dalat station is the last in Vietnam to retain its original French art deco architecture; the coloured-glass windows remain intact. Its steep pitched roofs could handle the heaviest of alpine snowfalls for which, presumably, they were designed. The waiting room, formerly segregated by race, is in good condition.

The station was opened in 1938, five years after the completion of the rack-and-pinion track from Saigon, and was closed in 1964. Despite the fact it is virtually unused, the building is surprisingly well maintained and beds of geraniums flourish under the sun and the careful hand of an unseen gardener. In 1991, a 7-km stretch to the village of Trai Mat was reopened and every day a small Russian-built diesel car makes the journey (daily at 0800, 0930, 1100, 1400, 1530, US$5 return, 30 minutes), minimum six people. There is also an old steam engine, which is occasionally fired up, and a Renault diesel car.

Lam Dong Museum
① *4 Hung Vuong St, T63-382239, Tue-Sat 0730-1130, 1330-1630, 4000d.*

The museum contains extensive tribal artefacts from the local Lam Dong Province tribes as well as natural history exhibits and old photos from when Dalat was founded up to the modern day. Particularly interesting are the ancient Dong Son relics and artifacts from Funnan-era temples recently discovered in Cat Tien National Park. At the time of this writing the museum was temporarily housed in the palace above the museum. The museum below will reopen in 2011 with extensive renovations and new collections.

Thien Vuong Pagoda
① *4 km south of the centre of town, at the end of Khe Sanh St.*

Begun in the 1950s, this stark pagoda has recently been expanded and renovated. In the main sanctuary are three massive bronze-coloured, sandalwood standing figures with Sakyamuni, the historic Buddha, in the centre. The pagoda, though in no way artistically significant, is popular with local visitors and stalls nearby sell local jams, artichoke tea, cordials and dried mushrooms.

Hunting Lodge (Dinh 1)

Emperor Bao Dai also had a hunting lodge that used to be a museum. East of the town centre, Dinh 1 sported 1930s furniture, antique telephone switchboards, and although it was not sumptuous, nevertheless had a feel of authenticity. It has now closed and the talk is of it reopening as a casino.

Waterfalls

Cam Ly Waterfall ⓘ *2 km from the centre of town, T63-382 4145, daily 0700-1700, 6000d,* is the closest waterfall to Dalat town centre. It is pleasant enough but should be avoided during the dry season, as it is the overflow for the sewerage system in Dalat and smells vile. As if added in perverse humour, a new concert amphitheatre sprays fountains of putrid river water, timed to the performers' music. **Datanla Falls** ⓘ *along a track, 5 km out of town on Highway 20 towards HCMC, T63-383 1804, 0700-1700, 5000d,* the path leads steeply downwards into a forested ravine; it is an easy hike there, but tiring on the return journey. However, the **Alpine Coaster**, a toboggan on rails (T63-383 1804, 35,000d return), makes the journey faster and easier. The falls – really a cascade – are hardly spectacular, but few people come here except at weekends so it is usually peaceful.

    Prenn Falls ⓘ *12 km from Dalat, on the route to HCMC, next to the road, T63-353 0785, 0700-1700, 10,000d,* the falls were dedicated to Queen Sirikit of Thailand when she visited them in 1959. Though it underwent renovations a few years ago, the falls began to suffer pollution and degredation in 2010 because dredged silt from Xuan Huong lake in Dalat was being dumped at the source of the falls. The falls are not that good but there is a pleasant rope bridge that can be crossed and pleasant views of the surrounding area.

Dalat cable car (Cáp Treo)

ⓘ *It starts south of town off 3 April Rd, T63-383 7938, 35,000d single, 50,000d return, 0730-1700 and is widely popular with both locals and tourists.*

The journey from top to bottom takes about 15 minutes and leads to a Thien Vien Truc Lam Pagoda and Paradise Lake.

Lake of Sighs and Valley of Love

ⓘ *The Lake of Sighs is 5 km northeast of Dalat (5000d) and the Valley of Love is 5 km due north (6000d). Because of the cool climate, it is very pleasant to reach the lakes, forests and waterfalls around Dalat by bicycle. In fact a day spent travelling is probably more enjoyable than the sights themselves.*

The lake is said by some to be named after the sighs of the girls being courted by handsome young men from the military academy in Dalat. Another unlikely theory is that the name was coined after a young Vietnamese maiden, Mai Nuong, drowned herself in the lake in the 18th century. The story is that her lover, Hoang Tung, had joined the army to fight the Chinese who were mounting one of their periodic invasions of the country, and had thoughtlessly failed to tell her. Devastated, and thinking that Hoang Tung no longer loved her; she committed suicide in the lake. Not long ago the lake was surrounded by thick forest; today it is a thin wood. The area is busy at weekends.

    The Valley of Love does not refer to a Jimi Hendrix or other psychedelic-era song but to **Thung Lung Tinh Yeu** ⓘ *8000d or free if you take a path to the side.* Boats can be hired on the lake here; there is also horse riding and a few refreshment stands.

Trai Mat

ⓘ *7 km from the centre of Dalat. By motorbike, follow Tran Hung Dao St which becomes Hung Vuong St, past SOS Village on the left, and keep going. Every day a small Russian-built diesel railway car makes the return journey (US$5 return, 30 mins) at 0800, 0930, 1100, 1400, 1530.*

Trai Mat Village is home to the local Coho tribe and can be reached by train from Dalat. In 1991 a 7-km stretch of track from Dalat railway station to the village of Trai Mat was reopened after nearly 20 years of closure. The journey to Trai Mat village takes you near the Lake of Sighs and past immaculately tended vegetable gardens; no space on the valley floors or sides is wasted and the high-intensity agriculture is a marvellous sight. Trai Mat is a prosperous market village with piles of produce from the surrounding area. Walk 300m up the road and to the left a narrow lane leads down to Chua Linh Phuoc, an attractive Buddhist temple more than 50 years old. It is notable for its huge Buddha and mosaic-adorned pillars. The mosaics are made of broken rice bowls and fragments of beer bottle. Just outside of Trai Mat is the flower garden of professor Jan Sook Kim, who is a world-renowned expert on the cultivation and growing of orchids.

Lang Ga (Chicken Village)

ⓘ *Just off the Dalat–HCMC road, 18 km from Dalat, Highway 20.*

This is a pleasant village of the Coho tribe of which the most noticeable sight is a 5-m-high concrete chicken in the middle of the village. There are numerous different stories as to why it was built with the more popular one being that it was constructed in honour of a local village wench who was tragically killed while searching for a nine-clawed chicken in the surrounding mountains to give to her fiancé for an engagement present. The local officials at the end of the war asked the inhabitants what they would like and were asked for the concrete chicken. The other version of the story of its origin is that it was built to commemorate the heroic peasant chicken farmers.

There are several weaving shops in the village that provide good-quality products at a fraction of what they would cost in Dalat or Ho Chi Minh City. Do stop and talk to the women who do the weaving; some of them speak excellent English learnt from visitors. They will show you the black bridal shawl with a red stripe (black for the wedding and red for good luck).

Lat village and Langbian Mountain

ⓘ *You pass through the Lat village to reach Langbian Mountain. The main gate is normally open 0800-1700, 7000d.*

The village itself is a mixture of old and new – there are traditional wooden stilt houses that are opposite new two- to three-storey houses. The village itself has to a large degree lost its traditional ways (there was a charming tradition in which the local Lat teenagers would bathe in the local rivers au natural. This was practised until the mid-1990s when the voyeuristic Vietnamese put a stop to it).

Langbian Mountain itself is the highest mountain in southern Vietnam at just over 2000 m. It housed an American radar listening post during the war. Nowadays it is visited primarily for its stunning vistas of the surrounding areas and also for its abundant wildlife, in particular birds. It is a trek to get to the top and sensible walking shoes would be appropriate.

For the first 20 km out of Dalat on Highway 20 to Ho Chi Minh City the land is forested. But as the road descends on to the Bao Loc Plateau the forest is replaced by tea plantations and fruit orchards. Many of the farmers on the plateau settled here after fleeing from the north following partition in 1954. At the centre of the plateau is the town of Bao (180 km from Ho Chi Minh City, 120 km from Dalat). About 20 km north of Bao Loc are the **Dambri Falls** ① *Jul-Nov only*, considered the most impressive in southern Vietnam and worth an excursion for those who have time. To get there take *xe ôm* from Bao.

Nam Cat Tien National Park
① *50,000d. Guides can be hired and accommodation is available. Take tough, long-sleeved and long-legged clothing, jungle boots and leech socks if possible and plenty of insect repellent.* This newly created national park is about 150 km north of Ho Chi Minh City en route for Dalat. About 50 km south of Bao Loc (at the small town of Tan Phu) turn off Highway 20 to Nam Cat Tien, which is about 25 km down a rough road (not well signposted). The park is one of the last surviving areas of natural bamboo and dipterocarp forest in southern Vietnam. It is also one of the few places where populations of large mammals can be found in Vietnam – tiger, elephant, bear and the last few (possibly only four or five) remaining Javan rhino (see page 477). There are also 300 species of bird, smaller mammals, reptiles and butterflies. The park is managed by 20 rangers who besides helping protect the flora and fauna also conduct research and show visitors around. They do not speak English.

South to Ho Chi Minh City
Beyond Nam Cat Tien, Highway 20 works its way down from the plateau through scrub bamboo forest towards the rolling landscape around Ho Chi Minh City, heavily cultivated with rubber and fruit trees. About 30 km before Highway 20 joins Highway 1 the road crosses **Tri An Lake**. Fishermen live in floating houses on the lake; besides fishing in conventional ways they also keep fish in cages under their houses. The road between Dalat and Ho Chi Minh City is good. At the important industrial centre of Bien Hoa, 26 km northeast of Ho Chi Minh City, a road runs south to the resort town of Vung Tau, see page 291.

Dalat to Buon Ma Thuot

Southwest of Dalat at Nam Ban is **Thac Voi** (Elephant waterfall), an impressive fall that you can clamber close to; up and down rocks to an outdoor 'shower'. Driving northwest to Buon Ma Thuot you will pass acres and acres of land that has been burned for the growing of new crops, casting an enormous scar on the landscape. Although this is illegal it is out of control in this part of the southern Central Highlands. From Lak Lake, south of Buon Ma Thuot, towards the city there is not one hill or slope untouched by deforestation; the odd tree and a couple of stumps remain.

Buon Ma Thuot → *For listings, see pages 252-264.*

Buon Ma Thuot is the provincial capital of Daklak Province. The city has changed from being a sleepy backwater town (similar to Kontum) to a thriving modern city within the last 15 years. Buon Ma Thuot has now surpassed its illustrious and renowned neighbour of Dalat to be the main centre for tea and coffee production, and the area has become the second largest producer of coffee in the world. The creation of the Trung Nguyen coffee empire in 1997 and the subsequent franchise of the names have meant that Trung Nguyen coffee shops are to be found everywhere in Vietnam (from the smallest communes to all the main cities). This has led to an unprecedented level of domestic coffee consumption. With the revenues that they have received it is pleasant to see that the money has to a great part been reinvested in the community (there are new schools, roads, hospitals

Buon Ma Thuot

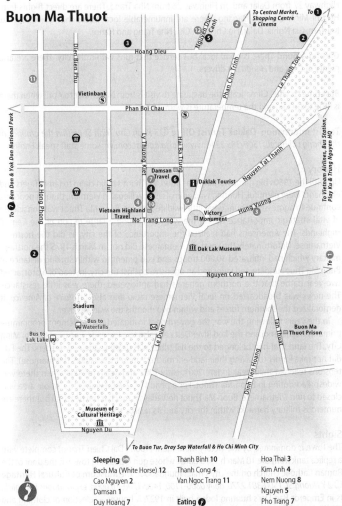

To Central Market, Shopping Centre & Cinema

To ①

To ②

To Ban Don & Yok Don National Park

To ⑦

To ①

To Vietnam Airlines, Bus Station, Play Ku & Trung Nguyen HQ

To Buon Tur, Dray Sap Waterfall & Ho Chi Minh City

Sleeping
Bach Ma (White Horse) **12**
Cao Nguyen **2**
Damsan **1**
Duy Hoang **7**
Gia Din Guesthouse **3**
Thang Loi **9**

Thanh Binh **10**
Thanh Cong **4**
Van Ngoc Trang **11**

Eating
Banh Mi Hanoi **2**
Bon Trieu **6**

Hoa Thai **3**
Kim Anh **4**
Nem Nuong **8**
Nguyen **5**
Pho Trang **7**
Polang Café **1**

N

100 metres
100 yards

aplenty). There is also a sports complex to rival any to be found in Ho Chi Minh City or Hanoi. Although it is a sprawling modern city, the heart of the city is located on the four streets that radiate out from the Thang Loi Hotel.

Ins and outs

Getting there Buon Ma Thuot is located on Highway 14 and can also be reached by Highway 27 from Dalat and on Highway 26 from Nha Trang. There are direct flights from Ho Chi Minh City and Danang. There are innumerable local buses that go to Play Ku, Kontum, Gia Nghia, Dalat, Ho Chi Minh City, Nha Trang and Hanoi.

Getting around There is good local bus service that runs within the city. There are also plenty of taxis and *Honda ôm* drivers.

Best time to visit Climatically the best time to visit is from November to April when there is little to no rain and the temperature is warm to hot.

Tourist information **Daklak Tourist Office** ⓘ *3 Phan Chu Trinh St (within the grounds of the Thang Loi Hotel), T500-385 2246, www.daklaktourist.com.vn; some staff speak English.*

History

Up until the 1950s big game hunting was Buon Ma Thuot's main claim to fame. Tigers and elephants were plentiful. Hunting wild animals is now illegal in Vietnam, though poachers continue to aggressively hunt what little wildlife remains. Buon Ma Thuot was considered of vital strategic importance during the war, dominating a large region of the Central Highlands. The Americans had realized the importance of the city, as did the northern Vietnamese. Unfortunately the southern Vietnamese did not. In March 1975 the northern military which had infiltrated 30,000 troops and equipment to within striking distance of Buon Ma Thuot undetected launched an offensive against the city. Instead of a protracted two-year battle that the northern generals had anticipated, there was little resistance. The news was broadcasted on local Vietnamese radio and also on *Voice of America*. It demoralized the southern forces and within two months the war was over.

In the years following the war, the government instigated a resettlement programme primarily from Hanoi and the Red River Delta but also to a lesser degree from Ho Chi Minh City. The land that had belonged to the hill tribes was given to the new settlers. The Ede did not take kindly to having their land encroached upon by outsiders (Vietnamese). The tensions reached their peak in late 2001, early 2002 and again in 2004 when there was widespread rioting in Buon Ma Thuot. For a period of several weeks the whole area was closed to non-Vietnamese. Buon Ma Thuot nowadays is much more peaceful but there are numerous military barracks within the city and its nearby suburbs.

Sights

The town is dominated by the Victory Monument (Tuong Dai Chien Thang) complete with a replica tank from the 10 March 1975 battle whose gun is pointing towards the door of the Roman Catholic church on the city's main roundabout. The **Museum of Cultural Heritage** ⓘ *2 Y Ngong St, T500-381 2770, daily 0800-1100, 1400-1700, 10,000d; explanations in English,* is in Emperor Bao Dai's hunting lodge built in 1927. It houses a selection of clothing and artefacts from some of the hill tribes, an Ede longhouse model, an Ede seat, rice and wine jars. There is a map showing Daklak Province onto which many of the ethnic minority villages are marked. There's also a photo of the Ban Don elephant race. A new museum complex is under construction and should be open by the time you read this.

The **Dak Lak Museum** ① *1 Le Duan St, T500-381 2770, Mon-Fri 0800-1100, 1400-1700, entry included with entrance to the Museum of Cultural Heritage*, is a dull museum recording revolution acts and the first battle between the north and south on the 10 March 1975.

At **Buon Ma Thuot prison** ① *18 Tan Thuat St, daily 0730-1700, free; no signs in English*, you can visit guardrooms, watchtowers and tiny cells that housed revolutionary prisoners from the 1930s to the 1970s; the whole complex has been completely renovated. The governor's former residence now houses a small museum containing photos of prison life and also some of the more illustrious prisoners and items that were used to hide secret information.

Not really a sight, but if you are passing, you should stop by the headquarters of the **Trung Nguyen coffee empire** ① *268 Nguyen Tat Thanh St, www.trungnguyen.com.vn*, and pop your head around the door to see what money buys in terms of interior decor. Coffee can be bought at a kiosk next to the main entrance.

Around Buon Ma Thuot → *For listings, see pages 252-264.*

Dray Sap, Dray Nur and Gia Long waterfalls
① *20 km south of Buon Ma Thuot, 2 km off Highway 14 heading in the direction of HCMC, T500-385 0123, daily 0700-1700, 8000d for Dray Sap and Dray Nur, 6000d for Gia Long.*
The best view of Gia Long is from the north side but you can't cross from the south to view it. In the wet season it may occasionally be closed, as the paths are too treacherous to use. There are two paths to take, one down by the river and the other on the high ground. The waterfalls consist of several different waterfalls all next to each other. They form a 100-m wide cascade and are particularly stunning in the wet season and justify the name of 'waterfall of smoke', although Dray Nur and Dray Sap are impressive even in the dry season. There's a café, and toilets at the entrance on the public bus side at Dray Nur and Dray Sap. These waterfalls originate from the Cu Yang Sin Mountain. The Krong Ana and the Krong No merge to form the Serepok River.

At the entrance to Dray Sap you will see an Ede ceremonial structure and staircase. The staircase is the female visitors' entrance also used by male guests from other families. The length of wood must have an odd number of steps carved on it as these are lucky numbers. The two breasts at the top of the ladder indicate a matrilineal society; the young moon shape indicates growth in the future. The ceremonial structure consists of a bronze pot at the base (a precious object belonging to the family) topped by a bird's head (a symbol of the Ede); on top of the bird's head is a canoe symbolizing the community's way of life. A jar of rice wine indicating wealth stands on the canoe; above that flames and a stove are carved into the wood to indicate the cooking area and food.

The serene **Lak Lake** is about 50 km southeast of Buon Ma Thuot. Take Highway 27 (the Dalat road) turn right down a track just before a sign advising 'Dalat 156 km'. It is an attraction in its own right but all the more compelling a visit on account of the surrounding **Mnong villages**. Early-morning mists hang above the calm waters and mingle with the columns of woodsmoke rising from the longhouses. The M'nong Rlam at Buon Jun have been influenced by the Ede and so live in longhouses. However, most M'nong such as M'nong Chil, Noong, Gar and Bu-dang live in straw and mud- or wood-thatched homes. The lake can be explored by dugout. The canoes are painstakingly hollowed out from tree trunks by axe. The M'nong have been famed as elephant catchers for hundreds of years, although the elephants are now used for tourist rides rather than in their traditional role for dragging logs from the forest. It is possible to stay overnight at a M'nong village, **Buon Jun** (Buon means village), indeed it is the only way to watch the elephants taking their evening wallow in the cool waters and to appreciate the tranquility of sunrise over the lake. The M'nong number about 50,000 and are matriarchal. An evening supping with your hosts, sharing rice wine and sleeping in the simplicity of a M'nong longhouse is an ideal introduction to these genial people. Between 1600 and 1730 every evening you can watch the men bring back the fish of the day to the lakeshore; the children are eager to help on the shore, buffalos are bathing and pigs are snorting around in the vegetation. Sup a beer at one of the cafés along the lake front as the sun sets. ▸▸ *For staying in a longhouse see Sleeping, Around Buon Ma Thuot, page 255.*

Unfortunately, Lak Lake has been developed as a tourist attraction and Buon Jun is rather touristy now. For those going on a tour there is little choice as to where to go, but for the independent traveller on a motorbike there are plenty of villages, both ethnic Vietnamese and minority, to visit, but do not expect any English to be spoken.

Yet another of Bao Dai's hunting lodges overlooks the lake about 3 km from Buon Jun. Whatever his other faults, the last emperor was blessed with a good eye for location. The building looks nothing like a palace now, having long ago been stripped of the precious woods with which it was panelled. A quick climb to the top of the stairs inside, however, brings its reward in the form of superb views of the lake and surrounding plateau.

The best Ede village to visit is **Buon Tur**. Apart from the odd TV aerial, life has remained unchanged in this community of 20 stilt houses and, despite the efforts of the government to stop it, Ede is still taught in school. Visitors used to be able to stay overnight in the village, but the local police have put a stop to this practice. This is for our own safety, they explain, "because the doors on Ede houses have no locks," but failing to mention the underlying political tension in the region.

Ban Don

Ban Don is the village at the centre of tourist operations in the area and is very touristy now. It is 7 km from the Yok Don National Park entrance, see below, and 43 km from Buon Ma Thuot. The locals speak Ede, Mnong and Laotian. Until 1992, when elephant catching was outlawed and the national park was set up, there used to be some 400 elephant catchers in the surrounding area. There's a restaurant at the entrance to the village, dozens of stalls selling tack and a bamboo bridge crossing (6000d) to an island where an unfortunate set of animals are (illegally) kept in far-too-small cages.

There is an old house (Nha San Co), built in 1883, that is lined with interesting elephant-catching equipment, for example a lasso and rope made from buffalo hide. There's also a bottle of rice wine with a deer foetus costing US$238. It was the home of N'thu Knul, the first elephant catcher in the village. In 1861 he caught a white elephant and presented it to the King of Thailand who renamed him Khun Junop – hero of the elephant king.

If you are lucky you may be able to visit the house of Ama Cong who has long lived between Ban Don and the national park. Ninety-something-year old Ama Cong is the last Mnong wild elephant catcher and is the nephew of N'thu Knul. He learnt to catch elephants from the age of 14. In 1938 he caught two tiger cubs and sold them for two dong to Emperor Bao Dai who kept them at his villa in Buon Ma Thuot. A surprisingly tall man, he lives with his fourth wife and 10-year-old daughter. From an early age, Ama Cong combined the leaf of the trong tree with brown sweet rice wine to create a very potent potion that is used to treat insomnia, loss of appetite and male virility. Ama Cong wine is, of course, heartily drunk by the local men and all visitors; it is, without doubt, absolutely lethal!

Near the village is the cemetery with the fascinating and highly unusual tombs of elephant catchers. Many are decorated with elephant tusk sculptures. A large tomb with Laotian influence is, in fact, the grave of a M'nong Bu-dang. See Tour operators, page 262, for companies that offer elephant trekking and trekking outside the national park.

Yok Don National Park

ⓘ *Yok Don National Park, Buon Don District, T500-378 3049, yokdonecotourism@vnn.vn. Tour guide section Mr Hung T090-519 7501 (mob), daily 0700-2200. Tours range from elephant riding (US$40 for 2 hrs) to elephant trekking (US$190 for 2 people for 3 days) to animal spotting by night (US$70), to riverboat rides (US$20 for 1 hr) to trekking (US$15 for 3 hrs). There is an additional entry fee to the park, for under US$1. Accommodation is available (see Sleeping, page 256).*

A 115,545-ha wildlife reserve about 40 km northwest of Buon Ma Thuot, Yok Don National Park (Vuon Quoc Gia Yok Don) contains at least 63 species of mammals, 17 of which are on the worldwide endangered list, and 250 species of bird, and is thought to be the home of several rare white elephants. There are known to be around 50 Asian elephants, 10 tigers, Samba deer, giant muntjac, leopard, the recently discovered golden jackal and green peafowl. The park is surprisingly flat – save Yok Don Mountain in the middle at 482 m and Yok Da Mountain (482 m) further north – and is, surprisingly, a less-than-dense deciduous forest which makes it easy to trek on an elephant though few wild animals congregate where elephant treks occur. There are 120 species of tree and 854 species of flora. Within its boundaries, also, there are 25 villages of different ethnic tribes who maintain a number of domesticated elephants. Trekking deep into the park and staying in tents near Yok Don Mountain is probably the only chance of seeing wildlife of any great rarity but, alas, the rare become rarer with each passing year. The less adventurous (or those with smaller elephant-trekking budgets) will have to make do with one-hour rides or simply watching one of the village's elephants at work. Note that the rainy season is from April to October.

Play Ku (Pleiku) → *For listings, see pages 252-264.*

Play Ku is the provincial capital of Gia Lai Province. It is located in a valley at the bottom of a local mountain, Ham Rong, that is clear from 12 km away. It is a modern, thriving, bustling town. The area around Play Ku is more cultivated than that of Kontum. Rubber, pepper, coffee and tea plantations abound and rice and watermelon are grown. The city itself is sprawling although there are six main streets on which you'll find all that you will need in terms of restaurants, shops, internet cafés and hotels. There was fierce fighting here during the American War. According to government statistics which are not always accurate, there are some 300,000 Gia-rai and some 150,000 Ba-na living in the province.

Ins and outs

Getting there Play Ku is just off Highway 14 and is 197 km from Buon Ma Thuot. It has a modern domestic airport that is 10 minutes' drive from the city centre with direct flights from Danang and Ho Chi Minh City. Plenty of local buses plough the routes to Kontum, Buon Ma Thuot and Tuy Hoa. There are also local buses to Ho Chi Minh City and to Hanoi.

Getting around Starting from **Laly Hotel** most of the city and sights are within walking distance. There are a few taxis available, a local bus service that will take you within the city and surrounding environs and *Honda ôm* drivers are plentiful.

Best time to visit Climatically the best time to visit is from November to April. It is warm with little to no rain.

Tourist information **Gia Lai Tourist** ① *215 Hung Vuong St (on the ground floor of the Hung Vuong Hotel), T59-387 4571, www.gialaitourist.com, daily 0730-1100, 1330-1630.* Ms Nga in the office speaks good English and is helpful and knowledgeable as is Mr Hai, the managing director. There has been much criticism of the company's exclusive control of the visits to ethnic minorities. Mr Hai explains that the money that tourists pay is divided between the village fund, the chief of the village, the owners of the house visitors stay in, Gia Lai Tourist and government tax. Foreigners are otherwise not permitted to travel independently outside the city and major highways in Gia Lai.

History

The town, with a population of 187,000, is located high on the Play Ku Plateau, one of many such structural features in the Central Highlands. It is the capital of Gia Lai Province which, with a population density of just 34 people per sq km, is one of the most sparsely inhabited areas of Vietnam. Historically, this was a densely forested part of the country and it remains home to a large number of ethnic minorities. Play Ku was the headquarters to two Corps, one of the four military tactical zones into which South Vietnam was divided during the war. John Vann (see Neil Sheehan's *Bright Shining Lie*) controlled massive B-52 bombing raids against the encroaching NVA from here until his death in a helicopter crash in June 1972. After the American departure in 1973, the South Vietnamese heavily fortified the town. The encroaching NVA decided to strike Buon Ma Thuot instead and soon controlled most of the highland region. President Thieu ordered his troops to withdraw and in doing so they torched Play Ku. This is the main reason there are very few old buildings here.

Sights

The town itself has little to offer the tourist; during the monsoon the side streets turn into muddy torrents and chill damp pervades guesthouse rooms. The **Gia Lai Provincial**

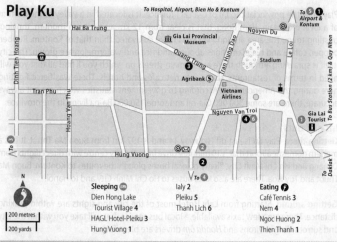

Play Ku

Sleeping 🛏
Dien Hong Lake
Tourist Village 4
HAGL Hotel-Pleiku 5
Hung Vuong 1

Ialy 2
Pleiku 5
Thanh Lich 6

Eating 🍴
Café Tennis 3
Nem 4
Ngoc Huong 2
Thien Thanh 1

200 metres
200 yards

Museum ⓘ *28 Quang Trung St, T59-382 4520, Mon-Fri 0730-1100, 1330-1630, 10,000d, Vietnamese signs only*, houses artefacts from the local minorities and from the war.

There are a number of places to visit on the Kontum road (hire a car or *Honda ôm*) **Bien Ho**, 5 km north of Play Ku, is a large **volcanic lake** and the main source of water for Play Ku, so no fishing or swimming. A raised platform on a promontory jutting out into the lake is a good place from which to appreciate the beauty and peace of the setting.

About 2 km further is the turn left to the once-spectacular **Yaly Falls**. Now that there is a hydroelectric plant to which the water is diverted there is not much to see, but along the road are several **Gia-rai villages** that are worth a visit, but a guide and permit is required and Gia Lai Tourist will only permit a visit to Plei Fun. **Plei Fun** is about 37 km along the Yaly road; around 16 km out of Play Ku you will pass a very colourful pink-patterned Rong house on the left-hand side. In the graveyard, tiled or wooden roofs which shelter the worldly possessions of the deceased – bottles, bowls, even the odd bicycle, cover the graves. Carved hardwood statues guard the graves, a peculiarly Gia-rai tradition. These are part of the grave abandonment ceremony and the statues represent minority life. Saplings are planted around the grave and will eventually grow to cover them. Until five year's ago the Gia-rai would reopen coffins to place their newly dead in them but the government forbade the practice on hygiene grounds. In 2010 there was a spectacularly coloured grave topped with carved metal figures and surrounded by numerous statues.

Trips to the Ba-na villages of **Dektu**, **Deron**, **DeDoa** and **Dekop**, 35 km east of Play Ku, can be arranged. At Dektu the government built a well next to the *rong* house (traditional communal lodge) but the Ba-na believe the water here is artificial and so have covered the well up. The jar on the pedestal in front of the *rong* represents the running water from the stream (ie real water). Inside the *rong* you will see drums, rice jars and truncated parts of buffalo that are sacrificed at harvest time. Here the graves are modern metal ones.

Tours for war veterans and those interested in war history can be arranged around Play Ku. Sites include Camp Enari, the former headquarters of 4th US infantry division, Hanzel Airstrip on Dragon Mountain, Camp Pleine, the base of US Special Services, the Catecka Teal Plantation, a US operational area, the 1st Cavalry Division base on Honcong Mountain, the Phoenix Airstrip near Dak To, the Airbase of 4th division at An Khe and Radcliff, the 1st Cavalry division base.

It is possible to reach Cambodia via the international border crossing at Le Thanh. Cámbodian visas should be available on arrival although it is safer to arrange a visa in Ho Chi Minh City or Hanoi. ▶▶ *See Transport, page 262.*

Kontum → *For listings, see pages 252-264.*

Kontum, although being one of the larger provinces within Vietnam, is the least populated and one of the poorest. It was created in 1991 when it was decided to break up Gia Lai Province. The town is 49 km north of Play Ku with a population of 36,000, many of whom are from ethnic minorities.

The town itself is a small, sleepy market town and in itself is not remarkable except that it houses the **Wooden Church**, **Tan Huong Church** and the **Bishop's Seminary**. These alone are worth a trip to Kontum.

Ins and outs

Getting there Kontum is situated just off Highway 14 and is 44 km north of Play Ku. There are numerous local buses that plough the route from Play Ku and to a lesser degree from

Buon Ma Thuot and Quy Nhon. Kontum does not have an airport but shares the airport with Play Ku, an hour's drive away. Twelve kilometres south of Kontum the road crosses the **Chu Pao Pass**. There is nothing to see in particular, but commanding views over the Kontum Plateau. The road descends past sugar cane plantations before crossing the Dakbla River. It is also possible to get to Kontum from Laos at the Bo-Y border crossing.

Getting around Starting from **Dakbla Hotel 1** most of the city and sights are within walking distance. There are a few taxis available and also a few *Honda ôm* drivers. It is possible to rent cars and bikes from the tourist office.

Best time to visit Climatically the best time to visit is from November to April. It is warm with little to no rain. The main festival is on 14 November to celebrate the life of Bishop Cuenot.

Tourist information **Kontum Tourist Office** ① *2 Phan Dinh Phung St (ground floor of the Dakbla Hotel 1), T60-386 1626, www.kontumtourism.com, daily 0700-1100, 1300-1700*. The staff are very knowledgeable.

History

The French Bishop Stephen Theodore Cuenot founded Kontum in the mid-1800s. He was a missionary priest endeavouring to convert the local tribes to Christianity. He succeeded, as many of the inhabitants are Christian. He was arrested on Emperor Tu Duc's orders (the Emperor did not like missionaries) and died in Binh Dinh prison on 14 November 1861, a day before the beheading instructions arrived. He was beatified Saint Etienne-Theodore Cuenot in 1909. His wooden church remain almost unchanged since that time.

In more recent years the area was the scene of some of the fiercest fighting during the American war.

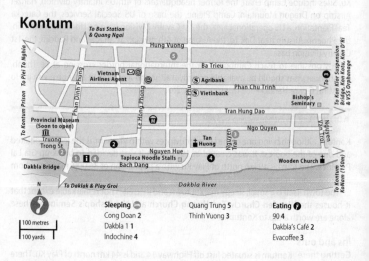

Kontum

To Bus Station & Quang Ngai

Hung Vuong 5

Ba Trieu

Phan Chu Trinh

Agribank

Vietinbank

Vietnam Airlines Agent

Phan Dinh Phung

To Plei Tha

To Kontum Prison   To Plei Nghia

Le Hong Phong

Tran Phu

Bishop's Seminary

To Kon Klor Suspension Bridge, Kon Kotu, Kon D'Ri & VSS Orphenage

Tran Hung Dao

Provincial Museum (Soon to open)

Truong Trong St

Ngo Quyen

Tan Huong

Nguyen Trai

Van Troi

Nguyen Hue

Tapioca Noodle Stalls

Bach Dang

Wooden Church

Dakbla Bridge

To Daklak & Play Groi

Dakbla River

To Kontum KoNam (150m)

N

100 metres
100 yards

Sleeping 🛏		Eating 🍴
Cong Doan **2**	Quang Trung **5**	90 **4**
Dakbla 1 **1**	Thinh Vuong **3**	Dakbla's Café **2**
Indochine **4**		Evacoffee **3**

Sights

The main sights within Kontum are the Wooden Church, Tan Huong Church, the Bishop's Seminary, a soon-to-open provinicial museum on the riverfront, surrounding Ba-na villages, and Kontum prison. **Tan Huong Church** ① *92 Nguyen Hué St (if the church is shut ask in the office adjacent and they will gladly open it).* The whitewashed façade bears an interesting depiction of St George and the dragon. It is not immediately evident that the church is built on stilts, but crouch down and look under one of the little arches that run along the side and the stilts, joists and floorboards are clear. The glass in the windows is all old, as the rippling indicates, although one of the two stained-glass windows over the altar has required a little patching up. Unfortunately the roof is a modern replacement, but the original style of fishscale tiling can still be seen in the tower. The interior of the church is exquisite, with dark wooden columns and a fine vaulted ceiling made of wattle and daub. The altar is a new, but rather fine addition, made of a jackfruit tree, as is the lectern. The original building was erected in 1853 and then rebuilt in 1860 following a fire. The current church dates from 1906.

Further east on the same street is the superb **Wooden Church**. Built by the French with Ba-na labour in 1913, it remains largely unaltered, with the original wooden frame and wooden doors. Unfortunately the windows are modern tinted-glass and the paintings on them depicting scenes from Christ's life as well as a couple of Old Testament scenes with Moses are a little crude. In the grounds stands a statue of Stephen Theodore Cuenot, the first Roman Catholic bishop of East Cochin China diocese. There is also an orphanage that is run by the church in the grounds that welcomes visitors.

The architecturally remarkable and prominent **Bishop's Seminary** is set in lovely gardens with pink and white frangipani trees. It was completed in 1935; the seminary was founded by French missionary Martial Jannin Phuoc. The upstairs **exhibition room** ① *Mon-Sat 0800-1130, by donation,* displays an eclectic collection of instruments, photos and scale models; some signs are in English.

Kontum prison ① *500 m along Truong Trong St, daily 0800-1100, 1400-1700, under US$1,* was built in 1915 and was home to several prominent revolutionaries. It was abandoned by the French in 1933 and later left to collapse. There is a small museum in some new buildings and a memorial depicting malnourished prisoners. The labels are in Vietnamese only.

There are scores of **Ba-na villages** around Kontum that can be reached by motorbike, and at least one that is easily accessible on foot. **Plei To Nghia** is at the westerly end of Phan Chu Trinh Street down a dusty track. Wattle and daub houses, mostly on stilts, can be seen and the long low white building on short stilts at the vilage entrance is the church. In the evening the elderly folk of the village go for communal prayers while the young people gather at the foot of their longhouses for a sunset chat. In and around the village are small fields heavily fortified with thorns and barbed wire, which seems a little strange considering the Ba-na do not lock their doors. In fact the defence is not against poachers but the village's large population of rooting, snuffling, pot-bellied pigs. Every family has a few pigs that roam loose. The pigs are sometimes given names and recognize the voice of their owner, coming when called.

Most houses are on stilts, with the animals living underneath. They are built from wattle and daub around a wooden frame, although brick is starting to appear as it is cheaper than declining wood resources, and modern tile is beginning to replace the lovely old fishscale tiling. Considering the tiny spaces in which most Vietnamese live, these houses are positively palatial. There is a large living room in the centre, a kitchen (with no chimney) at one end and bedroom at the other. **Kon D'Ri** (Kon Jori) is a fine example of a community almost untouched community almost untouched by modern life (apart from Celine Dion's voice competing with the cows and cockerels!). A perfect *rong* communal house dominates the hamlet, and all other dwellings in the village are made from bamboo, or mud and reeds. The Ba-na *rong* is instantly recognizable by its tall thatched roof. The height of the roof is meant to indicate the significance of the building and make it visible to all. It is a focal point of the village for meetings of the village elders, weddings and other communal events. The stilt house close by is in fact a small Roman Catholic church. Nearby **Kon Kotu** is similar. To get there follow Nguyen Hué Street and turn right into Tran Hung Dao Street, cross the suspension bridge (Kon Klor Bridge) over the Dakbla River (built in 1997 after a flood washed the old one away). After a few hundred metres turn left and continue for 3 km bearing left for Kon Kotu and right for Kon D'Ri. A private orphanage, simply titled "VS5 " is run in the area by Teresa Lung and her siblings, themselves orphans. Visitors are welcomed (contact lungdang2002@yahoo.com).

A more lively Ba-na community can be found at **Kontum KoNam** (turn right off Nguyen Hue past the wooden church). Here the stilt houses are crowded close together and the village bustles with activity.

Twenty kilometres from Kontum it's possible to visit the Gia-rai villages of Plei RoLay, Plei Bua and Plei Weh. Forty kilometres from Kontum you can visit Kon Biu, a Xo-dang village, 7 km further on is Kon Cheoleo, a Jolong village (there are only 15 known Jolong villages in Vietnam; their language is similar to Ba-na). The Xo-dang build the entrance to the *rong* on the east and west in harmony with the sun, unlike the Ba-na. The Xo-dang play the drums to ask for rain. It's also possible to visit Kon Hongor, a Ba-na Ro Ngao community (there are only 4000 Ro Ngao in Kontum Province).

The border crossing at **Bo-Y** is open to foreigners crossing into Laos. Lao visas should be available on arrival but it is safer to have obtained them beforehand.

Kontum to Hoi An

North of Dak To between Plei Kan and Dak Nay are Katu villages that speak a Mon-Khmer language. North of Dak Glei, you will pass through the most lush forests anywhere in Vietnam on the Lo-Xo Pass. Wild, dark green and luxuriant jungle tumbles down mountains carpeting the area in a thick, abundant forest. It is extremely beautiful and the height of the jungle-clad mountains are awe-inspiring. To the east of the road is the Ngoc Linh Nature Reserve and the towering Ngoc Linh peak at 2116 m. There is a riot of ferns, waterfalls and astoundingly beautiful scenery all around.

⊙ Dalat and the Central Highlands listings

For Sleeping and Eating price codes and other relevant information, see Essentials pages 26-31

● Sleeping

Dalat *p235, maps p234 and p236*
LL Ana Mandara Villas Dalat Resort & Spa, Le Lai St, T63-355 5888, www. anamandararesortdalat.com. This is a very special place and unique in Vietnam. The previous owners **Six Senses** restored 17

French hillside villas built in the 1920s and 1930s. Each of the villas has a couple of bedrooms, a living room and dining room; guests have dedicated butlers. The furnishings are reminiscent of Shaker-style furniture; the beds are heavenly; the baths are on feet. **Nine Restaurant & Bar** at Villa 9 has beautiful tilework and a large central fireplace. French-style shutters open on to a small terrace. The heated pool, buried amid the secluded hillside villas, is lovely; a night swim in the cool air is invigorating and at night the air is enveloped with the smell of pine. There's a luxurious spa on site and a city excursion in a 1930s Citroen is a must. **LL-L Sofitel Dalat Palace**, 12 Tran Phu St, T63-382 5444, www.sofitel.com/1744. This rambling old building, built in 1922 and restored to its former glory in 1995, is a wonderful hotel. Those that knew it before restoration will be amazed: the renovation is superb: curtains, furniture, statues, gilt mirrors and chandeliers adorn the rooms which are tastefully arranged as the French do best. The view over Xuan Huong Lake to the hills beyond is lovely and the extensive grounds of the hotel are beautifully laid out. One of the finest hotels in Vietnam with 43 rooms (opt for an enormous one with a balcony overlooking the lake), 3 restaurants and 3 bars. Service at the **Rabelais** restaurant is superb and for a true French colonial experience splurge on tea and cakes in the afternoons. The hotel offers guests special green fees on the nearby golf course; located in the eaves of the hotel, **L'Apothiquaire** spa offers a chocolate wrap, and there's a gym and tennis courts.

AL-C Hang Nga (Tree House), Huynh Thuc Khang St, T63-382 2070. If you fancy a fantasy night in a mushroom, a tree or a giraffe then this is the place for you. Prices have risen and the rooms tend to be ones visited by curious tourists and the furniture is sturdily made and not too comfortable.

A Mercure Dalat Hotel Du Parc (formerly **Novotel Dalat**), 7 Tran Phu St, T63-382 5777, www.mercure.com. The original hotel opened as the Hotel Du Parc in 1932 and was completely restored in 1995. It is opposite the post office and near the Sofitel with which it shares its management and many facilities. Rooms are nicely restored and comfortably furnished, now including complementary Wi-Fi. Meals are served at the atmospheric **Café de la Poste** across the street.

A Resort Hoang Anh Dalat, 3 Nguyen Du St, T63-381 0826. The huge rooms are arranged in villas with 10-14 rooms in each villa block. This is a large complex near the train station and so a little out of town although there is a courtesy bus available. A swimming pool is under construction.

A Saigon-Dalat Hotel, 2 Hoang Van Thu, T63-355 6789, www.saigondalathotel.com. The government-owned Saigon-Dalat is one of the largest in the city. The striking white exterior with bright orange, alpine-style roof is visible throughout western Dalat. The hotel has 2 restaurants and a bar, plus the **Moulin Rouge Restaurant** across the street.

C Empress Hotel, 5 Nguyen Thai Hoc St, T63-383 3888, empresdl@hcm.vnn.vn. This is a particularly attractive hotel in a lovely position overlooking the lake. All rooms are arranged around a small courtyard which traps the sun and is a great place for breakfast or to pen a postcard. The rooms are large with very comfortable beds and the more expensive ones have luxurious bathrooms – try and get a room upgrade. Attentive and courteous staff. A great value hotel and one with the best view of Xuan Huong Lake.

C Golf 3 Hotel, 4 Nguyen Thi Minh Khai St, T63-382 6042, golf3.dalat@vinagolf. vn. Smart, centrally located hotel with comfortable rooms; cheaper rooms have showers only. It has a good range of facilities – bar, restaurant, massage, nightclub and karaoke. The location by Dalat market is excellent. One drawback though is that because it is so near to the market the rooms facing the street are noisy. Breakfast is included.

D Golf 1, 11 Dinh Tien Hoang St, opposite the golf course, T63-382 4082, golf1.dalat@ vinagolf.vn. For a long time it was surpassed by **Golf 2** and **Golf 3** and was allowed to fall into a state of disrepair. Now, however, it is very popular and boasts 36 rooms. The staff are friendly and helpful and the service and facilities are good (massage and restaurant – popular with tourists and locals). Good value for money. As it is popular it is advisable to book in advance.

DMimosa, 170 Phan Dinh Phung St, T63-382 2656. A bit like all the other unremarkable **Dalat Tourist** hotels in this area, fairly central, but not terribly quiet at the front, with 30 clean rooms with soft beds that have showers, fridge and TV. The exterior needs considerable attention. Minimal English is spoken.

EAnh Dao, 50-52 Hoa Binh Sq, T63-382 3577. A small hotel with rooms which have en suite facilities, TV and phone. The rooms themselves are somewhat drab and the beds not too comfortable. The cheapest rooms have no windows; the better ones have city view and bathtubs in the bathrooms. The staff are friendly and helpful enough and some speak good English.

EDreams Hotel, 5 Hai Thuong St, T63-383 3748. Though 10 years old, this immaculate hotel looks brand new. The top floor has a jacuzzi, sauna and stream room, and there is free Wi-Fi throughout.

FDinh 2, 12 Tran Hung Dao St, T63-382 2092. Formerly the residence of the French Governor General set in lovely gardens dominated by pine trees and with fantastic views of the lake. There are 3 buildings with 22 rooms in all in a beautiful setting about 2 km from the centre. The spacious rooms with wooden floors, TV and fridge have fireplaces and large bathrooms with tubs. There's a restaurant on site.

FHoa Binh 1 (Peace Hotel 1), 64 Truong Cong Dinh St, T63-382 2787, peace12@hcm.vnn.vn. In a good location and one of the better low-cost places with 16 rooms including 5 at the back around a small yard, quiet but not much view. Rooms at the front have a view but can be a bit noisy. The rooms have TV, fan and mosquito nets. A friendly place with an all-day café.

FHoa Binh 2 (Peace Hotel 2), 67 Truong Cong Dinh St, T63-382 2982, peace12@hcm.vnn.vn. Diagonally opposite its sister hotel, this is rather an attractive 1930s building. It's clean and some rooms have small balconies.

F-GPhuong Hanh 1, 7/1 Hai Thuong St, T63-356 0528 and **Phuong Hanh 2**, 80-82, 3/2 St, T63-382 8213, phuonghanhhotel@gmail.com. There are a variety of sizes and prices among the clean rooms that have mosquito nets, fans, TV and fridge. The cheapest rooms don't have windows; those in the upper price bracket have bathrooms. You may want to avoid the main road rooms.

Nam Cat Tien National Park p242

EPark Guesthouse and Bungalows, T/F61-379 1228. The **Park** offers basic accommodation with fan and or a/c, cold showers and semi-operational TV. Wi-Fi may also be available. There is a very basic restaurant on site and several small restaurants outside the entrance that provide reasonable food and snacks.

Buon Ma Thuot p242, map p243

CBach Ma (White Horse Hotel), 7-11 Nguyen Duc Canh St, T500-381 5656,. Independently run hotel in a modern building. Rooms are spacious with desks and enormous cupboards; some bathrooms have tubs; some rooms do not have windows. For US$5 more you can get a room with a window and a sitting room. The staff are helpful and some have a good understanding of English.

CDamsan Hotel, 212-214 Nguyen Cong Tru St, T500-385 1234, www.damsanhotel.com.vn. A good hotel with a pool and tennis court and large restaurant. Service is good and rooms are comfortable. There's a lovely balconied coffee shop and bar, Da Quy, opposite.

ECao Nguyen Hotel, 65 Phan Chu Trinh St, T500-3851913. Modern hotel with a good range of facilities. There are 6 large suites that are well worth the additional US$5 surcharge. The staff are friendly and helpful and speak reasonable English. The restaurant is bigger than the one at the **Thang Loi Hotel** and provides a reasonable selection of food.

EThanh Cong Hotel, 51 Ly Thuong Kiet St, T500-385 8243, www.daklaktourist.com.vn. The more expensive rooms have a/c, TV, fridge and enjoy free coffee. Rooms are big and there's a very popular restaurant on site.

E Thang Loi Hotel, 1 Phan Chu Trinh St, T500-385 7615, www.daklaktourist.com.vn. Modern hotel in a prime location opposite the victory monument. The rooms are all large and come with en suite facilities. The more spacious rooms on the 2nd floor are equipped with a large bathroom with separate shower cubicle. The staff speak good English. The food is fresh, well presented, good value and plentiful. ATM on site.

F Duy Hoang Hotel, 30 Ly Thuong Kiet St, T500-385 8020. Spacious, well-furnished rooms with en suite facilities and a/c. Cheaper rooms have fan and shared bathrooms. Staff are efficient and friendly and have a reasonable grasp of English. Excellent value for money.

F Gia Dinh Guesthouse, 01 Hung Vuong St, Buon Ma Thuot. T500-812148, A quiet, family-run guesthouse with all the standard amenities like a/c, cable TV and hot water.

F Thanh Binh, 24 Ly Thuong Kiet St, T500-385 3812. Clean rooms with a/c, TV, and fridge; cheaper rooms may not have windows but have fan and TV; good value.

F Van Ngoc Trang, 269 Le Hong Phong St, T500-385 3945, khachsanvanngoctrang@yahoo.com. 5 rooms with fan and 9 with a/c that are newly built to a high standard. All rooms have hot water and bathtub, some have a/c. English is not spoken.

Around Buon Ma Thuot *p245*

C-D Bao Dai Villa, Lak Lake, T500-358 6184, www.daklaktourist.com.vn. Opt for the massive King's Room with portraits on the wall for a unique stay in the area. All 6 rooms have modern comforts and bathtubs. The villa is surrounded by beautiful magnolia trees. The restaurant features old black and white photos of the emperor and his elephant team.

D Lak Lake Resort, Lien Son village, near Buon Jun, Lak Lake, T500-358 6184, www.daklaktourist.com.vn. There are 32 rooms with balconies in a great position overlooking the lake. Rooms have TV, a/c and bathtubs. Breakfast is included. There's a branch of **Daklak Tourist** on site.

G Buon Jun longhouse, Buon Jun village, Lak Lake. Contact **Daklak Tourist** at the entrance to the village, T500-358 6184, laklake@daklaktourist.com.vn, for arrangements. It costs US$5 to stay in a longhouse excluding food (US$5 lunch; US$3 breakfast). Longhouses vary between traditional wooden ones to concrete ones. If you don't like creepy crawlies opt for the concrete ones. Those nearer the lake are noisier. The communal bathrooms in the village could be a lot cleaner.

G Lak Lake Resort Longhouse, in the grounds of the **Lak Lake Resort**, see above. This longhouse is specifically for guests. It is the same price as the village longhouses but the bathrooms are cleaner.

Ban Don *p246*

D-E Sinh Thai Tourism Facility, Krong Na Commune. Situated on the shores of a man-made lake, this is a good option with 11 a/c rooms and 10 fan rooms plus numerous longhouses. There's a restaurant on site and further developments are planned. It's very peaceful and lovely to watch the elephants bathing close to dusk but you'd need your own transport or ring for a pick up. Vietnamese guests receive big discounts.

E Biet Dien Hotel, in the centre of the village, T500-395 4299. Bungalows with private bathroom and longhouses with shared bathroom.

F Ban Don Tourist, Buon N'Rech, Ea Huar commune, Buon Don district, 1 km from the main road near the entrance to Yok Don National Park, T500-385 4903/091-343 5642 (mob), www.bandontour.com.vn. Thatched huts in gardens with en suite shower rooms with Western toilets. Mosquito nets provided. The restaurant serves good food, especially the fish and rice cooked in bamboo cane. Ama Cong is available.

Yok Don National Park *p247*

E Park Guesthouse, T500-378 3049, yokdonecotourism@vnn.vn. Park HQ has rooms with 2 beds, a/c, fan, hot showers, TV with minimal reception and Wi-Fi.

F Camping, available at US$7 per tent.

Play Ku (Pleiku) *p247, map p248*

C-D HAGL Hotel-Pleiku (Hoang Anh Gia Lai Hotel), 1 Phu Dong St, T59-371 8459, www.hagl.com.vn. This new hotel has 120 nicely furnished superior and deluxe rooms that are spacious with bathtubs in the bathrooms and fantastic views of the entire city. There is a Vietnamese and Western restaurant, massage centre, tennis court, gym and internet.

E Dien Hong Lake Tourist Village, Ho Dien Hong, T59-371 6450, dienhonglake@gialaitourist.com. 20 clean rooms with mosquito nets and bathtubs in bungalows set along an artificial stretch of water. Close by is an artificial lake with some under-utilized pedaloes and some caged animals. Vietnamese guests receive big discounts.

E Ialy Hotel, 89 Hung Vuong St, T59-382 4843, ialyhotel@dng.vnn.vn. Excellent location opposite the main post office. Rooms are a reasonable size with en suite facilities, coffee table and chairs, a/c, satellite TV. The staff are friendly enough. No English is spoken. Breakfast is included and there's an ATM in the lobby. Vietnamese guests receive a large discount.

E Pleiku Hotel, 124 Le Loi St, T59-382 4628, pleikuhotel@gialaitourist.com. Newly renovated, the rooms are modern and tastefully decorated with en suite facilities, satellite TV and a/c. The restaurant is basic by satisfactory. Some staff speak English.

F-G Hung Vuong Hotel, 215 Hung Vuong St, T59-382 4270, hungvuonghotel@gialaitourist.com. The rooms are tastefully decorated and have en suite facilities, satellite TV and a/c. The ground floor houses the Gia Lai tourist office.

G Thanh Lich Hotel, 86 Nguyen Van Troi St, T59-382 4674, thanhlichhotel@gialaitourist.

com. Surprisingly, the cheaper rooms are nicer than the more expensive ones, some of which smell. Don't get a room on the street, it's very, very noisy.

Kontum *p249, map p250*

C-D Indochine (Dong Duong) Hotel, 30 Bach Dang St, T60-386 3335, indochinevn@kontumtourism.com. The views from this new hotel are fantastic. You can look right up the river to the mountains beyond. Decent-sized rooms with mod-cons including hairdryer. A riverfront pool was due to open. The breakfasts could be better.

E Dakbla 1 Hotel, 2 Phan Dinh Phung St (it is the first building on the right as you cross the bridge into Kontum), T60-386 3333. Set amid attractive grounds, there is a small restaurant and jetty on the riverbank. Staff are friendly and helpful and have a basic understanding of English and French. The restaurant on the ground floor next to Kontum tourist office provides good food at a reasonable price. Carpeted rooms have minibars, satellite TV, a/c, hot water, and en suite bathrooms. Vietnamese guests stay half-price.

E Quang Trung Hotel, 168 Ba Trieu St, T60-386 2249. This Soviet-style hotel gives large discounts to Vietnamese customers. Some English is spoken.

E-F Thinh Vuong, 16B Nguyen Trai St, T60-391 4729. The more expensive bedrooms have living area, fridge, TV and bathtubs in the windowless bathrooms; the treadmill and internet are free. Cheaper rooms are quite spacious but the double beds are for 2 slim folk. Run by a friendly family.

F Cong Doan (Trade Union Hotel), 163 Nguyen Hue St, T60-391 1279. An extremely empty hotel, the top-floor rooms have a pleasant view of Dakbla River and the surrounding countryside and are equipped with a/c, satellite TV, hot water and en suite bathroom. The lower and cheaper rooms have a fan and en suite facilities. The staff do not speak any foreign languages but appear to understand English very well.

🍴 Eating

Dalat *p235, maps p234 and p236*
In the evening, street stalls line Nguyen Thi Minh Khai St, leading to Dalat market, which is itself the ideal place to buy picnic provisions. There are lakeside cafés and restaurants that may look attractive places to eat but they serve indifferent food.

♔♔♔ Le Rabelais, Sofitel Dalat Palace, 12 Tran Phu St, T63-382 5444. A superb dining room with views down to the lake. It serves French specialities with starters around US$12 and main courses US$25. The staff are attentive and knowledgeable. Excellent wine list. Please note that smart dress is required (if you turn up in shorts and a T-shirt you will be politely asked to reattire yourselves in more suitable clothing). Recommended.

♔♔♔ Nine Restaurant & Bar, at Villa 9, Ana Mandara Villas Dalat Resort & Spa, Le Lai St, T63-355 5888, www.anamandararesortdalat. com. Wonderfully hearty and also delicate food served up in the elegant dining room. Staff are very attentive. Recommended.

♔♔-♔ Le Café de la Poste, 12 Tran Phu St. Adjacent to the Sofitel and under the same management. International comfort food at near-Western prices in an airy and cool building. The 3-course lunch menu is great value. The staff look a little uncomfortable in French-style outfits. A pool table dominates the café. Upstairs is a Vietnamese restaurant.

♔♔-♔ Empress Restaurant, Empress Hotel, see Sleeping, above. Open all day specializing in Chinese fare but with a good selection of Vietnamese and Western food. Ideal breakfast setting as it is possible to have breakfast alfresco around the fountain in the courtyard of the hotel.

♔ Da Quy (Wild Sunflower), 49 Truong Cong Dinh St, T63-351 0883. This sweet little family-run business is very friendly and a delightful place to eat with maroon checked tablecloths and a tidy atmosphere. The menu is varied; try the sautéed beef and snow peas.

♔ Dong A Family Restaurant, 82 Phung St, T63-382 1033. Vegetarian, Vietnamese and Western dishes in this well-known place.

♔ Hoa Binh 1, 67 Truong Cong Dinh St. An all-day eatery serving standard backpacker fare – fried noodles, vegetarian dishes and pancakes at low prices.

♔ Long Hoa, 6 3 Thang 2, T63-382 2934. In the best traditions of French family restaurants, this place has delicious food with fish, meat and venison and super breakfasts. The chicken soup and beefsteak are recommended. Sample Madam's home-made strawberry wine; initially it tastes like sherry, later revealing a strawberry liqueur taste. Service is erratic; don't be surprised if your main course arrives with your starter. Fairly priced.

♔ Tau Cao, 217 Phung St, close to the Mimosa Hotel, T63-382 0104. This Chinese rice noodle restaurant serves up steaming soups with or without *wan tun*.

Cafés
Stop and Go Café, 2A Ly Tu Trong St, T63-382 8458. A café and art gallery run by the locally distinguished poet, Mr Duy Viet. Viet was born in the house, which fills with the early morning sunlight. Sit inside or on the terrace as he bustles around rustling up breakfast pulling out volumes of visitors' books and his own collected works. The garden is an attractively overrun wilderness.

Stalls
There are *pho* and *banh mi* (bread) stalls on Tang Bat Ho St in front of Phu Hoa Hotel. Noodle soup, filled baguettes and pastries available from early morning until late in this little side street.

Buon Ma Thuot *p242, map p243*
♔♔-♔ Thang Loi Restaurant, Thang Loi Hotel, 1 Phan Chu Trinh St. This is arguably the best restaurant in town. Set on the ground floor of the hotel it overlooks Liberty Sq. It has a good selection of Vietnamese and international cuisine (their chips are

particularly good) and plenty of noodle and rice dishes and fruit. Prices are reasonable and the service is friendly and efficient.

¶¶–¶ White Horse Restaurant, White Horse Hotel, 7-11 Nguyen Duc Canh St, T50-381 5656. It has a good selection of food to choose from but specializes in seafood. Reasonable prices, friendly and efficient service. Fans in the restaurant mean it is pleasantly cool.

¶ Bon Trieu, 33 Hai Ba Trung St, T50-385 2994. The steamed squid with ginger is very tasty but its beef in vinegar, cooked at the table, is even better.

¶ Hoa Thai, 70 Hoang Dieu St, T50-385 5456. Serves good Vietnamese and Chinese food. Service is friendly and it's good value. They have a basic understanding of English (when ordering your food your best bet is to pick and point). Menu is in Vietnamese with no prices.

¶ Kim Anh, 26 Ly Thuong Kiet, T50-385 9576. A *nem* shop selling delicious roll-your-own spring rolls.

¶ Nem Nuong Restaurants, east side of Ly Thuong Kiet St, between Quang Truong and No Trang Long streets. *Nem nuong* are roll-it-yourself fresh spring rolls with grilled meats. Inbetween the most popular budget accommodations in town are several eateries specializing in this must-try meal.

¶ Nguyen, Nguyen Duc Canh, diagonally opposite White Horse Hotel. 0630-0930 only. Clean and modern. Arguably the best *pho* in town (this is proven by how busy it is).

¶ Pho Trang, 138 Nguyen Thi Dinh St, T50-386 8282. Highway 14, 6.5 km from Buon Ma Thuot on the way to the waterfalls on the right-hand side with reddish-brown signage. A hearty filling *pho* is served.

Cafés

Buon Ma Thuot is one of the coffee capitals of the world, so there are lots of nice cafés with great coffee. Many are located west of Phan Chu Trinh Street in the neighborhoods around the Sports Center.

Banh Mi Hanoi, 123-125 Le Hong Phong St, T50-385 3609, and also 55 Le Thanh Ton St, T50-386 1888. Bakery selling a good selection of snacks, muffins, savoury croissants, sandwiches, drinks and chocolates all at reasonable prices. Friendly staff. A good place to stock up on picnic provisions.

Polang Café, G26 Tran Khanh Du St, T50-395 3322. This has a giant female Ede ladder leading up to its 2nd floor where you can drink coffee overlooking the street (*polang* means the flower of the kapok tree in Ede). They also have a refreshing range of fruit juices – strawberry and seaweed (!), tamarind juice – and a very palatable rum tea.

Around Buon Ma Thuot *p245*

¶ Lak Resort floating restaurant, Lien Son village, near Buon Jun, Lak Lake, T500-358 6184. This restaurant juts out into the lake and is a pleasant place for a meal and a few beers in the shade with a cooling breeze. The US$6 set menu with 6 or 7 dishes is good value and the food is good.

Play Ku (Pleiku) *p247, map p248*

¶ Nem, 64 Nguyen Van Troi St, T59-387 4352. This basic and very popular restaurant serves up heaps and heaps of wonderful do-it-yourself spring rolls. Roll to stuffing point. Recommended.

¶ Ngoc Huong Restaurant, 76 Hung Vuong St, T59-382 2795. Good northern Vietnamese food. Good-sized portions and cheap. Bring a phrasebook as the staff speak only Vietnamese.

¶ Thien Thanh Restaurant, 22 Pham Van Dong St, off Le Loi past the Ialy Hotel, T59-382 7011. A modern restaurant that is tastefully decorated serving up a good selection of Vietnamese and international cuisine. The outdoor seating area has great views over the surrounding countryside. The food is plentiful, fresh and good value for money.

Cafés

Café Tennis, 61 Quang Trung St, T59-387 4352. A sheltered plant-filled compound next to the courts that would be a perfect place for refreshment after a visit to the museum that is virtually opposite.

Kontum *p249, map p250*

There are many restaurants and cafés along **Nguyen Hue St** all of which are much of a muchness in terms of food, quality, choice, presentation and value. Tapioca noodles – *banh canh mi* – are excellent in Kontum.

†† Dakbla Restaurant, Dakbla 1 Hotel, 2 Phung St, T60-386 3333. Good selection of both Vietnamese and international cuisine. Quality and presentation are good and the service is friendly albeit a tad slow. The restaurant looks out onto the hotel courtyard.

† 90 Restaurant, 65 Nguyen Hue St, T60-862594. Modern restaurant with reasonable facilities. Friendly and helpful staff. They have a good selection of food at reasonable prices.

† Dakbla's Café, 168 Nguyen Hue St, T60-386 2584, vandakbla@yahoo.com. Modern restaurant filled with ethnic minority artefacts, it has the most interesting decor in the region. The pleasant staff are conversant in several languages (English, French and German) and there's a good selection of food at reasonable prices.

Cafés

Evacoffee, 1 Phan Chu Trinh St, T60-386 2944, evacoffee@gmail.com. A cool hideaway amid plants, sculptures and wooden furniture. Kick back with a fruit smoothie or a tipple. Very chic.

🟠 Bars and clubs

Dalat *p235, maps p234 and p236*
Chez Moi, back of the **Hai San Hotel**, Nguyen Thi Minh Khai St. This is the in vogue destination for all the hip folk in Dalat. Large, good selection of drinks and cheap. It has a large bar which gets full in the evenings. Entry 30,000d.

Golf 3 Bar, 4 Nguyen Thi Minh Khai St, T63-382 6042. Open 2000-2400. Located in the basement opposite the nightclub, it has several pool tables and has a good selection of drinks and a reasonable selection of bar food. Good value for money.

Larry's Bar, Sofitel Dalat Palace, see Sleeping, page 253. 1600-2400. A rustic look for this basement bar with comfortable chairs, a pool table and TV room. It was named after Larry Hillblum of DHL fame, who in 1994 spent a fortune renovating the **Sofitel**, **Mercure** and the golf course. Good selection of drinks and bar food available.

Sports Café, Empress Hotel, see Sleeping, above. Open-air bar with good views over Xuan Huong Lake. A good selection of drinks and a reasonable selection of bar food. Good value for money.

Thanh Thuy (**Bluewater Restaurant**), 2 Nguyen Thai Hoc St, on the lakeshore, T63-353 1668. Closes 2300. Lovely setting and good for an evening drink (take a jacket) to admire the coloured reflections on the water but food is not its forte.

Buon Ma Thuot *p242, map p243*
There are innumerable bars and cafés dotted along **Hai Ba Trung** and **Ly Thuong Kiet** streets, and surrounding the Sports Center. They tend to be of the Vietnamese variety but have a reasonable selection of drinks available and are cheap. Better stocked bars are in the **Bach Ma**, **Cao Nguyen** and **Thang Loi** hotels (see Sleeping, above).

Play Ku (Pleiku) *p247, map p248*
The best options are the hotel bars.

Kontum *p249, map p250*
Bars tend to be of the Vietnamese variety and are primarily along Nguyen Hue St. There are a few in town. For a cold beer or spirit your best choice is one of the hotels or **Evacoffee**.

✪ Entertainment

Buon Ma Thuot *p242, map p243*
Provincial Cultural Centre 2,
Hung Vuong St (with an amusement park
in the evenings).

✪ Festivals and events

Dec-Mar is when most of the festivals of
the local tribes take place. For specific
information contact the provincial
tourist offices.

Dalat *p235, maps p234 and p236*
Dec or Jan Celebrates the flower capital of
Vietnam in peak season.

Buon Ma Thuot *p242, map p243*
10 Mar Marks the fall of Buon Ma Thuot on
10 Mar 1975.

Kontum *p249, map p250*
14 Nov Festival to celebrate Bishop Cuenot.

✪ Shopping

Dalat *p235, maps p234 and p236*
Dalat produces some of the best handmade
silk paintings in Vietnam. During your stay
in Vietnam you are bound to see shops
selling them. The original place to develop
this was XQ in Dalat. It is possible to see how
these works of art are produced at the XQ
Historical Village on the north side of town
and the XQ showroom at the central market.

Local produce is plentiful and cheap and
can be purchased in Dalat market. Dalat
wine is the national standard and comes
in red and white. Artichoke teas, jams and
dried mushrooms are also a local favourite.
Lamdong Foodstuffs, Dalat wine showroom, 3 Nam Ky Khoi Nghia St, T63-382
7852, sells bottles of the local wine.

Buon Ma Thuot *p242, map p243*
Tea and coffee are the main items that are
purchased here. This is also one of the only
cities in Vietnam where authentic Central
Highlands hill tribe handicrafts can be
purchased in abundance.

Play Ku (Pleiku) *p247, map p248*
Play Ku has a surprisingly good selection
of shops and products. Coffee, tea and
pepper are plentiful. It is also known for its
quality of furniture (leading to rapid local
deforestation). Most of the shops are along
Hung Vuong St, Pham Van Dong St, Thong
Nhat and also Nguyen Van Troi St.

▲ Activities and tours

Dalat *p235, maps p234 and p236*
Golf
Dalat Palace Golf Club, 1 Phu Dong
Thien Vuong St, T63-382 3507, www.
dalatpalacegolf.vn. Originally built for
Emperor Bao Dai as a 9-hole course in
1922, it was rebuilt in 1994 as an 18-hole
championship golf course measuring
7009 yds. Rated by some, including Gordon
Simmonds, as the finest in Vietnam and
one of the best in the region, it overlooks
Xuan Huong Lake. Green fees start at US$55,
include caddie fee. **Sofitel** and **Mercure**
guests enjoy a 30% discount. Golf lessons
are available.

Pedaloes
Pedaloes on Xuan Huong Lake are available
by **Thuy Ta** restaurant, 45,000d per hr for
2 people.

Swimming
There is an open-air swimming pool on Phu
Dong Thien Vuong St (Hu Boi Nuoc Nong)
next to the Dalat Flower Garden. Open Mon-
Wed 1400-1900, Thu 1400-1800, Sat and Sun
0900-1800, 20,000d per hr.

Therapies
L'Apothiquaire, T63-382 5444,
www.lapothiquaire.com. In the eaves of the
Sofitel Dalat Palace. Open 1000-2100.

Tour operators

Dalat Toserco, No7, 3 Thang 2 St, T63-382 2125. It also provides budget trans-portation and a good selection of tours. It is slightly more expensive than **Sinh Café**.

Dalat Travel Bureau, 1 Nguyen Thi Minh Khai, T63-351 0104, www.dalattourist.com. vn. It is the state-run travel company for Lam Dong Province. Tours include: city, trekking, canyoning, rock climbing, exploring and biking; the majority of these tours cost upwards of US$20 per person.

Hardy Dalat, 57 Truong Cong Dinh St, T63-383 6840. A variety of trekking tours, abseiling, canyoning, mountain biking, horseriding, 2-day sightseeing trips to Nha Trang, 2-day trip to Nam Cat Tien National Park, birdwatching and longer wildlife spotting trips into the jungle.

Highland Holiday Tour, 49 Truong Cong Dinh Street, T090-284 8967, haitours@gmail. com. Recommended by CNN, **Highland Holiday's** guides are trained and graduated from a 4-year university tourism program.

Phattire Adventures, 73 Truong Cong Dinh St, T63-382 9422, www.phattireventures. com. Canyoning, from US$24; rock climbing, US$30; mountain biking, from US$32; trekking from US$17; kayaking US$27.

Sinh Tourist, 4a Bui Thi Xuan St, T63-382 2663, www.thesinhtourist.vn. Part of the nationwide **Sinh Tourist** tour operators. Primarily provides cheap travel to HCMC and Nha Trang. It can also arrange local tours and hotel bookings for you (bear in mind that they are located next to the hotel that they own so you will be offered a room there first). City sightseeing tour US$15; Langbian mountain hiking tour, US$15; elephant riding US$20; 3-day trip to Nam Cat Tien, US$100; a Central Highland tour, US$100 per day, all-inclusive except food.

Buon Ma Thuot *p242, map p243*
Sport

Daklak Water Park, on Highway 14, 5 km from the centre, T500-395 0403. It has several water chutes and splash pools and swimming pools. Daily 0730-1930, 30,000d per adult and 20,000d per child.

Sports Complex, just off Nguyen Tat Thanh St about 1 km from the centre of town. It has badminton courts and a fitness centre. Normally open from 0800-2000.

Tennis Courts, Damsan Hotel and 3 Le Duan St (Youth Court/Cultural House).

Tour operators

For kayaking, mountain bike riding and overnight stays with the local tribes.

Daklak Tourist, 3 Phan Chu Trinh St (in the grounds of the **Thang Loi Hotel**), T500-385 2246, www.daklaktourist.com.vn. Some staff speak English and French. It has a well-written website. Tours include 2-day tours to Lak Lake with elephant riding and canoe paddling, US$50 for 2; rafting and hiking, US$20 per person; guided cycling US$20 per person and homestay at Lak Lake, from US$10-30. Longer tours and other variations are arranged.

Damsan Travel, 35 Hai Ba Trung St, T500-385 0123, tuankiet117@yahoo.com. Tours include trips to waterfalls, Lak Lake, Ban Don, Yok Don National Park. A tour guide costs US$15 a day; elephant ride US$40 for 2 per hr; a dug-out, US$20 for 2 per hr. The company can arrange visa extensions and purchase air and bus tickets.

Vietnam Highland Travel, 1st floor, 24 Ly Thuong Kiet St, T500-385 5009, highlandco@dng.vnn.vn. A recommended tour operator running a range of good, fun tours across the Central Highlands area.

Around Buon Ma Thuot *p245*
Tour operators

Daklak Tourist, at the entrance to Buon Jun village, T500-358 6184, laklake@ daklaktourist.com.vn. It will organize, trekking, elephant riding (US$40), bicycling (10,000d per hr), fishing, canoeing (US$10) and a gong music and dancing show. There is also a branch at the Lak Resort where tours can be arranged. Bicycles rented from here are 40,000d per day.

Lak Lake Tourist Service, T500-358 6280/ 090-537 1633 (mob). Mr Duc is the manager and works at the main restaurant that visitors eat at but he speaks no English. It offers an array of services in the area.

Ban Don p246
Tour operators
Ban Don Tourist Center, Krong Na Commune, T500-321 1200. Situated in 1400 ha and on the shores of the man-made Dak Minh lake. It charges US$40 for a 3-hr elephant ride; US$20 for a dug-out canoe.
Biet Dien Tourist, Ban Don village; at the entrance of the village, T500-378 3020, offers elephant rides around the village and in Yok Don for US$20 per hr.

Play Ku (Pleiku) p247, map p248
Tour operators
Gia Lia Tourist, 215 Hung Vuong St (on the ground floor of the **Hung Vuong Hotel**), T59-387 4571, www.gialaitourist.com. It arranges tours to the local hill tribes, treks, tours of Yaly Hydro Electric power station, elephant rides (US$30 for 2), tours of the former battle sites and can arrange all your transportation requirements. Trips to the Ba-na villages of Dektu, Deron, DeDoa and Dekop, cost US$20 each for 1-5 people or US$10 for 1 village; to Plei Phun Gia-rai village, US$10. Former battlefield site tours including the La Drang Valley (from US$60) and trekking tours of up to 6 days staying in tents or longhouses are possible (from US$204).

Kontum p249, map p250
Kayaking and trekking
Kayaking, trekking and overnight stays with ethnic minorities can be arranged by Kontum Tourist (see below).

Therapies
Dong Phuong, 63 Dao Duy Ta St, T60-324 0357. Daily 0700-2300. A massage centre with steam bath, sauna and jacuzzi. A 1½-hr VIP massage is US$9.

Tour operators
Kontum Tourist, 2 Phan Dinh Phung St (ground floor of the **Dakbla Hotel**), T60-386 1626, www.kontumtourism.com. The office arranges kayaking along the river, visits and overnight stays in the local Ba-na and Gia-rai villages, trekking and visits to the former battle sites and Ho Chi Minh Trail; it can also arrange tours starting and finishing from Danang, HCMC or Buon Ma Thuot. Prices range from US$25 for up to 4 people in a car for a local trip to US$155 for a trip to HCMC.
Highland Ecotours, T90-511 2037 (mob), www.vietnamhighlands.com. Mr Huynh speaks good English and is courteous and helpful. Formerly the manager of **Kontum Tourist**, Mr Nguyen Do Huynh now runs a private company offering river boat trips and hilltribe trecks in the surrounding province.

⊙ Transport

Dalat p235, maps p234 and p236
Air
The government has expressed aspirations for international status for the airport in the near future.

   Vietnam Airlines, No 2 and No 40 Ho Tung Mau St, T63-383 3499. Daily 0730-1130, 1330-1630. Closes 30 mins earlier at the weekend. An airline bus leaves 2 hrs before every flight from the **Airport Hotel**, No 40 Ho Tung Mau St. Returning after flight arrivals, 20,000d one way, 30 mins.

Bus and Open Tour Bus
There are plenty of local buses that plough the inter provincial routes of **Buon Ma Thuot**, **Play Ku**, **Kontum**, **Nha Trang**, **HCMC**, **Gia Nghia**, **Phan Rang**, **Phan Thiet**, **Danang**. Buses to Lak Lake, 5 hrs, 50,000d. Open Tour Bus companies (**Phuong Trang**, **Sinh Tourist** and **Dalat Toserco**, see Tour operators, above) operate daily trips to **HCMC**, 7 hrs, **Nha Trang**, 7 hrs, and **Mui Ne**, 8 hrs. Prices are so competitive that the Open Tour Bus is now cheaper than the public bus.

Phuong Trang, 11A Le Quy Don St, T63-358 5858. Phuong Trang dominates southern Vietnam's bus services, and rightly so. The new Phuong Trang bus station below the cable car station is impressive, but more so is the top-quality service.

Car
It is possible to hire cars and taxis in Dalat. Many of the tour operators have cars for hire and there are many taxis. **Mai Linh Dalat**, 44/8 Hai Ba Trung St, T63-351 1511.

Motorbikes and bicycles
Xe ôms are ubiquitous. **Easy riders** (http://dalat-easyrider.com), English-speaking bike riders, congregate in front of the **Hoa Binh 1** although they are likely to find you and follow you in the street. There are so many claiming to be one that you just need to find one, work out a plan and negotiate a fair price. The **Dalat Travel Bureau**, see tour operators, above, rents motorbikes for US$5 a day; bicycles US$3.

Train
Daily services run the 7 km between Dalat and **Trai Mat**, see page 241.

Nam Cat Tien National Park *p242*
Tour operators in Dalat and HCMC offer trips to Nam Cat Tien, see Dalat tour operators, page 261, and HCMC tour operators, page 344.

Buon Ma Thuot *p242, map p243*
Air
Vietnam Airlines, 67 Nguyen Tat Thanh St, T500-395 4442 (Inside Buon Ma Thuot Airport Hotel), 0730-1130, 1330-1630.

Bus
The bus station is 5 km from the Victory monument on Nguyen Chi Thanh St, Km 4, T500-387 6789. Regular connections to **Kontum** (241 km), **Play Ku** (197 km), **Nha Trang** (197 km), **Dalat** (217 km). There are also daily buses to **HCMC** and **Hanoi**.

Car
Your hotel can arrange a car or you can visit **Daklak Tourist**. **Damsan Travel** also hires out cars for around US$65 a day.

Motorbike
Damsan Travel rents motorbikes for US$8 a day.

Taxi
Mai Linh Taxi, 188 Nguyen Tat Thanh, T500-381 3813, operates in town and also from the bus station. A taxi to and from the airport is US$5.

Around Buon Ma Thuot *p245*
Bus
There are hourly buses to and from Buon Ma Thuot to **Lak Lake**, 20,000d. Hourly buses to and from **Krong Kno** for the Dray Sap waterfall, 10000d. Buses to **Dalat** from Lak Lake, 5 hrs, 100,000d.

Play Ku (Pleiku) *p247, map p248*
Air
Vietnam Airlines, 55 Quang Trung St, T59-382 4660/382 3058.

Bus
There are regular connections by local bus to **Kontum** (44 km), **Buon Ma Thuot** (197 km), **Quy Nhon** (186 km). There are also buses to **HCMC** and **Hanoi**. **Gia Lai Tourist** runs buses to HCMC at 1830. It also runs transport to the border at **Le Thanh** where there is transport to **Ban Lung**, 70 km away. From Stung Treng, it is 210 km to a bridge crossing the border into Laos at Voen Kham; from here it is 180 km to Pakse. **Gia Lai Tourist** also plans to run buses to the Laos border, 130 km away, at **Bo-Y**.

Car
Arrange car hire through your hotel or with **Gia Lai Tourist** or **Pleiku Taxi**, 11B Nguyen Van Troi St, T59-757575. The cost from Play Ku to **Buon Ma Thuot** is about US$50. It is a 5½-hr drive.

Taxi
Mai inh Taxi, 5B Phan Dinh Phung St,
T59-371 8899, www.mailinh.vn.

Kontum *p249, map p250*
Air
Vietnam Airlines, has a sales agent at
129 Ba Trieu St, T60-386 2282.

Bus
There are daily departures from the bus
station at 281 Phan Dinh Phung St,
T60-386 2265, at 0700 and 0800 to **Play Ku**,
Buon Ma Thuot and **Quy Nhon**, 100,000d
per person. A bus runs from Quy Nhon via
Kontum to **Laos** via the border at Bo-Y,
see below, US$10, 3 times a week.

Car and motorbike
Kontum Tourist rents cars and motorbikes.
The latter costs US$8 a day. It will also
organize transport to the border at Bo-Y
(80 km, 1½ hrs) where you can cross to
Phu Kua in Laos (nearest town **Attapeu**).

⊙ Directory

Dalat *p235, maps p234 and p236*
Banks BIDV, 42 Hoa Binh Sq. Vietinbank,
46-48 Hoa Binh Sq. Mon-Fri 0700-1000,
1300-1600, Sat until 1100. It has a bureau de
change, ATM and cashes TCs. **Hospitals**
4 Pham Ngoc Thach St, T63-382 2154.
Well-equipped hospital. The doctors speak
English and French. **Internet** There are
internet cafés along Nguyen Chi Thanh
St, heading from Hoa Binh Sq to Xuan
Huong Lake. Most cafés, hotels and tourist
restaurants offer free Wi-Fi. **Post office
and telephone** 14 Tran Phu St, opposite
Novotel Hotel. Offers the full spectrum of
facilities – fax, internet, IDD, Poste Restante.

Buon Ma Thuot *p242, map p243*
Banks Asia Commercial Bank, 60-
62 Le Hong Phong St, T500-381 0198.
Vietcombank, 92-94 Y Jut St. Offers a good
selection of facilities including cashing of
TCs and also a bureau de change facilities.
Hospitals Daklak Polyclinic, 2 Mai Hac De
St, T500-385 3953. Buon Ma Thuot Health
Service, 235 Xo Viet Nghe Tinh St, T500-385
8561. **Internet** 36 Ly Thuong Kiet St, 2000-
3000d per hr. Most hotels and cafés provide
free Wi-Fi.**Post office and telephone**
6 Le Duan St, T500-385 3716. Offers the
full spectrum of facilities (fax, internet, IDD,
poste restante, etc).

Play Ku (Pleiku) *p247, map p248*
Banks Agribank, 12 Tran Hung Dao St.
Cashes TCs and also operates a bureau de
change service. Mon-Fri 0830-1600. There is
also an ATM in the lobby of the Ialy Hotel.
Hospitals Tran Hung Dao St. It is better
equipped then Kontum and facilities are
open 24 hrs (look for the sign **Cuu Cap**).
Internet The best place is the post office
(opposite the Ialy Hotel). There are also a
couple of places near the Pleiku Hotel.
Post office 69 Hung Vuong St (opposite
the Ialy Hotel). It provides internet access
and long-distance phone calls.

Kontum *p249, map p250*
Bank The Agribank, 88 Tran Phu St, does
not cash TCs or change currencies other
than dong and US dollars. ATM outside
Vietinbank, 90 Tran Phu St. **Hospitals**
Located on the corner of Phan Dinh Phung
St and Ba Trieu St. Basic medical facilities.
Internet The post office and also across
the street, 4000d per hr. Most hotels and
cafés offer free Wi-Fi. **Post office** 205 Le
Hong Phong St.

Footprint Mini Atlas
Vietnam

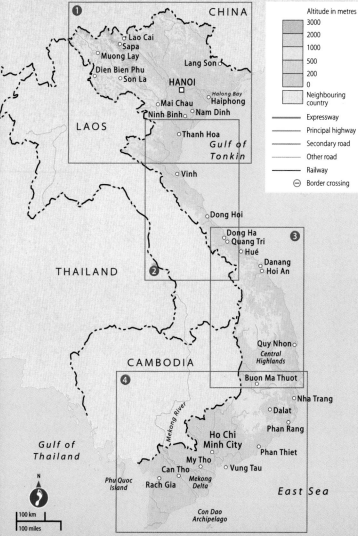

Map 1

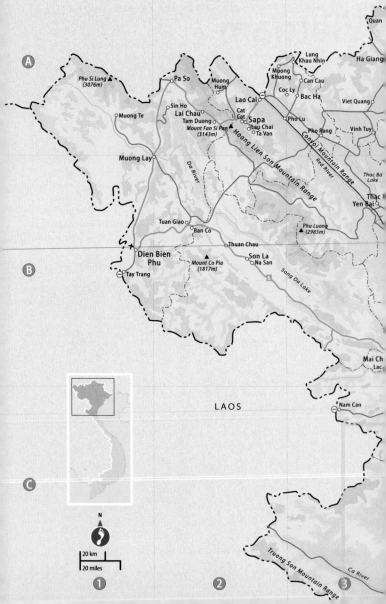

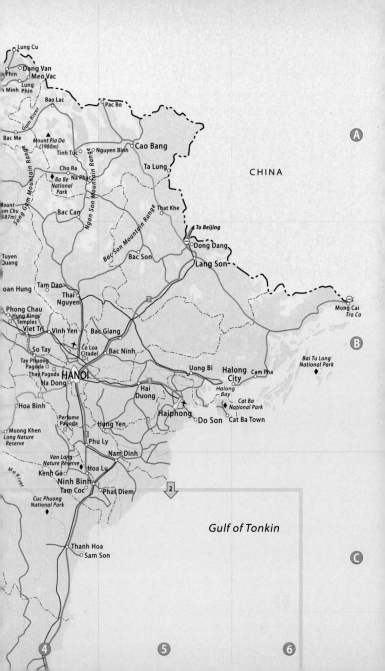

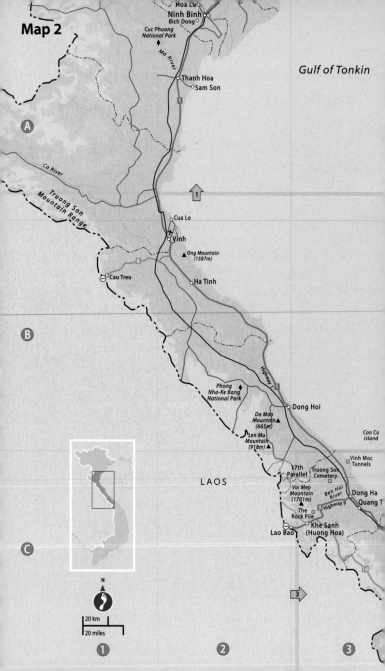

Map 3

Map 4

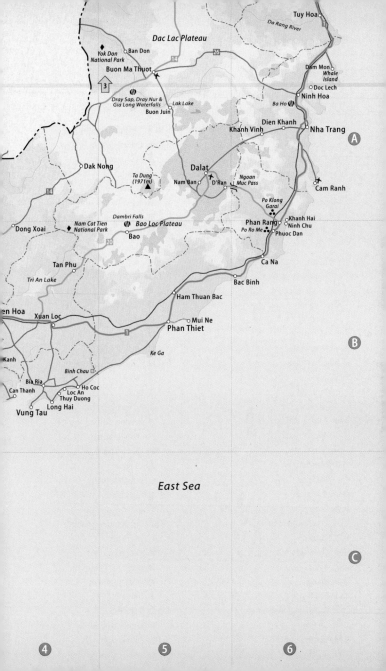

Map symbols

□	Capital city	▬	Building
○	Other city, town	■	Sight
⌁	International border	▮†♦	Cathedral, church
⌁	Regional border	♨	Chinese temple
⊖	Customs	🛕	Hindu temple
⬭	Contours (approx)	⚶	Meru
▲	Mountain, volcano	🕌	Mosque
⇌	Mountain pass	⚐	Stupa
⊥⊥⊥	Escarpment	✡	Synagogue
⌣	Glacier	ⓘ	Tourist office
⬚	Salt flat	🏛	Museum
🪨	Rocks	⊠	Post office
⩊	Seasonal marshland	Ⓟ	Police
⬚	Beach, sandbank	Ⓢ	Bank
⑈	Waterfall	@	Internet
⌒	Reef	♩	Telephone
═══	Motorway	⬠	Market
───	Main road	✚	Medical services
───	Minor road	Ⓟ	Parking
⌂⌂⌂	Track	⛽	Petrol
⋯⋯	Footpath	⛳	Golf
───	Railway	∴	Archaeological site
⊢▬	Railway with station	♦	National park,
✈	Airport		wildlife reserve
🚌	Bus station	❀	Viewing point
Ⓜ	Metro station	▲	Campsite
─ ─ ─	Cable car	⌂	Refuge, lodge
┽┽┽┽	Funicular	🏰	Castle, fort
⚓	Ferry	⚑	Diving
▭▭▭	Pedestrianized street	†♦♦	Deciduous, coniferous,
Σ Ι	Tunnel		palm trees
→	One way-street	❋	Mangrove
‖‖‖‖	Steps	⌂	Hide
⊰⊱	Bridge	♠	Vineyard, winery
▂▂▲	Fortified wall	⚗	Distillery
⬚	Park, garden, stadium	⋈	Shipwreck
●	Sleeping	✕	Historic battlefield
❷	Eating	⬗	Related map
❶	Bars & clubs		

Nha Trang and around

→ *Colour map 4, A6.*

Nha Trang is Vietnam's only real seaside city. It nestles amid the protective embrace of the surrounding hills and islands. The long golden beach, which only a very few years ago was remarkably empty, fills up quickly these days, and it is easy to see why. The light has a beautifully radiant quality and the air is clear; the colours are vivid, particularly the blues of the sea, sky and fishing boats berthed on the river.

An important Cham settlement, Nha Trang retains distinguished and well-preserved Cham towers. It is a centuries-old fishing town established in the sheltered mouth of the Cai Estuary. A port which can handle small coastal traders was built here in 1924. Its clear waters and offshore islands won wide acclaim in the 1960s and its new-found prosperity is based firmly on tourism with big name chain hotels opening along its shores. ▶▶ *For listings, see pages 277-284.*

Ins and outs

Getting there Nha Trang's airport is 34 km away at Cam Ranh. There is an airport bus service, 40 minutes, 40,000d or taxis, US$10-15. Some hotels arrange transfers. There are flights from Hanoi, Ho Chi Minh City and Danang. The town is on the main north-south railway line and there are trains to Ho Chi Minh City and Hanoi (and stops between). The main bus terminal is west of the town centre. *Xe ôms* take passengers into town. ▶▶ *See Transport, page 283.*

Getting around Nha Trang is negotiable on foot – just. But there are bicycles and motorbikes for hire everywhere and the usual cyclos. Some hotels and the tour companies have cars for out-of-town excursions.

Tourist information Khanh Hoa Tours ① *1 Tran Hung Dao St, T58-352 6753, www. nhatrangtourist.com.vn, daily 0700-1130, 1330-1700,* the official city tour office, can arrange visa extensions, car and boat hire and tours of the area. It's also a **Vietnam Airlines** booking office. It's not that helpful; plenty of the tour operators in town have good information.

Safety There have been a reports of revellers being mugged at night and men being relieved of their wallets by attractive women. Don't carry huge sums of money or your valuables with you on a night out. We've also received reports about money going missing during massage sessions.

Background

Word has spread, and Nha Trang's days as an undiscovered treasure are over. It is a firmly established favourite of Vietnamese as well as foreign visitors and Nha Trangites of all backgrounds and persuasions endeavour to ease the dollar from the traveller's sweaty paw. Nevertheless, there is a permanent relaxed holiday atmosphere, the streets are not crowded and the motorbikes still cruise at a leisurely pace.

The name Nha Trang is thought to be derived from the Cham word *yakram*, meaning bamboo river, and the surrounding area was a focal point of the Cham Kingdom – some of the country's best-preserved Cham towers lie close by. Nha Trang was besieged for nine months during the Tay Son rebellion in the late 18th century (see page 272), before eventually falling to the rebel troops. There are, in reality, two Nha Trangs: popular Nha Trang, which is a seaside town consisting of a long, palm and casuarina-fringed beach and one or two streets running parallel to it, and commercial Nha Trang to the north of Yersin Street, which is a bustling city with an attractive array of Chinese shophouses.

Nha Trang → For listings, see pages 277-284.

The beach

The beach and beachside promenade have been spruced up in recent years and it is now a pleasant place to relax although there are the occasional hawkers. Beach beds cost 25,000d per session; the nicest being in front of the Sailing Club and La Louisiane. There are fixed thatched umbrellas in the sand and public toilets.

Cham Ponagar temple complex

ⓘ *0600-1800, 15000d. The best time to visit the towers is late afternoon, 1600-1700.*

On a hill just outside the city is the Cham Ponagar Temple complex, known locally as Thap Ba. Originally the complex consisted of eight towers, four of which remain. Their stylistic differences indicate they were built at different times between the seventh and 12th centuries. The largest (at 23 m high) was built in AD 817 and contains a statue of Lady Thien Y-ana, also known as Ponagar (who was the beautiful wife of Prince Bac Hai), as well as a fine and very large lingam. She taught the people of the area weaving and new agricultural techniques, and they built the tower in her honour. The other towers are dedicated to gods: the central tower to Cri Cambhu (which has become a fertility temple for childless couples); the northwest tower to Sandhaka (woodcutter and foster-father to Lady Thien Y-ana); and the south tower to Ganeca (Lady Thien Y-ana's daughter).

To get to the temple complex you can either walk or catch a cyclo. Follow 2 Thang 4 Street north out of town; Cham Ponagar is just over the second of two bridges (Xom Bong bridge), a couple of kilometres from the city centre.

Cai River estuary and fishing boats

En route to the towers, the road crosses the Cai River estuary where there is a diversity of craft including Nha Trang's elegant fleet of blue fishing boats, lined with red and complete with painted eyes for spotting the fish, and coracles (*cái thúng*) for getting to the boats and mechanical fish traps. The traps take the form of nets which are supported by long arms; the arms are hinged to a platform on stilts and are raised and lowered by wires connected to a capstan which is turned, sometimes by hand but more commonly by foot.

Long Son Pagoda

ⓘ *23 Thang 10 St.*

The best-known pagoda in Nha Trang is the Long Son Pagoda, built in 1963. Inside the sanctuary is an unusual image of the Buddha, backlit with natural light. Murals depicting the *jataka* stories decorate the upper walls. To the right of the sanctuary, stairs lead up to a 9-m-high white Buddha, perched on a hill top, from where there are fine views. Before reaching the white pagoda, take a left on the stairs. Through an arch behind the pagoda you'll see a 14-m-long reclining Buddha. Commissioned in 2003, it is an impressive sight.

The pagoda commemorates the monks and nuns who died demonstrating against the Diem government – in particular those who, through self-immolation, brought the despotic nature of the Diem regime and its human rights abuses to the attention of the public.

Nha Trang

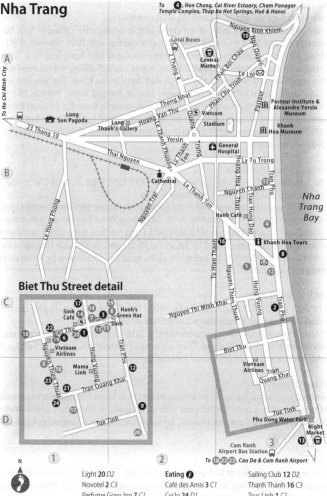

N

300 metres
300 yards

Sleeping 🛏
52 Tran Phu **19** *C2*
Backpacker's House **5** *D1*
Bao Dai's Villas **23** *D3*
Blue House **1** *C3*
Evason Ana Mandara **18** *D3*
36 Tram Phu **4** *B3*
La Suisse **17** *D1*

Light **20** *D2*
Novotel **2** *C3*
Perfume Grass Inn **7** *C1*
Que Huong
  (Que Thao) **8** *C2*
Sao Mai **10** *D1*
Sao Xanh (Blue Star) **11** *C1*
Sheraton **13** *B3*
Sofitel Vinpearl Resort
  & Spa **22** *D3*
T78 **12** *C3*
Truc Linh **14** *C1*

Eating 🍴
Café des Amis **3** *C1*
Cyclo **24** *D1*
Gia **21** *D1*
Good Morning
  Vietnam **6** *C1*
Hai Dao **4** *A2*
La Bella Napoli **8** *C1*
La Mancha **23** *D1*
Lac Canh **10** *A3*
Louisiane Brewhouse **9** *D2*
Omar's **13** *D3*
Paramount **2** *C3*

Sailing Club **12** *D2*
Thanh Thanh **16** *C3*
Truc Linh **1** *C1*
Truc Linh 2 **22** *C1*
Truc Linh 3 **17** *C1*

Bars & clubs 🍸
Blue Gecko **18** *C1*
Crazy Kim **19** *C1*
Guava **20** *C1*
Rainbow **14** *C1*
Shorty's **15** *C1*
Why Not **7** *D1*

Nha Trang Cathedral

ⓘ *Mass Mon-Sat 0500 and 1630, Sun 0500, 0700, and 1630.*

Granite-coloured (though built of concrete) and imposing, the cathedral was built between 1928 and 1933 on a small rock outcrop. It was not until 1961, however, that the building was consecrated as a cathedral for the diocese of Nha Trang and Ninh Thuan. The cathedral has a single, crenellated tower, a fine, vaulted ceiling, with stained glass in the upper sections of its windows and pierced metal in the lower. The windows over the altar depict Jesus with Mary and Joseph, Joan of Arc and Sainte Thérèse. Like the windows in Dalat and Danang cathedrals they were made in Grenoble by Louis Balmet. Fourteen rather fine pictures depict the stations of the cross: they look French but there is no attribution and no one seems sure of their provenance. The path to the cathedral runs off Nguyen Trai Street.

Alexandre Yersin Museum

ⓘ *10 Tran Phu St, T58-382 9540, Mon-Fri 0700-1130, 1330-1700, 26,000d. The curator is helpful, friendly and speaks fluent French and English.*

The Yersin Museum is contained within the colonnaded **Pasteur Institute** founded by the great scientist's protégé, Dr Alexandre Yersin. Swiss-born Yersin first arrived in Vietnam in 1891 and spent much of the rest of his life in Nha Trang (see box, page 269). The museum contains the lab equipment used by Yersin, his library and stereoscope through which visitors can see in 3-D the black-and-white slides, including shots taken by Yersin on his visits to the highlands.

Khanh Hoa Museum

ⓘ *16 Tran Phu St, T58-382 2277, Tue-Fri 0800-1100, 1400-1700, free. English-speaking curators will be pleased to show you around and should be tipped.*

The Khanh Hoa Museum, which was renovated in 2010, contains a Dongson bronze drum and a Palaeolithic stone xylophone. There is a room of ethnographics and, of course, a Ho Chi Minh room which contains several items of interest.

Central market

The **Cho Dam** (central market) close to Nguyen Hong Son Street is a good place to wander and browse and it is quite well-stocked with useful items. In the vicinity of the market, along **Phan Boi Chau Street**, for example, are some bustling streets with old colonial-style shuttered houses.

Long Thanh's gallery

ⓘ *126 Hoang Van Thu St, not far from the railway station, T58-382 4875, www.longthanhart. com, open 0900-1900. Long Thanh is willing by pre-arrangement to meet photographers and organize photographic expeditions.*

Long Thanh is one of Vietnam's most distinguished photographers and many of his famous pictures are taken in and around his native Nha Trang. He works only in black and white and his sensitive photographs capture the full gamut of human emotions. His outstanding images include cheerful children (often Cham) frolicking in the rain, young women and wistful old people who have witnessed generations of change in a single lifetime. Long Thanh has won a series of international awards and recognition for his work. His style is distinctive and many have tried to copy his technique. He speaks English and welcomes visitors to his gallery.

Alexandre Yersin

Alexandre John Emille Yersin was born in 1863 in Canton Vaud, Switzerland. He enrolled at the University of Lausanne and completed his medical education in Paris where he became an assistant to Louis Pasteur. In 1888, Yersin adopted French citizenship. To the astonishment of all he became a ship's doctor; he visited the Far East and in 1891 landed in Nha Trang.

Two years later, as part of his exploration of Vietnam he 'discovered' the Dalat Plateau which he recommended for development as a hill resort owing to its beauty and temperate climate. The following year, in 1894, he was urged to visit Hong Kong to assist in an outbreak of the plague. He identified the baccilus which was named *Yersinia pestis*.

In 1895 he set up a laboratory in Nha Trang which, in 1902, became a Pasteur Institute, the first to be established outside France. Here he developed an anti-serum for the treatment of plague. He established a cattle farm for the production of serum and vaccines and for the improvement of breeding stock at Suoi Dau, 25 km south of Nha Trang. Yersin was responsible for the introduction to Vietnam of commercial crops such as coffee, rubber and the cinchona (quinine) tree.

In his retirement he indulged his passions – astrology, photography and observation of the hydrographic conditions of Nha Trang Bay.

Yersin died in 1943 and was buried at Suoi Dau. His tombstone, simply engraved 'Alexandre Yersin 1863-1943', can be seen today at Suoi Dau. Take Highway 1, 25 km south of Nha Trang, look for the sign 'Tombeau de Alexandre Yersin'. The key to the gate is kept with a local family. The tomb is 1.5 km from the gate.

Around Nha Trang → For listings, see pages 277-284.

The islands
ⓘ *The best known are the tours run by Mama Hanh's/Hanh's Green Hat and Mama Linh. These tours (see page 282) depart at 0900. They have established 100,000d as the benchmark price for a day trip, which should include a seafood lunch and snorkelling equipment: cold beers (not unreasonably) cost extra. It is also possible to charter your own boat. From Cau Da pier, boats can be taken to the islands in Nha Trang Bay. Prices vary according to the number of passengers.*

On **Mieu Island** you can visit the **Tri Nguyen Aquarium** ⓘ *35,000d*, a series of tanks in which fish and crustacea are reared, ostensibly for scientific purposes but, as the adjacent restaurant makes plain, it is the science of the tummy that is being served. Not a particularly noteworthy trip.

Other nearby islands are **Hon Mun** ⓘ *40,000d*, and **Hon Mot**. Hon Tam is now off limits due to the building of a resort. The islands are usually a bit of an anticlimax for, as so often in Vietnam, to travel is better than to arrive; it's often a case of lovely boat trip, disappointing beach. The best part is anchoring offshore and jumping into the exquisitely cool water while your skipper prepares a sumptuous seafood feast and the beers chill in the ice bucket. These islands are sometimes known as the **Salangane islands** after the sea swallows that nest here in such profusion. The sea swallow (*yen* in Vietnamese) produces the highly prized bird's nest from which the famous soup is made (see box, page 30). **Hon Yen** (Swallow Island) is out of bounds and strictly government controlled, presumably to deter any would-be private nest collectors.

West of Nha Trang to Dalat

The road rises sharply out of the plain, past banana plantations and water pipes. The Ngoan Muc Pass is spectacular and you pass the Da Nhim power station. Above D'Ran the landscape gives way to pine trees. In 2007, a new 54-km road from Nha Trang to Dalat opened, cutting the journey by 80 km and passing through the Bidup National Park of the Ba (Lady) Mountain. The road linked route 723 of Lam Dong Province to Provincial Route 2 of Khanh Hoa Province.

North of Nha Trang

From Cham Ponagar (see page 266) proceed a few hundred metres north then turn off to the right down to the sea; from Nha Trang take Tran Phu street north and over the new bridge, follow the new road around the coast until you see the promontory. **Hon Chong** (Husband Rocks) are perched at the end of the promontory which has a large, rather pudgy indentation in it – said to have been made by the hand of a male giant. It looks more like a paw print and is disfigured with graffiti. The rocks are quite fun and safe for children to scramble about on. There are numerous shacks selling drinks here and the appeal of the whole area is distinctly Vietnamese.

North of Hon Chong is the attractive **Hon Chong Bay**. The water of the bay is clear and calm and the beach sandy, gently shelving and good for children. The bay is rather more sheltered than Nha Trang Bay itself so may be safe for swimming when Nha Trang is too rough. But do look out for rocks, particularly towards the ends of the bay. There are now a few guesthouses and restaurants here.

Thap Ba Hot Springs ① T58-383 5335, www.thapbahotspring.com.vn, charges vary for the different baths and services, aren't far from the Cai River; go a short distance past Ponagar and turn left, then carry on for couple of kilometres. A soak in mineral water or mud bath is supposed to do you good. As the literature says, "you feel so freshly even it is hotly". Baths and pools of differing sizes for singles, couples and groups. The water is 40°C.

Twenty kilometres north up Highway 1, followed by a 2-km hike will bring you to **Ba Ho**, the name given to a sequence of three pools and rapids to be found in a remote and attractive woodland setting. Huge granite boulders have been sculpted and smoothed by the dashing torrent, but it is easy enough to find a lazy pool to soak in.

Some 40 km north of Nha Trang – turn right off Highway 1 at Ninh Hoa – is the beach area of **Doc Lech**. Take a taxi or hire a car from your hotel. The beach here is gentler and more protected than Hon Chong, which would appear to make it suitable for young children. The sea is quite beautiful with multicoloured boats bobbing on the small waves and the beach is dotted with fishing baskets. Doc Lech is very popular with groups of Vietnamese holiday makers. Given that it is a long haul from Nha Trang it is probably best to go only mid-week out of the holiday season. There are guesthouses and restaurants (See Sleeping, page 278). On the way you will pass workers on the salt flats.

Ninh Van Bay, north of Nha Trang, is accessed from the private speedboat dock of the Evason group where they have a luxurious island hideaway. North of Doc Lech, off a long peninsula accessed by Dam Mon, is **Whale Island**, an island resort offering relaxation, diving and boat trips. ►► See Sleeping, page 278.

Quy Nhon and around → Colour map 3, C3.

Quy Nhon, the capital of Binh Dinh Province, has a population of nearly 250,000 and is situated on a spur just 10 km off Highway 1. The town, established by royal decree in 1898, is taking a breather after a flurry of economic growth based on the export of logs and smuggling but it is growing in popularity after a number of high-end resorts and low-key places have found their home here. A seaside town, it has reasonable swimming off the sandy **Quy Nhon Beach** and a number of sights in the vicinity. Take local advice about swimming, however, as a number of shark attacks were reported in 2010. A leper colony was founded here in 1929 by a French priest, Paul Maheu, and patients and their families were cared for by nuns. The colony survives (at the western end of Nguyen Hue Street) but is now run by the health department. The **Binh Dinh Tourism Company** ⓘ *10 Nguyen Hue St, T56-389 2524,* offers tourist information.

Walk or bicycle northwest on Tran Hung Dao Street, past the bus station, and after 2 km turn right onto Thap Doi Street to Thap Doi Cham towers, a short distance along this street. The area around Quy Nhon was a focus of the Cham Empire, and a number of monuments (13, it is said) have survived the intervening years.

Tay Son District is famous as the place where three brothers led a peasant revolt in 1771 (see box, page 272). To get there take a bus from the station on Tay Son Street and it is about 50 km from Quy Nhon off Highway 19, running west towards Play Ku. The Vietnamese have a penchant for celebrating the exploits of the poor and the weak, and those of the Tay Son brothers are displayed in the **Quang Trung Museum** in Kien My village, Binh Thanh commune, approximately 45 km from Quy Nhon. It is dedicated to Nguyen Hue, a national hero of the 18th century who was one of the three brothers who led the Tay Son insurrection.

Hoang De Citadel (also known as **Cha Ban**) is about 27 km north of Quy Nhon. Originally a Cham capital which was repeatedly attacked by the Vietnamese, it was taken over by the Tay Son brothers in the 18th century and made the capital of their short-lived kingdom. Not much remains except some **Cham ruins**, within the citadel walls, in the vicinity of the old capital.

Quang Ngai → *Colour map 3, B3.*

Quang Ngai is a modest provincial capital on Highway 1, situated on the south bank of the Tra Khuc River and 130 km from Danang. Few people stay here as facilities are still pretty basic. Its greatest claim to fame is its proximity to **Son My** – the site of the **My Lai massacre** (see box, page 273). There is an extensive **market** running north from the bus station, along Ngo Quyen Street (just east of Quang Trung Street or Highway 1). Also in the city is a citadel built during the reign of Gia Long (1802-1820).

Son My (My Lai)

ⓘ *13 km from Quang Ngai, 10,000d to contribute to the upkeep of the memorial. Motorbikes and taxis can take the track to Son My from the main road.*

Just over 1 km north of town on Highway 1, soon after crossing the bridge over the Tra Khuc River, is a plaque indicating the way to Son My. Turn right, and continue for 12 km to the subdistrict of Son My where one of the worst, and certainly the most publicized, atrocities committed by US troops during the Vietnam War occurred (see box, page 273). The massacre of innocent Vietnamese villagers is better known as the My Lai Massacre – after one of the four hamlets of Son My. In the centre of the village of Son My is a memorial with a military cemetery 400 m beyond. There is an exhibition of contemporary US military photos of the massacre and a reconstruction of an underground bomb shelter; the creek where many villagers were dumped after being shot has been preserved.

Tay Son Rebellion (1771-1788)

At the time of the Tay Son rebellion in 1771, Vietnam was in turmoil and conditions in the countryside were deteriorating to the point of famine. The three Tay Son brothers found a rich lode of dissatisfaction among the peasantry, which they successfully mined. Exploiting the latent discontent, they redistributed property from hostile mandarins to the peasants and raised a motley army of clerks, cattle-dealers, farmers, hill people, even scholars, to fight the Trinh and Nguyen lords. Brilliant strategists and demonstrating considerable leadership skills, the brothers and their supporters swept through the country extending the area under their control south as far as Saigon and north to Trinh.

The Chinese, sensing that the disorder and dissent caused by the conflict gave them an opportunity to bring the entire nation under their control, sent a 200,000-strong army southwards in 1788. In the same year, the most intelligent (by all accounts) of the brothers, Nguyen Hue, proclaimed himself emperor under the name of Quang Trung and began to prepare for battle against the cursed Chinese. On the fifth day of Tet in 1789, the brothers attacked the Chinese near Thang Long catching them unawares as they celebrated the New Year. (The Viet Cong were to do the same during the Tet Offensive nearly 200 years later.)

With great military skill, they routed the enemy, who fled in panic back towards China. Rather than face capture, one of the Chinese generals committed suicide. This victory at the Battle of Dong Da is regarded as one of the greatest in the annals of Vietnamese history. Quang Trung, having saved the nation from the Chinese, had visions of recreating the great Nam Viet Empire of the second century BC, and of invading China. Among the reforms that he introduced were a degree of land reform, a wider programme of education, and a fairer system of taxation. He even tried to get all peasants to carry identity cards with the slogan 'the great trust of the empire' emblazoned on them. These greater visions were not to be, however: Quang Trung died suddenly in 1792, failing to provide the dynastic continuity that was necessary if Vietnam was to survive the impending French arrival.

As a postscript to the Tay Son rebellion, in 1802 the new Emperor Gia Long ordered his soldiers to exhume the body of the last of the brothers and urinate upon it in front of the deceased's wife and son. They were then torn apart by four elephants. Quang Trung and the other Tay Son brothers – like many former nationalist and peasant leaders – are revered by the Vietnamese and honoured by the communists.

South of Nha Trang

Cau Da is a small fishing port 5 km south of Nha Trang along the beach road (Tran Phu). **Bao Dai's Villas**, yet another villa belonging to the last emperor of Vietnam, is attractively sited on a small promontory outside Cau Da with magnificent views on all sides. It is now a hotel (see Sleeping, page 279).

Cau Da is also home to the **Institute of Oceanography** ① *T58-359 0036, haiduong@dng. vnn.vn, daily 0730-1130, 1330-1630, 20,000d*, built in 1923, it is the only institute of its kind in Vietnam: it contains a selection of poorly displayed marine fauna in pickling jars and glass cases in its 'biodiversity' room and in the front courtyard are tanks of live fish – including sharks, turtles and seahorses. There is an aquarium containing weird and wonderful marine

Son My (My Lai) massacre

The massacre at Son My was a turning point in the American public's view of the war, and the role that the USA was playing. Were American forces defending Vietnam and the world from the evils of communism? Or were they merely shoring up a despotic government which had lost all legitimacy among the population it ostensibly served?

The massacre occurred on the morning of 16 March 1968. Units from the 23rd Infantry Division were dropped into the village of Son My. The area was regarded as an area of intense communist presence – so much so that soldiers referred to the villages as Pinkville. Only two weeks beforehand, six soldiers had been killed after stumbling into a mine field. The leader of the platoon that was charged with the job of investigating the hamlet of My Lai was 2nd Lieutenant William Calley. Under his orders, 347 people, all unarmed and many women and children, were massacred. Some of Calley's men refused to participate, but most did.

Neil Sheehan, in his book *A Bright Shining Lie*, wrote: "One soldier missed a baby lying on the ground twice with a .45 pistol as his comrades laughed at his marksmanship. He stood over the child and fired a third time. The soldiers beat women with rifle butts and raped some and sodomized others before shooting them. They shot the water buffalos, the pigs, and the chickens. They threw the dead animals into the wells to poison the water. They tossed satchel charges into the bomb shelters under the houses. A lot of the inhabitants had fled into the shelters. Those who leaped out to escape the explosives were gunned down. All of the houses were put to the torch".

In total, more than 500 people were killed at Son My; most in the hamlet of My Lai, but another 90 at another hamlet (by another platoon) in the same village.

The story of the massacre was filed by Seymour Hersh, but not until November 1969 – 20 months later. The subsequent court-martial only convicted Calley, who was by all accounts a sadist. He was sentenced to life imprisonment, but had served only three years before President Nixon intervened on his behalf (he was personally convicted of the murder of 22 of the victims). As Sheehan argues, the massacre was, in some regards, not surprising. The nature of the war had led to the killing and maiming of countless unarmed and innocent peasants; it was often done from a distance. In the minds of most generals, every Vietnamese was a potential communist; from this position it was only a small step to believing that all Vietnamese were legitimate targets.

life from the Vietnamese coastal shelf. Also on display is the impressive 18-m-long skeleton of a whale excavated in 1994 and the skeleton of a dugong (sea cow). There is a new display of machinery from the oil drilling industry. The institute conducts research and tries to promote marine conservation but wages an uphill struggle against the powerful fishing industry, which dynamites and trawls its way through the bay with little heed for tomorrow.

Cam Ranh Bay

Cam Ranh Bay, one of the world's largest natural harbours, lies 34 km south of Nha Trang. Highway 1 skirts around the bay – once an important US naval base and subsequently taken over by the Soviets. In fact the Soviets, or at least the Russians, were here before the Americans: they used it for re-provisioning during the Russo-Japanese war of 1904, which they emphatically lost. After re-unification in 1975, the Vietnamese allowed the Soviets

My Lai – rewriting history

It was thought that pretty much everything that happened that awful day in My Lai was known. Thirty years ago Hugh C Thompson Jr and Lawrence Colburn received medals for heroism under enemy fire, but in 1998 the US Army corrected an oversight: there was no enemy in My Lai; or rather, the enemy was the US.

Thompson, a 24-year-old helicopter pilot, Colburn, his gunner, and a third man, Glenn U Andreotta (who was later killed in action) stopped the My Lai massacre before more people were killed. Thompson spotted women and children hiding in a bunker and put his helicopter down between them and advancing American soldiers. He called up another chopper and between them they evacuated the 10 civilians. At the same time Thompson reported the massacre to his CO who called off all action in the sector, thus ending the killing.

On 7 March 1998, at the Vietnam Veterans Memorial in Washington, the two survivors, Thompson and Colburn, were awarded the highest medal for bravery not involving conflict with an enemy.

to use this fine natural harbour once again as part-payment for the support (political and financial) they were receiving. However, from the late 1980s, the former Soviet fleet began to wind down its presence here as Cold War tensions in the area eased and economic pressures forced the former USSR to reduce military expenditure. Now the port is almost deserted.

Cam Ranh is also a centre for Vietnam's salt industry; for miles around the scenery is white with salt pans (looking like wintry paddy fields) producing pure, crystalline sea salt. There is a modest **Cao Dai Church** near the intersection of Highway 1 and the road leading towards the Bay (Da Bac Street). Continuing east along Da Bac Street, the road leads to a thriving fish market (down a pair of narrow alleys) and then to a busy boatyard producing small fishing vessels. At 120 Da Bac Street is **Chua Phuoc Hai**, an attractive little Buddhist temple.

Nha Trang's airport is now here and there is a new coastal road linking the city to the airport. The views are truly magnificent of white sands and perfect blue seas – and are even more staggering from the air. Hotel development has already started on the stretch from Cam Rang to Nha Trang. In addition to the **Diamond Bay Resort & Golf**, the **Sailing Club** group (of Nha Trang and Mui Ne fame) has broken ground already.

Phan Rang and around → *For listings, see pages 277-284. Colour map 4, A6.*

Phan Rang was once the capital of Champa, when it was known as Panduranga, and there are a number of **Cham towers** (**Thap Cham**) nearby. The town and surrounding area are still home to a small population of Cham but few tourists stop in the small seaside town of about 150,000 people and the capital of Ninh Thuan Province. Open Tour Buses stop beneath Po Klong Garai and there are plenty of *xe ôms*.

Phan Rang

Phan Rang divides into three loosely connected areas: Phan Rang town itself, the beach area – Ninh Chu – and Thap Cham, the Cham tower and railway station. The towers make an interesting visit and can be done as a comfortable side excursion on the drive from Nha Trang to Phan Thiet, see below. (For the route from Phan Rang to Dalat, see page 276.) The beach, while gloriously unspoilt, lacks decent sleeping.

In the centre of town, at 305 Thong Nhat Street (Highway 1), is a large salmon-pink **pagoda** with fine roof decoration. South from the pagoda, opposite 326 Thong Nhat Street, is the entrance to **Phan Rang Market** (Cho Phan Rang). The beach, south of town, is beautiful and a few developers have begun to work on it but so far with a spectacular lack of success.

Po Klong Garai

ⓘ *5000d. Bicycle or take a xe ôm (US$1-2) or local bus on Highway 27 towards Dalat; 2 km beyond the village of Thap Cham turn right when a concrete water tank comes into view. The towers are visible a short distance along this track.*

Thap Cham is the name of a small village that boasts a railway station and the towers of Po Klong Garai, a group of three Cham towers on the road towards Dalat, 6 km from Phan Rang. Other than My Son, they are perhaps the best Cham relics in the country and are in good condition. Built during the 13th century, they are located on a cactus- and boulder-strewn hill with commanding views over the surrounding countryside. To the north you can see the remains of Thanh Son, the former US airbase. Raised up on a brick base, the towers have been extensively renovated. Apart from the renovations there is no sign of cement at all, the cohesion of the red bricks being one of the ingenious mysteries of the Cham. The central tower has a figure of dancing Siva over the main entrance. The door jambs are made of what looks like polished sandstone on which are ancient Cham engravings. Tucked inside the dimly lit main chamber full of incense smoke, is Siva's vehicle, the bull Nandi and other statues.

Nearby is the **railway station**, a very neat and orderly affair. The platform is attractively decorated with plants and there are good views of the towers.

Po Ro Me

ⓘ *The towers are a 1-km walk from the car park by the road. This is the only path as the hill is strewn with cactus. Ask for Thap Cham Po Ro Me. There are no tickets but please do tip the custodian; he keeps a visitors' book which he treats with great reverence.*

Po Ro Me is another group of more recently constructed Cham buildings – indeed the last Cham towers to be built – which can be seen in the distance from Po Klong Garai, rising up from the valley floor. To get there drive south on Highway 1 from Phan Rang towards Ho Chi Minh City; turn right by a sign to Ho Tan Giang which is 200 m past the Ninh Phuoc post office. It is a further 5-7 km from here; keep asking for directions.

There used to be three towers but only one remains; a lingam and yoni have been positioned on the site of one former tower. The towers were built during the reign of King Po Ro Me, the last king of independent Champa (1627-1651), who died a prisoner of the Vietnamese. His statue sits inside the remaining tower. With his manifold arms it is hard not to regard the statue as a depiction of Siva but the Cham custodian is adamant on this point.

Cham bricks are notable for their lightness. This is because (unlike the reproduction bricks of today which lie around) the clay was mixed with rice husks before firing. Indeed a close inspection shows the porous nature of the original bricks this produced. Roughly 10% of the tower has been rebuilt using modern brick.

An interesting feature of this (as with other Cham towers) are the curvaceous flowing lines achieved despite the use of rectangular brick. Quite whether the bricks were made to this pattern and carefully assembled as a jigsaw or whether they were carved into shape once finished it is hard to say.

King Po Ro Me had two wives. A statue of his second wife (Tha Kachanh) sits next to him in the tower. She was from the Rhade minority group. The statue of the king's first wife sits in a small hut behind the tower. Her fault of course was her inability to have children. Sadly the statues here are replacements for the originals, which were stolen in 1993 and 1994.

Finally, there is a third group of Cham towers, in poor condition, 16 km north of town right at the side of Highway 1.

Cham villages

The surrounding Cham villages are of some interest notably for the different style of houses (built of a very primitive looking wattle and daub) and for the appearance and dress of the people (women wearing sarongs, for instance). The village of **Phuoc Dan** (off Highway 1, turn to the right a short way before Ninh Phuoc post office), is notable for its Cham pottery. Rather heavy (in weight and texture) but simple in design and decoration it is moulded mostly into Etruscan-looking urns and vases. These are piled up and covered in firewood which is in turn heaped with rice husks and ignited. The husks prevent combustion and the wood converts to charcoal baking the pots slowly overnight. Pots near the charcoal are black and those in the centre emerge red, all being to some degree rather attractively mottled. These earthernware pieces make striking and unusual gifts and can be bought very cheaply.

Tuan Tu is a small Cham village, about 5 km south of Phan Rang. Like most Cham these villagers have renounced Hinduism in favour of Islam and their names reflect this, boys are called Mo Ham Mat, Su Le Man and so on.

Ninh Chu Beach

About 6-7 km northeast of Phan Rang is **Ninh Chu Beach**. Overall it's not a bad beach – at least it's fairly quiet. There are several cafés which rent chairs and umbrellas in addition to selling drinks. For accommodation there's a variety of odds and ends including some local guesthouses and there is a windy and inexpensive restaurant on the beach.

Ca Na

This is just a wide place in the road between Phan Thiet and Phan Rang with a 3-km-long beach and fishing grounds. It's about 36 km south of Phan Rang, nestled between boulder-strewn hills to the west and wild rocky surf to the east. There are a couple of small restaurants selling decent road-food and drinks and a couple of guesthouses that are as close to the highway as they are to the beach. It's worth a stop for noodles and a quick walk up the hill to see the small pagoda that is visible from the road, and maybe a stroll on the beach.

Phan Rang to Dalat

The 100-km trip between Phan Rang and Dalat is spectacular but sometimes uncomfortable by bus. The narrow strip of land between the highlands and the coast is an area of intensive rice, tobacco and grape cultivation. Winding upwards, the road passes under a massive pipe carrying water from the mountains down to the turbines of a hydropower plant in the valley. It then works its way through the dramatic Ngoan Muc Pass to the Dalat Plateau.

In 2007 a new, more direct road was opened between Dalat and Nha Trang shortening the journey time, see West of Nha Trang to Dalat, page 270.

For Sleeping and Eating price codes and other relevant information, see Essentials pages 26-31.

● Sleeping

Nha Trang *p266, map p267*

There has been a considerable increase in the number of hotel rooms available in Nha Trang and ever bigger hotels are being built. Rooms in the more popular hotels get snapped up quickly; book ahead.

LL Evason Ana Mandara, Tran Phu St, T58-352 2222, www.sixsenses.com. Nha Trang's finest beach resort and, despite the increasing competition, still the loveliest resort in Vietnam, where those who can afford it relax in unashamed and exquisite luxury. Simple but elegant designs are set against cool woods, wafting fans and icy a/c. The resort has 74 rooms in sea view or garden villas that are all beautifully furnished with special touches and new outdoor bathtubs. Every conceivable facilitiy is available in this enchanting retreat, including 2 pools, a tennis court, an enlarged gym, bicycles and restaurants. For those wanting further pampering there is the Six Senses Spa, see Activities and tours, page 282.

LL-L Hon Tam Resort, T58-352 3100, www. hontamresort.vn. This resort has colonised Hon Tam Island. Non-guests can now only visit on a special package. Watersports, a kids' club and traditional craft classes are available.

LL-AL Sheraton Nha Trang Hotel & Spa, 26-28 Tran Phu St, T58-388 0000, www. sheraton.com/nhatrang. New hotel with spaceship penthouse suite on the roof. It's all lovely and stylish but the view from the Feast restaurant on the 1st floor is obscured by coaches, the pool is as choppy as the sea mid afternoon and in shade from mid afternoon, but it's the top chain place to stay with Swiss sleeper beds, baths with ocean view and stylish decor. There are 6 restaurants and bars. The views are outstanding from the higher floors.

LL-AL Sofitel Vinpearl Resort & Spa, 7 Tran Phu St, T58-359 8188, www. vinpearlland.com. The resort itself is on Hon Tre Island, the address given is the reception and ferry jetty. The resort has 400 rooms and a huge range of facilities including a Qi Spa (with excellent facilities) and a gigantic swimming pool, said to be the largest in Asia and clearly visible from the air. The scale and the investment has been colossal and will not suit everyone. The rooms are opulent, beautifully finished in dark woods and marble. However, 'hill view' rooms face a blank quarry wall so try to get 'sea view'.

A Novotel Nha Trang, 50 Tran Phu St, T58-625 6900, www.novotel-nhatrang. com. Super smart rooms in this new hotel overlooking the beach.

A-B The Light Hotel, 86B Tran Phu St, T58-625 2333, www.thelighthotel.com.vn. This is in a great location opposite Louisiane Restaurant. Views are incredible and there's a small pool streetside. Music blares in the afternoon but all in all it's a good choice. Staff are very helpful.

B-D 52 Tran Phu, 52 Tran Phu St, T58-352 4228, www.52tranphuhotel.com. 46 rooms in this newly rebuilt 4-storey seafront hotel. Guestrooms are clean and comfortable. With breakfast included its great value for money.

C Que Huong, 60 Tran Phu St, T58-352 5047, www.quehuonghotel.com.vn. A 5-storey hotel with 56 rooms built on the site of the old one. Rooms have small balconies with sea view. There's a nice swimming pool and restaurant. It's clean, friendly and the price includes breakfast. ATM on site.

C-D La Suisse Hotel, 34 Tran Quang Khai St, T58-352 4353, www.lasuissehotel.com. This is an excellent new hotel with 24 rooms on 5 floors offering excellent value for money. The best rooms (VIP) are large and have attractive balconies with sea view. Breakfast included. All rooms have bathtubs.

C-E Perfume Grass Inn (Que Thao), 4A Biet Thu St, T58-352 4286, www.perfume-grass.

com. This well-run and super friendly family hotel now has 21 rooms. Restaurant and internet service downstairs. Good value for money. Book in advance.

C-G T78, 44 Tran Phu St, T58-352 3445. Formerly the **Grand** and now named with a code which tells us it is a government guesthouse. This impressive, large French colonial mansion that gloriously dominates the seafront has 20 spacious, elegant rooms overlooking the sea with a/c, TV and fridge and 52 cheaper rooms at the back. 12 rooms have fan. There are few staff so don't expect full service but this is a good place to stay; it's like being inside a real 'Cluedo' mansion.

D-E 36 Tran Phu, 36 Tran Phu St, T58-352 4590. A military-run establishment in an art deco building clad with dark wooden shutters. All 64 rooms have a/c with hot water. It's well kept and there's a restaurant. Price negotiable and depends on season. Not much English spoken.

D-E Sao Xanh (Blue Star), 1B Biet Thu St, T58-352 5447, quangc@dng.vnn.vn. Another popular, clean and friendly family-run hotel. 28 rooms, free coffee, Wi-Fi and bananas; more expensive rooms have seaview, bathtubs; breakfast is included. Near the beach and in a popular area.

D-F Backpacker's House, 54G Nguyen Thien Thuat St, T58-352 4500, www.backpackershouse.net. A super clean and bright new place with dorms and private rooms with cable TV and DVD players set up in a courtyard along with the attached **Green Apple Restaurant** and hangout joint. Tours also arranged. A dollar from each booking is invested in the **Anh Dao Orphanage** (http://heartsofnamfoundation.com)

E-G Blue House, 12/8 Hung Vuong St, T58-382 4505, ngovietthuy57@yahoo.com.vn. Down a little alley in a quiet setting. 16 a/c and cheaper fan rooms in a small, neat blue building. Friendly, warm welcome and excellent value for money.

E-G Sao Mai, 99A Nguyen Thien Thuat St, T58-352 6412, saomaiht1@dng.vnn.vn. Popular with travellers. A/c and cheaper fan rooms as well as dorm beds; hot water and kept clean. There's also the **Sao Mai 2**.

F Truc Linh, 27B Hung Vuong St, T58-352 2201, www.truclinhrest.com. Best known for its restaurant, this establishment, with an elevator, is popular with budget travellers. The 14 rooms have a/c, hot water, TV and minibar and some have sea view. Try to opt for a room with external windows.

North of Nha Trang p270

Thanks to the new Tran Phu bridge and extension of Tran Phu St to the north of Nha Trang it is now an easy 4-km ride to get to **Hon Chong Beach**. Consequently all sorts of new guesthouses and cafés are opening in what was previously just a fishing village.

LL Evason Hideaway & Six Senses Spa at Ana Mandara, Ninh Van Bay, 30 km north of Nha Trang (it is 20 km to the boat launch at Pearl Farm and then 10 km offshore to the island), T58-372 8222, www.sixsenses.com. Beach Villas, Rock Villas and Hilltop Villas are laid out in the full dramatic curve of Ninh Van Bay. You can't get more exceptionally luxurious than this; the Rock Villas are perched on rocks at the tip of the bay with bathrooms overlooking the sea and fronted by small infinity pools from where you can gaze out into the bay. The resort is large; from the Rock Villas to the main restaurant is an enormous hike and it's boiling. Beach Villas are more centrally located. While your days away in the herb garden, Six Senses Spa, library, bar and wine cave and be attended by your personal butler. It's highly romantic, very secluded and very expensive; the food is exceptional. The resort is 1 hr ahead of real time which is far too confusing.

L Ki-em Art House, Dong Khoi, Ninh Hai, Ninh Hoa, on Doc Lech Beach, T58-367 0952, www.ki-em.com/resort/. A small resort of 9 bungalows on the beach with gardens and an art gallery. Price is full board.

AL-A White Sand Doc Let Resort & Spa, Ninh Hai Village, Ninh Hoa, T58-367 0670, www.whitesandresort.com.vn. A Doc Lech resort with smart nicely furnished rooms in villa buildings set in a complex along the beach. There's a spa, pool, sauna, tennis court, pool table and watersports. There's also a kids' play area and campground.

B-C Whale Island Resort, T58-384 0501, www.iledelabaleine.com. Bungalows right on this island beach, 2½ hrs north of Nha Trang. The price includes breakfasts. Transfers to Nha Trang and from Nha Trang, twice daily. Activities include diving (**Rainbow Divers**), windsurfing, canoeing and catamaran sailing and there's plenty of wildlife to observe too.

E Jungle Beach Resort, Ninh Phuoc, Ninh Hoa, T58-362 2384, www.junglebeachvietnam.com. North of Nha Trang is this bay backed by mountains and this communal campsite. Guests sleep in bamboo huts or newer accommodation and meals are eaten at communal tables. The price is per person and includes 3 meals a day. Ring the owners to check availability as it can often be full. If you want the basic beach hut experience right on the sands next to the sea, this will be perfect for you.

Quy Nhon *p270*
LL-AL Life Wellness Resort Quy Nhon, Ghenh Rang, Bai Dai Beach, T56-384 0132, www.life-resorts.com. The resort, the first in Vietnam by Life Resorts, is inspired by Cham architecture with 63 rooms all facing the sea. It offers spa treatments, wellness activities and **Life Cuisine**.
AL-A Resort Hoang Anh Quy Nhon, 1 Han Mac Tu St, T56-374 7000, www.hagl.com. vn. A resort of 150 well-appointed rooms that are on the beach with swimming pools, tennis courts, a gym, and massage centre.
F Barbara's Backpackers, T56-389 2921. Dorms and private rooms for budget travellers with attached café. Great place to pick up lots of information.

Quang Ngai *p271*
B-D Petro Song Tra, 2 Quang Trung St, T55-382 2665. Outside of the main centre but with good facilities and Wi-Fi.

E Nha Khach Uy Ban, 54 Hung Vuong St, T55-382 2873. Situated west of the post office, with a/c and a restaurant.

South of Nha Trang *p272*
A-D Bao Dai's Villas, Tran Phu St (just before Cau Da village), T58-359 0147, http://baodaivillas.khatoco.com. Several villas of former Emperor Bao Dai, with magnificent views over the harbour and outlying islands, sited on a small promontory, with large elegant a/c rooms. There are an additional 40 rooms in assorted buildings that lack the scale and elegance, not surprisingly, of the emperor's own quarters. Overrun with sightseers during holiday periods. Now featuring 'the emperor's new dress' dressing-up photo sessions for a fee.

Phan Rang and around *p274*
D Thong Nhat, 343 Thong Nhat St, T68-382 7201, thongnhathotel_pr@hcm.vnn.vn. One of the mini-hotels with 34 rooms and all the modern conveniences but little charm or character. Clean but overpriced, restaurant and the usual karaoke, sauna and massage paraphernalia. Price includes breakfast.

Ninh Chu Beach *p276*
C-D Den Gion Ninh Chu Resort, T68-387 4047. This is a sort of fantasy place which has presumably cost someone a huge amount of money. It is vast with acres of land and attractive bungalows There's a pool, tennis court and restaurant. Camping is possible in the grounds.

Eating

Nha Trang *p266, map p267*
There are a number of seafood restaurants and cafés along the beach road and a wide range of restaurants elsewhere, particularly Indian and Italian. A local speciality is *nem nuong* which is grilled pork wrapped in rice paper with salad leaves and *bun*, fresh rice noodles. The bread in Nha Trang is excellent.

♨-♨ Ana Mandara, Tran Phu St, T58-352 4705. The Ana Mandara has 2 restaurants – the Ana Pavilion, which is open-air and open until the last guest leaves, and the Beach Restaurant, which offers a buffet and à la carte options. The food at this resort is always plentiful and exquisite. Highly recommended.

♨-♨ Gia, 30 Tran Quang Khai St, T58-352 5220. New Vietnamese restaurant in pretty, lantern-lit courtyard with exceptional service. The lemongrass beef with rice vermicelli was delicious.

♨-♨ Good Morning Vietnam, 19B Biet Thu St, T58-352 2071. 1000-2300. Popular Italian restaurant that is strong on pasta and part of a small chain. Vegetarians are catered for.

♨-♨ La Bella Napoli, 6/0 Hung Vuong St, T58-352 7299, labellanapoli@hotmail.com. This good Italian has moved from the beach near the now demolished war memorial to the backpacker quarter.

♨-♨ La Mancha, 78 Nguyen Thien Tuat St, T58-352 7978. 1100-2400. Great atmosphere, with Spanish and sangria decor, barbecued meat on the street. Garlic galore and great dishes but not served together (ie tapas style) and sadly the chorizo is not real. Nonetheless, highly recommended.

♨-♨ Louisiane Brewhouse, 29 Tran Phu St, T58-352 1948, www.louisianebrewhouse.com.vn. Opposite the turning for the old airport. 0700-0100. This place has been transformed into a restaurant and brewery but has maintained its swimming pool so is popular with families for lunch and has a great seating area. Serves a range of Western dishes and seafood; the fish menu is enormous. You can eat facing the beach, the pool or on converted beer barrels.

♨-♨ Sailing Club, 72-74 Tran Phu St, T58-352 4628, sailingnt@dng.vnn.vn. 0700-2300. Although best known as a bar, this busy and attractive beachfront area also includes several restaurants: Japanese, Italian and global cuisine (Casa Italia, Taj Mahal and Sandals). None is cheap but all serve good food and represent decent value.

♨ Café des Amis, 2D Biet Thu St, T58-352 1009. Good for breakfast, vegetarian and seafood. Not cheap and portions are not generous but tasty and nice to sit outside.

♨ Chau Café, 42 Hung Vuong St, T58-352 6336. A diverse menu includes Vietnamese and Indian dishes. Miss Chau, the lady owner and her sisters are friendly and helpful.

♨ Cyclo, 130 Nguyen Thien Thuat St, T58-352 4208, khuongthuy@hotmail.com. 0700-2400. A really outstanding little family-run restaurant. Italian and Vietnamese dishes. Real attention to detail in the bamboo decor and cooking.

♨ Hai Dao, 304 2 Thang 4 St, T58-382 2995. North of town on the way to Ponagar Towers and a great place to stop off for lunch on the way back from sightseeing. Located on an island from where there are views over the river and the Cham towers. The food is good and the seafood recommended, but service is erratic.

♨ Lac Canh, 44 Nguyen Binh Khiem St, T58-382 1391. Specializes in beef, squid and prawns which you barbecue at your table. Also excellent fish and a special eel dish: eel mixed with vermicelli. Smoky atmosphere and it can be hard to get a table. Highly recommended.

♨ Omar's, 96A/8 Tran Phu St, T58-352 2459. A popular Indian restaurant near the beach. Indian chef, excellent and filling food and friendly service.

♨ Paramount Coffee & Bar, 58 Tran Phu St, T58-352 1278. Popular people-watching spot. It's more elegant on the outside than in, which is where you'll want to be.

♨ Thanh Thanh, 10 Nguyen Thien Thuat St, T58-382 4413. Specializes in Italian food. Rather charming with its oil lamps.

♨ Truc Linh 1, 11 Biet Thu St, T58-352 6742. Deservedly popular with sensible prices. Good fruit shake and op la (fried eggs). Service a little slow but plenty to observe while waiting. There's also Truc Linh 2, at 18 Biet Thu St, T58-352 1089, and Truc Linh 3, at 80 Hung Vuong St, T58-352 5259. Nos 2 and 3 are recommended as the best.

Stalls

For excellent and inexpensive beefsteak there are a couple of *Bo Ne* restaurants at the western end of Hoang Van Thu St (that is, away from the beach) that serve beef napoleon and chips. A little way from the centre but worth a visit.

Quy Nhon *p270*

🍴 **Sao Bien Restaurant**, 50 km south of Quy Nhon is the small town of Song Cau, 2 km north of which is this restaurant. Recommended for its crab.

Phan Rang and around *p274*

There are no cafés or restaurants catering to backpackers. There are, however, quite a few *pho* stands and *bia hoi* joints on the west end of **Quang Trung St**, as well as some rice stalls near the bus station and the usual local cafés scattered around town.

🍴 **Hai Nam**, 17 Le Hong Phong, near the market, T68-382 5331. Serves excellent chicken and rice.

🍸 Bars and clubs

Nha Trang *p266, map p267*

Blue Gecko, 42 Biet Thu St, T58-352 3893. Lacks the buzz of the beach bars. Pool table.
Crazy Kim, 19 Biet Thu St, T58-381 6072. Open until late. A busy, popular and lively bar in the heart of a popular part of town. Pool, table tennis, food. Super bakery.
Guava, 17 Biet Thu St, T58-352 4140. 1100-2400. Stylish relaxing café, cocktail bar and lounge bar with garden and with a striking orange front. Good music and bar games.
The Rainbow, 90a Hung Vuong St, T58-352 4351. 0600-2400. This popular bar, run by **Rainbow Divers**, is a current hotspot. Dive information on site too. They've got draft Guinness and other imported beers and provide food in the shape of burgers and pizzas and excellent and generously portioned sushi. Service can be slack though.
Sailing Club, 74-76 Tran Phu St, T58-352 4628. Open until late. Lively bar, especially

on Sat nights when a wide spectrum of locals and visitors congregate to enjoy pool, cold beer, dancing and music.
Shorty's, 5 Biet Thu St, T58-381 0985. Open until 0200. The building here has been redeveloped. There's a bar with a pool table and an interesting menu that includes shepherd's pie and burgers. Second-hand books for sale.
Why Not, 24 Tran Quang Khai St, T58-352 2652. 0900-0400. Brown-cushioned seating on a big terracotta-tiled terrace makes this place an ideal spot for people-watching. There's an inside bar too and pool table. Happy hour is 1600-2300. The bar staff could be quicker on the uptake though.

🛍 Shopping

Nha Trang *p266, map p267*

A number of shops have opened up in the Biet Thu St area selling clothes, jewellery, gifts and handicrafts.
Amart… & more, 13 Biet Thu St. Open 0630-2230. Well-positioned mini-supermarket.
Shorty's, 5 Biet Thu St, T58-352 4057. Has a range of second-hand books which are also sold by boys who lug them around in boxes.
Sunsport, 97 Nguyen Thien Thuat St. Sells sportswear, bags and trainers and flip flops. Recommended.

▲ Activities and tours

Nha Trang *p266, map p267*
Cookery classes
The **Ana Mandara Resort** offers a morning market tour and cookery class. Recommended.

Diving
The Evason Hideway, Ninh Van Bay, has opened a PADI dive centre and are working with the Marine Protected Area Authority in Nha Trang to improve fishing practices in the area and to enlarge the protected area.

Rainbow Divers, 90A Hung Vuong St, T58-352 4351, www.divevietnam.com. It runs a full range of training and courses including the National Geographic dive courses. **Rainbow Divers** receives good reports regarding its equipment and focus on safety. Qualified instructors speak a variety of European languages. Top professional operation. Rainbow also operates out of Whale Island Resort, see page 279.

Fishing
Boats and equipment can be hired from Cau Da Pier; contact **Khanh Hoa Tours**, 1 Tran Hung Dao St, T58-352 6753, www.nhatrangtourist.com.vn, for more information.

Theme parks, waterparks and watersports
The **Evason Ana Mandara Resort**, see Sleeping, above, offers windsurfing, parasailing, hobiecats and fishing.
Phu Dong Amusement and Waterpark, aka **Nha Trang Waterpark**, beach front, Tran Phu St, T58-828883. Tue, Thu, Sat and Sun 0900-1700. If the sea is too rough the children might find the waterpark entertaining. Modest selection of rides.
Vinpearl Land, Tre Island, T58-359 8123, www.vinpearlland.com. This amusement and water park with an artificial mountain and Horror Cave is wildly popular with the Vietnamese. Its Hollywood-style sign can be seen from the shore, creating an eyesore. You can take the ferry (0830-2200) from the Phu Quy tourist jetty at 7 Tran Phu St, 80,000d or private taxi boat. The cable car is 4 km long and runs Mon-Fri 0800-2200, Sat, Sun 0800-2230, 9 mins, 50,000d, children 20,000d. A 300,000d card gets you entrance, rides and cable car ride (210,000d for children)There's a food village and disco on site too. Unfortunately, the light pollution from this rapidly expanding development is horrendous and dominates the night sky in Nha Trang.

Therapies
Six Senses Spa, Ana Mandara Resort, see Sleeping, above, www.sixsenses.com. Offers an array of treatments – Japanese and Vichy showers, hot tubs and massages, exfoliations using fruit body smoothers in beautiful and luscious surroundings. All too good not to indulge. 2007 saw the resort introduce Lifestyle programmes for vitality, stress management and meditation that include tailored spa treatments. 5-day lifestyle packages are US$990 not including accommodation.
Súspa, 93AB Nguyen Thien Thuat St, T58-352 3242, www.suspa.vn.

Tour operators
As so often happens in Vietnam, every café and guesthouse offers tours in the name of some company or other but in the end everyone gets lumped in together.

A number of boat captains and their wives are keen to cash in on the island trip trade and for those seeking a little more solitude in Nha Trang Bay or something a little less routine it may be preferable to charter a boat to see the islands – but establish exactly what the terms are before setting sail as some hapless travellers have been charged extortionate sums for their lunch.

Some tour operators can arrange trips to Buon Ma Thuot and the Central Highlands. **Khanh Hoa Tours**, 1 Tran Hung Dao St, T58-352 6753, www.nhatrangtourist.com.vn. Daily 0700-1130, 1330-1700. Official city tour office. See also page 265.
Mama Hanh/Hanh's Green Hat, 2C Biet Thu St, T58-352 6494, www.biendaotour.com. Boat trips (US$5 including lunch and pick-up from hotel, excluding entrance fees and Con Se Tre village fees). **Mama Hanh** also offers half-day and 1-day tours for US$14. Also other local tours, fishing tours, car, motorbike and bicycle hire.
Mama Linh, 144 Hung Vuong St, T58-352 2844, mamalinhvn@yahoo.com. Organizes boat trips 100,000d and sells minibus tickets to Hoi An, Phan Thiet, HCMC and Dalat. Not as helpful as Mama Hanh.

Sanest Tourist, 86 Tran Phu St, T58-352 8008, www.yensaokhanhhoa.com.vn. Parading as Khanh Hoa tourist office; it isn't but it's more helpful.

Sinh Tourist (formerly Sinh Café), 2A Biet Thu St, T58-352 1981, www.thesinhtouristvn. Offers the usual Sinh Café formula and Open Tour tickets to Nha Trang, Hoi An, Mui Ne, HCMC, Dalat, Hué and Hanoi. **Sinh Tourist** buses arrive and depart from here. It offers the island tour, a Central Highlands tour, city tour and arranges transport to Doc Lech Beach (49 km from Nha Trang), Monkey Island (14 km away) and Ba Ho Waterfalls (22 km away).

⊙ Transport

Nha Trang *p266, map p267*
Air
Connections with **HCMC**, **Hanoi** and **Danang**. Hotels can arrange bus transfers from the airport at Cam Ranh, 34 km away, 30 mins. The airport bus costs 80,000d from the airport and 40,000d from Nha Trang, and arrives at the bus station (T58-352 2589), 200 m from the main road signposted 'Bus Station to Cam Ranh Airport', 2 hrs before every flight. Taxis wait at the bus station to transport passengers to hotels. A taxi from the airport to town costs 260,000d. The airport has a restaurant and PO.

Airline offices Vietnam Airlines, 91 Nguyen Thien Thuat St, T58-352 6768.

Bicycles
Bicycles can be hired from almost every hotel and café in Nha Trang for around 20,000d per day.

Bus and Open Tour Bus
The long-distance bus station (*ben xe lien tinh*) is west out of town at 23 Thang 10 St (23 October St) and has connections with **HCMC**, **Phan Rang**, **Danang**, **Quy Nhon**, **Buon Ma Thuot**, **Dalat**, **Hué** and **Vinh**. Note that inter-province buses do not go into Nha Trang, they drop off at junctions on Highway

1 from where a *xe ôm* will deliver you to your destination. Open Tour Buses arrive at and depart from their relevant operator's café (see Tour operators, above).

Car hire
From **Vien Dong Hotel**, 1 Tran Hung Dao St. **Khanh Hoa Tours**. See also the tour operators listed above.

Motorbike
Motorbikes can be hired from almost every hotel and every café in Nha Trang.

Taxi
Mai Linh, T58-391 0910. **Nha Trang Taxi**, T58-382 6000. From Cam Ranh Airport to town, 260,000d.

Train
The station is a yellow building with blue shutters on Thai Nguyen St, T58-382 0666. Open 0700-1130, 1330-1700, 1800-2200. There are train connections with **Hanoi** and **HCMC** and all stops between the two.

Quy Nhon *p270*
Air
The airport is 35 km to the north. Connections with **HCMC** and **Danang**. Take a motorbike or taxi to the airport.

Bus
The bus station is on Tay Son St. Express buses leave for **Hanoi**, **HCMC**, **Nha Trang**, **Danang**, **Dalat**, **Hué**.

Train
The station is just over 1 km northwest of the town centre, on Hoang Hoa Tham St, which runs off Tran Hung Dao St. Express trains do not stop here. To catch the express, take the shuttle train to Dieu Tri, 10 km away.

Quang Ngai *p271*
Bus
The bus station is on Le Thanh Ton St south of the centre.

Train

The station is about 3 km west of town. There are regular connections with **Hanoi** and **HCMC** and all stops between the two.

Phan Rang and around p274
Bus

The bus station is on the east side of Thong Nhat, near the post office. Local buses, however, leave from the south side of town. Regular connections with **HCMC**, **Dalat** and **Nha Trang**.

Train

The closest stop is **Thap Cham**, about 5 km west of town, T68-388 8084. Train tickets can also be booked in Phan Thiet town.

❶ Directory

Nha Trang p266, map p267
Banks Vietcombank, 17 Quang Trung St. Will change most major currencies, cash, TCs (2% commission), and arrange cash advances on some credit cards. There's a Vietcombank exchange bureau at 8A Biet

Thu St. **Agribank**, 2 Huong Vuong St, with ATM. **Hospitals** General Hospital, 19 Yersin St, T58-382 2168. **Internet** There are internet cafés all over town, particularly in Biet Thu St and Hong Vuong St. Hugo.net, 1E Huong Vuong St. **Post office** GPO, 1 Hung Vuong St.

Quy Nhon p270
Banks Vietcombank, 152 Le Loi St. Changes US dollars, cash and TCs. **Hospitals** General Hospital, 102 Nguyen Hue St, T56-382 2722. **Internet** 245 Le Hong Phong St. **Post office** Phan Boi Chau St.

Quang Ngai p271
Banks Vietcombank, 45 Hung Vuong St. **Internet** 141 Hung Vuong St. **Post office** 80 Phan Dinh Phung St.

Phan Rang and around p274
Banks Bank, 540 Thong Nhat St. **Post office** 217 Thong Nhat St, the north end near the turn-off to Ninh Chu.

Phan Thiet and Mui Ne

→ Colour map 4, B5.

Phan Thiet is a fishing town at the mouth of the Ca Ty River. Despite its modest appearance and unassuming nature it is the administrative capital of Binh Thuan Province. For the traveller the real attraction lies east of town in the form of the 20-km sweep of golden sand of Mui Ne. Here can be found Vietnam's finest collection of coastal resorts with some excellent watersports and two of the country's most attractive golf courses. Overdevelopment is a real issue, though. Water and electricity are intermittently available at budget accommodations, though luxury resorts usually have reserves. Both pollution and seasonal erosion, augmented by development, detract from the beach during busy season. Road safety has also become a serious concern with several foreign fatalities (and many more locals) in 2009 and 2010, as both passengers and pedestrians. ▶▶ *For listings, see pages 286-290.*

Ins and outs

Getting there The drive from Ho Chi Minh City takes five to six hours. The north-south Open Tour Buses all divert to Mui Ne and drop off/pick up from every hotel along the beach. The express buses stop at the station in Phan Thiet and it is easy to take a motorbike taxi from there to Mui Ne. Hiring a car from Ho Chi Minh City is approximately US$75. From Nha Trang the journey is about as long, though much lengthier if stopping off to see the Cham Towers in Phan Rang. There are also rail connections from Phan Thiet to the mainline station at Muong Man, 12 km from Phan Thiet. A new line connects Ho Chi Minh City directly with Phan Thiet, leaving Phan Thiet daily at 1345 and 2235 Sat and Sun. All other city connections are available via the Muong Man station.

Getting about Both motorbike taxis and Mai Linh car taxis abound in the town and along the Mui Ne strip. ▸▸ *See Transport, page 290.*

Best time to visit The weather in Phan Thiet always seems nice. It is, of course, better in the dry season, December through April. Phan Thiet is most popular with overseas visitors (and the growing number of package tour operators) in the Christmas to Easter period when prices at the some of the better hotels rise by 20% or more. From December to March, Mui Ne loses portions of its beach to the sea.

Tourist information **Binh Thuan Tourist** ① *82 Trung Trac St, T62-381 6821, www.binhthuan-tourist.com*, arranges tours and car rentals.

Phan Thiet

Phan Thiet's 18-hole **golf course**, designed by Nick Faldo, is regarded by golfers as one of the best in Vietnam. Golfers come from all around the region to play it.

The most distinctive landmark in town is the municipal **water tower** completed in 1934. It is an elegant structure with a pagoda-like roof; built by the infamous "Red Prince" and first president of Laos. The tower icon features in the logos of many local businesses and agencies. There are a few **Ho Chi Minh relics**, including a **museum** on Nguyen Truong To Street and the **Duc Thanh school** next door, where Ho Chi Minh taught in 1911, but otherwise nothing of interest at the museum.

The **Van Thuy Thu Temple** ① *20A Ngu Ong St, 0730-1130 and 1400-1700, 5000d*, is the oldest whale temple (built in 1762) in Vietnam. The temple houses more than 100 whale skeletons, including one specimen more than 22m in length. Like all whale temples, it was originally built by the sea, but as sea levels have receded, this temple is now stranded in the middle of the neighborhood.

Mui Ne

Mui Ne (or Cape Ne) is the name of the famous sandy cape and the small fishing village that lies at its end. Mui Ne's claims to fame are its *nuoc mam* (fish sauce) and its **beaches** where it is possible to do a host of watersports including kiteboarding for which it is justly famous. Body boarding and surfing are better December to January when there are more waves. The wind dies down at the end of April, and May has virtually no wind. The cape is dominated by some impressive **sand dunes**; some are golden but in other parts quite red, a reflection of the underlying geology. Around the village visitors may notice a strong smell of rotting fish. This is the unfortunate but inevitable by-product of fish sauce fermenting in wooden barrels. The *nuoc mam* of Phan Thiet is made from anchovies, as *cá com* on the label testifies. The process takes a year but to Vietnamese palates it is worth every day. *Nuoc mam* from Phan Thiet is regarded highly but not as reverentially as that from the southern island of Phu Quoc.

There are still significant numbers of Cham (50,000) and Ra-glai (30,000) minorities, who until a century ago, were the dominnt groups in the region. There are many relics of the Champa kingdom here in Binh Thuan Province, the best and easiest to find being

Po Shanu, two Cham towers dating from the late eighth century on a hill on the Mui Ne road. They are now somewhat broken down but the road leading up to them makes a nice evening ride; you can watch the sun set and from this vantage point you'll see the physical make-up of the coastal plain and estuaries to the south and the central highlands to the north. Driving up the long climb towards Mui Ne the towers are on the right-hand side of the road and quite unmissable. Like Cham towers elsewhere in this part of the country they were constructed of brick bound together with resin of the *day* tree. Once the tower was completed timber was piled around it and ignited; the heat from the flames melted the resin, which solidified on cooling.

Hon Rom

Hon Rom, about 15 km by motorbike or bicycle from Mui Ne, is the name of the undeveloped bay north of Mui Ne and is accessible only from Mui Ne. North of Hon Rom is Suoi Noc, Binh Thien Village and Turtle Island. The **Full Moon Beach Resort** at Mui Ne is planning to open Full Moon Villas and Jibe's II at Suoi Noc.

◉ Phan Thiet and Mui Ne listings

For Sleeping and Eating price codes and other relevant information, see Essentials pages 26-31.

● Sleeping

Phan Thiet *p285*

AL Novotel Phan Thiet Ocean Dunes & Golf Resort, 1 Ton Duc Thang St, T62-382 2393, www.accorhotels.com. On the beach just outside Phan Thiet, this is set behind lovely gardens. 123 comfortable rooms (although some of these are showing their age) in a bland building and new well-appointed villas with beach views. Good facilities, 2 pools, 2 restaurants with tasty food , bar, tennis courts and gym. Guests enjoy a 30% discount on green fees at the adjacent 18-hole champion golf course, the **Ocean Dunes Golf Club**.

Mui Ne *p285*

High season is dry season, Nov-May, when prices rise by around 20%. Many of the resorts also raise their prices at weekends. Weekends tend to be busier as Mui Ne is a popular escape for expats from HCMC. There has been a great construction boom and there are now many places to stay at a range of prices. Fortunately supply has kept up with demand so Mui Ne offers good value. Advisable to

book ahead as the popular places fill up fast particularly around Christmas and Tet and Vietnamese public holidays.

LL Victoria Phan Thiet Beach Resort & Spa, T62-381 3000, www.victoriahotels-asia.com. Part of the French-run Victoria Group, the resort has 59 upgraded thatched bungalows with new outdoor rain showers and 3 villas, built in country-house style in an attractive landscaped setting. It is well equipped with restaurants, bar, 2 pools, sports facilities, a children's club and a spa.

L-AL Seahorse Resort & Spa, T62-384 7507, www.seahorseresortvn.com. Tastefully decorated and designed bungalows and rooms set around a large pool. There's also a kids' pool and tennis court. A lavish buffet breakfast is included.

AL Bamboo Village, T62-384 7007, www.bamboovillageresortvn.com. Attractive, simple hexagonal bamboo huts and larger thatched villas and lodges in a lovely shady spot at the top of the beach. More expensive rooms have a/c and hot-water showers. An excellent restaurant and attractive pool.

AL Blue Ocean Resort & Spa (Bien Xanh Resort), T62-384 7322, www.blueoceanresort.com. The low-key sea view bungalows are not much bigger than the standard rooms at this new resort with a lovely pool, landscaped garden area and thatched umbrellas planted on the beach.

AL Coco Beach (Hai Duong), T62-384 7111-3, www.cocobeach.net. The European owners live here and the place is well run. Not luxurious but friendly and impeccably kept. 28 wooden bungalows and 3 wooden, 2-bedroom 'villas' facing the beach. Beautiful setting, lovely pool and relaxing. Excellent restaurant and a beachclub. **Coco Beach** was the first resort on Mui Ne and it is pleasing how, despite (or because of) a little competition, it remains easily among the best. Price includes a decent buffet breakfast. There are 2 restaurants, the French **Champa** is open Tue-Sun 1500-2200 only, but beach club is open all day.

A Saigon Mui Ne, T62-384 7303, www.saigonmuineresort.com. This is a **Saigontourist** resort, perfectly professional but lacking flair and imagination. Bungalows, pool, jacuzzi, restaurant, spa, fitness centre and kiteboarding classes.

A Sailing Club, T62-384 7440, www.sailingclubvietnam.com. This is a gorgeous resort. Designed in the most charming style its bungalows and rooms are simple and cool and surrounded by dense and glorious vegetation. For inspiration and good taste it ranks among the best in Vietnam. Its pool has been extended and the bathrooms for the superior rooms enlarged. It has an excellent restaurant (a branch of **Sandals** in Saigon) and bar. A good buffet breakfast is included. Western owned and managed it is a beacon of excellence from which one hopes the whole Vietnamese tourist industry will draw inspiration.

A Swiss Village Resort, T62-384 7480, www.svr-vn.com.The cheapest rooms are in the hotel, the most expensive are in large, seafront villas. It has every conceivable amenity from conference rooms and a post office to tennis court, swimming pool, massage and sauna.

B The Beach Resort, T62-384 7626, www.thebeachresort.com.vn. A very attractive resort with 40 rooms set in luscious gardens with a lovely pool surrounded by tip top shrubbery and thatched umbrellas on the beach. Good value.

B Full Moon Beach, T62-384 7008, www.windsurf-vietnam.com. Visitors are assured of a friendly reception by the French and Vietnamese couple who own and run the place. Accommodation is in a variety of types: some rooms are spacious, others a little cramped, some brick, some bamboo. The most attractive rooms have a sea view and constant breeze. There is a good restaurant.

B Thuy Thuy, T62-384 7357, T091-816 0637 (mob), thuythuyresort2000@yahoo.com. Just 7 pleasant a/c bungalows with TV run by the friendly Elaine. Newer bungalows are a bit more expensive but the originals are perfectly comfortable. Set on the 'wrong' side of the road (ie away from the beach) this is nevertheless a rather charming and nicely run little place. Guests have the highest praise for it. Attractive swimming pool.

B-C Sea Breeze, T62-384 7373, www.muineseabreeze.com.vn This far north the beach is getting a bit narrow and the road is a little close to some of the rooms for comfort. Although they are slightly pricier, insist on a sea-view room, of which there are 2 categories. The place is well kept, clean and comfortable. Breakfast included. Motorbike and bike rental.

C Mui Ne Resort (Sinh Tourist), T62-384 7542, This recommended resort has packed the narrow site with 48 rooms and brick-built bungalows, rather like a crowded **Sinh Tourist** tour bus though the prices aren't as cheap as they once were. It has a nice pool. Bar and restaurant for guests and for those waiting for their bus to come along.

D Small Garden (Vuon Nho) Resort, T62-387 4012, nguyengrimm@yahoo.com. Run by a Vietnamese family, it consists of simple bamboo hut accommodation in well-cared-for gardens near the road and new small a/c concrete bungalows nearer the beach. Although lacking in amenities it is in a good part of the beach with plenty of cafés and restaurants nearby.

E Hiep Hoa, T62-384 7262, T090-812 4149 (mob), hiephoatourism@yahoo.com. This is an attractive place. Now with 15 a/c rooms. It's quiet, clean and with its own stretch of beach. Popular and should be booked in advance. Its rates are excellent value for Mui Ne; they go down in the low season.

🍴 Eating

Mui Ne *p285*
Mui Ne hotel restaurants tend to be expensive compared with the restaurants and cafés on the opposite side of the road. Of the hotel restaurants the Sailing Club, Sea Horse and Coco Beach stand out. Many hotels do good barbecues at the weekend.
🍴 **Forest Restaurant**, 7 Nguyen Dinh Chieu St, T62-384 7589, www.forestrestaurant.com. Local dishes and lots of seafood, this garden-jungle setting puts on live music and dance shows throughout the evening.
🍴 **Good Morning Vietnam**, T62-384 7585, www.goodmorningviet.com. Part of the branch chain of Italian restaurants. Usually packed and reliable in quality and service. They run a pick-up service to bring customers from more distant ends of the beach. Claimed 'MSG free zone'.
🍴 **Luna D'Autonno**, T62-384 7591. One of the best Italian restaurants in Indochina. A most inspired menu goes way beyond the standard pizzas and pasta with daily fish specials and BBQs. Huge portions and a good wine list.
🍴 **Jibe's Beach Club**, T62-384 7405. 0700-late. Popular chill-out bar serving burgers, salads and food with an Italian bent. This bar has matured with age and now suits career adults rather than rowdy backpackers. Come for the Sat night BBQ.
🍴 **Shree Ganesh** 57 Nguyen Dinh Chieu, T62-374 1330. This popular Omar's franchise serves North Indian and Tandoori cuisine. One of the best in Mui Ne.
🍴 **Sunset**, T62-384 7605. Good Vietnamese food, especially fish. Efficient service and excellent value.

🍸 Bars and cafés

Mui Ne *p285*
Joe's Cafe, 139 Nguyen Dinh Chieu St, T62-374 3447. A cosy, American-style café serving Bobby Brewer's coffee and American comfort food. Open 24 hrs with free Wi-Fi.
Pogo, www.thepogobar.com. Just down from Sinh Tourist with cocktails, movies, beer and local and international food
Sankara, 78 Nguyen Dinh Chieu St , T62-374 1122, www.sankaravietnam.com. This chic new beachside bar with pool has made a lot of noise since its much-anticipated opening in 2009. The place to see and be seen on weekends and holidays.
Snow, 109 Nguyen Dinh Chieu St, T62-374 3123. A stylish a/c Russian-owned bar with an extensive cocktails list and great sushi.
Wax, 68 Nguyen Dinh Chieu St, T62-384 7001. Located beside the beach at Windchamp Resort, Wax is dance-part central, especially during holidays.

🛍 Shopping

Mui Ne *p285*
There is now a large selection of shops in Mui Ne spanning the west end of the beach. Almost anything can be found, from beachwear, water sports equipment, peals and jewelry, lacquerware to crocodile leather. For a certified goldsmith who uses local gems, check out **Tinh & Sabine's** gold shop.

⛰ Activities and tours

Phan Thiet *p285*
Golf
Ocean Dunes Golf Club, 1 Ton Duc Thang St, T62-382 3366, www.oceandunesgolf. vn. This Nick Faldo-designed 18-hole, 6147-m course is highly regarded. It has a fully equipped club house with bar and restaurant, pro-shop and locker rooms. Green fees start at US$55 and go up to US$165 for walk-in seeking unlimited play (including caddie fees).

Tennis
Novotel Ocean Dunes & Golf Resort,
1 Ton Duc Thang St, T62-822 393, www.
accorhotels-asia.com. On the beach just
outside Phan Thiet.

Mui Ne *p285*
Classic car rides
Chasseur Blanc, T62-374 1222, T091-821
0876 (mob), www.chasseurblanc.com. Tours
in an old Citroën, US jeep or motorbikes with
sidecars to remote areas in the locality. Run
by Christophe Laville who was the activities
manager at the **Victoria Phan Thiet** for
more than 3 years and thus has done a fair
amount of exploring. Prices round US$35
per person per tour to a local sight. There's a
bar and garden restaurant in the attractively
designed and decorated building.

Golf
Forester Mini Golf, 7 Nguyen Dinh Chieu
St, T62-384 7589, www.forestrestaurant.
com. This 9-hole course is designed to look
like terraced rice paddies, nestled between
hilltribe stilt houses, the **Forester Spa**, and
the family-friendly **Docking Bar**.
Sea Links Golf & Country Club, T62-374
1666, www.sealinksvietnam.com. This 18-
hole course has breathtaking 270-degree
views of Mui Ne's coast. The property has
been expanded to include a luxury hotel,
villas, and has plans to develop a private
beach, luxury hotel and shopping centre.

Therapies
Lotus Day Spa, Sailing Club, T62-384 7440,
www.sailingclubvietnam.com. Massage
treatments are available in special cabins
in the **Sailing Club** grounds.
The Village, Victoria Phan Thiet Beach
Resort & Spa, see Sleeping, above. The
hotel's own on-site centre.

Watersports
Mui Ne is the water sports capital of
Vietnam. The waters can be crowded
with wind surfers and kite boarders. The
combination of powerful wind and waves
enables good kite surfers to get airborne for
several seconds at a time. Equipment and
training is offered by numerous centers.
Jibe's Beach Club, T62-384 7405, T091-316
2005 (mob), www.windsurf-vietnam.com.
The original centre which is part of and
close to **Full Moon Beach Resort**. Jibe's is
the importer of sea kayaks, windsurfers,
surfboards, sailboats, SUP (stand-up paddle)
and kitesurf equipment. Equipment is
available for purchase or for hire by the hr,
day or week. Hourly windsurf lessons are
US$45 and hourly kitesurf lessons are US$50;
US$7.50 surfboard hire; boogie board hire
US$2.50; kayaking US$5 per hr per person. It
also does a range of swimming costumes for
those who forgot to pack theirs.
Storm, T62-384 7442 www.
stormkiteboarding.com, has a station at the
beachfront of the **Sailing Club**. There are
also 2 **Storm** shops in town. Kiteboarding
lessons, starting at US$99; equipment hire
starting at US$30 per hr, surf lesson US$45
per hr; surf hire US$15 per hr.
Windchimes, Saigon-Mui Ne and **Bamboo
Village Resorts**,T90-972 0017, www.
kitesurfing-vietnam.com, is another major
provider of lessons and gear rentals.

Tour operators
Au Viet Travel, 53 Nguyen Dinh Chieu,
T62-374 3033, T090-879 6914 (mob), www.
go2vietnam.de. Excellent bikes for rent.
Hanh, Newly located in the Cat Trang
(White Sand Dunes Hotel) across from
Sankara, T62-384 7347. Buses to Dalat, HCMC
and Nha Trang. Exchange services too.
Sinh Tourist, 144 Nguyen Dinh Chieu St,
T62-384 7542, muine@thesinhtourist.vn. A
branch of the tour operator good for Open
Tour Bus tickets and local tours to the sand
dunes, fishing village and Phan Thiet city
tour. Transport rented.
Victor Tours, 121A Nguyen Dinh Chieu,
across from **Full Moon Resort**, T98-959 1599.
Victor Tours offers a full range of tour to
all the local sites and books bus transport

throughout Vietnam. Customs tours and unique outings are also available.

⊖ Transport

Phan Thiet and Mui Ne *p284*
Bicycles and motorbikes
Xe ôms are abundant in Phan Thiet town. Bikes (US$3 per day) and motorbikes (normally US$5-10 per day) can be rented from hotels or tour operators, see **Victor Tours**, tour operators, above, and are the best way to explore the vicinity.

Bus and Open Tour Bus
The bus station is on the east side of town next to the 19/4 Hotel. Connections with all neighbouring towns. A local bus plies the nearby Phan Thiet Coop supermarket to **Mui Ne** route, as do taxis. **Phuong Trang** and **Sinh Tourist** Open Tour Buses drop off and pick up from all resorts on **Mui Ne**. The Sinh Tourist bus departs from its resort and Phuong Trang from its central office. To **Nha Trang** and **HCMC** twice a day at 1300 and 2345 (also 0800 to HCMC), US$4.5, 5½ hrs, both journeys. To **Dalat**, 0700, US$6, 7 hrs. Phuong Trang, 97 Nguyen Dinh Chieu St, T62-374 3113, www.phuongtrangdalat.com. This Dalat-based company has emerged as the leader in Vietnam, with the most reliable, trustworthy and comfortable services anywhere south of Hué.

Car
Binh Thuan Tourist, 82 Trung Trac St, can arrange car hire, as can most hotels. A private car to HCMC will cost US$80.

Taxi
Travelling from one end of the strip to another can cost up to 100,000d. A taxi from Phan Thiet to Mui Ne is around US$6-7.

A *xe ôm* charges 10,000d for 1 km or more along the Mui Ne strip.
Mai Linh, T62-389 8989. These are as reliable as can be expected in Vietnam and found throughout Mui Ne.

Train
The Phan Thiet train station connects with the old station at **Muong Man**, 12 km to the west, on its way to Saigon. Trains leave Phan Thiet daily at 1345 and 2235.on weekends. From Muong Man there are also slow trains north to **Hanoi**. Transport to and from the Muong Man station should be arranged in advance as drivers are known to extort stranded travelers here. A taxi from Mui Ne to Muong Man for the train is 250,000d on the meter, 45 mins; don't agree to a non-metered fare. It's safest to catch the train connection in and out of Phan Thiet.
The trip from Phan Thiet to **HCMC** is a comfortable and scenic route. Even better, it's now faster and cheaper than the Open Tour Buses. The train takes just under 5 hrs, while buses take 5½-6 hrs. Train tickets vary from 70,000d-85,000d.

⊙ Directory

Mui Ne *p285*
Banks There are no banks in Mui Ne but a couple of ATMs; the **Saigon Mui Ne Resort** has one, there's one at **Wind Champ** resort, and there is one in front of the **Ocean Star Resort** that is next to the **Sailing Club**.
Hospitals Polyclinic, next to Swiss Resort, T62-384749, T091-821 0504 (mob), open 1130-1330, 1730-2100. An-Phuoc Hospital, 235 Tran Phu St, Ward Phu Trinh, T62-383 1056. in Phan Thiet is the best hospital in the province. **Internet** Coco Café is the best traditional internet café, located across from Full Moon Resort. Most Resorts and large restaurants or bars offer free Wi-Fi.

Phan Thiet *p285*
Banks Vietinbank, 2 Nguyen Tat Thanh St, near the Victory Monument, cashes TCs. For best rates, change at the bank or gold stores in town. Hotels and restaurants are a rip-off.
Post office Intersection of Nguyen Tat Thanh and Ton Duc Thang streets.

Vung Tau and around

→ Colour map 4, B4.

Vung Tau is the hub of the country's oil industry, a significant port and home to a major fishing fleet. Despite earlier successes it is now rather a downmarket seaside resort and, as gas is piped ashore to power stations and processing plants, it is becoming a sort of oriental Teesside, an image enhanced by Vung Tau's greyhound racing track. Up the coast are the resorts of Long Hai and the hot springs at Binh Chau. It's popular with Australian visitors and expats.
▶▶ For listings, see pages 295-298.

Ins and outs

Getting there Vung Tau is a painless two- to three-hour road journey from Ho Chi Minh City. The bus and minibus stations are both relatively central and there are regular connections from Ho Chi Minh City. The hydrofoil service from central Ho Chi Minh City takes one hour. To get to Long Hai, take the Vung Tau bus, get off at Ba Ria and catch a *xe ôm* from there.

Getting around Vung Tau has the normal fleet of *Honda ôms* and a good number of taxis but rather few cyclos. Distances within town are quite short and much can be covered on foot: from the hydrofoil to central hotels, for example. ▶▶ *See Transport, page 298.*

Tourist information There is a **tourist office** ① *207 Vo Thi Sau St, T64-385 6445, www. vungtautourist.com.vn.*

History

Before the 17th century, Vung Tau was under the control of the Khmer kings of Cambodia. A large dam and reservoir to the north was built by one of the Cambodian kings to water his horses and elephants. In the 17th century, the Vietnamese annexed the surrounding territory, and later still the French gained control. The town began to develop as a seaside resort at the beginning of the 20th century when roads linking it to Saigon were constructed. At this time it was known as Cap Saint-Jacques and considered a fine resort by the French; adequate, at least, for the Governor General of Indochina to build himself a retreat here.

Vung Tau is situated on a rocky and hilly promontory that juts into the sea. This is the last piece of solid coastal geology until Hon Chong near Cambodia, which gives some indication of the vast expanse of mud of the Saigon and Mekong river deltas that lie to the south. The town nestles between two hills, Nui Lon (Big Mountain) to the north and Nui Nho (Small Mountain) to the south. It is now a popular resort town for Vietnamese day trippers and enjoys a relatively high level of prosperity, its wealth based on oil, trade and its role as provincial capital of Ba Ria-Vung Tau Province.

Oil was found off the coast of Vung Tau in the 1970s and after 1975 the Russians moved in to help develop the fields. Then, in what now seem the heady days of the early 1990s, British, Japanese and Canadian oil companies poured vast sums of money into the search for more of the black stuff. But, with the exception of relatively minor gas deposits, not much was found and most oilmen have packed their kitbags and gone to prospect in more promising strata. Some cling on but more from inertia than any real sense of optimism. As a result the construction boom and easy riches which poured into the town have come to an end. In addition the Russians are also moving away: from 5000 in 1996 the contingent was down to 1000 in 1998 and are now no more than a couple of hundred.

Sadly for Vung Tau the development of other coastal resort towns means very few foreign tourists now ever reach Vung Tau. Nearby Long Hai, for instance, is packed with visitors every weekend for the simple reason that it has clean sandy beaches. But Vung Tau should not be dismissed lightly; it is a short hydrofoil ride from Ho Chi Minh City and a good place to take a non-beachy seaside break. With its cooling breezes and quiet streets it is pleasantly relaxing after the stresses of Ho Chi Minh City.

Sights and beaches → *For listings, see pages 295-298.*

Being a beach resort one would expect good beaches but with the exception of Bai Sau (Back Beach) they are poor – narrow, with little or no sand, no coral and second-rate swimming. Even the Back Beach can be a grubby affair: it is narrow and not particularly clean and the colour of the water is not inviting. In the town itself is **Bai Truoc** (Front Beach), lined with kiosks and restaurants and really not a beach at all. Freighters moor offshore and the bay and beach are home to Vung Tau's fishing fleet. South from town, taking the coast road (Halong Street), is **Bai Dua** (Pineapple Beach, formerly Roches Noires Beach) and a collection of guesthouses and hotels. Again, the beach is poor. At Bai Dua there are two temples, one with a **large Buddha** looking out to sea. Also at Bai Dua is **Niet Ban Tinh Xa**, a pagoda built on a hill in 1971. It is said to be one of the largest temples in Vietnam, and contains a 5000-kg bronze bell and a 12-m-long reclining Buddha.

Around the headland is a small cove with good surf – **Mui Nghinh Phong** (formerly Au Vents Beach); swimming can be dangerous here. Northeast from the headland, on Thuy Van Street, and just past the **island pagoda of Hon Ba**, is the longest stretch of sand – **Bai Sau** (**Back Beach**). Bai Sau is about 2 km southeast from the centre of town, taking Hoang Hoa Tham Street. This is a beach in the usual sense of the word, comprising 5 km of sand. It is exposed to the wind and the East Sea and the surf is usually good, sometimes ferocious. Overlooking the East Sea at the south end of Bai Sau is a **giant statue of Jesus** with arms outstretched – not on the same scale as that in Rio de Janeiro but impressive nevertheless. Behind the figure, on Small Mountain, Nui Nho, is a **lighthouse** built in 1910 which can be reached either from Halong Street (near the **Hai Au Hotel**) up Hem 150 or from the southern end of Bai Sau. It is a pleasant walk or motorbike ride in the late afternoon. Many local people do the walk for exercise. At a shade under 200 m it is sufficiently high to be cooler than sea level and there are good views of the town, bays and sea.

North of town, **Bach Dinh** (Villa Blanche) ⓘ *12 Tran Phu St (the coast road), daily 0700-1700, 5000d*, was built in the early part of the 20th century as a summer residence for Governor General Paul Doumer on the site of an old fort. King Thanh Thai was kept here from 1906-1917 prior to being sent into exile on the island of Réunion, and it was later used by President Thieu. The house is now a museum housing a sample of what the Vietnamese call the Hon Cau ceramics but what the rest of the world calls the Vung Tau ceramics. Whatever, these are Ching Dynasty ceramics salvaged in 1990-1991 from a Chinese trading junk which sank near Con Dao Island around 1690. The ceramics were auctioned at Christies in Amsterdam for US$7.3 million in 1992. The find was highly significant not only for its size, consisting of 48,000 pieces, but also because it represents some of the first pieces of standing as opposed to flat ceramics to come from China. The collection here consists of vases, goblets and small statues; some are encrusted with coral and some retain their original elegant blue and white glaze.

Bai Dau Beach is 3 km northwest of town at the fishing village of Ben Dinh (now geared primarily to the demands of domestic tourists). Again, the beach is nothing special, but it is the quietest spot on the peninsula. The pagoda on the hill here is called **Hung Thang Tu**.

Although there are numerous pagodas and churches in Vung Tau none is particularly noteworthy. At the south end of Tran Hung Dao Boulevard is a massive and rather crude **statue of General Tran Hung Dao** who defeated a Chinese invasion force in the mid-13th century. On the way to Bai Sau, is the 100-year-old **Linh Son Co Tu Pagoda** ① *104 Hoang Hoa Tham St*. Not far away on the other side of the road from the Linh Son Pagoda is the **Lang Ca Ong (Whale Dedication Temple)** ① *77A Hoang Hoa Tham St*, adorned in red and

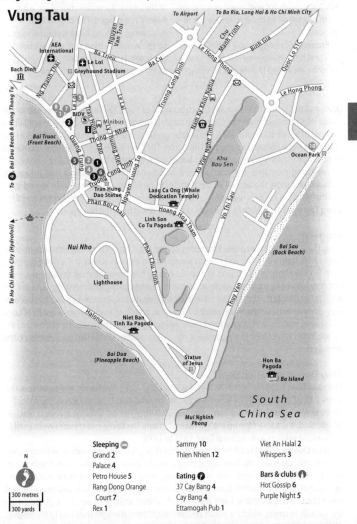

Vung Tau

Sleeping 🛏
Grand **2**
Palace **4**
Petro House **5**
Rang Dong Orange
Court **7**
Rex **1**

Sammy **10**
Thien Nhien **12**

Eating 🍴
37 Cay Bang **4**
Cay Bang **4**
Ettamogah Pub **1**

Viet An Halal **2**
Whispers **3**

Bars & clubs 🍸
Hot Gossip **6**
Purple Night **5**

gold, and dedicated to the whale, the patron god of Vung Tau fishermen (worship of the whale was inherited from the Cham, see box, above). It was built in 1911 and contains a number of whale skeletons displayed in cabinets behind the main altar. The cabinet to the right of the altar contains a skeleton dating from 1931, while the central skeleton is believed to date from 1848. Whale and dolphin bones are brought to the temple and worshipped before being cremated: they are credited with saving drowning sailors and fishermen. Photographs show the annual Whale Dedication ceremony. The Vietnamese regard large sea mammals as big fish: the whale is *cá voi* (jumbo fish) and the dolphin *cá heo* (pig fish). **Vung Tau market** ① *Nam Ky Khoi Nghia St*, is just down from the bus station.

Long Hai

Long Hai is a small town a few kilometres up the coast from Vung Tau, although in order to get here from Vung Tau you have to retreat inland as far as Ba Ria. It is a two-hour drive from Ho Chi Minh City. Glimpses of the sea can be had from the road through the trees, but only just. Long expanses of clean sand and beaches far superior to Vung Tau's are the main attraction, but although the town itself is rather shabby, in recent years it has become very popular with Vietnamese tourists. Along the stretch of road that runs north of Long Hai several resorts have opened and more will surely follow. The character building of the Palace Hotel has closed but opposite it runs a brand new swimming pool complex and tennis court.

Thuy Duong and Minh Danh

The road from Long Hai winds its merry way around rocky headlands and passing within a few feet of small, sandy beaches; watch out for sand that is blown across the road. The caves at **Minh Danh** ① *5 km from Long Hai, 20,000d if you are unlucky*, are soon reached. Signposted, it is a scramble up the hill to reach them. The caves and crevices were used by communist soldiers as a hide-out from 1948 to 1975.

Thuy Duong is soon reached, some 5 km from Long Hai. This amounts to nothing except a few hotels, cafés and shelters. But at weekends the place comes alive with families from Ho Chi Minh City, Bien Hoa and, one suspects, Vung Tau. The beaches here are superb, gently shelving and golden; there is lovely swimming, it's safe for kids and peaceful mid-week but there is no shade. Even at weekends a short walk will take you well away from the crowds to coves, which romantic couples might have thought they had to themselves.

Loc An and Ho Coc

After Thuy Duong, the new coastal road soon reaches Loc An, 8 km further on and then tiny Ho Coc. The beach here is long and wide, another idyllic place for swimming and relaxing (it will be cleaner if you don't swim directly in front of the resorts). This is a true escape as the landscape is wild and almost wholly undeveloped. During the week you can have the place almost to yourself but at the weekend a crush of trippers descends.

Binh Chau hot springs

ⓘ *T64-387 1131, www.saigonbinhchauecoresort.com, daily 0500-1900, part of an eco-resort, prices vary.*

A further 10 km or so east are the hot springs at Binh Chau. Here you can immerse yourself in a communal or a private pool, although be careful where you bathe: in places the sulphurous water bubbles out of springs at 82°C. See for yourself by buying an egg and cooking it. Other baths range from 37-60°C. There's a hotel here, foreign exchange bureau, restaurant, changing rooms, tennis, basketball and volleyball courts plus jacuzzi, steambath, karaoke and fishing.

Towards Phan Thiet, Ke Ga and Tien Thanh → *For listings, see pages 295-298.*

From Binh Chau to Phan Thiet you will pass dozens of dragonfruit plantations – the upright plants look as if they have long cactus hair; you will also pass ox and cart on the road and in the fields and remote hamlets in an area continuing a traditional way of life.

Some 25 km before Phan Thiet is the rock and sand bay of Ke Ga dominated by a tall thin French lighthouse built in 1899. The rocks in this area are an unusual phallic shape. The **Princess d'Annam Resort** has found seclusion here, see Sleeping, page 297. Nearby are the **Blue World Resort**, **Rock Garden Spa Resort**, and a host of others. Around 18 km south of Phan Thiet, the red sand dunes that characterize the area start appearing and cows wander on the roads.

⊚ Vung Tau and around listings

For Sleeping and Eating price codes and other relevant information, see Essentials pages 26-31.

⊜ Sleeping

Vung Tau *p291, map p293*
For much of the year there are many more rooms than customers and discounts can usually be negotiated although prices do tend to rise in the summer holidays when Vietnamese families pour into town. Vietnamese work outings tend to head for Vung Tau and many hotels place more emphasis on massage and karaoke than on a decent night's sleep. There are hundreds of guesthouses on both sides of the road at Bai Sau (Back Beach).

There are a number of smaller hotels and guesthouses in **Bai Dua**, a quiet, almost Mediterranean, enclave.
L-A Palace, 1 Nguyen Trai St, T64-385 6411, www.palacehotel.com.vn. Renovated and expanded. Comfortable rooms and efficient staff make this a popular hotel. Nice pool under the shade of a tamarind tree. Always worth phoning ahead to see if they have any special deals. A good breakfast included.
AL Rang Dong Orange Court, 5 Le Qui Don St, T64-385 4933, www. rangdongorangecourt.com. Comfortable, serviced apartment complex, apartments available by the day or for longer stays. Large pool, tennis court and all rooms come with fully equipped kitchen.

AL-A Grand, 2 Nguyen Du St, T64-385 6888, www.grand.oscvn.com. It is great to see what an excellent job has been done restoring this hotel to its former condition. It occupies a position overlooking the sea, so deserves no less. The rooms are comfortable and kept clean and there's a pool.

A-C Rex, 1 Le Quy Don St, T64-385 2135, http://rexhotelvungtau.com. Not far from the sea and good views from the upper floors; restaurant and swimming pool.

A-C Sammy, 157 Thuy Van St, Bai Sau, T64-385 4756, http://sammyhotelvt.com. Large hotel and easily the best along the Back Beach with decent service, good views, business facilities and good Chinese restaurant; customers get use of the Ocean Park pool opposite at reduced prices.

B-C Petro House Hotel, 63 Tran Hung Dao St, T64-385 2014, petro.htl@hcm.vnn.vn. 71 rooms and suites. Central, comfortable and full of amenities including a decent pool, a business centre and Ma Maison, a good French restaurant. Generally regarded as the best in town.

E Thien Nhien, 145A Thuy Van St, Bai Sau, T64-385 3481. A/c and fan rooms, hot water, balcony, kept spick and span.

Long Hai p294

AL Anoasis Beach Resort, 2-3 km east of Long Hai, T64-386 8227, www.anoasisresort. com.vn. It consists of 46 bungalows and villas in a park setting with fantastic views over the sea. Scenically, it is one of the most appealing of all Vietnam's resorts. It is attractively finished and everything is on a generous scale: each bungalow has a bath big enough for 2, comfortable and beautifully designed furnishings. It is equipped with a pool, its own private beach, tennis court and jetty.

AL Long Hai Beach Resort, T64-366 1355, www.longhaibeachresort.com. 200 m north of Anoasis, the Long Hai Beach Resort has 110 red-roofed villa rooms tastefully designed with very nice balconies and set in a complex with gardens overlooking the sea.

Thuy Duong and Minh Danh p294

AL-C Thuy Duong Resort, Phuoc Hai, T64-388 6215, www.thuyduongresort.com.vn. The majority of this resort is set on the other side of the road away from the beach. There are 100 comfortable rooms and bungalows, beachside villas with pool, tennis court and restaurants. The beach cafés don't look much but the food is plentiful, cheap and good.

Loc An and Ho Coc p295

L-AL Ho Tram Beach Resort & Spa, Ho Tram, Phuoc Thuan Ward, Xuyen Moc District, T64-378 1525, www.hotramresort. com. 50 km north of Vung Tau on the new Ba Ria coastal road and 7 km further on from the Loc An Resort. This lovely smart resort is on the beach amid casuarinas. It has a pool, spa and tennis courts.

L-A Saigon Ho Coc Beach Resort, T64-387 8175, www.saigonbinhchauecoresort.com. 20 bungalows with fans and 2 rooms with a/c on the beach. The food is mediocre at the Sao Bien restaurant; a new restaurant building is under construction.

C-D Loc An Resort, Loc An, T64-388 6377, www.locanresort.com. Friendly family running a 25-room resort. Cheaper and less com-fortable rooms are in the main building. The 1st-rate rooms are nicely decorated with bamboo furniture. The resort is set on a lagoon with a boat connection to the beach (0600-1800). BBQ, pool, bicycles, rowing boats, coracles and ball games available.

D-E Vên Vên, T64-379 1121. This small hotel with very welcoming staff has 12 rooms with showers, TVs, fans and a/c set back from the beach behind the road. Breakfast is included. The restaurant is open all day.

Binh Chau hot springs p295

LL-C Binh Chau Ecotourist Resort, T64-387 1131, www.saigonbinhchauecoresort.com. A variety of clean rooms in 117 villas with various prices set among the grounds of the hot springs complex. Entry to the baths is free with 24-hr access for residents.

Towards Phan Thiet, Ke Ga and Tien Thanh p295

LL Princess d'Annam Resort, Hon Lan, Tan Thanh Commune, Ham Thuan Nam District, T62-368 2222, www.princessannam.com. This uber-luxurious resort boasts colonial-style villas situated around 8 communal pools designed by Singapore resorts architect Tan Hock Beng. There are 36 superior villas, 18 deluxe villas and 3 executive, 2-storey villas with private pools that are contained within compounds with a private garden and outdoor bathroom. All rooms have a TV, DVD player, mini-bars, etc. There's a French restaurant, cigar lounge, library, bar, a vast spa with a Moroccan-style inner courtyard, a gym and a landscaped ginger garden.

🍴 Eating

Vung Tau p291, map p293
Restaurants in town are often attached to hotels but there are plenty of independents.

Owing to the power of the expat pocket, prices tend to be a little higher in town (Front Beach) than elsewhere. All the bars and cafés that were along the beach front have been swept away. The better ones have popped up in new locations.

🍴 37 Cay Bang, 37 Tran Phu St, Bai Dau, T64-383 2123. Same name and concept (see below); a no-frills, good seafood derivative.

🍴-🍴 Cay Bang, 69 Tran Phu St, Bai Dau, T64-383 8522. Vung Tau's most celebrated seafood restaurant and well worth a detour. People travel for miles just for this. It's packed on Sun, busy the rest of the week. Crab, prawn, squid and fish specialities in a rough-and-ready setting over the sea.

🍴-🍴 Whispers, 15 Nguyen Trai St, T64-385 6028. Extensive Western menu and excellent food, including imported beef. The Sunday roast is recommended.

🍴 Ettamogah Pub, 6 Nguyen Du St, T64-351 0173, ettamogah@hcm.vnn.vn. Now in a new location behind the **Grand** and **Palace** hotels. Serves substantial breakfasts and decent bar food throughout the day.

🍴 Viet An Halal, 40 Quang Trung St (despite the address, it's actually just around the corner at 11 Ba Cu St), T64-385 3735. A range of excellent curries for around the US$3 mark prepared by an Indian/Vietnamese chef; still popular with the expat community but not quite as good as it was.

🍸 Bars and clubs

Vung Tau p291, map p293
Ettamogah Pub, 6 Nguyen Du St, T64-351 0173. A friendly, ever-popular, Australian-run bar frequented by expats. Motorbikes can be rented. See also Eating, above.
Hot Gossip, 436 Truong Cong Dinh St, is just around the corner. Also with a pool table.
Purple Night, 1B Hoang Dieu St, T64-381 0243. Also moved to a new location it remains a good night-time hangout.

🎉 Festivals and events

Vung Tau p291, map p293
Whale festival (Le Nghinh Ong) (16th day of the 8th lunar month), fishermen make offerings starting on the beach and then processing in great splendour and dignity to the Lang Ca Ong (Whale) Temple at 77A Hoang Hoa Tham St. See box, page 294.

🛍 Shopping

Vung Tau p291, map p293
Ba Cu St, north of Le Loi, has a good selection of clothes and shoes and is regarded as Vung Tau's shopping belt.

🏔 Activities and tours

Vung Tau p291, map p293
Greyhound racing
15 Le Loi St, T64-380 7309. This has been operating in Vietnam for several years. There are 12 races every Sat evening 1915-2230. The track and stand are modern and maintained to the highest standards, a great evening's entertainment.

Tennis

There are courts in many of the main hotels: Grand, Palace, Rang Dong Orange Court, etc (see Sleeping, above).

Tour operators

OSC Tours, 2 Le Loi St, T64-385 2603, www.oscvn.com. The Oil Services Company, a large, well-established state-run operation that can provide just about every service from issuing visas to car hire.

⊖ Transport

Vung Tau p291, map p293
Bus

Vung Tau bus station is at 192 Nam Ky Khoi Nghia St, sandwiched between Nam Ky Khoi Nghia and Xo Viet Nghe Tinh streets. Regular connections with **HCMC**, 2½ hrs, 25,000d, **Bien Hoa** and **Binh Khanh**.

Boat

There are 3 'competing' companies which operate hydrofoils from the Ha Long St jetty to **HCMC**: Petro Express, on the jetty, T64-351 1914, 1st service 0630 and then 14 services until 1700 and vice versa 180,000d. Greenlines, T64-381 0202, http://greenlines.com.vn. 15 departures daily 0630-1700. Under 6s travel for free. Same price. Vina Express, T64-385 6565, vinaexpress@hcm.vnn.vn. From 0600-1630 both ways, 6 departures daily, 1 hr 15 mins. Same price.

To **Con Dao** from Cau Da wharf. 2 trips every 10 days, 1700, 13 hrs.

Taxi

A taxi or car chartered from a hotel should cost no more than US$25-30 to **HCMC**, 2 hrs. Mai Linh Taxi, T64-382 2266.

Long Hai p294
Boat

Catch the Vung Tau hydrofoil from **HCMC** and take a taxi or motorbike from there.

Bus

Some direct services from **HCMC** but it's probably quicker to take the Vung Tau bus, get off at Ba Ria and catch a *xe ôm* from there, about 15 km, 30 mins.

Loc An and Ho Coc p295
Bus

Buses from Ba Ria stop at Bong Trang, catch *Minsk ôm* from there to Ho Coc. Some HCMC travel cafés organize day trips (3-3½ hrs) from **HCMC** by car.

⊙ Directory

Vung Tau p291, map p293
Banks BIDV, 72 Tran Hung Dao St. Changes TCs and cash. **Hospitals** AEA International, 1 Nguyen Thanh Thai St, T64-385 8776; Le Loi Hospital, 22 Le Loi St. **Internet** In all hotels. **Post office** PetroVietnam Towers on Le Loi St.

Long Hai p294
Banks Agribank, 103 Nam Ky Khoi Nghia St. Vietcombank, 27 Tran Hung Dao St. **Post office** 408 Le Hong Phong St.

Con Dao

→ *Colour map 4, A3.*

Con Dao, a name given to the 14 islands that make up this tiny archipelago, is Vietnam's last untouched wilderness with possibilities for wildlife viewing but not for too much longer. A few years ago the government approved a tourism strategy that would see it attracting 500,000 to 700,000 tourists a year by 2020. The biggest and only permanently settled island is Con Son with a population of approximately 6000 people. ➤➤ *For listings see page 302.*

Ins and outs

Getting there There are now three flights a day to Con Dao from Ho Chi Minh City.
➡ *See Transport, page 302.*

Best time to visit Between June and September is sea turtle nesting season (records show that the 1st and 15th of the month are best) although good weather is not guaranteed. February to April can be incredibly windy. The wet season lasts from May to November.

History

The Portuguese arrived on Con Dao in 1516 but it wasn't until 1702 that a trading post was set up here by the East India Trading Company. Because of the millions of sea birds that inhabited it, it was then called Bird Island. In 1773, it became the home of Nguyen Anh and many mandarin families who fled there after being defeated by the armies of the Tay Son. In 1832, the Con Dao archipelago was handed over to the French by Emperor Tu Duc. Prisons were built in 1862 by Admiral Bonard in which the French incarcerated their more obstinate political prisoners. Up to 12,000 people could be held in the completed prisons. The Con Dao prisons were later used by the government of South Vietnam to hold political prisoners. In 113 years of prison existence 200,000 people were incarcerated here and one tenth of those people died in prison. Remarkably, 153 prisoners volunteered to stay on in Con Son to live after 1975.

Now targeted as the next hot tourist destination the province is to spend US$23 million upgrading the islands' infrastructure. US-based MH Golden Sands is to develop a tourism, commercial and convention complex worth US$30-50 million near the airport. A Japanese project is in the pipeline and Indochina Capital has invested in an Evason resort.

Sights

The combination of its mountains and islands, cultural diversity as well as its biodiversity, make Con Dao quite special. It is also one of Vietnam's last relatively pristine areas. There are just a few main roads around Con Son and an unbelievable lack of traffic. The main hotels face out onto Con Son Bay behind the coastal road. The colourful fishing boats that used to bob and work the sea here have been moved to Ben Dam port in the west of the island. Here you can see the docked squid boats if the timing is right.

The prison system operated between 1862 and 1975, first by the French and then by the Americans. **Prison Phu Hai**, which backs on to parts of the **Saigon Con Dao Resort**, was built in 1862 and is the largest prison on the islands with 10 detention rooms and 20 punishment cells. The chapel inside was built by the Americans in 1963. Next door is **Phu Son Prison** built in 1916. The third prison, **Phu Tho**, plus **Camp Phu Tuong** and **Camp Phu Phong** (built in 1962) contained the infamous 'tiger cages' where prisoners were chained and tortured; the enclosures still stand. Metal bars were placed across the roofs of the cells and guards would throw excrement and lime onto the prisoners. In addition, many prisoners were outside in areas known as 'sun-bathing compartments'. Not content on limiting torture methods, a cow manure enclosure was used to dunk prisoners in sewage up to 3 m deep. American-style tiger enclosures were built in 1971 at **Camp Phu Binh**. In total there were 504 tiger cages. Beyond the prisons, inland, is the **Hang Duong cemetery** where many of the victims of the prison are buried. The grave of Le Hong Phong, the very first General Secretary of the Communist Party in Vietnam (1935-1936) and Vo Thi Sau (1933-1952) can be seen among them. A tour of the prisons and cemetery costs 50,000d per person and is arranged through the museum, see below.

Vo Thi Sau

Vo Thi Sau was born Ba Ria in 1933 and was executed in Con Dao in 1952. At the age of 14 this Vietnamese revolutionary heroine developed an interest in politics and a passionate hatred for the French.

In 1949 she obtained three hand-grenades and, with one, killed a French soldier and injured 20 others. She became a messenger and supplied food and ammunition to the Viet Minh.

In 1950 she tried to assassinate a village headman working for the French but the hand-grenade failed to go off. She was caught, tortured and sentenced to death. She was executed on 23 January 1952 at the age of 18.

There is a **museum (Bao Tang Tong Ho Tinh)** ① *Mon-Sat 0700-1130, 1330-1700, 1000d,* in the town of Con Dao in the house of the former prison governor (built 1862) containing artefacts relating to the island's past. Con Dao museum has an interesting display of old photographs, and can arrange walking tours of the old prisons.

Opposite the museum is **Wharf 914**, the main ferry access point to the islands, so-called because of the number of prisoners who died building it.

There is a small museum and explanatory displays at the **National Park office headquarters** ① *see below, Mon-Fri 0700-1130, 1330-1700, Sat 0730-1100, 1400-1630.*

Con Dao National Park

① *29 Vo Thi Sau St, T64-383 0650, www.condaopark.com.vn. There are a number of activities that can be organized in the national park, from snorkelling and swimming, to forest walks and birdwatching. Diving is available to see some of Con Dao's underwater features, such as its caves, as well as the coral reefs. The national park will rent out snorkelling gear and you can also rent one of their speedboats if you are in a group that can share the cost.*

In 1984 the forests on all 14 islands of the Con Dao archipelago were given official protection, and in 1993, 80% of the land area was designated a national park. In 1998 the park boundaries were expanded to include the surrounding sea.

Con Dao is a special place ecologically, though it is not the most diverse protected area in Vietnam. In 1995, with support from the World Wildlife Fund, the park began a sea-turtle conservation project. Con Dao is the most important sea-turtle nesting site in Vietnam, with several hundred female green turtles (*Chelonia mydas*) coming ashore to lay their eggs every year. Occasionally the hawksbill turtle visits too. Park staff attach a tag to every turtle in order to identify returning turtles, and move the turtles' eggs if they are in danger of being flooded at high tide. The rest of the year the turtles migrate long distances. Recently, a turtle tagged in Con Dao was found in a fishing village in Cambodia – unfortunately the tag was insufficient protection to prevent it being eaten. Also in 1995, park staff identified the presence of dugongs (sea cows), which are mammals that feed on seagrass and can live to more than 70 years. Unfortunately, before the park was established dugongs were caught for meat so now the population in Con Dao is small and endangered.

The coral reefs surrounding the islands are among the most diverse in the country. Scientists have identified more than 200 species of coral and coral fish. In November 1997, typhoon *Linda* struck the islands and many of Con Dao's coral reefs were damaged.

In the forests scientists have identified more than 1000 plant species, of which several are unique to Con Dao and include many valuable medicinal and timber species. Bird life is also significant with rare species such as the pied imperial pigeon (*Ducula bicolor*) – Con

Turtles

Although the turtle is a symbol of longevity in Vietnam, its marine turtle population is under threat. In the last 30 years their numbers have declined. In an attempt to save the world's five species, all threatened with extinction according to the World Conservation Union (IUCN), the Ministry of Fisheries has launched a plan with IUCN to save the creature. Most of the turtles, the hawksbill (*Eretmochelys imbricata*), green (*Chelonia mydas*), loggerhead (*Caretta caretta*), Olive Ridley (*Lepidochelys olivacea*) and leatherback (*Dermochelys coriacea*) nest on the Con Dao islands. With populations of not more than 300 in total for all species in Vietnam they have faced decimation because of poaching, egg collecting and illegal trading of stuffed animals and products such as jewellery and ornaments. In a 2004 study by TRAFFIC, the wildlife trade monitoring network, more than 28,000 items made of mainly hawksbill tortoiseshell were being sold in Vietnam.

Dao is the only place in Vietnam where you can see this bird – the red-billed tropicbird (*Phaethon aethereus*) – found on only a few islands in the world – and the brown booby (*Sula leucogaster*) – a rare sea bird that inhabits the park's most remote island, Hon Trung (Egg Island). Egg Island, a speedboat ride northeast of Con Son, is a rugged outcrop hosting thousands of seabirds including sooty and crested terns, white-bellied sea eagles, and the rare, in Vietnam, masked booby. Most of the threats to the islands' natural resources come from development in the form of new roads, houses and the new fishing port built in Ben Dam Bay – an area of once-beautiful coral reef and mangrove forest.

Beaches and bays

Ong Dung Beach can be reached by walking across Con Son Island downhill on a track through the jungle. Plenty of birds can be seen if you trek at the right time of day. You can snorkel around 300 m offshore. There is a forest protection centre at the bay where you can buy food and drink and hire snorkelling gear and a boat. See also Sleeping, below. **Bai Nhat Beach**, just before Ben Dam Bay, is a beautiful wild stretch of sand where good swimming is possible. North of Con Son is **Tre Lon Island**, said to be one of the best places in the archipelago to see coral reefs and reef fish; this was also used as an isolated French prison. Le Duan, former General Secretary of the Communist Party, was imprisoned here from 1931-1936. Close to the airport is one of the island's best and most wild beaches at **Dam Trau**. Golden sands in a tight curved bay backed by casuarinas can be found here but there are no island views. Signposted 'Mieu Cau' on the left just before the airport, it is a 15-minute walk, passing a pagoda flanked by two white horses.

    Bay Canh Island is a major sea turtle nesting site; there is also a functioning French-built lighthouse dating from 1883. If you are interested in seeing the turtles arrange to stay overnight through the national park. **Cau Island**, east of Bay Canh Island is the only other island in the archipelago with fresh water. It harbours the swifts that make the nests and turtles that come to lay their eggs. It was also an isolated French prison at one time. Pham Van Dong, a former prime minster of both North Vietnam and the reunited Vietnam (1955-1987), was incarcerated here for seven years, from 1929 to 1936.

    For swimming, **Lo Voi Beach**, east of the hotels, is good for swimming as is **An Hai Beach** at the other end of the bay. Birdwatching is also possible around the freshwater lake – **Quang Trung** – swamps and tree-covered sand dunes near the park headquarters. Spotters could see the Brahminy kite (*Haliastur Indus*), white-bellied sea eagle, Javan pond heron and cinnamon bittern. On the way to **Ong Dung** you can see the white-rumped shama, greater racket-tailed drongo, the rare pied imperial pigeon and the even rarer red-billed tropicbird.

At Dat Doc, east of Con Son, is a very attractive and pristine bay backed by a sheer cliff face. The **Evason Hideaway & Six Senses Spa** company have built here.

◉ Con Dao listings

For Sleeping and Eating price codes and other relevant information, see Essentials pages 26-31.

● Sleeping

Con Dao *p298*
LL Evason Hideaway & Six Senses Con Dao, Dat Doc Beach, www.sixsenses.com. 35 hotel villas and 15 private residential bungalows plus a Six Senses Spa should be open by the time you read this.
A-B Saigon Con Dao, 18 Ton Duc Thang St, T64-383 0336, www.saigoncondao.com. These buildings on the seafront have had an upgrade and rooms are nicely furnished.
A-C Con Dao Resort, 8 Nguyen Duc Thuan St, T64-383 0939, www.condaoresort.com. vn. At present, this is the best resort on the island. There are 41 rooms including some in villas on the beach. The rooms feature a/c bathtubs, TV and balconies. There's a pool and a tennis court. There's also a restaurant – the **Du Gong**. Staff can arrange walking and motorbike tours of the area.
E Phi Yen Guest House, 34 Ton Duc Thang St, T64-383 0168. A state hotel opposite the fishing port where no English is spoken. Some rooms have a/c and others just have fans. There's a restaurant on site.

Camping
National Park Campsite, T64-383 0437. There are 3 rooms on Canh Island with beds and running water. Free.

❼ Eating

Con Dao *p298*
¶¶-¶ **Poulo Condore Restaurant.** Staff at the Poulo Condore are friendly and efficient.

▲ Activities and tours

Con Dao *p298*
Boat tours
The National Park organizes boat tours for depending on the number of people and the weather. These include trips to Hon Tre Lon, Hon Tre No, Hon Bay Canh and Hon Cau as well as points around Con Son Island.

❸ Transport

Con Dao *p298*
Air
Con Dao Airport, T64-383 1973. Weekly schedules vary throughout the year.
ATC tourism company has an office at 30 Le Loi St, District 1, HCMC, T8-3827 9717, www.condao.com, and offers packages. **Saigontourist**, www.saigontourist.net, also sells tickets and books accommodation.

Boat
The journey can be made by *Con Dao 9* or *Con Dao 10*. The journey to **Vung Tau** leaves at 1700, 13 hrs. Tickets can only be purchased a few days in advance when the departure day has been confirmed (this is every 10 days and subject to weather conditions; it is also subject to demand). The journey is overnight and a bunk bed is included in the price. Contact the shipping office at 2 Le Loi St, Vung Tau, T64-838 684; on Con Dao contact T064-830 619.

❻ Directory

Con Dao *p298*
Bank Vietinbank with ATM. **Post office** 48 Nguyen Hue St, T64-383 0123.

Contents

306 Ins and outs
308 History
309 Contemporary Ho
    Chi Minh City

310 Sights
310 City centre
320 Pham Ngu Lao
321 Cholon (Chinatown)
323 Outer Ho Chi Minh City
325 Around Ho Chi Minh City

328 Listings
328 Sleeping
332 Eating
338 Bars and clubs
339 Entertainment
340 Shopping
343 Activities and tours
345 Transport
349 Directory

Footprint features

304 Don't miss…
318 Buddhist martyrs:
        self-immolation as protest
319 Betel nut
347 On the move

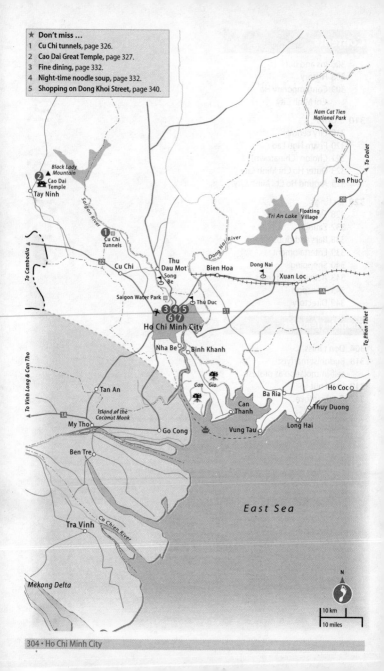

★ **Don't miss ...**
1 Cu Chi tunnels, page 326.
2 Cao Dai Great Temple, page 327.
3 Fine dining, page 332.
4 Night-time noodle soup, page 332.
5 Shopping on Dong Khoi Street, page 340.

Nam Cat Tien
National Park

To Dalat

Black Lady
Mountain

Cao Dai
Temple

Tay Ninh

Saigon River

Tri An Lake

Floating
Village

Tan Phu

Dong Nai River

Cu Chi
Tunnels

To Cambodia

Cu Chi

Thu
Dau Mot

Bien Hoa

Dong Nai

Xuan Loc

Song
Be

Saigon Water Park

Thu Duc

Ho Chi Minh City

To Phan Thiet

Nha Be

Binh Khanh

To Vinh Long & Can Tho

Tan An

Can
Gio

Ba Ria

Ho Coc

Island of the
Coconut Monk

Can
Thanh

Thuy Duong

My Tho

Go Cong

Vung Tau

Long Hai

Ben Tre

East Sea

Tra Vinh

Co Chien River

Mekong Delta

N

10 km
10 miles

Ho Chi Minh City, Pearl of the Orient, is the largest city in Vietnam. It is also the nation's foremost commercial and industrial centre. It is frenetic, exciting, riddled with traffic and enlivened by great shops, bars and restaurants. Founded as a Khmer trading and fishing port on the west bank of the Dong Nai River, it fell into Vietnamese hands in the late 17th century.

Early in the 18th century the Nguyen emperors established Gia Dinh Citadel, which was destroyed by French naval forces in 1859. Rebuilt as a French colonial city it was named Saigon (Soai-gon – 'wood of the kapok tree') and became capital of French Cochin China.

During the 1960s and early 1970s Saigon boomed and flourished under the American occupation (it was the seat of the South Vietnam government) until the fall or liberation – depending upon your point of view. Officially Ho Chi Minh City (HCMC) since 1975, it remains to most the bi-syllabic, familiar, old 'Saigon'.

The most dynamic city in one of the most rapidly growing economies in the world; Ho Chi Minh City today is a place of remorseless and relentless activity. Despite government restrictions thousands of young men and women make their way here every week in search of a better life. They come in droves to work, study, meet, marry and live. The city is growing at a prodigious rate: 25 years ago Tan Son Nhat, the airport, was right out at the edge of the city; it has been an inner suburb for years, long ago leapfrogged by the sprawl that is pushing outwards into former paddy fields with astonishing speed. The former swamps of District 2 across the river are developing at the fastest rate. The Thu Thiem bridge now links District 1 and District 2 under the Saigon River and the east-west highway linking HCMC to District 2. The brand new tarmac tongue to My Tho, making access to the Delta quicker and more comfortable, opened in early 2009.

Getting there

Ho Chi Minh City (HCMC) may not be Vietnam's capital, but it is the economic powerhouse of the country and the largest city. Reflecting its premier economic position, it is well connected with the wider world – indeed, more airlines fly into here than into Hanoi; it is also connected to all the domestic airports bar one. **Tan Son Nhat Airport** is 30-40 minutes from the centre. By taxi the cost is around US$6-7. Taxi drivers may try to demand a flat fee in US dollars but you should insist on using the meter, which is the law, and pay in dong. The official flat fare to downtown organized through a desk at the airport is US$8.

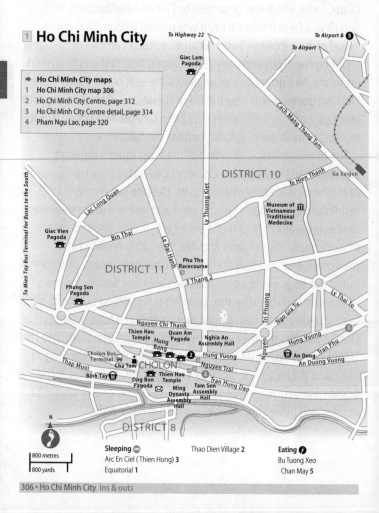

1 Ho Chi Minh City

To Highway 22   To Airport & 5
To Airport

→ Ho Chi Minh City maps
1 Ho Chi Minh City map 306
2 Ho Chi Minh City Centre, page 312
3 Ho Chi Minh City Centre detail, page 314
4 Pham Ngu Lao, page 320

Giac Lam Pagoda

DISTRICT 10

Cach Mang Thang Tam

Ga Saigon

To Hien Thanh

Museum of Vietnamese Traditional Medecine

Ly Thuong Kiet

Lac Long Quan

Giac Vien Pagoda

Bin Thai

Le Dai Hanh

Phu Tho Racecourse

3 Thang 2

DISTRICT 11

Phung Son Pagoda

Ly Thai To

Ngo Gia Tu

Tri Phuong

Hung Vuong

Nguyen Chi Thanh

Thien Hau Temple   Quan Am Pagoda   Nghia An Assembly Hall

Hung Bang

Cholon Bus Terminal   Cha Tam   CHOLON   Hung Vuong

Thap Muoi   Ong Bon Pagoda   Thien Hau Temple   Nguyen Trai

An Dong   Tran Phu

An Duong Vuong

Binh Tay   Ming Dynasty Assembly Hall   Tam Son Assembly Hall   Tran Hung Dao

DISTRICT 8

N

800 metres
800 yards

Sleeping
Arc En Ciel (Thien Hong) 3
Equatorial 1

Thao Dien Village 2

Eating
Bu Tuong Xeo
Chan May 5

The **railway station** is northwest of the city centre and there are regular daily connections with Hanoi and all stops on the line north. As well as international air connections, there are bus services to Phnom Penh (Cambodia). Buses for destinations within the country leave from two main city **bus terminals** and connect Ho Chi Minh City with many larger towns in the central and northern regions, and with most places in the Mekong Delta. With the ring road around Ho Chi Minh City, few long-distance public buses actually come into town. To avoid an additional 45-minute journey, try to catch a bus heading to Ben Xe Mien Dong or join the large number of visitors who arrive in Ho Chi Minh City on one or other of the many competing **Open Tour Buses**. ▸▸ See Transport, page 347.

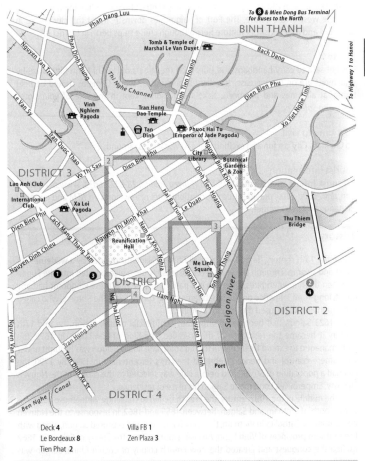

Deck **4**
Le Bordeaux **8**
Tien Phat **2**
Villa FB **1**
Zen Plaza **3**

Getting around

Ho Chi Minh City has abundant transport – which is fortunate, because it is a hot, large and increasingly polluted city. Metered taxis, motorcycle taxis and a handful of cyclos vie for business in a healthy spirit of competition. Many tourists who prefer some level of independence opt to hire (or even, buy) a bicycle or motorbike. ▶▶ *See Tour operators, page 344.*

Orientation

Virtually all of Ho Chi Minh City lies to the west of the Saigon River. The eastern side of the river, District 2, is for the most part marshy, poor and rather squalid, although a growing expat city has evolved. Most visitors to the city head straight for hotels in Districts 1 (the historic centre) or 3. Many will arrive on buses in De Tham or Pham Ngu Lao streets, the backpacker area, in District 1, not far from the city centre. Cholon or Chinatown (District 5) is a mile west of the centre. The Port of Saigon lies downstream of the city centre in districts 4 and 8. Few visitors venture here although cruise ships berth in District 4.

Safety

It is not safe to carry handbags and purses on the streets of Ho Chi Minh City. Drive-by snatchings are on the increase. Jewellery should not be worn. Cameras should be held tightly at all times and passports, tickets and money kept in the safe of your hotel. ▶▶ *See also Safety, page 38.*

Best time to visit

Ho Chi Minh City is a fun and exciting place to visit all year around.

Tourist information

A **Tourist Information Center** ① *92-96 Nguyen Hue St, T8-8322 6033, www.ticvietnam. com, daily 0800-2100*, provides free information, hotel reservations, an ATM and currency exchange and free internet.

History

Before the 15th century, Saigon was a small Khmer village surrounded by a wilderness of forest and swamp. Through the years it had ostensibly been incorporated into the Funan and then the Khmer empires, although it is hard to believe that these kingdoms had any direct, long-term influence on the inhabitants of the community. The Khmers, who called the region *Prei Nokor*, used the area for hunting.

By 1623 Saigon had become an important commercial centre, and in the mid-17th century it became the residence of the so-called Vice-King of Cambodia. In 1698, the Viets managed to extend their control this far south and finally Saigon was brought under Vietnamese control and hence celebrated the city's tercentenary in 1998. By 1790, the city had a population of 50,000 and before Hué was selected as the capital of the Nguyen Dynasty, Emperor Gia Long made Saigon his place of residence.

In the middle of the 19th century, the French began to challenge Vietnamese authority in the south of Vietnam and Saigon. Between 1859 and 1862, in response to the Nguyen persecution of Catholics in Vietnam, the French attacked and captured Saigon, along with the southern provinces of Vinh Long, An Giang and Ha Tien. The Treaty of Saigon in 1862 ratified the conquest and created the new French colony of Cochin China. Saigon was developed in French style: wide, tree-lined boulevards, street-side cafés, elegant French architecture, boutiques and the smell of baking baguettes. The map of French Saigon in the 1930s was a city that owed more to Haussmann than Vietnamese geomancers.

Contemporary Ho Chi Minh City

The population of Ho Chi Minh City today is officially more than seven million and rising fast as the rural poor are lured by the tales of streets paved with gold. Actual numbers are thought to be considerably higher when all the recent migrants without residence cards are added. But it has been a roller-coaster ride over the last 40 years. During the course of the Vietnam War, as refugees spilled in from a devastated countryside, the population of Saigon almost doubled from 2.4 million in 1965 to around 4.5 million by 1975. With reunification in 1976, the new communist authorities pursued a policy of depopulation, believing that the city had become too large, that it was parasitic and was preying on the surrounding countryside. Certainly, most of the jobs were in the service sector, and were linked to the United States' presence. For example, Saigon had 56,000 registered prostitutes alone (and many, many, more unregistered), most of them country girls.

Vietnam's economic reforms are most in evidence in Ho Chi Minh City and the average annual income here, at US$2800, is more than double the national average (US$1000). It is here that the highest concentration of Hoa (ethnic Chinese) is to be found – numbering around 380,000 – and, although once persecuted for their economic success (see page 456), they still have the greatest economic influence and acumen. Most of Ho Chi Minh City's ethnic Chinese live in the district of Cholon, and from there control two-thirds of small-scale commercial enterprises. The reforms have encouraged the Hoa to begin investing in business again. Drawing on their links with fellow Chinese in Taiwan, Hong Kong, Bangkok and among the overseas Vietnamese, they are viewed by the government as crucial in improving prospects for the economy. The reforms have also brought economic inefficiencies into the open. Although the changes have brought wealth to a few, and increased the range of goods on sale, they have also created a much clearer division between the haves and the have-nots.

In its short history Saigon has had a number of keepers. Each has rebuilt the city in their own style. First the Khmer, then the early Vietnamese, followed by the French who tore it all down and started from scratch and were succeeded by the Americans and the 'Puppet' Regime, and finally the communist north who engineered society rather than the buildings, locking the urban fabric in a time warp.

Under the current regime, best described as crony capitalist, the city is once more being rebuilt. Ever larger holes are being torn in the heart of central Ho Chi Minh City. Whereas a few years ago it was common to see buildings disappear, now whole blocks fall to the wrecker's ball. From the holes left behind, concrete, steel and glass monuments emerge. There is, of course, a difference from earlier periods of remodelling of the city. Then, it was conducted on a human scale and the largest buildings, though grand, were on a scale that was in keeping with the dimensions of the streets and ordinary shophouses. French buildings in Dong Khoi Street, for example, were consistent with the Vietnamese way of life: street-level trading with a few residential floors above. Now glitzy modern buildings on an altogether vaster scale dwarf every building from an earlier age. The latest overblown development is Times Square opposite the Grand Hotel on Dong Khoi St.

Ho Chi Minh City is divided, administratively, into 12 urban districts, or *quan*, and nine suburban districts, or *huyen*. These are further sub-divided into wards and the wards into neighbourhoods; each district and ward has its own People's Committee or local government who guard and protect their responsibilities and rights jealously and maintain a high degree of administrative autonomy. A city-wide People's Committee, elected every four years, oversees the functioning of the entire metropolis.

The future growth of Ho Chi Minh City will focus mostly on the southern and eastern sides. Saigon port did extend right up into the heart of the city into District 4 but has been relocated to Cat Lai and Hiep Phuoc in the suburbs. It is almost certain that in the coming years the valuable riverfront sites will be developed into desirable flats and offices – rather like London's Docklands. To the south, Saigon South, a huge new flank of the city is rising out of the marsh and mangrove. A site of 1336 ha has so far been converted from swamp into 'executive homes' and international schools; the infrastructure that will support the livelihoods of hundreds of thousands of people is materializing out of nothing. It may sound like propaganda but the fact is that parcels of what was recently disregarded wasteland are now changing hands for millions of dollars. Serious investors and land speculators are moving in and the city is expanding fast. Land prices in District 2, the marshy area to the east of the Saigon River, soared to previously unimaginable heights as speculators snapped up land in advance of the construction of new river crossings.

Sights

All the sights of Central Ho Chi Minh City can be reached on foot in no more than 30 minutes from the major hotel areas of Nguyen Hue, Dong Khoi and Ton Duc Thang streets. Visiting all the sights described below will take several days, not that we would particularly recommend visiting them all. Quite a good first port of call, however, is the **Panorama 33 Café** on the 33rd floor of **Saigon Trade Center** ① *37 Ton Duc Thang St, Mon-Fri 1100-2400, Sat-Sun 0900-2400*. From this vantage point you can see the whole city stretching before you, and its position and layout in relation to the river and surrounding swampland becomes strikingly clear. Another good spot to survey the river and downtown building work, is Chique, 15th floor, Landmark Building, 5B Ton Duc Thang St, 1400-2300. Its interior isn't chic but the views are front row. ►► *For listings, see page 328-350.*

City centre

The core of Ho Chi Minh City is, in many respects, the most interesting and historical. Remember, of course, that 'historical' here has a very different meaning from that in Hanoi. In Ho Chi Minh City a 100-year-old building is ancient – and, alas, increasingly rare. Still, a saunter down **Dong Khoi Street**, in District 1, the old rue Catinat can still give one an impression of life in a more elegant and less frenzied era. Much remains on a small and personal scale and within a 100-m radius of just about anywhere on Dong Khoi or Thai Van Lung streets there are dozens of cafés, restaurants and increasingly snazzy boutiques. However, the character of the street has altered with the opening of luxury chain names and will alter further with the completion of the Times Square mega hotel development. A little bit of Graham Greene history was lost in 2010 when the Givral Café in the Eden Centre, which featured in *A Quiet American*, was closed as Vincom Towers built another tower block on Lam Son Square.

Lam Son Square and around

The once-impressive, French-era **Opera House (Nha Hat Thanh Pho)** ① *7 Lam Son Sq, T8-3832 2009, nhahat_ghvk@hcm.fpt.vn*, dominates Lam Son Square. It was built in 1897 to the design of French architect Ferret Eugene and restored in 1998. It once housed the National Assembly; nowadays, when it is open, it provides a varied programme of events, for example, traditional theatre, contemporary dance and gymnastics.

North of the Opera House is the repainted **Continental Hotel**, built in 1880 and an integral part of the city's history. Graham Greene stayed here and the hotel features in the novel *The Quiet American*. Old journalists' haunt **Continental Shelf** was "a famous verandah where correspondents, spies, speculators, traffickers, intellectuals and soldiers used to meet during the war to glean information and pick up secret reports, half false, half true or half disclosed. All of this is more than enough for it to be known as Radio Catinat". It has a delightful enclosed garden ("I sometimes went there for a late evening drink among the frangipani and hibiscus blossom ... It was the reverse of the frenzy of the war, and a good place to think," wrote war journalist Jon Swain).

The **Continental** lines **Dong Khoi Street** (formerly the bar-lined Tu Do Street, the old Rue Catinat), which stretches from Cong Xa Paris down to the river. All the shops specialize in, or sell a mix of silk clothes and accessories, jewellery, lacquerware and household goods. Facing the **Continental**, also adjoining Dong Khoi Street, is the opulent **Hotel Caravelle**, which houses boutique shops selling luxury goods. The **Caravelle** opened for business in 1959. The famous **Saigon Saigon** bar on the 10th floor was a favourite spot for wartime reporters and during the 1960s the *Associated Press*, *NBC*, *CBS*, the *New York Times* and *Washington Post* based their offices here. The press escaped casualties when, on 25 August 1964, a bomb exploded in room 514, on a floor mostly used by foreign reporters. The hotel suffered damage and there were injuries but the journalists were all out in the field. It was renamed **Doc Lap** (Independence Hotel) in 1975 but not before a Vietnamese tank trundled down the rue Catinat to Place Garnier (now Lam Son Square) and aimed its turret at the hotel; to this day nobody knows why it did not fire. During the filming of Graham Greene's *The Quiet American*, actors Michael Caine and Brendan Fraser stayed at the hotel.

At the northwest end of Nguyen Hue Boulevard is the yellow and white **City Hall**, formerly the French **Hôtel de Ville** built in 1897 and now the Ho Chi Minh City People's Committee building, which overlooks a **statue of Bac Ho** (Uncle Ho) offering comfort, or perhaps advice, to a child. This is a favourite spot for Vietnamese to have their photograph taken, especially newly-weds who believe old Ho confers some sort of blessing.

South of City Hall, the **Rex Hotel**, a pre-Liberation favourite with US officers, stands at the intersection of Le Loi and Nguyen Hue boulevards. This was the scene of the daily 'Five O'Clock Follies' where the military briefed an increasingly sceptical press corps during the Vietnam War. Fully renovated and smartly expanding, the crown on the fifth-floor terrace of the **Rex** (a good place to have a beer) is rotating once again following a number of years of immobility. Some maintain that it symbolizes Ho Chi Minh City's newly discovered (or rediscovered) vitality.

On weekend evenings thousands of young Saigon men and women and young families cruise up and down Nguyen Hue and Le Loi boulevards and Dong Khoi Street on motorbikes; this whirl of people and machines is known as *chay long rong* 'cruising' or *song voi*, 'living fast'. There are now so many motorbikes on the streets of Ho Chi Minh City that intersections seem lethally confused. Miraculously, the riders miss each other (most of the time) while pedestrians safely make their way through waves of machines (see box, page 25).

Ho Chi Minh City maps

1 Ho Chi Minh City, page 306
2 **Ho Chi Minh City Centre, page 312**
3 Ho Chi Minh City Centre detail, page 314
4 Pham Ngu Lao, page 320

Sleeping 🛏
Lavender 9
Legend 3
Miss Loi's
 Guesthouse 11
New World 4
Sofitel Plaza Saigon 7

Eating 🍴
An Vien & Tous les Jours 16
Au Parc 22
Blue Ginger 3
Com Nieu Saigon 17
Cooku'nest Café 12
Hoa Vien 4
Hoi An 5

La Camargue 21
La Fenêtre Soleil 9
Mandarin 8
Tib 14

Bars & clubs 🍸
Lush 2

400 metres
400 yards

Notre Dame Cathedral

ⓘ *Visiting times are described as being 0500-1100 and 1500-1730. Communion is celebrated here 7 times on Sun (drawing congregations Western churches can only dream of) and 3 times on weekdays.*

North up Dong Khoi Street, in the middle of **Cong Xa Paris** (Paris Square), is the imposing, austere red-brick, twin-spired Notre Dame Cathedral, overlooking a grassed square in which a statue of the Virgin Mary stands holding an orb. The statue was the subject of intense scrutiny in 2006 as it was said that it had shed tears. The cathedral was built between 1877 and 1880 and is said to be on the site of an ancient pagoda. A number of the homeless sleep under its walls at night; unfortunately the signs asking Vietnamese men not to treat the walls as a public urinal do not deter this unpleasant but widespread practice. Mass times are a spectacle as crowds, unable to squeeze through the doors, listen to the service while perched on their parked motorbikes in rows eight or nine deep.

General Post Office

ⓘ *2 Cong Xa Paris, daily 0730-1930.*

Facing onto the Paris Square is the General Post Office, built in the 1880s in French style, it is a particularly distinguished building. The front façade has attractive cornices with French and Khmer motifs and the names of notable French men of letters and science. Inside, the high, vaulted ceiling and fans create a deliciously cool atmosphere in which to scribble a postcard. Note the old wall-map of Cochin China that has miraculously survived. The enormous portrait of Ho Chi Minh, hanging at the end of the hall, completes the sense of grandeur.

Reunification Hall

ⓘ *135 Nam Ky Khoi Nghia St, T8-3822 3652, daily 0730-1100, 1300-1600, 15,000d, brochure 10000d, documentary 50,000d. The guides are friendly, but their English is not always very good. Tours every 10 mins. The hall is sometimes closed for state occasions.*

Ngo Dinh Diem's **Presidential Palace**, now renamed Reunification Hall, or the **Thong Nhat Conference Hall**, is in a large park to the southeast of Nguyen Thi Minh Khai Street and southwest of Nam Ky Khoi Nghia Street. The residence of the French governor was built on this site in 1868 and was later renamed the Presidential Palace. In February 1962, a pair of planes took off to attack Viet Cong emplacements – piloted by two of the south's finest airmen – but they turned back to bomb the Presidential Palace in a futile attempt to assassinate President Diem. The president, who held office between 1955-1963, escaped with his family to the cellar, but the palace had to be demolished and replaced with a new building. (Diem was later assassinated after a military coup.) One of the two pilots, Nguyen Thanh Trung is a Vice President of **Vietnam Airlines** and still flies government officials around every couple of months to keep his pilot's licence current. One of the most memorable photographs taken during the war was of a North Vietnamese Army (NVA) tank crashing through the gates of the Palace on 30 April 1975 – symbolizing the end of South Vietnam and its government. The President of South Vietnam, General Duong Van Minh, along with his entire cabinet, was arrested in the Palace shortly afterwards. The hall has been preserved as it was found in 1975 and visitors can take a guided tour. In the **Vice President's Guest Room**, there is a lacquered painting of the Temple of Literature in Hanoi, while the **Presenting of Credentials Room** contains a fine 40-piece lacquer work showing diplomats presenting their credentials during the Le Dynasty (15th century). In the basement there are operations rooms, military maps, radios and other paraphernalia.

3 Ho Chi Minh City centre detail

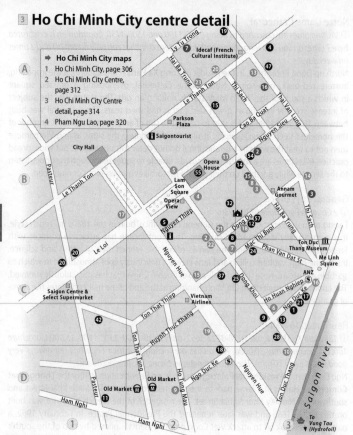

➡ **Ho Chi Minh City maps**
1 Ho Chi Minh City, page 306
2 Ho Chi Minh City Centre, page 312
3 Ho Chi Minh City Centre detail, page 314
4 Pham Ngu Lao, page 320

Ly Tu Trong
Idecaf (French Cultural Institute)
Hai Ba Trung
Le Thanh Ton
Thi Sach
Cao Ba Quat
Thai Van Lung
Nguyen Sieu
Parkson Plaza
Saigontourist
City Hall
Pasteur
Le Thanh Ton
Opera House
Lam Son Square
Annam Gourmet
Opera View
Nguyen Thiep
Dong Du
Ton Duc Thang Museum
Mac Thi Buoi
Phan Van Dat St
Me Linh Square
Le Loi
Saigon Centre & Select Supermarket
Ton That Thiep
Vietnam Airlines
Dong Khoi
Ho Huan Nghiep
Ngo Duc Ke
ANZ
Huynh Thuc Khang
Ton That Tung
Pasteur
Old Market
Old Market
Ho Tung Mau
Ngo Duc Ke
Nguyen Hue
Ton Duc Thang
Saigon River
Ham Nghi
Ham Nghi
To Vung Tau ▼ (Hydrofoil)

100 metres
100 yards

Sleeping
A & EM **23** A2
Bong Sen **2** B2
Bong Sen Annexe **3** B3
Caravelle **4** B2
Catina Saigon **22** C2
Continental **5** B2
Duxton **19** C2
Grand **6** C3
Ho Sen **14** B3
Huong Sen **7** C2

Khach San 69 **8** B3
Majestic **10** D3
Orchid **13** A3
Palace **15** C2
Park Hyatt Saigon **11** B2
Renaissance Riverside **16** C3
Rex **17** B1
Saigon **18** B3
Sheraton **21** B2
Spring **20** A2
Tan Hai Long **9** D2

Eating
13 Ngo Duc Ke **1** C3
Al Fresco's **57** B3

Ashoka **4** A3
Augustin's **5** B2
Bombay **8** B2
Hoang Yen **17** C3
Indian Curry-Rice **32** B2
Jaspas **9** C3
Juice **24** C3
Kem Bach Dang **20** C1
Kita **18** D2
La Cantine on the 6 **13** C3
La Fourchette **21** C3
Le Jardin **19** A2
Mogambo **11** D1
Maxim's Nam An **28** C3
Pacharan **14** B3
Pho 24 **25** C3
Qucina & Q Bar **55** B2

Refinery, Huo Tuc & Vasco's **15** A2
Saigon Indian & Warda **37** C2
Temple Club **42** C1
Wild Horse Saloon **47** A3
Wrap & Roll **54** C3
Zanzbar **12** B3

Bars & clubs
Alibi **16** A3
Apocalypse Now **3** B3
Blue Gecko **7** A2
Storm-P **2** B3
Xu **35** B3

In essence, it is a 1960s-style building filled with 1960s-style official furnishings that now look very kitsch. Not only was the building designed according to the principles of Chinese geomancy but the colour of the carpets – lurid mustard yellow in one room – was also chosen depending on whether it was to calm or stimulate users of the rooms. Visitors are shown an interesting film about the Revolution and some fascinating photographs and memorabilia from the era. A replica of the tank that bulldozed through the gates of the compound heralding the end of South Vietnam is displayed in the forecourt.

War Remnants Museum
ⓘ *28 Vo Van Tan St, Q3, T8-3930 6325, daily 0730-1200, 1330-1700, 15,000d.*
All the horrors of the Vietnam War from the nation's perspective – photographs of atrocities and action, bombs, military tanks and planes and deformed foetuses – are piled up in a new museum building. In the courtyard are tanks, bombs and helicopters, while the new museum, arranged in five new sections, records man's inhumanity. The display covers the Son My (My Lai) massacre on 16 March 1968 (see box, page 273), the effects of napalm and phosphorous, and the after-effects of Agent Orange defoliation (this is particularly disturbing, with bottled malformed human foetuses). There's also a new feature on Senator John Kerry's Vietnam involvement. Unsurprisingly, there is no record of North Vietnamese atrocities to US and South Vietnamese troops. This museum has gone through some interesting name changes in recent years. It began life as the Exhibition House of American and Chinese War Crimes. In 1990, 'Chinese' was dropped from the name, and in 1994 'American' was too. Since 1996 it has simply been called the War Remnants Museum.

Archbishop's Palace
ⓘ *330 Nguyen Dinh Chieu St and corner of Tran Quoc Thao St.*
Around this area are a number of very fine French-era buildings still standing; some have been allowed to fall into decay but others have been well maintained. In particular the Archbishop's Palace and the high schools, **Le Qui Don** ⓘ *2 Le Qui Don St*, and **Marie Curie** ⓘ *Nam Ky Khoi Nghia St*. All have had extensions built in recent years, but at least the schools (unlike the archbishop) have attempted to blend the new buildings in with the old. The palace is believed to be the oldest house in Ho Chi Minh City, built in 1790 (although not originally on this spot) for the then French bishop of Adran, Pierre Pigneau de Behaine.

Xa Loi Pagoda
ⓘ *89 Ba Huyen Thanh Quan St, daily 0630-1100, 1430-1700.*
Ho Chi Minh City has close to 200 pagodas – far too many for most visitors to see. Many of the finest are in Cholon (see page 321), although there is a selection closer to the main hotel area in central Ho Chi Minh City. The Xa Loi Pagoda is not far from the War Remnants Museum and is surrounded by food stalls. Built in 1956, the pagoda contains a multi-storeyed tower, which is particularly revered, as it houses a relic of the Buddha. The main sanctuary contains a large, bronze-gilded Buddha in an attitude of meditation. Around the walls are a series of silk paintings depicting the previous lives of the Buddha (with an explanation of each life to the right of the entrance into the sanctuary). The pagoda is historically, rather than artistically, important as it became a focus of dissent against the Diem regime (see box, page 318).

Le Duan Street

North of the cathedral is Le Duan Street, the former corridor of power with Ngo Dinh Diem's Palace at one end, the zoo at the other and the former embassies of the three major powers, France, the USA and the UK, in between. Quite who was aping who and who was the puppet and who was the master was a tangled question. Nearest the Reunification Hall is the compound of the **French Consulate**. A block away is the **former US Embassy**. After diplomatic ties were resumed in 1995 the Americans lost little time in demolishing the 1960s building which held so many bad memories. The US Consulate General now stands on this site. Outside, a queue of hopeful visa supplicants forms every day come rain or shine. This office has the distinction of being the busiest overseas US mission for marriage visas, a title for which it vies closely with the US Embassy in Manila. A **memorial** outside, on the corner of Mac Dinh Chi Street, records the attack by Viet Cong special forces during the Tet offensive of 1968 and the final victory in 1975. On the other side of the road, a little further northeast at 25 Le Duan, is the **former British Embassy**, erected in the late 1950s, now the British Consulate General and British Council. At 2 Le Duan Street is the **Museum of Ho Chi Minh Campaign (Bao Tang Quan Doi)** ① *T8-3822 9387, Tue-Sun 0730-1100, 1330-1630, 15,000d,* with a tank and warplane in the front compound. It contains an indifferent display of photographs and articles of war.

Botanical Gardens and Zoo

① *2 Nguyen Binh Khiem St, T8-3829 3728, daily 0700-2000, entrance to gardens and zoo, 12,000d.*

At the end of Le Duan Street are the Botanical Gardens which run alongside Nguyen Binh Khiem Street at the point where the Thi Nghe channel flows into the Saigon River. The gardens were established in 1864 by French botanist Jean-Batiste Louis Pierre; by the 1970s they had a collection of nearly 2000 species, and a particularly fine display of orchids. With the dislocations of the immediate postwar years, the gardens went into decline, a situation from which they are still trying to recover. In the south quarter of the gardens is a mediocre zoo with a rather moth-eaten collection of animals which form a backdrop to smartly dressed Vietnamese families posing for photographs.

Museum of Vietnamese History

① *2 Nguyen Binh Khiem St, T8-3829 8146, www.baotanglichsuvn.com, Tue-Sun 0800-1130, 1330-1700,15,000d. Photography permit, 32,000d. Labels in English and French. Water puppet shows (see also page 339) are held here daily 0900, 1000, 1100, 1400, 1500 and 1600, 15 mins, US$2.*

The history museum (Bao Tang Lich Su Viet Nam) is an elegant building constructed in 1928 and is pagodaesque in style. It displays a wide range of artefacts from the prehistoric (300,000 years ago) and the Dongson periods (3500 BC-AD 100), right through to the birth of the Vietnamese Communist Party in 1930. Particularly impressive are the Cham sculptures, of which the standing bronze Buddha, dating from the fourth to sixth century, is probably the finest. There is also a delicately carved Devi (Goddess) dating from the 10th century as well as pieces such as the head of Shiva, Hindu destroyer and creator, from the eighth to ninth century and Ganesh, elephant-headed son of Shiva and Parvati, also dating from the eighth to ninth century.

There are also representative pieces from the Chen-la, Funan, Khmer, Oc-eo and Han Chinese periods, and from the various Vietnamese dynasties together with some hill tribe artefacts. Labelling is in English, French and Vietnamese.

Other highlights include the wooden stakes planted in the Bach Dang riverbed for repelling the war ships of the Mongol Yuan in the 13th century, a beautiful Phoenix head from the Tran dynasty (13th to 14th century) and an Hgor (big drum) from the Jarai people, made from the skin of two elephants. It belonged to the Potauoui (King of Fire) family in Ajunpa district, Gia Lai Province. There are some fine sandstone sculptures too including an incredibly smooth linga from Long An Province (seventh to eighth century) in the Mekong Delta. The linga represents the cult of Siva and signifies gender, energy, fertility and potency.

Near the History Museum is the **Memorial Temple** ① *Tue-Sun 0800-1130, 1300-1600*, constructed in 1928 and dedicated to famous Vietnamese.

Ho Chi Minh City Museum and around

① *65 Ly Tu Trong St, T8-3829 9741, www.hcmc-museum.edu.vn, daily 0800-1700, 15,000d.*
This museum includes a mixed bag of displays concerning the revolution, with a display of photographs, a few pieces of hardware (helicopter, anti-aircraft guns) in the back compound, and some memorabilia. Other exhibits chart the development of the city and its economy. The building itself is historically important. Dominating a prominent intersection, the grey-white classical French-designed building was built as a museum before it became the palace for the governor of Cochin China in 1890. After the 1945 revolution it was used for administrative offices before returning to the French as the High Commissioner's residence in September 1945. During the War, Ngo Dinh Diem resided here under its new name as Southern Governor's Palace; during the reign of Nguyen Van Thieu (1967-1975), it operated as the supreme court.

Southwest from the museum on the corner of Ly Tu Trong Street and Nam Ky Khoi Nghia is the National Library.

Mariamman Hindu Temple

① *45 Truong Dinh St.*
Although clearly Hindu, with a statue of Mariamman flanked by Maduraiveeran and Pechiamman, the temple is largely frequented by Chinese worshippers, providing the strange sight of Chinese Vietnamese clasping incense sticks and prostrating themselves in front of a Hindu deity, as they would to a Buddha image. The Chinese have always been pragmatic when it comes to religions.

Ben Thanh Market (Cho Ben Thanh)

A large, covered central market, Ben Thanh Market faces a statue of Tran Nguyen Han (a Le Dynasty general) at a large and chaotic roundabout, the Ben Thanh gyratory system, which marks the intersection of Le Loi, Ham Nghi and Tran Hung Dao streets. Ben Thanh is well stocked with clothes (cheap souvenir T-shirts), household goods, a wide range of soap, shampoo and sun cream, a good choice of souvenirs, lacquerware, embroidery and so on, as well as some terrific lines in food, including cold meats, fresh and dried fruits. It is not cheap (most local people window-shop here and purchase elsewhere) but the quality is high and the selection probably without equal. It is a terrific experience just to wander through and marvel at the range of produce on offer, all the more so now most of the beggars have been eased out. Outside the north gate (*cua Bac*) on Le Thanh Ton Street are some tempting displays of fruit (the oranges and apples are imported) and cut flowers.

The **Ben Thanh Night Market** has flourished since 2003. Starting at dusk and open until after midnight the night market is Ho Chi Minh City's attempt to recreate Bangkok's Patpong market. As the sun sinks and the main market closes stalls spring up in the

Buddhist martyrs: self-immolation as protest

In August 1963 there was a demonstration of 15,000 people at the Xa Loi Pagoda, with speakers denouncing the Diem regime and telling jokes about Diem's sister-in-law, Madame Nhu (who was later to call monks "hooligans in robes"). Two nights later, ARVN special forces (from Roman Catholic families) raided the pagoda, battering down the gate, wounding 30 and killing seven people. Soon afterwards Diem declared martial law. The pagoda became a focus of discontent, with several monks committing suicide through self-immolation to protest against the Diem regime.

The first monk to immolate himself was 66-year-old Thich Quang Du, from Hué. On 11 June 1963, his companions poured petrol over him and set him alight as he sat in the lotus position. Pedestrians prostrated themselves at the sight; even

a policeman threw himself to the ground in reverence. The next day, the picture of the monk in flames filled the front pages of newspapers around the world. Some 30 monks and nuns followed Thich's example in protesting against the Diem government and US involvement in South Vietnam. Two young US protesters also followed suit, one committing suicide by self-immolation outside the Pentagon and the other next to the UN, both in November 1968.

Madame Nhu, a Catholic, is reported as having said after the monks' death: "Let them burn, and we shall clap our hands." Within five months Diem had been killed in a military coup.

In May 1993, a Vietnamese man immolated himself at the Thien Mu Pagoda in Hué – the pagoda where the first monk-martyr was based (see page 187).

---

surrounding streets. Clothes and cheap jewellery and an abundance of food stalls are the key attractions. The clear fact is that every night and often way beyond midnight the night market remains well and truly open. This may not sound unusual to new visitors but as the city authorities have been engaged in a tireless war against open-air eating for the past half dozen years the fact that it is now possible to sit in the open and eat well and cheaply is a positive achievement.

Opposite the south gate of Ben Thanh Market is a swirling current of traffic negotiating (by and large successfully) the Benh Thanh gyratory system, one of Ho Chi Minh City's busiest roundabouts and immediately to the south of that is the central (local) bus station. You can obtain a highly useful map inside the station and attempt to ask questions but very little English is spoken. Buses are air-conditioned too.

Ho Chi Minh City has a number of markets, but this one and the Binh Tay Market in Cholon (see page 323) are the largest. Many of the markets are surprisingly well stocked for a country that not too long ago was close to economic collapse.

Fine Arts Museum

ⓘ 97A Pho Duc Chinh St, T8-3829 4441, daily 0900-1700, 10,000d. Not everything is labelled and what is labelled is not in English

The so-called Fine Arts Museum (Bao Tang My Thuat), housed in an impressive cream-coloured mansion is a distinctly unimpressive and unloved collection of dusty works of art. The third floor contains artefacts from the ancient civilizations of Oc-eo through to the Cham era. More recent collections include some attractive Dong Nai ceramics of the early 20th century. Highlights include a 12th-century sculpture of kala, a monster guarding the temple,

Betel nut

Betel nut has been a stimulant for the Vietnamese for hundreds of years. The ingredients combine the egg-shaped betel palm (*Areca catechu*) nut (*cau*) with Piper betel vine leaves (*trau*) and lime. When chewed (known as *An trau*) the ingredients stain the mouth and lips and red juice can often be seen dribbling down the chins of users. It often stains teeth black due to the polyphenol in the nut and leaf, which

is considered attractive. The origin of the substance lies in Vietnamese legend and its use is found at weddings where a betel quid (a combination of powdered betel nut, betel leaves, lime and other flavourings) is laid out for guests. The areca nut is also a customary wedding gift given to the bride's family by the bridegroom's family. Betel and areca nuts are also presented at Tet (Lunar New Year).

from My Son. It is a fanged beast with a big protuberance for a nose, bulging eyes and forest-thick eyebrows. Hindu god sculptures are made of soft sandstone: Laksmi, found in Soc Trang in the Mekong Delta (seventh to eighth century) is the goddess of beauty and good fortune. A line of funeral statues (gaunt-looking, wooden folk) made by the Tay Nguyen people in the early 20th century in the central Highlands, line a corridor. These figures are crafted by the living as substitutes of their late relatives.

Part of the second floor is devoted to more recent events. Lacquered pictures appear, such as the interior of Cu Chi by Quach Phong (1997). There's a small collection of propaganda art posters (undated) and a vast bronze mural of the nation indicating anti-American sentiment by Nguyen Sang (undated). Some of the most interesting work is by Americans who have produced work that reflects on the war – namely montage and photographs. The ground floor is given over to temporary exhibitions.

The building itself is worthy of note having been built in the early 20th century by a Chinese man whose fortune was made by selling empty bottles.

Phung Son Tu Pagoda
ⓘ *338 Nguyen Cong Tru St.*

This is a small temple built just after the Second World War by Fukien Chinese; its most notable features are the wonderful painted entrance doors with their fearsome armed warriors. Incense spirals hang in the open well of the pagoda, which is dedicated to Ong Bon, the Guardian of Happiness and Virtue.

The **War Surplus Market (Dan Sinh)** ⓘ *Yersin between Nguyen Thai Binh St and Nguyen Cong Tru St*, is not far from the Phung Son Tu Pagoda. Merchandise on sale includes dog tags and military clothing and equipment (not all of it authentic). The market is popular with Western visitors looking for mementoes of their visit, so bargain particularly hard.

Old Market and riverside

The Old Market is on Ton That Dam Street, running between Ham Nghi Street and Ton That Thiep Street. It is the centre for the sale of black market goods (particularly consumer electronics) – now openly displayed. There is also a good range of foodstalls and fruit sellers. Close by is the old and rather splendid **Hong Kong and Shanghai Bank building** ⓘ *Ben Chuong Duong St*. It no longer houses the HSBC bank, which returned to Vietnam in 1994; this is now to be found on Dong Khoi Street facing the cathedral. Nguyen Tat Thanh Street runs south from here over the Ben Nghe Channel to **Dragon**

House Wharf, at the confluence of the Ben Nghe Channel and the Saigon River. The former customs building, dating from 1863, has been converted into the **Ho Chi Minh Museum** ⓘ *1 Nguyen Tat Thanh St, 0730-1130, 1330-1630, 10,000d*, (predominantly on the first floor), celebrating the life and exploits of Ho Chi Minh, mostly through pictures and the odd piece of memorabilia. School children are brought here to learn about their country's recent history, and people of all ages have their photographs taken with a portrait of Bac Ho in the background.

A short distance north up Ton Duc Thang Street from the broad Me Linh Square (in the centre of which is an imposing statue of Vietnamese hero Tran Hung Dao) is the rarely visited **Ton Duc Thang Museum** ⓘ *5 Ton Duc Thang St, T8-3829 7542, Tue-Sun 0730-1130, 1330-1700, free*. Opened in 1989, it is dedicated to the life of Ton Duc Thang or Bac (Uncle) Ton. Bac Ton, a comrade who fought with Ho Chi Minh, was appointed President of Vietnam following Ho's death, remaining in office until his own death in 1980. The museum contains an array of photographs and other memorabilia.

Pham Ngu Lao

Most backpackers arriving overland in Ho Chi Minh City are dropped off in this bustling district, a 10- to 15-minute walk from downtown. Those arriving by air tend to head straight here too. The countless hotels, guesthouses and rooms to rent open and close and change name or owner with remarkable speed. The area is littered with restaurants, cafés, bars, email services, laundries, tour agencies and money changers, all fiercely competitive; there are mini-supermarkets and shops selling rucksacks, footwear, CDs, DVDs, pirated software and ethnic knick-knacks.

> ➡ **Ho Chi Minh City maps**
> 1 Ho Chi Minh City map, page 306
> 2 Ho Chi Minh City Centre, page 312
> 3 Ho Chi Minh City Centre detail, page 314
> 4 Pham Ngu Lao, page 320

④ Pham Ngu Lao

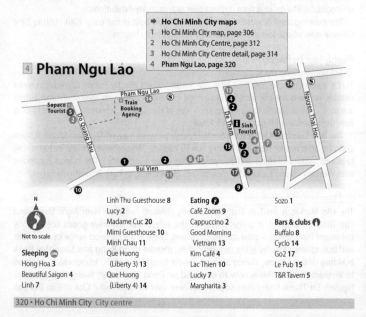

N
Not to scale

Sleeping 🛏
Hong Hoa **3**
Beautiful Saigon **4**
Linh **7**

Linh Thu Guesthouse **8**
Lucy **2**
Madame Cuc **20**
Mimi Guesthouse **10**
Minh Chau **11**
Que Huong
  (Liberty 3) **13**
Que Huong
  (Liberty 4) **14**

Eating 🍴
Café Zoom **9**
Cappuccino **2**
Good Morning
  Vietnam **13**
Kim Café **4**
Lac Thien **10**
Lucky **7**
Margharita **3**

Sozo **1**

Bars & clubs 🍸
Buffalo **8**
Cyclo **14**
Go2 **17**
Le Pub **15**
T&R Tavern **5**

Cholon (Chinatown)

This is the heart of Ho Chi Minh City's Chinese community. Cholon is an area of commerce and trade; not global but nevertheless international. In typical Chinese style it is dominated by small and medium-size businesses and this shows in the buildings' shop fronts (look for the Chinese characters on signs over the door). The Chinese do less on the pavements than the Vietnamese and this is apparent on a tour through Cholon. Cholon is home to a great many temples and pagodas – some of which are described below. As one would expect from a Chinese trading district, there is plenty of fabric for sale in the markets.

Cho lon or 'big market' or Chinatown, is inhabited predominantly by Vietnamese of Chinese origin. However, since 1975 the authorities have alienated many Chinese, causing hundreds of thousands to leave the country. In making their escape many have died – either through drowning, as their perilously small and overladen craft foundered, or at the hands of pirates in the East Sea. In total, between 1977 and 1982, 709,570 refugees were recorded by the UNHCR as having fled Vietnam. By the late 1980s, the flow of boat people was being driven more by economic, rather than political, forces; there was little chance of making good in a country as poor, and in an economy as moribund, as that of Vietnam. Even with this flow of Chinese out of the country, there is still a large population of Chinese Vietnamese living in Cholon, an area which encompasses District 5 to the southwest of the city centre. Cholon appears to the casual visitor to be the most populated, noisiest and in general the most vigorous part of Ho Chi Minh City, if not of Vietnam. It is here that entrepreneurial talent and private funds are concentrated; both resources that the government are keen to mobilize in their attempts to reinvigorate the economy.

Cholon is worth visiting not only for the bustle and activity, but also because the temples and assembly halls found here are the finest in Ho Chi Minh City. As with any town in Southeast Asia boasting a sizeable Chinese population, the early settlers established meeting rooms which offered social, cultural and spiritual support to members of a dialect group. These assembly halls (*hoi quan*) are most common in Hoi An and Cholon. There are temples in the buildings which attract Vietnamese as well as Chinese worshippers, and indeed today serve little of their former purpose. The elderly meet here occasionally for a natter and a cup of tea.

Nghia An Assembly Hall
ⓘ *678 Nguyen Trai St, not far from the Arc en Ciel Hotel.*
A magnificent, carved, gold-painted wooden boat hangs over the entrance to the Nghia An Assembly Hall. To the left, on entering the temple, is a larger-than-life representation of Quan Cong's horse and groom. (Quan Cong was a loyal military man who lived in China in the third century.) At the main altar are three figures in glass cases: the central red-faced figure with a green cloak is Quan Cong himself; to the left and right are his trusty companions, General Chau Xuong (very fierce) and the mandarin Quan Binh respectively. On leaving, note the fine gold figures of guardians on the inside of the door panels.

Tam Son Assembly Hall
ⓘ *118 Trieu Quang Phuc St, just off Nguyen Trai St.*
The temple, built in the 19th century by Fukien immigrants, is frequented by childless women as it is dedicated to Chua Thai Sanh, the Goddess of Fertility. It is an uncluttered, 'pure' example of a Chinese/Vietnamese pagoda – peaceful and quiet. Like Nghia An Hoi Quan, the temple contains figures of Quan Cong, his horse and two companions.

Thien Hau Temples
① *710 and 802 Nguyen Trai St.*

The Thien Hau Temple at 710 Nguyen Trai Street is one of the largest in the city. Constructed in the early 19th century, it is Chinese in inspiration and is dedicated to the worship of both the Buddha and to the Goddess Thien Hau, the goddess of the sea and the protector of sailors. Thien Hau was born in China and as a girl saved her father from drowning, but not her brother. Thien Hau's festival is marked here on the 23rd day of the third lunar month. One enormous incense urn and an incinerator can be seen through the main doors. Inside, the principal altar supports the gilded form of Thien Hau, with a boat to one side. Silk paintings depicting religious scenes decorate the walls. By far the most interesting part of the pagoda is the roof, which can be best seen from the small open courtyard. It must be one of the finest and most richly ornamented in Vietnam, with the high-relief frieze depicting episodes from the Legends of the Three Kingdoms. In the post-1975 era, many would-be refugees prayed here for safe deliverance before casting themselves adrift on the East Sea. A number of those who survived the perilous voyage sent offerings to the merciful goddess and the temple has been well maintained since. On busy days it is very smoky. Look up on leaving to see over the front door a picture of a boiling sea peppered with sinking boats. A benign Thien An looks down mercifully from a cloud. The temple has its own shop stocked with joss sticks, paper offerings and temple tat. Most people seem to buy their gear from the vendors outside who presumably don't have to pass on any 'overhead' costs. The shop also sells chilled water and Coca Cola.

A **second temple** dedicated to Thien Hau is a couple of blocks away at 802 Nguyen Trai St. This was built by migrants from Fukien Province in China in the 1730s although the building on the site today is not old. The roof can be seen from the road and in addition to the normal dragons are some curious models of what appear to be miniature Chinese landscapes carried by bowed men. Inside it is less busy than the first Thien Hau temple but on good days worshippers hurry from one image of Thien Hau (depicted here with a black face) to another waving burning joss sticks in front of her. Whatever happens in these temples is not religious in the sense of worshipping a god but more a superstition, entreating the spirits for good fortune (hence the lottery ticket sellers outside) or asking them to stave off bad luck. Note that these are not pagodas in the sense that they are not a place for the worship of Buddha and you will see no Buddhist monks here and have no sense of serene or enlightened calm. This temple has some nicely carved stone pillars of entwined dragons and on the wall to the right of the altars is a frieze of a boat being swamped by a tsunami. The walls are festooned with calendars from local Chinese restaurants and gold shops.

Ming Dynasty Assembly Hall
① *380 Tran Hung Dao St.*

The Ming Dynasty Assembly Hall (Dinh Minh Huong Gia Thanh) was built by the Cantonese community which arrived in Saigon via Hoi An in the 18th century. The assembly hall was built in 1789 to the dedication and worship of the Ming Dynasty although the building we see today dates largely from an extensive renovation carried out in the 1960s. There is some old furniture, a heavy-marble topped table and chairs which arrived in 1850 from China. It appears that the Vietnamese Emperor Gia Long used the Chinese community for cordial relations with the Chinese royal court and one of the community, a man called Trinh Hoai Duc was appointed Vietnamese ambassador to the Middle Dynasty. In the main hall there are three altars which, following imperial tradition, are: the central altar dedicated to the royal family (Ming Dynasty in this case), the right-hand altar dedicated to two mandarin officers (military) and the left-hand altar dedicated to two mandarin officers (civil).

The hall behind is dedicated to the memory of the Vuong family who built the hall and whose descendants have lived here ever since. The custodian is in fact the third generation of this family and he will explain the complexities in broken English or polished French. There is, in addition, a small side chapel where childless women can seek divine intercession from a local deity, Ba Me Sanh.

Quan Am Pagoda
ⓘ *12 Lao Tu St (just off Luong Nhu Hoc St).*
The Quan Am Pagoda is thought to be one of the oldest in the city. Its roof supports four sets of impressive mosaic-encrusted figures, while inside, the main building is fronted with old, gold and lacquer panels of guardian spirits. The main altar supports a seated statue of A-Pho, the Holy Mother. In front of the main altar is a white ceramic statue of Quan Am, the Goddess of Purity and Motherhood (Goddess of Mercy) – see page 61. The pagoda complex also contains a series of courtyards and altars dedicated to a range of deities and spirits. Outside, hawkers sell caged birds and vast quantities of incense sticks to pilgrims.

Binh Tay Market
The Binh Tay Market, sandwiched between Thap Muoi and Phan Van Khoe streets, is one of the most colourful and exciting markets in Ho Chi Minh City, with a wonderful array of noises, smells and colours. It sprawls over a large area and is contained in what looks like a rather decayed Forbidden Palace. Beware of pickpockets here. A new high-rise market – the five-storey **An Dong Market** – opened at the end of 1991 in Cholon. It was built with an investment of US$5 million from local ethnic Chinese businessmen.

Outer Ho Chi Minh City

Outer Ho Chi Minh City includes a clutch of scattered pagodas in several districts, namely Districts 3, 10, 11 and Binh Thanh. All are accessible by cyclo, moto or taxi. There's also a new museum of traditional medicine in District 10.

Phung Son Pagoda
ⓘ *A 40-min walk or 8-min motorbike ride from the Binh Tay Market, set back from the road at 1408 3 Thang 2 Blvd.*
The Phung Son Pagoda, also known as **Go Pagoda**, was built at the beginning of the 19th century on the site of an earlier Cambodian structure and has been rebuilt several times. At one time, it was decided to move the pagoda, and all the temple valuables were loaded on to the back of a white elephant. The beast stumbled and the valuables tumbled out into the pond that surrounds the temple. This was taken as a sign from the gods that the pagoda was to stay where it was. In the sanctuary, there is a large, seated, gilded Buddha, surrounded by a variety of other figures from several Asian and Southeast Asian countries. This, being a pagoda, has a very different atmosphere from the temples of Chinatown. There is no frenzied scrum in front of the altars and only a few whisps of smoke. Monks sit in contemplation.

Giac Vien Pagoda

ⓘ *At the end of a narrow and rather seedy 400-m-long alley running off Lac Long Quan St (just after No 247). There is a also a temple down here of no interest whatsoever, the pagoda is right at the end.*

Giac Vien Pagoda (Buddha's Complete Enlightenment) is similar in layout, content and inspiration to Giac Lam Pagoda (see below). Visiting just one of the two pagodas would be enough for most visitors. The Giac Vien Pagoda was built in 1771 and dedicated to the worship of the Emperor Gia Long. Although restored, Giac Vien remains one of the best-preserved temples in Vietnam. It is lavishly decorated, with more than 100 carvings of various divinities and spirits, dominated by a large gilded image of the Buddha of the Past (Amitabha or *A Di Da Phat* in Vietnamese). It is everything a pagoda should be: demons and gods jump out around every corner, a confusion of fantastic characters. With the smoke and smells, the richness of colour and the darkness, it's an assault on the senses. Among the decorations, note the 'Buddha lamp', funerary tablets and urns with photographs of the deceased. Outside there is a small pavilion in which the ashes of the dead are stored in small urns.

Giac Lam Pagoda

ⓘ *118 Lac Long Quan St, Ward 10, Q Tan Binh, T8-865 3933, about 2 km northeast of Giac Vien Pagoda, through an arch and down a short track about 300 m from the intersection with Le Dai Hanh St. Near the intersection is a modern 7-storey tower and beyond a giant Buddha statue which is also modern. Daily 0500-1200, 1400-2100.*

The Giac Lam Pagoda (Forest of Enlightenment) was built in 1744 and is the oldest pagoda in Ho Chi Minh City. There is a sacred Bodhi tree in the temple courtyard and the pagoda is set among fruit trees and vegetable plots. Inside Giac Lam it feels, initially, like a rather cluttered private house. In one section, there are rows of funerary tablets with pictures of the deceased – a rather moving display of man's mortality. The main altar is impressive, with layers of Buddhas, dominated by the gilded form of the Buddha of the Past. Note the 49-Buddha oil lamp with little scraps of paper tucked in. On these scraps are the names of the mourned. The number seven is very important in Buddhism and most towers have seven storeys. Behind the main temple in the section with the funerary tablets is a bust of Ho Chi Minh. At the very back of the pagoda is a hall with murals showing scenes of torture from hell. Each sin is punished in a very specific and appropriate way. The monks are very friendly and will probably offer tea. Some speak good English and French as well as having detailed knowledge of the history of the pagoda. It is a small haven of peace. An unusual feature is the use of blue and white porcelain plates to decorate the roof and some of the small towers in the garden facing the pagoda. These towers are the burial places of former head monks.

Phuoc Hai Tu (Emperor of Jade Pagoda) and around

ⓘ *73 Mai Thi Luu St off Dien Bien Phu St, 0700-1800.*

The Phuoc Hai Tu can be found, nestling behind low pink walls, just before the Thi Nghe Channel. Women sell birds that are set free to gain merit, and a pond to the right contains large turtles. The Emperor of Jade is the supreme god of the Taoists, although this temple, built in 1900, contains a wide range of other deities. These include the archangel Michael of the Buddhists, a Sakyamuni (historic) Buddha, statues of the two generals who tamed the Green Dragon (representing the east) and the White Dragon (representing the west), to the left and right of the first altar respectively, and Quan Am (see page 61). The Hall of Ten Hells in the left-hand sanctuary has reliefs depicting the 1000 tortures of hell.

Nearby, the architecturally interesting **city library** ⓘ *3 Nguyen Dinh Chieu*, has a cool, modern façade; there is a memorial at the front of the building.

Tran Hung Dao Temple
ⓘ *Near the Emperor of Jade Pagoda at 34 Vo Thi Sau St, daily 0700-1100, 1430-1700.*
The small Tran Hung Dao Temple, built in 1932, was dedicated to the worship of the victorious 13th-century General Hung Dao and contains a series of bas-reliefs depicting the general's successes, along with weapons and carved dragons. In the front courtyard is a larger-than-life bronze statue of this hero of Vietnamese nationalism.

Vinh Nghiem Pagoda
ⓘ *To the west, on Nguyen Van Troi St, and just to the south of the Thi Nghe Channel.*
Another modern pagoda, the Vinh Nghiem Pagoda, was completed in 1967 and is one of the largest in Vietnam. Built in the Japanese style, it displays a classic seven-storey pagoda in a large and airy sanctuary. On either side of the entrance are two fearsome warriors; inside is a large Japanese-style Buddha in an attitude of meditation, flanked by two goddesses. Along the walls are a series of scrolls depicting the *jataka* tales, with rather quaint (and difficult to interpret) explanations in English.

Tomb and Temple of Marshal Le Van Duyet
ⓘ *126 Dinh Tien Hoang St, a 10- to 15-min cyclo ride across the Thi Nghe Channel and almost into the suburbs, 0500-1800.*
Le Van Duyet was a highly respected Vietnamese soldier who put down the Tay Son Rebellion (see page 272) and who died in 1831. The pagoda was renovated in 1937 – a plaque on the left lists those who made donations to the renovation fund. The main sanctuary contains a weird assortment of objects: a stuffed tiger, a miniature mountain, whale baleen, spears and other weapons of war. Much of the collection is made up of the Marshal's personal possessions. In front of the temple is the tomb itself, surrounded by a low wall and flanked by two guardian lions and two lotus buds. The pagoda's attractive roof is best seen from the tomb.

Museum of Vietnamese Traditional Medicine
ⓘ *41 Hoang Du Khuong St, District 10, T8-386 42430, www.fitomuseum.com.vn, open daily 0830-1730.*
A fascinating exploration into traditional medicine with 3000 exhibits including instruments, manuscripts, ceramic jars and model of a 19th-century pharmacy.

Around Ho Chi Minh City

Unlike Hanoi, which is so rich in sights to visit on a day out, the Ho Chi Minh City region is woefully under-endowed. The **Cu Chi Tunnels** (see below) are the most popular day trip, followed closely by an excursion to the Mekong Delta, especially **My Tho** (see page 356). It is possible to get to the coast and back in a day, **Vung Tau** (see page 291), **Long Hai** (see page 294) and **Ho Coc** (see page 295) being the obvious candidates. Ho Chi Minh City does, on the other hand, have several out-of-town sports facilities with three **golf courses** and the exhilarating **Saigon Water Park** all within less than an hour's drive (see page 344).

Cu Chi Tunnels

① Most visitors reach Cu Chi on a tour or charter a car and include a visit to Tay Ninh – see below. Regular buses leave for Cu Chi town from the Mien Tay station (Cholon) and the Ham Nghi station; from Cu Chi it is necessary to take a Honda ôm to the tunnels or the infrequent Ben Suc bus, 10 km. It is also possible to take a motorbike from Ho Chi Minh City and back but the road (now the Bangkok to Ho Chi Minh City highway) is becoming increasingly dangerous with fast and heavy traffic. Go up Cach Mang Thang Tam St, which turns into Highway 22. Continue to Cu Chi. Go over the flyover and take the next turning to the right which is signed to the Cu Chi Tunnels. From here the tunnels are quite badly signed and you will almost certainly need to ask. Daily 0700-1630, 75,000d.

Cu Chi Tunnels are about 40 km northwest of Ho Chi Minh City. Cu Chi town is on the main road to Tay Ninh and the Cao Dai temple and both the tunnels and the temple can be visited in a single day trip. Dug by the Viet Minh, who began work in 1948, they were later expanded by the People's Liberation Armed Forces (PLAF, or Viet Cong, VC, see page 417) and used for storage and refuge, and contained sleeping quarters, hospitals and schools. Between 1960 and 1970, 200 km of tunnels were built. At the height of their usage, some 300,000 were living underground. The width of the tunnel entry at ground level was 22 cm by 30 cm. The tunnels are too narrow for most Westerners, but a short section of the 250 km of tunnels has been especially widened to allow tourists to share the experience. Tall or large people might still find it a claustrophobic squeeze.

Cu Chi was one of the most fervently communist of the districts around Ho Chi Minh City and the tunnels were used as the base from which the PLAF mounted the operations of the Tet Offensive in 1968. Communist cadres were active in this area of rubber plantations, even before the Second World War. Vann and Ramsey, two American soldiers, were to notice the difference between this area and other parts of the south in the early 1960s: "No children laughed and shouted for gum and candy in these hamlets. Everyone, adult and child, had a cold look" (*A Bright Shining Lie*, Sheehan 1989).

When the Americans first discovered this underground base on their doorstep (Dong Du GI base was nearby) they would simply pump CS gas down the tunnel openings and then set explosives. They also pumped river water in and used German Shepherd dogs to smell out air holes. The VC, however, smothered the holes in garlic to deter the dogs. They also used cotton from the cotton tree – kapok – to stifle the smoke from cooking; 40,000 VC were killed in the tunnels in 10 years. Later, realizing that the tunnels might also yield valuable intelligence, volunteer 'tunnel rats' were sent into the earth to capture prisoners.

Cu Chi district was a free-fire zone and was assaulted using the full battery of ecological warfare. Defoliants were sprayed and 20 tonne Rome Ploughs carved up the area in the search for tunnels. It was said that even a crow flying over Cu Chi district had to carry its own lunch. Later it was also carpet bombed with 50,000 tonnes dropped on the area in 10 years.

At **Cu Chi 1** (Ben Dinh) *① 75,000d*, visitors are shown a somewhat antique but nevertheless interesting film of the tunnels during the war before being taken into the tunnels and seeing some of the rooms and the booby traps the GIs encountered. The VC survived on just cassava for up to three months and at both places you will be invited to taste some dipped in salt, sesame, sugar and peanuts. You will also be invited to a firing range to try your hand with ancient AK47s at a buck a bang.

Cu Chi 2 (Ben Duoc), has a temple, the **Ben Duoc Temple**, in memory of the 50,000 Saigon dead; the exterior is covered in mosaic murals. It stands in front of a rather beautiful sculpture of a tear called *Symbol of the Country's Spiritual Soul*.

Near the tunnels is the Cu Chi graveyard for patriots with 8000 graves. It has a very interesting large and striking bas-relief of war images along the perimeter of the entrance to the cemetery.

Cao Dai Great Temple

ⓘ *Ceremonies are held each day at 0600, 1200, 1800 and 2400, visitors can watch from the cathedral's balcony. Visitors should not enter the central portion of the nave – keep to the side aisles – and also should not wander in and out during services. If you go in at the beginning of the service you should stay until the end (1 hr). Photography is allowed. Take a tour, or charter a car in Ho Chi Minh City. Regular buses leave for Tay Ninh, via Cu Chi, from Mien Tay station (2½ hrs) or motorbike.*

Tay Ninh, the home of the temple, is 96 km northwest of Ho Chi Minh City and 64 km further on from Cu Chi town. It can be visited on a day trip from the city and can easily be combined with a visit to the Cu Chi tunnels. The idiosyncratic Cao Dai Great Temple, the 'cathedral' of the Cao Dai religion (see page 474 for background on Cao Daism), is the main reason to visit the town.

The Cao Dai Great Temple, built in 1880, is set within a very large complex of schools and administrative buildings, all washed in pastel yellow. The twin-towered cathedral is European in inspiration but with distinct oriental features. On the façade are figures of Cao Dai saints in high relief and at the entrance is a painting depicting Victor Hugo flanked by the Vietnamese poet Nguyen Binh Khiem and the Chinese nationalist Sun Yat Sen. The latter holds an inkstone, symbolizing, strangely, the link between Confucianism and Christianity. Novelist Graham Greene in *The Quiet American* called it "The Walt Disney Fantasia of the East". Monsieur Ferry, an acquaintance of Norman Lewis, described the cathedral in even more outlandish terms, saying it "looked like a fantasy from the brain of Disney, and all the faiths of the Orient had been ransacked to create the pompous ritual…". Lewis himself was clearly unimpressed with the structure and the religion, writing in *A Dragon Apparent* that "This cathedral must be the most outrageously vulgar building ever to have been erected with serious intent".

After removing shoes and hats, women enter the cathedral through a door to the left, men to the right, and they then proceed down their respective aisles towards the altar, usually accompanied by a Cao Dai priest dressed in white with a black turban. During services they don red, blue and yellow robes signifying Confucianism, Taoism and Buddhism respectively. The men in coloured robes sporting an embroidered divine eye on their costumes are more senior. During services, on the balcony at the back of the cathedral, a group of men play a stringed instrument called a Dan Co between their feet using a bow; women sing as they play.

Two rows of pink pillars entwined with green dragons line the nave, leading up to the main altar which supports a large globe on which is painted a single staring eye – the divine, all-seeing-eye. The roof is blue and dotted with clouds, representing the heavens, and the walls are pierced by open, lattice-work windows with the divine eye as the centrepiece to the window design. At the back of the cathedral is a sculpture of Pham Com Tac, the last pope and one of the religion's founders who died in 1957. He stands on flowers surrounded by huge brown snakes and is flanked by his two assistants; one is the leader of spirits, the other leader of materialism.

There are nine columns and nine steps to the cathedral representing the nine steps to heaven. Above the altar is the Cao Dai pantheon: at the top in the centre is Sakyamuni Buddha. Next to him on the left is Lao Tzu, master of Taosim. Left of Lao Tzu, is Quan Am,

Goddess of Mercy, sitting on a lotus blossom. On the other side of the Buddha statue is Confucius. Right of the sage is the red-faced Chinese God of War and Soldiers, Quan Cong. Below Sakyamuni Buddha is the poet and leader of the Chinese saints, Li Ti Pei. Below him is Jesus and below Christ is Jiang Zhia, master of Geniism.

About 500 m from the cathedral (turn right when facing the main façade) is the **Doan Ket**, a formal garden.

The town of Tay Ninh also has a good **market** and some **Cham temples** 1 km to the southwest of the town.

Black Lady Mountain (Nui Ba Den)
ⓘ *Buses go from the bus station on Cach Mang Tam Tang St by the western edge of Tan Son Nhat Airport. From Tay Ninh to Nui Ba Den go by Honda ôm. There is now a cable car to the summit.*
Also known as *Nui Ba Den*, Black Lady Mountain is 10 km to the northeast of Tay Ninh and 106 km from Ho Chi Minh City. The peak rises dramatically from the plain to a height of almost 1000 m and can be seen in the distance, to the right, on entering Tay Ninh. The Black Lady was a certain Ly Thi Huong who, while her lover was bravely fighting the occupying forces, was ordered to marry the son of a local mandarin. Rather than complying, she threw herself from the mountain. Another version of this story is that she was kidnapped by local scoundrels. A number of shrines to the Black Woman are located on the mountain, and pilgrims still visit the site. Fierce battles were also fought here between the French and Americans, and the Viet Minh. There are excellent views of the surrounding plain from the summit.

Border crossings to Cambodia
The province of Tay Ninh borders Cambodia and, before the 17th century, was part of the Khmer Kingdom. Between 1975 and December 1978, soldiers of Pol Pot's Khmer Rouge periodically attacked villages in this province, killing the men and raping the women. Ostensibly, it was in order to stop these incursions that the Vietnamese army invaded Cambodia on Christmas Day 1978, taking Phnom Penh by January 1979.

Travellers taking the bus to Phnom Penh from Ho Chi Minh City cross at **Moc Bai** (Bavet in Cambodia). Cambodian visas are available at the border; Vietnamese visas are not. There is also an underutilised crossing at **Xa Mát** in Tay Ninh Province (Trapeang Phlong) in Cambodia. Neither visas are available at the border.

◉ Ho Chi Minh City listings

For Sleeping and Eating price codes and other relevant information, see Essentials pages 26-31.

● Sleeping

City centre *p310, maps p306, p312 and p314*
LL Park Hyatt Saigon, 2 Lam Son Sq, T8-3824 1234, www.saigon.park.hyatt.com. This striking hotel is in a class of its own. It exudes elegance and style and its location north of the Opera House is unrivalled.

Works of art are hung in the lobby, rooms are classically furnished in French colonial style but with modern touches; the pool area is lovely; the wonderful lounge area features a baby grand piano and there are a number of very good restaurants that incorporate jaw-dropping displays of floor-to-ceiling wines in a glass display. **Square One**, see page 333, is an excellent restaurant with open kitchens and displays. There's also a fitness centre and spa.

LL-L Hotel Catina Saigon, 109 Dong Khoi St, T8-3829 6296, www.hotelcatina.com.vn. This newcomer is brilliantly positioned on Dong Khoi with lovely, light rooms.

LL-L Majestic, 1 Dong Khoi St, T8-3829 5517, www.majesticsaigon.com. Built in 1925, the hotel has character and charm and has been tastefully restored and expanded. There's a restaurant and small but nicely shaded pool. More expensive and large rooms have superb views over the river (quieter rooms at the back have pool view); from the new **M Bar** on the top floor there are magnificent views of the riverfront, especially at night.

LL-L Renaissance Riverside, 8-15 Ton Duc Thang St, T8-3822 0033, www.marriott. com. Despite its 21 floors and 319 rooms and suites this is, in style and feel, almost a boutique hotel. Very well run, comfortable and popular with its customers. It also has Vietnam's highest atrium. Several excellent restaurants including **Kabin** Chinese restaurant and attractive pool. Executive floors provide breakfast and all-day snacks.

LL-L Sheraton, 88 Dong Khoi St, T8-3827 2828, www.sheraton.com/saigon. This tall, glass-clad hotel has certainly proved popular since it opened in late 2003. There is very good lunch and dinner on offer at the **Saigon Café**, and **Level 23**, with its brilliant views across HCMC, is recommended for a night-time drink. The hotel, with modern, stylish rooms is sandwiched into a down-town street and boasts boutique shops, a gorgeous pool, a spa and tennis courts.

LL-L Sofitel Plaza Saigon, 17 Le Duan St, T8-3824 1555, www.sofitel.com. A smart, fashionable and comfortable hotel with a delicious roof-top pool surrounded by frangipani plants. Superior rooms aren't too big but bathrooms are attractive. **L'Olivier** is a good restaurant.

LL-AL Caravelle, 19 Lam Son Sq, T8-3823 4999, www.caravellehotel.com. Central and one of HCMC's top hotels. It incorporates the old **Air France Caravelle** hotel onto which it added a modern tower in 1998 and this gives it an attractive historical dimension. Very comfortable with 335 rooms, fitted out with all the mod cons, many with incredible views and well-trained and friendly staff. Breakfast is sumptuous and filling and **Restaurant Nineteen**, see page 333, serves a fantastic buffet lunch and dinner. **Saigon Saigon**, see page 339, the roof-top bar, draws the crowds until the early hours. A suite of boutique shops plus a pool and **Qi Spa** complete the luxury experience.

LL-AL Legend, 2A-4A Ton Duc Thang St, T8-3823 3333, www.legendsaigon.com. The hotel boasts HCMC's most opulent foyer. Popular with businessmen, it overlooks the river and offers a full range of restaurants, business facilities, a pool and health club. A very fine hotel with 283 rooms.

LL-AL New World, 76 Le Lai St, T8-3822 8888, www.newworldsaigon.com. Over the years this has proved the most popular hotel with visiting businessmen. It has efficient, friendly English-speaking staff, a large attractive pool and gym and good business facilities. There are 538 guestrooms, Chinese and Western restaurants, nightclub, patisserie and bakery, dry-cleaning service and ATM. The Executive Floor offers excellent value with breakfast, afternoon tea and refreshments available all day.

L-AL Duxton, 63 Nguyen Hue Blvd, T8-3822 2999, www.duxton.com.au The **Duxton** is a very attractively appointed and well-finished hotel and popular with Japanese visitors. It has 198 finely decorated rooms, health club, pool and a restaurant and is well located in the heart of downtown.

L-AL Rex, 141 Nguyen Hue Blvd, T8-3829 2185, www.rexhotelvietnam.com. A historically important hotel in the heart of HCMC with unusual interior decor and a new fabulous side extension that has become the principal entrance. The original lobby is decorated entirely in wood, furnished with numerous wicker chairs, and dominated by the ceiling, a vast replica of a Dongson Drum, see page 461, while the new wing is a vast cathedral of glass and marble New wing premium rooms are very smart; the Governor's Suite has a unique view of City Hall. Cheaper 'Superior' rooms in the old wing have small bathtub and are interior facing. 'Deluxe' rooms are double the size but those on the main road are noisy. Interior deluxe do not enjoy private balconies. There's a small rooftop pool awkwardly accessed through the rooftop terrace bar that's a regular pull. The new extension has created an attractive interior patio garden, the **Rose Garden**, with an open kitchen. It's a real draw and escapes the street noise.

L-AL Saigon, 41-47 Dong Du St, T8-3829 9734, www.saigonhotel.com.vn. Opposite the mosque in a good central location. Some rooms are a bit dark and small, but it's popular and clean.

L-A Huong Sen, 66-70 Dong Khoi St, T8-3829 1415, www.huongsenhotel.com.vn. This central hotel is popular with tour groups and good value on this street. A roof-top bar on the 7th floor is a nice place for a beer.

L-A Lavender Hotel, 208-210 Le Thanh Ton St, T8-2222 8888, www.lavenderhotel.com.vn. In an excellent location. The standard rooms are small but nicely furnished so you may want to opt for a superior. Helpful staff. Internet access and breakfast included.

L-A Palace, 56-66 Nguyen Hue Blvd, T8-3829 2860, www.palacesaigon.com. Saigontourist-run hotel with some decent-sized rooms. It's very central with a restaurant and small roof-top pool.

AL Grand, 8 Dong Khoi St, T8-3823 0163, www.grandhotel.vn. A 1930s building in the heart of the shopping district that might look more comfortable on Brighton's seafront than in HCMC. It was renovated 10 years ago but the stained glass and marble staircase have largely survived the process. A huge, modern featureless wing has been added. Lovely pool (try to get a pool-side room) and a very reasonably priced restaurant. It is to be upgraded to 5 stars in 2011 with a major expansion underway.

AL-A Bong Sen, 117-123 Dong Khoi St, T8-3829 1516, www.hotelbongsen.com. A **Saigontourist** well-run and upgraded hotel in a perfect location in the heart of the shopping district. It is very good value for the location but standard rooms are very small. All superior rooms have bathtubs. Few rooms have views. There is a restaurant and the **Green Leaf** café.

AL-A Continental, 132-134, Dong Khoi St, T8-3829 9201, www.continentalhotel.com.vn. Built in 1880 and renovated in 1989, the **Continental** has an air of faded colonial splendour and its large but still-dated rooms need upgrading. The exterior has had a lick of paint. (A US$10 million renovation has been approved.) The hotel has a couple of restaurants, a business centre, fitness room and a pool. Probably in an attempt to stamp out the theft of souvenirs, you can purchase every item in the room. Don't opt for the balconied rooms overlooking Lam Son Square if you value your sleep.

A Bong Sen Hotel Annex, 61-63 Hai Ba Trung St, T8-3823 5818, www.hotelbongsen.com. Sister hotel of the **Bong Sen**, this is a well-managed hotel with standard a/c rooms and a restaurant.

A-C Ho Sen, 4B-4C Thi Sach St, T8-3823 2281, www.hosenhotel.com.vn. This bland-looking hotel in a very central location is a good find. Rooms are very quiet, fairly spacious and comfortable with TVs. Staff are friendly and helpful and will store luggage.

A-C Spring, 44-46 Le Thanh Ton St, T8-3829 7362, www.springhotelvietnam.com. Central, comfortable, charming and helpful staff; book well in advance if you want to stay in this well-run family hotel that is excellent value; breakfast included. Recommended.

B Asian, 150 Dong Khoi St, T8-3829 6979, asianhotel@hcm.fpt.vn. Rooms with a/c and satellite TV are a little small. There's a restaurant and breakfast and Wi-Fi is included. The location is central.

B-C Tan Hai Long 3, 65 Ho Tung Mau St, T8-3915 1888, www.thlhotelgroup.com.

A well-positioned hotel with small rooms, good-sized bathrooms and good service. However, check the a/c unit in your room for noise before choosing.

B-D Orchid, 29A Thai Van Lung St, T8-3823 1809, www.orchid-hotel.com. In a good, central spot, surrounded by restaurants and bars, worth taking a look at. Rooms have a/c and satellite TV. Discounts for longer stays.

C A&EM Hotel, 60 Le Thanh Ton St, T8-3825 8529, www.a-emhotels.com. These are trying to be boutique hotels and there are flourishes but some rooms are a tad scruffy around the edges. Offers standards and deluxe – the difference being that the standards have no computer and no bathtub and no room to swing a cat. Opt for the much bigger deluxes. This A&EM is in a great location

D Khach San 69, 69 Hai Ba Trung St, T8-3829 1513, hotel69haibatrung@yahoo.com. vn. Central location with clean a/c rooms that back onto HCMC's Indian mosque. It's an ancient hotel but spotless and staff are super polite. Possibly the cheapest accommodation in the heart of downtown.

Pham Ngu Lao *p320, map p320*

AL-A Que Huong (Liberty 4), 265 Pham Ngu Lao St, T8-3836 4556, www.libertyhotels.com.vn. A perfectly comfortable hotel. It has had to moderate its prices which means it is now possibly fair value but priced way too high for this area. Breakfast is included.

AL-B Que Huong (Liberty 3), 187 Pham Ngu Lao St, T8-3836 9522, www.libertyhotels. com.vn. Less popular with travellers than previously as there is now more choice; cheapest rooms are on the upper floors; rather noisy.

B-D Beautiful Saigon, 62 Bui Vien St, T8-3836 4852, www.beautifulsaigonhotel. com. A new addition to the backpacker zone replacing an old hotel, this is more for the flashpackers and welcome it is too. Very nice smart and tidy rooms all with mod cons, Wi-Fi and breakfast at fair prices and

recommended by happy guests.

D-E Hong Hoa, 185/28 Pham Ngu Lao St, T8-3836 1915, www.honghoavn.com. A well-run family hotel with 9 rooms, all a/c, hot water and private bathroom. Conveniently, the downstairs has banks of free email terminals and a supermarket.

E Linh, 40/10 Bui Vien St, T8-3836 9641, hotelinh@hotmail.com. A well-priced, clean, friendly, family-run hotel with a/c and hot water. Attracts some long-stay guests. Cheaper rooms have small windows.

E Mimi Guesthouse, 40/5 Bui Vien St, T8-3836 9645, mimihotel405@yahoo.fr. 10 rooms with private bathroom, a/c, TV and Wi-Fi in rooms and hot water. Motorbikes, bikes and internet.

E Minh Chau, 75 Bui Vien St, T8-3836 7588, minhchauhotel@hcm.vnn.vn. Some a/c, hot water and private bathrooms. It is spotlessly clean and run by 2 sisters; it has been recommended by lone women travellers. Free internet but breakfast not included.

E-F Hotel Madame Cuc, 64 Bui Vien St, T8-3836 5073, 127 Cong Quynh St, T8-3836 8761, and 184 Cong Quynh St, T8-3836 1679, www.madamcuchotels.com. The reception staff at No 64 could be a lot friendlier. Rooms are quite small but the US$20 room is the bargain of the place.

E-F Linh Thu Guesthouse, 72 Bui Vien St, T8-3836 8421, linhthu_72bv@yahoo.com.vn. Fan rooms with bathroom and some more expensive a/c rooms too. Free internet and breakfast included.

Apartments

Those intending to stay a month or more might consider a furnished apartment:

Lucy Hotel, 61 Do Quang Dau St, T8-3838 9636, www.lucysaigon.com. US$450-480 per month including laundry, water and internet; often full.

Cholon *p321, map p306*
Few people stay in Cholon, but it does have the best pagodas in HCMC and is only a short cyclo ride from the centre of town.

A-C Arc en Ciel (Thien Hong), 52-56 Tan Da St, Q5, T8-3855 1662. This is the best hotel in Cholon. It boasts 4 restaurants and a rooftop bar that affords views over the district. Standard rooms are carpeted with TV and minibar but do not have much of a view and the bathroom is small. Some standard rooms enjoy bathtubs, others do not. Superior rooms have adequate-sized bathrooms.

Outer Ho Chi Minh City *p323, maps p306 and p312*

These hotels are a little out of the centre – around 10-30 mins' walk or a short taxi ride.
LL-AL Thao Dien Village, 195 Nguyen Van Huong St, Thao Dien Ward, Q2, T8-3744 6458, www.thaodienvillage.com. A stylish boutique hotel and spa resort in the expat enclave. Lovely to escape the hustle of downtown. Popular restaurants too.
L-A Equatorial, 242 Tran Binh Trong St, Q5, T8-3839 7777, www.equatorial.com. This hotel is in a rather out-of-the-way location between Cholon and downtown HCMC but there is a free shuttle at scheduled times. It is a marble-cool oasis of calm with charming staff. The 333 rooms are tastefully furnished and there are restaurants, a gym and pool.
E Miss Loi's Guesthouse, 178/20 Co Giang St, T8-3836 7973, missloi@hcm.fpt.vn. Cheap and cheerful, well kept, some a/c, breakfast included, popular. US$300-400 per month.

🍴 Eating

HCMC has a rich culinary tradition and, as home to people from most of the world's imagined corners, its cooking is diverse. You could quite easily eat a different national cuisine every night for several weeks. French food is well represented and there are many restaurants from neighbouring Asian countries especially Japan, Korea, China and Thailand. The area between **Le Thanh Ton** and **Hai Ba Trung** streets has become a 'Little Tokyo' and 'Little Seoul' on account of the number of Japanese and Korean restaurants. HCMC, it is said, has the

cheapest Japanese food in the world.
Pham Ngu Lao, the backpacker area, is chock-a-block with low-cost restaurants many of which are just as good as the more expensive places elsewhere. Do not overlook street-side stalls whose staples consist of *pho* (noodle soup), *bánh xeo* (savoury pancakes), *cha giò* (spring rolls) and *banh mi pate* (baguettes stuffed with pâté and salad), all usually fresh and very cheap. The major hotels all have gourmet shops selling bread and pastries. Eating out is an informal business; suits are not necessary anywhere, and in Pham Ngu Lao expect shorts and sandals.

The Ben Thanh night market (see page 317) is a major draw for Vietnamese and overseas visitors. Stalls are set up at dusk and traffic suppressed. There is a good range of inexpensive foodstall dishes and lots of noodles; it stays open until around 2300.

City centre *p310, maps p306, p312 and p314*

🍴🍴🍴 **An Vien**, 178A Hai Ba Trung St, T8-3824 3877. Open 1200-2300. This excellent and intimate restaurant is on 3 floors. Each room is small and furnished in Vietnamese style. The food – Vietnamese – is excellent; it serves some of the most fragrant rice in Vietnam. Service is attentive but discreet.
🍴🍴🍴 **Dynasty**, New World Hotel, see Sleeping, page 329, T8-3822 8888. A long Chinese menu and excellent lunchtime dim sun.
🍴🍴🍴 **Hoi An**, 11 Le Thanh Ton St, T8-3823 7694. Open 1730-2300. This is a sister (and almost neighbouring) restaurant of **Mandarin** (see below). The building is a good replica of a Hoi An house, a theme that is repeated in the decor and staff uniforms. Service and food (Vietnamese) are good although the clientele are mostly tourists, so do not expect good value for money.
🍴🍴🍴 **Kabin**, Renaissance Riverside Hotel, see Sleeping, page 329, T8-3822 0033. One of HCMC's best Chinese restaurants; it sometimes features chefs from China.
🍴🍴🍴 **Mandarin**, 11A Ngo Van Nam St, T8-3822 9783. Open 1130-1400, 1730-2300. One of

the finest restaurants in HCMC serving up a culinary mix of exquisite flavours from across the country amid elegant decor including stunning, richly coloured silk tablecloths. The food is delicious but it's not very Vietnamese and the service is a little over the top.

MMM Maxim's Nam An, 13-17 Dong Khoi St, T8-3829 6676. Open 1000-2300. Massive menu; the food receives mixed reviews but the floorshows at 2000 are widely acclaimed and reservations are wise.

MMM Qucina, 7 Lam Son Sq, T8-3824 6325. Mon-Sat 1800-2300. Smart and stylish Italian restaurant serving divine cuisine. It's attached to the popular **Q Bar** under the Opera House.

MMM Square One, Park Hyatt Saigon, 2 Lam Son Sq, T8-3824 1234. Open1200-1430, 1800-2230. Charming, efficient and friendly staff manage an extensive menu of Vietnamese seafood. Sit out or in among the gorgeous carved screens dividing the eating and cooking stations. There are 5 show kitchens – Western Grill, Vietnamese steam and woks, seafood, a dessert counter and a juice and tea area. Dine amid the fish tanks and admire the floor-to-ceiling wine bottles – 1500 perfectly stacked up. Try the Nha Trang oysters and the signature spicy rolls that are an interesting twist on an old classic; avoid the tasteless white ice cream and don't overdose on the sherbert on the dessert menu.

MMM-MM La Camargue, 191 Hai Ba Trung St, Q3, T8-3520 4888. Open 1800-2300. One of HCMC's longest-standing restaurants and bars it has remained consistently one of the most successful and popular places in town but it has had to move from its central French villa to one hidden further out of downtown. There's still an upstairs open-air terrace restaurant serving excellent food from an international menu with a strong French influence.

MMM-MM Pacharan, 97 Hai Ba Trung St, T8-3825 6024. Open 1100-late. A hit from the beginning, this Spanish restaurant is nearly full every night with happy and satisfied

customers. The open-air rooftop bar that overlooks the **Park Hyatt Hotel** is a winner when there's a cool breeze blowing through the terrace. Fans of Spanish fare will love the (expensive) Iberian cured ham from rare, semi-wild acorn-fed black-footed pigs as well as staples such as anchovies, olives, mushrooms and prawns; all the tapas are beautifully presented. Don't forget to have a tipple of one of the numerous *vinos tintos* lining the wall of the bar.

MMM-MM Restaurant Nineteen, Caravelle Hotel, see Sleeping, page 329, T8-3823 4999. Open 1130-1430, 1745-2200. A buffet of Japanese sushi, Chinese dim sum, seafood, a range of hot dishes, cheeses and puddings galore. Weekends are especially extravagant with excellent roast beef. The free-flow of wine makes it an epicurean delight and tremendous value for money.

MMM-MM Temple Club, 29 Ton That Thiep St, T8-3829 9244. Open 1100-1400, 1830-2230. This is a most beautifully furnished club and restaurant open to non-members in French-colonial style and the effect is striking. Tasty Vietnamese dishes are excellent value. There's a very pleasant club area in which to meet and have a drink. The restaurant is popular so it's wise to book.

MMM-M Zanzbar, 41 Dong Du St, T8-3822 7375. Enormous portions of surf and turf. Dine outside on the mini terrace when the heat is hotting up.

MM Augustin, 10 Nguyen Thiep St, T90-866 8081. Mon-Sat 1130-1400, 1800-2230. Fairly priced and some of the best, unstuffy French cooking in HCMC; tables are pretty closely packed and there is a congenial atmosphere at this small and central restaurant. Try the excellent gratinée onion soup and baked clams.

MM Blue Ginger (Saigon Times Club), 37 Nam Ky Khoi Nghia St, T8-3829 8676. Open 0700-1430 and 1700-2200. A gorgeous restaurant in style, welcome and comfort, it offers a feast of Vietnamese food for diners with more than 100 dishes on its menu. Dine indoors in the cellar-like restaurant or outdoors in a small courtyard accompanied by charming staff offering courteous and discrete service.

Hoa Vien, 28 bis Mac Dinh Chi St, T8-3829 0585. Open 0900-2400. An amazing and vast Czech bierkeller boasting HCMC's first microbrewery. Freshly brewed dark and light beer available by the litre or in smaller measures. Grilled mackerel, pork and sausages all are very useful for soaking up the alcohol.

Jaspas, 33 Dong Khoi St, T8-3822 9926. Open 0830-late. This welcoming restaurant in the heart of the shopping district serves up a superlative, unmissable melt-in-the-mouth raw tuna encrusted with sesame. Come back to try other tantalizingly good starters such as salt and pepper squid and goat's cheese parcels. For mains there's lamb shank, blackened barrimundi seared in cajun spices and *spanikopita* for vegetarians. If you have any room left tuck into the apple and blueberry crumble with vanilla ice cream.

La Cantine on the 6, 6 Dong Khoi St, T8-3823 8866, www.lacantine.vn. Opt for the street-front **Cafe Bistro** for excellent people-watching opportunities and opt for the great-value express lunches or bistro dinners. English is not well spoken by staff.

La Fourchette, 9 Ngo Duc Ke St, T8-3829 8143. Open 1200-1430, 1830-2230. A truly excellent and authentic little French bistro. Warm welcome, well-prepared dishes, generous portions and local steak as tender as any import. Booking advised. Recommended.

Le Jardin, 31 Thai Van Lung St, T8-3825 8465. Mon-Sat 1100-1400, 1800-2100. Excellent little French café, part of the **French Cultural Institute**. Eat inside or in the garden and indulge in the good food.

The Refinery, 74 Hai Ba Trung St, T8-3823 0509. Open 1100-2300. This former opium factory (through the arch and on the left) is a little understated in its reincarnation. The herb-encrusted steak and grilled barramundi are delicious but the seared tuna with lentil salad is

outstanding. Braised rabbit and duck and apple tagine with raisin and butter couscous are other menu offerings. Admire the original fleur-de-lys tiles and photos of the working factory while you wait.

Saigon Indian, 1st floor, 73 Mac Thi Buoi St, T8-3824 5671. Open 1115-1430, 1730-2230. Proving to be a very popular Indian restaurant it has a wide range of dishes from north and south with tandoori dishes and plenty of vegetarian options. Delicious garlic naan bread.

Tib, 187 Hai Ba Trung St, Q3, T8-3829 7242. Open 1100-1400, 1700-2200. This is a little pocket of Hué in HCMC furnished in the dark wood so favoured by the area but is more of an Imperial lite. There's an extensive menu, which includes a good selection of Hué specialities and the food is good. The atmosphere is convivial and the restaurant, which is down an alley off the main road, is popular with Vietnamese families. The incredible wine stock is a bonus.

Wild Horse Saloon, 8A/1D1 Thai Van Lung St, T8-3825 1901, www.wildhorsesteakhouse. com. 1000-1400, 1600-2330. Unmissable with its monumental beer barrel façade, this Tex Mex (which has turned more low-key on its theme) is a popular spot for a good old Sun roast. Dine at solid wood tables on pastas, burgers, Mexican meatballs, crab cakes or Texas-style rack of lamb. The Sun roast of pork, chicken, beef or lamb is served with boiled vegetables, roast potato, gravy, stuffing, crackling and apple sauce. The separate bar area, entered by a massive, cut-out beer barrel, shows sport TV.

Al Fresco's, 27 Dong Du St, T8-3822 7317. Open 0830-1400, 1830-2300. Opened in late 2003 and sister of the famous Hanoi restaurant, it has had a huge success from its first day. The Australian-run restaurant specializes in ribs, steak, pizzas, hamburgers and Mexican dishes which are all excellent and highly popular. It serves giant portions: think before ordering the rack of ribs. Book or be prepared to wait. Delivery available.

Ashoka, 17A/10 Le Thanh Ton St, T8-3823 1372. Open 1100-1400, 1700-2230. Delicious food from an extensive menu at this beacon of Indian cuisine. Its set lunch lists 11 options with a further, extraordinary 19 curry dishes. Highlights in the low-lit, comfortably a/c restaurant are mutton *shami* kebab, prawn vindaloo and *kadhai* fish – barbecued chunks of fresh fish cooked in *kadhai* (a traditional Indian-style wok with Peshwari ground spices and sautéd with onion and tomatoes).

Hoa Tuc, 74 Hai Ba Trung St, T8-3825 1676. Open 1000-2230. A new addition to this popular courtyard dining space. Dine amid the art deco accents on soft shell crab or a salad of pink pomelo, squid and crab with herbs. The desserts are tantalizing. Try the Earl Grey tea custard. Portions a tad on the small side. Cooking classes available.

Kita, 39 Nguyen Hue St, T8-3821 5300. Open 0730-2200, Sun 0730-1600. A bright and breezy café in a French colonial corner building serving top salads, soups, and sandwiches. Popular with the expat crowd. Try for the balconies on the upper floors.

Spice, 27C Le Quy Don St, T8-3930 7873. Open 1100-1400 and 1730-2230. This is an excellent Thai restaurant and is very popular, especially with the younger set. Prices are reasonable and the food is authentically Thai. Welcoming and friendly service and an entertaining menu with horoscopes.

Villa FB, 79 Suong Nguyet Anh St, T8-6290 6571, www.villafb.com. Open 0700-2300. This might be all style over substance in an oriental chic that is trying too hard. Raining walls of glass and choreographed black and white furniture evoke sleek Saigon but a crab dish came with real crab plus crabsticks; unforgivable. Menu options are tempting and there are few other options in this part of town stufffed with a growing number of hotels.

Warda, 71/7 Mac Thi Buoi St, T8-3823 3822, www.wardavn.com. Open Mon-Sat 0900-2400, Sun 1500-2400. A Bedouin tent huddles over plump pumpkin-coloured cushions on sofas amid a few shisha pipes at the end of this buzzy alley. The menu options are tantalizing and this is a wonderful way to break from Vietnamese menus. It's a meat-lovers paradise but vegetarians are not ignored.

13 Ngo Duc Ke, 15 Ngo Duc Ke St, T8-3823 9314. Open 0600-2230. Fresh, well cooked, honest Vietnamese fare, chicken in lemon grass (no skin, no bone) is a great favourite and the beef (*bo luc lac*) melts in the mouth. Popular with locals, expats and travellers. Vegetarians, soup lovers and squid eaters are catered for too.

Au Parc, 23 Han Thuyen St, T8-3829 2772. Open Mon-Sat 0730-2230, Sun 0800-1700. Facing on to the park in front of the old Presidential Palace this attractive café serves snacks and light meals including sandwiches, salads, juices and drinks; it also does a good Sun brunch; lovely spot for a leisurely breakfast Delivery available.

Bombay, 59 Dong Du St, T090-386 3114. Open for lunch and carries on until around 2100. Almost opposite the mosque; a long-established and informal restaurant serving excellent curries and very good paratha.

Com Nieu Saigon, 19 Tu Xuong St, Q3, T8-3932 2799. Open 1000-2200. Well known for the theatricals which accompany the serving of the speciality baked rice: one waiter smashes the earthenware pot before tossing the contents across the room to his nimble-fingered colleague standing by your table. Deserves attention for its excellent food and a good selection of soups.

Hoang Yen, 5-7 Ngo Duc Ke St, T8-3823 1101. Open 1000-2200. Utterly plain setting and decor but absolutely fabulous Vietnamese dishes, as the throngs of local lunchtime customers testify. Soups and chicken dishes are ravishing.

Indian Curry-Rice Restaurant, 66 Dong Du St, T8-3823 2159. Open 1000-2000. A small, canteen-like restaurant behind the down-town mosque. Enter the compound and walk to the right and around the back. The aroma will greet you before you see the superb spread of vegetarian and meat curries and stuffed bread – pots, pans and stoves all on view. A curry extravangaza of chicken, fish, goat, beef, cuttlefish, shrimp and crab served with yellow rice by the very friendly staff will provide a filling meal.

¶ **Juice**, 49 Mac Thi Buoi St, T8-3829 6900. Open 0730-2200. Hidden away in a tiny outlet, **Juice** offers dozens of scrummy options from sandwiches, bagels and paninis (and more types of bread) to healthy smoothies. Its modern comfy seating, attentive staff and large portions attract working expats and Vietnamese for lunchtime meetings.

¶ **Mogambo**, 50 Pasteur St, T8-3825 1311. Open 0730-2300. The bar and restaurant serves cold beer, excellent burgers, steaks, pies and fries. Popular with American expats and now in a new location.

¶ **Pho 24**, 71-73 Dong Khoi St, www.pho24. com.vn. Convenient and quick pho from this noodle soup chain.

¶ **Pho Hoa Pasteur**, 260C Pasteur St. Open 0600-2400. Probably the best known of all *pho* restaurants and packed with customers and dizzying aromas. The *pho*, which is good, and costs more than average comes in 10 options and is served in the small restaurant with tables tightly arranged. Chinese bread and wedding cake (*banh xu xe*) provide the only alternative in this specialist restaurant.

¶ **Wrap & Roll**, 62 Hai Ba Trung St, T8-3822 2166. Open 0730-2230. This is the Vietnamese equivalent of a **Wagamama's**. It has a plethora of options at bargain prices including wrap your own spring rolls, *banh xeo*, soups, desserts and smoothies. The mint-green walls match the modern finish; the branding, prices and substance is pulling in the punters – young Vietnamese and expats alike.

Cafés, bakeries and foodstalls

Cooku'nest Café, 13 Tu Xuong St, Q3, T8-2241 2043. This kooky venue looks like it has been hoiked off an Alpine slope. It's a pine cabin equipped with cuckoo clock. Sit upstairs on the floor next to tiny tables and mingle with the local student gang. There's live music every night. Wi-Fi available.

La Fenêtre Soleil, 2nd floor, 135 Le Thanh Ton St (entrance at 125 Nam Ky Khoi Nghia St), T8-3822 5209. Open Mon-Sat, café 0900-1900, bar 1900-2400. Don't be put off by the slightly grimy side entrance; clamber up into the boho-Indochine world of this gorgeous café/bar, artfully cluttered with antiques, lamps, comfy sofas and home-made cakes, muffins, smoothies and other delights. The high-energy drinks of mint, passionfruit, and ginger juice are lovely. Highly recommended.

Kem Bach Dang, 26-28 Le Loi Blvd. On opposite corners of Pasteur St. A very popular café serving fruit juice, shakes and ice cream. Try the coconut ice cream (*kem dua*) served in a coconut.

Tous les Jours, 180 Hai Ba Trung St, Q3, and also in several other locations including Diamond Plaza, T8-3823 8302. Open 0600-2300. A smorgasbord of cakes and pastries awaits the hungry visitor.

Pham Ngu Lao *p320, map p320*

Nearly all these restaurants are open all day every day from early or mid-morning until 2230 or later – when the last customer leaves, as they like to say. All are geared to Westerners and their habits and tastes and in just about all of them there will be at least one person who speaks English and French. Most tend to be cheap but prices have risen in recent times; do check

¶¶¶ **Good Morning Vietnam**, 197 De Tham St, T8-3837 1894. Open 0900-2400. One of the popular chain of Italian restaurants in southern Vietnam. Italian owned and run and serving up Italian flavours. Their pizzas are delicious and salads are good.

¶ **Bobby Brewers Coffee**, 45 Bui Vien St, Pham Ngu Lao, T8-3920 4090, www. bobbybrewers.com. Western-style coffee bar with burgers and baguettes. 5 movies a day shown too.

¶ **Cafe Zoom**, 169A De Tham St, T1222 993585, www.vietnamvespaadventure. com. Laid-back vibe and venue serving top burgers and fries.

¶ **Cappuccino**, 258 De Tham St, T8-3837 4114, and 86 Bui Vien St, T8-3920 3134. Open 0800-2300. Running since 1992, with a good range of well-prepared Italian food at sensible prices: pizzas, pasta, a very good lasagne and zabaglione. Wine by the glass – either French or Dalat wine. The Bui Vien branch is particularly good.

¶ **Kim Café**, 268 De Tham St, T8-3836 8122. Open from early till late. Wide range of food, popular with travellers and expats. One of the best-value breakfasts in the country.

¶ **Lac Thien**, 207 Bui Vien St, T090-445 6103. Open 0800-2300. Vietnamese food. This outpost of the well-known **Lac Thien** in Hué is run by the same family. *Banh xeo* (savoury pancake) is a major feature of the menu.

¶ **Lucky** or **May Man**, 224 De Tham St, T8-3836 7277. Italian food (Japanese upstairs), bar and breakfasts. Good value and popular.

¶ **Margherita**, 175/1 Pham Ngu Lao St, T8-3837 0760. Open 0700-1300, 1500-2400. Serves good Italian at reasonable prices.

¶ **Sozo**, 176 Bui Vien, T8-6271 9176, www. sozocentre.com. As well as coffees of every shade, this place serves bagels, and excellent cookies with proceeds going to charity.

¶ **Zen Plaza**, 54-56 Nguyen Trai St, close to Pham Ngu Lao, T8-3925 0339. Open 1000-2200. Sushi lovers will want to come here for a good feed washed down by the plum wine. It is convenient for the backpacker district. The set menus are excellent value.

Cholon *p321, map p306*

The Chinese seem to prefer eating in cavernous restaurants or at street side noodle stands. Cholon has more of the latter.

¶¶¶ **Tien Phat**, 18 Ky Hoa St, Q9, T8-3853 6217. Conveniently located near the temples of Cholon. Open for breakfast and lunch. Specializes in dim sum. A good selection of freshly prepared dim sum is nice with hot tea.

Outer Ho Chi Minh City *p323, map p306*

¶¶¶ **The Deck,** 38 Nguyen U Di, An Phu, Q2, T8-3744 6322, www.thedecksaigon.com. A very popular expat nightspot with tables on a decking right on the Saigon River. The food, rich in meats and fish is, in the main, delicious and creative. It's an elegant spot and a big draw in the area.

¶¶¶-¶¶ **Le Bordeaux**, 72 D2 St, Cu Xa Van Thanh Bac, Q Binh Thanh, T8-3899 9831, www.restaurant-lebordeaux.com.vn. Mon 1830-2130, Tue-Sat 1130-1330, 1830-2130. Rather a tragedy that it is in such an awkward location. If you can find it you are in for a treat. Lovely decor and warm atmosphere, receives the highest accolades for its French cuisine but it is not cheap.

¶ **Bo Tuong Xeo Chan May** (formerly **Luong Son**) 65 Nguyen Van Sang St, Tan Nhi Ward, Tan Phu District, near the airport, T8-3812 1820. Open 0900-2200. Noisy, smoky, chaotic and usually packed, this large, restaurant that has had to move from downtown specializes in *bo tung xeo* (sliced beef barbecued at the table served with mustard sauce – the name also refers to a gruesome torture, ask Vietnamese friends for details). The beef, barbecued squid and other delicacies are superb. This restaurant is also the place to sample unusual dishes such as scorpion, porcupine, fried cricket, coconut worm and cockerel's testicles.

Foodstalls

362-376 Hai Ba Trung St, just north of Tan Dinh market. Everyone has their favourite but these restaurants serve excellent chicken rice (*com ga*), **No 381, Hong Phat**, is good. All charge just over US$2 for steamed chicken and rice (*com gà hap*) with soup.

Anh Thu, 49 Dinh Cong Trang St, and other stalls nearby on the south side of Tan Dinh market serve *cha gio, banh xeo, bi cuon* and other Vietnamese street food.

Nguyen Trai St (extreme east end of the street, by the **New World Hotel** roundabout). Late night *pho* is available from stalls in this area.

Tran Cao Van St, east of Cong Truong Quoc Te, Q3. The restaurants and stalls here serve delicious noodles of all kinds, especially noodle soup with duck (*my vit*).

Vietnamese cafés

Vietnamese tend to prefer non-alcoholic drinks and huge numbers of cafés exist to cater to this market. Young romantic couples sit in virtual darkness listening to Vietnamese love songs all too often played at a deafening volume while sipping coffee. The furniture tends to be rather small for the Western frame but these cafés are an agreeable way of relaxing after dinner in a more typically Vietnamese setting.

Bars and clubs

Along with the influx of foreigners and the freeing up of Vietnamese society has come a rapid increase in the number of bars in HCMC and they cater to just about all tastes – drink, music and company-wise. At one time hotel bars were just about the only safe and legal place for foreigners to drink but now they are beginning to look much the same as hotel bars the world over. The rooftop bar at the **Rex Hotel** is an exception.

Bar opening times can be a little difficult to predict as it depends entirely upon the whim of the local police. Some stay open until 0200-0300 but at other times the police shut them down at 2400. The **Pham Ngu Lao** area has a few bars, most have pool tables, and tend to be busy later at night and tend to stay open longer than those in the centre.

Alibi, 11 Thai Van Lung St, T8-3822 3240. Goes on after hours and is a magnet for tourists and expats. There's a small terrace to escape the inner heat.

Apocalypse Now, 2BCD Thi Sach St, T8-3825 6124. Open 2100-0300. Free admission for Westerners. Gets going after 2300 and stays open very late if the police permit. Each night crowds of tourists go in search of a legend, or in search of something. It remains one of the most popular and successful bars and clubs in HCMC and draws a very wide cross section of punters of all ages and nationalities. The crowded dancefloor gets very sticky; the ceiling is decorated with helicopter reliefs – the fans revolving as if they were the helicopter blades. There's quite a large outside area at the back where it's possible to strike up a conversation.

Blue Gecko, 31 Ly Tu Trong St, T8-3824 3483. It has been adopted by HCMC's Australian community so expect cold beer and Australian flags above the pool table.

The Cage, 3A Ton Duc Thang St. Fashionable new clubby hangout for the young and beautiful. Guest DJs spin the tunes for the city's clubbing denizens. Drinks are expensive.

Cyclo Bar, 163 Pham Ngu Lao St, T8-3920 1567. 0700-2400. A welcome addition to this neighbourhood. Inexpensive drinks and light meals from breakfast onwards.

The Hi Fi, Level 2, 38 Nguyen Hue St, www.thehifi.asia. Good central spot for catching live acts.

Le Pub, 175/22 Pham Ngu Lao St, T8-3837 7679, www.lepub.org. Like its Hanoi counterpart, a great meeting place for a beer and good slap-up nosh. You can sit out front and watch the world go by.

Lush, 2 Ly Tu Trong St, T8-3824 2496. Quite an impressive set-up for HCMC with an outdoor area for hanging, funky indoors area for drinking and a balcony for watching. There's also a pool table and when the DJs start spinning the dance floor gets packed especially on Fri and Sat.

Q Bar, 7 Lam Son Sq, under the **Opera House**, T8-3823 3479. 1800 till the small hours, police permitting. The most sophisticated of HCMC's bars with striking decor and design and haunt of a wide cross-section of HCMC society: the sophisticated, intelligent, witty, rich, handsome, cute, curvaceous, camp, glittering and famous are all to be found here. **Qucina**, Q Bar's Italian restaurant, is attached and meals can be served at the bar.

Rex Hotel Bar, see Sleeping, above. An open-air rooftop bar which has a kitsch revolving crown. There are good views, cooling breeze, snacks and meals – and a link with history.

Saigon Saigon, 10th floor of the **Caravelle Hotel**, 19 Lam Son Sq, T8-3824 3999. It is breezy and cool, has large comfortable chairs in which to loll and superb views by day and by night. Excellent cocktails but they're not cheap.

Sax n' Art, 28 Le Loi St, T8-3822 8472. Open 1700-2400. A new jazz club for the city in a central location with nightly performances. Popular with tourists and locals.

Storm-P, 28 Cao Ba Quat, T8-3822 1539. HCMC's Scandinavian bar, popular with Danes and Swedes (not to mention the odd Scot or 2). Friendly staff to chat to at the bar and a few Danish dishes for the homesick.

Vasco's, 74/7D Hai Ba Trung St, T8-3824 2888. Open 1600-2400. A hugely popular expat spot now in its new courtyard setting.

Xu Restaurant Lounge, Level 1, 71-75 Hai Ba Trung St, T8-3824 8468, www.xusaigon. com. Excuse the strange alleyway entrance and climb the steps to this bar, which is trying for a modern London feel and is certainly an ultra-cool refuge away from the hurly-burly of downtown. However, the proximity of the restaurant and its harsh lighting is a little stark. The impossibly glamorous bar staff are friendly and some seating is more comfortable than others. Choose your drinks wisely; avoid the sake-tinis but the passionfruit caprioska slips down a treat.

In Pham Ngu Lao, the **Go2** and **Buffalo** cluster are the junction of De Tham and Bui Vien streets is always busy and for much later night jinks, move to the **T&R Tavern** on Do Quang Dau St.

🎭 Entertainment

Cinemas
Diamond Plaza has a cinema on the 13th floor of this shopping centre which screens English-language films.
French Cultural Institute (Idecaf), 31 Thai Van Lung St, T8-3829 5451, www.idecaf.gov. vn. French films are screened here.
Galaxy, 116 Nguyen Du St, T8-3823 5235, www.galaxycine.vn shows English-language movies on 3 big screens.

Traditional music and opera
Conservatory of Music (Nhac Vien Thanh Pho Ho Chi Minh), 112 Nguyen Du St, T8-3824 3774, www.hcmcchoir.com. Traditional Vietnamese music and classical music concerts are performed by the young students who study music here and sometimes by local and visiting musicians.
Opera House, Lam Son Sq, T8-3832 2009. Infrequent concerts are held here. Consult the *Vietnam News* and other local publications for upcoming events or visit the ticket office. Ticket prices vary. Also consult www.hbso.org.vn for the city's ballet symphony orchestra and opera.
TrucMai House, 104 Pham Viet Chanh St, Ward 19, Q Binh Thanh, T8-3840 1762, www.trucmaimusic.com. Dinh Linh and his wife Tuyet Mai perform home concerts, introduce you to the traditional instruments and allow you to try some of them. This is a very interesting and worthwhile experience. **Buffalo Tours**, www.buffalotours.com, offers this as a tour.

Water puppetry
Golden Dragon Water Puppet Theatre, 55B Nguyen Thi Minh Khai St, T8-3930 2196, www.thaiduongtheatre.com. A new 50-min performance daily at 1830 and 2000.
Museum of Vietnamese History, 2 Nguyen Binh Khiem St, T8-3829 8146, www.baotanglichsuvn.com. There are daily 15-min water puppetry performances in the tiny theatre in an outdoor, covered part of

the museum, see page 316. The advantage of this performance over the Hanoi theatre is that the audience can get closer to the puppetry and there is better light and more room for manoeuvre when taking photos.

O Shopping

Antiques

Most shops are on **Dong Khoi, Mac Thi Buoi** and **Ngo Duc Ke** streets. For the knowledgeable, there are bargains to be found, especially Chinese and Vietnamese ceramics – however you will need an export permit to get them out of the country (see page 33). Also available are old watches, colonial bric-à-brac, lacquerware and carvings, etc. For the less touristy stuff, visitors would be advised to spend an hour or so browsing the treasure trove shops in **Le Cong Trieu St** (aka Antique St). It runs between Nam Ky Khoi Nghia and Pho Duc Chinh streets just south of Ben Thanh Market. Among the bric-a-brac and tat are some interesting items of furniture, statuary, stamps, candlesticks, fans, badges and ceramics. Bargaining is the order of the day and some pretty good deals can be struck.

Art and gifts

HCMC has acquired something of a reputation for its galleries and a number of artists have a considerable international following. There are countless shops which do nothing but reproduce works of art and are willing to turn their hand to anything. They will produce an oil portrait from a crumpled passport photograph, paint a stately home from a postcard or a grand master from a photograph in a magazine. There is also a lot of colourful 'original' work cheaply available around **Pham Ngu Lao** and the **Dong Khoi** area.

Ancient/Apricot, 50-52 Mac Thi Buoi St, T8-3822 7962, www.apricotgallery.com.vn. This specializes in famous artists and commands high prices.

Dogma, 175 De Tham St, www.dogma. vietnam.com. Sells propaganda posters, funky T-shirts and postcards.
Duc Minh Art Gallery, 31c Le Quy Don St, Q3, T8-3933 0498, ducminh-art@hcm.vnn. vn. Daily 0900-1200, 1400-1800. A small gallery with a few interesting works. Those by Tran Long are still lifes and portraits with a photographic-like quality.
Gaya, 1 Nguyen Van Trang St, corner of Le Lai St, T8-3925 2495, www.gayavietnam. com. Open 0900-2100. A 3-storey shop with heavenly items: exquisitely embroidered tablecloths, bamboo bowls, ceramics and large home items such as screens; also gorgeous and unusual silk designer clothes by, among others, Romyda Keth, based in Cambodia. If you like an item but it does not fit they will take your measurements but it could take a fortnight to make.
Hanoi Gallery, 43 Le Loi Blvd, T098-203 8803 (mob). Like its counterpart in Hanoi it sells propaganda posters.
Lotus, 25 Dong Khoi St, T8-3824 8977. Old propaganda posters galore.
Lotus Gallery, 47 Dong Khoi St, T8-3829 2695, www.lotusgallery.com. Another expensive gallery at the top end of the market. Many are members of the Vietnam Fine Arts Association and many have exhibited around the world.
Mosaique, 98 Mac Thi Buoi St, T8-3823 4634, www.mosaiquedecoration.com. Open 0900-2100. Like its sister store in Hanoi, this boutique, which is rather like entering a cavern, is a home accessories parlour. Upstairs exquisitely embroidered wall hangings and table runners are displayed.
Nagu, 132-134 Dong Khoi St (next to the Park Hyatt), www.zantoc.com. Delicate embroidered silk products among other fashion, home and giftware.
Nguyen Freres, 2 Dong Khoi St, T8-3823 9459, www.nguyenfreres.com. An absolute Aladdin's cave. Don't miss this – even if it's just to potter among the collectable items.
Saigon Kitsch, 43 Ton That Tiep St, www. saigonkitsch.com. 0900-2000. This is

the place to come for communist kitsch ranging from big propaganda art posters to placemats and mugs – there is some essential buying here for those who like this kind of thing. Also retro bags and funky jewellery on sale.

Bicycles
From the stalls along **Le Thanh Ton St** close to the Ben Thanh Market and Vo Thi Sau west of the junction with Pham Ngoc Thach St. US$40 for a Vietnamese bike, at least US$70 for a better-built Chinese one.

Books, magazines and maps
All foreigners around Pham Ngu Lao and De Tham streets are game to the numerous booksellers who hawk mountains of pirate books under their arms and stagger from table to table. The latest bestsellers together with enduring classics (ie *The Quiet American*) can be picked up for a couple of dollars.
Artbook, 43 Dong Khoi St, T8-3910 3518, www.artbookvn.com. For art, architecture and coffeetable books.
Bookazine, 28 Dong Khoi St. A decent range of English-language books.
Fahasa, 40 Nguyen Hue Blvd, T8-3912 5358, www.fahasasg.com. A very large store with dozens of English titles and magazines.

Western newspapers and magazines
Sold in the main hotels. Same day *Bangkok Post* and *The Nation* newspapers (English-language Thai papers), and up-to-date *Financial Times*, *Straits Times*, *South China Morning Post*, *Newsweek* and *The Economist*, available from larger bookshops.

Maps
HCMC has the best selection of maps in Vietnam, at stalls on Le Loi Blvd between Dong Khoi St and Nguyen Hue Blvd. Bargain hard – the bookshops are probably cheaper.

Clothing, silk and *ao dai*
Dong Khoi, with its many excellent boutiques, is the street that most Western and Japanese women head straight for. Vietnamese silk and traditional dresses (*ao dai*) are to be found in the shops on Dong Khoi St and in Ben Thanh Market. A number of shops in De Tham St sell woven and embroidered goods including bags and clothes.
Ipa Nima, 77-79 Dong Khoi St and in the **New World Hotel**, T8-3822 3277, www.ipa-nima.com. Sister branch of the Hanoi store with the sparkling and alluring products and must- have accessories for new seasons.
Khaisilk, 107 Dong Khoi, T8-3829 1146. **Khaisilk** belongs to Mr Khai's growing empire (see box, page 86). He has a dozen shops around Vietnam. Beautifully made, quality silk products from dresses to scarves to ties can be found in this luxury outlet.
Mai's, 132-134 Dong Khoi St, T8-3827 2733, www.mailam.com.vn. One of the most exciting designers working in Vietnam, see box, page 86.
Song, 76D Le Thanh Ton St, T8-3824 6986, www.valeriegregorimckenzie.com. Open 0900-2000. A beautiful clothes emporium. It's hard to resist buying something from this shop. Lovely, flowing summer dresses from designer Valerie Gregori McKenzie plus other stylish and unique pieces plus accessories and cookbooks. Recommended.

Department stores
Diamond Department Store, Diamond Plaza 1st-4th floor, 34 Le Duan St, T8-3822 5500. Open 1000-1000. HCMC's central a/c department store set over a couple of floors. It sells luxury goods, clothes with some Western brands, watches, bags and perfumes. There is also a small supermarket inside. A bowling alley complex and cinema dominate the top floor.
Hung Vuong Plaza, 126 Hung Vuong St, Q5 is the largest department store in Vietnam.
The Opera View, 161 Dong Khoi St, corner of Le Loi. Opened in mid-2007, it houses Louis Vuitton, Burberry and the like.

Parkson Plaza, 35 Bis - 45 Le Thanh Ton St. A new high-end department store.

Foodstores

Shops specializing in Western staples such as cornflakes, peanut butter and Marmite, abound on Ham Nghi St around Nos 62 and 64 (**Kim Thanh**). You'll also find baby products, nappies, etc at a price.

Annam Gourmet Hai Ba Trung, 16-18 Hai Ba Trung St, T8-3822 9332, www.annam-gourmet.com. Mon-Sat 0800-2100, Sun 1000-2000. Local organic vegetables and other international delicacies at this new culinary emporium.

Circle K Vietnam, 49 Dong Du St. A mini store for basic goods.

Select Supermarket, Saigon Centre, 65 Le Loi Blvd, is a fairly decent-sized store where you can buy alcohol and all manner of processed and Western foods.

Handicrafts

Handicrafts include embroidered and woven fabrics and mother-of-pearl inlaid screens. There are dozens of shops along Dong Khoi St and Nguyen Hue Blvd.

East Meets West, 24 Le Loi Blvd. Nicely made handicrafts, reasonably priced.

Mai Handicrafts, 298 Nguyen Trong Tuyen St, Q Tan Binh, T8-3844 0988. A little way out of town but sells an interesting selection of goods, fabrics and handmade paper all made by disadvantaged people in small income-generating schemes.

Ceramics

Vietnam has a ceramics tradition going back hundreds of years. There has been a renaissance of this art in the past decade. Shops selling new and antique (or antique-looking ceramics) abound on the main shopping streets of **Dong Khoi** and **Le Thanh Ton**. There is a lot of traditional Chinese-looking blue and white and also very attractive celadon green, often with a crackled glaze. There are many other styles and finishes as local craftsmen brush the

dust off old ideas and come up with new ones. **Nga Shop**, see Lacquerware, below, has a good range.

Lacquerware

Vietnamese lacquerware has a long history, and a reputation of sorts (see page 463). Visitors to the workshop can witness the production process and, of course, buy the products if they wish. Lacquerware is available from many of the handicraft shops on Nguyen Hue Blvd and Dong Khoi St. Also from the **Lamson Lacquerware Factory**, 106 Nguyen Van Troi St (opposite Omni Hotel). Accepts Visa and MasterCard.

Duy Tan, 41 Ton That Thiep St, T8-382 3614. Open 1100-2000. Pretty ceramics and lacquerware.

Cong Ty 27-7, Handicapped Handicrafts, 153 Xo Viet Nghe Tinh St, T8-3840 8211, http://www.27-7.com.vn/handicraft/html/about.asp. Lacquerware and its fascinating process can be seen and bought at this outlet on the outskirts of the city. All tour operators will know where it is.

Nga Shop, 49-57 Dong Du St, T8-3823 8356, www.huongngafinearts.vn. **Nga** has become one of the best-known lacquer stores as a result of her high-quality designs. Other top-quality rosewood and ceramic handicrafts suitable for souvenirs are available.

Home furnishings and furniture

This is a new industry in Vietnam and one that has grown from nowhere to becoming very significant in global terms. Interestingly, now that Vietnam has just about cut down all its own trees, timber is imported from Borneo and Cambodia. How much comes from 'sustainable' sources no one knows – whatever they might try to tell you. One thing is certain: one heck of a lot comes from plundered forests.

Red Door Deco, 31 Le Thanh Ton St. Stylish, innovative and well-made furniture, fabrics and ornaments.

Linen

Good-quality linen table cloths and sheets are avaliable from shops on **Dong Khoi** and **Le Thanh Ton** streets.

Jewellery

Jewellery is another industry that has flourished in recent years and there is something to suit most tastes. At the cheaper end there is a cluster of gold and jewellery shops around **Ben Thanh Market** and and also in the **International Trade Centre** on Nam Ky Khoi Nghia St. In these stalls because skilled labour is so cheap one rarely pays more than the weight of the item in silver or gold. At the higher end **Therese**, with a shop in the **Caravelle Hotel**, has established an international reputation.

Outdoor gear

Vietnam produces a range of equipment for climbing and camping, such as walking boots, fleeces and rucksacks. Top-quality brand-name goods can be bought cheaply, especially from around **Pham Ngu Lao** and **De Tham** streets.

War surplus

From **Dan Sinh Market**, Yersin St, between Nguyen Thai Binh St and Nguyen Cong Tru St.

▲▲ Activities and tours

Bowling

Diamond Superbowl is on the 4th floor of **Diamond Plaza**, 34 Le Duan St, right behind the cathedral, T8-3825 7778, ext 12. 24 lanes on the top floor, which also has a fast-food outlet, video games and plenty of pool tables.
Superbowl, 43A Truong Son St, Q Tan Binh, T8-3848 8888. An enormous complex just outside the airport with 32 lanes, video arcades and fast-food outlets.

Cookery classes

Saigon Cooking Class, held at the new **Hoa Tuc** (see Eating), 74 Hai Ba Trung St, T8-3825 8485, www.saigoncookingclass.com. Children, aged 7 and above, are welcome.
Vietnam Cookery Center, 362/8 Ung Van Khiem St, Q Binh Thanh, T8-3512 2764, www.vietnamcookery.com. Offers short and in-depth courses for adults and children.

Golf

Bochang Dong Nai Golf Resort, Dong Nai Province, 50 km north of HCMC up Highway 1, T61-386 6288, http://dongnaigolf.com.vn. A very attractive 27-hole golf course with restaurant and bar and accommodation.
Golf Vietnam and Country Club, Long Thanh My Ward, Q9, T8-6280 0124, http://vietnamgolfcc.com. An internationally owned 36-hole course with an east and west course, just north of the city. The complex also has tennis and badminton courts, a boating lake and children's playground. On-site accommodation is available.
Song Be Golf Resort, 77 Binh Duong Blvd, Lai Thieu, Q Thuan An, Binh Duong Province, 22 km from HCMC on Highway 13, T650-375 6660, http://songbegolf.com. An attractive golf resort set in 100 ha of land with lakes and tree-lined fairways. For non-golfers there are tennis courts, a gym, sauna and children's playground.

Racing

Phu Tho Racecourse, 2 Le Dai Hanh St, Q11, T8-3962 4319, http://horseracing.vietnamracing.net. Races on Sat and Sun afternoons starting at 1200. Both the winner and the 2nd horse have to be selected to collect. The course has been reopened with financing from an interested Chinese entrepreneur and Britons plan to introduce new breeding stock to Vietnam. Beware pickpockets.

Swimming

Some hotels allow non-residents to use their pool for a fee. Decent pools are at the **Sofitel Plaza**, **Grand** and **Caravelle**.

International Club, 285B Cach Mang Thang Tam St, Q10, T8-3865 7695.

Lan Anh Club, almost next door to the International Club at 291 Cach Mang Thang Tam St, T8-3862 7144. Pleasant with a nice pool and tennis courts.

Saigon Water Park, Go Dua Bridge, Kha Van Can St, Q Thu Duc, T8-3897 0456, Mon-Fri 0900-1700, Sat and Sun 0900-2000. Admission is charged according to height. A little way out but is enormous fun. It has a variety of water slides of varying degrees of excitement and a child's pool on a 5-ha site. It is hugely popular with the Vietnamese.

Tennis

Tennis is possible at the **Rex Hotel** and **New World Hotel**, see Sleeping, above.

Lan Anh Club, 291 Cach Mang Thang Tam St. 20,000d per hr.

Therapies

L'Apothiquaire, 61-63 Le Thanh Ton St, T8-3822 1218, www.lapothiquaire.com. Massages, chocolate therapy, spa packages and slimming treatments in this lovely spa.

Qi Salon and Spa, Caravelle Hotel, www.qispa.com.vn. You can indulge in everything from a 20-min Indian head massage to a blow-out 5-hr Qi Special.

Vespa tours

Vietnam Vespa Adventures, **Cafe Zoom**, 169A De Tham St, T8-3920 3897, www.vietnamvespaadventure.com. Half-day tours of the city, 3-day tours to Mui Ne and 8-day tours to Dalat and Nha Trang. The city tours are fun, insightful and recommended. Led by Oz veteran Walter Pearson.

Tour operators

Many operators run cheap tours to and through the Mekong Delta (starting from US$10 for a day trip) and should be your

1st port of call for trips to the south as local buses will eat in to your holiday time. These trips are also useful if you want to see some of the delta but work your way into Cambodia via Chau Doc. Trips to Phu Quoc overland and back via a flight are also arranged. TNK can also book trips to the Long Tan battle memorial cross and Nui Dat battlefield for those interested in ANZAC involvement in the Second Indochina War.

Ann Tours, 58 Ton That Tung St, T8-3925 3636, www.anntours.com. Generally excellent with knowledgeable guides.

Asia Pacific Travel, 127 Ban Co St, District 3, T8-3833 4083, www.asiapacifictravel.vn. Affordable small-group adventure travel and a wide selection of tours.

Asian Trails, 5th floor, 21 Nguyen Trung Ngan St, Q1, T8-3910 2871, www.asiantrails.info. Experienced operators offering various package tours across Asia.

Buffalo Tours, Satra House, Suite 601, 58 Dong Khoi St, T8-3827 9170, www.buffalotours.com. Organizes trips to the Mekong Delta, city tours, the Cu Chi tunnels and Cao Dai Temple and arranges a home concert in HCMC with a family who have mastered and perform traditional Vietnamese instruments; this latter trip is a delightful way to spend an evening. Staff are helpful. Good countrywide operator with longstanding reputation.

Cuu Long Tourist, 190 Cong Quynh St, T8-3920 0339, cuulongtouristnet@hcm.vnn.vn, www.cuulongtourist.com. Tours and homestays from Vinh Long in the Mekong Delta. **Cuu Long** has a monopoly on the homestays here and so you will need to book through its office here or in Vinh Long. 10-hr day trips to Vinh Long can be organized.

Delta Adventure Tours, 267 De Tham St, T8-920 2112, www.deltaadventuretours.com. Slow and express bus and boat tours through the Mekong Delta to Phnom Penh, Cambodia at very good prices.

Exotissimo, 64 Dong Du St, T8-3827 2911, www.exotissimo.com. An efficient agency that can handle all travel needs of visitors to

Vietnam. Its excursions are well guided.
Fiditour, 129 Nguyen Hue Blvd, T8-3914
1516, www.fiditour.vn. Reasonably priced
tour organizer with polite and helpful staff.
Visa service and money exchange.
Handspan, F7, Titan Building, 18A Nam
Quoc Cang St, T8-3925 7605, www.
handspan.com. Wide range of tours with a
commitment to sustainable tourism.
Kim Travel, 270 De Tham St, T8-3920 5552,
www.kimtravel.com. Organizes minibuses
to Nha Trang, Dalat, etc and tours of the
Mekong; good source of information.
Saigontourist, 45 Le Thanh Ton St, T8-3829
8914, www.saigontourist.net. City and
Mekong Delta tours. Longstanding operator.
SinhBalo, 283/20 Pham Ngu Lao, T8-3837
6765, www.sinhbalo.com. Mr Sinh, formerly
of **Sinh Café**, is a recommended tour
operator organizing tours including cycling,
adventure and cross-country tours.
Sinh Tourist (formerly Sinh Café),
246-248 De Tham St, T8-3838 9597, www.
thesinhtourist.vn. **Sinh Tourist** now has
branches and agents in all main towns in
Vietnam. Its tours are generally good value
and its open ticket is excellent value. For
many people, especially budget travellers,
Sinh is the first port of call. It is tempting
to tour the entire country with them as
it makes travelling easy. Like many other
tour operators, trips to the Mekong Delta
(from180,000d) and onwards to Cambodia
are organized (from 580,000d). It also offers
round trip bus and plane journeys to Phnom
Penh and Siem Reap. The company also
deals with visa extensions, flight, train and
hotel bookings and car rentals. Children
under 2 are free; 2- to 5-year-olds are
charged 75% of the full price. Beware that
there are numerous copycat **Sinh Cafés**;
make sure you know which ones are the
real deal as many of the fake Sinhs are to be
avoided. This one is the HQ.
TM Brother's Café, 230 De Tham St, T8-3837
7764, tmbrothertours@yahoo.com. The
genuine version is a reliable Open Tour
Bus operator. It also runs trips around the

Mekong Delta, bus services to Delta towns,
and trips on to Cambodia; also to Phu Quoc
by land and ferry (US$29).
TNK Travel, 222 De Tham St, 40 Bui Vien St
and 161 Pham Ngu Lao St, T8-3920 4766,
www.tnktravel.com.vn. Open Tour Bus trips
as well as trips to the Mekong Delta and on
to Cambodia. Very helpful.
Vidotour, 145 Nam Ky Khoi Nghia St, Q3, T8-
3933 0457, www.vidotourtravel.com. One of
the most efficient organizers of group travel
in the country. Its website contains useful
travel news on Indochina.

⊖ Transport

HCMC will get a much-needed mass rapid
transit system in the next 5 years with 22
stations in the downtown area and there are
plans to eventually move the international
airport to a site east of HCMC.

Air
Airport information
Tan Son Nhat Airport, 49 Troung Son, Tan
Binh, T8-3844 8358, www.saigonairport.com,
is 30 mins northwest of the city, depending
on the traffic. The new international terminal
opened in 2007; the old terminal building is
now the domestic terminal.

Airport facilities include banks and ATMs
and 2 locker rooms from US$1 a bag for
10 hrs (T8-3848 5383, 0700-2230 daily),
a **Vietnam Airlines** desk, a post office,
information desk. **Lost and found** T8-3844
6665 ext 7461.

Official taxis from the Saigon Airport
Corporation (T8-3866 6666) to the city
centre cost 140,000d. By doing it this way
you avoid the hordes of taxi drivers who will
swamp you as you exit.

Bus No 152 runs from the airport to town
every 50 mins, 30 mins, 6000d one way. The
bus goes to Pham Ngu Lao backpacker area
and then to Benh Thanh Market and on to
Dong Khoi St.

HCMC is connected to every airport in the
country except Dien Bien Phu. For **Vietnam**

Airlines routes, see Essentials, page 21.

Flights to **Con Dao** are 3 times daily, 55 mins.

Airline offices

AirAsia, 254 De Tham St, T8-3838 9810, www.airasia.com. **Air France**, 130 Dong Khoi St, T8-3829 0981, www.airfrance.com. **Bangkok Airways**, Unit 103, Saigon Trade Center, 37 Ton Duc Thang St, T8-3910 4490, www.bangkokair.com. **Cathay Pacific**, 72-74 Nguyen Thi Minh Khai St, T8-3822 3203, www.cathaypacific.com. **Emirate Airlines**, 170-172 Nam Ky Khoi Nghia, Q3, T8-3930 2939, www.emirates.com. **Eva Air**, 2A-4A, Ton Duc Thang St, T8-3844 5211, www.evaair.com. **Gulf Air**, 18 Dang Thi Nhu St, Q1, T8-3915 7614, www.gulfair.com. **JAL**, www.jal.co.jp. **Jetstar**, 112 Hong Ha, Q Tan Binh, T8-3845 0092, www.jetstar.com. **Lao Airlines**, www.laoairlines.com. **Lufthansa**, 19-25 Nguyen Hue Blvd, T8-3829 8529, www.lufthansa.com. **Malaysia**, Saigon Trade Center, 37 Ton Duc Thang St, T8-3829 2529, www.malaysiaairlines.com. **Qantas**, HT&T Vietnam, Level 2, Ben Thanh TSC Building, 186-188 Le Thanh Ton St, T8-3910 5373, www.qantas.com.au. **Qatar**, Suite 8, Petro Vietnam Tower, 1-5 Le Duan St, T8-3827 3777, www.qatarairways.com. **Singapore Airlines**, 29 Le Duan St, T8-3823 1588, www.singaporeair.com. **Thai Airways**, 29 Le Duan St, T8-3822 3365, www.thaiairways.com.vn. **Tiger Airways**, T1206 0114, www.tigerairways.com. **Vietnam Airlines**, 6th floor, Sun Wah Tower, 115 Nguyen Hue St, T8-3832 0320, www.vietnamairlines.com. Mon-Fri 0800-1830, Sat 0800-1200, 1330-1700.

Bicycle and motorbike

If staying in HCMC for any length of time it might be a good idea to buy a bicycle (see Shopping, above, and page 25). Alternatively, bikes can be hired for around US$3 a day in Pham Ngu Lao.

Motorbikes can be hired from some of the cheaper hotels and travel cafés, especially in Pham Ngu Lao St for around US$5-10 per day depending on the age, manual or automatic model, and model of the bike. Bikes should always be parked in the roped-off compounds (*Gui xe*) that are all over town; they will be looked after for a small charge (12,000d – always get a ticket).

Bus
Local

The bus service in HCMC has now become more reliable and frequent: it is really quite a useful means of getting about. The buses are green or yellow and are a safer and cheaper (even in some cases more convenient) alternative to any other modes of transport in HCMC. They run at intervals of 10-20 mins – depending on the time of day. In rush hours they are jammed with passengers and can run late. There are bus stops every 500 m. The same price – 3000d per person – applies to all routes.

All these buses start from or stop by the Ben Thanh bus station opposite Ben Thanh Market, T8-3821 4444. A free map of all bus routes can also be obtained here in the chaotic waiting room. Buses depart here for Vung Tau and Cu Chi.

No 1 Saigon – China Town (Cho Binh Tay). From the bus stop, you can walk to Cho Lon Bus Station (Ben Xe Cho Lon), 86 Trang Tu, Q5, T8-3855 7719, where there are buses to **Tien Giang**, **Long An** and **Ben Tre**), 0500-2130.

No 2 Saigon – Western Coach Station (Ben Xe Mien Tay), 137 Hung Vuong, Q Binh Chanh, T8-3877 6593. Buses to the south and **Mekong Delta**, 0445-1900.

No 26 Ben Thanh Market – Eastern Coach Station (Ben Xe Mien Dong), 227/6 Highway 13, Q Binh Thanh, T8-3877 6593. Buses to provinces in the north and **Vung Tau**, 0500-1930.

No 28 Ben Thanh Market – Tan Son Nhat (a bit misleading – it stops beside Super Bowl, 700 m from the airport), 0530-1840.

No 152 Ben Thanh Market – Tan Son Nhat Airport (straight to the airport – very often empty), 0615-1900.

On the move

Traffic in Ho Chi Minh City is out of control. In fact, traffic in Vietnam is madder than it has ever been, but at last officials have decided to act.

By 2013 the economic power-house is to get six metro stations to shuffle commuters in and out from the suburbs. This is not a year too late. Ho Chi Minh City throbs with eight million people, four million motorbikes and more than 400,000 cars contributing to a polluted pool and traffic gridlock in rush hour. An additional one million motorbikes and 60,000 cars commute in on a daily basis. (In comparison, London is home to 7.5 million people and 2.5 million cars.)

Restrictions on buying a motorbike were lifted in 2006 after a three-year ban to try to reduce the number of bikes on the road and although the city introduced more buses – some 3300 in the same three-year period – more than 750,000 new motos swerved onto the roads.

There are 20,000 accidents every year and 40 deaths a day according to the Ministry of Transport (see also box, page 25).

But it's the train that is the future in Vietnam. Heavy investment is to be made in railways, partly to reduce traffic on the roads, officials say. Not only are the Japanese involved in a brand new north-south railway but they are in talks with city officials to build an urban railway system using mass rapid transit trains. Six US\$6bn subway routes covering 107 km are under construction: The first underground section will run 2.6 km from Ben Thanh Market to Ba Son Shipyard. Three tramlines including one from Cholon to Mien Tay bus station will be built.

A new express north-south railway project costing US\$32.6 billion has been cancelled. The government said it would not serve the majority of the population and local people could not afford the fares.

Long distance

With the completion of a new ring road around HCMC, long-distance public buses, unless specifically signed Saigon or 'Ben Xe Ben Thanh' do not come into the city. Passengers are dropped off on the ring road at Binh Phuoc bridge. From here it is a 45-min *xe ôm* journey into town. Therefore always try to catch a bus heading into the town centre, such as one of the Open Tour Buses. A fleet of a/c buses connects central HCMC with the bus terminals, 3000d. These connecting buses depart from the bus station opposite Ben Thanh Market.

From **Mien Dong Terminal**, north of the city, buses north to **Dalat**, **Hué**, **Danang** and all significant points on the road to Hanoi. The **Hoang Long** bus company runs 11 deluxe buses daily to **Hanoi**, T8-2243 8990, with comfortable beds, 690,000d one way, including all meals and drinks, 36 hrs.

Also an office at 47 Pham Ngu Lao, T8-915 1818, https://hoanglongasia.com.

From **Mien Tay Terminal**, some distance southwest of town, buses south to the **Mekong Delta** towns. There is also a bus station in **Cholon** which serves destinations such as **Long An**, **My Thuan**, **Ben Luc** and **My Tho**.

Minibus

Minibuses for **Vung Tau** depart from Ham Nghi St – hop in quickly as they are not meant to pick up passengers in town. **Mai Linh Express**, 201 Pham Ngu Lao, T8-3920 2929, www.mailinh.vn, runs minivans or small coaches to the Mekong Delta and other southern Vietnam destinations.

Open Tour Bus

Numerous Open Tour Buses start their journey from HCMC with first stops being either **Dalat**, **Mui Ne** or **Nha Trang**. See under Tour operators, page 344.

International bus

Many tour operators run tours and transport to Cambodia (see Tour operators, page 344) crossing the border at **Moc Bai**. Visas for Cambodia can be bought at the border for around US$25. **Mai Linh**, T8-3920 2929, runs to **Phnom Penh**, 0630, 0830, 1300, 1430, US$11, 6 hrs from 201 Pham Ngu Lao. **Sapaco Tourist**, 309-327 Pham Ngu Lao St, T8-3920 3623, www.sapacotourist.com, runs buses from Pham Ngu Lao to **Phnom Penh** from 0600-1400, 8 daily, US$12, 6 hrs; at 0600 to **Siem Reap**, US$20, 12 hrs. Buses return at 0700 from Siem Reap and between 0600-1500 from Phnom Penh to HCMC. TNK runs daily buses (0800-1400) hourly to **Phnom Penh**, US$12. Or take a tour with a company like **Sinh** that will ensure you see a bit of the Mekong Delta before ending up in Phnom Penh.

Cyclos

Cyclos are a peaceful way to get around the city. They can be hired by the hour (approximately 250,000d per hr) or to reach a specific destination. Some drivers speak English. Each tends to have his own patch which is jealously guarded. Expect to pay more outside the major hotels – it is worth walking around the corner.

Cyclos are much rarer now but can be found waiting in tourist spots. Some visitors complain of cyclo drivers in HCMC 'forgetting' the agreed price (though Hanoi is worse). Cyclos are being banned from more and more streets in the centre of HCMC, which may involve a longer and more expensive journey. This is the excuse trotted out every time (particularly if extra money is demanded) and it is invariably true. If taking a tour agree a time and price and point to watches and agree on the start time. One scam involves drivers arguing you have used up more than the agreed time and shouting in the street that you are

pulling a fast one. Do not be humiliated into offering more than the agreed price because of the shouting.

Hydrofoil

There are 2 or 3 'competing' companies which operate hydrofoils from the wharf at the end of Ham Nghi St in HCMC to Halong St jetty in Vung Tau.

Greenlines, office on the jetty and at 51 Ham Nghi, T8-3821 5609, www. taucanhngam.com, 180,000d; children 90,000d. Same deal as Petro Express.

Petro Express, on the jetty. First service 0630 and then 4 services until 1645-1700. **Vina Express**, www.vinaexpress.com.vn. 13 services a day from 0630-1645.

Taxi

HCMC has quite a large fleet of meter taxis. There are more than 14 taxi companies fighting bitterly for trade. Competition has brought down prices so they are now reasonably inexpensive and for 2 or more are cheaper than cyclos or *xe ôm*.

All taxis are metered, ensure it is set after you get in. Prices start at between 12,000d-15,000d for the first 1.5-2 km reducing after that to, for example, 8500d with **Vinasun**, cheaper than, say, **SaigonTourist**. The standard of vehicle and service vary widely. All taxis are numbered; in the event of forgotten luggage or other problems ring the company and quote the number of your taxi.

Taxi tips Taxi scams, especially in HCMC and Hanoi, are rife beyond belief. If the meter is 'not working' (which is illegal) get out and get another cab, otherwise you will be ripped off. If the meter starts doubling and tripling, ask to stop and get out and pay the fare or, if you know the city and the fare for your trip, get out and pay the fare you think it should have been. If you can, avoid taxis hovering outside late-night establishments. Walk away from the place and hail a cab on the road or walk to a hotel with a taxi rank. If you think you have been overcharged and you are arriving at a hotel or restaurant, get out and ask the establishment staff to help.

Take only taxis listed below (Vinataxi, Mai Linh and Vinasun are the best):

Mai Linh Taxi (green and white, note that the Deluxe version is more expensive), T8-3822 2666, www.mailinh.vn. Saigontourist, T8-3845 0912. Vinasun (white), T8-3827 2727. Vinataxi (yellow), T8-3811 1111.

Motorcycle taxis

Honda or *xe ôm* are the quickest way to get around town and cheaper than cyclos; agree a price and hop on the back. *Xe ôm* drivers can be recognized by their baseball caps, and tendency to chain smoke; they hang around on most street corners. Short journeys should be around 10-15,000d but you may end up paying more.

Train

The station (*Nha ga*) is 2 km from the centre of the city at 1 Nguyen Thong St, Q3, T8-3931 2795. Facilities for the traveller are much improved and include a/c waiting room, post office and bank (no TCs). Regular daily connections with **Hanoi** and all points north. Trains take between 29½ and 42½ hrs to reach Hanoi; hard and soft berths are available. Sleepers should be booked in advance. (See Essentials, page 23, for more information on rail travel.)

There is now a **Train Booking Agency** at 275c Pham Ngu Lao St, T8-3836 7640, 0730-1830, which saves an unnecessary journey out to the station. Alternatively, for a small fee, most travel agents will obtain tickets. The railway timetable can be seen online at www.vr.com.vn.

ⓘ Directory

Banks

There are now dozens of ATMs in shops, hotels and banks. Remember to take your passport if cashing TCs and withdrawing money from a card.

ANZ Bank, 2 Ngo Duc Ke St, T8-3829 9319, www.anz.com/vietnam. 2% commission charged on cashing TCs into US dollars or dong, ATM. **HSBC, Hong Kong** and **Shanghai Bank**, 235 Dong Khoi St, T8-3829 2288. Provides all financial services, 2% commission on TCs, ATM. **Sacombank**, 11-213 Pham Ngu Lao St, Q1, T8-3837 1526.

Embassies and consulates

Australia, Landmark Building, 5B Ton Duc Thang St, T8-3521 8100, www.hcmc.vietnam. embassy.gov.au. **Cambodia**, 41 Phung Khac Khoan St, T8-3829 2751. **Canada**, 235 Dong Khoi St, T8-3827 9899, www. canadainternational.gc.ca. **China**, 39 Nguyen Thi Minh Khai St, T8-3829 2457. **France**, 27 Nguyen Thi Minh Khai St, T8-3520 6800, www.consulfrance-hcm.org. **Germany**, 126 Nguyen Dinh Chieu St, Q3, T8-3829 2455. **Italy**, 91 Nguyen Huu Canh St, Binh Thanh District, T8-3514 4937, www.ambhanoi.esteri. it. **Japan**, 13-17 Nguyen Hue Blvd, T8-3822 5314. **Laos**, 9B Pasteur St, T8-3829 7667. **Malaysia**, 2 Ngo Duc Ke St, T8-3829 9023. **Netherlands**, Saigon Tower, 29 Le Duan St, T8-3823 5932, http://www.mfa.nl/hcm-en. **New Zealand**, Suite 909, Metropole Building, 235 Dong Khoi St, T8-3822 6907. **Singapore**, 65 Le Loi Blvd, T8-3822 5174, www.mfa.gov. sg/hochiminhcity/. **Sweden**, 8A/11D1 Thai Van Lung St, T8-3823 6800. **Switzerland**, 42 Giang Minh St, T8-3744 6996. **Thailand**, 77 Tran Quoc Thao St, Q3, T8-3932 7637. **UK**, 25 Le Duan St, T8-3829 8433. **USA**, 4 Le Duan St, T8-3520 4200, http://hochiminh.usconsulate.gov.

Hospitals

Cho Ray Hospital, 201B Nguyen Chi Thanh Blvd, Q5, T8-3855 3137, www.choray.org. vn. **Colombia-Gia Dinh International Clinic**, 1 No Trang Long St, Q Binh Thanh, T8-3803 1104. American-run emergency clinic with medivac and General Practice services. **Colombia Asia** (Saigon International Clinic), 8 Alexander de Rhodes St, T8-3823 8455, www.columbiaasia.com. International doctors. **French Vietnam Hospital**, 6 Nguyen Luong Bang St, Saigon South, Q7, T8-5411 3333, www.fvhospital.com. **Family Medical Practice Ho Chi Minh City**, Diamond Plaza, 34 Le Duan St, T8-3822 7848, www.vietnammedicalpractice.com. Well-equipped practice, 24-hr emergency service and an evacuation service; Australian and European doctors. Also provides a useful major and minor disease outbreak service on its website. **International SOS**, 167 Nam Ky Khoi Nghia St, Q3, T8-3829 8424, www.internationalsos.com. Comprehensive 24-hr medical and dental service and medical evacuating.

Immigration office
Immigration office, 254 Nguyen Trai St, T8-3832 2300. Changes visa to specify overland exit via Moc Bai if travelling to Cambodia, or for overland travel to Laos or China. Also for visa extensions but a tour operator offering this service could save you time and hassle.

Internet
There are a number of internet cafés in the Pham Ngu Lao area. Virtually all hotels and guesthouses in the city offer email services and Wi-Fi.

Laundry
There are several places that will do your laundry around Pham Ngu Lao St.

Police
Police, 161 Nguyen Du St. The police will not resolve anything but if you are the victim of a robbery or crime you will need a crime report for an insurance claim. Do not even think about attending a police station without a translator.

Post office and telephone
GPO, 2 Cong Xa Paris (facing the cathedral), 0630-2100. Telex, telegram and international telephone services available. **Vinaphone** and **Mobiphone**, the local mobile phone providers, both have offices around the general PO building for the sale of pre-pay sim cards. Much cheaper than using an overseas sim card in Vietnam. You can also buy **mobicards** from Shop & Go JSC, 74A Hai Ba Trung St, near the Park Hyatt and from other outlets displaying the stickers.

Contents

354 Ins and outs

356 My Tho and around
356 My Tho
357 Around My Tho
358 Ben Tre
359 Vinh Long
360 Tra Vinh
361 Sa Dec
363 Cao Lanh
364 Listings

370 Can Tho and around
370 Can Tho
372 Soc Trang
373 Bac Lieu
374 Ca Mau
375 Listings

380 Chau Doc and around
381 Chau Doc
381 Around Chau Doc
384 Long Xuyen
385 Rach Gia
386 Ha Tien
388 Around Ha Tien
389 Listings

395 Phu Quoc Island
397 Listings

Footprint features

352 Don't miss…
355 Hydrology of the Mekong Delta
365 Mekong homestays

Mekong Delta

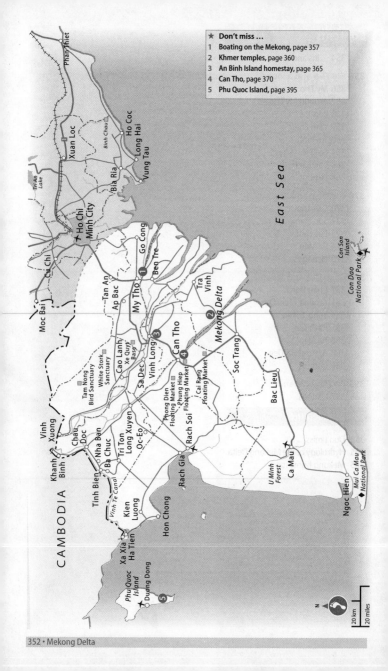

★ **Don't miss ...**
1 Boating on the Mekong, page 357
2 Khmer temples, page 360
3 An Binh Island homestay, page 365
4 Can Tho, page 370
5 Phu Quoc Island, page 395

East Sea

Con Son Island

Con Dao National Park

Phan Thiet

Ho Coc
Long Hai
Vung Tau
Bia Ria
Xuan Loc
Binh Chau

Tri An Lake

Ho Chi Minh City
Cu Chi
Moc Bai

Go Cong
Ben Tre
My Tho
Tan An
Ap Bac

Mekong Delta

Tra Vinh

Can Tho

Cao Lanh
Xe Quyt Bassi
Vinh Long
Sa Dec

Tam Nong Bird Sanctuary
White Stork Sanctuary

Phong Dien Floating Market
Phung Hiep

Cai Rang Floating Market

Soc Trang

Bac Lieu

CAMBODIA

Vinh Xuong
Khanh Binh
Chau Doc
Nha Ban
Tri Ton
Long Xuyen
Oc-Eo
Ba Chuc

Rach Soi
Rach Gia

Ca Mau
U Minh Forest

Ngoc Hien

Mui Ca Mau National Park

Tinh Bien
Vinh Te Canal
Kien Luong
Xa Xia
Ha Tien
Hon Chong

Phu Quoc Island
Duong Dong
5

N

20 km
20 miles

The Mekong Delta is the rice basket of Vietnam. At its verdant best the delta is a riot of greens. Pale green rice seedlings deepen in shade as they sprout ever taller. Palm trees and orchards make up an unbroken horizon of green. As the morning sun climbs, all greens pass through a spectrum of hues not to be seen elsewhere; and in the horizontal rays of the setting sun, all colours bloom briefly in ravishing intensity.

But at its muddy worst the paddy fields ooze with slime and sticky clay. Grey sky, hostile clouds and incessant rain make daily life a misery while the murky rising waters, the source of all the natural wealth of the delta, sweep hundreds each year to a wretched death.

Formal sights are thin on the ground in the Mekong Delta and travel can be slow, involving ferry crossings and boat rides although year on year new bridges are being built linking hitherto remote islands to main lines of communication. But herein lies the first contradiction of the delta, for the journey is often more fun than the destination. Boat trips along canals, down rivers and around islands hold more appeal than many of the towns and the main roads that are straggled with mile upon mile of homes and small, and increasingly large, industry. Driving past paddy fields or cycling through orchards is often more enchanting than the official tourist stops.

Ins and outs

Getting there

Follow Highway 1 from Ho Chi Minh City and it will take you as far as Can Tho passing through Vinh Long and My Tho along the way. There are several highways throughout the region linking the major towns. Highway 1 from Ho Chi Minh City goes to My Tho, Vinh Long and ends in Can Tho. Highways 80 and 50 are reasonably good and Highway 91 is improving. The road is relatively good from Ho Chi Minh City to Can Tho, Long Xuyen and Chau Doc, but beyond these towns roads are narrow and pot-holed and travel is generally slow, although it is improving. Roads, however, are dangerous, especially for motorbike drivers – so much so that the large number of placards that used to dot the Mekong warning against the dangers of HIV have, in the main, been replaced with billboards warning of the dangers of driving too fast.

Ferry crossings slow travel down still further and if travelling by bus expect long waits in queues (private cars push straight to the front). The huge My Thuan suspension bridge, a major Australian aid project just outside Vinh Long, has eliminated one ferry trip and made the journey quicker and smoother. Other new bridges have opened – My Tho and Ben Tre, once an island province and backwater, are now linked. In Chau Doc a new bridge links the city to Con Tien village and thus connects to a road to the Cambodian border at Khanh Binh but this is not yet an international border crossing. A 2.7-km bridge over the Hau River linking up Highway 1 in Vinh Long Province to Can Tho city opened in April 2010. Some ferries do still cross to and from Can Tho from the ferry piers. Public long-distance boat services have ceased from Can Tho. The **Victoria** hotel chain operates a boat service for its guests between Chau Doc and Phnom Penh.

It is possible to fly from Ho Chi Minh City to Phu Quoc Island and Rach Gia daily and sometimes to Ca Mau. Currently there are flights from Hanoi to Can Tho.

Ho Chi Minh City tour operators run tours to Can Tho, My Tho and Chau Doc and agents within these towns run tours to surrounding sights and organize onward transport. Many local and Ho Chi Minh City operators also arrange boat and bus transport to Phnom Penh, Cambodia. ▶▶ *See also Tour operators, pages 87, 367, 378 and 392, and Transport, pages 368, 379 and 393.*

Getting around

There are the ubiquitous *Honda ôms* and also, in the major towns, taxis, *xe lôi* and public bus services are plentiful and efficient. Also there are many river taxis available and – not used anywhere else in Vietnam – the sampan.

Best time to visit

The months December to May are when the Mekong Delta is at its best. During the monsoon from June to November the weather is poor with constant background drizzle interrupted by bursts of torrential rain. In October flooding may interrupt movement particularly in the remoter areas and around Chau Doc and Dong Thap Province.

Background

The region has had a restless history. Conflict between Cambodians and Vietnamese for ownership of the wide plains resulted in ultimate Viet supremacy although important Khmer relics remain. But it was during the French and American wars that the Mekong Delta produced many of the most fervent fighters for independence.

Hydrology of the Mekong Delta

Thw Mekong River enters Vietnam in two branches known traditionally as the Mekong and the Bassac but now called the Tien and the Hau. Over the 200-km journey to the sea they divide to form nine mouths, the so-called Nine Dragons or *Cuu Long*.

In response to the rains of the Southwest monsoon, river levels begin to rise in June, usually reaching a peak in October and falling to normal in December. This seasonal pattern is ideal for rice growing, around which the whole way of life of the delta has evolved.

The Mekong has a unique natural flood regulator in the form of Cambodia's great lake, the Tonlé Sap. As river levels rise the water backs up into the vast lake which more than doubles in size, preventing more serious flooding in the Mekong Delta. Nevertheless, the Tien and Hau still burst their banks and water inundates the huge Plain of Reeds (*Dong Thap Muoi*) and the Rach Gia Depression, home to thousands of water birds.

The annual flood has always been regarded as a blessing bringing, as it does, fertile silt and flushing out salinity and acidity from the soil. Since the 1990s, however, frequent serious flooding has made this annual event less benign and an increasingly serious problem.

From 1705 onwards Vietnamese emperors began building canals to improve navigation in the delta. This task was taken up enthusiastically by the French in order to open up new areas of the delta to rice cultivation and export. Interestingly it is thought the canals built prior to 1975 had little effect on flooding.

Since 1975 a number of new canals have been built in Cambodia and Vietnam and old ones deepened. The purpose of some of these predominantly west–east canals is to carry irrigation water to drier parts. Their effect has been to speed up the flow of water across the delta from about 17 days to five. Peak flows across the border from Cambodia have tripled in 30 years, partly as a result of deforestation and urbanization upriver.

In addition, the road network of the delta has been developed and roads raised above the normal high-water levels. This has the effect of trapping floodwater, preventing it from reaching the Gulf of Thailand or East Sea and prolonging floods. Many canals have gates to prevent the inundation of sea water; the gates also hinder the outflow of floodwaters.

Information taken from a paper by Quang M Nguyen

The Mekong Delta or Cuu Long (Nine Dragons) is Vietnam's rice bowl and, before the partition of the country in 1954, rice was traded from the south where there was a rice surplus, to the north where there was a rice deficit, as well as internationally. Even prior to the creation of French Cochin China in the 19th century, rice was being transported from here to Hué, the imperial capital. The delta covers 67,000 sq km, of which about half is cultivated. Rice yields are in fact generally lower than in the north, but the huge area under cultivation and the larger size of farms means that both individual households and the region produce a surplus for export. In the Mekong Delta there is nearly three times as much rice land per person as there is in the north. It is this that accounts for the relative wealth of the region.

The Mekong Delta was not opened up to agriculture on an extensive scale until the late 19th and early 20th centuries. Initially it seems that this was a spontaneous process: peasants, responding to the market incentives introduced by the French, slowly began to push the frontier of cultivation southwards into this wilderness area. The process gathered pace when the French colonial government began to construct canals and drainage projects to open more land to wet rice agriculture. By the 1930s the population of the delta had reached 4.5 million with 2,200,000 ha of land under rice cultivation. The Mekong Delta, along with the Irrawaddy (Burma) and Chao Phraya (Thailand) became one of the great rice exporting areas of Southeast Asia, shipping over 1.2 million tonnes annually.

Given their proximity to prosperous Ho Chi Minh City the inhabitants of the Mekong Delta might have expected some of the benefits of development to trickle their way: in this they have largely been disappointed. Most of the Mekong Delta provinces are trying and to a degree securing investment into their respective provinces. Be it hotels, cafés, karaoke in Ha Tien to canning and storage plants in Can Tho, they are trying to improve their collective lot. The main problem that they face is that everyone knows that each year during the monsoon season wide areas of the Mekong flood. The government is slowly but surely building up river defences against the annual floods but it is a laborious process. Tourist services are improving year on year.

My Tho and around

→ *Colour map 4, B3.*
My Tho is an important riverside market town, 5 km off the main highway to Vinh Long, and is the capital of Tien Giang Province. It is the stepping-off point for boat trips to islands in the Tien River. Visitors enjoy the chance to wander among abundant fruit orchards and witness at first hand local industries. My Tho is 71 km southwest of Ho Chi Minh City on the banks of the Tien River, a distributary of the Mekong. The drive from Ho Chi Minh City is dispiriting, nose-to-tail traffic and virtually uninterrupted ribbon development testify to the population pressure in so much of this land. The town has had a turbulent history: it was Khmer until the 17th century, when the advancing Vietnamese took control of the surrounding area. In the 18th century Thai forces annexed the territory, before being driven out in 1784. Finally, the French gained control in 1862. Around My Tho are the northern delta towns of Ben Tre, Vinh Long, Tra Vinh, Sa Dec and Cao Lanh. ▶▶ *For listings, see pages 364-369.*

Ins and outs
Getting there and around The much-improved Highway 1 is the main route from Ho Chi Minh City to My Tho. There is an efficient public bus service, taxis aplenty, a few river taxis and boats and *Honda ôm.* ▶▶ *See Transport, page 368.*

Tourist information Tien Giang Tourist ⓘ *8 30 Thang 4 St on the river, Ward 1, T730-387 3184, www.tiengiangtourist.com.* It has improved its services and attitude a good deal. Competition has opened up in the area but it has a near monopoly on the popular boat trips. The staff are friendly and helpful and have a good command of several languages.

My Tho → *For listings, see pages 364-369. Colour map 4, B3.*

On the corner of Nguyen Trai Street and Hung Vuong Street, and five minutes' walk from the central market, is **My Tho church** painted with a yellow wash with a newer, white campanile. The **central market** covers a large area from Le Loi Street down to the river. The river is the most enjoyable spot to watch My Tho life go by.

It is a long walk to **Vinh Trang Pagoda** ① *60 Nguyen Trung Trac St, daily 0900-1200, 1400-1700 (best to go by bicycle or* Honda ôm*).* The entrance to the temple is through an ornate porcelain-encrusted gate. The pagoda was built in 1849 and displays a mixture of architectural styles: Chinese, Vietnamese and colonial. The façade is almost fairytale in inspiration. Two huge new statues of the Buddha now dominate the area.

There has been a flurry of municipal activity in the past couple of years not much of it beneficial. All the bustling cafés along Trung Trac Street by the side of the small Bao Dinh River have been swept away and in their place is a broad, scorched pavement devoid of any shade. The saving grace, however is the new corner café from where you can idly pass the time watching the river and passing motorbikes.

Around My Tho

The islands
There are four islands in the Tien River between My Tho and Ben Tre: Dragon, Tortoise, Phoenix and Unicorn. The best way of getting to them is to take a tour. A vast pier and boat service centre has been built on 30 Thang 4 Street where all the tour operators are

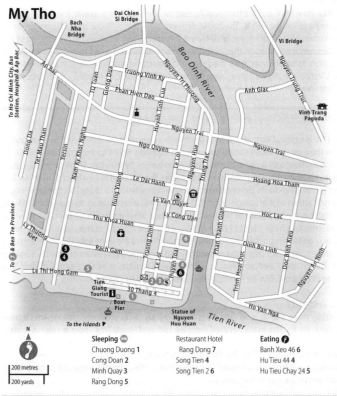

My Tho

Sleeping	Restaurant Hotel	Eating
Chuong Duong **1**	Rang Dong **7**	Banh Xeo 46 **6**
Cong Doan **2**	Song Tien **4**	Hu Tieu 44 **4**
Minh Quay **3**	Song Tien 2 **6**	Hu Tieu Chay 24 **5**
Rang Dong **5**		

now concentrated. To avoid the hundreds of visitors now descending on these islands, go in the afternoon after the tour buses have gone. Hiring a private boat (US$10) is not recommended due to the lack of insurance, the communication difficulties and lack of explanations. Prices vary according to the number of people and which islands you choose to visit. ▶▶ *See Tour operators, page 367.*

Immediately opposite My Tho is Dragon Island, **Tan Long Island**. It is pleasant to wander along its narrow paths. Tan Long is noted for its longan production but there are many other fruits to sample as well as honey and rice whisky.

The Island of the Coconut Monk, also known as **Con Phung** (**Phoenix Island**), is about 3 km from My Tho. The 'Coconut Monk' established a retreat on this island shortly after the end of the Second World War where he developed a new 'religion', a fusion of Buddhism and Christianity. He is said to have meditated for three years on a stone slab, eating nothing but coconuts – hence the name. Persecuted by both the South Vietnamese government and by the communists, the monastery has fallen into disuse.

Unicorn Island is a garden of Eden – stuffed with longan, durian, roses, pomelo and a host of other fruit trees. Honey is made on this island too.

Ap Bac
Not far from My Tho is the hamlet of Ap Bac, the site of the communists' first major military victory against the ARVN. The battle demonstrated that without direct US involvement the communists could never be defeated. John Paul Vann was harsh in his criticism of the tactics and motivation of the South Vietnamese Army who failed to dislodge a weak VC position. As he observed from the air, almost speechless with rage, he realized how feeble his Vietnamese ally was; an opinion that few senior US officers heeded – to their cost (see *Bright Shining Lie* by Neil Sheehan).

Ben Tre → *For listings, see pages 364-369. Colour map 4, B3.*

Ben Tre is a typical Vietnamese delta town with a charming riverfront feel. The small bridge over the river is wooden slatted but with iron supports. Bountiful fruit stalls are laid out on the waterfront and locals sell potted plants on barges by the river. Small cargo ships pass dilapidated shacks falling into the muddy waters. Ben Tre used to be a bit of a cul-de-sac but this is changing due to the opening of the new bridge linking it to My Tho. Consequently, it doesn't attract a lot of foreign or, for that matter, Vietnamese visitors. Its main claim to fame is that it is the birthplace of Nguyen Dinh Chieu, a blind and patriotic poet. The province is essentially a huge island of mud at one of the nine mouths of the Mekong. It depends heavily on farming, fishing and coconuts although there are some light industries engaged in processing the local farm output and refining sugar. During the wars of resistance against the French and Americans, Ben Tre earned itself a reputation as a staunch Viet Minh/Viet Cong stronghold. Ben Tre in recent years has improved its tourism facilities.

Ins and outs
Getting there and around Ben Tre is no longer an island province; a bridge links it from just outside My Tho. In the city itself there are taxis and *Honda ôms*. There are also river taxis.

Tourist information **Ben Tre Tourist** ① *16 Hai Ba Trung St, T75-382 2392, www.bentre tourist.vn,* is friendly and helpful. The tours that it offers are not particularly cheap but it does provide a reasonable selection.

Sights

Vien Minh Pagoda is located on Nguyen Dinh Chieu Street and is the centre for the association of Buddhists in Ben Tre Province. It was originally made of wood but was rebuilt using concrete in 1958.

At **Binh Phu** village, 2 km from downtown, you can see rice wine being made. **Phu Le** village also makes rice wine.

Nguyen Dinh Chieu Temple is 36 km from the town centre in An Duc village. The temple is dedicated to the poet Nguyen Dinh Chieu who is Ben Tre's most famous son. It is well kept and photogenic and worth a visit. The monks are friendly and helpful.

Vinh Long → *For listings, see pages 364-369. Colour map 4, B3.*

Vinh Long is a rather ramshackle, but nonetheless clean, riverside town on the banks of the Co Chien River and is the capital of Vinh Long Province. It is the launch pad for lovely boat trips through An Binh Island via the small floating market at Cai Be. An Binh is the centre of the Mekong homestay industry (see box, page 365).

At sunset families cluster along the river promenade to fly colourful kites in animal shapes. In the mornings, puppies and watermelons are for sale along Hung Dao Vuong Street and teenagers play ball and throw home-made shuttlecocks in the afternoons along Hung Vuong Street.

Vinh Long was one of the focal points in the spread of Christianity in the Mekong Delta and there is a cathedral and Roman Catholic seminary in town. The richly stocked and well-ordered Cho Vinh Long (central market), is on 1 Thang 5 Street down from the **Cuu Long** hotel and stretches back to near the local bus station. A new market building has also been built opposite the existing market. There is a Cao Dai church not far from the second bridge leading into town from Ho Chi Minh City and My Tho, visible on the right-hand side. In the countryside around Vinh Long you will see dozens of egg-shaped brick mounds – these are

Vinh Long at the end of the 19th century
Source: *The French in Indochina*, first published in 1884

terracotta-coloured kilns for the brick works and are an attractive sight. Vinh Long makes a reasonable stopping-off point on the road to Long Xuyen, Rach Gia and Ha Tien.

Ins and outs

Getting there and around The road runs direct from Ho Chi Minh City via the My Thuan bridge. There are good connections to all other Mekong towns. There is a good bus service and *Honda ôms*. ➤➤ *See Transport, page 368.*

Tourist information Cuu Long Tourist ① *No 1, 1 Thang 5 St, T70-382 3616, http:// cuulongtourist.com, daily 0700-1700.* Ask for Mr Phu, he is helpful, and has a good understanding of English and French. This is one of the friendlier and more helpful of the state-run companies and runs tours and homestays. ➤➤ *See Tour operators, page 368.*

Sights

The **river trips** taking in the islands and orchards around Vinh Long are as charming as any in the delta, but getting there can be expensive. See tour operators, page 367. Local boatmen are prepared to risk a fine and take tourists for one-tenth of the operators' charge. **Binh Hoa Phuoc Island** and An Binh, generally collectively known as An Binh, make a pleasant side trip, see also Sleeping. There is a **floating market** at Cai Be, about 10 km from Vinh Long. This is not quite so spectacular as the floating markets around Can Tho (see page 372) but nevertheless make for a diverting morning's trip.

An Binh Island, just a 10-minute ferry ride from Phan Boi Chau Street, represents a great example of delta landscape. The island can be explored either by boat, paddling down narrow canals, or by following the dirt tracks and crossing monkey bridges on foot. Monkey bridges are those single bamboo poles with, if you are lucky, a flimsy handrail which is there for psychological reassurance rather than to stop you from falling off. But don't worry, the water is warm and usually shallow and the mud soft. On the island is the ancient **Tien Chau Pagoda** and a *nuoc mam* (**fish sauce factory**).

The **Vinh Long Museum** ① *T70-382 3181, daily 0800-1100 and 1330-1630, Fri-Sun 1800-2100, free,* displays photographs of the war including the devastation of the town in 1968, some weaponry and a room dedicated to Ho Chi Minh.

The **Van Thieu Mieu Temple** ① *0500-1100, 1300-1900,* a charming mustard yellow cluster of buildings is 2 km from town along Tran Phu Street. In the first building to the right on entering the complex is an altar dedicated to Confucius.

The Khmer Temples at Tra Vinh (see below) can be visited on a day trip from Vinh Long.

Tra Vinh → *For listings, see pages 364-369. Colour map 4, C3.*

Tra Vinh is the capital of the province of the same name and has a large Khmer population – 300,000 people (30% of the province's population) are Khmer, and at the last count there were 140 Khmer temples. The large Khmer population is a bit of an enigma, for while Khmer people can be found across the Mekong Delta the concentration is highest in this, the most distant Mekong province from Cambodia. For whatever reason, Tra Vinh established itself as a centre of population some 500 years ago; then, as Vietnamese settlers began fanning across the delta displacing the Khmer, the population of this area remained firmly rooted creating a little pocket of Cambodian ethnicity and culture far from home. The modern market building, adorned with a huge picture of Ho Chi Minh, is the pivot of the city.

Ins and outs

Getting there and around The road is direct from Vinh Long and then follow the signs. There are quite a few taxis, plenty of *Honda ôm* and a reasonable domestic bus service. As the majority of town is shaded thanks to the tree-lined boulevards most people walk. »See Transport, page 369.

Tourist information Tra Vinh Tourist ⓘ*64-66 Le Loi St, T74-385 8556, travinhtourist@ yahoo.com*, owns the **Cuu Long Hotel** and is friendly and helpful. City tour by moto from US$18.

Background

For those interested in religious edifices Tra Vinh is the place to visit. In one of the more obscure surveys undertaken to calculate the number of religious buildings per head of population it was found that with more than 140 Khmer temples, 50 Vietnamese pagodas, five Chinese pagodas, seven mosques and 14 churches serving a town of only 70,000 souls Tra Vinh was the outright winner by miles.

So many attractive buildings coupled with the tree-lined boulevards – some trees are well over 30 m tall – make this one of the more attractive cities in the Delta. It is well worth an overnight stay here to recharge the batteries.

Sights

The **market** is on the central square between Dien Bien Phu Street – the town's main thoroughfare – and the Tra Vinh River, which is a relatively small branch of the Mekong compared with most Delta towns. A walk through the market and along the river bank makes a pleasant late afternoon or early evening stroll. Otherwise there is not a lot to do in Tra Vinh, although it's a nice enough place to spend some time. The **Ong Met Pagoda** on Dien Bien Phu Street north of the town centre dates back to the mid-16th century. It is a gilded Chinese-style temple where the monks will be only too happy to ply you with tea and practice their English, although the building itself is fairly unremarkable.

Around Tra Vinh

The two best reasons to come to Tra Vinh are to see the storks and the Khmer temples. Fortunately, these can be combined at the nearby **Hang Pagoda**, also known as Ao Ban Om, about 5 km south of town amd 300 m off the main road. It is not particularly special architecturally, but the sight of the hundreds of storks that rest in the grounds and wheel around the pointed roofs at dawn and dusk (1600-1800) is truly spectacular.

There's also the **Bao Tang Van Hoa Dan Toc Khmer** (0700-1100, 1300-1700) a small collection of artefacts next to the square-shaped lotus filled pond of Ba Om just south of town (there are plans for a hotel here). Labels are in Vietnamese and Khmer only; naga heads, Hanuman masks and musical instruments feature. Opposite is the **Chua Angkorajaborey (Ang)** or Chua Van Minh in Vietnamese dating from AD 990, which is rather peaceful.

Sa Dec → *For listings, see pages 364-369. Colour map 4, B2.*

Sa Dec's biggest claim to fame is that it was the birthplace of French novelist Marguerite Duras, and the town's three main avenues – Nguyen Hue, Tran Hung Dao and Hung Vuong garlanded with fragrant frangipani – together with some attractive colonial villas betray the French influence on this relatively young town. Sa Dec is also renowned for its flowers and bonsai trees. There are many flower nurseries on the fringes of the city. It is untouched by tourism and offers an untainted insight into life in one of the last attractive towns of the delta.

The town was formerly the capital of Dong Thap Province, a privilege that was snatched by Cao Lanh in 1984 but a responsibility that Sa Dec is better off without. It is a small and friendly town about 20 km west of Vinh Long. The delightful journey between the two towns passes brick kilns, and bikers transporting their wares (namely tropical fish in bottles and dogs).

Ins and outs

Getting there The most direct route is by crossing My Thuan Bridge and following the signs to Sa Dec. Local options include taxis, *Honda ôm* and sampans. ►► *See Transport, page 369.*

Tourist information There is no tourist information in Sa Dec. **Dong Thap Tourist Company** keeps some leaflets at the Sa Dec Hotel, and has a contact at the Huynh Thuy Le House (see below) but its main office is in Cao Lanh.

Sights

Sa Dec's bustling riverside market on Nguyen Hue Street is worth a visit. Many of the scenes from the film adaptation of Duras' novel *The Lover* were filmed in front of the shop terraces and merchants' houses here. Sit in one of the many riverside cafés to watch the world float by – which presumably, as a young woman, is what Duras did.

Duras' lover **Huynh Thuy Le's house** ① *Nha Co Huynh Thuy Le, 255A Nguyen Hue St, Ward 2, T67-377 3937, huynhthuyle@dongthaptourist.com, Mon-Sat 0730-1700, Sun 0830-1700, 10,000d,* is a lovely Sino-influenced building on the main street. There are stunning gold-leaf carved animal figures framing arches and the centrepiece is a golden shrine to Chinese warrior Quan Cong. The Ancient House was built in 1895 and restored in 1917. There are photographs of the Huynh family (he later married and had five daughters and three sons; he died in 1972), Duras and the Sa Dec school. The building was a police station and cared for from 1975-2006. The two friendly women who run the place, Xuan and Tuyen, speak French and English will offer you tea and crystallised ginger; this is a wonderful way to pass the afternoon. Reserved lunch and dinner is possible, as is a stay in the house. **Duras' childhood home** is not across the river as some guidebooks say; it no longer exists. She lived in a house near the Ecole de Sa Dec (now Truong Vuong primary school on the corner of Hung Vuong and Ho Xuan Huong St), which is pictured inside the Nha Co Huynh Thuy Le.

Phuoc Hung Pagoda ① *75/5 Hung Vuong St,* is a splendid Chinese-style pagoda constructed in 1838 when Sa Dec was a humble one-road village. Surrounded by ornamental gardens, lotus ponds and cypress trees, the main temple to the right is decorated with fabulous animals assembled from pieces of porcelain rice bowls. Inside are some marvellous wooden statues of Buddhist figures made in 1838 by the venerable sculptor Cam. There are also some superbly preserved gilded wooden beams and two antique prayer tocsins. The smaller one was made in 1888 and its resounding mellow tone changes with the weather. The West Hall contains a valuable copy of the 101 volume Great Buddhist Canon. There are also some very interesting and ancient photos of dead devotees and of pagoda life in the past.

A few kilometres west of Sa Dec is the **Tu Ton Rose Garden (Vuon Hong Tu Ton)** ① *28 Vuon Hong St, Khom 3, Ward 3, T67-376 1685, 0600-2000, free.* The garden is next to a lemon yellow building with yellow gates. This 6000-ha nursery borders the river and is home to more than 40 varieties of rose and 540 other types of plant, from medicinal herbs to exotic orchids. Wander amid the potted hibiscus, beds of roses and bougainvillea and enjoy the visiting butterflies. The garden can be reached either on foot or by taking a *Honda ôm* to Tan Qui Don village.

Cao Lanh → For listings, see pages 364-369. Colour map 4, B2.

Cao Lanh for many years was a small, underdeveloped Mekong town. However, since becoming the capital of Dong Thap Province, an honour previously bestowed on Sa Dec, it has changed and has become a thriving market town. It also benefits from being the closest main city to, Xeo Quit base (Rung Cham forest), and Tram Chim Nature Reserve, all of which are main tourist attractions. In fact, the excursions are the only real reason to visit Cao Lanh, particularly if you are a bird lover or a Ho Chi Minh biographer.

Ins and outs
Getting there By car/bus from Ho Chi Minh City it is a three-hour drive. There are a few taxis, *Honda ôm*, river taxis and sampans. ▸▸ *See Transport, page 369.*

Tourist information **Dong Thap Tourist Co** ⓘ *2 Doc Binh Kieu St, T67-385 5637, www. dongthaptourist.com, Mon-Sat 0700-1130, 1330-1700.* Some staff have a reasonable command of English and are helpful and provide excellent value for the services it provides.

Sights
To the northeast along Nguyen Hue Street is the **war memorial**, containing the graves of Vietnamese who fell in the war with the USA. The **tomb of Ho Chi Minh's father** ⓘ *Nguyen Sinh Sac (Tham Quan Khu Di Tich Nguyen Sinh Sac), next to Quan Nam restaurant at 137 Pham Huu Lau St, open 0700-1130, 1330-1700, 8000d,* set under a shell structure and sits in front of a lotus pond. A small stilt-house museum sits in the tranquil grounds.

The vast **Plain of Reeds** (**Dong Thap Muoi**) is a swamp that extends for miles north towards Cambodia, particularly in the late monsoon season (September to November). It is an important wildlife habitat (see below) but in the wet season, when the water levels rise, getting about on dry land can be a real problem. Extraordinarily, the Vietnamese have not adapted the stilt house solution used by the Khmer and every year get flooded out. In the rural districts houses are built on the highest land available and in a good year the floor will be just inches above the lapping water. At these times all transport is by boat. When the sky is grey the scene is desolate and the isolation of the plain can truly feel like the end of the Earth has been reached.

Tower Mound (**Go Thap**) is the best place from which to get a view of the immensity and beauty of the surrounding Plain of Reeds. There was a watchtower here although no one seems sure if it was 10-storeys high or the last in a chain of 10 towers. There are earthworks from which General Duong and Admiral Kieu conducted their resistance against the French between 1861 and 1866.

Tam Nong Bird Sanctuary (**Tram Chim**) is an 8000-ha reserve 45 km northwest of Cao Lanh (T67-382 7436). It contains 182 species of bird at various times of year, but most spectacular is the red-headed crane (sarus), rarest of the world's 15 crane species. Between August and November these spectacular creatures migrate across the nearby Cambodian border to avoid the floods (cranes feed on land), but at any other time, and particularly at dawn and dusk, they are a magnificent sight. Floating rice is grown in the area around the bird sanctuary and although the acreage planted diminishes each year this is another of nature's truly prodigious feats. The leaves float on the surface while the roots are anchored in mud as much as 4-5 m below; but as so much energy goes into growing the stalk little is left over for the ears of rice, so yields are low.

About 20 km east of Cao Lanh – 6 km off the main road at My Long where it is signposted to the on-site restaurant – **Xeo Quit Base** ① T67-350 4733, kdtxeoquit@yahoo.com.vn, 0730-1700, 5000d for entrance and boat trip, Nguyen Thanh Nguyen is the only English-speaking guide at the site; T91-827 3125, he requires 1-2 days' notice. Xeo Qiut was home to Viet Cong generals who planned the war from the safety of the base. There was so little vegetation cover here that fast-growing eucalyptus trees were planted; but even these took three years to provide sufficient cover to conceal humans. As the waterlogged ground prevented tunnelling, waterproof chambers sealed with plastic and resin were sunk into the mud. Stocked with rice, water and candles communist cadres coordinated their resistance strategy from here for almost 15 years. Despite frequent land and air raids the US forces never succeeded in finding or damaging the base. There is a restaurant at the site.

◉ My Tho and around listings

For Sleeping and Eating price codes and other relevant information, see Essentials pages 26-31.

◉ Sleeping

My Tho p356, map p357

C Song Tien, 33 Trung Trac St, T730-397 7883, www.tiengiangtourist.com. Undergone a remarkable transformation into a very nice 20-room hotel boasting large beds and bathtubs on legs. Price includes breakfast and now the best place in town.

C Song Tien 2, 101 Trung Trac St, T730-387 2009. This hotel was undergoing an extensive refurbishment in 2010.

C-D Chuong Duong, No 10, 30 Thang 4 St, T730-387 0875, www.chuongduonghotel. com. My Tho's newest hotel occupies a prime riverside location in front of the erstwhile hydrofoil ferry. The staff are eager to please. All rooms are en suite, have a/c, satellite TV and minibar but are beginning to show their age. They also all overlook the river. The in-house restaurant provides good food.

C-D Minh Quan, 69 30 Thang 4 St, T730-397 9979, minhquanhotel@gmail.com. A new presence on the riverside road offering comfortable rooms with Wi-Fi and breakfast in a very convenient location.

E-F Restaurant Hotel Rang Dong, 40/5, Section 3, ward 6, Le Thi Hong Gam St, T730-397 0085, www.rangdonghotel.net. About 1 km out of town on the riverfront but in an inconvenient location. This is the new sister hotel to the town centre Rang Dong. The best rooms are those with balconies overlooking the Mekong.

F Rang Dong, No 25, 30 Thang 4 St, T730-387 4400, www.rangdonghotel.net. Private hotel, near river with a/c, TV and hot water.

F-G Cong Doan, No 61, 30 Thang 4 St, T730-387 4324, congdoantourist.tgg@vnn. vn. Clean hotel with 5 fan rooms that are cheaper than the 18 with a/c. Good views and location for the boat trips.

Ben Tre p358

C-D Hung Vuong, 148-166 Hung Vuong St, T75-382 2408. Spacious a/c rooms (39 in total) with huge bathtubs feature in this waterfront hotel that is in a great location. Each room has 2 beds plus TV, fridge and balcony. Restaurant; breakfast is included. Some English is spoken.

F Cong Doan, 36 Hai Ba Trung St, T75-382 5082. All rooms with a/c, TV and bathrooms. No English spoken and much patience required at reception.

Mekong homestays

Facing Vinh Long town in the Co Chien River, a tributary of the Mekong, is a large island known as An Binh that is further sliced into smaller islands by ribbons of canals. **Cuu Long Tourist** runs several homestays on the island – a wonderful way to immerse yourself in local life.

The accommodation is basic with camp beds, shared bathrooms and mosquito nets and a home-cooked dinner of the fruits of the delta (elephant ear fish with abundant greens including mint and spring rolls and beef cooked in coconut). Sunset and drinks in patios or terraces or riverfront lookouts chatting with the owner completes the night. A dawn paddle in the Mekong, surrounded by floating water hyacinth and watching the sun rise is the reward for early risers. These tranquil islands are stuffed with fruit-bearing trees and flowers. Travel is by sampan or you can walk down the winding paths that link the communities. During your stay you will take tea and fruit at a traditional house, see rice cakes and popcorn being made, and visit a brick factory and watch terracotta pots being created close to the unusually shaped kilns that dot this area of the delta. Costs are US$49 per person or US$60 for two. Short of time? The four-hour tour costs US$25 for two people.

Vinh Long p359

For homestays, see box, above.

C-D Cuu Long (B), No 1, 1 Thang 5 St (ie No 1 May St), T70-382 3616, www. cuulongtourist.com. Set back from the river, in the centre of action. 34 comfortable a/c rooms; price includes breakfast (over the road at the **Phuy Thuong Restaurant**). The **Hoa Vien Club** in grounds next to the hotel is also good for a drink.

E Van Tram Nha Tro, No 4, 1 Thang 5 St, T70-382 3820. A small friendly place, close to the centre of the action, with 5 small and large a/c rooms with TV. Tours to An Binh offered that are cheaper than **Cuu Long Tourist** at US$24 for 2.

E-F Nam Phuong, 11 Le Loi St, T70-382 2226, khachsannamphuongvl@yahoo.com. These comfortable rooms have a/c and hot water; clean and cheap and very friendly service. There's a big co-op mart nearby. Bikes to rent too.

F Phung Hoang 1, 2H Hung Vuong St, T70-382 5185, ksphunghoang@yahoo.com. Very friendly service at this mini hotel. Clean rooms with varying facilities; cheaper rooms come with fan. Recommended.

Tra Vinh p360

C-E Cuu Long, 999 Nguyen Thi Minh Khai St, T74-386 2615. About 2 km out of town, a modern hotel with a good choice of facilities. The rooms are well equipped with a/c, satellite TV, and en suite facilities. The restaurant provides a good selection of food at reasonable prices. The friendly, helpful staff have a good understanding of English. Although it is 2 km from town if you are planning to stay overnight in Tra Vinh then this hotel is recommended. Wi-Fi and breakfast included.

F Tra Vinh Palace, 3 Le Thanh To St, T74-386 4999. A comfortable and quiet hotel with very large rooms 10 mins' walk from the central market. Staff are helpful. Wi-Fi available. The sister hotel, **Tra Vinh Palace 2** has cheaper rooms (**F**) and is a few streets away.

F-G Duy Thanh, 6 Dien Bien Phu St, T74-385 8034. Diagonally opposite the market and main roundabout. Windowless rooms smell and so it's worth forking out the extra 80,000d for a window and some air. Friendly reception.

Sa Dec p361

D Nha Co Huynh Thuy Le, 255A Nguyen Hue St, Ward 2, T67-377 3937. Run by **Dong Thap Tourist**, this lovely home has 4 fan rooms with 2 single beds in each and would be the most enjoyable way to spend time in Sa Dec. The 2 front rooms are much more attractive than the plain 2 back rooms with stained-glass windows and carved wooden doors. The shared bathroom is at the back with cold water. The price includes breakfast and dinner. See also Eating, below.

D-F Bong Hong, 251A Nguyen Sinh Sac St, T67-386 8287, bonghonghotel@yahoo.com.vn. A short distance before the bus station on Highway 80 leading into town. Some good-value a/c rooms with TV and fridge. Cheaper rooms have fan and cold water only. Breakfast not included. Tennis court on site.

D-F Sa Dec, 108/5A (499) Hung Vuong St, T67-386 1430, sadechotel@yahoo.com.vn. More expensive rooms come equipped with a/c, hot water, TV and a fridge; cheaper ones make do with a fan and warm water showers. Somewhat run down and unloved but clean. Breakfast included except for fan rooms. Closer to the river than the **Bong Hong**.

Cao Lanh p363

B-E Song Tra, 178 Nguyen Hue St, T67-385 2624, www.dongthaptourist.com. Cao Lanh's best hotel with a good location in the town. The rooms are tastefully decorated and come equipped with a/c, satellite TV and en suite facilities. The staff are helpful and friendly, with a decent grasp of English. The restaurant is reasonable. See Eating, below.

D-E Hoa Binh, east of town on Highway 30 towards My Tho, opposite the striking war memorial, T67-385 1469. All a/c, some nice rooms. Friendly and helpful staff. The rooms come equipped with a/c, phone, satellite TV, minibar and en suite facilities. The restaurant on the ground floor provides a reasonable selection of food. If it were not for the fact that it is a little way out of town it would be the best hotel. Wi-Fi available.

E-F Xuan Mai, 33 Le Quy Don St, T67-385 2852. Clean and spacious hotel; all rooms with a/c, fridge and bath but breakfast is not included. One of the better restaurants in town. The staff are friendly and helpful, the rooms tastefully decorated and there's internet and Wi-Fi access.

F-G Binh Minh Hotel, 157 Hung Vuong St, T67-385 3423. A good little hotel but note that it's actual entrance is not on Hung Vuong, it is just around the corner from the Vespa/Piaggio garage on Do Cong Tuong St. The owner, a local schoolteacher, is friendly and helpful. If you are travelling on a budget then this would be a good choice. Fan and a/c rooms.

⦿ Eating

My Tho p356, map p357

A speciality of the area is *hu tieu my tho*, a spicy soup of vermicelli, sliced pork, dried shrimps and fresh herbs. Sadly most of the good cheap restaurants have been cleared away from **Trung Trac St** but some remain. At night noodle stalls spring up on the pavement of **Le Loi St** by the junction with Le Dai Han.

¶ Banh Xeo 46, 11 Trung Trac St. Serves *bánh xèo*, savoury pancakes filled with beansprouts, mushrooms and prawns; delicious.

¶ Hu Tieu 44, 44 Nam Ky Khoi Nghia St. 0500-1200. Specializes in *hu tieu my tho*. At 16,000d for a good-sized bowl filled to the top with hot *hu tieu my tho*, it is unbeatable.

¶ Hu Tieu Chay 24, 24 Nam Ky Khoi Nghia St. It is the vegetarian equivalent of Hu Tieu 44 and is even cheaper than the meat variety.

¶ Lac Hong, 63, 30 Thang 4 St, is the latest place to be seen. Sip your coffee in the cool and watch the world go by.

Ben Tre p358

Most of the hotels have restaurants; there is a floating restaurant on the river but it has moved from its town centre location to 1 km upstream because, they say, it's a prettier location; not so. The best option is local noodle and rice stands. The hotel restaurants are open all day. The choice is adequate.

Dong Khoi Hotel, see Sleeping, above. The restaurant, next to the hotel, has a good selection. English spoken.

Nha Hang Noi Ben Tre, Hung Vuong, T75-382 2492. 0700-2200. A variety of dishes plus karaoke on this large boat overlooking the banks of the river in its new location. It's not within walking distance.

Vinh Long *p359*

It is remarkably difficult to find anything to eat in Vinh Long apart from the bountiful fruit in the market. There are a few restaurants along 1 Thang 5 St, just beyond **Cuu Long Hotel (A)**.

Nem Nuong, 12 1 Thang 5 St. Open all day. Sells grilled meat with noodles.

Phuong Thuy Restaurant, No 1, 1 Thang 5 St, T70-382 4786. 0600-2100. A 'stilt' restaurant on the river with Vietnamese and Western dishes and welcoming service. Cuttlefish and shrimp feature strongly.

Cafés

Hoa Nang Cafe, 1 Thang 5 St. A great spot for a sunset drink, and for morning coffee when it is exceptionally busy.

Tra Vinh *p360*

Cuu Long, see Sleeping, above. Restaurant has a good selection of food.

Tuy Huong, 8 Dien Bien Phu St. Opposite the market; good, simple Vietnamese dishes.

Viet Hoa, 80 Tran Phu St. Walk through the garage to sample the squid, shrimp and crab dishes. English menu.

Sa Dec *p361*

Cay Sung, 2/4 Hung Vuong St. Open all day. It serves a good selection of rice dishes. The *duong chau* (fried rice) in particular is good. There is a menu in English available. The food is well presented and piping hot.

Thuy Com, 439 Hung Vuong St, T67-386 1644. Serves excellent *dong chau*. The menu is in English and there is a variety of food.

Nha Co Huynh Thuy Le, 255A Nguyen Hue St, Ward 2, T67-377 3937. Run by **Dong Thap Tourist**, reserve a day in advance for the chance to dine in the home of Marguerite Duras' lover. Attended to by Xuan and Tuyen who are guides at the house, dine on spring rolls, fried fish, lotus salad, noodles, fried vegetables with pork and fruit. Lunch and dinner menus are US$6 each for 5 courses.

Cao Lanh *p363*

The restaurants in Song Tra, Xuan Mai and Hoa Binh hotels are all open for breakfast, lunch and dinner. There is not much difference in their quality, presentation choice and value. The highlight, however, is the attractively presented weekend buffet in the **Song Tra Hotel** garden (see Sleeping, above), on Sat and Sun nights.

A Chau, Ly Thuong Kiet St. 0800-2100. Specializes in fried pancakes.

Hong Nhien, 143 Hung Vuong St, behind the **Song Tra Hotel**. Serves *com tam* and *hu tieu* in a simple set up.

O Shopping

Ben Tre *p358*

The main items to buy are coconuts and related coconut-made products. They might not be too versatile but they are very pretty and make ideal novelty presents for friends and family at home. The gift cabinet in the **Dong Khoi** hotel has the best selection of coconut-related items.

▲ Activities and tours

My Tho *p356, map p357*

Tour operators

Ben Tre Tourist, 8, 30 Thang 4 St, T730-387 5070, www.bentretourist.vn. Although this company operates island tours from My Tho, it would be best to use its specialist knowledge of Ben Tre province. Escape the My Tho crowds with homestays at Cai Mon and take a tour to the gardens and canals of this neigbouring province.

Chuong Duong Tourist, next to the hotel, T730-387 0875, cdhoteltravel@vnn.vn. Offers the same tour as Tien Giang Tourist for the same price but for 3 hrs.

Tien Giang Tourist, Dockside location is at No 8, 30 Thang 4 St, T730-387 3184, www.tiengiangtourist.com. Dinner with traditional music on the Mekong for US$28. Canoe hire is US$50 per hr for 2 people and a boat is US$12 for 1½ hrs.

Ben Tre *p358*
Tour operators
Tours of the islands in the Tien River from Ben Tre cost half the price of those leaving from My Tho and include taking a horse and cart. The 4-hr Ben Tre ecological tour will take you to see local agricultural industries.
Ben Tre Tourist, 16 Hai Ba Trung St, T75-382 2392, www.bentretourist.vn. Daily 0700-1100, 1300-1700. Island tour, US$8 for 2; Ben Tre ecological tour, US$11 for 2. Bicycles can be rented for US$0.60 per hr or US$1.90 per day. There's also a motorboat for rent for US$5.60 per hr.

Vinh Long *p359*
Tour operators
Cuu Long Tourist, No 1, 1 Thang 5 St, T70-382 3616, www.cuulongtourist.com. Trips to An Binh Island include a visit to the floating market of Cai Be. A tour of the area including homestay, dinner and breakfast can be arranged (see box, page 365). A day trip to Cai Be passing the floating market, is possible as is the arrangement from HCMC.
Mekong Travel, No 8, 30 Thang 5 St, T70-383 6252, www.mekongtravel.com.vn. Breaking the monopoly of Cuu Long Tourist is this new company offering the same homestay and floating market options.

Tra Vinh *p360*
Tra Vinh Tourist, 64-66 Le Loi St, T74-385 8556, travinhtourist@yahoo.com.

Sa Dec *p361*
Dong Thap Tourist, is based at the Huynh Thuy Le Old House, T67-377 3937, www.dongthaptourist.com. Trips to Xeo Quit and Cao Lanh organized.

Cao Lanh *p363*
Birdwatching at the nearby sanctuaries is the most common activity. It is also possible to hire boats from **Dong Thap Tourist Company**, 2 Doc Binh Kieu St, T67-385 5637. Dong Thap also organizes trips to the mausoleum of Nguyen Sinh Sac, Xeo Quit, Sa Dec and the Gao Giong Eco-tourism Zone.

⊖ Transport

My Tho *p356, map p357*
Boat
As in all Mekong Delta towns, local travel is often by boat to visit the orchards, islands and remoter places.

Bus
Local On land there are xe ôms.
Long distance The bus station (Ben Xe My Tho) is 3-4 km from town on Ap Bac St towards HCMC with regular connections every 30 mins from 0430 to **HCMC**'s Mien Tay station (2 hrs); **Vinh Long** (2½ hrs); and **Cao Lanh** (2½ hrs). There are also buses to **Can Tho** and **Chau Doc**.

Ben Tre *p358*
Car
Ben Tre is 70 km from **My Tho**, 32 km from **Can Tho**, and 147 km from **HCMC** via the My Thuan toll bridge. It is possible to travel from Ben Tre to **Vinh Long** along route 60 then 57, which takes 1 hr to the ferry crossing from Long Ho (15,000d). This tarmacked route passes plenty of small bridges and village life.

Vinh Long *p359*
Bus
The local bus station is on 3 Thang 2 St, between Hung Dao Vuong and Hung Vuong in the centre of town with services to Sa Dec

and Can Tho. The long-distance bus station is at Dinh Tien Hoang St, Ward 8 for connections with **HCMC**'s Mien Tay station. Links with **My Tho**, **Long Xuyen**, Tra Vinh, **Rach Gia**, and other Mekong Delta destinations.

Tra Vinh *p360*
Bus
The bus station is on Nguyen Dang St, about 500 m south of town. Regular connections with **Vinh Long**.

Sa Dec *p361*
Bus
The bus station is about 500 m southeast of town on the main road just before the bridge. Buses to **Vinh Long** and **Long Xuyen** leave from here. The town is 143 km from HCMC and 102 km from Chau Doc, and 20 km from Vinh Long along Highway 80.

Taxi
Vina Taxi, T67-386 6666.

Cao Lanh *p363*
Bus
The bus station is located at the corner of Ton That Tung and Doc Binh Kieu St. Connections with all delta towns. To **HCMC** from the bus station on Vo Thi Sau St and Nguyen Van Troi St.

⦿ Directory

My Tho *p356, map p357*
Banks EXIM, Le Van Duyet St, T730-387 9374. Offers a bureau de change service as does the **Incombank**, on Nam Ky Khoi Nghia St. There's also a Visa and Plus ATM at the Truong Luong Restaurant just outside My Tho that is used by tour operators and ATMs on 30 Thang 4 St. **BIDV** ATM next to the post office. **Hospitals** 2 Hung Vuong St, T730-387 2360. **Internet** The post office and Choung Dong hotel offer internet and there's Wi-Fi at the Lac Hong café. **Post office** 2 Truong Dinh St. Facilities for international telephone calls, 0700-1130, 1330-1700.

Ben Tre *p358*
Banks Cong Thuong Bank, 142 Nguyen Dinh Chieu St, T75-382 2507. It offers a bureau de change service and cashes TCs. **Agribank**, on the corner of Le Lai and Dong Khoi St, has a Visa ATM. **Hospitals** Nguyen Dinh Chieu Hospital, 109 Doan Hoang Minh St. **Post office** 3 Dong Khoi St, T75-382 2264, 0700-1100, 1300-1700. It also has internet access.

Vinh Long *p359*
Banks Agribank, 47 1 Thang 5 St. With ATM. There's a Visa ATM next to the Cuu Long B hotel. **Hospitals** 301 Tran Phu St, Ward 4, T70-382 3520. **Internet** The post office and Cuu Long (B) offer internet access and there are a couple of email places on Ly Thuong Kiet St. **Post office** 12c Hoang Thai Hieu St, T70-382 5888. 0600-2100.

Tra Vinh *p360*
Banks Vietinbank, 15A Dien Binh Phu St, has a bureau de change service and also cash advances off Visa and MasterCard. ATM too. Sacombank, 40 Dien Bien Phu St with ATM. **Hospitals** 27 Dien Binh Phu, Ward 6, T74-386 2458. **Internet** At the post office and 83 Le Loi St. **Post office** Corner of Hung Vuong St and Ngo Quyen St has internet.

Sa Dec *p361*
Banks Agribank, 77 Ly Thuong Kiet St, off Tran Hung Dao St. **Sacombank**, 6-7Nguyen Sinh Sac St. **Hospitals** Ap Hoa Khanh, Ward 2, T67-386 1964. **Post office** 90 Hung Vuong St, Ward 2, T67-386 1025. Internet service.

Cao Lanh *p363*
Banks Vietinbank, corner of Nguyen Hue and Ly Thuong Kiet St with ATM. Sacombank, 43 Ly Thuong Kiet St. **Hospitals** Dong Thap Hospital, Ap 3 Xa My Tan Thi Xa Cao Lanh, T67-385 1130. **Internet** Xuan Mai hotel. **Post office** 83-85 Nguyen Hue St, T67-389 8989.

Can Tho and around

→ *Colour map 4, B2.*

Can Tho is a large and rapidly growing commercial city situated in the heart of the Mekong Delta. Lying chiefly on the west bank of the Can Tho River it is the capital of Can Tho Province, the largest city in the delta, and the region's principal transport hub, with roads and canals running to most other important towns. It is also one of the most welcoming of the delta towns and is the launch pad for trips to see some of the region's floating markets. South of Can Tho are the towns of Soc Trang, Bac Lieu and Ca Mau. ▶▶ *For listings, see pages 375-380.*

Can Tho → *For listings, see pages 375-380. Colour map 4, B2.*

A small settlement was established at Can Tho at the end of the 18th century, although the town did not prosper until the French took control of the Delta a century later and rice production for export began to take off. Despite the city's rapid recent growth there are still strong vestiges of French influence apparent in the broad boulevards flanked by flame trees, as well as many elegant buildings. Can Tho was also an important US base. Paul Theroux in *The Great Railway Bazaar* wrote: "Can Tho was once the home of thousands of GIs. With the brothels and bars closed, it had the abandoned look of an unused fairground after a busy summer. In a matter of time, very few years, there will be little evidence that the Americans were ever there. There are poisoned rice fields between the straggling fingers of the Mekong Delta and there are hundreds of blond and fuzzy-haired children, but in a generation even these unusual features will change."

Ins and outs
Getting there Virtually all visitors arrive by road. With the My Thuan Bridge (near Vinh Long) and the new bridge linking Vinh Long and Can Tho, journey times have fallen.▶▶ *See Transport, page 379.*

Getting around Quite a lot of Can Tho can be explored on foot. *Xe lôi* the Mekong cyclo is no longer able to trade between 0600-1800 due to traffic problems but a motorbike taxi can be picked up. Some of the sites, the floating markets for instance, are best visited by boat. There are also river taxis and an efficient public bus service.

Best time to visit As in all the other Mekong cities the best time is from December to April when the temperatures are warm and there is no rain. May to November is the monsoon season and as such it is prone to flooding (although it does fare better than other cities).

Background Can Tho has its own university, founded in 1966 and also a famous rice research institute, located at O Mon, 25 km away on Highway 91. Like the **International Rice Research Institute (IRRI)**, its more famous counterpart at Los Baños in the Philippines (and to which it is attached), one of the Can Tho institute's key functions is developing rice hybrids that will flourish in the varied conditions of the delta. Near the coast, rice has to be tolerant of salt and tidal flooding. In Dong Thap Province, near Cambodia, floating rice grows stalks of 4-5 m in order to keep its head above the annual flood. The task of the agronomists is to produce varieties which flourish in these diverse environments and at the same time produce decent yields.

Sights

Hai Ba Trung Street, alongside the river, is the heart of the town; at dusk families stroll in the park here in their Sunday best. Opposite the park is **Chua Ong Pagoda** ① *34 Hai Ba Trung St*, dating from 1894 and built by Chinese from Guangzhou. Unusually for a Chinese temple it is not free-standing but part of a terrace of buildings. The right-hand side of the pagoda is dedicated to the Goddess of Fortune, while the left-hand side belongs to General Ma Tien, who, to judge from his unsmiling statue, is fierce and warlike and not to be trifled with. The layout is a combination of typical pagoda – with a small open courtyard for the incense smoke to escape – and typical meeting house, complete with its language school, of the overseas Chinese in Southeast Asia.

The bustling market that used to operate on Hai Ba Trung Street along the bank of the river, and gave the town a bit of character, has been moved 1 km downriver. A new riverside promenade has been created. There's also a new crafts market building with a riverside restaurant, see Eating, page 377.

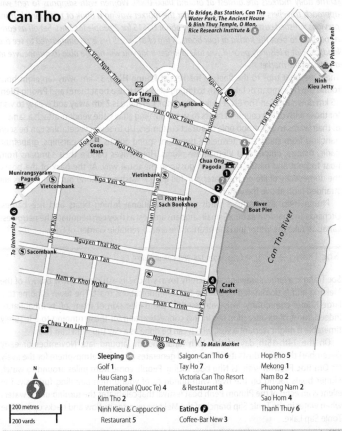

Can Tho

To Bridge, Bus Station, Can Tho Water Park, The Ancient House & Binh Thuy Temple, O Mon, Rice Research Institute & ⑧

To Phnom Penh

Ninh Kieu Jetty

Xo Viet Nghe Tinh

Ngo Gia Tu

Hai Ba Trung

Bao Tang Can Tho

Agribank

Tran Quoc Toan

Ly Thuong Kiet

Hoa Binh

Coop Mast

Ngo Quyen

Thu Khoa Huan

Munirangsyaram Pagoda

Vietcombank

Ngo Van So

Vietinbank

Phan Dinh Phung

Phat Hanh Sach Bookshop

Chua Ong Pagoda

River Boat Pier

Dong Khoi

Nguyen Thai Hoc

Vo Van Tan

Can Tho River

Sacombank

Nam Ky Khoi Nghia

Phan B Chau

Craft Market

Phan C Trinh

Hai Ba Trung

Chau Van Liem

Ngo Duc Ke

To Main Market

To University & ⑥

N

200 metres
200 yards

Sleeping 🛏
Golf 1
Hau Giang 3
International (Quoc Te) 4
Kim Tho 2
Ninh Kieu & Cappuccino Restaurant 5

Saigon-Can Tho 6
Tay Ho 7
Victoria Can Tho Resort & Restaurant 8

Eating 🍴
Coffee-Bar New 3

Hop Pho 5
Mekong 1
Nam Bo 2
Phuong Nam 2
Sao Hom 4
Thanh Thuy 6

The **Munirang-syaram Pagoda** ⓘ *36 Hoa Binh Blvd (southwest of post office)*, was built just after the Vietnam War and is a Khmer Hinayana Buddhist sanctuary. **Bao Tang Can Tho** ⓘ *Hoa Binh St, Tue-Thu 0800-1100, 1400-1700, Sat-Sun 0800-1100, 1830-2100*, in an impressive building, is the local history museum.

The **Can Tho Water Park (Cong Vien Nuoc Can Tho)** ⓘ *near the Hotel Victoria Can Tho at Tran Van Kheu, T710-376 3343, Mon-Fri 0845-1800, Sat-Sun 0740-1900, 40,000d*, provides liquid fun on slides and in pools.

Binh Thuy Temple, 7 km north along the road to Long Xuyen, dates from the mid-19th century; festivals are held here in the middle of the fourth and 12th lunar months. Nearby, 500 m down Bui Huu Nghia Road, opposite Binh Thuy temple, visit **Nha Co Binh Thuy** aka the **ancient house** ⓘ *10,000d to go inside the house; ask the owners*, (also known as Vuon Lan if you get a moto to take you there), which was used as a setting in the film *The Lover*.

Floating markets

ⓘ *The daily markets are busiest at around 0600-0900. Women with sampans to rent will approach travellers in Hai Ba Trung St near the market waving a book of testimonials from previous satisfied customers. Expect to pay about US$15 for 2 people for 3 hrs. Set off as early as possible to beat the flotilla of tour boats. A trip of at least 5 hrs is recommended to see the landscape at a leisurely pace. If you take a larger boat you will not be able to manoeuvre in and out of the market.*

There are boat trips to the floating markets at **Phung Hiep**, 33 km away (an eight-hour round trip by sampan or take a bus to Phung Hiep and rent a boat there) and **Phong Dien**, 15 km down the Can Tho River (a five-hour trip). **Cai Rang** is 7 km away and is easy to visit for those with only a couple of hours to spare. Bustling affairs, the vendors attach a sample of their wares to a bamboo pole to attract customers. Up to seven vegetables can be seen dangling from staffs – wintermelon, pumpkin, spring onions, giant parsnips, grapefruit, garlic, mango, onions and Vietnamese plums. Housewives paddle their sampans from boat to boat and barter, haggle and gossip in the usual way. At the back of the boats, the domesticity of life on the water is in full glare – washing is hung out and motors are stranded high above the water.

Phung Hiep also features yards making traditional fishing boats and rice barges. Orchards and gardens abound, small sampans are best as they can negotiate the narrowest canals to take the visitor into the heart of the area, a veritable Garden of Eden.

Soc Trang → *For listings, see pages 375-380. Colour map 4, C3.*

Soc Trang is a large, sprawling and scruffy town which sits astride a narrow branch of the Mekong and is dominated by a huge telecommunications mast. The town is home to a large Khmer community, as is witnessed by the darker skin of many of its inhabitants. Indeed, most of its attraction lies in this connection and for those running to a leisurely timetable it might warrant a visit, which can be done as a day trip from Can Tho.

On the 14th-15th day of the 10th lunar month (around late November or early December) the town dusts itself down and generates a carnival atmosphere for the lively **Oc Om Boc Festival** with its Nho boat racing. People come from miles around to watch Khmer boats racing on the river, with hundreds of young men paddling furiously. The event is an echo of the Phnom Penh boat festival that celebrates the turning of the waters when water in the Tonlé Sap branch of the Mekong reverses its flow and backs up into the Tonlé Sap Lake.

Ins and outs

Getting there The most direct route is to head to Can Tho and then follow the signs along Highway 1A. ▶▶ *See Transport, page 379.*

Best time to visit December to April is the best time to visit but if possible try and plan your trip to coincide with the festival.

Tourist information Soc Trang Tourist ⓘ *131 Nguyen Chi Thanh St, T79-382 2292, www.soctrangtourism.com.*

History

Soc Trang, along with its neighbours of Tra Vinh and Bac Lieu is home to many Khmer and Chinese. Soc Trang and Bac Lieu have the largest concentrations of Khmer in Vietnam. The city was founded in the late 1700s. Many of the stunning temples date from the early 1800s.

Sights

At the top end of town on Nguyen Thi Minh Khai Street is the **Kleang Pagoda**, a temple built in traditional Cambodian style, perched on a two-level terrace. Vivid colours adorn the windows and doors while inside sits a fine golden Sakyamuni statue. Opposite the pagoda is the **Khmer Museum** ⓘ *Mon-Sat 0730-1100, 1330-1700, free,* in which musical instruments, traditional clothing and agricultural tools form the rather uninspired display.

About 3 km out of town (follow Le Hong Phong Street and fork right after the fire station) is the **Matoc Pagoda** or **Chua Doi** (or Maha Tup as it is properly called in Khmer). The main pagoda is on the right and is decorated with superb, brightly coloured murals; it has been restored with donations from the Vietnamese and Khmer diaspora. Buddhists have worshipped on this holy site for over 400 years, but the pagoda's current incarnation is relatively modern. The chief attraction of the place, megachirop- teraphobes excepted, is the fruit bat. Thousands of these enormous mammals roost in the trees behind the pagoda and at dusk are an impressive sight as they fly off en masse to find food, literally blackening the sky. Also behind the pagoda are the monks' living quarters and the tombs of some five-toed pigs, which have special significance for this community. Look carefully at the picture on the grave!

Bac Lieu → *For listings, see pages 375-380. Colour map 4, C2.*

Bac Lieu is a small and pretty riverside city and the provincial capital of Bac Lieu Province. It is not as rich in rice production as other Mekong provinces on account of its proximity to the sea, so the enterprizing locals have salt farms instead. They also make a living out of oysters and fishing. New hotels and buildings are being erected and they are trying to capture some of the lucrative Tra Vinh market (there are many Khmer living here and several temples). Bac Lieu has a bird sanctuary that has large numbers of white herons.

Ins and outs

Getting there It is 56 km from Soc Trang, 113 km from Can Tho, 287 km from Ho Chi Minh City and 67 km from Ca Mau. The roads have improved but it is a long drive. ▶▶ *See Transport, page 379.*

Tourist information **Bac Lieu Tourist Company** ⓘ *2 Hoang Van Thu St, T781-382 4272, www.baclieutourist.com*, has a reasonable selection of quite moderately priced tours and is eager to help but only basic English is spoken. The office is closed Saturday afternoons and Sundays.

History

The earliest inhabitants were part of the Funan Empire (see Oc-Eo, page 386). There is a Cham Stupa dating from AD 892 in Vinh Hung. It is somewhat overgrown with vegetation but if you are in the neighbourhood it is quite interesting. Life has always been hard in the province due to saltwater intrusion.

Sights

The **bird sanctuary**, 3 km southwest of town, is home to a large white heron population. The best times to visit are December and January. The birds nest in January and then migrate and do not return until late May. Do apply plenty of mosquito repellent as the place is inundated with biting insects.

Xiem Can Temple (Komphir Sakor Prekchru) ⓘ *12 km west of Bac Lieu, free to enter but alms would be appreciated*, is a pretty Khmer temple complex. It was built in 1887 and a small group of monks still resides here.

Hoi Binh Moi Temple (Resay Vongsaphuth lethmay) is one of the newer temples as it was constructed in 1952. A recent addition (1990) is the ossuary tower. There is a small monastic school attached to the temple.

Ca Mau → *For listings, see pages 375-380. Colour map 4, C2.*

Ca Mau is the provincial capital of Ca Mau Province, Vietnam's most southerly province and is a huge, ugly, cluttered urban sprawl. The province consists primarily of the U Minh cajeput forest and swamp, both of which are the largest in Vietnam. Right at the tip of the country is the new Mui Ca Mau National Park. Apart from a reasonable selection of churches and pagodas Ca Mau's main interest is for botanists and ornithologists.

Ins and outs

Getting there and around There are seasonal direct flights from Ho Chi Minh City, bus connections and a boat from Rach Gia. The city has plenty of taxis and river taxis and a public bus service. ▸▸ *See Transport, page 379.*

Best time to visit This is somewhat complex as in the dry season U Minh Forest is liable to forest fires and the whole area is very dry. In the monsoon season flooding occurs on a regular basis. December to February should be the best months to visit.

Tourist information Minh Hai Tourist ⓘ *91 Phan Dinh Phung St, T780-383 1828, www.dulichminhai.com, Mon-Fri 0730-1100, 1330-1700, Sat 0730-1100*, is a well-run and professional travel agency offering the full spectrum of services. Very little English is spoken.

History

The first attempt at cultivation was in the 17th century. It has been on and off ever since. The main problems facing those trying to cultivate the area is the presence of the saline swamp and mangrove forest. Fishing is still the mainstay of the local economy. The

U Minh Forest was a favoured hiding place for the Viet Cong troops during the war. A large quantity of chemical defoliant was dropped to destroy the forest. Eucalyptus trees were planted as they proved resilient to Agent Orange and other defoliants.

Sights

A **Cao Dai Temple** is located on Phan Ngoc Hien street. Although not as large as the main one in Tay Ninh it is still an impressive structure. It houses quite a few monks and is thriving. The monks will be happy to explain Cao Daism.

The **U Minh Forest** is the main reason most people visit Ca Mau. The U Minh Forest was a favoured hiding place for the Viet Cong troops during the war. Despite the chemical damage and the huge postwar deforestation to make way for shrimp farms there are still trees and large numbers of birds to be seen and it is a favourite destination for ornithologists. It is also of interest to botanists. **Minh Hai Tourist** operates an all-day tour of the forest and mangrove swamps for US$52 per person including tour guide, car and ticket. Note that tours may be off limits from May to October due to forest fires.

The **Mui Ca Mau National Park**, at the southern edge of the country, has been named a UNESCO World Biosphere Reserve. The 41,862-ha park of mangrove and mudflats is home to hundreds of animals and birds. Some of the birds include the Far Eastern curlew, Chinese egret, and black-headed ibis. **Minh Hai Tourist** arranges tours for US$73 for two including tour guide, speedboat and ticket.

◉ Can Tho and around listings

For Sleeping and Eating price codes and other relevant information, see Essentials pages 26-31.

◉ Sleeping

Can Tho *p370, map p371*

LL Victoria Can Tho Resort, Cai Khe ward, T710-381 0111, www.victoriahotels.asia. A 92-room riverside hotel set in lovely, well-tended garden on its own little peninsula. It is Victoria Hotel 'French colonial' style at its best with a breezy open reception area and emphasis on comfort and plenty of genuine period features. It has a pool, spa pavilion, tennis court and restaurant. The staff are multilingual and helpful. The a/c rooms are well decorated and have satellite TV, Wi-Fi, en suite facilities, decent-sized bathtub, well-stocked minibar and electronic safe in the room. Even if you decide to stay in a more centrally and somewhat cheaper hotel then a visit to the grounds and one of the restaurants would be a pleasant experience. The hotel offers a complimentary boat shuttle to the town centre.

L-AL Golf Hotel, 2 Hai Ba Trung St, T710-381 2210, www.vinagolf.vn. No longer the tallest hotel in town with its 10 floors. The services and facilities are on a par with the better hotels in HCMC and Hanoi but it always seems empty. The staff are friendly. The rooms are well equipped with all mod cons en suite. The restaurants provide fine dining and the views from the **Windy Sky Bar** (8th floor) are superb. The swimming 'fool' on site is a draw. ATM on site.

A-C Kim Tho, 14 Ngo Gia Tu St, T710-322 2228, www.kimtho.com. The closest thing to boutique hotel in the delta with low-slung beds and white linens. Don't bother paying extra for a room with a views. Choose a standard with a bathtub. The standout attraction is the roof-top café with fabulous views. Includes breakfast.

A-C Ninh Kieu, 2 Hai Ba Trung St, T710-382 1171, www.ninhkieuhotel.vn. Lovely position on the river and a popular venue, in the wedding season for Can Tho's classier wedding receptions. Parts of the hotel have undergone renovation; there are now 97 rooms, 3 floating restaurants, a bar, tennis courts and sauna. The rooms have a/c and en suite facilities and those in the older, unrenovated building are cheaper (buildings A1 and A2). Rooms in A3 are large and comfortable. The staff are friendly.

B-C Saigon-Can Tho, 55 Phan Dinh Phung St, T710-382 5831, www.saigoncantho.com. vn. A/c, comfortable, central business hotel in the competent hands of **Saigontourist**. The staff are friendly and helpful. The rooms are well equipped with a/c, satellite TV, en suite facilities and minibar. There's a currency exchange, free internet and Wi-Fi for guests, sauna and breakfast included.

C-D International (Quoc Te), 12 Hai Ba Trung St, T710-382 2079, http:// canthotourist.vn. This hotel, heavy in appearance, overlooks the river with a good if rather soulless restaurant. The a/c rooms are somewhat drab and a coat of paint would not go amiss on the outside. But, that being said, the rooms are large and reasonably equipped with satellite TV and en suite facilities; bathrooms have tubsl. Breakfast and Wi-Fi included.

E-F Tay Ho, 42 Hai Ba Trung St, T710-382 3392, tay_ho@hotmail.com. This lovely place has a variety of rooms and a great public balcony that can be enjoyed by those paying for back rooms. All rooms now have private bathrooms. River view rooms, inevitably, cost more. The staff are friendly.

F Hau Giang, 27 Chau Van Liem St, T710-382 1950. 70 a/c rooms all with hot water, TV and fridge. Breakfast and Wi-Fi is included. Used by backpacker tour groups from HCMC, good value. No English spoken.

Soc Trang *p372*

E-G Khanh Hung, 15 Tran Hung Dao St, T79-382 1026. A/c and fan rooms, hot water, satellite TV, some very nice rooms, friendly; restaurant on the premises. Recommended. No English spoken.

F Phong Lan, 124 Dong Khoi St, T79-382 1619. A/c, hot water, some rooms have a balcony overlooking the river.

F-G Phong Lan 2, 133 Nguyen Chi Thanh St, T79-382 1757. Reasonable hotel, next to **Soc Trang Tourist**, offering comfortable rooms with Wi-Fi and TV. Restaurant also. Some English spoken.

Bac Lieu *p373*

D-E Bac Lieu Hotel, 4-6 Hoang Van Thu St, T781-382 2437, baclieuhotel@yahoo. com. A good little 3-star hotel. The location is central, near the river. The rooms are reasonably well equipped with a/c, satellite TV and en suite facilities. The staff are friendly and helpful. English is spoken. The restaurant has a reasonable selection on offer and is cheap.

D-E Cong Tu Bac Lieu, 13 Dien Bien Phu St, T781-395 3304. A stunning French colonial home that has undergone a sprucing up. Its ochre front with duck egg blue shutters looks out over the river. There's fanciful stucco work and beautiful tiling throughout. Linger in the café or the restaurant compound behind. ATM on site.

Ca Mau *p374*

C-F Quoc Te, 179 Phan Ngoc Hien St, T780-366 6666, www.hotelquocte.com. The pick of the bunch for the Ca Mau hotels. They have nice rooms to cater for all budgets. The staff are very friendly and helpful and speak good English. The facilities include Wi-Fi and a restaurant that closes at 2200 serving Western and Vietnamese food.

D-E Hoang Gia, 27-29 Tran Hung Dao St, ward 5, T780-381 9999. A clean, quiet and pleasant hotel.

F Ca Mau Hotel, 20 Phan Ngoc Hien St, T780-383 1165. All the rooms have a/c and are pleasantly equipped with en suite facilities. Good location, modern and the staff are friendly and helpful. The restaurant is open all day and is reasonable. Some English is spoken.

F Song Hung Hotel, 28 Phan Ngoc Hien St, T780-382 2822. Good location. Plesant modern rooms with en suite and a/c. Helpful staff but no English spoken.

F-G Quoc Nam, 23 Phan Boi Chau St, T780-382 7514. Charming little hotel with an excellent café on top offering great views of Ca Mau. Good value for money. Helpful staff but cars may have difficulty pulling up because of the narrow road by the river.

🍴 Eating

Can Tho *p370, map p371*

Hai Ba Trung St by the river offers a good range of excellent and very well-priced little restaurants, and the riverside setting is an attractive one.

🍴🍴-🍴🍴 **Victoria Can Tho Spices**, see Sleeping, above. Excellent location on the river bank where it's possible to dine alfresco or inside its elegant restaurant. The food is delicious and the service is excellent. Try the deep-fried elephant fish in Mekong style or the seared tuna with mint on a pomelo sauce or duck leg confit on a passion fruit sauce. The hot chocolate cake is a treat.

🍴🍴-🍴 **Sao Hom**, Nha Long Cho Co, T710-381 5616, http://saohom.transmekong.com. This new and very busy restaurant on the riverfront serves plentiful food and provides very good service. Watching the river life and the floating pleasure palaces at night is a good way to spend an evening meal here. Shame about the illuminated billboards on the opposite bank. This place is popular with large tour groups that alter the character of the restaurant when they swarm in.

🍴 **Coffee-Bar New**, 1 Ngo Quyen St. The latest youth hangout serving up coffee, food and loud music. The perfect people-watching spot opposite the old market area.

🍴 **Hop Pho**, 4-6 Ngo Gia Tu, T710-381 5208, Open from 0630. New kid on the block, Hop Pho is all grey and black lines under umbrellas amid water features. It's a stylish hangout with abundant Vietnamese food. Try the avocado and durian ice cream.

🍴 **Mekong**, 38 Hai Ba Trung St. Perfectly good little place near the river in this popular restaurant strip. Serves decent Vietnamese fare at reasonable prices.

🍴 **Nam Bo**, 50 Hai Ba Trung St, T710-382 3908. Excellent little place serving tasty Vietnamese and French dishes in an attractive French house on the corner of the street; try to get a table on the balcony. The set menu is 170,000d. Small café downstairs.

🍴 **Ninh Kieu**, 2 Hai Ba Trung St. Part of the hotel complex. On the river, good seafood and some Western dishes. Popular local venue for wedding parties.

🍴 **Phuong Nam**, 48 Hai Ba Trung St, T71-812077. Similar to the nextdoor **Nam Bo**, good food, less stylish, a popular travellers' haunt and reasonable prices.

🍴 **Thanh Thuy**, No 149, 30 Thang 4, T710-384 0207. A popular goat hotpot restaurant run by a French Canadian and his Vietnamese wife. Goat, in Vietnam, particularly stewed testicles or testicle rice wine, is popular with men who believe that a good helping will boost their sexual potency. Any mention of goat normally results in giggles.

Soc Trang *p372*

Soc Trang has no outstanding eateries, but several restaurants on **Hai Ba Trung St** do simple and cheap rice dishes. **Khanh Hung Hotel** offers a range of good food. **Phong Lan Hotel** has some Western dishes on a largely Vietnamese menu.

Bac Lieu *p373*

Bac Lieu hotel, see page 376, has reasonable restaurants for breakfast, lunch and dinner.

🍴 **Cong Tu Bac Lieu**. This compound is popular all day. Serves up Vietnamese food in the surrounds of a colonial mansion.

🍴 **Hai Ho**, 103/4 Highway 1A, Ward 7, T781-395 2026. Open for breakfast, lunch and dinner. A clean restaurant with a reasonable selection of Western and Vietnamese dishes. The service is friendly although staff don't understand any English.

Ca Mau *p374*

There are also plenty of very cheap restaurants close to the market on Ly Bon St.

¶ **Hu Tieu Nam Vang**, 2C Tran Hung Dao St, diagonally opposite **Hoang Gia** hotel. Cheap and friendly and serving hu tieu.

¶ **Sao Mai Cafe in the Sao Mai Hotel**, a few doors down from Trieu Phat. Serves *banh mi*, *bo* and *pho bo*.

¶ **Trieu Phat**, 26 Phan Ngoc Hien St. Serves *com* and *hu tieu*.

◑ Bars and clubs

Can Tho *p370, map p371*

The **Golf Can Tho Hotel** and **Victoria Can Tho Hotel** have well-stocked bars (see Sleeping, above). The latest draw for young locals is **Coffee-Bar New** in the centre of town. It's got karaoke too and stays open until 0100.

✹ Festivals and events

Soc Trang *p372*

For details of the **Oc Om Boc festival**, see page 372.

Bac Lieu *p373*

The main festival is the **Ngo boat racing** held at the same time as the Soc Trang Om Boc festival (see above and page 372) but it is overlooked in favour of the Soc Trang festival. If you wish to see the races in a more relaxed atmosphere then visit Bac Lieu.

◯ Shopping

Can Tho *p370, map p371*

Coop Mart, corner of Ngo Quyen and Hoa Binh Sts. Open 0800-2200 and stocked with hundreds of items. Useful for picnics.
Phat Hanh Sach, 29 Phan Dinh St. A bookshop which also sells local maps.

Soc Trang *p372*

Soc Trang is renowned for the beautiful, locally made gold statues; a bargain for the quality on offer.

▲ Activities and tours

Can Tho *p370, map p371*
Boat trips

Trans Mekong, 97/10 Ngo Quyen, P An Cu, T710-382 9540, www.transmekong. com. Operates the *Bassac*, a converted 24-m wooden rice barge that can sleep 12 passengers in 6 a/c cabins with private bathrooms. Prices include dinner and breakfast, entry tickets to visited sites, a French- or English-speaking guide on board and access to a small boat, *Bassac II*, catering for 24 guests. The **Victoria Can Tho** operates the *Lady Hau*, an upmarket converted rice barge for trips to the floating markets, US$50 per person (minimum 4 people). **Can Tho Tourist** operate trips.

Cookery classes

The **Victoria Can Tho** (see Sleeping, above) offers a Vietnamese cooking class in the hotel, in a rice field, at the 'Ancient House' or on its boat the *Lady Hau* with a trip to the local market from US$38 (minimum 2 people).

Swimming

The **Victoria Can Tho** (see Sleeping, above) has a pool open to the public for US$6.

Tennis

Tennis courts are available at the **Golf Hotel** and **Victoria Can Tho** (see Sleeping, above).

Therapies

The **Victoria Can Tho** boasts several massage cabins on the riverfront offering a host of treatments. Open to non-guests.

Tour operators

Can Tho Tourist, 20 Hai Ba Trung St, T710-382 1852, http://canthotourist.vn. It's quite expensive and organizes tours in small boats and powerful boats – the latter not the best way to see the delta. The staff are helpful and knowledgeable. Tours include trips to Cai Rang, Phong Dien and Phung Hiep floating markets, to Soc Trang, city tours (328,000d), canal tours, bicycle tours, trekking tours, stork sanctuary tour and homestays that involve working with farmers in the fields. General boat tours also arranged. It charges US$60 for a 1 night tour for 2 including floating market and bike tour.

Victoria Can Tho, T710-381 0111, www. victoriahotels.asia. Expensive tours to see delta sights; city tour; floating markets and Soc Trang offered. The *Lady Hau* cruises to Cai Rang floating market (breakfast on board). Sunset cruises also possible.

Soc Trang *p372*
Tour operators
See Soc Trang Tourist, page 373.

Bac Lieu *p373*
Tour operators
See Bac Lieu Tourist Company, page 374.

Ca Mau *p374*
The main activities are botanical and bird-watching trips to U Minh Forest and the Mui Ca Mau National Park.

Tour operators
See Minh Hai Tourist, page 374.

☉ Transport

Can Tho *p370, map p371*
Air
Vietnam Airlines, 66 Chau Van Liem St. The airport is situated about 7 km from the city centre. Flights to **Hanoi**. A taxi from the airport is 40,000-50,000d.

Bicycle
Bikes can be hired for US$4 a day from **Can Tho Tourist**, see Tour operators, above.

Boat
A bridge has been built to Can Tho but ferries will still operate for direct routing as the bridge is 10 km from Can Tho. There are no public boats leaving Can Tho.

Bus
The bus station is about 2 km northwest of town along Nguyen Trai St, at the intersection with Hung Vuong St. *Xe-ôm* is 10,000d into town. Hourly connections to **HCMC**'s Mien Tay terminal, 4-5 hrs, 80,000d (**Phuong Trang** bus company, T710-376 9768, provides a good service), and other towns in the Mekong Delta: **Rach Gia**, 0400-1800, 5 hrs, 60,000d; **Chau Doc**, 8 daily, 4 hrs, 55,000d; **Long Xuyen**, 6 daily, 33,000d; **My Tho**, hourly, 55,000d; **Vinh Long**, hourly, 55,000d; **Ca Mau**, hourly, 65,000d; **Soc Trang**, 35,000d. Can Tho Tourist, see Tour operators above, will book a ticket for you for 10,000d and includes transfer from your hotel to the bus station.

Cars
Cars with drivers can be hired from larger hotels.

Taxi
Mai Linh Taxi, T710-382 8282.

Soc Trang *p372*
Bus
Buses to **Ca Mau**, **Can Tho**, **Rach Gia** and **HCMC**.

Motorbike
Soc Trang is normally reached on Highway 1 from **Can Tho** but it's possible to get here from **Tra Vinh** by a single ferry crossing (there are several per hr) but note it's not a car ferry.

Bac Lieu *p373*
Bus
Buses go to **Soc Trang**, **Can Tho**, **HCMC**, **Ca Mau** and **Long Xuyen** from the station on Hai Ba Trung St

Ca Mau *p374*
Air
The airport is located at 93 Ly Thuong Kiet St heading out of town. Flights to **HCMC**.

Boat
It is possible to take a daily ferry (3 times a day) from Ca Mau to **Rach Gia**, from Ferry

Pier B (located off Cao Thang St near the floating market), 100,000d.

Travelling by road up to Rach Gia, there is a river crossing, the Tac Cau Ferry (20,000d, moto 10,000d) after which there is a brand new road up to Rach Gia.

Bus

Ca Mau is almost at the end of Highway 1A. Bac Lieu, Soc Trang and onwards connection to Can Tho are along Highway 1A. Rach Gia is reached by Highway 63. Good bus connections to **Can Tho**, **Bac Lieu**, **Soc Trang** and **Rach Gia**. The bus service to **HCMC** takes 11 hrs by regular bus and 8 hrs by express, daily 0530-1030.

❶ Directory

Can Tho *p370, map p371*
Banks These are all the way along Phan Dinh Phung St. BIDV, 29-31 Chau Van Liem St. Visa and MasterCard ATM. Vietinbank, 9 Phan Dinh Phung St, at the corner with Ngo Quyen. Changes TCs, Visa ATM. Agriank, 3 Phan Dinh Phung St. Sacombank, 99 Vo Van Tan St. Visa and MasterCard ATM. Vietcombank, 7 Hoa Binh Blvd, T710-

382 0445. Bureau de change service.
Hospitals 4 Chau Van Liem St, T710-382 0071. **Internet** Pizza_CT, 9 Chau Van Liem St. Alternatively, the big hotels (see Sleeping, above) have email facilities. **Post office** 2 Hoa Binh Blvd, T710-382 7280.

Soc Trang *p372*
Banks Vietcombank, 27 Hai Ba Trung St.
Hospitals 15 Pasteur St, T79-382 5201.
Internet Available in the post office. 0700-2000. **Post office** 2 Tran Hung Dao St.

Bac Lieu *p373*
Banks BIDV, Lo 42-44, Hoa Binh Blvd, Ward 3. **Hospitals** 128 Nguyen Hue St, Ward 3, T781-382 2297. **Internet** At the post office. **Post office** Tran Phu St, Ward 3.

Ca Mau *p374*
Banks Incombank, Hung Vuong St, opposite the main post office. Bureau de change, credit card cash advances.
Hospitals Ca Mau Hospital, Phan Anh Dao St, Khom 1, T780-383 1015. **Internet** The main post office is the best place. **Post office** 3 Luu Tan Tai St, Ward 5.

Chau Doc and around

→ *Colour map 4, B2.*
Chau Doc was once an attractive bustling riverside town (formerly called Chau Phu) in An Giang Province on the west bank of the Hau or Bassac River and bordering Cambodia. It is still a bustling market town but no longer so appealing. The town is an important trading and marketing centre for the surrounding agricultural communities. One of its biggest attractions is the nearby Nui Sam (Sam Mountain), which is dotted with pagodas and tombs and from whose summit superb views of the plains below can be enjoyed. Around Chau Doc are the towns of Rach Gia, Ha Tien and, capital of the province, Long Xuyen. ►► *For listings, see pages 389-395.*

Ins and outs

Getting there Chau Doc is an increasingly important border crossing into Cambodia. There are connections by boat with Phnom Penh as well as by road. It is also possible (but expensive) to get to Chau Doc by boat from Can Tho (private charter only or by the Victoria Hotel group boat for guests only). Road connections with Can Tho, Vinh Long and Ho Chi Minh City are good. ►► *See Transport, page 393.*

Getting around Chau Doc itself is easily small enough to explore on foot. By means of a bridge or sampan crossing, some nearby Cham villages can be reached and explored on foot too. Nui Sam, the nearby sacred mountain, can be reached by motorbike or bus.

Best time to visit Chau Doc suffers not only from the universal Mekong problem of the monsoon floods, but also from the fact that Nui Sam is one of the holiest sites in southern Vietnam and, as such, attracts vast numbers of pilgrims on auspicious days. From a climatic viewpoint then the best time to visit is December to April.

Tourist information Tour operators in town are a good source of information.➺ *See Tour operators page 392.*

History
Until the mid-18th century Chau Doc was part of Cambodia: it was given to the Nguyen lord, Nguyen Phuc Khoat, after he had helped to put down a local insurrection. The area still supports a large Khmer population, as well as the largest Cham settlement in the Delta. Cambodia's influence can be seen in the tendency for women to wear the *kramar*, Cambodia's famous chequered scarf, instead of the *non lá* conical hat, and in the people's darker skin, indicating Khmer blood. Chau Doc district (it was a separate province for a while) is the seat of the **Hoa Hao religion**, which claims about one to 1.5 million adherents and was founded in the village of Hoa Hao in 1939.

Chau Doc → *For listings, see pages 389-395. Colour map 4, B2.*

A large market sprawls from the riverfront down and along Le Cong Thanh Doc, Phu Thu, Bach Dang and Chi Lang streets. It sells fresh produce and black-market goods smuggled across from Cambodia. Near the market and the river, at the intersection of Tran Hung Dao Street and Nguyen Van Thoai Street, is the **Chau Phu Pagoda**. Built in 1926, it is dedicated to Thai Ngoc Hau, a former local mandarin. The pagoda is rather dilapidated, but has some fine carved pillars, which miraculously are still standing. A **Cao Dai temple**, which welcomes visitors, stands on Louise Street.

The **Vinh Te Canal**, north of town, is 90 km long and is a considerable feat of engineering, begun in 1819 and finished in 1824 using 80,000 workers. Its purpose was twofold: navigation and defence from the Cambodians. So impressed was Emperor Minh Mang in the achievement of its builder, Nguyen Van Thoai (or Thoai Ngoc Hau), that he named the canal after Thoai's wife, Chau Thi Vinh Te.

Around Chau Doc → *For listings, see pages 389-395.*

Easily visited from Chau Doc is the holy mountain, Nui Sam, covered in pagodas. Across the river you can boat over to Cham villages and see the floating fish farms. South of Chau Doc the road passes the sorrowful Ba Chuc ossuary. There are also three international border crossings to Cambodia, two to the southwest and one to the north of Chau Doc.

Nui Sam (Sam Mountain)
ⓘ *Take a bus (there is a stop at the foot of the mountain) or xe lôi.*
Nui Sam lies about 5 km southwest of town and is one reason to visit Chau Doc. This mountain was designated a 'Famed Beauty Spot' in 1980 by the Ministry of Culture. It

is one of the holiest sites in southern Vietnam. Rising from the flood plain, Nui Sam is a favourite spot for Vietnamese tourists who throng here, especially at festival time.

The mountain, really a barren, rock-strewn hill, can be seen at the end of the continuation of Nguyen Van Thoai Street. It is literally honeycombed with tombs, sanctuaries and temples. Most visitors come only to see Tay An Pagoda, Lady Xu Temple, and the tomb of Thoai Ngoc Hau (see above). But it is possible to walk or drive right up the hill for good views of the surrounding countryside: from the summit it is easy to appreciate that this is some of the most fertile land in Vietnam. At the top is a military base formerly occupied by American soldiers and now by Vietnamese watching their Cambodian flank. Near the top the **Victoria Hotel** group has built a hotel used for conferences only.

The **Tay An Pagoda** is at the foot of the hill, facing the road. Built originally in 1847, it has been extended twice and now represents an eclectic mixture of styles – Chinese, Islamic, perhaps even Italian. The pagoda contains a bewildering display of more than 200 statues. A short distance on from the pagoda, to the right, past shops and stalls, is the **Chua Xu**. This temple was originally constructed in the late 19th century, and then rebuilt in 1972. It is rather a featureless building, though highly revered by the Vietnamese and honours the holy Lady Xu whose statue is enshrined in the new multi-roofed pagoda. The 23rd to the 25th of the fourth lunar month is the period when the holy Lady is commemorated, during which time, hundreds of Vietnamese flock to see her being washed and reclothed. Lady Xu is a major pilgrimage for traders and business from Ho Chi Minh City and the south, all hoping that sales will thereby soar and profits leap. On the other side of the road is the **tomb of Thoai Ngoc Hau** (1761-1829); an enormous head of the man graces the entranceway. Thoai is a local hero having played a role in the resistance against the French but more for his engineering feats in canal building and draining swamps. He is also known as Nguyen Van Thoai and this name is given to one of Chau Doc's streets. The real reason to come here is to watch the pilgrims and to climb the hill.

Chau Doc

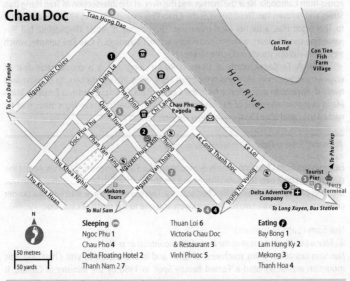

Sleeping
Ngoc Phu 1
Chau Phu 4
Delta Floating Hotel 2
Thanh Nam 2 7

Thuan Loi 6
Victoria Chau Doc
& Restaurant 3
Vinh Phuoc 5

Eating
Bay Bong 1
Lam Hung Ky 2
Mekong 3
Thanh Hoa 4

Hang Pagoda, a 200-year-old temple situated halfway up Nui Sam, is worth visiting for several reasons. In the first level of the temple are some vivid cartoon drawings of the tortures of hell. The second level is built at the mouth of a cave which last century was home to a woman named Thich Gieu Thien. Her likeness and tomb can be seen in the first pagoda. Fed up with her lazy and abusive husband she left her home in Cholon and came to live in this cave, as an ascetic supposedly waited on by two snakes.

Nui Sam is the most expensive burial site in southern Vietnam. Wealthy Vietnamese and Chinese believe it is a most propitious last resting place. This is why the lower flanks are given over almost entirely to tombs. Demand for burial plots has reached such levels that a new complex is being developed to help ease the demands on the land at Sam Mountain.

Cham villages

There are a number of Cham villages around Chau Doc. **Phu Hiep**, **Con Tien** and **Chau Giang** are on the opposite bank of the Hau River. There are several mosques in the villages as the Cham in this part of Vietnam are Muslim. At **Chau Phong** visitors can enjoy homestays. To reach the villages, take a sampan from the ferry terminal near the **Victoria Chau Doc Hotel**.

A visit to the **floating fish farm villages** (some 3000 floating houses), such as **Con Tien**, is a worthwhile and informative experience. A floating farm will have some 150,000 carp contained in a 6-m-deep iron cage beneath the house. Fish are worth around 600d for a baby and up to 25,000d for 500 g for a five-month-old fish. Catfish and mullet are also raised. (Chau Doc has a catfish monument on the riverfront promenade). When the fish are ready for sale, boats with nets under them are used to transport the fish to Long Xuyen.

Border crossings to Cambodia

It is possible to cross the border to Cambodia north of Chau Doc at the **Vinh Xuong** (Omsano in Cambodia) boat crossing; just south of Chau Doc at **Tinh Bien** near Nha Ban (Phnom Den, Takeo, on the Cambodian side), and at **Xà Xía**, near Ha Tien (Prek Chak in Cambodia). It is possible to exit at Vinh Xuong and get a Cambodian visa but it's not possible to get a Vietnamese visa to enter Vietnam. At Tinh Bien you can buy a Cambodian visa but not a Vietnamese visa on entering. (Xe ôm to Tinh Bien from Chau Doc, US$6; private transfer, US$40.) At Xà Xía, you can get a Cambodian visa for US$25 but not a Vietnamese visa. There is a Vietnam consulate in Sihanoukville.

Chau Doc to Ha Tien

Ha Tien can be reached either by boat or by road. The road is in a pitiful state but can be traversed by 4WD, Minsk or bicycle. Nevertheless, it is well worth attempting as it means the south coast can be reached without trailing back the 38 km to Long Xuyen. Also, the scenery as the road skirts the Cambodian border is beautiful and the local way of life little changed in hundreds of years. The road passes **Ba Chuc ossuary** where the bones of 1000 Vietnamese killed in 1978 by the Khmer Rouge are displayed in a glass-sided memorial. Skulls are also stacked up in a glass-sided memorial, and each section is categorized by gender and by age – from children to grandparents. Nearby, there is a house in a small row of shops where photographs of the massacre are displayed; they are grisly and abhorrent.

An alternative route to Ha Tien is to follow Highway 91 to Nha Ban town. Turn right and follow the signs to Tri Ton town (along the way you drive through the Plain of Reeds, pass Cam Mountain and also various Khmer temples that are beautiful and thankfully tourist free. Upon arrival in Tri Ton town (some of the shops have signs in Khmer script) turn right and head for the Vam Ray ferry. Once across the Ha Tien-Rach Gia canal you are on Highway 80. Turn left to Rach Gia and right to Ha Tien.

Long Xuyen → *For listings, see pages 389-395. Colour map 4, C3.*

Sprawling for miles along the west bank of the Bassac or Hau River is Long Xuyen, capital of An Giang Province. Driving along the dazzling new dual carriageways into town one anticipates something rather splendid but Long Xuyen disappoints for there is nothing of any interest at the end. It is rather surprising that such a large town can so spectacularly fail to produce anything of real note. The town is not mired in poverty but agreeably well off. In fact there is an attractive sense of civic pride and this is demonstrated in the 'cared for' feel of the place and in its new university which is notable for its well-regarded faculty of agriculture.

Rice fields predominate and small villages huddle under the shade of fruit trees. The architecture is traditional and modest in scale: houses retain their pitched tile roofs and incorporate plenty of wood. The region remains isolated, for the time being, from the demands of the 21st century, so life proceeds at the pace its people have been familiar with for a hundred years. The roads are narrow, traffic is light and for visitors with time to spare a tour by bicycle or on motorbike is easily the best way to see the area.

Ins and outs

Getting there and around The quickest way is direct from Ho Chi Minh City with one ferry crossing at Long Xuyen itself. There are plenty of taxis, an efficient local bus service and a plethora of *Honda ôm* drivers. ▶▶ *See Transport, page 393.*

Tourist information An Giang Tourimex ① *80 Tran Hung Dao St, T76-384 1036, http://www.angiangtourimex.com/aboutus.htm.*

History

Long Xuyen was once the main centre for the Hoa Hao religious sect. They believed in simplicity and as such built no structures. Up until 1956 they had their own militia and were, along with the Cao Dai sect, a major military force in the south. Long Xuyen has two main claims to fame. Firstly, nearby Ong Ho Island was the birthplace of Ton Duc Thang, who, when he worked in the Bason Shipyard in Saigon, agitated against the French. As a result he served a term on Con Dao Island. In 1946 he went to Hanoi and became friends with Ho Chi Minh. Upon the latter's death in 1969 Ton Duc Thang became president of North Vietnam and, in 1975, was the first president of united Vietnam.

Sights

The large **Roman Catholic Cathedral** ① *Hung Vuong St*, is visible from out of town; two clasped hands form the spire. It was completed shortly before reunification in 1975.

A short walk away is **Quan Thanh Pagoda** ① *8 Le Minh Nguyen St*, which contains lively murals on the entrance wall and the figure of General Quan Cong and his two mandarin companions General Chau Xuong and Mandarin Quan Binh at the altar. Also on Le Minh Nguyen Street, close to the intersection with Huynh Thi Huong Street, is the **Dinh Than My Phuoc Pagoda**. Note the roof and the murals on the wooden walls near the altar.

An Giang Museum ① *77 Thoai Ngoc Hau St, T76-384 1251, 0730-1030, 1400-1630*, is a pleasant enough museum. Primarily geared to the life and times of Ton Duc Thang it also houses relics from Oc-Eo but probably of more interest is a display showing the changing ways of life from the 1930s until the present day .

On the outskirts of town on Tran Hung Dao Street travelling towards Chau Doc (just after the second bridge, about 500 m), the **Cao Dai church** is worth visiting, especially if you are unable to see the Cao Dai temple at Tay Ninh.

Ong Ho Island is a pleasant trip up the Hau River for fans of Bac Ton (Uncle Ton). Boats leave from the riverfront.

Rach Gia → For listings, see pages 389-395. Colour map 4, B2.

Rach Gia has undergone somewhat of a transformation in recent years. It has gone from being a rather unpleasant little town to a thriving port with a new urban development on reclaimed land at Lan Bien on the coast south of the city. Already an entry point for goods, both smuggled and legal, from Thailand, the port has grown in significance as trade with neighbouring ASEAN countries has developed. The centre of the town is in fact an island at the mouth of the Cai Lon River. There are a number of pagodas to visit. The wharf area is interesting and the bustling fish market displays the wealth of the seas here. Some attractive colonial architecture survives.

Rach Gia is the capital of Kien Giang Province. The wealth of the province is based on rice, seafood and trade. *Nuoc mam*, the renowned Vietnamese fish sauce, is also produced here.

Ins and outs

Getting there There are daily flights from Ho Chi Minh City and Phu Quoc. In the peak season it is advisable to book well in advance as the flights tend to fill up fast. There are good road connections with Ha Tien, Long Xuyen, Can Tho. There are also boats to Phu Quoc. ▶ See Transport, page 394.

Tourist information **Kien Giang Travel Co** ① 5 Le Loi St, T77-386 7687, nguyendaihokg@ gmail.com, is the government tourist office and is helpful and friendly but little English is spoken. See also Tour operators for other sources of information.

History

As the straight blue lines on any good map will show, several highly impressive canals converge on Rach Gia. Nguyen Van Thoai, builder of the Chau Doc to Ha Tien canal, built the straight-as-an-arrow Long Xuyen to Rach Gia canal in 1822. Highway 80, along which most visitors drive to Rach Gia, runs alongside the canal. It was formerly named the Thoai canal in honour of its builder but maps today simply call it the Cai San canal. The O Mon canal was built by the French in 1896 and in 1955 the Rach Soi–Kien Luong canal was built to transport clinker from Kien Luong plant to the Thu Duc cement works on the outskirts of Saigon.

Sights

Rach Gia's pagodas include the **Phat Lon Pagoda**, which is on the mainland north of town just off Quang Trung Street, and the **Nguyen Trung Truc Temple**, which is not far away at 18 Nguyen Cong Tru Street, close to the port. The latter is dedicated to the 19th-century Vietnamese resistance leader of the same name. Nguyen Trung Truc was active in Cochin China during the 1860s, and led the raid that resulted in the attack on the French warship *Esperance*. As the French closed in, he retreated to the island of Phu Quoc. From here, the

French only managed to dislodge him after threatening to kill his mother. He gave himself up and was executed at the market place in Rach Gia on 27 October 1868. His statue also dominates the main small city park at the top of Le Loi street and the riverbank.

Tam Bao Temple dates from the 18th century but was rebuilt in 1917. During the First Indochina War it was used to conceal Viet Minh nationalists who published a newspaper from here. There is the small **Rach Gia Museum** ① *27 Nguyen Van Troi St, T77-386 3727, Mon-Fri 0700-1100, free,* which houses a good selection of pottery and artefacts from Oc-Eo in a lovely old building. It was undergoing repairs at the time of publication.

Oc-Eo

① *The site is near the village of Tan Hoi and is only accessible by boat. Hire a small boat (the approach canal is very shallow and narrow) from the river front beyond the Vinh Tan Van Market, northeast along Bach Dang St. The trip takes several hours. Entrance 60,000d*

Oc-Eo is an ancient city about 10 km inland from Rach Gia. It is of great interest and significance to archaeologists, but there is not a great deal for the visitor to see bar a pile of stones on which sits a small bamboo shrine. The site is overseen by an elderly custodian who lives adjacent to it. This port city of the ancient kingdom of Funan (see page 386) was at its height between the first and sixth centuries AD. Excavations have shown that buildings were constructed on piles and the city was interlinked by a complex network of irrigation and transport canals. Like many of the ancient empires of the region, Oc-Eo built its wealth on controlling trade between the East (China) and the West (India and the Mediterranean). Vessels from Malaya, Indonesia and Persia docked here. No sculpture has yet been found, but a gold medallion with the profile of the Roman emperor Antonius Pius (AD 152) has been unearthed

Ha Tien → *For listings, see pages 389-395. Colour map 4, B1.*

Ha Tien used to be a quaint small town with a tranquil pace of life and an attractive US-built pontoon bridge that carried bikers and pedestrians across to the opposite bank of the river. It has quite rapidly become a sprawling urban mess with ugly hotels cluttering the riverbank and construction running rampant with no regard to aesthetic. The boom has no doubt been helped by the opening of the border with Cambodia at Xà Xía. Step back off the main thoroughfare and you will find vestiges of the quaint appeal that once made this city worth visiting. After the drive from either Chau Doc or Rach Gia a drink on the stilted café is a relaxing way to pass the afternoon.

Ins and outs

Getting there Ha Tien can be reached by road from Chau Doc, Rach Gia and also by ferry from Phu Quoc Island. The first 20 km before Ha Tien on Highway 80 and the first 10 km out of Rach Gia are interesting. The rest of the journey is monotonous. It can also be reached by crossing the border from Cambodia at Xà Xía. See border crossings with Cambodia, page 383. In the town itself there are one or two taxis and plenty of *Honda ôm* drivers. ▶▶ *See Transport, page 394.*

Tourist information Ha Tien Tourism Coop Ltd ① *1 Phuong Thanh St, T77-395 9598, hatientourism@gmail.com.* Run by the helpful Marie, this new private tourism service is a great boon for tourists, especially those coming in from Cambodia. Boat and bus tickets and free internet for guests. There's also food.

History

Ha Tien's history is strongly coloured by its proximity to Cambodia, to which the area belonged until the 18th century. The numerical and agricultural superiority of the Vietnamese allowed them to gradually displace the Khmer occupants and eventually military might, under Mac Cuu, prevailed. But it is not an argument the Khmer are prepared to walk away from, as their incursions into the area in the late 1970s showed, and bitter resentments remain on both sides of the border. Unfortunately, the floating pontoon built by US army engineers was dismantled a few years ago.

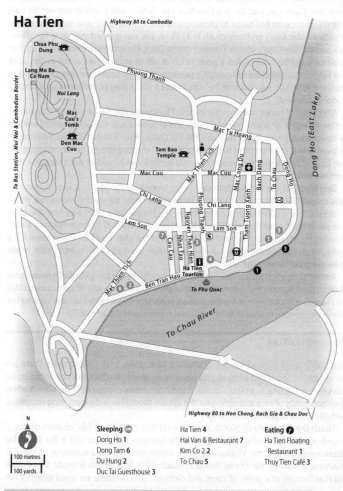

Ha Tien

Highway 80 to Cambodia

To Bus Station, Mui Nai & Cambodian Border

Chua Phu Dung

Lang Mo Ba Co Nam

Nui Lang

Mac Cuu's Tomb

Den Mac Cuu

Phuong Thanh

Mac Tu Hoang

Tam Bao Temple

Mac Thien Tich

Mac Cuu

Mac Cuu

Mac Cong Du

Bach Dang

To Chau

Chi Lang

Chi Lang

Phuong Thanh

Tham Tuong Xanh

Dong Ho (East Lake)

Lam Son

Lam Son

Nguyen Than Hien

Nhat Tao

Cau Cau

Mac Thien Tich

Ben Tran Hau

Ha Tien Tourism

To Phu Quoc

To Chau River

Highway 80 to Hon Chong, Rach Gia & Chau Doc

N

100 metres
100 yards

Sleeping
Dong Ho 1
Dong Tam 6
Du Hung 2
Duc Tai Guesthouse 3

Ha Tien 4
Hai Van & Restaurant 7
Kim Co 2
To Chau 5

Eating
Ha Tien Floating Restaurant 1
Thuy Tien Café 3

Sights

Despite its colourful history, modern Ha Tien does not contain a great deal of interest to the visitor and apart from a handful of buildings there is little of architectural merit.

There are a number of pagodas in town. The **Tam Bao Temple**, at 328 Phuong Thanh Street, was founded in the 18th century, as too was **Chua Phu Dung** (**Phu Dung Pagoda**) which can be found a short distance along a path to the northwest just off Phuong Thanh Street. A lengthy story is attached to this temple, the 'Cotton Rose Hibiscus Pagoda'. In 1730, newly widowed Nguyen Nghi fled invaders from Laos and landed in Ha Tien with his son and 10-year-old daughter, Phu Cu (the ancient form of Phu Dung with the same floral meaning). Nguyen Nghi was soon appointed Professor of Literature and Poetry to Duke Mac Cuu's son, Mac Tu (see Den Mac Cuu, below) and privately tutored his own little daughter, who had taken to dressing as a boy in order to be able to attend school. After Duke Mac Cuu's untimely death in 1735 his son was granted the name Mac Thien Tich and the title Great Admiral Commander-in-Chief, Plenipotentiary Minister of Ha Tien Province. Later he inaugurated a poetry club at which young Phu Cu, still in the guise of a boy, declaimed exquisitely, setting passions ablaze. Surreptitious investigations put the Great Admiral's mind at rest: 'he' was in fact a girl. A long poetic romance and royal wedding followed.

After years of happy marriage the angelic Phu Cu one day begged her husband to let her break with their poetic love of the past and become a nun. The Great Admiral realized he could not but comply. He built the Phu Cu, Cotton Rose Hibiscus Pagoda, wherein his beloved wife spent the rest of her life in prayer and contemplation. The towering pagoda was built so high that it served as a constant reminder and could, in due course, be seen from his own tomb.

Den Mac Cuu, the temple dedicated to the worship of the Mac Cuu and his clan, was built in 1898-1902. Mac Cuu was provincial governor under the waning Khmer rule and in 1708 established a Vietnamese protectorate. The temple lies a short way from the town and sits at the foot of Nui Lang (Tomb Mountain). To the left of the altar house is a map showing the location of the tombs of members of the clan. Mac Cuu's own tomb lies a short distance up the hill along a path leading from the right of the temple, from where there are good views of the sea.

Around the back of Nui Lang (a short drive, or longish trek) is **Lang Mo Ba Co Nam** (tomb of Great Aunt Number Five), an honorary title given to the three-year-old daughter of Mac Cuu who was buried alive. It has become an important shrine to Vietnamese seeking her divine intercession in time of family crisis and is more visited than Mac Cuu's tomb.

Around Ha Tien

Mui Nai ① *small entrance fee*, lies in a 'tourist park' about 5 km west of town. There are some nicely wooded hills and a muddy beach from where Phu Quoc Island and Cambodia can be seen. The beach gets very crowded and litter-strewn during public holidays. It offers the opportunity of rock scrambling for the nimble-footed but is disappointing compared with the sandy beach at Hon Chong.

Thach Dong Pagoda ① *5000d*, 3 km from Ha Tien, and a short hike up from the road, is dedicated to the goddess Quan Am; at the bottom of the mountain is **Bia Cam Thu** (Monument of Hate; the Vietnamese don't mince their words) a memorial to the 130 Vietnamese slain by the Khmer Rouge in March 1978. The temple is inside a limestone hill that consists of a series of caves and clefts in the rock. There are good views of the surrounding, remarkably flat, country. About 2 km beyond Thach Dong Pagoda is the **Cambodian border** at Xà Xía, see page 383.

Hon Chong is a popular and well known beach area about 30 km east of Ha Tien. Unlike Ha Tien, Hon Chong has miles of beach which can get dirty and littered although it is much nicer than Ha Tien but not a patch on Phu Quoc. The beach area is undeveloped apart from a string of cafés set back behind the casuarina trees with chairs and hammocks where you can sup a beer. Apart from the beach its main claim to fame is the **holy grotto** and the interesting limestone formations **Hon Phu Tu** (Father and Son rocks), which lie 100 m or so offshore. To get to Hon Chong by car, turn south off Highway 80 at Kien Luong, 18 km, or take a bus to Kien Luong, or *xe ôm* to Hon Chong (130,000d, 20 minutes); it's very dusty. Once in Hon Chong, boats are available to the grotto and to Ngo Island.

Follow the path through **Chua Hang** (Hang Pagoda) , to the beach. The temple with its Buddha of 100 hands loses much of its religious significance and atmosphere at holiday times (notably Tet) when noisy throngs of trippers file through on their way to the beach.

◎ Chau Doc and around listings

For Sleeping and Eating price codes and other relevant information, see Essentials pages 26-31.

◉ Sleeping

Chau Doc *p381, map p382*
LL-L Victoria Chau Doc, 32 Le Loi St, T76-386 5010, www.victoriahotels-asia.com. The old building was entirely renovated by this excellent French hotel group, to produce a lovely hotel right on the river. It is comfortable, equipped with a pool and all mod cons. Its outdoor terrace is the perfect place to drink and watch the hustle and bustle on the Mekong. The hotel group runs a speedboat to and from Phnom Penh.
C Chau Pho, Trung Nu Vuong St, Ward B, T76-356 4139, www.chauphohotel.com. This 38-room hotel is very comfortable and quiet but the occasional lack of hot water shouldn't happen at these prices; it's a 10-min walk from the town centre. Breakfast is included and has improved. Wi-Fi available.
E Delta Floating Hotel, 443 Le Loi St (Casu Lo Heo), Phu Hiep Ward, next to the Chau Doc Tourist Pier, T76-355 0838. These 10 rooms on the water are small and airless and overpriced but some have balconies and they feature mosquito nets. There's a café and restaurant on the adjacent floating boats and it would be a novel way to spend

the night in Chau Doc but note that river traffic starts very early on the Mekong.
E Thuan Loi, 18 Tran Hung Dao St, T76-386 6134, hotelthuanloi@hcm.vnn.vn. A/c and good river views, clean and friendly. The expanded and attractively designed restaurant enjoys a great location right on the river and is recommended especially in the late afternoon for coffee. This is a highly popular place; reserve in advance if possible.
E-F Ngoc Phu (formerly Chau Doc), 17 Doc Phu Thu St, T76-386 6484. The staff are friendly although very little English is spoken. The rooms (a/c or fan) are large, clean and equipped with basic facilities.
E-F Thanh Nam 2, 10 Quang Trung St, T76-321 2616, thanhnam2hotel@yahoo.com. Rooms are nicer here than the Vinh Phuoc if you can stand the bright green floor tiles. There are 10 rooms; those with a/c are slightly more expensive.
E-G Vinh Phuoc, 12-14 Quang Trung St, T76-356 3013, vinhphuochotel@yahoo.com. A/c rooms are slightly more expensive than fan rooms.

Nui Sam *p381*
Almost every café near Sam Mountain has a room for rent and you can get good value by shopping around and bargaining hard.

C-D Ben Da Sam Mountain Resort, Highway 91, T76-386 1745. This resort consists of 4 hotels, a restaurant and bar. The staff speak good English. If you want a little bit of luxury then this would be the place to stay. Sam Mountain is 5 mins' walk away.

Cham villages *p383*
F Cham Communities Based Tourism Village, T76-395 2541, sodulichangiang@ vnn.vn. Contact **Ang Giang Tourism** to have the opportunity to stay in Chau Phong, a Cham village close to Chau Doc.

Long Xuyen *p384*
C-D Dong Xuyen Hotel, 9A Luong Van Cu St, T76-384 1365, longxuyenhotel@hcm. vnn.vn. The rooms all come equipped with a/c, en suite facilities, minibar. The hotel itself has massage, steam bath and jacuzzi. The staff speak good English and are helpful.
D Long Xuyen, 19 Nguyen Van Cung St, T76-384 1927, longxuyenhotel@hcm.vnn.vn. A/c, hot water, restaurant. Cheaper than the **Dong Xuyen** hotel. The staff are friendly and the rooms are adequate.

Rach Gia *p385*
E Hong Nam, Lo B1, Ly Thai To St, T77-387 3090, opposite the market area and convenient for the bus station. Rooms are comfortable but make sure you ask for a room on the interior; the ones facing the street suffer a bit from noise.
E Kim Co, 141 Nguyen Hung Son St, T77-387 9610, www.kimcohotel.com. The pastel shades of this hotel are incongruous in the surrounding streets. Still, it's well located. Breakfast not included. Wi-Fi available.
E-F Hoang Gia 2, 32 Le Thanh Ton St, T77-392 0980, www.hoanggiahotels.com.vn. Located near the bus station with smartly decorated rooms.

Ha Tien *p386, map p387*
C-E Ha Tien Hotel, 36 Tran Hau St, T77-385 1563. In a convenient location close to the ferry station with a nice alfresco restaurant.

However, the 30 rooms are a little lacklustre despite it being a new hotel and are a tad overpriced; those with balconies cost more.
E Dong Tam, 83 Tran Hau St, T77-395 0555, www.dongtamhotel.com. A less professional outfit than the sister hotel the **Du Hung**. Staff refuse to serve Vietnamese coffee because they think you won't like it; bizarre.
E Du Hung, 27A Tran Hau St, T77-395 1555, www.dongtamhotel.com. A recommended hotel with spacious rooms and all facilities close to the ferry station.
E Kim Co 2, 21-23 Tran Hau St, T77-395 7957, www.kimcohotel.com. A good central option on the main strip.
E-G Hai Van, 55 Lam Son St, T77-385 2872. This new hotel with attached restaurant offers a comfortable rooms a few block backs from the hustle, bustle and building works on Tran Hau Street.
F Dong Ho, 2 Tran Hau St, T77-385 2141. This yellow-shuttered building is on the quiet and quaint riverside of Ha Tien. Rooms are brighter and a little smarter than at neighbouring **To Chau** although they are basic. Those with a balcony overlooking the river and pontoon bridge are a must. All the rooms have twin beds, en suite bathrooms. Some a/c is available.
F To Chau, 56 Dong Ho St, T77-385 2148. A small hotel on the riverfront with views that commend it. Rooms are very large but also very spartan. They all come equipped with a/c, TV, minibar and en suite facilities with hot water. Try and opt for a room with a view of the To Chau River as it'll have a balcony. The owner and his family are friendly but they only speak a little English.
G Duc Tai Guesthouse, 9 Phuong Thanh St, T77-385 2405. At the end of the street is the main market for Ha Tien. If you are an early riser then this hotel would suit you well. Rooms are en suite and basically furnished with a/c or fans.

Hon Chong *p389*
B-C Hon Trem Resort, T77-385 4331, www.kiengiangtourist.com.vn. Built in the most

fantastic location overlooking the bay at Hon Chong, it is rather under utilized. Rooms enjoy beautiful views that can be seen from the bed through the floor-to-ceiling windows. The massage centre is a little unloved but there's plans for a pool. Opt for a villa over the rooms in the ugly block at the foot of the hill on which the resort is perched. There's no beach to access here which is disappointing. Bikes can be rented.
D-E My Lan, opposite Duong Beach on the other side of the road, T77-375 9044, mylanhotel@vnn.vn. A secure, gated hotel with excellent-value large, clean rooms on the beach road. The rooms are in smart, new bungalows with TV, ceiling fan, a/c and shower units. The 24-hr restaurant does a good breakfast. The menu is not in English but some staff speak basic English.

D-E Green Hill Guest House, 905 Hon Chong, Binh An, T77-385 4369. A friendly, clean and comfortable white guesthouse perched on a hill with excellent views of the bay from the spacious top bedrooms.

🍴 Eating

Chau Doc *p381, map p382*

🍴🍴-🍴 **La Bassac**, in Victoria Chau Doc, see Sleeping, above. The extravagant French and Vietnamese menus at this riverside restaurant outstrip the decor which has the air of a conservatory. Ignoring this, tuck into delicious meals of duck, rack of lamb or prawns. You won't be disappointed.

🍴 **Bay Bong**, 22 Thung Dang Le St, T76-386 7271. Specializes in hot pots and soups and also offers a good choice of fresh fish. The staff are friendly.

🍴 **Lam Hung Ky**, 71 Chi Lang St. Excellent freshly prepared and cooked food. There's a wide range of food stalls in the market area.

🍴 **Mekong**, 41 Le Loi St, T76-386 7381, opposite **Victoria Chau Doc**, open for lunch and dinner. It is located in a lovingly restored French villa. Good selection of food and the staff are friendly.

🍴 **Thanh Hoa**, Trung Nu Vuong St. Choose from the dozens of shellfish aquariums and platters at this buzzing restaurant.

🍴 **Vinh Phuoc**, see Sleeping, above. 0630-2230. Pretty standard Western and Vietnamese food with good, friendly service.

Long Xuyen *p384*

All the hotels have restaurants.

🍴 **Long Xuyen**, corner of Nguyen Trai and Hai Ba Trung St. Good Chinese and Western food. Specializes in seafood.

Rach Gia *p385*

🍴 **Hai Au**, 2 Nguyen Trung Truc St, T77-386 3740. Good choice of food, well presented with decent-sized portions in a smart building with a lovely outdoor terraced area covered in creepers overlooking the river.

🍴 **Sen Hong Hoan Hi**, G20-21 Huynh Thuc Khang St, T77-325 4447, just around the corner from the bus station is a cosy and popular place, lit with fairy lights, to kick back with a coffee or fruit shake waiting for your departure.

🍴 **Valentine**, 37 Hung Vuong St. Comfortable restaurant offering up plenty of sautéed dishes as well as omelettes and shellfish and steamed fish dishes.

🍴 **Vinh Hong 2**, 194 Lam Quang Ky St, T77-387 7870. Preferred choice for the locals. Vietnamese fare only but well cooked, well presented and cheap.

Cafés

There is a good selection on **Nguyen Trung Truc**, **Nguyen Thai Hoc** and **Tran Hung Dao** Sts. **Cafe Yumi**, corner of Lac Hong and Pham Hung Sts, and **Cafe Ja**, corner of Le Van Huu and Bui Huy Bich Sts behind Citimart are 2 smart hangouts in the new district of Lan Bien on reclaimed land. These are the latest hangouts for young Vietnamese. At the centre of the coastal strip is the Lac Hong Park where you'll find stalls, cafés and the **Lagoon Seafood Center** as well as dozens of folk flying colourful kites.

Ha Tien p386, map p387

There are numerous food stalls along the river and Ben Tran Hau and Dong Ho streets. ¶¶–¶ **Hai Van**, 55 Lam Son St, T77-385 2872. This restaurant has moved from its popular riverside spot to be at the back end of a hotel of the same name and has smartened up its appearance. It serves up a reasonable selection of Chinese, Vietnamese and international cuisine.

¶ **Ha Tien Floating Restaurant**, T77-395 9939. Quite a nice surprise for Ha Tien with Australian beef on the menu. There's a huge menu of chicken, frog and eel as well as fish. Popular with local businesspeople.

Cafés

Thanh Nam, Tran Hau St. Great smoothies and is a good for people-watching.
Thuy Tien Café, Nguyen Van Hai St. This is the pick of the bunch. A small, stilted affair overlooking the river and the pontoon bridge. It's a wooden café from where you can sit and watch the world go by.

Hon Chong p389

Relax Bar. Traveller friendly shack on the beach offering food, drinks, information and transfer to Phu Quoc.

🟠 Bars and clubs

Chau Doc p381, map p382
Victoria Chau Doc, see Sleeping, above, has a bar and a pool table.

🟤 Festivals and events

Chau Doc p381, map p382
On all almost every weekend there is one festival or another. The busiest festivals are centred on Tet, 4 months after Tet and the mid-autumn **moon festival**.

Long Xuyen p384
20 Aug There are big celebrations on the birthday of Ton Duc Thang.

Rach Gia p385
Apart from the main festival they have occasional processions to thank Ca Ong, the God of the Sea, for protecting them.

🔺 Activities and tours

Chau Doc p381, map p382
Swimming
There is a swimming pool at the Victoria Chau Doc.

Therapies
A massage and fitness centre can be found at the **Victoria Chau Doc**. All the services are available to the general public.

Tour operators
Chau Doc Tourist Pier, next to the Victoria hotel, T76-355 0949, btdlcd@vnn.vn. Offers slow boat tours for US$10 per person or speedboat tours for US$50 per person in the area.
Delta Adventure Co, 55 Bis Le Loi St, T76-355 0838, www.kimtravel.com. Organizes speedboats to Phnom Penh and runs a floating hotel. You might even be able to book a local tour if you can find someone behind reception that speaks English.
Mekong Tours, Vinh Phuoc Hotel, and at 14 Nguyen Huu Canh St, T76-386 8222, and at the **Thanh Nam 2** hotel where they are particularly helpful, www.mekongtours.net. Local trips include the fish farms, floating markets and Cham village. Organizes delta trips, city tours, Mekong homestays,trips to Phu Quoc and boat trips to Phnom Penh (US$10, departs 0700, 8-10 hrs or express boat, US$25, departs 0800, 5 hrs; Cambodian visas can be bought at the border). A/c and public buses also booked; air ticketing; Open Bus ticketing (to Can Tho hourly, US$5, 3 hrs; to Ha Tien, US$7, 3 hrs; to HCMC hourly, US$9, 6 hrs); and visa applications. Onward bus transport to Can Tho and HCMC can include tour stops on the way (from US$16-37). You need to ask exactly what your payment includes and whether any

accommodation included is individual or shared. Private express boat transfer to My Tho, US$450; slow boat to Can Tho, 4½ hrs, US$180, 6 people maximum.

Victoria Chau Doc, 32 Le Loi St, T76-386 5010, www.victoriahotels-asia.com. Tours to Nui Sam, the city and a very interesting tour to the floating market, fish farms and Muslim village, cooking class, Tra Su forest tour, farming tour and Le Jarai cruise tour. Minimum 2 people for all tours.

Long Xuyen *p384*
Tour operators
See **An Giang Tourimex**, page 384.

Rach Gia *p385*
Tour operators
Kien Giang Travel Co, 5 Le Loi St, T77-386 7687. Mon-Fri 0700-1100, 1300-1500. Sat 0700-1100.
Kiengiang Tourist Public Company, 11 Ly Tu Trong St, T77-396 2024. Professional and helpful and a smarter outfit than the government-run **Kien Giang Travel**. More English spoken too. Offers tours to Ha Tien and Phu Quoc.

Ha Tien *p386, map p387*
Ha Tien Tourism Coop Ltd, 1 Phuong Thanh St, T77-395 9598, hatientourism@ gmail.com. Organizes boat tickets to Phu Quoc for US$9 and US$10. Open buses to HCMC, US$10 at 0900, 1130, 2200. Also to Can Tho, Chau Doc, Vinh Long, My Tho and Rach Gia. 3-day Mekong tours ending in HCMC offered from US$55. Organizes buses to Cambodia at 1200 and 1600: to Kep, US$12; to Kampot US$15; to Sihanoukville, US$20; to Phnom Penh at 1200 and 0600, US$18. Cambodian visa organized, US$25. These trips do not involve a change of bus. Vietnam visa extensions also organized.

Chau Doc *p381, map p382*
Bicycle and motorbike
Mekong Tours rents bikes for US$2 a day and motorbikes for US$10.

Boat
There are daily departures to **Phnom Penh**. A couple of tour operators in town organize boat tickets, see Tour operators, above. **Victoria Hotel** speedboats go to Phnom Penh. Boats for hotel guests depart for Phnom Penh at 0700, returning 1330, US$100.

Make sure you have a valid Vietnamese visa if you are entering the country as these cannot be issued at the border crossing; Cambodian visas can be bought at all the nearby crossings. For other Cambodian border crossings, see page 383.

Bus
The new station is 3 km south from the town centre T76-386 7171. No English is spoken at the ticket office. Minibuses stop in town on Quang Trung St. Connections with **HCMC** (6 hrs), hourly, 0600-2400, 75,000d; **Tra Vinh**, 62,000d; **Ca Mau**, 81,000d; **Long Xuyen** (1½ hrs), 18,000d; **Can Tho**, every 30 mins, 0400-1700, 44,000d; **Rach Gia**, 38,000d; and **Ha Tien** (from 0600, every 3 hrs, 4 hrs, US$5) and other destinations in the delta. A *xe-ôm* from town is 15,000-20,000d.

There is an uncomfortable 10-hr bus ride from Chau Doc to **Phnom Penh** via **Moc Bai**, see page 383.

Mekong Tours, see Tour operators, runs a bus to **Phnom Penh** via **Tinh Bien** (see border crossings to Cambodia, page 383) at 0815, 5 hrs, US$25 with no change of bus.

See also under Tour operators for domestic and international bus transport.

Long Xuyen *p384*
Bus
The station is 1.5 km east of town at 414 Tran Hung Dao St. Minibuses stop on Hung

Vuong St, not far from the cathedral. There are regular connections with **HCMC** (6-7 hrs), **Chau Doc** (1½ hrs), **Can Tho**, **Vinh Long** and other destinations in the delta. Some private minibus companies offer a faster and more comfortable service than the regular buses.

Car

The most direct route to Long Xuyen from **HCMC** is to cross the My Thuan Bridge near Vinh Long. Alternatively, it's a pleasant drive on Highway 91 from **Can Tho** via O Mon. It is also possible to get here from **Cao Lanh** by taking 2 small ferries. For those who know the way, this is possibly the quickest and certainly the most scenic route back to HCMC.

Rach Gia *p385*
Air

Daily connections with **Phu Quoc Island**, 40 mins, and **HCMC**, 50 mins. The airport is at Rach Soi about 10 km south of Rach Gia. *Xe ôm* from the airport, 50,000d; taxi 80,000d.

Airline offices Vietnam Airlines, 16 Nguyen Trung Truc St, T77-392 4320.

Boat

Daily connections to **Phu Quoc**, departing from the ferry terminal on Nguyen Cong Tru St. A variety of ferry companies including **Superdong** ferries, T77-387 7742, **Duong Dong Express**, T77-387 9765, www. duongdongexpress.com.vn, and **Savanna** leave daily at 0745-0800 arriving 1030 and 1300; 270,000d, 200,000d for children. The ferries no longer arrive at An Thoi in the southern part of the island.

From the **Rach Meo** ferry terminal, 2 km south of town on Ngo Quyen St close to the junction with Nguyen Van Cu St, boats go to **Vinh Thuan** and **Ca Mau**, 0800, 100,000d. Travellers have reported overcrowding on the ferries, others have reported unlicensed boats in and out of Phu Quoc; highly dangerous.

Bus

There are 2 stations; the city centre terminal at Nguyen Binh Kiem St and a terminal at Rach Soi, 7 km south of town near the airport. From the 1st bus station, connections to **HCMC**, 8 hrs, **Can Tho**, **Vinh Long**, **Ha Tien** and **Long Xuyen**. Mai Linh and Phung Trang companies operate express buses to **HCMC**, 5 hrs, 115,000d. From the 2nd bus station, services to **Chau Doc** and **HCMC**.

Taxi

Mai Linh wait at the Nguyen Truc Trac city park. Taxi Phuong Trinh, 26 Nguyen Van Troi St, T77-387 8787.

Ha Tien *p386, map p387*
Bicycle

Ha Tien Tourism Coop Ltd rents bikes for 50,000d a day and motorbikes for 150,000d.

Boat

The ferry wharf is opposite the Ha Tien hotel. Ferries to **Phu Quoc** leave at 0800-0830 (120,000d) and at 1000, 100,000d. Note that the 1000 service arrives at **Nam Ninh** where there are few public transport options.

Bus

The bus station is on the way to the Cambodia border on Highway 80 north of town. There are buses to **HCMC**, at 0700, 0800 and 0900, 10-12 hrs, 100,000d; and connections with **Rach Gia**, 4 hrs, 38,000d; **Chau Doc**, 52,000d; **Can Tho**, 83,000d; as well as other Delta towns. Reliable **Mai Linh** runs to **Rach Gia**, 45,000d. *Footprint* has news of scams involving illegally operated buses running out of Ha Tien and the Cambodia border. Make sure you buy a ticket at the real Ha Tien bus station. All real buses provide tickets in Vietnam. (Phong Ve means ticket office in Vietnamese). Ha Tien bus station is new with a ticket office. *Xe ôms* wait outside. *Xe ôm* to the Cambodia border, 30,000d; into town, 10,000d.

The **Ha Tien Service Tourism Co** wil transfer to the border for US$10. See border crossings to Cambodia, page 383.

A new road 5 km outside Ha Tien takes you to Tinh Bien and on to Chau Doc, shortening the Ha Tien-Chau Doc route.

⊙ Directory

Chau Doc *p381, map p382*
Banks Vietinbank, 68-70 Nguyen Huu Canh St with ATM. BIDV, 7-9 Nguyen Huu Canh St, has a Visa ATM. Vietcombank, 1 Hung Vuong St. **Hospitals** Located opposite the Victoria Chau Doc Hotel, 5 Le Loi St, T76-356 0851. **Internet** Available in the post office and also in Victoria Chau Doc Hotel. Fast connection at Internet, 30 Nguyen Huu Canh St. **Post office** 73 Le Loi St, open 0700-2000.

Long Xuyen *p384*
Banks Vietcombank, 1 Hung Vuong St (at the junction of Hung Vuong and Nguyen Thi Minh Khai St). **Hospitals** 2 Le Loi, T76-385 2989. **Internet** There are plenty of internet cafés, many of which are dotted along Hung

Vuong St. **Post office** The main post office is at 106 Tran Hung Dao St (quite a way over the Hoang Dieu Bridge).

Rach Gia *p385*
Banks Sacombank, 37 Nguyen Hung Son St with ATM. There are ATMs and banks around the city. **Hospitals** 46 Le Loi, T77-386 3328. **Internet** Apart from the post office there is a selection along Nguyen Trung Truc St and at 72 Nguyen Van Troi St. **Post office** 1 Duong Mau Than St, T77-386 2551. Internet and 171 international dialling services.

Ha Tien *p386, map p387*
Banks Agribank is located on 37 Lam Son St on the corner of Phung Thanh St with a currency exchange and ATM. Sacombank, 16 Tran Hau St; ATM. **Hospitals** On the corner of Mac Cuu and Bach Dang Sts, T77-385 2666. **Internet** In the main post office and at Ha Tien Tourism. **Post office** 3 To Chau St, T77-385 2182.

Phu Quoc Island

→*Colour map 4, B1.*
Phu Quoc is Vietnam's largest island, lying off the southwest coast of Vietnam. The island remains largely undeveloped with beautiful sandy beaches along much of its coastline and forested hills inland. Most of the beaches benefit from crystal-clear waters making it perfect for swimming and a place well worth visiting for those with some time to spend in southern Vietnam. The island's remoteness and lack of infrastructure has meant that it is only recently that tourism has started developing and the pace of development has been slower than in other parts of the country owing to the lack of power and water supplies to much of the island.

However, Phu Quoc is set to expand at a phenomenal rate as multi-million dollar projects have been given the green light The island's status as a remote, undeveloped bolt hole, is over. Phu Quoc's northernmost tip lies just outside Cambodian territorial waters and, like other parts of present-day Vietnam in this area, it has been fought over, claimed and reclaimed by Thai, Khmer and Viet. At the moment some of the island is reserved for military use and hence certain areas are restricted but, despite this, there remains plenty to explore. ▸▸ For listings, see pages 397-400.

Ins and outs
Getting there You can get to Phu Quoc by boat from Rach Gia or Ha Tien or by plane from Rach Gia and Ho Chi Minh City. Most hotels will provide a free pick-up service from the airport if accommodation is booked in advance. The same does not apply to transfers from the ferry port. *Xe ôm* drivers meet the ferries. ▸▸ *See Transport, page 400.*

Getting around While some of the island's roads are surfaced many are still dirt tracks and so the best way to get around the entire island is by motorbike (see Transport, page 400), although this could prove desperately hot and dusty. There are plenty of motorbike taxis and motorbikes are easily available and cheap to hire. The only problem that visitors are likely to encounter is the very limited signposting which can make some places pretty hard to find without some form of local assistance. Cars with drivers at fairly reasonable costs are available. Ask at hotels.

Tourist information Most of the resorts are very happy to arrange tours and they are a good source of up-to-date information. There are several tour operators which will provide plenty of information, see Tour operators.

History
Historically, the island is renowned for its small part in the triumph of the Nguyen Dynasty. In 1765 Pigneau de Behaine was sent here as a young seminarist to train Roman Catholic missionaries; by chance he was on the island when Nguyen Anh (son of emperor-to-be Gia Long) arrived, fleeing the Tay Son. Pigneau's role in the rise of the Nguyen Dynasty is described on page 189. Another link between the island and Vietnamese history is that it was here, in 1919, that the civil servant Ngo Van Chieu communed with the spirit world and made contact with the Supreme Being, leading to the establishment of the Cao Dai religion.

Phu Quoc Island

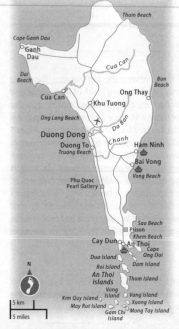

Around the island
Duong Dong is the main town on the island and many of the hotels and resorts are near here on Truong Beach. Millions of fish can be seen laid out to dry on land and on tables – all destined for the pot. Before being bottled they are fermented. At the Khai Hoan **fish sauce factory** ① *free*, huge barrels act as vats, each containing fish and salt. If the sauce is made in concrete vats, the taste is lost and so the sauce is cheaper.

The **Coi Nguon Museum** ① *149 Tran Hung Dao St, T77-398 0206, www.coi nguonphuquoc.com, daily 0700-1700, 1 English-speaking guide*, displays a huge amount of island creatures, fishing paraphernalia, old currency and Chinese ceramics from shipwrecked boats. The guide could not explain, however, how a private collector has amassed such a large haul of natural and man-made treasures.

About 10 km south of Dong Duong is the **Phu Quoc Pearl Gallery** ① *T91-399 3202, 0800-1800*. Just offshore 10,000 South Sea pearls are collected each year. A video demonstrates the farming operation and the tasting of pearl meat and the pearl process is illustrated in the gallery. Jewellery is for sale. Some 100 m south of the pearl farm on the coastal road there are two **whale dedication temples**, Lang Ca Ong. In front of one is a crude whale/dolphin statue.

Ganh Dau, at the northwest tip, is 35 km from Duong Dong. The townsfolk speak Khmer because refugees escaping the Khmer Rouge came here and settled with the locals. The Cambodian coast is 4-5 km away and can be seen, as can the last island of Vietnam. (The Cambodians actually claim Phu Quoc as their own). The beach has a few palms and rocks to clamber on and there is a restaurant. **Dai Beach**, south of Ganh Danh, is a strip of white sand backed by casuarinas overlooking Turtle Island. The water is clear but there are no facilities. Inland from here the area is heavily forested but the wood is protected by law. In this part of the island fish are laid out to dry on large trestle-tables or on the ground for use as fertilizer. South of Dai Beach is **Ong Lang Beach** where there are a couple of resorts, see Sleeping.

The dazzling white sands of **Sao Beach** on the southeast coast are stunning and worth visiting by motorbike. There are a couple of restaurants at the back of the beach.

The inland streams and waterfalls (**Da Ban** and **Chanh** streams) are not very dramatic in the dry season but still provide a relaxing place to swim and walk in the forests.

One of the biggest draws are the boat trips around the **An Thoi islands**, scattered islands, like chips off a block, off the southern coast, which offer opportunities for swimming, snorkelling, diving and fishing. It is also possible to stop off to visit an interesting fishing village at **Thom Island**.

◉ Phu Quoc Island listings

For Sleeping and Eating price codes and other relevant information, see Essentials pages 26-31.

◉ Sleeping

During peak periods such as Christmas and Tet it is advisable to book accommodation well in advance. Representatives from different resorts meet flights, providing free transfers and touting for business. Most of the resorts lie along the west coast on Long Beach to the south of Duong Dong and are within a few kilometres of the airport. Others are on On Lang Beach.

LL-AL La Veranda, Tran Hung Dao St, Long Beach, T77-398 2988, www.laverandaresort. com. A beautiful luxury resort with rooms and villas set in luscious gardens leading on to the main beach on the island. All rooms are beautifully furnished and come with TVs, DVD players and wireless internet. Deluxe rooms and villas come with gorgeous 4-poster beds and drapes. There's a spa, pool and the delicious food of the **Peppertree Restaurant**. The service is exceptional.

LL-A Cassia Cottage, T77-384 8395, Long Beach, www.cassiacottage.com. A small resort set in front of a small length of beach and focused around a pool. Families will love the inflatable water toys collection. Cooking classes and volleyball are offered for the active. Rooms (with no TV) are lovely with bathrooms. Diners can eat in the garden.

L-AL Chen La Resort & Spa, Ong Lang Beach, T77-399 5895, www.chenla-resort. com. A very inviting resort with lovely villas set back from the white-sand beach with alfresco bathrooms. Smaller-roomed semi-detached bungalows face the sea. The golden sands are dotted with umbrellas, and there's an infinity pool, spa, watersports and atmospheric restaurant.

L-A Saigon Phu Quoc Resort, 1 Trang Hung Dao St, Long Beach, T77-384 6999, www.vietnamphuquoc.com. Well-finished a/c bungalows set on a hillside garden overlooking the sea. The resort has good facilities including a decent pool, tennis court, internet access and a reasonably priced restaurant serving international food.

AL-B Mango Bay, Ong Lang Beach, T90-338 2207, www.mangobayphuquoc. com. A small and exclusive environmentally friendly private resort in tropical gardens located on the beach close to pepper farms. A perfect spot. Bungalows are made from rammed earth and come with fans and coconut doorknobs and are kitted out with bamboo furniture and tiled floors. There are also fishermen's huts and rooms, with a wonderful, large communal veranda. Some have outdoor bathrooms in bamboo-enclosed patios which are very attractive. The restaurant provides a mixture of Vietnamese and Western food at reasonable prices. Price includes breakfast.

A-B Mai House Resort, Long Beach, T77-384 7003, maihouseresort@yahoo.com. This is a really lovely resort run by Tuyet Mai and Gerard Bezardin set in large gardens in front of a slice of beach. The 20 bungalows feature 4-poster beds, bathrooms and balconies. Sea-view rooms are bigger. The restaurant (with Wi-Fi access) overlooks the beach.

A-B Tropicana Resort, Long Beach, T77-384 7127, tropicana_vn@yahoo.com. The resort has high-quality wooden bungalows set in a tropical garden next to the beach with a pool but some of the bungalows and the garden are looking unloved compared to the gardens of neighbouring resorts; they've even neglected to put a sign up to the resort on the main road. Prices vary according to facilities although the beachfront balconied bungalows are overpriced. The resort has

one of the best restaurants, a well-stocked bar and internet access.

A-C Bo Resort, Ong Lang Beach, T77-986 142/3, www.boresort.com. This feels like a great escape with 18 stilted bungalows set on a hillside amid flourishing gardens. Rooms come with large rustic bathrooms and alfresco showers. There's no road access to the wild stretch of beach where there are pines, hammocks, kayaks and a beach bar. There's Wi-Fi in the restaurant/bar and candlelight at night. The owners are warm and friendly.

A-C Thien Hai Son, 68 Tran Hung Dao St, Long Beach, T77-398 3044, www. phuquocthienhaison.com. This is a pleasant resort with comfortable rooms but characterless. There's only a thin strip of beach out front. A last resort if nicer properties are booked up.

B-D Kim Hoa Resort, 88/2 Tran Hung Dao St, Long Beach, T77-384 7039, www. kimhoaresort.com. This resort that has expanded to offer 72 rooms: typical wooden bungalows are right on a strip of sand in front of the resort as well as garden rooms, pool view rooms and rooms in a block away from the beach; these are the cheapest. One of the oldest resorts on the island.

B-D Sao Bien, Tran Hung Dao St, Long Beach, T77-398 2161, www.seastarresort. com. Spacious but spartan rooms at this resort with 38 bungalows of mixed price and a long stretch of beach. Garden rooms at the rear of the property are cheaper than

CHEN LA
RESORT & SPA

PHU QUOC ISLAND
VIET NAM

www.chenla-resort.com

those nearer the beachfront. Cheapest are those in a hotel block. Wi-Fi at reception and restaurant only.

C-D Thang Loi, Ong Lang Beach, T77-398 5002, www.phuquoc.de. Wooden bungalows with fans, set in a remote coconut plantation north of Duong Dong. It has a good bar and restaurant with friendly German owners. There is a library, music and great food including *weiner schnitzel*. A jetty has been built out over the sea. Closed May-Sep. Breakfast not included.

C-E Beach Club, Long Beach, T77-398 0998, www.beachclubvietnam.com. Luscious golden sands and thatched beach umbrellas at this small resort, the furthest from the town and thus not conveniently located. If you don't want to leave the resort and kick back for a while this is perfect. If you want more activity, choose a resort closer to town. The 6 rooms and 4 bungalows are all close to the sea. It's good value and so always booked up. Reserve well in advance.

D Freedomland, Ong Lang Beach, 10 mins' walk from beach, T77-399 4891, www.freedomlandphuquoc.com. Run by Peter, this resort creates a community vibe as all guests eat together at the large dinner table. Bungalows are scattered around the grounds. 4 of the rooms have private bathroom and 4 share. Boat and motos can be rented.

F Kim Phung, Tran Hung Dao St, Duong Dong, T77-398 1727. This is a basic but clean town hotel with rooms in a little courtyard out back. It would be fine and convenient for those with no budget for a resort break. It's on the main strip amid the restaurants and dive operators.

🍴 Eating

The food on Phu Quoc is generally very good, especially the fish and seafood. On the street in Duong Dong try the delicious *gio cuong* (fresh spring rolls) but do be aware that some of the market stalls appear to cook using water taken straight from the river.

Most of the resorts mentioned have beachfront restaurants.

🍴-🍴 **Ocean Bar & Grill & Winestore**, 60 Tran Hung Dao St, T77-399 4268, winestore.pq@gmail.com. The owner of this place gives the biggest welcome in Phu Quoc. Friendly ambience, tasty and varied Vietnamese and pan-Asian dishes and a great view of the sunset for an early dinner.

🍴-🍴 **Pepper's**, 89 Tran Hung Dao St, T77-384 8773. A popular Italian restaurant set away from the beach. Service is a bit slack though.

🍴 **Buddy's**, 26 Nguyen Trai St, T77-399 4181. Western-style café with roadside view serving up ice cream at 20,000d per scoop.

🍴 **German B**, 5 Tran Hung Dao St. A conveniently located German bakery and café on the main road. Service is friendly and efficient.

🍴 **La Craft & Cafe**, 11 Tran Hung Dao St, T90-820 1102. A tiny streetside caff serving yoghurts, shakes and breakfasts on cute black-lacquered furniture under beige umbrellas. It's opposite the market entrance.

🍴 **My Lan**, Sao Beach, T77-384 4447, dungmyt@yahoo.com. Daily 0600-2100. A gorgeous setting on a gorgeous beach. Tables are under thatched roofs. Sit back and enjoy a beer with fresh seafood dishes.

🍸 Bars and clubs

The Dog Bar, 88 Tran Hung Dao St, near the **Thien Hai Son Resort**, T90-381 4688. Well-located beer den with cold drinks, pool and sports TV.

🛍 Shopping

If you have Vietnamese friends or family and return without a bottle of the fish sauce you will be in trouble. However, you cannot take the sauce on a **Vietnam Airlines** flight.

Apart from the fish sauce there is a surprisingly good choice of goods to buy. Do remember, however, that no matter how pretty the coral ornaments and ashtrays may look, they are cut from living coral.

▲▲ Activities and tours

Watersports are available at the hotels. Also cycling tours, boat tours and walking.

Diving
Rainbow Divers, Tran Hung Dao St, close to the market, T91-723 9433 (mob), www.divevietnam.com Long-standing operation with a very good reputation.

Tour operators
Discovery Tour, 32 Tran Hung Dao St, Duong Dong, T77-384 6587, www.phuquoctravel.com.vn. Daily 0700-1800.
Ha Tien Tourism Coop Ltd, 37A Tran Hung Dao St, Duong Dong, T77-398 2888, hatientourism@gmail.com. Branch office of the one in Ha Tien that is run by the on-the-ball and helpful Marie. Sells boat tickets and has free internet for customers.
John's Tours, New Star Café, 143 Tran Hung Dao St, T91-910 7086, www.johnislandtours.com. Run by John Tran out of the **New Star Café** (next to the alley to **La Veranda**) and various kiosks on the beach as well as hotel desks. Snorkelling, squid fishing, island tours and car hire can be arranged. Prices from US$15. Car hire with driver also arranged.
Tony Travel, 100 Tran Hung Dao St or based at the **Rainbow Divers** office on Tran Hung Dao St opposite the market, T913-197334, tonytravelpq@yahoo.com.vn. Kiosks on the beach too. Tony speaks fluent English. In his stable are island tours, snorkelling to the south and north islands, deep-sea fishing excursions, car and motorbike rental and hotel and transport reservations. Prices from US$15. Snorkelling tours make sure you're fitted with a mask and snorkel properly.

⊖ Transport

Air
There are daily flights to **HCMC** and **Rach Gia**.
   Airline offices Vietnam Airlines, 122 Nguyen Trung Truc St, Duong Dong, T77-399667.

Boat
Ferries leave from Bai Vong port in the southeastern part of the island and Ham Ninh in the east. An Thoi port in the south is closed for renovation. See also Getting there, page 395, for details.
   Superdong, 1 Tran Hung Dao St, Duong Dong, T77-348 6180, to **Rach Gia** from Bai Vong at 1300 arriving 1535. 270,000d.
   Duong Dong Express, www.duongdongexpress.com.vn, leaves for **Rach Gia** at 1245 arriving 1515, 270,000d; children 200,000d.
   Savanna, 36 Tran Hung Dao St, T77-399 2999, at Bai Vong, T77-399 2555. Leaves at 1305 arriving **Rach Gia** at 1535, 270,000d.
   Vinashin, 21 Nguyen Trai St, T77-260 0155, leaves 0810.
   Cawaco from Ham Ninh to Ha Tien at 0830 arriving 1000, 160,000d. Also departs Bai Vong 1400 arriving 1520. Bus picks up from agents, at 1200, 20,000d, for the **Bai Vong** departure. No public transport to Ham Ninh; taxi 160,000d.

Cars, bicycles and motorbikes
Cars, motorbikes and bicycles can be rented from resorts.

Taxis
Mai Linh, No 10 30 Thang 4 St, Duong Dong, T77-397 9797.
Sasco, 379 Nguyen Trung Truc St, T77-399 5599. Taxis from the airport to Ong Lang are around US$15 and from the port, US$8.

⊙ Directory

Banks Agribank, 2 Tran Hung Dao St, Duong Dong, also cashes TCs; ATM. **Phu Quoc Bank**, Duong Dong, cashes TCs. Vietcombank, 0700-1100, 1300-1700, has Visa and MasterCard ATM. **Hospitals** The hospital is in Khu Pho, 1 Duong Dong, T77-384 8075. **Internet** Available at resorts; some have Wi-Fi. Terminals at John's Tours, New Star Café, 143 Tran Hung Dao St. **Post office** Phu Quoc Post Office, 2 Tran Hung Dao St Duong Dong, 0645-2030.

Contents

402 History

434 Modern Vietnam

443 Economy

448 Culture

470 Religion

475 Land and environment

482 Books

486 Films

Footprint features

404 Patriot games: Vietnamese
street names
406 Nguyen Trai
407 Vietnamese dynasties
410 A Spanish account of Champa
circa 1595
414 Ho Chi Minh: 'He who
enlightens'
416 Ho Chi Minh pseudonyms
422 A war glossary
424 The Anzacs in Vietnam
425 The war in figures
428 A nation at sea: the boat people
436 Getting our children out of
Vietnam: a personal story
442 Cyber-dissidents
451 Visiting minorities: house rules
452 Rite of passage: from baby
to infant
461 Brilliance in bronze: rain
drums of Dongson
465 Modern Vietnamese art
472 In Siddharta's footsteps:
a short history of Buddhism
478 The Mekong: mother river of
Southeast Asia
480 Temperatures, humidity and
rainfall by place

Background

History

Vietnam prehistory

The earliest record of humans in Vietnam is from an archaeological site on Do Mountain, in the northern Thanh Hoa Province. The remains discovered here have been dated to the Lower Palaeolithic (early Stone Age). So far, all early human remains have been unearthed in North Vietnam, invariably in association with limestone cliff dwellings. Unusually, tools are made of basalt rather than flint, the more common material found at similar sites in other parts of the world.

Archaeological excavations have shown that between 5000 BC and 3000 BC, two important Mesolithic cultures occupied North Vietnam: these are referred to as the **Hoa Binh** and **Bac Son** cultures after the principal excavation sites in Tonkin. Refined stone implements and distinctive hand axes with polished edges (known as Bacsonian axes) are characteristic of the two cultures. These early inhabitants of Vietnam were probably small, dark-skinned and of Melanesian or Austronesian stock.

There are 2000 years of recorded Vietnamese history and another 2000 years of legend. The Vietnamese people trace their origins back to 15 tribal groups known as the **Lac Viet** who settled in what is now North Vietnam at the beginning of the Bronze Age. Here they established an agrarian kingdom known as Van-lang that seems to have vanished during the third century BC.

A problem with early **French archaeological studies** in Vietnam was that most of the scholars were either Sinologists or Indologists. In consequence, they looked to Vietnam as a receptacle of Chinese or Indian cultural influences and spent little time uncovering those aspects of culture, art and life that were indigenous in origin and inspiration. The French archaeologist Bezacier for example, expressed the generally held view that 'Vietnamese' history only began in the seventh century AD. Such sites as Hoa Binh, Dong Son and Oc-Eo, which pre-date the seventh century, were regarded as essentially Chinese or Indonesian, their only 'Vietnamese-ness' being their location. This perspective was more often than not based on faulty and slapdash scholarship, and reflected the prevailing view that Southeast Asian art was basically derivative.

Pre-colonial history

The beginning of Vietnamese recorded history coincides with the start of **Chinese cultural hegemony** over the north, in the second century BC. The Chinese dominated Vietnam for more than 1000 years until the 10th century AD and the cultural legacy is still very much in evidence, making Vietnam distinctive in Southeast Asia. Even after the 10th century, and despite breaking away from Chinese political domination, Vietnam was still overshadowed and greatly influenced by its illustrious neighbour to the north. Nonetheless, the fact that Vietnam could shrug off 1000 years of Chinese subjugation and emerge with a distinct cultural heritage and language says a lot for Vietnam's strength of national identity. Indeed, it might be argued, as William Duiker, an expert on Ho Chi Minh, does, that the Vietnamese nation "has been formed in the crucible of its historic resistance to Chinese conquest and assimilation".

Ly Dynasty

The Ly Dynasty (1009-1225) was the first independent Vietnamese dynasty. Its capital, Thang Long, was at the site of present day Hanoi and the dynasty based its system of government and social relations closely upon the Chinese Confucianist model (see page 471). The Vietnamese owe a considerable debt to the Chinese – mainly in the spheres of government, philosophy and the arts – but they have always been determined to maintain their independence. Vietnamese Confucianist scholars were unsparing in their criticism of Chinese imperialism. Continuous Chinese invasions, all ultimately futile, served to cement an enmity between the two countries, which is still in evidence today – despite their having normalized diplomatic relations in October 1991.

The first Ly emperor, and one of Vietnam's great kings, was Ly Cong Uan who was born in AD 974. He is usually known by his posthumous title, **Ly Thai To**, and reigned for 19 years from 1009-1028. Ly Cong Uan was raised and educated by monks and acceded to the throne when, as the commander of the palace guard in Hoa Lu (the capital of Vietnam before Thang Long or Hanoi) and with the support of his great patron, the monk Van Hanh, he managed to gain the support of the Buddhist establishment and many local lords. During his reign, he enjoyed a reputation not just as a great soldier, but also as a devout man who paid attention to the interests and wellbeing of his people. He also seemed, if the contemporary records are to be believed, to have been remarkably sensitive to those he ruled. He tried to re-establish the harmony between ruler and ruled which had suffered during the previous years and he even sent his son to live outside the walls of the palace so that he could gain a taste of ordinary life and an understanding of ordinary people. As he approached death he is said to have increasingly retired from everyday life, preparing himself for the everlasting.

Ly Cong Uan was succeeded by his son, Ly Phat Ma, who is better known as **Ly Thai Tong** (reigned 1028-1054). Ly Phat Ma had been prepared for kingship since birth and he proved to be an excellent ruler during his long reign. It is hard to generalize about this period in Vietnamese history because Ly Phat Ma adapted his pattern of rule no less than six times during his reign. Early on he challenged the establishment, contending for example that good governance was not merely a consequence of following best practice (which the logic of bureaucratic Confucianism would maintain) but depended upon good kingship – in other words, depended upon the qualities of the man at the helm. Later he was more of an establishment figure, holding much greater store by the institutions of kingship. Perhaps his greatest military success was the mounting of a campaign to defeat the Cham in 1044 from which he returned with shiploads of plunder. His greatest artistic legacy was the construction of the One Pillar Pagoda or Chua Mot Cot in Hanoi (see page 60).

Ly Phat Ma was succeeded by his son, Ly Nhat Ton, posthumously known as **Ly Thanh Tong** (reigned 1054-1072). History is not as kind about Ly Thanh Tong as it is about his two forebears. Nonetheless he did challenge the might of the Chinese along Vietnam's northern borders – largely successfully – and like his father also mounted a campaign against Champa (see page 409) in 1069. Indeed his expedition against the Cham mirrored his father's in most respects and, like his father, he won. (But unlike his father, he did not execute the Cham king.) Records indicate that he spent a great deal of time trying to father a son and worked his way through numerous concubines and a great deal of incense in the process. At last, after much labour (on his part, and probably on the mother's too, although the texts do not say as much), a son was born to a concubine of common blood in 1066 and named Ly Can Duc.

Patriot games: Vietnamese street names

Like other countries that have experienced a revolution, the Vietnamese authorities have spent considerable time expunging street names honouring men and women who lack the necessary revolutionary credentials. Most obviously, Saigon had its name changed to Ho Chi Minh City following reunification in 1975. Most towns have the same street names and most are in memory of former patriots:

Dien Bien Phu Site of the communists' famous victory against the French in 1954 (see page 108).

Duy Tan 11th Nguyen emperor (1907-1916) until exiled to Réunion by the French for his opposition to colonial rule. Killed in an aircrash in Africa in 1945, his remains were interred in Hué in 1987.

Hai Ba Trung The renowned Trung sisters who led a rebellion against Chinese overlords in AD 40 (see box, page 66).

Ham Nghi The young emperor who joined the resistance against the French in 1885 at the age of 13 and thus gave it legitimacy.

Hoang Van Thu Leader of the Vietnamese Communist Party, executed by the French, 1944.

Le Duan Secretary-General of Lao Dong from 1959.

Le Lai Brother-in-arms of Emperor Le Loi. Le Lai saved Viet forces by dressing in the Emperor's clothes and drawing away surrounding Chinese troops.

Le Loi (Le Thai To) Leader of a revolt which, in 1426, resulted in the liberation of Vietnam from Ming Chinese overlords. Born into a wealthy family he had a life-long concern for the poor. Founder of the Le Dynasty, he ruled 1426-1433.

Le Thanh Ton(g) A successor to Le Loi, ruled 1460-1498, poet king, and cartographer he established an efficient administration on strict Confucian lines and an enlightened legal code; literature and the arts flourished.

Ly Thuong Kiet Military commander who led campaigns against the Chinese and Cham during the 11th century, and gained a reputation as a brilliant strategist. He died at the age of 70 in 1105.

Ly Can Duc was proclaimed emperor in 1072 when he was only six years old and, surprisingly, remained king until he died in 1127. During the early years of his reign the kingdom faced a succession of crises, largely due to the fact that his young age meant that there was no paramount leader. His death marks the end of the Ly Dynasty for he left no heir and the crown passed to the maternal clan of his nephew. There followed a period of instability and it was not until 1225 that a new dynasty – the Tran Dynasty – managed to subdue the various competing cliques and bring a semblance of order to the country.

Tran Dynasty

Scholars do not know a great deal about the four generations of kings of the Tran Dynasty. It seems that they established the habit of marrying within the clan, and each king took queens who were either their cousins or, in one case, a half-sister. Such a long period of intermarriage, one imagines, would have had some far-reaching genetic consequences, although ironically the collapse of the dynasty seems to have been brought about after one foolish king decided to marry outside the Tran clan. The great achievement of the Tran Dynasty was to resist the expansionist tendencies of the Mongol forces who conquered

Nguyen Du (1765-1820) Ambassador to Peking, courtier and Vietnam's most famous poet, wrote *The Tale of Kieu* (see page 486).

Nguyen Hue Tay Son brother who routed the Chinese at the Battle of Dong Da. Later became Emperor Quang Trung (see page 407).

Nguyen Thai Hoc Leader of the Vietnam Quoc Dan Dang Party (VNQDD) and the leader of the Yen Bai uprisings; captured by the French and guillotined on 17 June 1930 at the age of 28.

Nguyen Trai Emperor Le Loi's advisor and a skilled poet, he advised Le Loi to concentrate on political and moral struggle: "Better to conquer hearts than citadels."

Nguyen Van Troi Viet Cong hero who in 1963 tried, unsuccessfully, to assassinate Robert McNamara by blowing up a bridge in Saigon. He was executed.

Phan Boi Chau A committed anti-colonialist from the age of 19, he travelled to China and Japan to organize resistance to the French. Captured in Shanghai in 1925 he was extradited to Hanoi and sentenced to life imprisonment. Public pressure led to his amnesty in the same year and he spent the rest of his life in Hué where he died in 1940.

Quang Trung Leader of the Tay Son peasant rebellion of 1771; defeated both the Siamese (Thais) and the Chinese (see box, page 272).

Ton Duc Thang Became President of the Socialist Republic of Vietnam; he took part in a mutiny aboard a French ship along with other Vietnamese shipmates in the Black Sea in support of the Russian Revolution.

Tran Hung Dao A 13th-century hero who fought and defeated the Yuan Chinese. Regarded as one of Vietnam's great military leaders and strategists, also a man of letters writing the classic *Binh Thu Yeu Luoc* in 1284.

Tran Nguyen Han A 15th-century general who fought heroically against the Ming Chinese occupiers.

Tran Phu The first Secretary General of the Communist Party of Indochina, killed by the French in 1931 at the age of 27.

30 Thang 4 Street Commemorates capture of Saigon by communists on 30 April 1975.

China in the 1250s and then set their sights on Vietnam. In 1284 a huge Mongol-Yuan force, consisting of no fewer than four armies, massed on the border to crush the Vietnamese. Fortunately the Tran were blessed with a group of brave and resourceful princes, the most notable of whom was Tran Quoc Tuan, better known – and now immortalized in street names in just about every Vietnamese town – as Tran Hung Dao. Although the invading forces captured Thang Long (Hanoi) they never managed to defeat the Vietnamese in a decisive battle and in the end the forces of the Tran Dynasty were victorious.

Le Dynasty and the emergence of Vietnam

Le Loi

During its struggle with the Cham, nascent Dai Viet had to contend with the weight of Ming Chinese oppression from the north, often in concert with their Cham allies. Despite 1000 years of Chinese domination and centuries of internal dynastic squabbles the Viet retained a strong sense of national identity and were quick to respond to charismatic leadership. As so often in Vietnam's history one man was able to harness nationalistic

Nguyen Trai

Our country, Dai Viet, has long been A land of ancient culture, With its own rivers and mountains, ways and customs, Different from those of the North.

(Opening lines of *Proclamation of Victory Over the Invaders*.)

Nguyen Trai, mandarin, poet and nationalist, rose to prominence as an adviser to Le Loi during the 10-year campaign to eject the Ming from Dai Viet. His famous counsel "better to win hearts than citadels" (which mirrors similar advice during a war over 500 years later) was heeded by Le Loi who aroused patriotic fervour in his compatriots to achieve victory on the battlefield. It was on Nguyen Trai's suggestion that 100,000 defeated Ming troops were given food and boats to make their way home. After the war, Nguyen Trai accepted and later resigned a court post. He was a prolific composer of verse, which is considered some of the finest in the national annals.

On an overnight visit to Nguyen Trai, Emperor Le Thai Tong (Le Loi's son and heir) died unexpectedly. Scheming courtiers were able to fix the blame on Nguyen Trai who in 1442, along with three generations of his family, were executed, a punishment known as *tru di tam tôc*.

sentiment and mould the country's discontent into a powerful fighting force: in 1426 it was Le Loi. Together with the brilliant tactician **Nguyen Trai** (see box, above), Le Loi led a campaign to remove the Chinese from Vietnamese soil. Combining surprise, guerrilla tactics and Nguyen Trai's innovative and famous propaganda, designed to convince defending Ming of the futility of their position, the Viet won a resounding victory which led to the enlightened and artistically distinguished Le period. Le Loi's legendary victory lives on in popular form and is celebrated in the tale of the restored sword in water puppet performances across the country. Following his victory against the Ming he claimed the throne in 1428 and reigned until his death five years later.

Le Thanh Ton

With Le Loi's death the Le Dynasty worked its way through a succession of young kings who seemed to hold the throne barely long enough to warm the cushions before they were murdered. It was not until 1460 that a king of substance did accede: Le Thanh Ton (reigned 1460-1497). His reign was a period of great scholarship and artistic accomplishment. He established the system of rule that was to guide successive Vietnamese emperors for 500 years. He also mounted a series of military campaigns, some as far as Laos to the west.

Le expansion

The expansion of the Vietnamese state, under the Le, south from its heartland in the Tonkin Delta, followed the decline of the Cham Kingdom at the end of the 15th century. By the early 18th century the Cham were extinct as an identifiable political and military force and the Vietnamese advanced still further south into the Khmer- controlled territories of the Mekong Delta. This geographical over-extension and the sheer logistical impracticability of ruling from distant Hanoi, disseminating edicts and collecting taxes, led to the disintegration of the – ever tenuous – imperial rule. The old adage 'The edicts of the emperor stop at the village gate' was particularly apt more than 1000 km from the capital.

Vietnamese dynasties

Dynasty	Dates	Capital (province)
Hong Bang (legendary)	2876-258 BC	Phong Chau (Son Tay)
Thuc	257-207 BC	Loa Thanh (Vinh Phu)
Trieu	207-111 BC	Phien Ngung (S China)
under Chinese domination 111 BC-AD 23		
Trung Sisters	AD 40-43	Me Linh (Son Tay)
under Chinese domination AD 25-589		
Early Ly	544-602	various (Hanoi)
under Chinese domination AD 603-938		
Ngo	939-967	Co Loa (Vinh Phuc)
Dinh	968-980	Hoa Lu (Ninh Binh)
Early Le	980-1009	Hoa Lu (Ninh Binh)
Ly	1010-1225	Thang Long (Hanoi)
Tran	1225-1400	Thang Long (Hanoi)
Ho	1400-1407	Dong Do (Hanoi)
Post Tran	1407-1413	
under Chinese domination AD 1414-1427		
Le	1427-1788	Thang Long (Hanoi)
Mac	1527-1592	
Northern Trinh	1539-1787	Hanoi
Southern Nguyen	1558-1778	Hué
Quang Trung	1787-1792	
Nguyen of Tay Son	1788-1802	Saigon
Nguyen	1802-1945	Hué

From the 16th to 18th centuries there were up to four centres of power in Vietnam.
For a list of Nguyen Emperors see box, page 182.

Noble families, locally dominant, challenged the emperor's authority and the Le Dynasty gradually dissolved into internecine strife and regional fiefdoms, namely Trinh in the north and Nguyen in the south, a pattern that was to reassert itself some 300 years later. But although on paper the Vietnamese – now consisting of two dynastic houses, Trinh and Nguyen – appeared powerful, the people were mired in poverty.

There were numerous peasant rebellions in this period, of which the most serious was the **Tay Son Rebellion** of 1771 (see box, page 272). One of the three Tay Son brothers, Nguyen Hue, proclaimed himself **Emperor Quang Trung** in 1788, only to die four years later.

The death of Quang Trung paved the way for the establishment of the **Nguyen Dynasty** – the last Vietnamese dynasty – in 1802 when Emperor Gia Long ascended to the throne in Hué. Despite the fact that this period heralded the arrival of the French – leading to their eventual domination of Vietnam – it is regarded as a golden period in Vietnamese history. During the Nguyen Dynasty, Vietnam was unified as a single state and Hué emerged as the heart of the kingdom.

History of the non-Viet civilizations

Any history of Vietnam must include the non-Vietnamese peoples and civilizations. The central and southern parts of Vietnam have only relatively recently been dominated by the Viets. Before that, these lands were in the hands of people of Indian or Khmer origins.

Funan (AD 100-600)

According to Chinese sources, Funan was a Hindu kingdom founded in the first century AD with its capital, Vyadhapura, close to the Mekong River near the border with Cambodia. A local legend records that Kaundinya, a great Indian Brahmin, acting on a dream, sailed to the coast of Vietnam carrying with him a bow and arrow. When he arrived, Kaundinya shot the arrow and where it landed he established the capital of Funan. Following this act, Kaundinya married the princess Soma, daughter of the local King of the Nagas (giant water serpents). The legend symbolizes the union between Indian and local cultural traditions – the naga representing indigenous fertility rites and customs, and the arrow, the potency of the Hindu religion.

Oc-Eo

Funan built its wealth and power on its strategic location on the sea route between China and the islands to the south. Maritime technology at the time forced seafarers travelling between China and island Southeast Asia and India to stop and wait for the winds to change before they could continue on their way. This sometimes meant a stay of up to five months. The large port city of Oc-Eo (see page 386) offered a safe harbour for merchant vessels and the revenues generated enabled the kings of the empire to expand rice cultivation, dominate a host of surrounding vassal states as far away as the Malay coast and South Burma, and build a series of impressive temples, cities and irrigation works. Although the Chinese chronicler K'ang T'ai records that the Funanese were barbarians – "ugly, black, and frizzy-haired" – it is clear from Chinese court annals that they were artistically and technologically accomplished. It is recorded for example that one Chinese emperor was so impressed by the skill of some visiting musicians in AD 263 that he ordered the establishment of an institute of Funanese music.

Funan reached the peak of its powers in the fourth century and went into decline during the fifth century AD when improving maritime technology made Oc-Eo redundant as a haven for sailing vessels. No longer did merchants hug the coastline; ships were now large enough, and navigation skills sophisticated enough, to make the journey from South China to the Malacca Strait without landfall. By the mid-sixth century, Funan, having suffered from a drawn-out leadership crisis, was severely weakened. Neighbouring competing powers took advantage of this crisis, absorbing previously Funan-controlled lands. Irrigation works fell into disrepair as state control weakened and peasants left the fields to seek more productive lands elsewhere. The Cham ultimately conquered Funan, having lost both the economic wealth and the religious legitimacy on which its power had been based.

What is interesting about Funan is the degree to which it provided a model for future states in Southeast Asia. Funan's wealth was built on its links with the sea, and with its ability to exploit maritime trade. The later rulers of Champa, Langkasuka (Malaya), Srivijaya (Sumatra), and Malacca (Malaya) repeated this formula.

Champa (AD 200–1720) → *See also box, page 410.*

In South Vietnam, where the dynastic lords achieved hegemony only in the 18th century, the kingdom of Champa – or Lin-yi as the Chinese called it – was the most significant power. The kingdom evolved in the second century AD and was focused on the narrow ribbon of lowland that runs north-south down the Annamite coast with its various capitals near the present-day city of Danang. Chinese sources record that in AD 192 a local official, Kiu-lien, rejected Chinese authority and established an independent kingdom. From then on, Champa's history was one of conflict with its neighbour; when Imperial China was powerful, Champa was subservient and sent ambassadors and tributes in homage to the Chinese court; when it was weak, the rulers of Champa extended their own influence and ignored the Chinese.

The difficulty for scholars is to decide whether Champa had a single identity or whether it consisted of numerous mini-powers with no dominant centre. The accepted wisdom at the moment is that Champa was more diffuse than previously thought and that only rarely during its history is it possible to talk of Champa in singular terms. The endless shifting of the capital of Champa is taken to reflect the shifting centres of power that characterized this 'kingdom'.

Like Funan, Champa built its power on its position on the maritime trading route through Southeast Asia. During the fourth century, as Champa expanded into formerly Funan-controlled lands, they came under the influence of the Indian cultural traditions of the Funanese. These were enthusiastically embraced by Champa's rulers who tacked the suffix '-varman' onto their names (for example Bhadravarman) and adopted the Hindu-Buddhist cosmology. Though a powerful trading kingdom, Champa was geographically poorly endowed. The coastal strip between the Annamite highlands to the west, and the sea to the east, is narrow and the potential for extensive rice cultivation limited. This may explain why the Champa Empire was never more than a moderate power: it was unable to produce the agricultural surplus necessary to support an extensive court and army, and therefore could not compete with either the Khmers to the south nor with the Viets to the north. But the Cham were able to carve out a niche for themselves between the two, and to many art historians, their art and architecture represent the finest that Vietnam has ever produced (see pages 224). Remains are to be found on the central Vietnamese coast from Quang Tri in the north, to Ham Tan 800 km to the south.

For over 1000 years the Cham resisted the Chinese and the Vietnamese. But by the time Marco Polo wrote of the Cham, their power and prestige were much reduced: "The people are idolaters and pay a yearly tribute to the Great Kaan which consists of elephants and nothing but elephants. In the year of Christ 1285 ... the King had, between sons and daughters, 326 children. There are a very great number of elephants in that country, and they have lignaloes (eagle wood) in great abundance. They have also extensive forests of the wood called Bonús, which is jet black, of which chessmen and pencases are made. But there is nought more to tell, so let us proceed." After 1285, when invading Mongol hordes were repelled by the valiant Viets, Champa and Dai Viet enjoyed an uneasy peace maintained by the liberal flow of royal princesses south across the Col des Nuages (Hai Van Pass) in exchange for territory. During the peaceful reign of Che A-nan a Franciscan priest, Odoric of Pordenone, reported of Champa "'tis a very fine country, having a great store of victuals and of all good things". Of particular interest, he refers to the practice of suti, writing "When a man dies in this country, they burn his wife with him, for they say that she should live with him in the other world also". Clearly, some of the ancient Indian traditions continued.

A Spanish account of Champa circa 1595

This account of Champa is taken from an anonymous manuscript compiled in Manila about 1590-1595, possibly as part of the documentation assembled by Don Luis Perez das Marinas in justification of his scheme for the conquest of Indochina.

"It is a land fertile in foodstuffs and cows and oxen and very healthy in itself. It is not thickly populated and the people are swarthy and heathens. In this kingdom there is no money nor silver with which to sell anything; and in order to buy what they need, they exchange foodstuffs for cotton blankets and other things that they make for the purpose of buying and selling with each other. Nobody is allowed to go shod, save only the king, and nobody can be married with more than two wives.

Food and drink

These people do not eat anything properly cooked, but only in raw or putrid condition; and in order to digest these foods, they are great drinkers of very strong spirits, which they drink little by little and very frequently, thinking it no disgrace to fall down from drinking too much.

Seasons

They divide the year into six festivals, during the first of which the vast majority of his vassals pay tribute to the king. The king goes to a field, and there they assemble all these tributes, out of which they make alms to the souls of the dead and perform great obsequies and funeral rites in their memory.

The second festival also lasts two months and they spend the whole of this time singing to the exclusion of everything else, except when they are actually eating their meals. During these festivals the women, of whatsoever condition they be, have liberty to do what they like for the space of three days, during which they are not asked to account for their behaviour.

During the third festival they go to the seaside, where they stay fishing for another two months. They make merry, catching enough fish to last them for the year, pickling it in their jars, with just a little salt, and they eat it putrid in this manner. And they thrive very strong and lusty on this food.

When the king returns to the city, they display lights by night and day, putting on plays and races in public, in which the king participates. This is the fourth of their festivals.

The fifth is when the king goes hunting elephants, of which there are many in this land, taking with him the nobility and their female elephants; and the females go into the place where the wild elephants are, which follow the former into a little space which they have stockaded off for this purpose, and there they keep them for some days until they are tamed.

Champa saw a late flowering under King Binasuos who led numerous successful campaigns against the Viet, culminating in the sack of Hanoi in 1371. Subsequently, the treachery of a low-ranking officer led to Binasuos' death in 1390 and the military eclipse of the Cham by the Vietnamese. The demographic and economic superiority of the Viet coupled with their gradual drift south contributed most to the waning of the Cham Kingdom, but finally, in 1471 the Cham suffered a terrible defeat at the hands of the

The last festival which they celebrate is a tiger-hunt. The tigers come to eat the buffaloes that are tied to a tree in certain places. They place sentinels over them, so that when the tigers approach, the king is informed. And as soon as this news arrives the king gets ready with a great number of Indians and nets, and they do with the tigers what they do with the elephants, surrounding them at once and killing them there and then. It is the custom with these Indians that at the time when they are occupied with this hunt, the king and his wife send out 100 or more Indians along the roads, with express order that they should not return without filling two gold basins which they give them, full of human gall, which must be from people of their own nation and not foreigners; and these emissaries do as they are told, not sparing anyone they meet, whether of high or low degree. As soon as they can catch a person on the road, they tie him at once to a tree, and there they cut out the gall ... When all this is over the king and his wife bathe and wash with this human gall; and they say that in this way they cleanse themselves of their sins and their faults.

Justice

The justice of this people is peculiar, for they have no fixed criminal code, but only their personal opinions, and when the case is a serious one, they investigate it with two witnesses. Their oaths are made with fire and boiling oil, and those condemned to death are executed with extreme barbarity. Some are sentenced to be trampled to death by elephants; others are flogged to death; others are tortured for two or three days, during which time bits and pieces are cut out of their bodies with pincers until they die. And for very trifling and common offences, they cut off their feet, hands, arms and ears.

Death

They have another custom invented by the Devil himself, which is that when any leading personage dies, they cremate the body, after it has been kept for eight or 10 days until they have made the necessary preparations in accordance with the quality of the deceased, when they burn it in the field. When such a person dies, they seize all the household servants and keep them until the same day on which they burn the body of their master, and then they throw them alive into the flames, so that they can serve them therewith in the other ... Another custom which they have, which is a very harsh one for women, is that when the husband dies, they burn the wife with him. They say that this law was made to prevent wives from giving poisonous herbs to their husbands, for there are very great witchcrafts and knaveries in these lands. They say that if the wife realizes that her husband will not live any longer than her, she will take good care of his life and ease, and will not dare to kill him with poison.

Vietnamese. Some 60,000 of their soldiers were killed and another 36,000 captured and carried into captivity, including the King and 50 members of the royal family. The kingdom shrank to a small territory in the vicinity of Nha Trang that survived until 1720 when surviving members of the royal family and many subjects fled to Cambodia to escape from the advancing Vietnamese.

The colonial period

One of the key motivating factors that encouraged the **French** to undermine the authority of the Vietnamese emperors was their treatment of Roman Catholics. Jesuits had been in the country from as early as the 17th century – one of them, Alexandre de Rhodes, converted the Vietnamese writing system from Chinese characters to Romanized script (see page 466) – but persecution of Roman Catholics began only in the 1830s. Emperor Minh Mang issued an imperial edict outlawing the dissemination of Christianity as a heterodox creed in 1825. The first European priest to be executed was François Isidore Gagelin who was strangled by six soldiers as he knelt on a scaffold in Hué in 1833. Three days later, having been told that Christians believe they will come to life again, Minh Mang had the body exhumed to confirm the man's death. In 1840 Minh Mang actually read the Old Testament in Chinese translation, declaring it to be 'absurd'.

Yet, Christianity continued to spread as Buddhism declined and there was a continual stream of priests willing to risk their lives proselytizing. In addition, the economy was in disarray and natural disasters common. Poor Vietnamese saw Christianity as a way to break the shackles of their feudal existence. Fearing a peasants' revolt, the Emperor ordered the execution of 25 European priests, 300 Vietnamese priests, and 30,000 Vietnamese Catholics between 1848 and 1860. Provoked by these killings, the French attacked and took Saigon in 1859. In 1862 **Emperor Tu Duc** signed a treaty ceding the three southern provinces to the French, thereby creating the colony of **Cochin China**. This treaty of 1862 effectively paved the way for the eventual seizure by the French of the whole kingdom. The French, through weight of arms, also forced the Emperor to end the persecution of Christians in his kingdom. In retrospect, although many Christians did die cruelly, the degree of persecution was not on the scale of similar episodes elsewhere: Minh Mang's successors Thieu Tri (1841-1847) and Tu Duc (1847-1883), though both fervently anti-Christian, appreciated French military strength and the fact that they were searching for pretexts to intervene.

The **French conquest of the north** was motivated by a desire to control trade and the route to what were presumed to be the vast riches of China. In 1883 and 1884, the French forced the Emperor to sign treaties making Vietnam a French protectorate. In August 1883 for example, just after Tu Duc's death, a French fleet appeared off Hué to force concessions. François Harmand, a native affairs official on board one of the ships, threatened the Vietnamese by stating: "Imagine all that is terrible and it will still be less than reality ... the word 'Vietnam' will be erased from history." The emperor called on China for assistance and demanded that provinces resist French rule; but the imperial bidding proved ineffective, and in 1885 the **Treaty of Tientsin** recognized the French protectorates of Tonkin (North Vietnam) and Annam (Central Vietnam), to add to that of Cochin China (South Vietnam).

Resistance to the French: the prelude to revolution

Like other European powers in Southeast Asia, the French managed to achieve military victory with ease, but they failed to stifle Vietnamese nationalism. After 1900, as Chinese translations of the works of Rousseau, Voltaire and social Darwinists such as Herbert Spence began to find their way into the hands of the Vietnamese intelligentsia, so resistance grew. Foremost among these early nationalists were Phan Boi Chau (1867-1940) and Phan Chau Trinh (1871-1926) who wrote tracts calling for the expulsion of the French. But these men and others such as Prince Cuong De (1882-1951) were traditional nationalists, their beliefs rooted in Confucianism rather than revolutionary Marxism. Their efforts and perspectives were essentially in the tradition of the nationalists who had resisted Chinese domination over previous centuries.

Quoc Dan Dang (VNQDD), founded at the end of 1927, was the first nationalist party, while the first significant communist group was the **Indochina Communist Party (ICP)** established by **Ho Chi Minh** in 1930. Both the VNQDD and the ICP organized resistance to the French and there were numerous strikes and uprisings, particularly during the harsh years of the Great Depression. The Japanese 'occupation' from August 1940 (Vichy France permitted the Japanese full access to military facilities in exchange for allowing continued French administrative control) saw the creation of the **Viet Minh** to fight for the liberation of Vietnam from Japanese and French control.

The Vietnam wars

The First Indochina War (1945-1954)

The Vietnam War started in September 1945 in the south of the country and in 1946 in the north. These years marked the onset of fighting **between the Viet Minh and the French** and the period is usually referred to as the First Indochina War. The communists, who had organized against the Japanese, proclaimed the creation of the **Democratic Republic of Vietnam** (DRV) on 2 September 1945 when Ho Chi Minh read out the Vietnamese **Declaration of Independence** in Hanoi's Ba Dinh Square. Ironically, this document was modelled closely on the American Declaration of Independence. Indeed, the USA was favourably disposed towards the Viet Minh and Ho. Operatives of the OSS (the wartime precursor to the CIA) met Ho and supported his efforts during the war and afterwards Roosevelt's inclination was to prevent France claiming their colony back. Only Winston Churchill's persuasion changed his mind.

The French, although they had always insisted that Vietnam be returned to French rule, were in no position to force the issue. Instead, in the south, it was British troops (mainly Gurkhas) who helped the small force of French against the Viet Minh. Incredibly, the British also ordered the Japanese, who had only just capitulated, to help fight the Vietnamese. When 35,000 French reinforcements arrived, the issue in the south – at least superficially – was all but settled, with Ca Mau at the southern extremity of the country falling on 21 October. From that point, the war in the south became an underground battle of attrition, with the north providing support to their southern comrades.

In the north, the Viet Minh had to deal with 180,000 rampaging Nationalist Chinese troops, while preparing for the imminent arrival of a French force. Unable to confront both at the same time, and deciding that the French were probably the lesser of two evils, Ho Chi Minh decided to negotiate. He is said to have observed in private, that it was preferable to 'sniff French shit for a while than eat China's all our lives'. To make the DRV government more acceptable to the French, Ho proceeded cautiously, only nationalizing a few strategic industries, bringing moderates into the government, and actually dissolving the Indochina Communist Party (at least on paper) in November 1945. But in the same month Ho also said: "The French colonialists should know that the Vietnamese people do not wish to spill blood, that it loves peace. But if it must sacrifice millions of combatants, lead a resistance for long years to defend the independence of the country, and preserve its children from slavery, it will do so. It is certain the resistance will win."

Chinese withdrawal

In February 1946, the French and Chinese signed a treaty leading to the withdrawal of Chinese forces and shortly afterwards Ho concluded a treaty with French President de Gaulle's special emissary to Vietnam, Jean Sainteny, in which Vietnam was acknowledged

Ho Chi Minh: 'He who enlightens'

Ho Chi Minh, one of a number of pseudonyms Ho adopted during his life (see box, page 416), was born Nguyen Sinh Cung, or possibly Nguyen Van Thanh (Ho did not keep a diary during much of his life, so parts of his life are still a mystery), in Nghe An Province near Vinh on the 19 May 1890, and came from a poor scholar-gentry family. In the village, the family was aristocratic; beyond it they were little more than peasants. His father, though not a revolutionary, was a dissenter and rather than go to Hué to serve the French, he chose to work as a village school teacher. Ho must have been influenced by his father's implacable animosity towards the French, although Ho's early years are obscure. He went to Quoc Hoc College in Hué and then worked for a while as a teacher in Phan Thiet, a fishing village in South Annam.

In 1911, under the name Nguyen Tat Thanh, he travelled to Saigon and left the country as a messboy on the French ship *Amiral Latouche-Tréville*. He is said to have used the name 'Ba' so that he would not shame his family by accepting such lowly work. This marked the beginning of three years of travel during which he visited France, England, America (where the skyscrapers of Manhattan both amazed and appalled him) and North Africa. Seeing the colonialists on their own turf and reading such revolutionary literature as the French Communist Party newspaper *L'Humanité*, he was converted to communism. In Paris he mixed with leftists, wrote pamphlets and attended meetings of the French Socialist Party. He also took odd jobs: for a while he worked at the **Carlton Hotel** in London and became an assistant pastry chef under the legendary French chef Georges Escoffier.

An even more unlikely story emerges from Gavin Young's *A Wavering Grace* In the book he recounts an interview he conducted with Mae West in 1968 shortly after he had returned from reporting the Tet offensive. On hearing of Vietnam, Mae West innocently said that she "used to know someone *very*, very important there … His name was Ho … Ho … Ho something". At the time she was staying at the Carlton while starring in a London show, *Sex*. She confided to Young: "There was this waiter, cook, I don't know what he was. I know he had the slinkiest eyes though. We met in the corridor. We – well…" Young writes that "Her voice trailed off in a husky sigh…"

Gradually Ho became an even more committed communist, contributing articles to radical newspapers and working his way into the web of communist and leftist groups. At the same time he remained, curiously, a French cultural

as a 'free' (the Vietnamese word *doc lap* being translated as free, but not yet independent) state that was within the French Union and the Indochinese Federation.

It is interesting to note that in negotiating with the French, Ho was going against most of his supporters who argued for confrontation. But Ho, ever a pragmatist, believed at this stage that the Viet Minh were ill-trained and poorly armed and he appreciated the need for time to consolidate their position. The episode that is usually highlighted as the flashpoint that led to the resumption of hostilities was the French government's decision to open a customs house in Haiphong at the end of 1946. The Viet Minh forces resisted and the rest, as they say, is history. It seems that during the course of 1946 Ho changed his view of the best path to independence. Initially he asked: "Why should we sacrifice 50 or 100,000 men when we can achieve independence within five years through negotiation?" although he chauvinist, complaining for example about the intrusion of English words like *le manager* and *le challenger* (referring to boxing contests) into the French language. He even urged the French prime minister to ban foreign words from the French press. In 1923 he left France for Moscow and was trained as a communist activist – effectively a spy. From there, Ho travelled to Canton where he was instrumental in forming the Vietnamese communist movement. This culminated in the creation of the Indochina Communist Party in 1930. His movements during these years are scantily documented: he became a Buddhist monk in Siam (Thailand), was arrested in Hong Kong for subversive activities and received a six month sentence, travelled to China several times, and in 1940 even returned to Vietnam for a short period – his first visit for nearly 30 years. Despite his absence from the country, the French had already recognized the threat that he posed and sentenced him to death in absentia in 1930. He did not adopt the pseudonym by which he is now best known – Ho Chi Minh – until the early 1940s.

Ho was a consummate politician and, despite his revolutionary fervour, a great realist. He was also a charming man, and during his stay in France between June and October 1946 he made a great number of friends. Robert Shaplen in his book *The Lost Revolution* (1965) talks of his "wit, his oriental courtesy, his savoir-faire… above all his seeming sincerity and simplicity". He talked with farmers and fishermen and debated with priests; he impressed people wherever he travelled. He died in Hanoi at his house in the former governor's residence in 1969.

Since the demise of communism in the former Soviet Union, the Vietnamese leadership have been concerned that secrets about Ho's life might be gleaned from old comintern files in Moscow by nosy journalists. To thwart such an eventuality, they have, reportedly, sent a senior historian to scour the archives. To date, Ho's image remains largely untarnished – making him an exception amongst the tawdry league of former communist leaders. But a Moscow-based reporter has unearthed evidence implying Ho was married, challenging the official hagiography that paints Ho as a celibate who committed his entire life to the revolution. It takes a brave Vietnamese to challenge established 'fact'. In 1991, when the popular Vietnamese *Youth* or *Tuoi Tre* newspaper dared to suggest that Ho had married Tang Tuyet Minh in China in 1926, the editor was summarily dismissed from her post.

later came to the conclusion that it was necessary to fight for independence. The customs house episode might, therefore, be viewed as merely an excuse. The French claimed that 5000 Vietnamese were killed in the ensuing bombardment, versus five Frenchmen; the Vietnamese put the toll at 20,000.

In a pattern that was to become characteristic of the entire 25-year conflict, while the French controlled the cities, the Viet Minh were dominant in the countryside. By the end of 1949, with the success of the Chinese Revolution and the establishment of the Democratic People's Republic of Korea (North Korea) in 1948, the USA began to offer support to the French in an attempt to stem the 'Red Tide' that seemed to be sweeping across Asia. At this early stage, the odds appeared stacked against the Viet Minh, but Ho was confident that time was on their side. As he remarked to Sainteny "If we have to fight, we will fight.

You can kill 10 of my men for every one I kill of yours but even at those odds, I will win and you will lose". It also became increasingly clear that the French were not committed to negotiating a route to independence. A secret French report prepared in 1948 was obtained and published by the Viet Minh in which the High Commissioner, Monsieur Bollaert, wrote: "It is my impression that we must make a concession to Vietnam of the term, independence; but I am convinced that this word need never be interpreted in any light other than that of a religious verbalism."

Ho Chi Minh pseudonyms

Born	
1890	Nguyen Sinh Cung or Nguyen Van Thanh (Vinh)
1910	Van Ba (South Vietnam)
1911	Nguyen Tat Thanh (Saigon)
1913	Nguyen Tat Thanh (London)
1914	Nguyen Ai Quoc (Paris)
1924	Linh (Moscow)
1924	Ly Thuy (Moscow)
1925	Wang (Canton)
1927	Duong (Paris)
1928	Nguyen Lai, Nam Son, Thau Chin (Siam)
1942	Ho Chi Minh

Dien Bien Phu (1954) and the Geneva Agreement

The decisive battle of the First Indochina War was at Dien Bien Phu in the hills of the northwest, close to the border with Laos. At the end of 1953 the French, with American support, parachuted 16,000 men into the area in an attempt to protect Laos from Viet Minh incursions and to tempt them into open battle. The French in fact found themselves trapped, surrounded by Viet Minh and overlooked by artillery. There was some suggestion that the US might become involved, and even use tactical nuclear weapons, but this was not to be. In May 1954 the French surrendered – the most humiliating of French colonial defeats – effectively marking the end of the French presence in Indochina (for a fuller account of the battle see page 108). In July 1954, in Geneva, the French and Vietnamese agreed to divide the country along the 17th parallel, so creating two states – the communists occupying the north and the non- communists occupying the south. The border was kept open for 300 days and over that period about 900,000 – mostly Roman Catholic – Vietnamese travelled south. At the same time nearly 90,000 Viet Minh troops along with 43,000 civilians went north, although many Viet Minh remained in the south to continue the fight there.

The Second Indochina War (1954-1975)

The Vietnam War, but particularly the American part of that war, is probably the most minutely studied, reported, analysed and recorded in history. Yet, as with all wars, there is still large grey areas and continuing disagreement over important episodes. Most crucially, there is the question of whether the US might have won had their forces been given a free hand and were not forced, as some would have it, to fight with one hand tied behind their backs. This remains the view among many members of the US military.

Ngo Dinh Diem

At the time of the partition of Vietnam along the 17th parallel, the government in the south was chaotic and the communists could be fairly confident that in a short time their sympathizers would be victorious. This situation was to change with the rise of Ngo Dinh Diem. Born in Hué in 1901 to a Roman Catholic Confucian family, Diem wished to become a priest. He graduated at the top of his class from the French School of Administration and at the age of 32 was appointed to the post of minister of the interior at the court of Emperor Bao Dai. Here, according to the political scientist William Turley, "he worked with uncommon industry and integrity" only to resign in exasperation at court intrigues and French interference. He withdrew from political activity during the First Indochina War and in 1946 Ho Chi Minh offered him a post in the DRV government – an offer he declined.

Turley describes him as a man who was a creature of the past: "For Diem, the mandarin, political leadership meant rule by example, precept and paternalism. His Catholic upbringing reinforced rather than replaced the Confucian tendency to base authority on doctrine, morality and hierarchy. Utterly alien to him were the concepts of power-sharing and popular participation. He was the heir to a dying tradition, member of an elite that had been superbly prepared by birth, training, and experience to lead a Vietnam that no longer existed."

In July 1954 Diem returned from his self-imposed exile at the Maryknoll Seminary in New Jersey to become Premier of South Vietnam. It is usually alleged that the USA administration was behind his rise to power, although this has yet to be proved. He held two rigged elections (in October 1955, 450,000 registered voters cast 605,025 votes) that gave some legitimacy to his administration in American eyes. He proceeded to suppress all opposition in the country. His brutal brother, Ngo Dinh Nhu, was appointed to head the security forces and terrorized much of Vietnamese society.

During the period of Diem's premiership, opposition to his rule, particularly in the countryside, increased. This was because the military's campaign against the Viet Minh targeted – both directly and indirectly – many innocent peasants. At the same time, the nepotism and corruption that was endemic within the administration also turned many people into Viet Minh sympathizers. That said, Diem's campaign was successful in undermining the strength of the Communist Party in the south. While there were perhaps 50,000-60,000 party members in 1954, this figure had declined through widespread arrests and intimidation to only 5000 by 1959.

The erosion of the Party in the south gradually led, from 1959, to the north changing its strategy towards one of more overt military confrontation. The same year also saw the establishment of Group 559 which was charged with the task of setting up what was to become the Ho Chi Minh Trail, along which supplies and troops were moved from the north to the south. But, even at this stage, the Party's forces in the south were kept from open confrontation and many of its leaders were hoping for victory without having to resort to open warfare. There was no call for a 'People's War' and armed resistance was left largely to guerrillas belonging to the Cao Dai (see page 474) and Hoa Hao (Buddhist millenarian) sects. The establishment of the National Liberation Front of Vietnam in 1960 was an important political and organizational development towards creating a credible alternative to Diem – although it did not hold its first congress until 1962.

The escalation of the armed conflict (1959-1963)

Viet Cong

The armed conflict began to intensify from the beginning of 1961 when all the armed forces under the communists' control were unified under the banner of the **People's Liberation Armed Forces (PLAF)**. By this time the Americans were already using the term Viet Cong (or VC) to refer to communist troops. They reasoned that the victory at Dien Bien Phu had conferred almost heroic status on the name Viet Minh. American psychological warfare specialists therefore invented the term Viet Cong, an abbreviation of *Viet-nam*

Cong-san (or Vietnamese Communists) and persuaded the media in Saigon to begin substituting it for Viet Minh from 1956.

The election of **John F Kennedy** to the White House in January 1961 coincided with the communists' decision to widen the war in the south. In the same year Kennedy dispatched 400 special forces troops and 100 special military advisers to Vietnam, in flagrant contravention of the Geneva Agreement. With the cold war getting colder, and Soviet Premier Nikita Khrushchev confirming his support for wars of 'national liberation', Kennedy could not back down and by the end of 1962 there were 11,000 US personnel in South Vietnam. At the same time the NLF had around 23,000 troops at its disposal. Kennedy was still saying that: "In the final analysis, it's their war and they're the ones who have to win or lose it". But just months after the Bay of Pigs debacle in Cuba, Washington set out on the path that was ultimately to lead to America's first large-scale military defeat.

The bungling and incompetence of the forces of the south, the interference that US advisers and troops had to face, the misreading of the situation by US military commanders, and the skill – both military and political – of the communists, are most vividly recounted in Neil Sheehan's massive book, *A Bright Shining Lie* (see page 486). The conflict quickly escalated from 1959. The north infiltrated about 44,000 men and women into the south between then and 1964, while the number recruited in the south was between 60,000 and 100,000. In August 1959, the first consignment of arms was carried down the **Ho Chi Minh Trail** into South Vietnam. Meanwhile, Kennedy began supporting, arming and training the Army of the Republic of Vietnam (ARVN). The USA however, shied away from any large-scale, direct confrontation between its forces and the Viet Cong.

An important element in Diem's military strategy at this time was the establishment of **strategic hamlet**s, better known simply as 'hamleting'. This strategy was modelled on British anti-guerrilla warfare during Malaya's communist insurgency, and aimed to deny the communists any bases of support in the countryside while at the same time making it more difficult for communists to infiltrate the villages and 'propagandize' there. The villages which were ringed by barbed wire were labelled 'concentration camps' by the communists, and the often brutal, forced relocation that peasants had to endure probably turned even more of them into communist sympathizers. Of the 7000-8000 villages sealed in this way, only a fifth could ever have been considered watertight.

In January 1963 at **Ap Bac**, not far from the town of My Tho, the communists scored their first significant victory in the south. Facing 2000 well-armed ARVN troops, a force of just 300-400 PLAF inflicted heavy casualties and downed five helicopters. After this defeat, many American advisers drew the conclusion that if the communists were to be defeated, it could not be left to the ARVN alone – US troops would have to become directly involved. As Lieutenant Colonel John Vann, a US Army officer, remarked after the debacle to the American media (as cited in Neil Sheehan's *A Bright Shining Lie*): "A miserable damn performance. These people won't listen. They make the same goddam mistakes over and over again in the same way."

In mid-1963 a Buddhist monk from Hué committed suicide by dousing his body with petrol and setting it alight. This was the first of a number of **self-immolations**, suggesting that even in the early days the Diem regime was not only losing the military war but also the 'hearts and minds' war. He responded with characteristic heavy handedness by ransacking suspect pagodas. On 2 December 1963, Diem and his brother Nhu were both assassinated during an army coup.

Vietnam War

NORTH VIETNAM

CHINA

Dien Bien Phu

HANOI   Haiphong

LAOS

Sam Neua

Luang
Prabang   Phonsavanh

*Plain of
Jars*

*Gulf of
Tonkin*

VIENTIANE

THAILAND

Ho Chi Minh Trail

Demilitarized Zone
(22-7-54)

Khe Sanh   Quang Tri

Hamburger Hill   Hué

Danang

My Lai

Kontum

Pleiku

*Ia Drang
Valley*   Qui Nhon

CAMBODIA

SOUTH
VIETNAM

Ho Chi Minh Trail

Dalat

*Cam
Ranh
Bay*

PHNOM PENH   Tay
Ninh

Cu Chi   Bien Hoa

SAIGON   Vung
Tao

Sihanoukville   Can Tho   Ap Bac

East Sea

N

*Gulf of
Thailand*   Ca Mau

100 km
100 miles

The American war in Vietnam

The US decision to enter the war has been the subject of considerable disagreement. Until recently, the received wisdom was that the US administration had already taken the decision, and manufactured events to justify their later actions. However, the recent publication of numerous State Department, Presidential, CIA, Defence Department and National Security Council files – all dating from 1964 – has shed new light on events leading up to American intervention (these files are contained in the United States Government Printing Office's 1108-page-long *Vietnam 1964*).

In Roger Warner's *Back Fire* (1995), which deals largely with the CIA's secret war in Laos, he recounts a story of a war game commissioned by the Pentagon and played by the Rand Corporation in 1962. They were asked to play a week-long game simulating a 10-year conflict in Vietnam. At the end of the week, having committed 500,000 men, the US forces were bogged down, there was student unrest and the American population had lost confidence in their leaders and in the conduct of the war. When the game was played a year later but, on the insistence of the US Airforce, with much heavier aerial bombing, the conclusions were much the same. If only, if only …

By all accounts, **Lyndon Johnson** was a reluctant warrior. In the 1964 presidential campaign he repeatedly said: "We don't want our American boys to do the fighting for Asian boys". This was not just for public consumption. The files show that LBJ always doubted the wisdom of intervention. But he also believed that John F Kennedy had made a solemn pledge to help the South Vietnamese people, a pledge that he was morally obliged to keep. In most respects, LBJ was completely in agreement with Congress, together with sections of the American public, who were disquietened by events in South Vietnam. The Buddhist monk's self-immolation, broadcast on prime-time news, did not help matters.

It has usually been argued that the executive manufactured the **Gulf of Tonkin Incident** to force Congress and the public to approve an escalation of America's role in the conflict. It was reported that two American destroyers, the *USS Maddox* and *USS C Turner Joy*, were attacked without provocation in international waters on the 2 August 1964 by North Vietnamese patrol craft. The US responded by bombing shore installations while presenting the Gulf of Tonkin Resolution to an outraged Congress for approval. Only two Congressmen voted against the resolution and President Johnson's poll rating jumped from 42% to 72%. In reality, the *USS Maddox* had been involved in electronic intelligence gathering while supporting clandestine raids by South Vietnamese mercenaries – well inside North Vietnamese territorial waters. This deception only became apparent in 1971 when the **Pentagon papers**, documenting the circumstances behind the incident, were leaked to the *New York Times* (the Pentagon papers were commissioned by Defense Secretary McNamara in June 1967 and written by 36 Indochina experts).

But these events are not sufficient to argue that the incident was manufactured to allow LBJ to start an undeclared war against North Vietnam. On 4 August, Secretary of State Dean Rusk told the American representative at the United Nations that: "In no sense is this destroyer a pretext to make a big thing out of a little thing". Even as late as the end of 1964, the President was unconvinced by arguments that the US should become more deeply involved. On 31 August, McGeorge Bundy wrote in a memorandum to Johnson: "A still more drastic possibility which no one is discussing is the use of substantial US armed forces in operation against the Viet Cong. I myself believe that before we let this country go we should have a hard look at this grim alternative, and I do not at all think that it is a repetition of Korea."

But events overtook President Johnson, and by 1965 the US was firmly embarked on the road to defeat. In March 1965, he ordered the beginning of the air war against the north perhaps acting on Air Force General Curtis Le May's observation that "we are swatting flies when we should be going after the manure pile". **Operation Rolling Thunder**, the most intense bombing campaign any country had yet experienced, began in March 1965 and ran through to October 1968. In 3½ years, twice the tonnage of bombs was dropped on Vietnam (and Laos) as during the entire Second World War. During its peak in 1967, 12,000 sorties were being flown each month – a total of 108,000 were flown throughout 1967. North Vietnam claimed that 4000 out of its 5788 villages were hit. Most terrifying were the B-52s that dropped their bombs from such an altitude (17,000 m) that the attack could not even be heard until the bombs hit their targets. Each aircraft carried 20 tonnes of bombs. By the end of the American war in 1973, 14 million tonnes of all types of munitions had been used in Indochina, an explosive force representing 700 times that of the atomic bomb dropped on Hiroshima. As General Curtis Le May explained on 25 November 1965 – "We should bomb them back into the Stone Age". In the same month that Rolling Thunder commenced, marines landed at Danang to defend its airbase, and by June 1965 there were 74,000 US troops in Vietnam. Despite President Johnson's reluctance to commit the US to the conflict, events forced his hand. He realized that the undisciplined South Vietnamese could not prevent a communist victory. Adhering to the domino theory, and with his own and the US's reputation at stake, he had no choice. As Johnson is said to have remarked to his press secretary Bill Moyers: "I feel like a hitchhiker caught in a hail storm on a Texas highway. I can't win. I can't hide. And I can't make it stop."

Dispersal of the North's industry

In response to the bombing campaign, industry in the north was decentralized and dispersed to rural areas. Each province was envisaged as a self-sufficient production unit. The economic effect of this strategy was felt at the time in a considerable loss of productivity; a cost judged to be worth paying to protect the north's industrial base. In order to protect the population in the north, they too were relocated to the countryside. By the end of 1967 Hanoi's population was a mere 250,000 essential citizens – about a quarter of the pre-war figure. The same was true of other urban centres. What the primary US objective was in mounting the air war remains unclear. In part, it was designed to destroy the north's industrial base and its ability to wage war; to dampen the people's will to fight; to sow seeds of discontent; to force the leadership in the north to the negotiating table; and perhaps to punish those in the north for supporting their government. By October 1968 the US realized the bombing was having little effect and they called a halt. The legacy of Operation Rolling Thunder, though, would live on. Turley wrote: "... the bombing had destroyed virtually all industrial, transportation and communications facilities built since 1954, blotted out 10 to 15 years' potential economic growth, flattened three major cities and 12 of 29 province capitals, and triggered a decline in per capita agricultural output".

However, it was not just the bombing campaign that was undermining the north's industrial and agricultural base. Socialist policies in the countryside were labelling small land owners as 'landlords' – in effect, traitors to the revolutionary cause – thus alienating many farmers. In the cities, industrial policies were no less short-sighted. Though Ho's policies in the battlefield were driven by hard-headed pragmatism, in the field of economic development they were informed – tragically – by revolutionary fervour.

A war glossary

Agent Orange	herbicide used to defoliate forests
APC	armoured personnel carrier
ARVN	Army of the Republic of Vietnam; the army of the South
Body Count	the number of dead on a field of battle
BUFF	nickname for the B-52 bomber; stands for Big Ugly Fat Fellow or, more usually, Big Ugly Fat Fucker
COIN	counter-insurgency
DMZ	demilitarized zone; the border between North and South Vietnam at the 17th parallel
Dust-off	medical evacuation helicopter
DZ	parachute drop zone
FAC	forward air controller, an airborne spotter who directed bombers onto the target
Fire base	defence fortification for artillery, from which to support infantry
Fragging	to kill or attempt to kill with a fragmentation grenade; better known as the killing of US officers and NCOs by their own men. In 1970 one study reported 209 fraggings
Gook	slang, derogatory term for all Vietnamese
Grunt	slang for a US infantryman; the word comes from the 'grunt' emitted when shouldering a heavy pack
Huey	most commonly used helicopter, UH1
LZ	helicopter landing zone
Napalm	jellified fuel, the name derives from two of its constituents, naphthenic and palmitic acids. To be burnt by napalm after an attack was terrible and one of the most famous photo images

William Westmoreland, the general appointed to command the American effort, aimed to use the superior firepower and mobility of the US to 'search and destroy' PAVN forces. North Vietnamese bases in the south were to be identified using modern technology, jungle hideouts revealed by dumping chemical defoliants and then attacked with shells, bombs and by helicopter-borne troops. In 'free-fire zones' the army and air force were permitted to use whatever level of firepower they felt necessary to dislodge the enemy. 'Body counts' became the measure of success and collateral damage – or civilian casualties – was a cost that just had to be borne. As one field commander famously explained: 'We had to destroy the town to save it'. By 1968 the US had more than 500,000 troops in Vietnam, while **South Korean**, **Australian**, **New Zealand**, **Filipino** and **Thai** forces contributed another 90,000. The ARVN officially had 1.5 million men under arms (100,000 or more of these were 'flower' or phantom soldiers, the pay for whom was pocketed by officers in an increasingly corrupt ARVN). Ranged against this vastly superior force were perhaps 400,000 PAVN and National Liberation Front forces.

1964-1968: who was winning?

The leadership in the north tried to allay serious anxieties about their ability to defeat the American-backed south by emphasizing human over physical and material resources. **Desertions** from the ARVN were very high – there were 113,000 from the army in 1965 of the war (taken by Nick Ut) showed a naked local girl (Kim Phuc) running along a road at Trang Bang, northwest of Saigon after being burnt; the girl survived the attack by South Vietnamese aircraft and now lives in Canada

NLF	National Liberation Front
NVA	North Vietnamese Army
PAVN	People's Army of Vietnam
Phoenix	counter-insurgency programme established by the US after the Tet Offensive of 1968 (see page 425)
PLAF	People's Liberation Armed Forces;the army of the communist north
POW/MIA	prisoner of war/missing in action
Pungi stakes	sharpened bamboo stakes concealed in VC pits: accounted for 2% of US combat wounds
Purple Heart	medal awarded to US troops wounded in action
R&R	Rest & Recreation; leave
ROE	rules of engagement
Rome Plow	20 tonne bulldozer designed to clear forest. Equipped with a curved blade and sharp protruding spike it could split the largest trees
Tunnel Rats	US army volunteers who fought VC in the Cu Chi tunnels
VC, Charlie	Viet Cong (see page 417); US term for Vietnamese Communist; often shortened to Charlie from the phonetic alphabet, Victor Charlie
Viet Minh	Communist troops – later changed to Viet Cong (see above and page 417)
WP, Willy Pete	White phosphorous rocket used to mark a target

alone (200,000 in 1975) – and the PAVN did record a number of significant victories. The communists also had to deal with large numbers of desertions – 28,000 men in 1969. By 1967 world opinion, and even American public opinion, appeared to be swinging against the war. Within the US, **anti-war demonstrations** and 'teach-ins' were spreading, officials were losing confidence in the ability of the US to win the war, and the president's approval rating was sinking fast. As the US Secretary of Defense, Robert McNamara is quoted as saying in the *Pentagon Papers*: "... the picture of the world's greatest superpower killing or seriously injuring 1000 non-combatants a week, while trying to pound a tiny, backward nation into submission on an issue whose merits are hotly disputed, is not a pretty one".

But although the communists may have been winning the psychological and public opinion wars, they were increasingly hard-pressed to maintain this advantage on the ground. Continual American strikes against their bases, and the social and economic dislocations in the countryside, were making it more difficult for the communists to recruit supporters. At the same time, the fight against a vastly better equipped enemy was also taking its toll in sheer exhaustion. Despite what is now widely regarded as a generally misguided US military strategy in Vietnam, there were notable US successes (for example, the Phoenix Programme, see page 426). American GIs were always sceptical about the 'pacification' programmes that aimed to win the 'hearts and minds' war. GIs were fond of saying, 'If you've got them by the balls, their hearts and minds will follow'. At times,

The Anzacs in Vietnam

In April 1964, President Johnson called for "more flags" to help defend South Vietnam. Among the countries that responded to his call were Australia and New Zealand. Australia had military advisers in Vietnam from 1962, but in April 1965 sent the First Battalion Royal Australian Regiment. Until 1972 there were about 7000 Australian combat troops in Vietnam, based in the coastal province of Phuoc Tuy, not far from Saigon. There, operating as a self-contained unit in a Viet Cong-controlled zone, and with the support of two batteries of 105 mm artillery (one from New Zealand), the Australians fought one of the most effective campaigns of the entire war.

As US Army Chief of Staff, General Westmoreland said: "Aggressiveness, quick reaction, the good use of firepower, and old-fashioned Australian courage have produced outstanding results."

Of the battles fought by the Australians in Phuoc Tuy, one of the most significant was Long Tan, on 18 August 1966. Although caught out by the advance of 4000 Viet Cong, the Australians successfully responded to inflict heavy casualties: 17 dead against about 250 VC.

Following this they managed to expand control over large areas of the province, and then win the support of the local people. Unlike the Americans who adopted a policy of 'search and destroy', the Australians were more intent on a 'hearts and minds' strategy (COIN, or counter insurgency). Through various health, education and other civic action programmes, the Australians gained the confidence of many villagers, making it much harder for the VC to infiltrate rural areas of Phuoc Tuy.

This policy of gaining support of the local population was complemented by the highly effective use of small **Special Air Service** (SAS) teams who worked closely with the US Special Forces. Many of these men were transferred after fighting in the jungles of Borneo during the *Konfrontasi* between Malaysia and Indonesia. They came well trained in the art of jungle warfare and ended the war with the highest kill ratio of any similar unit: at least 500 VC dead, against none of their own to hostile fire. The Australians left Phuoc Tuy in late 1971, having lost 423 men. The ARVN were unable to fill the vacuum, and the Viet Cong quickly regained control of the area.

the US military and politicians appeared to view the average Vietnamese as inferior to the average American. This latent racism was reflected in General Westmoreland's remark that Vietnamese "don't think about death the way we do" and in the use by most US servicemen of the derogatory name "gook" to refer to Vietnamese.

At the same time as the Americans were trying to win 'hearts and minds', the Vietnamese were also busy indoctrinating their men and women, and the population in the 'occupied' south. In Bao Ninh's moving *The Sorrow of War* (1994), the main character, Kien, who fights with a scout unit describes the indoctrination that accompanied the soldiers from their barracks to the field: "Politics continuously. Politics in the morning, politics in the afternoon, politics again in the evening. 'We won, the enemy lost. The enemy will surely lose. The north had a good harvest, a bumper harvest. The people will rise up and welcome you. Those who don't just lack awareness. The world is divided into three camps.' More politics."

By 1967, the war had entered a period of military (though not political) stalemate. As Robert McNamara writes in his book *In Retrospect: the Tragedy and Lessons of Vietnam*, it

The war in figures

Killed (soldiers of the North)	1,100,000
Killed (soldiers of the South)	250,000
Vietnamese civilians	2,000,000

Americans:

Served	3,300,000
Killed	57,605
Captured	766 (651 returned)
Wounded	303,700
MIA	4993 (121 returned, 4872 declared dead)

Australians:

Killed	423
Wounded	2398

At height of the war:

Bombs dropped	1.2 million tonnes/year
Cost of bombs	US$14 bn/year
Area defoliated	2.2 million ha (1962-1971)
US air attacks	400,000/year
Refugees	585,000/year
Civilian casualties	130,000/month

was at this stage that he came to believe that Vietnam was "a problem with no solution". In retrospect, he argues that the US should have withdrawn in late 1963, and certainly by late 1967. Massive quantities of US arms and money were preventing the communists from making much headway in urban areas, while American and ARVN forces were ineffective in the countryside – although incessant bombing and ground assaults wreaked massive destruction. A black market of epic proportions developed in Saigon, as millions of dollars of assistance went astray. American journalist Stanley Karnow once remarked to a US official that "we could probably buy off the Vietcong at US$500 a head". The official replied that they had already calculated the costs, but came to "US$2500 a head".

The Tet Offensive, 1968: the beginning of the end

By mid-1967, the communist leadership in the north felt it was time for a further escalation of the war in the south to regain the initiative. They began to lay the groundwork for what was to become known as the Tet (or New Year) Offensive – perhaps the single most important series of battles during the American War in Vietnam. During the early morning of 1 February 1968, shortly after noisy celebrations had welcomed in the New Year, 84,000 communist troops – almost all Viet Cong – simultaneously attacked targets in 105 urban centres. Utterly surprising the US and South Vietnamese, the Tet Offensive had begun.

Preparations for the offensive had been laid over many months. Arms, ammunition and guerrillas were smuggled and infiltrated into urban areas and detailed planning was undertaken. Central to the strategy was a 'sideshow' at Khe Sanh. By mounting an attack on the marine outpost at **Khe Sanh**, the communists successfully convinced the American and Vietnamese commanders that another Dien Bien Phu was underway. General Westmoreland moved 50,000 US troops away from the cities and suburbs to prevent any such humiliating repetition of the French defeat. But Khe Sanh was just a diversion, a feint designed to draw attention away from the cities. In this the communists were successful; for days after the Tet offensive, Westmoreland and the South Vietnamese President Thieu thought Khe Sanh to be the real objective and the attacks in the cities the decoy.

The most interesting aspect of the Tet Offensive was that although it was a strategic victory for the communists, it was also a considerable tactical defeat. They may have occupied the US embassy in Saigon for a few hours but, except in Hué, communist forces were quickly repulsed by US and ARVN troops. The government in the south did not collapse nor did the ARVN. Cripplingly high casualties were inflicted on the communists – cadres at all echelons were killed – morale was undermined and it became clear that the cities would not rise up spontaneously to support the communists. Tet, in effect, put paid to the VC as an effective fighting force. The fight was now increasingly taken up by the North Vietnamese Army (NVA). This was to have profound effects on the government of South Vietnam after reunification in 1975; southern communists and what remained of the political wing of the VC – the government in waiting – were entirely overlooked as northern communists were given all the positions of political power, a process that continues. This caused intense bitterness at the time and also explains the continued mistrust of many southerners for Hanoi. Walt Rostow wrote in 1995 that "Tet was an utter military and political defeat for the communists in Vietnam", but adding "yet a political disaster in the United States". But this was not to matter; Westmoreland's request for more troops was turned down and US public support for the war slumped still further as they heard reported that the US embassy itself had been 'over-run'. Those who for years had been claiming it was only a matter of time before the communists were defeated seemed to be contradicted by the scale and intensity of the offensive. Even President Johnson was stunned by the VC's successes for he too had believed the US propaganda. As it turned out the VC incursion was by a 20-man unit from Sapper Battalion C-10 who were all killed in the action. Their mission was not to take the embassy but to 'make a psychological gesture'. In that regard at least, the mission must have exceeded the leadership's wildest expectations.

The **Phoenix Programme**, established in the wake of the Tet Offensive, aimed to destroy the communists' political infrastructure in the Mekong Delta. Named after the Vietnamese mythical bird the Phung Hoang, which could fly anywhere, the programme sent CIA-recruited and trained Counter Terror Teams – in effect assassination units – into the countryside. The teams were ordered to try and capture communist cadres; invariably they fired first and asked questions later. By 1971, it was estimated that the programme had led to the capture of 28,000 members of the VCI (Viet Cong Infrastructure), the death of 20,000 and the defection of a further 17,000. By the early 1970s the countryside in the Mekong Delta was more peaceful than it had been for years; towns that were previously strongholds of the Viet Cong had reverted to the control of the local authorities. Critics have questioned what proportion of those killed, captured and sometimes tortured were communist cadres, but even communist documents admit that it seriously undermined their support network in the area. In these terms, the Phoenix Programme was a great success.

The costs

The Tet Offensive concentrated American minds. The costs of the war by that time had been vast. The US budget deficit had risen to 3% of Gross National Product by 1968, inflation was accelerating, and thousands of young men had been killed for a cause that, to many, was becoming less clear by the month. Before the end of the year President Johnson had ended the bombing campaign. Negotiations began in Paris in 1969 to try and secure an honourable settlement for the US. Although the last American combat troops were not to leave until March 1973, the Tet Offensive marked the beginning of the end. It was from that date the Johnson administration began to search seriously for a way out of the conflict. The illegal bombing of Cambodia in 1969 and the resumption of the bombing of the north in 1972 (the most intensive of the entire conflict) were only flurries of action on the way to an inevitable US withdrawal.

The Paris Agreement (1972)

US Secretary of State **Henry Kissinger** records the afternoon of 8 October 1972, a Sunday, as the moment when he realized that the communists were willing to agree a peace treaty. There was a great deal to discuss, particularly whether the treaty would offer the prospect of peaceful reunification, or the continued existence of two states: a communist north, and non-communist south. Both sides tried to force the issue: the US mounted further attacks and at the same time strengthened and expanded the ARVN. They also tried to play the 'Madman Nixon' card, arguing that **President Richard Nixon** was such a vehement anti-communist that he might well resort to the ultimate deterrent, the nuclear bomb. It is true that the PAVN was losing men through desertion and had failed to recover its losses in the Tet Offensive. Bao Ninh in his book *The Sorrow of War* about Kinh, a scout with the PAVN, wrote: "The life of the B3 Infantrymen after the Paris Agreement was a series of long suffering days, followed by months of retreating and months of counter-attacking, withdrawal, then counter-attack. The path of war seemed endless, desperate, and leading nowhere."

But the communist leadership knew well that the Americans were committed to withdrawal – the only question was when, so they felt that time was on their side. By 1972, US troops in the south had declined to 95,000, the bulk of whom were support troops. The north gambled on a massive attack to defeat the ARVN and moved 200,000 men towards the demilitarized zone that marked the border between north and south. On 30 March the PAVN crossed into the south and quickly overran large sections of Quang Tri province. Simultaneous attacks were mounted in the west highlands, at Tay Ninh and in the Mekong Delta. For a while it looked as if the south would fall altogether. The US responded by mounting a succession of intense bombing raids that eventually forced the PAVN to retreat. The spring offensive may have failed, but like Tet, it was strategically important, for it demonstrated that without US support the ARVN was unlikely to be able to withstand a communist attack.

Both sides, by late 1972, were ready to compromise. Against the wishes of South Vietnam's President Nguyen Van Thieu, the US signed a treaty on 27 January 1973, the ceasefire going into effect on the same day. Before the signing, Nixon ordered the bombing of the north – the so-called Christmas Campaign. It lasted 11 days from 18 December (Christmas Day was a holiday) and was the most intensive of the war. With the ceasefire and President Thieu, however shaky, both in place, the US was finally able to back out of its nightmare and the last combat troops left in March 1973. As J William Fulbright, a highly influential member of the Senate and a strong critic of the US role in Vietnam, observed: "We [the US] have the power to do any damn fool thing we want, and we always seem to do it."

A nation at sea: the boat people

One of the most potent images of Vietnam during the 1970s and 80s was of foundering, overloaded vessels carrying 'boat people' to Hong Kong, Thailand, Malaysia and the Philippines. Beginning in 1976, but becoming a torrent from the late 1970s, these boat people initially fled political persecution. Later, most were economic migrants in search of a better life. Now the tragedy of the boat people is almost at an end and fast becoming a footnote in history as the last refugees are sent 'home' or onward to what they hope will be a better life.

Escaping the country was not easy. Many prospective boat people were caught by the authorities (often after having already paid the estimated US$500-3000 to secure a place on a boat), and sent to prison or to a re-education camp. Of those who embarked, it has been estimated that at least a third died at sea, from drowning or dehydration, and at the hands of pirates. The boats were usually small and poorly maintained, hardly seaworthy for a voyage across the East Sea. Captains rarely had charts (some did not even have an experienced sailor on board) and most had never ventured further afield than the coastal waters with which they were familiar.

By 1977, the exodus was so great that some freighters began to stop heaving-to to pick up refugees – a habit which, until then, had been sacrosanct among sailors. Malaysia instructed their coastal patrol vessels to force boats back out to sea – and in the first six months of 1979 they did just that to 267 vessels carrying an estimated 40,000 refugees. One boat drifted for days off Malaysia, with the passengers drinking their own urine, until they were picked up – but not before two children had died of dehydration. The Singapore and Malaysian governments adopted a policy of allowing boats to replenish their supplies, but not to land – forcing some vessels to sail all the way to Australia before they were assured of a welcome (over 8000 km). Cannibalism is also reported to have taken place; one boy who had only just survived being killed himself told a journalist: "After the body [of a boy] had been discovered, the boat master pulled it up out of the hold. Then he cut up the body. Everyone was issued a piece of meat about two fingers wide."

As numbers rose, so did the incidence of piracy – an age-old problem in the East Sea. Pirates, mostly Thai, realizing that the boats often carried families with all their possessions (usefully converted into portable gold) began to target the refugee boats. Some commentators have estimated that by the late 1970s, 30% of boats were being boarded, and the United Nations High Commissioner for Refugees (UNHCR) in 1981 reported that 81% of women had been raped. Sometimes the boats were boarded and plundered, the women raped, all the passengers murdered, and the boats sunk. Despite all these risks, Vietnamese continued to leave in huge numbers: by 1980 there were 350,000 awaiting resettlement in refugee camps in the countries of Southeast Asia and Hong Kong.

Most of these 'illegals' left from the south of Vietnam; identified with the

The Final Phase 1973-1975

The Paris Accord settled nothing; it simply provided a means by which the Americans could withdraw from Vietnam. It was never going to resolve the deep-seated differences between the two regimes and with only a brief lull, the war continued, this time without US troops. Thieu's government was probably in terminal decline even before the peace treaty was signed. Though ARVN forces were at their largest ever and, on paper, former regime, they were systematically persecuted – particularly if they also happened to be ethnic Chinese or *Hoa* (the Chinese 'invasion' of 1979 did not help matters). But as conditions worsened in the north, large numbers also began to sail from Ha Long Bay and Haiphong. Soon the process became semi-official, as local and regional authorities realized that fortunes could be made providing boats and escorts. Large freighters began to carry refugees; the *Hai Hong* (1600 tonnes), which finally docked in Malaysia, was carrying 2500 passengers who claimed they had left with the cognizance of the authorities.

The peak period of the crisis spanned the years 1976-1979, with 270,882 leaving the country in 1979 alone. The flow of refugees slowed during 1980 and 1981 to about 50,000 and until 1988 averaged about 10,000 each year. But in the late 1980s the numbers picked up once again, with most sailing for Hong Kong and leaving from the north. It seems that whereas the majority of those sailing in the first phase (1976-1981) were political refugees, the second phase of the exodus was driven by economic pressures. Daily wage rates in Vietnam at that time were only 3000 dong (US$0.25), so it is easy to see the attraction of leaving for healthier economic climes. With more than 40,000 refugees in camps in Hong Kong, the Hong Kong authorities began to forcibly repatriate (euphemistically termed 'orderly return') those screened as economic migrants at the end of 1989 when 51 were flown to Hanoi. Such was the international outcry as critics highlighted fears of persecution that the programme

was suspended. In May 1992, an agreement was reached between the British and Vietnamese governments to repatriate the 55,700 boat people living in camps in Hong Kong and the orderly return programme was quietly restarted. As part of their deal with China, the British government agreed to empty the camps before the handover date in 1997 (a target they failed to meet).

Ironically, the evidence is that those repatriated are doing well – better than those who never left the shores of Vietnam – and there is no real evidence of systematic persecution, despite the fears of such groups as Amnesty International. With the European Community and the UN offering assistance to returnees, they have set up businesses, enrolled on training courses and become embroiled in Vietnam's thrust for economic growth.

In early 1996, around 37,000 boat people were still living in camps in Hong Kong (mostly), Indonesia, Thailand, the Philippines and Japan. The difficulty is that those who are left are the least attractive to receiving countries. As Jahanshah Assadi of the UNHCR put it at the end of 1994, "Our Nobel Prize winners left a long time ago for the West", adding "What we have now is the bottom of the barrel." Even Vietnam is not enamoured with the idea of receiving ex-citizens who clearly do not wish to return. For the refugees themselves, they have been wasted years. As the UNHCR's Jean-Noel Wetterlauth said in 1996: "Leaving Vietnam was the project of their lives." Now they're going back with nothing to show for the years and the tears.

considerably stronger than the PAVN, many men were weakly committed to the cause of the south. Corruption was endemic, business was in recession, and political dissent was on the increase. The North's Central Committee formally decided to abandon the Paris Accord in October 1973; by the beginning of 1975 they were ready for the final offensive. It took only until April for the communists to achieve total victory. ARVN troops deserted in their thousands, and the only serious resistance was offered at Xuan Loc, less than 100 km from

Saigon. President Thieu resigned on 27 April. ARVN generals, along with their men, were attempting to flee as the PAVN advanced on Saigon. The end was quick: at 1045 on 30 April a T-54 tank (number 843) crashed its way through the gates of the Presidential Palace, symbolizing the end of the Second Indochina War. For the US, the aftermath of the war would lead to years of soul searching; for Vietnam, to stagnation and isolation. A senior State Department figure, George Ball, reflected afterwards that the war was "probably the greatest single error made by America in its history".

Legacy of the Vietnam War

The Vietnam War (or 'American War' to the Vietnamese) is such an enduring feature of the West's experience of the country that many visitors look out for legacies of the conflict. There is no shortage of physically deformed and crippled Vietnamese. Many men were badly injured during the war, but large numbers also received their injuries while serving in Cambodia (1979-1989). It is tempting to associate deformed children with the enduring effects of the pesticide **Agent Orange** (1.7 million tonnes had been used by 1973), although this has yet to be proven scientifically; American studies claim that there is no significant difference in congenital malformation. One thing is certain: Agent Orange is detectable today only in tiny isolated spots, often near former military bases where chemicals were dumped. No scientific survey has found lingering widespread effects.

Bomb damage
Bomb damage is most obvious from the air: well over five million tonnes of bombs were dropped on the country (north and south) and there are said to be 20 million bomb craters – the sort of statistic people like to recount, but no one can legitimately verify. Many craters have yet to be filled in and paddy fields are still pockmarked. Some farmers have used these holes in the ground to farm fish and to use as small reservoirs to irrigate vegetable plots. War scrap was one of the country's most valuable exports. The cities in the north are surprisingly devoid of obvious signs of the bombing campaigns; Hanoi remains remarkably intact. In Hué the Citadel and the Forbidden Palace were extensively damaged during the Tet offensive in 1968 although much has now been rebuilt.

Psychological effect of the war
Even harder to measure is the effect of the war on the Vietnamese psyche. Bao Ninh in *The Sorrow of War* writes of a driver with the PAVN who, talking with Kien, the book's main character, observes: "I'm simply a soldier like you who'll now have to live with broken dreams and with pain. But, my friend, our era is finished. After this hard-won victory, fighters like you, Kien, will never be normal again. You won't even speak with your normal voice, in the normal way again." Later in the book, Kien muses about the opportunities lost due to the war. Although the book is a fictional story, the underlying tale is one of truth:

"Still, even in the midst of my reminiscences I can't avoid admitting there seems little left for me to hope for. From my life before soldiering there remains sadly little. ... Those who survived continue to live. But that will has gone, that burning will which was once Vietnam's salvation. Where is the reward of enlightenment due to us for attaining our sacred war goals? Our history-making efforts for the next generations have been to no avail."

The Vietnamese Communist Party leadership still seem to be preoccupied by the conflict and school children are routinely shown war museums and Ho Chi Minh memorials. But despite the continuing propaganda offensive, people harbour surprisingly little animosity towards America or the West. Indeed, of all westerners, it is often Americans who are most warmly welcomed, particularly in the south.

But it must be remembered that about 60% of Vietnam's population has been born since the US left in 1973, so have no memory of the American occupation. Probably the least visible but most lasting of all the effects of the war is in the number of elderly widowed women and the number of middle aged women who never married.

The deeper source of antagonism is the continuing divide between the north and south. It was to be expected that the forces of the north would exact their revenge on their foes in the south and many were relieved that the predicted bloodbath didn't materialize. But few would have thought that this revenge would be so long lasting. The 250,000 southern dead are not mourned or honoured, or even acknowledged. Former soldiers are denied jobs and the government doesn't recognize the need for national reconciliation.

This is the multiple legacy of the War on Vietnam and the Vietnamese. The legacy on the US and Americans is more widely appreciated. The key question that still occupies the minds of many, though, is, was it worth it? Economic historian Walt Rostow, ex-Singaporean prime minister Lee Kuan Yew and others would probably answer 'yes'. If the US had not intervened, communism would have spread farther in Southeast Asia; more dominoes, in their view, would have fallen. In 1973, when the US withdrawal was agreed, Lee Kuan Yew observed that the countries of Southeast Asia were much more resilient and resistant to communism than they had been, say, at the time of the Tet offensive in 1968. The US presence in Vietnam allowed them to reach this state of affairs. Yet Robert McNamara in his book *In Retrospect: the Tragedy and Lessons of Vietnam*, and one of the architects of US policy, wrote:

"Although we sought to do the right thing – and believed we were doing the right thing – in my judgment, hindsight proves us wrong. We both overestimated the effects of South Vietnam's loss on the security of the West and failed to adhere to the fundamental principle that, in the final analysis, if the South Vietnamese were to be saved, they had to win the war themselves."

After the war

The Socialist Republic of Vietnam (SRV) was born from the ashes of the Vietnam War on 2 July 1976 when former North and South Vietnam were reunified. Hanoi was proclaimed as the capital of the new country. But few Vietnamese would have guessed that their emergent country would be cast by the US in the mould of a pariah state for almost 18 years. First President George Bush I, and then his successor Bill Clinton, eased the US trade embargo bit by bit in a dance of appeasement and procrastination, as they tried to comfort American business clamouring for a slice of the Vietnamese pie, while also trying to stay on the right side of the vociferous lobby in the US demanding more action on the MIA issue. Appropriately, the embargo, which was first imposed on the former North in May 1964, and then nationwide in 1975, was finally lifted a few days before the celebrations of Tet, Vietnamese New Year, on 4 February 1994.

On the morning of 30 April 1975, just before 1100, a T-54 tank crashed through the gates of the Presidential Palace in Saigon, symbolically marking the end of the Vietnam War. Twenty years later, the same tank – number 843 – became a symbol of the past as parades and celebrations, and a good deal of soul searching, marked the anniversary of the end of the War. To many Vietnamese, in retrospect, 1975 was more a beginning than an end: it was the beginning of a collective struggle to come to terms with the war, to build a nation, to reinvigorate the economy and to excise the ghosts of the past. Two decades after the armies of the South laid down their arms and the last US servicemen and officials frantically fled by helicopter to carriers waiting in the East Sea, the Vietnamese government is still trying, as they put it, to get people to recognize that 'Vietnam is a country, not a war'. A further 20 years from now, it may seem that only in 1995 did the war truly end.

Re-education camps

The newly formed Vietnam government ordered thousands of people to report for re-education camps in 1975. Those intended were ARVN members, ex-South Vietnam government members and those that had collaborated with the South regime including priests, artists, teachers and doctors. It was seen as a means of revenge and a way of indoctrinating the 'unbelievers' with communist propaganda. It was reported in the Indochina Newsletter in 1982 that some 80 camps existed with an estimated 100,000 still languishing in them seven years after the war ended. Detainees were initially told that they would be detained for between three days and one month. Those that were sent to the camp were forced to undertake physical labour and survived on very little food and without basic medical facilities all the while undergoing communist indoctrination.

The boat people

Many Vietnamese also fled, first illegally and then legally through the Orderly Departure Programme. See box, page 428.

Invasion of Cambodia

In April 1975, the Khmer Rouge took power in Cambodia. Border clashes with Vietnam erupted just a month after the Phnom Penh regime change but matters came to a head in 1977 when the Khmer Rouge accused Vietnam of seeking to incorporate Kampuchea into an Indochinese Federation. Hanoi's determination to oust Pol Pot only really became apparent on Christmas Day 1978, when 120,000 Vietnamese troops invaded. By 7 January they had installed a puppet government that proclaimed the foundation of the People's Republic of Kampuchea (PRK): Heng Samrin, a former member of the Khmer Rouge, was appointed president. The Vietnamese compared their invasion to the liberation of Uganda from Idi Amin – but for the rest of the world it was an unwelcome Christmas present. The new government was accorded scant recognition abroad, while the toppled government of Democratic Kampuchea retained the country's seat at the United Nations.

But the country's 'liberation' by Vietnam did not end the misery; in 1979 nearly half of Cambodia's population was in transit, either searching for their former homes or fleeing across the Thai border into refugee camps. The country reverted to a state of outright war again, for the Vietnamese were not greatly loved in Cambodia – especially by the Khmer Rouge. American political scientist Wayne Bert wrote: "The Vietnamese had long seen a special role for themselves in uniting and leading a greater Indochina Communist movement and the Cambodian Communists had seen with clarity that such a role for the Vietnamese could only be at the expense of their independence and prestige."

Under the Lon Nol and Khmer Rouge regimes, Vietnamese living in Cambodia were expelled or exterminated. Resentment had built up over the years Hanoi – exacerbated by the apparent ingratitude of the Khmer Rouge for Vietnamese assistance in fighting Lon Nol's US-supported Khmer Republic in the early 1970s. As relations between the Khmer Rouge and the Vietnamese deteriorated, the communist superpowers, China and the Soviet Union, polarised too – the former siding with Khmer Rouge and the latter with Hanoi.

The Vietnamese invasion had the full backing of Moscow, while the Chinese and Americans began their support for the anti-Vietnamese rebels.

Following the Vietnamese invasion, three main anti-Hanoi factions were formed. In June 1982 they banded together in an unholy alliance of convenience to fight the PRK and called themselves the Coalition Government of Democratic Kampuchea (CGDK), which was immediately recognized by the UN. The three factions of the CGDK were: The Communist Khmer Rouge whose field forces had recovered to at least 18,000 by the late 1980s. Supplied with weapons by China, they were concentrated in the Cardamom Mountains in the southwest and were also in control of some of the refugee camps along the Thai border. The National United Front for an Independent Neutral Peaceful and Co-operative Cambodia (Funcinpec) – known by most people as the Armée National Sihanoukiste (ANS). It was headed by Prince Sihanouk – although he spent most of his time exiled in Beijing; the group had fewer than 15,000 well-equipped troops – most of whom took orders from Khmer Rouge commanders. The anti-Communist Khmer People's National Liberation Front (KPNLF), headed by Son Sann, a former prime minister under Sihanouk. Its 5000 troops were reportedly ill-disciplined in comparison with the Khmer Rouge and the ANS.

The three CGDK factions were ranged against the 70,000 troops loyal to the government of President Heng Samrin and Prime Minister Hun Sen (previously a Khmer Rouge cadre.) they were backed by Vietnamese forces until September 1989.

In the late 1980s the Association of Southeast Asian Nations (ASEAN) – for which the Cambodian conflict had almost become its raison d'être – began steps to bring the warring factions together over the negotiating table. ASEAN countries were united in wanting the Vietnamese out of Cambodia. After Mikhail Gorbachev had come to power in the Soviet Union, Moscow's support for the Vietnamese presence in Cambodia gradually evaporated. Gorbachev began leaning on Vietnam as early as 1987, to withdraw its troops. Despite saying their presence in Cambodia was 'irreversible', Vietnam completed its withdrawal in September 1989, ending nearly 11 years of Hanoi's direct military involvement. The withdrawal led to an immediate upsurge in political and military activity, as forces of the exiled CGDK put increased pressure on the now weakened Phnom Penh regime to begin a round of power-sharing negotiations.

Border incursions with China

In February 1979 the Chinese marched into the far north of northern Vietnam justifying the invasion because of Vietnam's invasion of Cambodia, its treatment of Chinese in Vietnam, the ownership of the Paracel and Spratley Islands in the East Sea also claimed by China and a stand against Soviet expansion into Asia (Hanoi was strongly allied with the then USSR). They withdrew a month later following heavy casualties although both sides have claimed to be victorious. Vietnamese military hardware was far superior to the Chinese and their casualties were estimated to be between 20,000 and 60,000; Vietnamese casualties were around 15,000. In 1987 fighting again erupted on the Sino-Vietnamese border resulting in high casualties.

Modern Vietnam

Politics

The **Vietnamese Communist Party** (**VCP**) was established in Hong Kong in 1930 by Ho Chi Minh and arguably has been more successful than any other such party in Asia in mobilizing and maintaining support. While others have fallen, the VCP has managed to stay firmly in control. To enable them to get their message to a wider audience, the Communist Party of Vietnam have launched their own website, www.cpv.org.vn.

Vietnam is a one party state. In addition to the Communist Party the posts of president and prime minister were created when the constitution was revised in 1992. The president is head of state and the prime minister is head of the cabinet of ministries (including three deputies and 26 ministries), all nominated by the National Assembly. The current president is Nguyen Minh Triet and the current prime minister is Nguyen Tan Dung. Although the National Assembly is the highest instrument of state it can still be directed by the Communist Party. The vast majority of National Assembly members are also party members. Elections for the National Assembly are held every five years. The Communist Party is run by a politburo of 15 members. The head is the general secretary, currently Nong Duch Manh. The politburo, last elected in 2006 at the Tenth Party Congress, meets every five years and sets policy directions of the Party and the government. The Eleventh Party Congress is scheduled for 2011. In addition, there is a Central Committee made up of 161 members, who are also elected at the Party Congress.

In 1986, at the Sixth Party Congress, the VCP launched its economic reform programme known as *doi moi*, which was a momentous step in ideological terms (see page 445). However, although the programme has done much to free up the economy, the party has ensured that it retains ultimate political power. Marxism-Leninism and Ho Chi Minh thought are still taught to Vietnamese school children and even so-called 'reformers' in the leadership are not permitted to diverge from the party line. In this sense, while economic reforms have made considerable progress (but see below) – particularly in the south – there is a very definite sense that the limits of political reform have been reached, at least for the time being.

From the late 1990s to the first years of the new millennium there have been a number of arrests and trials of dissidents charged with what might appear to be fairly innocuous crimes (see The future of communism in Vietnam, page 441) and, although the economic reforms enacted since the mid-1980s are still in place, the party resolutely rejects any moves towards greater political pluralism.

Looking at the process of political succession in Vietnam and the impression is not one of a country led by young men and women with innovative ideas. Each year commentators consider the possibility of an infusion of new blood and reformist ideas but the Party Congress normally delivers more of the same: dyed-in-the-wool party followers who are more likely to maintain the status quo than challenge it along with just one or two reformers. The Asian economic crisis did, if anything, further slow down the pace of change. To conservative party members, the Asian crisis – and the political instability that it caused – were taken as warnings of what can happen if you reform too far and too fast. The latest change of faces in the leadership occurred during the Ninth Party Congress in April 2001. The key change was the appointment of 67-year-old Nong Duc Manh as party

Provinces

CHINA

Hà Giang
Cao Bang
Lai Châu
Lào Cai
Tuyên Quang
Bac Kan
Diên Biên Phu
Yên Bái
Lang Son
Son La
Phu Tho **11**
Bac Giang
Quang Ninh
2
1 **10 9**
8 **3**
Hòa Bình
7 **4**
6 5
Thanh Hóa

LAOS

Gulf of Tonkin

Nghê An

Hà Tinh

Quang Bình

THAILAND

Quang Tri

Thùa Thiên Huê

Dà Nang

Quang Nam

Quang Ngai

Kon Tum

Bình Dình

Gia Lai

Phú Yên

CAMBODIA

Dak Lak

Khánh Hòa

Bình Phuoc
Lâm Dong
Ninh Thuan
Tây Ninh **19**
Dong Nai
Bình Thuân
An Giang **17**
Long An **14**
15
13
Gulf of Thailand
Kien Giang
Cân Tho
Ben Tre
16
Kiên Giang
Trà Vinh
East Sea
18
Sóc Trang
Bac Lieu
Ca Mau

N

100 km
100 miles

Provinces

Hanoi **1**
Hà Tay **2**
Hai Phong **3**
Thái Bình **4**
Nam Dinh **5**
Ninh Bình **6**
Ha Nam **7**
Hung Yen **8**
Hai Duong **9**
Bac Ninh **10**
Vinh Phuc **11**
Thai Nguyen **12**
Ba Ria-Vung Tau **13**
Ho Chi Minh City **14**
Tien Giang **15**
Vinh Long **16**
Dong Tháp **17**
Hau Giang **18**
Binh Duong **19**

Getting our children out of Vietnam: a personal story

The following is a personal account by Ken Thompson and his wife Kim Chi. Ken flew in Vietnam and Laos as a Forward Air Controller (FAC). In Laos he was designated Raven 58.)

It was 1 April 1975. I was watching the news on television. The North Vietnamese had captured Qui Nhon. From my 26-month experience in the war zone of Vietnam, I knew that South Vietnam was going to fall and we, myself and my Vietnamese wife, had to decide now to go to Vietnam to get our children out or possibly never see them again.

We had not heard from them in over a year and did not know if they were still with their grandmother in Luong Phuoc (a village 90 miles northeast of Saigon), whether their village had already been overrun, or if they were already dead. It had been a longer time since we had heard from our son and we believed that he had been killed.

Before, the North Vietnamese had moved south and captured Hué and Danang, only to be pushed back. But now they had captured Qui Nhon. They had outflanked the South Vietnamese Army and would now push south to Saigon. The country was lost.

We decided right then to go. In six days, we had our passports, shots and visas and were on our way to Saigon. We had been trying to get our girls out of Vietnam for over three years. But government red tape prevented us. Before going, everyone thought that we would not come back alive. So we taped our last wills to the kitchen cabinets in our home in Milford Center, Ohio.

We took as much money as possible and borrowed whatever we could. On 3 April, we left our 10-month-old daughter, Thao, with my parents and went to Washington DC to get my passport and our visas. Then we flew to the Philippines. But we had more delays. First, the flight to Saigon was delayed because the President's Palace in Saigon was being bombed. Then, during the delay, my passport was stolen. We went to the American Embassy in Manila and applied for an emergency passport'. Realizing that Vietnam was about to fall to the North Vietnamese, the Emergency Passport was issued.

Finally, on 10 April 1975, we arrived in Saigon. We got a room in the Embassy Hotel and started to make enquiries about the status of the war. The police in Saigon told us that Luong Phuoc had been evacuated and the villagers were in Vung Tau, a former resort area turned into a refugee camp. Kim Chi went to Vung Tau to find our girls. They were not there and none of the villagers from Luong Phuoc was there. The police told us the village had been evacuated so they would not have to go to Luong Phuoc to get the girls.

We had to find someone to go for us. We could not go. I, being an American, and Kim Chi now being too westernized, would both be killed by the Viet Cong or stopped by the South Vietnamese Army. Our cousin, Ty, in Saigon agreed to go and search for the girls in Luong Phuoc.

Our search for the girls was the main topic of interest at the Embassy Hotel, as none of the other Americans or Vietnamese staying there expected us to ever find them. We had received word that Luong Phuoc was already cut off from Saigon. Ty had

general secretary, replacing the unpopular conservative Le Kha Phieu. Nong Duc Manh was re-elected as general secretary at the Tenth Party Congress in April 2006.

Nguyen Tan Dung was also re-elected and is now the country's prime minister. On his appointment as general secretary in 2001, Manh – who commentators are hoping will be a little more modern in his outlook than his predecessor – pledged to continue the modernization drive, reform the party and counter corruption. Nothing new there.

to go by boat in order to bypass the Viet Cong and arrived at Luong Phuoc to find Kim Chi's mother and the children. They left everything behind. Even then, they were stopped by the South Vietnamese Army and held for over an hour. The village came under attack by the North Vietnamese and Kim Chi's grandmother pushed the girls to the bottom of the boat and lay on top of them, yelling to the boatman to head for the sea. Under fire, they reached the safety of the ocean and headed south.

They reached Vung Tau and the following morning took a bus to Saigon. While waiting for the girls to arrive in Saigon, Kim Chi and I had been processing the papers required for their immigration to the US. However, on 20 April all that changed. The word had come down that all Vietnamese would be given refugee status if they accompanied an American out of Saigon. You could take anyone you wanted, just as long as you claimed they were a relative. (It really did not matter if they were or not. If an American thought that a Vietnamese should be given refugee status that was all that mattered.)

We arrived by bus at Tan San Nhut Airport while the outskirts of the city were being bombed by the North Vietnamese. After several hours, we boarded the Air Force C-141 Transport and flew to the Philippines where we slept on the gymnasium floor of the military base. We were there only four days before President Marcos kicked out all the refugees and we had to go to Guam where we were kept in a tent city constructed by the US Navy. Since we had most of our papers completed for the girls, Mai and Phuong (12 and seven years old), we were evacuated on 27 April 1975. We arrived in San Francisco on 28 April 1975, the day that Saigon fell to the North Vietnamese.

Nearly 15 years later, in 1989, Kim Chi returned to Vietnam to visit her mother. In 1995 she bought property near Luong Phuoc where we hope to eventually build a business.

(Footprint has managed to contact Ken and is pleased to report the following update. Ken's eldest daughter Mai has since married and has three children. She runs a property business with her husband in Columbus, Ohio, near to where Ken and Kim Chi live. The younger daughter, Phuong, has an engineering degree from Ohio State University and is working for a firm in Kentucky. She has one son who is in high school. Ken and Kim Chi had a further daugther in the US who trained with the Marine Corps and now works as a consultant for the military. She lives in Alexandria, Virginia, with her husband, also a Marine. Ken is a mathematical logician consultant for a professor at Indiana University.

Ken and Kim Chi returned to Vietnam in 1998 with their youngest daughter. Ken writes: "In 1998 while I was at our home, this gentleman came riding in on his bicycle. He knew I was there and wanted to come and see me. We sat down and had some tea as my wife translated for him. He was the former VC general whose troops I had bombed and who had tried to capture my wife during the war. We sat and talked and had a good time together.")

General Secretary Manh repeated his plan to tackle **corruption** at the Tenth Party Congress in the light of two high profile cases indicating that the authorities now mean business. In 2006 one case involving a minister for transport led his superior, the head of Transport Dao Dinh Binh to resign. Bui Tien Dun was sentenced to 13 years imprisonment along with others who were jailed for seven years in 2007. They had been accused of using US$760,000 of embezzled funds to place illegal bets on European football. Bui also was sentenced to a further seven years for bribery as he tried to cover up the bets.

Vietnam's former deputy trade minister was also convicted in 2007 of taking US$6000 bribes from textile companies who wanted to increase their US export quota above government-fixed figures (now no longer in place since Vietnam joined the WTO). He stood trial with 12 others, including his son and other high profile officials. He was sentenced to 14 years in prison; on appeal this was reduced to 12 years. Le Van Thang, former deputy director of the ministry's import-export department, was sentenced to 17 years for taking bribes.

For many westerners there is something strange about a leadership calling for economic reform and liberalization while, at the same time, refusing any degree of political pluralism. How long the VCP can maintain this charade, along with China, while other communist governments have long since fallen (with the hardly edifying exceptions of Cuba and North Korea), is a key question. Despite the reforms, the leadership is still divided over the road ahead. But the fact that debate is continuing, sometimes openly, suggests that there is disagreement over the necessity for political reform and the degree of economic reform that should be encouraged. One small chink in the armour is the proposed bill to allow referenda. The draft report indicates that referenda would be held on the principles of universality, equality, directness and secret ballot but that the subject of referenda would be decided by the party.

In the country as a whole there is virtually no political debate at all, certainly not in the open. There are two reasons for this apparently curious state of affairs. First there is a genuine fear of discussing something that is absolutely taboo. The police have a wide network of informers who report back on a regular basis and no one wants to accumulate black marks that make it difficult to get the local police reference required for a university place, passport or even a job. Second, and more importantly, is the booming economy. Since the 1990s, economic growth in Vietnam has been unprecedented. In 2006 the growth rate was 8.2% but this dropped to 5.3% in 2009. As every politician knows, the one thing that keeps people happy is rising income. Hence with not much to complain about most Vietnamese people are content with their political status quo.

Nevertheless it would be foolish to think that everyone was happy. That political tensions are bubbling somewhere beneath the surface of Vietnamese society became clear in 1997 with serious disturbances in the poor coastal northern province of Thai Binh, 80 km southeast of Hanoi. In May, 3000 local farmers began to stage protests in the provincial capital, complaining of corruption and excessive taxation. There were reports of rioting and some deaths – strenuously denied, at least at first, by officials. However, a lengthy report appeared in the army newspaper *Quan Doi Nhan Dan* in September detailing moral decline and corruption in the Party in the province. For people in Thai Binh, and many others living in rural areas, the reforms of the 1980s and 1990s have brought little benefit. People living in Ho Chi Minh City may tout mobile phones and drive cars and motorbikes, but in much of the rest of the country average monthly incomes are around US$50-80. The Party's greatest fear is that ordinary people might lose confidence in the leadership and in the system. The fact that many of those who demonstrated in Thai Binh were, apparently, war veterans didn't help either. Nor can the leadership have failed to remember that Thai Binh was at the centre of peasant disturbances against the French. A few months later riots broke out in prosperous and staunchly Roman Catholic Dong Nai, just north of Ho Chi Minh City. The catalyst to these disturbances was the seizure of church land by a corrupt Chairman of the People's Committee. The mob razed the Chairman's house and stoned the fire brigade. Clearly, pent up frustrations were seething beneath the surface for Highway 1 had to be closed for several days while the unrest continued. While the Dong Nai troubles went wholly unreported in Vietnam, a *Voice of Vietnam* broadcast admitted to them and went on to catalogue a list of previous civil disturbances, none of which was known to the outside world; it appears the purpose was to advise Western journalists that this was just another little local difficulty and not the beginning of the end of communist rule. But reports of disturbances continue to filter out of Vietnam. At the beginning of 2001 thousands of ethnic minorities rioted in the Central Highland provinces of Gia Lai and Dac Lac and the army had to be called in to re-impose order. All foreigners were banned from the Central Highlands.

Again in April 2004 violence between ethnic minorities and the government flared in the Central Highlands, resulting in 'unknown numbers of dead and injured and reports of people missing' according to Amnesty International. Once more the cause was religious freedom and land rights although the government persists in its implausible conspiracy theory about 'outside forces' and extremists in the US wanting to destabilize it; a pretext, some fear, for the use of the jackboot and the imprisonment of trouble makers. To its shame (not that they are aware of such a concept) the Cambodian government simply hands refugees – many of who are asylum seekers in the strictest meaning – straight back to the Vietnamese forces. Much of the border area is a no-go zone in both countries, neither country allowing representatives of UNHCR anywhere near.

In 2006 Brad Adams, Asia director at Human Rights Watch (HRW) said: "The Vietnamese government continues to persecute Montagnards once they are out of the sight of international observers. The international community should oppose their forced return to the Central Highlands as long as the authorities continue to persecute them." He continued: "Vietnamese officials continue to force Montagnard Christians to sign pledges renouncing their religion, despite the passage of new regulations banning such practices. Authorities in some areas restrict freedom of movement between villages – in particular for religious purposes not authorized by the government – and ban Christian gatherings in many areas unless they are presided over by officially recognized pastors."

HRW reports than more than 350 ethnic minority people from the Central Highlands have been jailed, charged under Vietnam's Penal Code.

In more recent years, others have been prepared to voice their views. In 2006 Bloc 8406, a pro-democracy group named after its founding date of 8 April 2006, was set up. Catholic priest Father Nguyen Van Ly, editor of the underground online magazine *Free Speech* and a founding member of Bloc 8406, was sentenced to eight years in jail for anti-government activity. Four others were also sentenced with him. His trial can be seen on You Tube, including images of him having his mouth covered up and being bundled out of the courtroom. In March 2007 Nguyen Van Dai and Le Thi Cong Nhan, two human rights lawyers, were arrested on the grounds of distributing material "dangerous to the State" and were sentenced to four and five years in prison respectively. See also page 442 on cyber-dissidents.

As well as Bloc 8406, other pro-democracy movements include the US-based Viet Tan Party, www.viettan.org, with offices also in Australia, France, Japan, and the People's Democratic Party, among others.

International relations

In terms of international relations, Vietnam's relationship with the countries of the **Association of Southeast Asian Nations (ASEAN)** have warmed markedly since the dark days of the early and mid-1980s and in mid-1995 Vietnam became the association's seventh – and first communist – member. The delicious irony of Vietnam joining ASEAN was that it was becoming part of an organization established to counteract the threat of communist Vietnam itself – although everyone was too polite to point this out. No longer is there a deep schism between the capitalist and communist countries of the region, either in terms of ideology or management. The main potential flashpoint concerns Vietnam's long-term historical enemy – China. The enmity and suspicion which underlies the relationship between the world's last two real communist powers stretches back over 2000 years. Indeed, one of the great attractions to Vietnam of joining ASEAN was the bulwark that it created against a potentially aggressive and actually economically ascendant China.

China and Vietnam, along with Malaysia, Taiwan, Brunei and the Philippines, all claim part (or all) of the East Sea's **Hoang Sa** (formerly **Spratly Islands**). These tiny islands, many no more than coral atolls, would have caused scarcely an international relations ripple were it not for the fact that they are thought to sit above huge oil reserves. Whoever can prove rights to the islands lays claim to this undersea wealth. Over the last decade China has been using its developing blue water navy to project its power southwards. This has led to skirmishes between Vietnamese and Chinese forces, and to diplomatic confrontation between China and just about all the other claimants. Although the parties are committed to settling the dispute without resort to force, most experts see the Spratly Islands as the key potential flashpoint in Southeast Asia – and one in which Vietnam is seen to be a central player. **Truong Sa** (formerly **Paracel Islands**) further north are similarly disputed by Vietnam and China.

Rapprochement with the USA

One of the keys to a lasting economic recovery was a normalization of relations with the US. From 1975 until early 1994 the US made it largely illegal for any American or American company to have business relations with Vietnam. The US, with the support of Japan and other Western nations, also blackballed attempts by Vietnam to gain membership to the IMF, World Bank and Asian Development Bank, thus cutting off access to the largest source of cheap credit. In the past, it has been the former Soviet Union and the countries of the Eastern Bloc that have filled the gap, providing billions of dollars of aid (US$6 billion 1986-1990), training and technical expertise. But in 1990 the Soviet Union halved its assistance to Vietnam, making it imperative that the government improve relations with the West and particularly the US.

In April 1991 the US opened an official office in Hanoi to assist in the search for Missing in Action (MIAs), the first such move since the end of the war, and in December 1992 allowed US companies to sign contracts to be implemented after the US trade embargo had been lifted. In 1992, both Australia and Japan lifted their embargoes on aid to Vietnam and the US also eased restrictions on humanitarian assistance. Support for a **full normalization of relations** was provided by French President Mitterand during his visit in February 1993, the first by a Western leader since the end of the war. He said that the US veto on IMF and World Bank assistance had "no reason for being there", and applauded Vietnam's economic reforms. He also pointed out to his hosts that respect for human rights was now a universal obligation, which did not go down quite so well. Nonetheless he saw his visit as marking the end of one chapter and the beginning of another.

This inexorable process towards normalization continued with the full lifting of the trade embargo on 4 February 1994 when President Bill Clinton announced the normalization of trade relations. Finally, on 11 July 1995 Bill Clinton declared the full normalization of relations between the two countries and a month later Secretary of State Warren Christopher opened the new American embassy in Hanoi. On 9 May 1997 Douglas 'Pete' Peterson, the first 'post-war' American ambassador to Vietnam and a former POW who spent six years of the war in the infamous 'Hanoi Hilton', took up his post in the capital.

The progress towards normalization was so slow because many Americans still harbour painful memories of the war. With large numbers of ordinary people continuing to believe that servicemen shot down and captured during the war and listed as MIAs were still languishing in jungle jails, presidents Bush and Clinton had to tread exceedingly carefully. In a sense, it was recognized long ago that the embargo no longer served American interests, it was just that the public were not yet ready to forgive and forget.

Even though the embargo is now a thing of the past, there are still the families of over 2000 American servicemen listed as Missing in Action who continue to hope that the remains of their loved ones might, some day, make their way back to the US. (The fact there are still an estimated 300,000 Vietnamese MIAs is, of course, of scant interest to the American media.) It was this, among other legacies of the war, which made progress towards a full normalization of diplomatic and commercial relations such a drawn-out business.

The normalization of trade relations between the two countries was agreed in a meeting between Vietnamese and US officials in July 1999 and marked the culmination of three years' discussions. But conservatives in the politburo prevented the agreement being signed into law worried, apparently, about the social and economic side effects of such reform. This did not happen until 28 November 2001 when Vietnam's National Assembly finally ratified the treaty. It has led to a substantial increase in bilateral trade. In 2003 the USA imported US$4.5 billion worth of Vietnamese goods, roughly four times more than it exported to Vietnam. And not only goods: by 2004 the US Consulate General in Ho Chi Minh City handled more applications for American visas than any other US mission in the world.

Recent progress

More good news came for Vietnam when it became the 150th member of the World Trade Organization in January 2007. The immediate effect was the lifting of import quotas from foreign countries thereby favouring Vietnamese exporters. Full benefits are expected to be realised when Vietnam hope to gains full market economy status in 2020. In June 2007 President Nguyen Minh Triet became the first president of Vietnam to visit the US. He met with George W Bush in Washington to discuss relations between the two countries; trade between the two former enemies now racks up US$9 billion a year. And, in October 2007, Vietnam was elected to the UN Security Council from 1 January 2008 as a non-permanent member for two years. In 2009, the International Bank for Reconstruction and Development loaned the country US$500 million a sign that Vietnam's economic growth is good.

The future of communism in Vietnam

In his book *Vietnam at the Crossroads*, BBC World Service commentator Michael Williams asks the question: "Does communism have a future in Vietnam?" He answers that "the short answer must be no, if one means by communism the classical Leninist doctrines and central planning". Instead some bastard form of communism has been in the process of evolving. As Williams adds: "Even party leaders no longer appear able to distinguish between communism and capitalism".

There is certainly **political opposition** and disenchantment in Vietnam. At present this is unfocused and dispersed. Poor people in the countryside, especially in the north,

Cyber-dissidents

Human Rights Watch (HRW) has condemned Vietnam for its witch-hunt of those trying to disseminate information about democracy via the internet and urges the release of cyber prisoners. Despite the amnesties mentioned below, Viet-nam continues to imprison those writing about democracy on the web. According to Amnesty International, Vietnam has asked internet café owners and Internet Service Providers (ISPs) to monitor activity.

Vietnam has imprisoned several internet dissidents on charges of espionage and disseminating propaganda against the state in the last 10 years and continues to hold trials for those it arrests. In 2010, Tran Huynh Duy Thuc, a former internet company owner and businessman and Nguyen Tien Trung, IT engineer and blogger were convicted of "activities aimed at overthrowing the people's administration". They were sentenced, along with to others, to between five and 16 years in prison

according to Amnesty International UK. Prior to that physician Dr Nguyen Dan Que was sentenced to 2½ years' imprisonment after he sent an email on state censorship of the media to the US. (He was later released in an amnesty in February 2005.) In 2003 Pham Hong Son was sentenced to 13 years' imprisonment plus three years' house arrest for, among other charges, translating an article from the US Embassy website in Vietnam entitled 'What is Democracy?'. (Pham Hong Son was released by amnesty in August 2006.) Journalist Nguyen Vu Binh was sentenced to seven years' imprisonment and three years' house arrest in 2002 after he provided the US Congress with written reports of human rights abuses. He was granted an amnesty in June 2007.

"Harsh prison sentences and vaguely worded charges of spying appear designed to intimidate not only government critics, but everyone in Vietnam who uses the internet," reported HRW.

resent the economic gains in the cities, particularly those of the south (see the section on serious disturbances, page 438, in Thai Binh). But this rump of latent discontent has little in common with those intellectual and middle class Vietnamese itching for more political freedom or those motivated entrepreneurs pressing for accelerated economic reforms or those Buddhist monks and Christians demanding freedom of worship and respect for human rights. Unless and until this loose broth of opposition groups coalesces, it is hard to see a coherent opposition movement evolving.

Nonetheless, each year a small number of brave, foolhardy or committed individuals challenge the authorities. Most are then arrested, tried, and imprisoned for various loosely defined crimes including anti-government activity. There is always the possibility that cataclysmic, and unpredictable, political change will occur. As one veteran, but anonymous, Central Committee member said in an interview at the end of 1991: "If the CPSU [Communist Party of the Soviet Union], which had been in power for 74 years, can fall to pieces in 72 hours, we have at least to raise that possibility in Vietnam." Major General Tran Cong Man highlighted these fears when he remarked that: "the collapse of the Soviet Union was a devastating blow for [Vietnam] … [It] was our support, ideologically and psychologically, also militarily and economically. It was our unique model. Now we find it was a false model".

The tensions between reform and control are constantly evident. A **press law** which came into effect in mid-1993 prohibits the publication of works "hostile to the socialist homeland, divulging state or [communist] party secrets, falsifying history or denying the gains of the revolution". Ly Quy Chung, a newspaper editor in Ho Chi Minh City, described the Vietnamese responding to the economic reforms "like animals being let out of their cage". But, he added, alluding to the tight control the VCP maintains over political debate, "Now we are free to graze around, but only inside the fences". The Party's attempts to control debate and the flow of information have extended to the internet. In 1997 a National Internet Control Board was established and all internet and email usage is strictly monitored. The authorities attempt to firewall topics relating to Vietnam in a hopeless attempt to censor incoming information. By 2004 a number of 'cyber- activists' were held on charges of disseminating information deemed injurious to national interests, see box page 442 and www.hrw.org/en/news/2010/05/26/vietnam-stop-cyber-attacks-against-online-critics. The government continues to crack down on blogs and websites it sees critical of the government, according to Human Rights Watch. Facebook has also been blocked. The Vietnamese cyber police clearly credit the information highway with greater influence than any surfer.

Economy

Partition and socialist reconstruction 1955-1975
When the French left North Vietnam in 1954 they abandoned a country with scarcely any industry. The north remained predominantly an agrarian society and just 1.5% of 'material output' (the Socialist equivalent of GDP) was accounted for by modern industries. These employed a few thousand workers out of a population of about 13 million. The French added to the pitiful state of the industrial sector by dismantling many of the (mostly textile) factories that did exist, shipping the machinery back to France.

With **independence**, the government in the north embraced a socialist strategy of reconstruction and development. In the countryside, agricultural production was collectivized. Adopting Maoist policies, land reform proceeded apace. Revolutionary cadres were trained to spot 'greedy, cruel and imperialist landlords', farmers of above average wealth who might themselves have owned tiny plots. Leaders of land reform brigades applied Chinese-inspired rules through people's tribunals and summary justice. An estimated 10,000 people died; Ho Chi Minh was opposed to the worst excesses and, although he failed to curb the zealots, land reform in Vietnam was a much less bloody affair than it was in China.

In industry, likewise, the means of production were nationalized, co-operatives were formed, and planning was directed from the centre. Although evidence is hard to come by, it seems that even as early as the mid-1960s both the agricultural and industrial sectors were experiencing shortages of key inputs and were suffering from poor planning and mismanagement. The various sectors of the economy were inadequately linked, and the need for consumer goods was largely met by imports from China. But it was just at this time that the US bombing campaign 'Rolling Thunder' began in earnest (see page 421), and this served to obscure these economic difficulties. It was not until the late 1970s that the desperate need to introduce reforms became apparent. The bombing campaign also led to massive destruction and caused the government in the north to decentralize activity to the countryside in order to protect what little industry there was from the American attacks.

Reunification and a stab at socialist reconstruction (1975-1979)

With the reunification of Vietnam in 1975, it seems that most leaders in the north thought that the re-integration of the two economies, as well as their re-invigoration, would be a fairly straightforward affair. As one of the Party leadership tellingly said during the Sixth Plenum at the end of 1979: "In the euphoria of victory which came so unexpectedly, we … somewhat lost sight of realities; everything seemed possible to achieve, and quickly." This is understandable when it is considered that the north had just defeated the most powerful nation on earth. But the war disguised two economies that were both chronically inefficient and poorly managed, albeit for different reasons and in different ways. The tragedy was that just as this fact was becoming clear, the Vietnamese government embarked on another military adventure; this time the invasion and subsequent occupation of Cambodia in December 1978. Shortly afterwards, Hanoi had to deploy troops again to counter the Chinese 'invasion' in 1979. As a result, the authorities never had the opportunity of diverting resources from the military to the civilian sectors.

Conditions in the south were no better than in the north. The US had been supporting levels of consumption far above those which domestic production could match, the shortfall being met through massive injections of aid. Following the communists' victory, this support was ended – overnight. The Americans left behind an economy and society scarred by the war: three million unemployed, 500,000 prostitutes, 100,000 drug addicts, 400,000 amputees and 800,000 orphans. Nor did many in the south welcome their 'liberation'. The programme of socialist transition that began after 1975 was strongly resisted by large sections of the population and never achieved its aims. As resistance grew, the government became more repressive, thus leading to the exodus of hundreds of thousands of Vietnamese, who became known as the Boat People (see page 428). Even as late as 1978, with the economy close to crisis, sections of the leadership were still maintaining that the problems were due to poor implementation, not to the fact that the policies were flawed. The key problem was bureaucratic centralism: if a factory wished to transport umbrellas from Tay Ninh to Ho Chi Minh city, less than 100 km apart, it was required to go through 17 agencies, obtain 15 seals, sign five contracts and pay numerous taxes.

The roots of economic reform (1979-1986)

In a bid to re-invigorate the economy, the Vietnamese government – like others throughout the communist and former communist world – has been introducing economic reforms. These date back to 1979 when a process of administrative decentralization was set in train. Farmers signed contracts with their collectives to deliver produce in return for access to land and inputs like fertilizers and pesticides, thereby returning many aspects of decision making to the farm level. Surplus production could be sold privately. Factories were made self-accounting, and workers' pay was linked to productivity. The reforms of 1979 also accepted a greater role for the private sector in marketing, agriculture and small-scale industry.

Unfortunately these reforms were generally unsuccessful in stimulating Vietnam's moribund economy. Agriculture performed reasonably, but industry continued to decline. Cadres at the regional and local levels often ignored directives from the centre and critical inputs needed to fuel growth were usually unavailable. Both national income and per capita incomes continued to shrink. The reform process is referred to as *doi moi* (renovation), the Vietnamese equivalent of Soviet perestroika. Implementation of *doi moi* has not been easy. In Neil Sheehan's *Two Cities: Hanoi and Saigon*, he asked one manager of a state enterprise: "What was worse ... fighting the French in Interzone Five ... or directing a state factory during *doi moi*?" The answer: "It was easier in Interzone Five."

Some commentators have argued that the economic reforms of 1979 showed that the Vietnamese government was forward-looking and prescient. However there is also considerable evidence to show that the pressure for reform was coming as much from the bottom as from the top. Farm households and agricultural cooperatives, it seems, were engaged in what became known as 'fence-breaking', bypassing the state planning system. The communist party, to some degree, was forced to follow where peasants had already gone. This raises the questions of how far Vietnam's command economy was truly commanding. Benedict Kerkvliet, for example, argues that: "Even at the height of state economic planning and control, there were social, economic and political activities in Vietnam that the state did not authorize. 'Pluralism' ... has been around in Vietnam for some time". Peasants in Vietnam devoted enormous efforts in time and energy to the cultivation of their small private plots and tried to bypass the collective system through what became known as *khóan chui* (sneaky contracts).

Doi moi: the reform economy (1986-present)

Recognizing that the limited reforms of 1979 were failing to have the desired effect, the VCP leadership embraced a further raft of changes following the **Sixth Congress in 1986**. At the time, the Party daily, *Nhan Dan* wrote that never had "morale been so eroded, confidence been so low or justice been so abused". Subsidies on consumer goods were reduced and wages increased partially to compensate. There was also limited monetary reform although prices were still centrally controlled. In late 1987 the central planning system was reformed. The net effect of these changes was to fuel inflation that remained high 1986-1988; in 1988 it was running at well over 100%.

Again, appreciating that the reforms were not having the desired effect, and with the advice of the IMF, a third series of changes were introduced in 1988 and 1989. The market mechanism was to be fully employed to determine wages, output and prices for the great majority of goods. The domestic currency, the dong, was further devalued to bring it into line with the black market rate and foreign investment actively encouraged.

But, with each series of reform measures, disquiet in some sections of the Party grows. For example, in 1993 government salary differentials were widened to better reflect responsibilities. Whereas under the old system the differential between the highest and lowest paid workers was only 3.5 to one, the gap under the new system is 13 to one. This may make good sense to World Bank economists, but it is hard to swallow for a party and leadership who have been raised on ideals of equality.

Until the Asian crisis was heralded with the collapse of the Thai baht at the beginning of July 1997, the Vietnamese economy had done well to ride some pretty serious **external shocks**. With the collapse of communism in Eastern Europe, around 200,000 migrant workers returned to the country and had to be reintegrated. The decline in aid and assistance from the former Soviet Union (which was only partially compensated by aid from Russia) and the corresponding precipitous decline in trade from US$1.8 billion (admittedly at the then unrealistic rouble exchange rate) in 1990 to US$85 million in 1991 illustrates the extent to which Vietnam had to re-orientate its economy in the face of global political and economic change. No longer able to rely on the Soviet Union to bail it out (although even before then the Vietnamese would lament that the Soviets were 'Americans without dollars'), the Vietnamese government took the drastic step of banning the import of all luxury consumer goods in October 1991 in an attempt to save valuable foreign exchange.

Economic challenges

Let's start with the good news: Vietnam's economy is resilient and growing fast, the population is comparatively well educated, it has good access to world markets and, as former Singapore Prime Minister Lee Kuan Yew put it, Vietnam also has that "vital intangible" necessary for Newly Industrializing Country-style rapid economic growth. Vietnam currently enjoys the highest rate of growth in one of the most economically dynamic regions in the world. This happy state of affairs is the product of a hard-working, underpaid labour force generating massive profits and of the switch from an agrarian economy to an industrial economy. In other words, 200 years after Britain, Vietnam is now undergoing its industrial revolution. Indeed industry and construction now account for 41% of Vietnam's economy with services accounting for an additional 38% and this figure is rising fast. Between 1992 and 1998 Vietnam was one of the 10 fastest growing economies in the world with an average growth of 8.4% per annum. During the period 2002-2004 the economy grew by an average of 7% per year. One of the driving forces has been the export of textiles – chiefly to the USA.

Not that it has always been this good. Not only did the Asian crisis put talk of Tiger economies on the back burner, but even before the crisis there were voices of caution. The gloss of the immediate post-*doi moi* years has dulled and people now accept that reforms will need to be both deeper and wider. For a start, many of the reforms apparently in place are not being implemented in the expected manner. Take the process of privatization introduced in 1993. By 1998, out of 5800 state-owned enterprises only 29 had been partially sold off. Foreign investors, who initially piled into the country thinking there was money to be made, then started shying away, daunted by the red tape, bureaucratic inertia and corruption. In 2000 a new Enterprise Law was enacted to kickstart reform by streamlining the approval system. At one level this was a clear improvement on what had gone before. After all, 84 types of licenses necessary to set up some private businesses were scrapped; but another 300 remain. Kazi Martin, the World Bank's head economist in Vietnam, diplomatically stated that he sees "a new-found willingness to unshackle the private sector" but many foreign investors are not so impressed. A related problem is that while there are technocrats who are skilled and knowledgeable about the demands of building a market economy, the Party leadership have very little understanding of what it takes – and it is the Party that ultimately calls the shots. In 1996 the Party Congress reaffirmed the state sector's 'leading role' in building the economy, granting just a supporting role to the private sector. Perhaps this explains the fact that while every official seems to accept the importance of reform – as one senior government economist put it in 2000, "if not, we will die" – few appear willing to put this into concrete action. However, investment has rapidly improved since 2001. From a foreign investment figure of US$3.2 billion in 2001 it reached US$7.8 billion in 2006 to US$11.5 billion in 2008. The greatest beneficiaries by are Ho Chi Minh City followed by Hanoi, Dong Nai and Binh Duong. By sector it is the service industry proving the overall winner with offices and apartments being the most heavily invested sector followed by hotels and tourism. For the extraordinary amount of development read the Hardhat report from Blackwell Media: http://www.blackwellmedia.com.

But Vietnam's problems do not begin and end with the reform programme. There are also many more rather more familiar challenges.

The population is growing rapidly in a country where there are 900 people for every square kilometre of agricultural land. As the World Bank has pointed out, this means "the country will have to develop on the basis of human resources rather than natural resources". But the human resources themselves need substantial 'upgrading'; despite rapid progress in poverty elimination, poverty in the countryside over large areas of the north and interior uplands remains the norm rather than the exception. Education and health facilities also require massive investment, not to mention the physical infrastructure including roads and power.

The numbers of **unemployed** are also being boosted by the reduction in the size of the army, which celebrated its 60th anniversary in 2005. By late 1997 the country's standing army had been cut by two-thirds from its strength in 1989, to 500,000. It now stands at 450,000. Preparation for civilian life for the hundreds of thousands demobilized seems perfunctory to say the least. As one former soldier, now a cyclo driver, recounted to a journalist from *The Economist*: "When I joined, I was told they would help me find a job later. But when I left, all they gave me was a set of clothes, a piece of cloth and a paper that said that I had fulfilled my requirements."

Foreign investors are put off by the archaic physical infrastructure compared to other Southeast Asian countries such as Thailand and Malaysia and also worry about the lack of legal, banking and accounting systems. Le Dang Doanh of Hanoi's Central Institute of Economic Management plainly stated that many of the new laws introduced since the late 1980s to deal with the economic reforms 'are words, not really laws'. Commercial law, for instance, barely exists in Vietnam, and some foreign companies are unwilling to throw money into a country that is, in legal terms, the equivalent of a black hole.

The country's **export base** is also still comparatively narrow: coal, oil, textiles, rice, footwear and marine products are the country's key exports. But this list grows all the time and in recent years items as diverse as coffee and computer programming and software have joined the more traditional ones. But economic growth has brought its own problems in the same way that has occurred in China.

Inequalities, both spatial and personal, are widening. Growth in agriculture is down, while industry is expanding. So, while the economies of Hanoi and Ho Chi Minh City have been growing annually, the countryside is lagging far behind. Over recent years rural incomes have fallen as rice prices and other agricultural commodities have remained depressed. This is drawing people in from the countryside, creating urban problems both socially (for instance, unemployed people living in poor conditions with a lack of educational facilities) and economically (such as strains on the physical infrastructure). These inequalities will widen further in the short to medium term as the process of industrialization continues apace.

As with industry, the leadership is reluctant to allow rural people to run their own businesses and lives, continually interfering and fine-tuning and without addressing the key shortages which are of credit, training, skills and management. As Bui Quang Toan, senior researcher at the National Institute of Agricultural Planning and Projection, explained to a journalist from the Far Eastern Economic Review: "Cooperatives should be free of politics, free of administrative control … the government must give up the idea that they can use cooperatives as a tool to manage the people." Nevertheless Vietnam has made dramatic strides at reducing poverty, including rural poverty.

Culture

People

Vietnam is home to a total of 54 ethnic groups including the Vietnamese themselves. The ethnic minorities vary in size from the Tay, with a population of about 1.3 million, to the Odu, who number only 300 individuals. Life has been hard for many of the minorities who have had to fight not only the French and Vietnamese but often each other in order to retain their territory and cultural identity. Traditions and customs have been eroded by outside influences such as Roman Catholicism and Communism although some of the less alien ideas have been successfully accommodated. Centuries of Viet population growth and decades of warfare have taken a heavy toll on minorities and their territories; increasingly, population pressure from the minority groups themselves poses a threat to their way of life.

Highland people: the Montagnards of Vietnam

The highland areas of Vietnam are among the most linguistically and culturally diverse in the world. In total, the highland peoples number around seven million. As elsewhere in Southeast Asia, a broad distinction can be drawn in Vietnam between the peoples of the lowlands and valleys and the peoples of the uplands. The former tend to be settled, cultivate wet rice and are fairly closely integrated into the wider Vietnamese state; in most instances they are Viet. The latter are often migratory, cultivate upland crops often using systems of shifting cultivation and are comparatively isolated from the state. The generic term for these diverse peoples of the highlands is Montagnard (from the French, Mountain People), in Vietnamese *nguoi thuong* (highland citizen) or, rather less politely, *moi* (savage or slave). As far as the highland peoples themselves are concerned, they identify with their village and tribal group and not as part of a wider grouping, as highland inhabitants.

The French attitude towards the Montagnards was often inconsistent. The authorities wanted to control them and sometimes succumbed to the pressure from French commercial interests to conscript them into the labour force, particularly on the plantations. But some officials were positively protective; one, Monsieur Sebatier, refused missionaries access to the territory under his control, destroyed bridges to prevent access and had three tribal wives. He recommended total withdrawal from their lands in order to protect their cultural integrity. In *A Dragon Apparent*, Norman Lewis provides a wonderful account of the Montagnards and their way of life and perceptively examines the relationship between them and the French.

Relations between the minorities and the Viet have not always been as good as they are officially portrayed. Recognizing and exploiting this mutual distrust and animosity, both the French and American armies recruited from among the minorities. In 1961 US Special Forces began organizing Montagnards into defence groups to prevent communist infiltration into the Central Highlands from the north. Since 1975 relations between minorities and Viet have improved but there is still hostility and in recent years this has flared into vicious fighting. Official publications paint a touching picture portraying the relationship between Viet and minority peoples. Thus we read "successive generations of Vietnamese, belonging to 54 ethnic groups, members of the great national community of Vietnam, have always stood side by side with one another, sharing weal and woe, shedding sweat and blood to defend and build up their homeland". This illusion has been shattered by recent events so the government is keen to stress its role in improving health, eradicating poverty and introducing a settled rather than a nomadic existence among the minorities. But one serious consequence of a sedentary way of life has been the narrowing, blunting and elimination of cultural differences. In recent years the government has come to regard the minorities as useful 'tourist fodder' – with a splash of colour, primitive villages and ethnic dances, they provide a taste of the 'mystical East', which much of the country otherwise lacks.

Potentially tourism is a more serious and insidious threat to the minorities' way of life than any they have yet had to face. A great deal has been written about cultural erosion by tourism and any visitor to a minority village should be aware of the extent to which he or she contributes to this process. Traditional means of livelihood are quickly abandoned when a higher living standard for less effort can be obtained from the tourist dollar. Long-standing societal and kinship ties are weakened by the intrusion of outsiders. Young people may question their society's values and traditions that may seem archaic, anachronistic and risible by comparison with those of the modern tourist. And dress and music lose all cultural significance and symbolism if they are allowed to become mere tourist attractions.

Nevertheless, this is an unavoidable consequence of Vietnam's decision to admit tourists to the highland areas. Perhaps fortunately, however, for the time being at least, many of the minorities are pretty inaccessible to the average traveller. Visitors can minimize their impact by acting in a sensitive way; it is, for example, perfectly obvious when someone does not want their photograph taken. See also box, page 451, for general advice on visiting minority villages. In addition, you can report to provincial tourism authorities on arrival to check the latest on areas where travel is permitted. But the minority areas of Vietnam are fascinating places and the immense variety of colours and styles of dress add greatly to the visitor's enjoyment.

Bahnar

This is a Mon-Khmer-speaking minority group concentrated in the central highland provinces of Gia Lai-Kon Tum, numbering about 174,000. Locally powerful from the 15th to 18th centuries, they were virtually annihilated by neighbouring groups during the 19th century. Roman Catholic missionaries influenced the Bahnar greatly and they came to identify closely with the French. Some conversions to Roman Catholicism were made but Christianity, where it remains, is usually just an adjunct to Bahnar animism. Bahnar houses are built on stilts and in each village there is a communal house, or *rông*, which is the focus of social life. When a baby reaches his or her first full month he or she has their ears pierced in a village ceremony equivalent to the Vietnamese *day thang* (see box, page 452); only then is a child considered a full member of the community. Their society gives men and women relatively equal status. Male and female heirs inherit wealth and the families of either husband or wife can arrange marriage. Bahnar practise both settled and shifting cultivation.

Coho

These are primarily found on the Lam Dong Plateau in Lam Dong Province (Dalat) with a population of about 100,000. Extended family groups live in longhouses or *buon*, sometimes up to 30 m long. Unusually, society is matrilineal and newly married men live with their wives' families. The children take their mother's name; if the wife dies young her smaller sister will take her place. Women wear tight-fitting blouses and skirts. Traditional shifting cultivation is giving way to settled agriculture.

Yao

The Yao live in northern Vietnam in the provinces bordering China, particularly in Lao Cai and Ha Giang. They number 6210,000 and include several sub-groupings, notably the Dao Quan Chet (Tight Trouser Dao), the Dao Tien (Money Dao) and the Dao Ao Dai (Long Dress Dao). As these names suggest, Yao people wear highly distinctive clothing although sometimes only on their wedding day. The **Dao Tien** or Money Dao of Hoa Binh and Son La provinces are unique among the Yao in that the women wear black skirts and leggings rather than trousers. A black jacket with red embroidered collar and cuffs, decorated at the back with coins (hence the name) together with a black red-tasselled turban and silver jewellery are also worn. By contrast men look rather plain in black jacket and trousers. Headgear tends to be elaborate and includes a range of shapes (from square to conical), fabrics (waxed hair to dried pumpkin fibres) and colours.

The women of many branches of Yao shave off their eyebrows and shave back their hair to the top of their head before putting on the turban; a hairless face and high forehead are traditionally regarded as attributes of feminine beauty.

Yao wedding customs are as complex as Yao clothing and vary with each group. Apart from parental consent, intending marriage partners must have compatible birthdays and the groom has to provide the bride's family with gifts worthy of their daughter. If he is unable to do this, a temporary marriage can take place but the outstanding presents must be produced and a permanent wedding celebrated before *their* daughter can marry.

The Yao live chiefly by farming: those in higher altitudes are swidden cultivators growing maize, cassava and rye. In the middle zone, shifting methods are again used to produce rice and maize, and on the valley floors sedentary farmers grow irrigated rice and rear livestock.

Spiritually the Yao have also opted for diversity; they worship Ban Vuong, their mythical progenitor, as well as their more immediate and real ancestors. The Yao also find room for elements of Taoism, and in some cases Buddhism and Confucianism, in their elaborate metaphysical lives. Never enter a Yao house unless invited; if tree branches are suspended above the gate to a village, guests are not welcome – reasons might include a post-natal but pre-naming period, sickness, death or special ceremony. Since the Yao worship the kitchen god, guests should not sit or stand immediately in front of the stove.

Ede

Primarily concentrated in the Central Highlands province of Dac Lac and numbering nearly 270,000, they came into early contact with the French and are regarded as one of the more 'progressive' groups, adapting to modern life with relative ease. Traditionally the Ede live in longhouses on stilts; accommodated under one roof is the matrilineal extended family or commune. The commune falls under the authority of an elderly, respected woman known as the *khoa sang* who is responsible for communal property, especially the gongs and jars, which feature in important festivals. Ede society is matrilocal in that after the girl's family selects a husband, he then comes to live with her. As part of the wedding festivities the two families solemnly agree that if one of the partners should break the wedding vow they will forfeit a minimum of one water buffalo, a maximum of a set of gongs. Wealth and property are inherited solely by daughters. Shifting cultivation is the traditional subsistence system, although this has given way in

Visiting minorities: house rules

Etiquette and customs vary between the minorities. However, the following are general rules of good behaviour that should be adhered to whenever possible.

1. Dress modestly without displaying too much flesh.
2. Ask permission before photographing anyone (old people, pregnant women and mothers with babies can object).
3. Only enter a house if invited.
4. Do not touch or photograph village shrines.
5. Do not smoke opium.
6. Avoid sitting or stepping on door sills.
7. Avoid displays of wealth and be sensitive when giving gifts (for children, pens are better than sweets).
8. Avoid introducing Western medicines.
9. Do not sit with the soles of your feet pointing at others (sit cross-legged).
10. If offered a cup of rice wine it is polite to down the first cup in one (what the Vietnamese call *tram phan tram* – 100%).

most areas to settled wet rice agriculture. Spiritually the Ede are polytheist: they number animism (recognizing the spirits of rice, soil, fire and water especially) and Christianity among their beliefs. See also page 245 for a description of the ceremonial structure and staircase at Dray Sap waterfall.

Giarai

Primarily found in Gia Lai and Kon Tum provinces (especially near Play Ku) and numbering 317,557, these are the largest group in the Central Highlands. They are settled cultivators and live in houses on stilts in villages called *ploi* or *bon*. The Giarai are animist and recognize the spiritual dimension of nature; ever since the seventh century they have had a flesh and blood King of Fire and King of Water whose spirit is invoked in rain ceremonies.

Hmong

These are widely spread across the highland areas of the country, but particularly near the Chinese border down to the 18th parallel. The Hmong number about 787,600 (over 1% of Vietnam's population) and live at higher altitudes, above 1500 m, than all other hill people. Comparatively recent migrants to Vietnam, the Hmong began to settle in the country during the 19th century after moving south from China. The Hmong language in its various dialects remained oral until the 1930s when a French priest attempted to Romanize it with a view to translating the Bible. A more successful attempt to create a written Hmong language was made in 1961 but has since fallen into disuse. Nevertheless – or perhaps because of this failure – the Hmong still preserve an extraordinarily rich oral tradition of legends, stories and histories. Hmong people are renowned for their beautiful folk songs. Each branch of the Hmong people preserves its own corpus of songs about love, work and festivals that are sung unaccompanied or with the accompaniment of the *khène*, a small bamboo pipe organ, a two-stringed violin, flutes, drums, gongs and jew's harps. Numerous Hmong dances also exist to celebrate various dates in the social calendar and to propitiate animist spirits.

They have played an important role in resisting both the French and the Vietnamese. Living at such high altitudes they tend to be one of the most isolated of all the hill people. Their way of life does not normally bring them into contact with the outside world that suits them well – the Hmong traders at Sapa are an exception. High in the hills, flooding

Rite of passage: from baby to infant

In a poor country like Vietnam, staying alive for long enough to see one's own first birthday has not always been easy. Fortunately, infant mortality levels have fallen drastically but remain high by Western standards. Perhaps not surprisingly therefore, Vietnamese families celebrate two important milestones in the early lives of their children.

Day thang, or full month, is celebrated exactly one month after birth. Traditionally, the mother remained in bed with her heavily swaddled baby for the first month keeping him or her away from sun, rain and demon spirits. At one month the child is beyond the hazardous neo-natal stage and the mother would leave her bed and go out of the house to introduce her baby to the village.

Today, the parents hold a small party for friends and neighbours.

Thoi noi is celebrated at the end of the first year; it marks the time the baby stops sleeping in the cot and, having reached a full year, it is also a thanksgiving that the child has reached the end of the most dangerous year of life. At the party the baby is presented with a tray on which are various items such as a pen, a mirror, scissors, some soil and food; whichever the baby takes first indicates its character and likely job: scissors for a tailor, pen for a teacher, soil for a farmer and so on. Babies are normally weaned at about this time. Some Vietnamese mothers use remarkably unsubtle but effective means for turning the baby from the breast, smearing the nipple with charcoal dust or Tiger Balm!

---

is not a problem so their houses are built on the ground, not raised up on stilts. Hmong villages are now increasingly found along the river valleys and roads as the government resettlement schemes aim to introduce them to a more sedentary form of agriculture. The Hmong practice slash-and-burn cultivation growing maize and dry rice. Traditionally opium has been a valuable cash crop. Although fields are often cleared on very steep and rocky slopes, the land is not terraced. There are a number of different groups among the Hmong including the White, Black, Red and Flower Hmong that are distinguishable by the colour of the women's clothes. Black Hmong wear almost entirely black clothing with remarkable pointed black turbans. White Hmong women wear white skirts and the Red Hmong tie their heads in a red scarf while the Flower Hmong wrap their hair (with hair extensions) around their head like a broad-brimmed hat. However, such numerous regional variations occur that even experts on ethnic minority cultures sometimes have problems trying to identify which branch of Hmong they have encountered. Serious social problems have occurred among the Hmong owing to opium addiction; with over 30% of the male population of some Hmong villages addicted, the drug has rendered many incapable of work, causing misery and malnutrition for their families and with the drug finding its way on to the streets of Vietnam's cities, the authorities have resolved to clamp down hard on opium production. This has had tragic consequences when the Hmong have tried to protect their livelihoods.

Muong

Numbering more than one million the Muong are the fourth largest ethnic minority in Vietnam. They live in the area between northern Thanh Hoa Province and Yen Bai but mainly in Hoa Binh Province. It is thought that the Muong are descended from the same stock as the Viets: their languages are similar and there are also close similarities in culture and religion. But whereas the Vietnamese came under strong Chinese cultural influence from the early centuries of the Christian era, the Muong did not. The Muong belong to the Viet-Muong language group; their language is closest to Vietnamese of all the ethnic minority languages. Muong practise wet and dry rice cultivation where possible, supplementing their income with cash crops such as manioc, tobacco and cotton. Weaving is still practised; items produced include pillowcases and blankets. Culturally the Muong are akin to the Thai Vietnamese ethnic minority and they live in stilt houses in small villages called *quel*; groupings of from three to 30 quel form a unit called a *muong*. Muong society is feudal in nature with each *muong* coming under the protection of a noble family (*lang*). The common people are not deemed worthy of family names so are all called Bui. Each year the members of a *muong* are required to labour for one day in fields belonging to the lang.

Marriages are arranged: girls, in particular, have no choice of spouse. Muong cultural life is rich, literature has been translated into Vietnamese and their legends, poems and songs are considered particularly fine.

Mnong
The Mnong number some 92,000 people and predominantly live in Dak Lak, Binh Phuoc and Binh Duong province with a smaller group living in Lam Dong province. The Mnong are hunter-gatherers and grow rice. The Mnong village is characterised by a longhouse on stilts although some groups live in normal sized stilt houses. Families are matrilineal and tradition sees the women bare topped and with distended earlobes. It is the Mnong who are the elephant catchers at Ban Don, see page 246.

Nung
Concentrated in Cao Bang and Lang Son provinces, adjacent to the Chinese border, the Nung number approximately 860,000 people. They are strongly influenced by the Chinese and most are Buddhist, but like both Vietnamese and Chinese the Nung practise ancestor worship too. In Nung houses a Buddhist altar is placed above the ancestor altar and, in deference to Buddhist teaching, they refrain from eating most types of meat. The Nung are settled agriculturalists and, where conditions permit, produce wet rice; all houses have their own garden in which fruit and vegetables are grown.

Tay
The Tay are the most populous ethnic minority in Vietnam; they number about 1.5 million and are found in the provinces of northwest Vietnam stretching from Quang Ninh east to Lao Cai. Tay society was traditionally feudal with powerful lords able to extract from the free and semi-free serfs' obligations such as droit de seigneur. Today Tay society is male dominated with important decisions being taken by men and eldest sons inheriting the bulk of the family's wealth.

Economically the Tay survive by farming and are highly regarded as wet rice cultivators, they are also noted for the production of fruits (pears, peaches, apricots and tangerines), herbs and spices. Diet is supplemented by animal and fish rearing and cash is raised by the production of handicrafts. The Tay live in houses on stilts, located in the river valleys. Tay architecture is quite similar in design to that of the Black Thai, but important differences may be identified, most notably the larger size of the Tay house, the deeper overhang of the thatched or (among more affluent Tay communities) tiled roof and the extent of the railed balcony which often encircles the entire house.

Like the Thai, Tay ancestors migrated south from southern China along with those of the Thai and they follow the three main religions of Buddhism, Confucianism and Taoism in addition to ancestor worship and animist beliefs. While Tay people have lived in close proximity to the Viet majority over a period of many centuries, their own language continues to be their primary means of communication. They hail from the Austro-Asian language family and specifically the Thai-Kadai language group. Tay literature has a long and distinguished history and much has been translated into Vietnamese. During the French colonial period missionaries Romanized Tay script.

Thai

Numbering more than one million this is the second largest ethnic minority in Vietnam and ethnically distinct from the Thais of modern-day Thailand. There are two main sub-groups, the Black (Thai Den), who are settled mainly in Son La, Lai Chan, Lao Cai and Yen Bai provinces and the White Thái, who are found predominantly in Hoa Binh, Son La, Thanh Hoa and Vinh Phu provinces, as well as many others, including the Red Thai (Thai Do). The use of these colour-based classifications has usually been linked to the colour of their clothes, particularly the colour of women's shirts. However, there has been some confusion over the origins of the terms and there is every reason to believe that it has nothing to do with the colour of their attire and is possibly linked to the distribution of the sub-groups near the Red and Black rivers. The confusion of names becomes even more perplexing when the Vietnamese names for the sub-groups of Thai people are translated into Thai. Some scholars have taken Thai Den (Black Thai) to be Thai Daeng – *daeng* being the Thai word for red, thereby muddling up the two groups. With the notable exception of the White Thai communities of Hoa Binh, traditional costume for the women of both the Black and White Thai generally features a coloured blouse with a row of silver buttons down the front, a long black skirt, a coloured waist sash and a black headscarf embroidered with intricate, predominantly red and yellow designs.

The traditional costume of the White Thai women of Hoa Binh comprises a long black skirt with fitted waistband embroidered with either a dragon or chicken motif together with a plain pastel coloured blouse and gold and maroon sash.

The Thai cover a large part of northwest Vietnam, in particular the valleys of the Red River and the Da and the Ma rivers, spilling over into Laos and Thailand. They arrived in Vietnam between the fourth and 11th centuries from southern China and linguistically they are part of the wider Thai-Kadai linguistic grouping. Residents of Lac village in Mai Chau claim to have communicated with visitors from Thailand by means of this shared heritage.

The Thai tend to occupy lowland areas and they compete directly with the Kinh (ethnic Vietnamese) for good quality farmland that can be irrigated. They are masters of wet rice cultivation producing high yields and often two harvests each year. Their irrigation works are ingenious and incorporate numerous labour-saving devices including river-powered water wheels that can raise water several metres. Thai villages (*ban*) consist of 40-50 houses on stilts; they are architecturally attractive, shaded by fruit trees and surrounded by verdant paddy fields. Commonly located by rivers, one of the highlights of a Thai village is its suspension footbridge. The Thai are excellent custodians of the land and their landscapes and villages are invariably very scenic.

Owing to their geographical proximity and agricultural similarities with the Kinh it is not surprising to see cultural assimilation – sometimes via marriage – and most Thai speak Vietnamese. It's also interesting to note the extent to which the Thai retain a distinctive cultural identity, most visibly in their dress.

When a Thai woman marries, her parents-in-law give her a hair extension (*can song*) and a silver hair pin (*khat pom*) that she is expected to wear (even in bed) for the duration of the marriage. There are two wedding ceremonies, the first at the bride's house where the couple live for one to three years, followed by a second when they move to the husband's house.

Sedang
Concentrated in Gia Lai and Kon Tum provinces and numbering about 127,000, the Sedang live in extended family longhouses and society is patriarchal. The Sedang practise both shifting agriculture and the cultivation of wet rice. A highly war-like people, they almost wiped out the Bahnar in the 19th century. Sedang thought nothing of kidnapping neighbouring tribesmen to sacrifice to the spirits; indeed the practice of kidnapping was subsequently put to commercial use and formed the basis of a slave trade with Siam (Thailand). Sedang villages, or *ploi*, are usually well defended (presumably for fear of reprisal) and are surrounded by thorn hedges supplemented with spears and stakes. Complex rules designed to prevent in-breeding limit the number of available marriage partners that sometimes results in late marriages.

Other groups
These are Hre (Hrê), in Quang Ngai and Binh Dinh provinces, numbering 113,000 and Stieng/Xtieng (Xtiêng) in Song Be province, with 66,788.

Viet (Kinh)
The 1999 census revealed that 86.2% of the population were ethnic Vietnamese. But with a well-run family planning campaign beginning to take effect in urban areas and higher fertility rates among the ethnic minorities it is likely that this figure will fall. The history of the Kinh is marked by a steady southwards progression from the Red River basin to the southern plains and Mekong Delta. Today the Kinh are concentrated into the two great river deltas, the coastal plains and the main cities. Only in the central and northern highland regions are they outnumbered by ethnic minorities. Kinh social cohesion and mastery of intensive wet rice cultivation has led to their numerical, and subsequently political and economic, dominance of the country. Ethnic Vietnamese are also in Cambodia where some have been settled for generations; recent Khmer Rouge attacks on Vietnamese villages have, however, caused many to flee to Vietnam.

Cham
With the over-running of Champa in 1471 (see page 409) Cham cultural and ethnic identity was diluted by the more numerous ethnic Vietnamese. The Cham were dispossessed of the more productive lands and found themselves in increasingly marginal territory. Economically eclipsed and strangers in their own land, Cham artistic creativity atrophied, their sculptural and architectural skills, once the glory of Vietnam, faded and decayed like so many Cham temples and towers. It is estimated that there are, today, 132,873 Cham people in Vietnam, chiefly in central and southern Vietnam in the coastal provinces extending south from Quy Nhon. Small communities are to be found in Ho Chi Minh City and in the Mekong Delta around Chau Doc. They are artistically the poor relations of their forebears but skills in weaving and music live on.

The Cham of the south are typically engaged in fishing, weaving and other small scale commercial activities; urban Cham are poor and live in slum neighbourhoods. Further north the Cham are wet or dry rice farmers according to local topography; they are noted for their skill in wet rice farming and small-scale hydraulic engineering.

In southern Vietnam the majority of Cham are Muslim, a comparatively newly acquired religion although familiar from earlier centuries when many became acquainted with Islamic tenets through traders from India and the Indonesian isles. In central Vietnam most Cham are Brahminist and the cult of the linga remains an important feature of spiritual life.

Hoa: ethnic Chinese

There are nearly one million ethnic Chinese or Hoa in Vietnam, 80% living in the south of the country. Before reunification in 1975 there were even more; hundreds of thousands left due to persecution by the authorities and a lack of economic opportunities since the process of socialist transformation was initiated. There are now large Vietnamese communities abroad, particularly in Australia, on the west coast of the US and in France. It has been estimated that the total Viet-kieu population numbers some two million. With the reforms of the 1980s, the authorities' view of the Chinese has changed; they now appreciate the crucial role they played, and could continue to play, in the economy. Before 1975, the Hoa controlled 80% of industry in the south and 50% of banking and finance. Today, ethnic Chinese in Vietnam can own and operate businesses and are once again allowed to join the communist party, the army and to enter university. The dark days of the mid- to late 1970s seem to be over.

Viet Kieu: overseas Vietnamese

Since 1988, overseas Vietnamese or Viet Kieu (most of whom are of Chinese extraction) have been allowed back to visit their relatives, in some cases helping to spread stories of untold wealth in the US, Australia and elsewhere. The largest community of overseas Vietnamese, about 1.1 million, live in the US. The next largest populations are resident in France (250,000) and Australia (160,000), with much smaller numbers in a host of other countries. In 1990, 40,000 returned to visit; in 2003, 340,000 returned 'home'. Amusingly, many from America come back for dental treatment as it is much cheaper in Vietnam.

Many Viet Kieu are former boat people (see box, page 428), while others left the country as part of the UN-administered Orderly Departure Programme that began in earnest in the late 1980s. A smaller number (and one wonders whether they are strictly classed as Viet Kieu) left Vietnam for one of the former COMECON countries at some point between the 1950s and 1980s either to study or to work. The largest number appear to have gone to East Germany from where many have returned to take up important political positions. Those fortunate enough to find themselves in dour East Germany at the time of reunification suddenly found themselves privileged to be citizens of one of the world's richest countries. In the upheavals occasioned by ridding Eastern Europe of communism they showed sound business acumen and carved out a pivotal position in the German tobacco smuggling industry.

In America the Viet Kieu have often shown enormous perseverance and grit. Take the small Texan shrimping town of Palacios. Today there are around 300 Americans of Vietnamese extraction, mostly Roman Catholics, living in and around Palacios. When the first settlers arrived in 1976 escaping from the defeated South, most had nothing. Many faced bigotry from racist elements in the local community who feared competition from foreigners. But they worked and saved and by the early 1980s some families had managed to buy shrimping boats for themselves. Another 10 years on and the most successful boats were owned and operated by Vietnamese. By that time, many of their children had been born and raised in the local community, they had gone through local schools (often winning the top scholastic prizes) and few questioned their credentials to be counted as Americans. There are Little Saigons in many countries but the most famous is in Los Angeles. From this social and economic hub the Vietnamese diaspora has set about cornering several industries. The nail manicure business is now virtually synonymous with the Vietnamese. In California and increasingly in other parts of the world, nail bars are Vietnamese owned; 'Hollywood Nails' appears to be the name of choice. In California, it seems, almost every block has a Vietnamese pharmacy and a *pho* restaurant selling noodles. And now shoppers in malls from Virginia to San José can sit down to a good bowl of *pho bo* (beef noodle soup), surely one of the more surprising outcomes of the Vietnam War.

As the Viet Kieu have discovered some measure of prosperity in the West, the Vietnamese government is anxious to welcome them back – or rather, welcome their money. So far, however, flows of investment for productive purposes have been rather disappointing and largely concentrated in the service sector, particularly in hotels and restaurants. Far more is thought to have been invested in land and property as overseas Vietnamese have, since 2000, been able to purchase property in their own name. (This, incidentally, has contributed to property speculation and a dizzy spiral of price increases that have made land prices in Ho Chi Minh City and Hanoi some of the most expensive in Asia.) Part of the problem is that many Viet Kieu were escaping from persecution in Vietnam and of all people continue to harbour doubts about a government that is, in essence, the same as the one they fled. On the government's side, they worry that the Viet Kieu may be a destabilizing influence, perhaps even a Fifth Column intent on undermining the supremacy of the Communist Party. Again the leadership have cause for concern as the most vocal opponents of the US policy of rapprochement have been Viet Kieu. Nor are the Overseas Vietnamese quite as rich as their ostentatious displays of wealth on the streets of Ho Chi Minh City and Hanoi would indicate. They do not have the economic muscle of the Overseas Chinese, for example, and in most cases have only been out of the country for less than 20 years, many having lost everything in their attempt to escape. Many young Viet Kieu have, however, equipped themselves with qualifications and skills overseas – often much needed in Vietnam – and can find lucrative employment back in Vietnam.

Art and architecture

Dongson culture

The first flourishing of Vietnamese art occurred with the emergence of the Dongson culture (named after a small town near Thanh Hoa where early excavations were focused) on the coast of Annam and Tonkin between 500 and 200 BC. The inspiration for the magnificent bronzes produced by the artists of Dongson originated from China: the decorative motifs have clear affinities with earlier Chinese bronzes. At the same time, the exceptional skill of production and decoration argues that these pieces represent among the first, and finest, of Southeast Asian works of art. This is most evident in the huge and glorious **bronze drums** which can be seen in museums in both Hanoi and Ho Chi Minh City.

Cham art

If there was ever a golden period in Vietnamese art and architecture, it was that of the former central Vietnamese **kingdom of Champa**, centred on the Annamite coast, which flowered in the 10th and 11th centuries. Tragically however, many of the 250 sites recorded in historical records have been pillaged or damaged and only 20 have survived the intervening centuries in a reasonable state of repair. Most famous are the sites of My Son and Dong Duong, south of Danang. Many of the finest works have been spirited out of the country to private collections and foreign museums while others were destroyed by bombing and artillery fire during the Vietnam War. Nonetheless, the world's finest collection – with some breathtakingly beautiful work – is to be found in Danang's **Museum of Champa Sculpture**.

The earliest Cham art belongs to the My Son E1 period (early eighth century). It shows stylistic similarities with Indian Sanchi and Gupta works, although even at this early stage in its development Cham art incorporated distinctive indigenous elements, most clearly seen in the naturalistic interpretation of human form. By the Dong Duong period (late ninth century), the Cham had developed a unique style of their own. Archaeologists recognize six periods of Cham art: My Son E1 (early eighth century), Hoa Lai (early ninth century), Dong Duong (late ninth century), Late Tra Kieu (late 10th century), Thap Mam (12th-13th century) and Po Klong Garai (13th-16th century).

The Cham Kingdom was ethnically and linguistically distinct, but was overrun by the Vietnamese in the 15th century. It might be argued, then, that their monuments and sculptures have little to do with Vietnam per se, but with a preceding dynasty.

Understanding Cham art: Hindu deities

The Museum of Champa Sculpture in Danang (see above) displays many pieces on the Hindu trinity, the three Gods that are widely seen as all-powerful: **Brahma, Vishnu** and **Siva**. While Brahma is regarded as the ultimate source of creation, Siva also has a creative role alongside his function as destroyer. Vishnu in contrast is seen as the preserver or protector of the universe. Vishnu and Siva are widely represented and have come to be seen as the most powerful and important.

Brahma Popularly Brahma is interpreted as the Creator in a trinity, alongside Vishnu as Preserver and Siva as Destroyer. In the literal sense the name Brahma is the masculine and personalized form of the neuter word Brahman.

In the early Vedic writing, Brahman represented the universal and impersonal principle that governed the universe. Gradually, as Vedic philosophy moved towards a monotheistic interpretation of the universe and its origins, this power was increasingly personalized. In the Upanishads, Brahman was seen as a universal and elemental creative spirit. Brahma, described in myths as having been born from a golden egg and then to have created the Earth, assumed the identity of the Vedic deity Prajapati and became identified as the creator.

By the fourth and fifth centuries AD, the height of the classical period of Hinduism, Brahma was seen as one of the trinity of Gods – Trimurti – in which Vishnu, Siva and Brahma represented three forms of the unmanifested supreme being. It is from Brahma that Hindu cosmology takes its structure. The basic cycle through which the whole cosmos passes is described as one day in the life of Brahma: the kalpa. It equals 4320 million years, with an equally long night. One year of Brahma's life, a cosmic year, lasts 360 days and nights. The universe is expected to last for 100 years of Brahma's life. Brahma is characteristically, shown with four faces, a fifth having been destroyed by the fire from Siva's third eye. In his four arms he usually holds a copy of the Vedas, a sceptre and a water jug or a bow. He is accompanied by the goose, symbolizing knowledge.

Sarasvati Seen by some Hindus as the 'active power' of Brahma, popularly thought of as his consort, Sarasvati has survived into the modern Hindu world as a far more important figure than Brahma himself. In popular worship Sarasvati represents the goddess of education and learning, worshipped in schools and colleges with gifts of fruit, flowers and incense. She represents 'the word' itself, which began to be deified as part of the process of the writing of the Vedas, which ascribed magical power to words. The development of her identity represented the rebirth of the concept of a mother goddess, which had been strong in the Indus Valley Civilization over 1000 years before and which may have been continued in popular ideas through the worship of female spirits.

In addition to her role as Brahma's wife, Sarasvati is also variously seen as the wife of Vishnu and Manu or as Daksha's daughter, among other interpretations. Normally white coloured, riding on a swan and carrying a book, she is often shown playing a vina. She may have many arms and heads, representing her role as patron of all the sciences and arts.

Vishnu is seen as the God with the human face. From the second century a new and passionate devotional worship of Vishnu's incarnation as Krishna developed in the South of India. He has 10 successive incarnations in animal and human form.

Rama and Krishna By far the most influential incarnations of Vishnu are those in which he was believed to take recognizable human form, especially as Rama (twice) and Krishna.

Lakshmi Commonly represented as Vishnu's wife, Lakshmi is widely worshipped as the goddess of wealth. Earlier representations of Vishnu's consorts portrayed her as Sridevi, often shown in statues on Vishnu's right, while Bhudevi, also known as Prithvi, who represented the earth, was on his left. Lakshmi is popularly shown in her own right as standing on a lotus flower, although eight forms of Lakshmi are recognized.

Hanuman The Ramayana tells how Hanuman, Rama's faithful servant, went across India and finally into the demon Ravana's forest home of Lanka at the head of his monkey army in search of the abducted Sita. He used his powers to jump the sea channel separating India from Sri Lanka and managed after a series of heroic and magical feats to find and rescue his master's wife. Whatever form he is shown in, he remains almost instantly recognizable.

Siva American professor of religion Wendy Doniger O'Flaherty argues that the key to the myths through which Siva's character is understood, lies in the explicit ambiguity of Siva as the great ascetic and at the same time as the erotic force of the universe.

Siva is interpreted as both creator and destroyer, the power through whom the universe evolves. He lives on Mount Kailasa with his wife Parvati (also known as Uma, Sati, Kali and Durga) and two sons, the elephant-headed Ganesh and the six-headed Karttikeya. Siva is normally accompanied by his 'vehicle', the bull (**Nandi** or **Nandin**).

Siva is also represented in Shaivite temples by the **linga**, literally meaning 'sign' or 'mark', but referring in this context to the sign of gender or phallus and yoni. On the one hand a symbol of energy, fertility and potency, as Siva's symbol it also represents the yogic power of sexual abstinence and penance. The linga has become the most important symbol of the cult of Siva. O'Flaherty suggests that the worship of the linga of Siva can be traced back to the pre-Vedic societies of the Indus Valley civilization (circa 2000 BC), but that it first appears in Hindu iconography in the second century BC. From that time a wide variety of myths appeared to explain the origin of linga worship.

Nandi Siva's vehicle, the bull, is one of the most widespread of sacred symbols of the ancient world and may represent a link with Rudra, sometimes represented as a bull in pre-Hindu India. Strength and virility are key attributes and pilgrims to Siva temples will often touch the Nandi's testicles on their way into the shrine.

Ganesh is one of Hinduism's most popular gods. He is seen as the great clearer of obstacles. Shown at gateways and on door lintels with his elephant head and pot belly, his image is revered.

Nagas and Naginis The multiple-hooded cobra head often seen in sculptures represents the fabulous snake gods the Nagas, though they may often be shown in other forms, even human. In South India it is particularly common to find statues of divine Nagas being worshipped. They are usually placed on uncultivated ground under trees in the hope and belief, as author Masson-Oursel puts it, that "if the snakes have their own domain left to them they are more likely to spare human beings". The Nagas and their wives, the Naginis, are often the agents of death in mythical stories.

Hué architecture

More characteristic of Vietnamese art and architecture are the pagodas and palaces at Hué (see page 180) and in and around Hanoi (page 51). But even this art and architecture is not really 'Vietnamese', as it is highly derivative, drawing heavily on Chinese prototypes. Certainly there are some features that are peculiarly Vietnamese, but unlike the other countries of mainland Southeast Asia, the Vietnamese artistic tradition is far less distinct. Vietnamese artistic endeavour was directed more towards literature than the plastic arts. In his art history of Indochina, French art historian Bernard Groslier – better known for his work on Angkor – writes, rather condescendingly: "From 1428 to 1769 Vietnamese art is bogged down in formulas. Despite the absorption of Champa, no foreign influence, save that of China, affected them. However, execution and technique greatly improved, so that some of the works take an honourable place among Chinese provincial products".

Contemporary Vietnamese art

The beginnings of contemporary or modern Vietnamese art can be traced back to the creation of the **École de Beaux Arts Indochine** in Hanoi in 1925. By this time there was an emerging westernized intelligentsia in Vietnam who had been schooled in French ways and taught to identify, at least in part, with French culture. Much of the early painting produced by students taught at the École de Beaux Arts Indochine was romantic, portraying an idyllic picture of Vietnamese life and landscape. It was also weak. However, by the 1930s a Vietnamese nationalist tone began to be expressed both in terms of subject matter and technique. For example, paintings on silk and lacquer became popular around this time.

In 1945, with the Declaration of Independence, the École de Beaux Arts Indochine closed, and art for art's sake came to an end. From this point, artists were strongly encouraged to join in the revolutionary project and, for example, paint posters of heroic workers, stoic peasants and brave soldiers. Painting landscapes or pictures of rural life was no longer on the agenda.

In 1950 a new **School of Fine Art** was established in Viet Bac with the sole remit of training revolutionary artists. Central control of art and artists became even more stringent after 1954 when many artists were sent away to re-education camps. Established artists like Bui Xuan Phai, for example, were no longer permitted either to exhibit or to teach so lacking were they in revolutionary credentials.

In 1957 a new premier art school was created in the capital: the **Hanoi School of Fine Arts**. Students were schooled in the methods and meanings of socialist-realism and Western art became, by definition, capitalist and decadent. But while the state saw to it that artists kept to the revolutionary line, fine art in North Vietnam never became so harsh and uncompromising as in China or the Soviet Union; there was always a romantic streak. In addition, the first director of the Hanoi School of Fine Arts, Nguyen Do Cung, encouraged his students to search for inspiration in traditional Vietnamese arts and crafts, in simple village designs and in archaeological artefacts. Old woodblock prints, for example, strongly influenced the artists of this period.

Brilliance in bronze: rain drums of Dongson

Of the artefacts associated with the Dongson culture, none is more technologically or artistically impressive than the huge bronze kettledrums that have been unearthed. Understandably, Vietnamese archaeologists have been keen to stress the 'Vietnamese-ness' of these objects, rejecting many of the suggestions made by Western scholars that they are of Chinese or Indian inspiration. As Professor Pham Huy Thong of the Academy of Sciences writes, Western studies are "marked by insufficient source material, prejudices and mere deductions", and that their "achievements [in understanding the drums] remain insignificant". He supports the view that these magnificent objects were products of the forebears of the Viet people. The jury on the issue remains out.

The squat, waisted, bronze Dongson drums show their makers to have been master casters of the first order. They can measure over 1 m in height and width and consist of a decorated tympanum, a convex upper section, waisted middle, and expanding lower section. Decoration is both geometric and naturalistic, most notably on the finely incised drumhead. An area of continuing debate concerns the function of the drums. They have usually been found associated with human remains and other precious objects, leading archaeologists to argue that they symbolized power and prestige and were treasured objects in the community. Also known as rain drums, they are sometimes surmounted with bronze figures of frogs (or toads). It is thought that the drums were used as magical instruments to summon rain, frogs being associated with rain. Other decorative motifs include dancers (again, possibly part of rain-making rites) and boats with feather-crowned passengers (perhaps taking the deceased to the Kingdom of the Dead). Other Dongson drums have been found as far east as the island of Alor in Nusa Tenggara, Indonesia, indicating possible trade links between northern Vietnam and the archipelago.

As if to stress the nationalist symbolism of the drum, an image of an ornate tympanum is used as an icon by Vietnamese television, and Vietnam Airlines prints the motif on their tickets.

With *doi moi* – economic reform – has come a greater degree of artistic freedom. Nguyen Van Linh, the late secretary-general of the Vietnamese Communist Party, talked of 'untying the strings', to give artists greater freedom of individual expression. The first exhibition of abstract art in Vietnam was held in 1992. Today there are numerous art galleries in Hanoi and Ho Chi Minh City and while artists still paint within limits set by the Communist Party, these have been considerably relaxed. Although artist Truong Tan incurred the wrath of the party in 2007 when his exhibit was rapidly withdrawn from a Goethe Institute-supported art show in Hanoi. Truong Tan had created a giant nappy out of police uniform pockets. The link between the absorption of the pockets of the policemen and that of a nappy was not missed by the authorities, especially in the current climate.

The Vietnamese Pagoda and Buddhist iconography

The pagoda or *chua* is a Buddhist temple and shows clear affinities with its Chinese equivalent. A Vietnamese pagoda is usually not a many-tiered tower but a single-storey structure. However, some pagodas do have a tower (*thap*), which in most cases was erected as a memorial to the founder of the pagoda. Most will have a sacred pond (often with sacred turtles), bell tower and yard. The main building – the pagoda itself – usually consists of a number of rooms. At the front are three main doors that are opened only for special festivals. Behind these doors are the front hall, outer hall and the inner or main altar hall, the former being at the lowest level, the altar hall at the highest. There will be Buddha statues, sometimes three: past, present and future. At the back of the pagoda are living quarters for monks or nuns, as well as gardens and other secular structures. Monks and nuns never serve in the same pagoda. While a temple may be dedicated to a hero, a mythical character or holy animal, a pagoda is an exclusively Buddhist place of worship.

Common pagoda characters and iconography

Avalokitesvara or Ti-Ts'ang Wang: the compassionate male Boddhisattva, usually depicted in an attitude of meditation with his attributes, a water flask and lotus. The figure is sometimes represented with four arms, in which case his attributes are a rosary and book, as well as the lotus and water flask. He is merciful and offers help and solace to those suffering the torments of hell.

Bodhisattvas: enlightened beings or future Buddhas who have renounced nirvana to remain on earth. They are in theory countless, although just a handful are usually represented, most easily recognizable to the devotee. Bodhisattvas are usually depicted as princes with rich robes and a crown or head-dress.

Buddha (Sakyamuni): the Buddha, or the historic Buddha; usually depicted seated on a throne or thrones (often a lotus) in one of the mudras or 'attitudes' of the Buddha, and clothed in the simple dress of an ascetic. Among the Buddha's features are elongated ear lobes, the *urna* or third 'eye' in the centre of the forehead, and tightly curled hair.

Buddha of the Past (Amitabha): central to the Pure Land faith. Adherents chant the Amitabha sutra, and on their death are transported to the Western Paradise where they are guided to nirvana. The Amitabha Buddha is merciful and wise. Recent interpretations can sometimes be identified by a very long right arm – so carved so that the Buddha can embrace all of humanity, and bring salvation to everyone.

Ch'eng-huang Yeh (City God): each town will have its own deity who controls the behaviour of the population. He also keeps the records of the dead and sends out his henchmen to collect people when their due date has arrived. He is therefore greatly feared. More generally, he controls the demons and therefore has some power over natural disasters like flood and pestilence.

Dragon (long/rong): not the evil destructive creature of Western mythology but divine and beneficial. Often associated with the emperor.

Fertility Goddesses: there are lots of these, of which the most famous is Quan Am. Other popular fertility goddesses can usually be identified by the children that they hold in their laps. Sometimes they are surrounded by attendants who hold infants, or are shown breast-feeding, teaching or playing with them.

Judges or Magistrates: these 10 men run the Ten Courts of the Afterworld and are usually arranged in two rows of five (often on either side of the hall). Their mission is to sentence the dead according to their role and life on earth. Each Judge is responsible for a different sin – murder, unfilial acts, arson, and so on – and having judged an individual passes them on to the next Judge. But just like the real world, sinners can have their sentences lightened by handing over money (Hell Money), so corruption works even here! Having passed through the hands of 10 Judges, the poor soul then arrives at the feet of **Mother Meng**. She gives the extirpated sinner the Soup of Oblivion, whereupon he or she forgets everything and is in a suitable state to be reborn in the real world.

Ong Tao: ascends to heaven at the end of the old year to inform God of the family's conduct during the previous 12 months. He is, therefore, fêted and petitioned for days before.

Patron deities: this includes a number of deities that look after the interests of particular groups of people, such as fishermen (see Thien Hau), actors, policemen and farmers.

Quan Am: Chinese Goddess of Mercy (Kuan-yin), often all-white, and usually depicted holding her adopted son in one arm and standing on a lotus leaf (the symbol of purity). Quan Am's husband is occasionally depicted as a parakeet (see page 61). Quan Am is sometimes represented as a man, and as a Bodhisattva – Avalokitesvara – the two are fused in a single representation.

Quan Cong and companions: usually red-faced and green-cloaked and accompanied by his two trusty companions, General Chau Xuong and the Mandarin Quan Binh and sometimes also with his horse and groom.

Swastika: running either left to right or vice versa, it is often complicated by various additions. The motif symbolizes the 'heart of the Buddha', 'long life' and 'ten thousand'. In Buddhist and Cao Dai temples, swastikas run in opposite directions. Cao Dai believers argue 'their' direction is in harmony with the movement of the universe.

Thien Hau Thanh Mau (also Ma Tsu): goddess of the sea and protector of sailors. She first appeared, so to speak, in Fukien province in China during the 11th century. Folklore has it that she was the daughter of a fisherman named Lin and that she died while a virgin. She appears to fishermen in times of extreme peril and saves their lives. Thien Hau Thanh Mau is usually represented seated, with a flattened crown. But the real giveaway are her two companions, who go by the great names of **Thousand-mile Eye** and **Follow the Wind Ear**. These are both tamed demons that the goddess uses to provide long range weather forecasts to fishermen. Thousand-mile Eye is red-skinned and peers towards the horizon, hand shading his eyes; Follow the Wind Ear is green skinned and is usually depicted cupping his hand to his ear as he listens for minor climatic changes. The three of them are usually seen, unsurprisingly, in coastal towns.

T'u-ti Kung or Fu-te Cheng-shen (Earth God): the Lord of the Earth is effectively a petty official and not to be greatly feared as he merely does the work of much more powerful gods. He keeps track of birth, deaths and marriages, as headmen do in real life. He is usually represented as an old man.

Yin-yang symbol: the Taoist symbol, a circle divided by an 'S' line, splitting the circle into dark and light halves, symbolizing the dualism of the world (see page 472).

Crafts

Lacquerware (son mai)

The art of making lacquerware is said to have been introduced into Vietnam after Emperor Le Thanh Ton (1443-1459) sent an emissary to the Chinese court to investigate the process. Lacquer is a resin from the son tree (*Rhus succedanea or R vernicifera*) that is then applied in numerous coats (usually 11) to wood (traditionally teak), leather, metal or porcelain. Prior to lacquering, the article must be sanded and coated with a fixative. The final coat is highly polished with coal powder. The piece may then be decorated with an incised design, painted, or inset with mother-of-pearl. If mother-of-pearl is to be used, appropriately shaped pieces of lacquer are chiselled out and the mother-of-pearl inset. This method is similar to that used in China, but different from Thailand and Burma. The designs in the north show Japanese influences, apparently because Japanese artists were employed as teachers at the École des Beaux Arts in Hanoi in the 1930s.

Non Lá conical hat

This cone-shaped hat is one of the most common and evocative sights in Vietnam's countryside. Worn by women (and occasionally men), it is usually woven from latania leaves. The poem hats of Hué are particularly well known (see Shopping, page 204). Although all peasants in Southeast Asia wear straw hats only the Vietnamese version is perfectly conical and as such instantly identifies the wearer. As well as providing protection from the weather it serves other functions such as fan and rice holder and can even be used for carrying water. It also makes an original lampshade, often to be seen hanging over a pool table in bars in Saigon. It is probably less versatile than its Cambodian equivalent, the *kramar* (cotton scarf), which acts as a sarong, towel, curtain, sheet and baby sling, among its other uses.

Ao dai

This garment exhibits more conspicuously what it was intended to hide. It is the national women's costume of Vietnam, literally, but prosaically it means 'long dress'. Ao dai consists of a long flowing tunic of diaphanous fabric worn over a pair of loose-fitting white pants; the front and rear sections of the tunic are split from the waist down. The modern design was created by a literary group called the *Tu Luc Van Doan* in 1932, based on ancient court costumes and Chinese dresses such as the chong san. In traditional society, decoration and complexity of design indicated the status of the wearer (for example, gold brocade and dragons were for the sole use of the emperor; purple for higher-ranked mandarins). The popularity of the *ao dai* is now worldwide and the annual Miss Ao Dai pageant at Long Beach attracts entrants from all over the US. Today *ao dai* is uniform for hotel receptionists and many office workers, particularly in Ho Chi Minh City but less so in cooler Hanoi. French designer Elian Lille said: "The first thing most people see when they come to Vietnam is the young students wearing a white *ao dai*, with their long hair clipped back and sitting very straight on their bicycles. It is exquisite."

Montagnard crafts

There are more than 50 ethnic minorities and their crafts are highly available. Textiles, jewellery and basketwork are the most widely available. The finely worked clothing of the Muong (with Dongson-derived motifs) and indigo-dyed cloth of the Bahnar are two examples of Montagnard crafts.

Drama and dance

Classical Vietnamese theatre, known as *hat boi* (hat = to sing; boi = gesture, pose), shows close links with the classical theatre of China. Emperor Tu Duc had a troupe of 150 female artists and employed stars from China via a series of extravagant productions. Since the partition of the country in 1954, there has developed what might be termed 'revolutionary realist' theatre and classical Vietnamese theatre is today almost defunct. However, the most original theatrical art form in Vietnam is *mua roi nuoc* or **water puppet theatre**. This seems to have originated in northern Vietnam during the early years of this millennium when it was associated with the harvest festival (at one time scholars thought water puppet theatre originated in China before being adopted in Vietnam). An inscription in Nam Ha province mentions a show put on in honour of King Ly Nhan Ton in 1121. By the time the French began to colonize Vietnam in the late 19th century it had spread to all of the major towns of the country.

Modern Vietnamese art

Contemporary art in Vietnam, as elsewhere in Southeast Asia, has recently benefited from an upsurge in interest from young Asian collectors with plenty of money. Exhibitions in Hong Kong, New York, Paris and London have helped bring contemporary Vietnamese art to a wider public. Galleries have opened in all Vietnam's major cities and although much of the work displayed is purely commercial, artists now have an opportunity to exhibit pictures which until recently were considered sub-versive. Vietnam has three art colleges, in Ho Chi Minh City, Hué and the School of Fine Arts in Hanoi, founded by the French in 1925.

Although most Vietnamese painting is still conservative in subject, idiom and medium, some painters of the younger generation, including Dao Hai Phong, Tran Trong Vu and Truong Tan, experiment with more abstract ideas and, in the more liberal artistic climate of the new millennium, their work is more expressive and less clichéd than that of 10 or 20 years ago. Even established artists such as Ly Quy Chung, Tran Luu Hau and Mai Long are taking advantage of their newly found artistic freedom to produce exciting experimental work; Trinh Cung and Tran Trong Vu are noted for their abstract paintings and Nguyen Thanh Binh's famous but faceless schoolgirls in *ao dais* hang in drawing rooms across Asia and Europe. The popularity of this theme has been seized upon by many lesser artists. Among the most respected artists of the older generation are Professor Nguyen Thu, Colonel Quang Tho and Diep Minh Chau, whose work draws heavily on traditional Vietnamese themes, particularly rural landscapes, but also episodes from recent history: the battle of Dien Bien Phu, life under American occupation and pencil sketches of Ho Chi Minh. Traditional art forms such as watercolour paintings on silk and lacquerwork are still popular.

For further information visit www.thavibu.com/vietnam and to see the latest in the world of art, visit Art Vietnam in Hanoi, www.artvietnamgallery.com.

As the name suggests, this form of theatre uses the surface of the water as the stage. Puppeteers, concealed behind a bamboo screen symbolizing an ancient village communal house, manipulate the characters while standing in a metre of water. The puppets – some over half a metre tall – are carved from water resistant *sung* wood that is also very lightweight and then painted in bright colours. Most need one puppeteer to manipulate them, but some require three or four. Plays are based on historical and religious themes: the origins of the Viet nation, legends, village life, and acts of heroism. Some include the use of fireworks – especially during battle scenes – while all performances are accompanied by folk opera singers and traditional instruments. Performances usually begin with the clown, Teu, taking the stage and he acts as a linking character between the various scenes.

The most famous and active troupe is based in Hanoi (see page 83), although in total there are about a dozen groups. Since the 1980s Vietnamese writers have turned their attention from revolutionary heroes to commentary on political and social issues of the day. Consequently, many plays have failed to see the light of day and those that have are often been badly mauled by the censoring committee's scissors; references to corrupt officials and policemen seldom make the transition from page to stage.

Chèo is another traditional theatre form developed from mime during the 11th century but is little practised now. Tuong is another traditional theatre based on Chinese opera and is characterized by stylized rules for singing, mime, dancing and the spoken word. Cai luong (reformed opera) derives from popular folk songs and remains a favourite in the south.

Language

The Vietnamese language has a reputation for being fiendishly difficult to master. Its origins are still the subject of dispute; at one time thought to be a Sino-Tibetan language (because it is tonal), it is now believed to be Austro-Asiatic and related to Mon-Khmer. Sometime after the ninth century, when Vietnam was under Chinese domination, Chinese ideograms were adapted for use with the Vietnamese language. This script – *chu nho* (scholar's script) – was used in all official correspondence and in literature right through to the early 20th century. Whether this replaced an earlier writing system is not known. As early Vietnamese nationalists tried to break away from Chinese cultural hegemony in the late 13th century, they devised their own script, based on Chinese ideograms but adapted to meet Vietnamese language needs. This became known as *chu nom* (vulgar script). So, while Chinese words formed the learned vocabulary of the intelligentsia (largely inaccessible to the man on the street or in the paddy field), non-Chinese words made up a parallel popular vocabulary.

Finally, in the 17th century, European missionaries under the tutelage of Father Alexandre de Rhodes created a system of Romanized writing: *quoc ngu* (national language). It is said that Rhodes initially thought Vietnamese sounded like the 'twittering of birds' (a view interestingly echoed by Graham Greene in *The Quiet American*: "To take an Annamite to bed with you is like taking a bird: they twitter and sing on your pillow") but had mastered the language in six months. The first quoc ngu dictionary (Vietnamese-Portuguese-Latin), *Dictionarium Annamiticum Lusitanum et Latinum*, was published in 1651. Quoc ngu uses marks – so-called diacritical marks – to indicate tonal differences. Initially it was ignored by the educated unless they were Roman Catholic and it was not until the early 20th century that its use became a mark of modernity among a broad spectrum of Vietnamese. Even then, engravings in the mausoleums and palaces of the royal family continued to use Chinese characters. It seems that the move from chu nom to quoc ngu, despite the fact that it was imposed by an occupying country, occurred as people realized how much easier it was to master. The first quoc ngu newspaper, *Gia Dinh Bao* (Gia Dinh Gazette), was published in 1865 and quoc ngu was adopted as the national script in 1920.

Standard Vietnamese is based on the language spoken by an educated person living in the vicinity of Hanoi. This has become, so to speak, Vietnam's equivalent of BBC English. There are also important regional dialects in the centre and south of the country and these differ from Standard Vietnamese in terms of tone and vocabulary, but use the same system of grammar.

For useful Vietnamese words and phrases, and food, drink and shopping phrases, see page 490.

Literature

In ancient Vietnam, texts were reproduced laboriously, by scribes, on paper made from the bark of the mulberry tree (*giay ban*). Examples exist in Ho Chi Minh City, Paris, Hanoi and Hué. Printing technology was introduced in the late 13th century, but due to the hot and humid climate no early examples exist.

Vietnam has a rich folk literature of fables, legends, proverbs and songs, most of which were transmitted by word of mouth. In the 17th and 18th centuries, satirical poems and, importantly, verse novels (truyen) appeared. These were memorized and recited by itinerant storytellers as they travelled from village to village.

Like much Vietnamese art, Vietnamese literature also owes a debt to China. Chinese characters and literary styles were duplicated and although a tradition of nom literature did evolve (nom being a hybrid script developed in the 13th century), Vietnamese efforts remained largely derivative. One exception was the scholarly **Nguyen Trai** (see box, page 406) who bridged the gap; he excelled in classical Chinese chu nho as well as producing some of the earliest surviving, and very fine, poetry and prose in the new chu nom script. An important distinction is between the literature of the intelligentsia (essentially Chinese) and that of the people (more individualistic). These latter nom works, dating from the 15th century onwards, were simpler and concerned with immediate problems and grievances. They can be viewed as the most Vietnamese of literary works and include Chinh Phu Ngam (Lament of a Soldier's Wife), an anti-war poem by Phan Huy Ich (1750-1822). The greatest Vietnamese literature was produced during the social and political upheavals of the 19th century: Truyen Kieu (The Tale of Kieu) written by Nguyen Du (1765-1820) is a classic of the period. This 3254-line story is regarded by most Vietnamese as their cultural statement par excellence (see the next section for a taster). Nguyen Du was one of the most skilled and learned mandarins of his time and was posted to China as Vietnam's Ambassador to the Middle Kingdom. On his return, Nguyen Du wrote the Truyen Kieu (or Kim Van Kieu), a celebration of Vietnamese culture, in the lines of which can be traced the essence of Vietnamese-ness.

French influence, and the spread of the Romanized Vietnamese script, led to the end of the Chinese literary tradition by the 1930s and its replacement by a far starker, freer, Western-derived style. Poetry of this period is known as Tho Moi (New Poetry). The communist period has seen restrictions on literary freedom and in recent years there have been numerous cases of authors and poets, together with journalists, being imprisoned owing to the critical nature of their work. Much of Vietnam's literature is allegorical (which people readily understand); this reflects a centuries-old intolerance of criticism by the mandarin and royal family. Although the Communist Party might be expected to approve of anti-royal sentiment in literature it seldom does, fearing that the Party itself is the true object of the writer's scorn.

Kieu: oriental Juliet or prototype Miss Saigon?

The tale of Kieu is a true story of pure love corrupted by greed and power. It also offers a fascinating glimpse into the Vietnamese mind and Vietnamese sexual mores. Kieu is in love with the young scholar Kim and early on in the story she displays her physical and moral qualities:

"A fragrant rose, she sparkled in full bloom, bemused his eyes, and kindled his desire. When waves of lust had seemed to sweep him off, his wooing turned to wanton liberties.She said: 'Treat not our love as just a game – please stay away from me and let me speak.What is a mere peach blossom that one shouldfence off the garden, thwart the bluebird's quest? But you've named me your bride – to serve her man, she must place chastity above all else.'"

But the overriding theme of the story is the ill-treatment of an innocent girl by a duplicitous and wicked world unopposed by Heaven. Unmoved by Kieu's sale into prostitution the fates actively oppose her wishes by keeping her alive when she attempts to kill herself.

Any respite in her tale of woe proves short-lived and joy turns quickly to pain. The story illustrates the hopelessness of women in a Confucianist, male-dominated world; Kieu likens herself to a raindrop with no control over where she will land. Early on in the story when Kim is away attending to family matters Kieu has to choose between Kim, to whom she has pledged herself, and her family. Such is the strength of family ties that she offers herself to be sold in marriage to raise money for her kith and kin:

"By what means could she save her flesh and blood? When evil strikes you bow to circumstance. As you must weigh and choose between your love and filial duty, which will turn the scale? She put aside all vows of love and troth – a child first pays the debts of birth and care."

Kieu gets married off to an elderly 'scholar' called Ma who is in fact a brothel keeper; but before removing her from her family he deflowers her. Kieu is now commercially less valuable but Ma believes he can remedy this:

"One smile of hers is worth pure gold – it's true. When she gets there, to pluck the maiden bud, princes and gentlefolk will push and shove. She'll bring at least three hundred liang, about what I have paid – net profit after that. A morsel dangles at my mouth – what Godserves up I crave, yet money hate to lose. A heavenly peach within a mortal's grasp: I'll bend the branch, pick it, and quench my thirst. How many flower-fanciers on Earth can really tell one flower from the next? Juice from pomegranite skin and cockscomb blood will heal it up and lend the virgin look. In dim half-light some yokel will be fooled: she'll fetch that much, and not one penny less."

Kieu's sorrows deepen; she becomes a concubine of a married brothel patron, Thuc. After a year of happiness together with Thuc his spurned wife, Hoan, decides to spoil the fun. Kieu ends up as a slave serving Thuc and Hoan. She laments her fate knowing full well the reason for it:

"I've had an ample share of life's foul dust, and now this swamp of mud proves twice as vile. Will fortune never let its victims go but in its snares and toils hold fast a rose? I sinned in some past life and have to pay: I'll pay as flowers must fade and jade must break."

She later commits her only earthly crime stealing a golden bell and silver gong from the shrine she is charged with keeping, and flees to seek sanctuary in a Buddhist temple. But when her crime comes to light she is sent to live with the Bac family that, again on the pretext of marriage, sells her to another brothel. This time she meets a free-spirited warlord Tu Hai:

"A towering hero, he outfought all foes with club or fist and knew all arts of war. Between the earth and heaven he lived free…"

who rescues her from the brothel. They become soul- and bed-mates until, after six months, Tu Hai's wanderlust and urge to fight take him away from her. He returns a year later victorious in battle. At this stage the story reaches a happy (and false) ending; Tu Hai sends his Captains out to round up all those who have crossed Kieu's path.

"Awesome is Heaven's law of recompense – one haul and all were caught, brought back to camp. Under a tent erected in the midst, Lord Tu and his fair lady took their seats. No sooner had the drum roll died away than guards checked names, led captives to the gate. 'Whether they have used you well or ill,' he said, 'pronounce yourself upon their just deserts.'"

Those who have shown Kieu kindness are rewarded while those who have harmed her are tortured. The exception is Hoan who, cruel though she was, Kieu releases (after torture) in a show of mercy following Hoan's plea "I have a woman's mind, a petty soul, and jealousy's a trait all humans share" – Kieu had been living with Hoan's husband for a year.

All is well for five years until another warlord, Lord Ho, flatters Kieu encouraging her to persuade Tu to put down his sword and make peace with the emperor. Guileless Kieu does so and "Lord Tu lets flags hang loose, watch-drums go dead. He slackened all defence – imperial spies / observed his camp and learned of its true state." All is lost: Tu is killed, Kieu has betrayed her hero and she is married off to a tribal chief. She throws herself into a river but yet again fails to die. Eventually Kieu, is reunited with Kim and her family:

"She glanced and saw her folks – they all were here: Father looked quite strong, and Mother spry; both sister Van and brother Quan grown up; and over there was Kim her love of yore."

Kieu and Kim hold a wedding feast and share a house but not a bed; Kim has sons by Van, Kieu's sister, and they all settle down to an untroubled life overseen by a more benevolent Heaven.

Huynh Sang Thong's translation (see page 486) is considered the finest and is accompanied by excellent notes, which explain the Vietnamese phrasing of the original and which set the story in context. Translation and commentary will bring Truyen Kieu to a wider and, one hopes, appreciative audience and help shed some light on what many Vietnamese regard as their most important cultural statement.

A Vietnamese account of the 'American' War

Most visitors to Vietnam, if they were not involved in the war themselves, gain their views from literature and films made by westerners, for westerners. It is rare for people to have access to Vietnamese literary perspectives on the war, partly because most that do exist are not translated and because, in comparison to the torrent of especially American accounts, there have been comparatively few written by Vietnamese. One of these few is Bao Ninh's moving and poetic *The Sorrow of War* which was first published in Vietnamese in 1991 under the title *Thân Phân Cua Tinh Yêu*. In Vietnam it was a huge success, no doubt prompting its translation into English by Frank Palmos. The English edition was published in 1994 and is now available in paperback, see page 485. This is not a romantic vision of war, a macho account relishing the fight nor once revelling in victory, but a deeply sad and melancholic book. Perhaps this is because Bao Ninh is recounting his story from the position of one who was there. He served with the Glorious 27th Youth Brigade, joining-up in 1969 at the age of 17. Of the 500 who went to war with the Glorious 27th, he was one of just 10 to survive the conflict. For those who want an alternative perspective, the book is recommended.

Banned books

Duong Thu Huong, who lives in Hanoi, is no stranger to censorship. She has criticized the regime and was imprisoned for a short term in 1991. Following publication of her third novel *Nhung Thien Duong* (*Paradise of the Blind*) about the 1953 land reforms, it was banned. Four of her books, which were extremely popular when sold in Vietnam, are now banned. Her books, written since 1991, including *Luu Ly* (*Memories of a Pure Spring*) have been published abroad.

Religion

Vietnam supports followers of all the major world religions, as well as those religions that are peculiarly Vietnamese: Theravada and Mahayana Buddhism, Protestant and Roman Catholic Christianity, Taoism, Confucianism, Islam, Cao Daism, Hoa Hao and Hinduism. In addition, spirit and ancestor worship (*To Tien*) are also practised. Confucianism, although not a formal religion, is probably the most pervasive doctrine of all. Nominal Christians and Buddhists will still pay attention to the moral and philosophic principles of Confucianism and it continues to play a central role in Vietnamese life.

Following the communist victory in 1975, the authorities moved quickly to curtail the influence of the various religions. Schools, hospitals and other institutions run by religious organizations were taken over by the state and many clergy either imprisoned and/or sent to re-education camps. The religious hierarchies were institutionalized, and proselytizing severely curtailed.

During the late 1980s and into the early 1990s some analysts identified an easing of the government's previously highly restrictive policies towards religious organizations. At the beginning of 1993, former General Secretary of the Vietnamese Communist Party, Do Muoi, even went so far as to make official visits to a Buddhist monastery and a Roman Catholic church. However it is clear the communist hierarchy is highly suspicious of priests and monks. They are well aware of the prominent role they played in South Vietnamese political dissension and are quick to crack down on any religious leader or organization that becomes involved in politics. In recent years this religious intolerance has been particularly manifest in the repression of the Montagnards in the Central Highlands, the closure of churches and imprisonment of church leaders, particularly protestant sects.

There is no question that more people today are attending Buddhist pagodas, Christian churches and Cao Dai temples. However, whether this rise in attendance at temples and churches actually means some sort of religious rebirth is questionable. Dang Nghiem Van, head of Hanoi's Institute of Religious Studies, poured scorn on the notion that young people are finding religion. They "are not religious," he said, "just superstitious. This isn't religion. It's decadence".

Mahayana Buddhism

Although there are both Theravada (also known as Hinayana) and Mahayana Buddhists in Vietnam, the latter are by far the more numerous. Buddhism was introduced into Vietnam in the second century AD: Indian pilgrims came by boat and brought the teachings of Theravada Buddhism, while Chinese monks came by land and introduced Mahayana Buddhism. In particular, the Chinese monk Mau Tu is credited with being the first person to introduce Mahayana Buddhism in AD 194-195.

Initially, Buddhism was very much the religion of the elite and did not impinge upon the common Vietnamese man or woman. It was not until the reign of Emperor Ly Anh Tong (1138-1175) that Buddhism was promoted as the state religion, nearly 1000 years after Mau Tu had arrived from China to spread the teachings of the Buddha. By that time it had begun to filter down to the village level, but as it did so it became increasingly syncretic; Buddhism became enmeshed with Confucianism, Taoism, spirituality, mysticism and animism. In the 15th century it also began to lose its position to Confucianism as the dominant religion of the court.

There has been a resurgence of Buddhism since the 1920s. It was the self-immolation of Buddhist monks in the 1960s which provided a focus of discontent against the government in the south (see box, page 318), and since the communist victory in 1975, monks have remained an important focus of dissent, hence the persecution of Buddhists during the early years following reunification. Mahayana Buddhists are concentrated in the centre and north of the country and the dominant sect is the Thien (Zen) meditation sect. Of the relatively small numbers of Theravada Buddhists, the majority are of Cambodian stock and are concentrated in the Mekong Delta. In Vietnam, Buddhism is intertwined with Confucianism and Taoism. See also box, above.

Confucianism

Although Confucianism is not strictly a religion, the teachings of the Chinese sage and philosopher Confucius (551-479 BC) form the basis on which Vietnamese life and government were based for much of the historic period. Even today, Confucianist perspectives are, possibly, more strongly in evidence than communist ones. Confucianism was introduced from China during the Bac Thuoc Period (111 BC-AD 938) when the Chinese dominated the country. The 'religion' enshrined the concept of imperial rule by the mandate of heaven, constraining social and political change.

In essence, Confucianism stresses the importance of family and lineage and the worship of ancestors. Men and women in positions of authority were required to provide role models for the 'ignorant', while the state, epitomized in the emperor, was likewise required to set an example and to provide conditions of stability and fairness for his people. Crucially, children had to observe filial piety. This set of norms, which were drawn from the experience of the human encounter at the practical level, were enshrined in the Forty-seven Rules for Teaching and Changing first issued in 1663. A key element of Confucianist thought is the Three Bonds (tam cuong) – the loyalty of ministers to the emperor, obedience of children to their parents and submission of wives to their husbands. Added to these are mutual reciprocity among friends and benevolence towards strangers. Not surprisingly the communists are antipathetic to such a hierarchical view of society although ironically Confucianism, which inculcates respect for the elderly and authority, unwittingly lends support to a politburo occupied by old men. In an essay entitled 'Confucianism and Marxism', Vietnamese scholar Nguyen Khac Vien explains why Marxism proved an acceptable doctrine to those accustomed to Confucian values: "Marxism was not baffling to Confucians in that it concentrated man's thoughts on political and social problems. By defining man as the total of his social relationships, Marxism hardly came as a shock to the Confucian scholar who had always considered the highest aim of man to be the fulfilment of his social obligations ... Bourgeois individualism, which puts personal interests ahead of those of society and petty bourgeois anarchism, which allows no social discipline whatsoever, are alien to both Confucianism and Marxism."

Taoism

Taoism was introduced from China into Vietnam at about the same time as Confucianism. It is based on the works of the Chinese philosophers Lao Tzu (circa sixth-fifth centuries BC) and Chuang Tzu (fourth century BC). Although not strictly a formal religion, it has had a significant influence on Buddhism (as it is practised in Vietnam) and on Confucianism. In reality, Taoism and Confucianism are two sides of the same coin: the Taoist side is poetry and spirituality; the Confucianist side, social ethics and the order of the world. Together they form a unity. Like Confucianism, it is not possible to give a figure to the number of followers of Taoism in Vietnam. It functions in conjunction with Confucianism and Buddhism and

In Siddhartha's footsteps: a short history of Buddhism

Buddhism was founded by Siddhartha Gautama, a prince of the Sakya tribe of Nepal, who probably lived from 563 to 483 BC. He achieved enlightenment and the word buddha means 'fully enlightened one', or 'one who has woken up'. Siddhartha Gautama is known by a number of names. In the West, he is usually referred to as The Buddha, ie the historic Buddha (but not just Buddha); more common in South-east Asia is Sakyamuni, or Sage of the Sakyas (referring to his tribal origins).

Over the centuries, the life of the Buddha has become part legend and the Jataka tales that recount his various lives are colourful and convoluted. But central to Buddhist belief is that he was born under a sal tree, that he achieved enlightenment under a bodhi tree in the Bodh Gaya Gardens, that he preached the First Sermon at Sarnath, and that he died at Kusinagara (all in India or Nepal).

The Buddha was born at Lumbini (in present-day Nepal) as Queen Maya was on her way to her parents' home. She had an auspicious dream before the child's birth of being impregnated by an elephant, whereupon a sage prophesied Siddhartha would become either a great king or a great spiritual leader. His father, being keen that the first option of the prophesy be fulfilled, brought him up in all the princely skills – at which Siddhartha excelled – and ensured that he only saw beautiful things, not the harsher elements of life.

Despite his father's efforts Siddhartha saw four things while travelling between palaces: a helpless old man, a very sick man, a corpse being carried by lamenting relatives, and an ascetic, calm and serene as he begged for food. The young prince renounced his princely origins and left home to study under a series of spiritual teachers. He finally discovered the path to enlightenment at the Bodh Gaya Gardens in India. He then proclaimed his thoughts to a small group of disciples at Sarnath, near Benares, and continued to preach

also often with Christianity, Cao Daism and Hoa Hao. Of all the world's religions, Taoism is perhaps the hardest to pin down. It has no formal code, no teachings and no creed. It is a cosmic religion. Even the word Tao is usually left untranslated or merely translated as 'The Way'. The inscrutability of it all is summed up in the writings of the Chinese poet Po Chu-i: "Those who speak know nothing, Those who know keep silence. These words, as I am told, were spoken by Lao Tzu. But if we are to believe that Lao Tzu was himself one who knew, how comes it that he wrote a book of five thousand words?"

Or to quote Chuang Tzu even more inscrutably: "Tao is beyond material existence ... it may be transmitted, but it cannot be received [possessed]. It may be attained, but cannot be seen. It exists prior to Heaven and Earth, and, indeed, for all eternity ... it is above the Zenith, but is not high; it is beneath the Nadir, but it is not low. It is prior to Heaven and Earth, but it is not ancient. It is older than the most ancient, but it is not old."

Central to Taoist belief is a world view based upon yin and yang, two primordial forces on which the creation and functioning of the world are based. The yin-yang is not specifically Taoist or Confucianist, but predates both and is associated with the first recorded Chinese ruler, Fu-hsi (2852-2738 BC). The well-known yin-yang symbol symbolizes the balance and equality between the great dualistic forces in the universe: dark and light, negative and positive, male and female. JC Cooper explains in *Taoism: the Way of the Mystic*, the symbolism of the black and white dots: "There is a point, or embryo, of black in the white and white in the black. This is essential to the symbolism since there is no being which and attract followers until he died at the age of 81 at Kusinagara.

In the First Sermon at the deer park in Sarnath, the Buddha preached the Four Truths, still seen as the root of Buddhist belief and experience: suffering exists; there is a cause of suffering; suffering can be ended; and to end suffering it is necessary to follow the 'Noble Eightfold Path' – right speech, livelihood, action, effort, mindfulness, concentration, opinion and intentionSoon after the Buddha began preaching, a monastic order – the Sangha – was established. As the monkhood evolved in India, it also began to fragment into different sects. An important change was the belief that the Buddha was transcendent: he had never been born, nor had he died; he had always existed and his life on earth had been mere illusion. The emergence of these new concepts helped to turn what up until then was an ethical code of conduct, into a religion. It eventually led

to a new Buddhist movement, Mahayana Buddhism, which split from the more traditional Theravada 'sect'.

Despite the division of Buddhism into two sects, the central tenets are common to both. Specifically, the principles pertaining to the Four Noble Truths, the Noble Eightfold Path, the Dependent Origination, the Law of Karma, and nirvana. In addition, the principles of non-violence and tolerance are also embraced by both sects. The differences between the two are of emphasis and interpretation. Theravada Buddhism is strictly based on the original Pali Canon, while the Mahayana tradition stems from later Sanskrit texts. Mahayana Buddhism also allows a broader interpretation of the doctrine. Other major differences are that while the Theravada tradition is more 'intellectual' and self-obsessed, stressing the attainment of wisdom and insight for oneself, Mahayana Buddhism emphasizes devotion and compassion.

does not contain within itself the germ of its opposite. There is no male without feminine characteristics and no female without its masculine attributes." Thus the dualism of the yin-yang is not absolute, but permeable.

To maintain balance and harmony in life it is necessary that a proper balance be maintained between yin (female) and yang (male). This is believed to be true both at the scale of the world and the nation, and also for an individual, for the human body is the world in microcosm. The root cause of illness is imbalance between the forces of yin and yang. Even foods have characters: 'hot' foods are yang and 'cold', yin. Implicit in this is the belief that there is a natural law underpinning all of life, a law upon which harmony ultimately rests. Taoism attempts to maintain this balance and thereby harmony. In this way, Taoism is a force promoting inertia, maintaining the status quo. Traditional relationships between fathers and sons, between siblings, within villages, and between the rulers and the ruled, are all rationalized in terms of maintaining balance and harmony. Forces for change – like communism and democracy – are resisted on the basis that they upset this balance.

Christianity

Christianity was first introduced into Vietnam in the 16th century by Roman Catholic missionaries from Portugal, Spain and France. The first Bishop of Vietnam was appointed in 1659 and by 1685 there were estimated to be 800,000 Roman Catholics in the country. For several centuries Christianity was discouraged, and at times, outlawed. Many Christians were executed and one of the reasons the French gave for annexing the country in the late 19th century was religious persecution. Today, 8-10% of the population are thought to be Roman Catholic; less than 1% are Protestant. This Christian population is served by around 2000 priests. Following reunification in 1975, many Roman Catholics in the former south were sent to re-education camps. They were perceived to be both staunchly pro-American and anti-communist and it was not until 1988 that many were returned to normal life.

Today, Roman Catholics are still viewed with suspicion by the state and priests felt to be drifting from purely religious concerns into any criticism of the state (seen as anti-government activity) are detained, such as Father Nguyen Van Ly, see page 439. And this is the key point: the Vietnamese remain tolerant and open in matters of religion and spirituality. It is the political overtones that come with any established religion that the authorities find impossible to accept. While memories of the role of the Roman Catholic church in the downfall of Polish communism linger relations between Hanoi and the Vatican are not warm and often strained and Rome finds it difficult to appoint bishops. However, in 2007 the prime minister became the first head of government to be received at the Vatican to discuss relations. More generally, the authorities have been slow to permit Vietnamese men to become ordained, and they have limited the production and flow of religious literature. Nevertheless centuries of existence in what for the Roman Catholic church has been the hostile environment of Vietnam has enabled it to reach an accommodation and degree of acceptance. Doubtless the brighter of the communist leaders realise the Roman Catholic church will be around long after their Party has disappeared.

Protestant sects have a much tougher time. This is partly due to the evangelical nature of much Protestantism that makes the authorities distinctly uneasy. Evangelical protestants have faced the brunt of the crackdowns in the last couple of years.

Islam and Hinduism

The only centres of Islam and Hinduism are among the Cham of the central coastal plain and Chau Doc. The Cham were converted to Islam by Muslim traders. There are several mosques in Ho Chi Minh City and Cholon, some of them built by Indians from Kerala.

Cao Daism

Cao Dai took root in southern Vietnam during the 1920s after Ngo Van Chieu, a civil servant, was visited by 'Cao Dai' or the 'Supreme Being' and was given the tenets of a new religion. Ngo received this spiritual visitation in 1919 on Phu Quoc Island. The Cao Dai later told Ngo in a seance that he was to be symbolized by a giant eye. The religion quickly gained the support of a large following of dispossessed peasants. It was both a religion and a nationalist movement. In terms of the former, it claimed to be a synthesis of Buddhism, Christianity, Taoism, Confucianism and Islam. Cao Dai 'saints' include Joan of Arc, the French writer Victor Hugo, Sir Winston Churchill, Sun Yat Sen, Moses and Brahma. Debates over doctrine are mediated through the spirits who are contacted on a regular basis through a strange wooden contraption called a *corbeille-à-bec* or planchette. The five Cao Dai commandments are: do not kill any living creature; do not covet; do not practise high living; do not be tempted; and do not slander by word. But, as well as being a religion, the movement also claimed that it would restore traditional Vietnamese attitudes and was anti-colonial and modestly subversive. Opportunist to a fault, Cao Dai followers sought the aid of the Japanese against the French, the Americans against the Viet Minh and the Viet Minh against the south. Following reunification in 1975, all Cao Dai lands were confiscated and their leadership emasculated. The centre of Cao Daism remains the Mekong Delta where – and despite the efforts of the communists – there are thought to be perhaps two million adherents and perhaps 1000 Cao Dai temples. The Cao Dai Great Temple is in the town of Tay Ninh, 100 km from Ho Chi Minh City (see page 327).

Hoa Hao

Hoa Hao is another Vietnamese religion that emerged in the Mekong Delta. It was founded by Huynh Phu So in 1939, a resident of Hoa Hao village in the province of Chau Doc. Effectively a schism of Buddhism, the sect discourages temple building and worship, maintaining that simplicity of worship is the key to better contact with God. There are thought to be perhaps 1-1.5 million adherents of Hoa Hao, predominantly in the Chau Doc area.

Land and environment

The regions of Vietnam

The name Vietnam is derived from that adopted in 1802 by Emperor Gia Long: Nam Viet. This means, literally, the Viet (the largest ethnic group) of the south (Nam), and substituted for the country's previous name, Annam. The country is S-shaped, covers a land area of 329,600 sq km and has a coastline of 3000 km. The most important economic zones, containing the main concentrations of population, are focused on two large deltaic areas. In the north, there are the ancient rice fields and settlements of the Red River, and in the south, the fertile alluvial plain of the Mekong. In between, the country narrows to less than 50 km wide, with only a thin ribbon of fertile lowland suited to intensive agriculture. Much of the interior, away from the coastal belt and the deltas, is mountainous. Here ethnic minorities (Montagnards), along with some lowland Vietnamese resettled in so-called New Economic Zones since 1975, eke out a living on thin and unproductive soils. The rugged terrain means that only 25% of the land is actually cultivated. Of the rest, 20-25% is forested and some of this is heavily degraded.

The French subdivided Vietnam into three regions, administering each separately: Tonkin or Bac Ky (the north region), Annam or Trung Ky (the central region) and Cochin China or Nam Ky (the south region). Although these administrative divisions have been abolished, the Vietnamese still recognize their country as consisting of three regions, distinct in terms of geography, history and culture. Their new names are Bac Bo (north), Trung Bo (centre) and Nam Bo (south).

Northern Highlands

Vietnam consists of five major geographical zones. In the far north are the northern highlands which ring the Red River Delta and form a natural barrier with China. The rugged mountains on the west border of this region – the Hoang Lien Son – exceed 3000 m in places. The tributaries of the Red River have cut deep, steep-sided gorges through the Hoang Lien Son, which are navigable by small boats. The eastern portion of this region, bordering the Gulf of Tonkin, is far less imposing; the mountain peaks of the west have diminished into foothills, allowing easy access to China. It was across these hills that the Chinese mounted their successive invasions of Vietnam, the last of which occurred as recently as 1979, see page 433.

Red River Delta

The second region lies in the embrace of the hills of the north. This, the Red River Delta, can legitimately claim to be the cultural and historical heart of the Viet nation. Hanoi lies at its core and it was here the first truly independent Vietnamese polity was established in AD 939 by Ngo Quyen. The delta covers almost 15,000 sq km and extends 240 km inland from the coast. Rice has been grown on the alluvial soils of the Red River for thousands of years. Yet despite the intricate web of canals, dykes and embankments, the Vietnamese have never been able to completely tame the river, and the delta is the victim of frequent and sometimes devastating floods. The area is very low-lying, rarely more than 3 m above sea level and often less than 1 m. The highwater mark is nearly 8 m above land level in some places. During the monsoon season, the tributaries of the Red River quickly become torrents rushing through the narrow gorges of the Hoang Lien Son, before emptying into the main channel that then bursts its banks. Although the region supports one of the highest agricultural population densities in the world, the inhabitants have frequently had to endure famines, most recently in 1989.

South of the Red River Delta

South of the Red River Delta region lie the central lowlands and the mountains of the Annamite Chain. The **Annam Highlands**, now known as **Truong Son Mountain Range**, form an important cultural divide between the Indianized nations of the west and the Sinicized cultures of the east. Its northern rugged extremity is in Thanh Hoa Province. From here the Truong Son stetches over 1200 km south, to peter out 80 km north of Ho Chi Minh City.

The highest peak is Ngoc Linh Mountain in Kon Tum Province at 2598 m. The Central Highlands form an upland plateau on which the hill resorts of **Buon Ma Thuot** and **Dalat** are situated. On the plateau, plantation agriculture and hill farms are interspersed with stands of bamboo and tropical forests. Once rich in wildlife, the plateau was a popular hunting ground during the colonial period.

Central coastal strip

To the east, the Annamite Chain falls off steeply, leaving only a narrow and fragmented band of lowland suitable for settlement: the central coastal strip. In places the mountains advance all the way to the coast, plunging into the sea as rock faces and making north-south communication difficult. At no point does the region extend more than 64 km inland, and it covers 6750 sq km. The soils are often rocky or saline, and irrigation is seldom possible. Nonetheless, the inhabitants have a history of sophisticated rice culture and it was here that the Champa Kingdom was established in the early centuries of the Christian era. These lowlands have also formed a conduit along which people have moved. Even today, the main north-south road and rail routes cut through the coastal lowlands.

Mekong Delta

Unlike the Red River Delta this region is not so prone to flooding and consequently rice production is more stable. The reason why flooding is less severe lies in the regulating effect of the Great Lake of Cambodia, the Tonlé Sap. During the rainy season, when the water flowing into the Mekong becomes too great for even this mighty river to absorb, rather than overflowing its banks, the water backs up into the Tonlé Sap, which quadruples in area. The Mekong Delta covers 67,000 sq km and is drained by five branches of the Mekong, which divides as it flows towards the sea. The vast delta is one of the great rice bowls of Asia producing nearly half of the country's rice and over the years has been cut into a patchwork by the canals that have been dug to expand irrigation and rice cultivation. Largely forested until the late 19th century, the French supported the settlement of the area by Vietnamese peasants, recognizing that it could become enormously productive. The deposition of silt by the rivers that cut through the delta, means that the shoreline is continually advancing, by up to 80 m each year in some places. To the north of the delta lies Ho Chi Minh City. See also boxes, pages 355 and 478.

Climate

Vietnam stretches more than 1800 km from north to south and the weather patterns in the two principal cities, Hanoi in the north and Ho Chi Minh City in the south, are very different. For the best time to visit, see page 16 and table, page 480. Average temperatures tend to rise the further south you go, while the seasonal variation in temperature decreases. The exceptions to this general rule of thumb are in the interior highland areas where the altitude means it is considerably colder.

North Vietnam
The seasons in the north are similar to those of South China. The winter is November to April, with temperatures averaging 16°C and little rainfall. The summer begins in May and lasts until October. During these months it can be very hot, with an average temperature of 30°C, along with heavy rainfall and the occasional violent typhoon.

Central Vietnam
Central Vietnam experiences a transitional climate, halfway between that in the south and in the north. Hué has a reputation for poor weather: it's often overcast and an umbrella is needed whatever the month, even in the short 'dry' season from February to April. Hué's annual rainfall is 3250 mm. See page 16 for the best time to visit.

South Vietnam
Temperatures in the south are fairly constant through the year (25°C-30°C) and the seasons are determined by the rains. The dry season runs from November to April (when there is virtually no rain whatsoever) and the wet season from May to October. The hottest period is during March and April, before the rains have broken. Typhoons are quite common in coastal areas between July and November.

Highland Areas
In the hill resorts of Dalat (1500 m), Buon Ma Thuot and Sapa nights are cool throughout the year and in the 'winter' months between October to March it can be distinctly chilly with temperatures falling to 4°C. Even in the hottest months of March and April the temperature rarely exceeds 26°C.

Flora and fauna

Together with overseas conservation agencies such as the Worldwide Fund for Nature (WWF), Vietnamese scientists have, in recent years, been enumerating and protecting their fauna and flora. The establishment of nature reserves began in 1962 with the gazetting of the Cuc Phuong National Park. Today there are a total of 87 reserves covering 3.3% of Vietnam's land area. However, some of them are too small to sustain sufficiently large

The Mekong: mother river of Southeast Asia

The Mekong River is one of the 12 great rivers of the world. It stretches 4500 km from its source on the Tibet Plateau in China to its mouth (or mouths) in the Mekong Delta of Vietnam. (On 11 April 1995 a Franco-British expedition announced that they had discovered the source of the Mekong – 5000 m high, at the head of the Rup-Sa Pass, and miles from anywhere. Each year, the river empties 475 billion cubic metres of water into the East Sea. Along its course it flows through Burma, Laos, Thailand, Cambodia and Vietnam – all countries constituting mainland Southeast Asia – as well as China. In both a symbolic and a physical sense it links the region. Bringing fertile silt to the land along its banks, but particularly to the Mekong Delta, the river contributes to Southeast Asia's agricultural wealth. In former times, a tributary of the Mekong that drains the Tonlé Sap (the Great Lake of Cambodia), provided the rice surplus on which the fabulous Angkor empire was founded. The Tonlé Sap acts like a great regulator, storing water in time of flood and then releasing it when levels recede.

The first European to explore the river was French naval officer Francis Garnier. His Mekong expedition (1866-1868) followed the great river upstream from its delta in Cochin China (southern Vietnam). Of the 9960 km that the trip covered, 506 km were 'discovered' for the first time. The motivation for the trip was to find a southern route into the Heavenly Kingdom – China. But they failed. The river is navigable only as far as the Lao-Cambodian border where the Khone rapids make it impassable. Nonetheless, the expedition report is one of the finest of its genre. Today the Mekong itself is perceived as a source of potential economic wealth, not just as a path to riches. The Mekong Secretariat was established in 1957 to harness the waters of the river for irrigation and hydropower. The Secretariat devised a grandiose plan with a succession of seven huge dams that would store 142 billion cubic metres of water, irrigate 4.3 million ha of riceland and generate 24,200MW of power. But the Vietnam War disrupted construction. Only Laos' Nam Ngum Dam on a tributary of the Mekong was ever built and even though this generates just 150MW of power, electricity exports to Thailand are one of Laos' largest export earners. Now that the countries of mainland Southeast Asia are on friendly terms once more, the Secretariat and its scheme have been given a new lease of life. But in the intervening years, fears about the environmental consequences of big dams have raised new questions. The Mekong Secretariat has moderated its plans and is now looking at less ambitious and less contentious ways to harness the Mekong River. See also box, page 355, on hydrology of the delta.

breeding populations of endangered species and many parks are quite heavily populated. For instance 80,000 people live, farm and hunt within the 22,000 ha Bach Ma National Park. Vietnamese scientists with support from outside agencies, in particular the WWF, have begun the important task of cataloguing and protecting Vietnam's wildlife.

The **Javan rhinoceros** is one of the rarest large mammals in the world and until recently was thought only to survive in the Ujung Kulon National Park in West Java, Indonesia. However in November 1988 it was reported that a Stieng tribesman had shot a female Javan rhino near the Dong Nai River around 130 km northeast of Saigon. When he tried to sell the horn and hide he was arrested and this set in train a search to discover if there were any more of the animals in the area. Researchers discovered that Viet Cong soldiers operating in the area during the war saw – and killed – a number of animals. One former revolutionary, Tran Ngoc Khanh, reported that he once saw a herd of 20 animals and that between 1952 and 1976 some 17 animals were shot by the soldiers. With the Viet Cong shooting the animals whenever they chanced upon them, and the Americans spraying tonnes of defoliant on the area, it is a wonder than any survived through to the end of the war. However, a study by George Schaller and three Vietnamese colleagues in 1989 found tracks, also near the Dong Nai River, and estimated that a population of 10-15 animals probably still survived in a 750 sq km area of bamboo and dipterocarp forest close to and including Nam Cat Tien National Park.

This remarkable find was followed by, if anything, an even more astonishing discovery: of two completely new species of mammal. In 1992 British scientist Dr John MacKinnon discovered the skeleton of an animal now known as the **Vu Quang ox** (*Pseudoryx nghetinhensis*) but known to locals as *sao la*. The Vu Quang ox was the first new large mammal species to be found in 50 years; scientists were amazed that a large mammal could exist on this crowded planet without their knowledge. In June 1994 the first live specimen (a young calf) was captured and shortly afterwards a second one was caught and taken to the Forestry Institute in Hanoi. Sadly, both died in captivity but in early 1995 a third was brought in alive. The animals look anything but ox-like, and have the appearance, grace and manner of a small deer. The government responded to the discovery by extending the Vu Quang Nature Reserve and banning hunting of *sao la*. Local ethnic minorities, who have long regarded *sao la* as a tasty and not uncommon animal, have therefore lost a valued source of food and no longer have a vested interest in the animal's survival. *Sao la* must rue the day they were 'discovered'. In 1993 a new species of deer that has been named the **giant muntjac** was also found in the Vu Quang Nature Reserve. The scientists have yet to see it alive but villagers prize its meat and are reported to trap it in quite large numbers.

Large rare mammals are confined to isolated pockets where the government does its best to protect them from hunters. On Cat Ba Island, the national park is home to the world's last wild troops of white-headed langur. In North Vietnam tigers have been hunted close to extinction and further south territorial battles rage between elephants and farmers. Rampaging elephants sometimes cause loss of life and are in turn decimated by enraged villagers.

Among the **larger mammals**, there are small numbers of tiger (around 200), leopard, clouded leopard, Indian elephant, Malayan sun bear, Himalayan black bear, sambar deer, gibbon and gaur (wild buffalo). These are rarely seen, except in zoos. There are frequent news reports of farmers maiming or killing elephants after their crops have been trampled or their huts flattened. The larger reptiles include two species of crocodile, the estuarine (*Crocodilus porosus*) and Siamese (*Crocodilus siamensis*). The former grows to a length of 5 m and has been reported to have killed and eaten humans. Among the larger snakes are the reticulated python (*Python reticulatus*) and the smaller Indian python (*Python molurus*), both non-venomous constrictors. Venomous snakes include two species of cobra (the king cobra and common cobra), two species of krait and six species of pit viper.

Given the difficulty of getting to Vietnam's more remote areas, the country is hardly a haven for amateur naturalists. Professional photographers and naturalists have been escorted to the country's wild areas but this is not an option for the average visitor. Getting there requires time and contacts. A wander around the markets of Vietnam reveals the variety and number of animals that end up in the cooking pot, including deer, bear, snakes, monkeys and turtles. The Chinese penchant for exotic foods (such gastronomic wonders as tigers' testicles and bear's foot) has also become a predilection of the Vietnamese and most animals are fair game.

Temperatures, humidity and rainfall by place

Hanoi

	Jan	Feb	Mar	Apr	May	Jun	Jul	Aug	Sep	Oct	Nov	Dec
Max (°C)	33	35	37	39	43	40	40	39	37	36	36	32
Min (°C)	3	5	9	10	15	20	22	21	16	12	7	5
Humidity (%)	80	84	88	87	83	83	83	85	85	81	81	81
Rainfall (mm)	18	26	48	81	194	236	302	325	262	47	47	20

Hué

	Jan	Feb	Mar	Apr	May	Jun	Jul	Aug	Sep	Oct	Nov	Dec
Max (°C)	35	36	30	40	40	40	39	39	38	36	35	32
Min (°C)	9	11	12	14	18	21	19	21	19	16	13	11
Humidity (%)	90	90	88	84	80	76	73	77	84	88	88	90
Rainfall (mm)	188	89	57	64	78	104	76	124	498	744	693	346

Danang

	Jan	Feb	Mar	Apr	May	Jun	Jul	Aug	Sep	Oct	Nov	Dec
Max (°C)	31	34	34	36	39	40	39	40	38	35	34	32
Min (°C)	15	15	16	19	20	19	21	22	21	19	17	15
Humidity (%)	78	78	80	81	80	79	78	79	82	84	83	79
Rainfall (mm)	50	18	31	40	61	47	42	53	162	322	359	174

Nha Trang

	Jan	Feb	Mar	Apr	May	Jun	Jul	Aug	Sep	Oct	Nov	Dec
Max (°C)	31	34	34	36	39	40	39	40	38	35	34	32
Min (°C)	15	15	16	19	20	19	21	22	21	19	17	15
Humidity (%)	78	78	80	81	80	79	78	79	82	84	83	79
Rainfall (mm)	50	18	31	40	61	47	42	53	162	322	359	174

Ho Chi Minh City

	Jan	Feb	Mar	Apr	May	Jun	Jul	Aug	Sep	Oct	Nov	Dec
Max (°C)	36	39	39	40	39	36	35	35	35	35	35	36
Min (°C)	14	16	17	20	22	20	19	20	21	20	14	13
Humidity (%)	74	71	71	74	80	84	84	85	86	83	82	78
Rainfall (mm)	14	5	12	50	221	315	296	274	332	264	115	51

Birds

Birds have, in general, suffered rather less than mammals from over-hunting and the effects of the war. There have been some casualties however: the eastern sarus crane of the Mekong Delta – a symbol of fidelity, longevity and good luck – disappeared entirely during the war. However, in 1985 a farmer reported seeing a single bird, and by 1990 there were over 500 pairs breeding on the now pacified former battlefields. A sarus crane reserve has been established in Dong Thap Province. For more on birdwatching holidays, see page 16. The best time of year for birding is November to May.

Among the more unusual birds are the snake bird (named after its habit of swimming with its body submerged and only its snake-like neck and head above the surface), the argus pheasant, which the Japanese believe to be the mythical phoenix, the little bastard quail of which the male hatches and rears the young. But what may come as the real surprise to many visitors to Vietnam is that it has the highest number of endemic bird species of any country in mainland Southeast Asia. There are currently 12 endemic species of bird that can only be seen in Vietnam which is one reason it is becoming a popular destination for overseas birdwatchers. In addition to these 12 endemics there are many more near endemics, bird species restricted to Vietnam and a few neighbouring countries, and other distinct subspecies that may well be considered endemic species in the future.

An incredible diversity of birds live in the forest and wetland habitats of **Nam Cat Tien National Park**, see page 242, including an estimated 230 species of birds. Endangered birds that can be found here include Germain's peacock pheasant, green peafowl and the highly elusive orange-necked partridge. You can hire a jeep at the park headquarters to visit areas further afield such as Bird Lake to look for visiting waders or Crocodile Lake where grey-headed fish eagle, lesser adjutant and Asian golden weaver may be seen, as well as the reintroduced Siamese crocodiles. During the walk through the forest to Crocodile Lake look out for bar-bellied and blue-rumped pitta, red-and-black and banded broadbill and orange-breasted trogon. Other interesting species at Cat Tien include scaly-breasted partridge, Siamese fireback, woolly-necked stork and grey-faced tit-babbler and white-bellied, great slaty, pale-headed and heart-spotted woodpecker. On the trails or the headquarters road, green-eared, blue-eared, lineated and – if you're lucky – red-vented barbet can often be seen perched high up in the roadside trees.

Twenty minutes by road from Dalat at **Langbian Mountain**, see page 241, the evergreen forests are home to many interesting birds including several endemic species. Key species to be found here include the silver pheasant, Indochinese cuckooshrike, Eurasian jay, mugimaki flycatcher, yellow-billed nuthatch and red crossbill. This is also the place to see three of Vietnam's most sought-after endemics: collared laughingthrush, Vietnamese cutia and Vietnamese greenfinch. Mount Langbian is best avoided at weekends and holidays when it is a popular destination for local tourists.

Tuyen Lam Lake, only 3 km from the centre of Dalat, is another hotspot for birders. Take a boat to far side of the lake where a track leads through the pines to areas of remnant tropical evergreen forest. With luck, the rare and endemic grey-crowned crocias, rediscovered in 1994 after not being seen for nearly 60 years, can be found. Other interesting species here include slender-billed oriole, maroon oriole, rufous- backed sibia, black-crowned parrotbill and orange-breasted, black-hooded and white- cheeked laughingthrush.

Ta Nung Valley, around 10 km from Dalat, holds pockets of remnant evergreen forest where many of the Dalat specialities can still be found including orange-breasted, black-hooded and white-cheeked laughing thrush, blue-winged minla, grey-crowned crocias, black-crowned parrotbill and black-throated sunbird.

At **Bach Ma National Park**, see page 198, more than 330 species of bird have been recorded. Species include the annam partridge, crested argus, Blyth's kingfisher, coral-billed ground cuckoo, ratchet-tailed treepie, sultan tit and Indochinese wren-babbler. Others include red-collared woodpecker, bar-bellied and blue-rumped pitta and white-winged magpie.

There are several good trails in the forested hills above the tourist resort of **Tam Dao**, which is 1½ hours by road from Hanoi. Specialities of Tam Dao include chestnut bulbul, grey laughingthrush, rufous-headed and short-tailed parrotbill and fork-tailed sunbird. In the winter months look out for red-flanked bluetail, black-breasted and Japanese thrush and Fujian niltava.

In **Cuc Phuong National Park**, see page 167, an area of limestone hills covered with large tracts of primary forest, key bird species include silver pheasant, red-collared woodpecker, pied falconet, white-winged magpie, limestone wren-babbler and bar-bellied, blue-rumped and eared pitta.

Books

Books on the region

Dingwall, Alastair, Traveller's Literary Companion: Southeast Asia (In Print: Brighton, 1994). Experts on Southeast Asian language and literature select extracts from novels and books by Western and regional writers. The extracts are annoyingly brief but give a good overview of what is available.

Dumarçay, Jacques, The Palaces of South-East Asia: Architecture and Customs (OUP: Singapore, 1991). A broad summary of palace art and architecture in both mainland and island Southeast Asia.

Fenton, James, All the Wrong Places: Adrift in the Politics of Asia (Penguin: London, 1988). British journalist James Fenton skilfully and entertainingly recounts his experiences in Vietnam, Cambodia and the Philippines.

Fraser-Lu, Sylvia, Handwoven Textiles of South-East Asia (OUP: Singapore, 1988). Well illustrated, large-format book with informative text.

Higham, Charles, The Archaeology of Mainland Southeast Asia from 10,000 BC to the Fall of Angkor (CUP: Cambridge, 1989). The best summary of changing views of the archaeology of the mainland.

Keyes, Charles F, The Golden Peninsula: Culture and Adaptation in Mainland Southeast Asia (Macmillan: New York, 1977). Academic yet readable summary of the threads of continuity and change in Southeast Asia's culture. The volume has been recently republished by Hawaii University Press, but not updated or revised.

King, Ben F and Dickinson EC, A Field Guide to the Birds of South-East Asia (Collins: London, 1975). Best regional guide to the birds of the region.

Osborne, Milton, Southeast Asia: An Introductory History (Allen & Unwin: Sydney, 1979). Good history, clearly written, published in a portable paperback edition. But a new revised edition is needed.

Rawson, Philip, The Art of Southeast Asia (Thames & Hudson: London, 1967). Portable general art history of Myanmar, Cambodia, Vietnam, Thailand, Laos, Java and Bali; rather superficial, but it's a good place to start.

Reid, Anthony, Southeast Asia in the Age of Commerce 1450-1680: the Lands Below the Winds (Yale University Press: New Haven, 1988). Perhaps the best history of everyday life in Southeast Asia, looking at such themes as physical well being, material culture and social organization.

Reid, Anthony, Southeast Asia in the Age of Commerce 1450-1680: Expansion and Crisis (Yale University Press: New Haven, 1993). Volume 2 in this excellent history of the region.

Rigg, Jonathan, Southeast Asia: A Region in Transition (Unwin Hyman: London, 1991). A thematic geography of the ASEAN region, providing an insight into some of the major issues affecting the region today.

Rigg, Jonathan, Southeast Asia: The Human Landscape of Modernization and Development (London: Routledge, 1997). A book that covers both the market and former command economies (Myanmar, Vietnam, Laos and Cambodia) of the region. It focuses on how people in the region have responded to the challenges of modernization.

SarDesai, DR, Southeast Asia: Past and Present (Macmillan: London, 1989). Skilful but at times frustratingly thin history of the region from the first century to the withdrawal of US forces from Vietnam.

Savage, Victor R, Western Impressions of Nature and Landscape in Southeast Asia (Singapore University Press: Singapore, 1984). Based on a geography PhD thesis, the book is a mine of quotations and observations from Western travellers.

Steinberg, DJ et al, *In Search of Southeast Asia: A Modern History* (University of Hawaii Press: Honolulu, 1987). The best standard history of the region; it examines and assesses general processes of change and their impacts from the arrival of the Europeans in the region.

Tarling, Nicholas, *Cambridge History of Southeast Asia* (CUP, 1992). Two volume edited study, long and expensive with contributions from most of the leading historians of the region. A thematic and regional approach is taken, not a country one, although the history is fairly conventional.

Waterson, Roxana, *The Living House: An Anthropology of Architecture in South-East Asia* (OUP: Singapore, 1990). An academic but extensively illustrated book on the region's architecture and how it links with lives and livelihoods. Fascinating material.

Books on Vietnam

Art and archaeology

Hejzlar, J, *The Art of Vietnam* (Hamlyn: London, 1973). The text is rather heavy going, but there are numerous photos.

Le Brusq, Arnauld and de Selva, Léonard, *Vietnam, A Travers L'Architecture Coloniale* (Patimoines et Medias, 1999). Available in German but not in English. A meticulously researched and fascinating guide to Vietnam's colonial architecture chronicling the evolution of the colonial cities and describing the history of many of Vietnam's public buildings erected during French rule. Superbly illustrated with contemporary colour photos, archive pictures and plans.

Parmentier, Henri with Mus, Paul and Aymonier, Etienne *Cham Sculpture in the Tourane Museum: Religious Ceremonies and Superstitions of Champa* (White Lotus, 2001). Reprint of a classic 1922 text by Parmentier who was responsible for assembling the Cham sculptures and after whom the museum in Danang was originally named.

Biography and autobiography

Fenn, Charles, *Ho Chi Minh: A Biographical Introduction* (Studio Vista: London, 1973).

Greene, Graham, *Ways of Escape* (1980). Autobiographical.

Ho Chi Minh, *Prison Diary* (Hanoi: Foreign Languages Publishing House). A collection of poems by Ho while he was incarcerated in China in 1942. They record his prison experiences and his yearning for home.

Page, Tim, *Derailed in Uncle Ho's Victory Garden* (Touchstone Books, 1995). War photojournalist Tim Page makes a return visit to Vietnam, amusing in places.

Tin, Bui, *Following Ho Chi Minh* (Hurst: London, 1995). Autobiographical account of a North Vietnamese Colonel's disillusionment with the communist regime following Ho Chi Minh's death. Western readers may find it rather self-congratulatory in tone but it's still an interesting read.

Culture

Crawford, Ann Caddell *Customs and Culture of Vietnam* (Charles Tuttle: Rutland, Vermont).

Hickey, Gerald, *Village in Vietnam* (Yale University Press: New Haven, 1964). Classic village study, only available second-hand.

Economics, politics and development

Beresford, Melanie, *Vietnam: Politics, Economics and Society* (Pinter: London, 1988). Academic account of social, economic and political developments to the mid-1980s; too early to include much discussion of economic reform programme.

Hayton, Bill, *Vietnam – Rising Dragon* (Yale University Press: 2010). A new, well-researched insightful account into Vietnam today that seeks to enlighten readers about the current economic and political structures and issues in this rapidly growing country. Hayton spent time as a BBC reporter in Hanoi.

Kemf, Elizabeth, *Month of Pure Light: The Re-greening of Vietnam* (The Women's Press: London, 1990). Account of the attempts to overcome the after-effects of US defoliation and replant the Vietnamese countryside; more light travelogue than objective book.

Nugent, Nicholas, *Vietnam: The Second Revolution* (In Print: London, 1996). A good summary of the main changes in Vietnam's economy and society. Also covers the more recent changes dating from the early 1990s.

Popkin, Samuel L, *The Rational Peasant: The Political Economy of Rural Society in Vietnam* (Berkeley: University of California Press, 1979). This book was written in response to James Scott's *The Moral Economy of the Peasant*. Popkin contests the view that traditional Southeast Asia (here, Vietnam) was a moral economy where village solidarity and community spirit were dominant.

Scott, James C, *The Moral Economy of the Peasant: Rebellion and Subsistence in Southeast Asia* (New Haven: Yale University Press, 1976). The classic historical study of the 'moral' economy of the peasant. Available as a portable paperback.

Templer, Robert, *Shadows and Wind: A View of Life in Modern Vietnam* (London: Little Brown, 1998). Templer was an Agence France Presse correspondent and this is his account of modern Vietnam and where it is headed. It is a downbeat picture of the country, one where bureaucratic inertia and political heavy handedness constrain progress, but is a fascinating read.

Turner, Robert F, *Vietnamese Communism: Its Origins and Development* (Hoover Institution Press: Stanford, 1975). Academic study of the rise of communism in Vietnam.

Williams, Michael C, *Vietnam at the Crossroads* (Pinter: London, 1992). Most recent survey of political and economic reforms by a senior BBC World Service commentator; lucid and informed.

Young, Marilyn, *The Vietnam Wars 1945-1990* (Harper Collins: New York, 1990). Good account of the origins, development and aftermath of the Vietnam wars.

History

Elliott, Mai, *Sacred Willow: Four Generations in the Life of a Vietnamese Family* (OUP: Oxford,

1999). Recounts the history of Vietnam through the life of the Duong family from the 19th century to the tragedy of Boat People. A story of Vietnam through Vietnamese eyes.

Marriott, Edward, *Claude and Madeline: A True Story of War, Espionage and Passion* (Picador 2005). This is an unputdownable tale of madness and bravado set in Vietnam and France.

Osborne, Roger, *The Deprat Affair: Ambition, Revenge and Deceit in French Indochina* (Jonathan Cape, 1999). An account of the extraordinary pickle into which Jacques Deprat, a brilliant young geologist, got himself. Whether he was guilty of professional deceit or not the book gives a useful insight into colonial society and mores in the first two decades of the 20th century.

Taylor, Keith Weller, *The Birth of Vietnam* (University of California Press: Berkeley, 1983) Academic history of early Vietnam from the third century BC to 10th century.

Wintle, Justin, *The Vietnam Wars* (Weidenfeld and Nicholson: London, 1991). Not just about *the* War, but about all of Vietnam's interminable conflicts.

Novels

Duras, Marguerite, *The Lover* (London: Flamingo, 1984). Now a film starring Jane March; this is the story of the illicit relationship between an expat French girl and a Chinese from Cholon set in the 1930s.

Greene, Graham, *The Quiet American* (Heinemann: London, 1954). What is remarkable about this novel is the way that it predicts America's experience in Vietnam. The two key figures are Alden Pyle, an idealistic young American, and Thomas Fowler, a hard-bitten and cynical British journalist. It is set in and around Saigon as the war between the French and the Viet Minh intensifies.

Grey, Anthony, *Saigon* (Pan: London, 1983). An entertaining novel.

Travel and geography

Garstin, Crosbie, *The Voyage from London to Indochina* (Heinemann, 1928). Hilarious and rather irreverent account of a journey through Vietnam.

Lewis, Norman, *A Dragon Apparent: Travels in Cambodia, Laos and Vietnam* (1951). One of the finest of all travel books.

Stewart, Lucretia, *Tiger Balm: Travels in Laos, Cambodia and Vietnam* (London: Chatto & Windus, 1998).

Theroux, Paul, *The Great Railway Bazaar* (Penguin: London, 1977). Theroux describes a graphic account of one American's attempt to travel by rail between Saigon and Hué.

Vu Tu Lap and **Taillard, Christian,** *An Atlas of Vietnam* (Reclus – La Documentation Française, 1994). Summary of the population and economy of Vietnam in maps.

Wintle, Justin, *Romancing Vietnam. Inside the Boat Country* (Penguin 1992). A humorous and unusual account of a writer's attempts to see as much of the real Vietnam as possible whilst surrounded and monitored by bureaucratic officials. It also gives an insight into a very changed Vietnam – in the 1980s – which a recent traveller may find hard to comprehend.

The Vietnamese wars

Cawthorne, Nigel, *The Bamboo Cage* (Leo Cooper, 1992). The story of MIAs and POWs.

Doyle, Jeff with **Grey, Jeffrey** and **Pierce, Peter,** *Australia's Vietnam War,* (A&M University Press, 2002). Australia's role in the Vietnam War is little known and this book examines Australia's motives for joining and contribution to America's war effort.

Fall, Bernard B, *Hell in a Very Small Place: The Siege of Dien Bien Phu* (Pall Mall Press, 1967).

Fitzgerald, Francis, *Fire in the Lake* (Vintage Books: New York, 1972). Pulitzer prize winner; a well-researched and readable account of the US involvement.

Harrison, James P, *The Endless War: Fifty Years of Struggle in Vietnam* (Free Press: New York, 1982).

Herr, Michael, *Dispatches* (Knopf: New York, 1977). An acclaimed account of the war written by a correspondent who experienced the conflict first hand.

Kaiser, David, *American Tragedy: Kennedy, Johnson and the Origins of the Vietnam War,* (Harvard University Press, 1999). This account is based on newly opened archives and provides a penetrating insight into America's involvement in Vietnam.

Karnow, Stanley, *Vietnam: A History* (Viking Press: New York, 1983 and 1991). A comprehensive and readable history; the best there is.

Kissinger, Henry, *The White House Years* (Little, Brown, 1979). Part one of the memoirs of America's best known diplomat. This covers the first Nixon term and ends with the Paris Peace Accord of 1973. Also, *Years of Upheaval* (Little, Brown, 1982). This covers the turbulent months from his visit to Hanoi in February 1973 to Nixon's resignation in August 1974. And, *Years of Renewal* (Simon and Schuster, 1999). The third and concluding volume of the memoirs covers the end of the Vietnam war and collapse of the South.

Lunn, Hugh, *Vietnam: A Reporter's War* (University of Queensland Press: St Lucia, Australia, 1985). Account of Australian reporter Hugh Lunn's year in Vietnam with Reuters between 1967 and 1968, including an account of the Tet Offensive.

McNamara, Robert S and **Mark, Brian Van de,** *In Retrospect: The Tragedy and Lessons of Vietnam* (Times/Random House: New York, 1995). McNamara was Secretary for Defense from 1961 to 1968 and this is his cathartic account of the war. Informed from the inside, he concludes that the war was a big mistake.

Mangold, Tom and **Penycate, John,** *The Tunnels of Cu Chi* (1985). Compelling account of the building of the tunnels and the Viet Cong who fought in them.

Mason, Robert, *Chickenhawk* (Penguin: Harmondsworth, 1984). Excellent autobiography of a helicopter pilot.

Ninh, Bao, *The Sorrow of War* (Secker & Warburg, London, 1993). Wartime novel by a North Vietnamese soldier, a wonderful account of emotions during and after the war.

Roth, Philip, *The Human Stain* (Jonathan Cape, 2000). Not, ostensibly, about the Vietnam War at all but it has an excellent account of American war vets coming to terms with their traumas and the country that shuns them.

Sheehan, Neil, *A Bright Shining Lie* (Jonathan Cape: London, 1989). A meticulously researched 850-page account of the Vietnam War, based around the life of John Paul Vann. Recommended.

Sheehan, Neil, *Two Cities: Hanoi and Saigon* (in US *After the War was Over*) (Jonathan Cape: London, 1992). A short but fascinating book that tries to link the past with the present in a part autobiography, part travelogue, part contemporary commentary.

SIPRI, *Ecological Consequences of the Second Indochina War* (Almqvist & Wiksell: Stockholm, 1976). Academic study of environmental side effects of war.

Swain, Jon, *River of Time* (Heinemann, 1996). A gripping account of this war correspondent's time throughout the Vietnam War. He expounds the interesting hypothesis that the reason the American generals were willing to sacrifice so many men was that they saw it as a rehearsal for a future war in Europe against the Red Army.

Turley, William S, *The Second Indochina War: A Short Political and Military History 1954-75* (Westview: Boulder, 1986). A clear, well-balanced academic account of the war.

Windrow, Martin, *The Last Valley: Dien Bien Phu and the French Defeat in Vietnam* (De Capo Press, 2004). A new, detailed and well regarded account of the battle in the north that heralded the end of French involvement in Indochina.

Young, Gavin, *A Wavering Grace: A Vietnamese Family in War and Peace* (London: Viking, 1997). An account of the war – Young was a reporter – told through the lives of a Vietnamese family.

Vietnamese literature in English

Nguyen Du, *The Tale of Kieu* (also known as *Truyen Kieu*) (Yale University Press: New Haven, 1983), translated by Huynh Sanh Thong. This is an early 19th-century Vietnamese classic and, for many, the masterpiece of Vietnamese poetry. It is also published in Vietnam (in English) by the Foreign Languages Publishing House. It tells the story of a beautiful girl and her doomed love affair with a soldier. See also page 467 for a detailed description of the work.

Films

Few countries have provided so much material for celluloid tales as Vietnam. The US movie houses cranked up for action in the post-Vietnam War era to provide some of the most harrowing, soul-searching and cinematically exciting films of the 20th century that focused on the US involvement in the war.

The better-known films on Vietnam are American as US filmakers have attempted to explain or come to terms with their country's disastrous involvement in Vietnam. Francis Ford Coppola's *Apocalypse Now* won two Oscars in 1979. Coppola substitutes Vietnam for the Africa of Joseph Conrad's *Heart of Darkness*; it remains the best known and most outstanding of all Vietnam films. *The Deer Hunter*, which stars Robert de Niro, won five Oscars in 1978. It charts the horrors into which three tough steelworkers were plunged in Vietnam. Stanley Kubrick's *Full Metal Jacket* (1987), followed GIs from Boot Camp to the Tet Offensive and was acclaimed as a "riveting condemnation of the Vietnam War". *Good Morning Vietnam* (1987) starred Robin Williams as an irreverent DJ working for the armed services radio. The comedy of the film is hilarious without trivializing the seriousness of the situation. Oliver Stone's trilogy of *Platoon* (1986), *Born on the Fourth of July* (1989) and *Heaven and Earth* (1993), is quite a contrast. The first two deal with the war from the perspective of the American soldier; *Platoon* examines the soldiers' experience in Vietnam; and *Born on the Fourth of July* explores adjusting to life after the war. *Heaven and Earth* looks at the war from the 1960s onwards from the perspective of a Vietnamese woman, Le Ly Hayslip, and the aftermath of war.

The film version of Graham Greene's novel of love, war, murder and betrayal, *The Quiet American*, was set in 1950s Saigon and was filmed in Vietnam in 2001. It was the first Hollywood blockbuster to be filmed in the country since the end of the war. It stars Sir Michael Caine as Times journalist Thomas Fowler, Brendan Fraser as American aid worker Alden Pyle and Do Thi Hai Yen as Phuong. The Hotel Continental, the social pivot of the time, is actually replicated on screen in the facing Hotel Caravelle across Lam Son Square (Place Garnier). The La Fontaine milk bar on Dong Khoi Street (Rue Catinat), frequented by Fowler's lover Phuong, is in present-day Ho Chi Minh City's Givral café and patisserie. The infamous double bomb scene in the Place Garnier in front of the Opera House and La Fontaine, a moment of epiphany for the jaded London hack, used hundreds of Vietnamese extras including mutilated Vietnam War victims. Hoi An doubled as the setting for the restaurant date between Pyle and Fowler – an engagement that Pyle would never make.

The 1990s was a decade that saw French-made films covering the French colonial era in Vietnam before they were forced to withdraw in 1954.

Three French films have captured the atmosphere of Vietnam at peace although with a frisson of tension never too far away: *Indochine* (directed by Régis Wargnier) won acclaim for its beautiful sets and scenery as well as an Oscar for Best Foreign Film in 1993. It is set in the 1930s and focuses on a mother (Catherine Deneuve), who runs a rubber plantation, and her adopted daughter, who both fall in love with the same man. It captures the vices and flaws of French colonial Vietnam before its demise. *L'Amant* (*The Lover*, 1992), directed by Jean-Jacques Annaud, charts the relationship of a young French girl (Jane March) with an older, Chinese businessman, in the colonial era; it was adapted from Margeurite Duras' book. The little-known but delightful *Scent of Green Papaya* (1993) by Tran Anh Hung is an account of family relationships and the secret love of the family's young servant. Set in Saigon in the 1950s, it was filmed entirely in a Paris studio.

Vietnamese-made films, however, have suffered arrested development. After the Second World War, Ho Chi Minh began making propaganda documentaries. In 1959 the first film was released – *On the Same River* – about a couple who were divided when the border along the 17th parallel was created in 1954.

Post-1975, when the country was reunified, all Vietnamese films were censored at the script stage and those that made it past the censor were state-funded. The tight grip of the Ministry of Culture suffocated any enterprising or criticial movie production. In 2002, the ministry reversed its policy on censorship of scripts and encouraged private film studios to open up. The turnaround, it said, was to encourage competition and investment to re-energize the industry. Since then, Vietnam has been undergoing a cinematic revolution.

However, judging from the persecutory response to Vietnamese actor Don Duong's role in the US movie *We Were Soldiers*, the day that Vietnamese film directors will be able to criticize the Vietnamese regime through the medium of film is a long way off. Don Duong angered national censors in 2002 by appearing in what the Vietnamese government saw as a movie with a pro-US stance. *We Were Soldiers* (directed by Randall Wallace) depicts the Battle of La Drang in the Central Highlands in 1965. Some 400 US troops, led by Lieutenant-Colonel Harold Moore (Mel Gibson), were completely swamped by 2000 North Vietnamese soliders commandeered by Nguyen Huu An (Duong). The authorities said the film of the first major battle between the two enemies, which saw severe casualties on both sides and bloody hand-to-hand combat, distorted history. Vietnam's National Film Censorship Council moved to ban the actor from appearing in productions and to fine him. Other officials branded him a traitor. Duong, 50, eventually emigrated to the US in 2003.

Director Le Hoang's *Gai Nhay* (*Bar Girls*), about sex, drugs and HIV, has rocked cinema audiences since it was released in 2003. HIV and drugs are serious social problems in Vietnam (see box, page 436). Produced by Ho Chi Minh's Liberation Studios, run by the army, the film about these contemporary social taboos suited the government as it documented the social evils of prostitution and drug addiction. It disturbingly portrays the grim lives of two working girls, Hoa (My Duyen) and Hanh (Minh Thu) and depicts gang rape and murder. It cost US$78,000 to make but raked in more than US$1 million at the box office and is Vietnam's biggest grossing movie.

It may have been pipped to the post, however, by the release of *The Rebel*, a US$1.5 million film made by Vietnamese-born Americans in Vietnam and released in 2006. Set in 1920s Vietnam, it tells of Vietnamese hired by their French colonial masters to hunt down rebels and uses some great martial arts action.

Luoi Troi (*Heaven's Net*), directed by Phi Tien Son, winner of a Vietnam Cinema Association Award and released in 2003, also marked a change in mood that heralds the end of propaganda-only films and a willingness to expose national problems, like the drug abuse and HIV in *Gai Nhay* and corruption in *Luoi Troi*. The latter film features the life of infamous mafia criminal Nam Cam who was blamed for a 15-year killing spree in Ho Chi Minh City. Top communist officials and local police officers were indicted at his 2003 trial. He was executed by firing squad in 2004. Three party officials were also given jail sentences in 2003.

Contents

490 Useful words
and phrases

495 Glossary

497 Index

503 Advertisers' index

504 Credits

Footnotes

Useful words and phrases

Vowel sounds

a	as in rather
ă	as in cut
â	as in hum
e	as in egg
ê	as in say
i	as in bin
y	as in be
o	as in saw
ô	as in so
ơ	as in blur
u	as in rule
ư	as in put

Consonant sounds

ch	as in child
-ch	as in eke (end position)
d	as in zip
đ	as in dad
g	as in gad
gi	as in zip
kh	as in king
ng	as in singer
nh	as in onion
ph	like an 'f'
r	like a 'z' in the North
	'r' in the South
th	as in ten
tr	as in train
x	like an 's'

Introductions

hello	xin chào
goodbye	tạm biệt, xin chào
please	làm ơn
thank you	càm ơn
sorry	xin lỗi

I'm glad to see you
Rất hân hạnh được gặp ông/bà

How are you?
Ông/bà khỏe không?

I'm fine, thanks
Càm ơn, tôi khoẻ

What's your name?
Ông/bà tên là gì?

My name is …
Tôi tên là …

This is my wife/husband
Đây là nhàtôi

daughter	con gái
son	con trai

What is your job?
Ông/bà làm nghề gì?

I'm a…	Tôi là…
businessman	thương gia
doctor	bác sĩ
nurse	y tá
teacher	giáo viên
student	học sinh
engineer	kỹ sư
journalist	nhá báo
lawyer	luật sư
secretary	thư ký
clerk	viên chức văn phòng
worker	công nhân
farmer	nông dân
scientist	khoa học gia
tourist	khách du lịch

Which country are you from?
Ông/bà là người nước nào?

I am English	Tôi là người Anh
American	Mỹ
Australian	Úc
Austrian	Áo
Chinese	Trung Quốc
Danish	Đan Mạch
Dutch	Hà Lan
French	Pháp
German	Đức
Indian	Ấn Độ
Italian	Ý
Japanese	Nhật
Korean	Hàn Quốc
Norwegian	Na Uy
Russian	Nga
Swedish	Thuy Diển
Swiss	Thụy Si

Numbers

1	một
2	hai
3	ba
4	bốn
5	năm
6	sáu
7	bảy
8	tám
9	chín
10	mười/ một chục
11	mười một
12	mười hai
15	mười lăm
20	hai mười

21	*hai muoi một*	
22	*hai muoi hai*	
30	*ba muoi*	
100	*một tram*	
101	*một tram le một*	
	or *một tram một*	
200	*hai trăm*	
1000	*một nghìn /một ngàn*	
10,000	*mười nghìn/mười ngàn*	
100,000	*một trăm nghìn*	
1,000,000	*một triệu*	

Date and time

morning	*buổi sáng*
noon	*trúa*
afternoon	*buổi chiều*
evening	*buổi tối*
night	*ban đêm*
day time	*ban ngày*
today	*hôm nay*
yesterday	*hôm qua*
tomorrow	*ngày mai*
Sunday	*chủ nhật*
Monday	*thứ hai*
Tuesday	*thứ ba*
Wednesday	*thứ tư*
Thursday	*thứ năm*
Friday	*thứ sáu*
Saturday	*thứ bảy*
month	*tháng*
January	*tháng giêng*
February	*tháng hai*
March	*tháng ba*
April	*tháng tư*
May	*tháng năm*
June	*tháng sáu*
July	*tháng bảy*
August	*tháng tám*
September	*tháng chín*
October	*tháng mười*
November	*tháng mười một*
December	*tháng mười hai*
spring	*mùa xuân*
summer	*mùa hạ/hè*
autumn	*mùa thu*
winter	*mùa đông*

Directions

Where is the …?	
	ở đâu …?

airport	*phi trường*
bus station	*bến xe*
church	*nhà thờ*
ferry station	*bến phà*
hospital	*bệnh viện*
market	*cho*
museum	*viên bao tàng*
pagoda	*chùa*
phamarcy	*hiệu thuốc tây*
police station	*tram canh sát*
post office	*buu diên*
railway station	*ga xe lửa*
school	*trường học*
toilet	*nam (men)*
	nu (women)
university	*trường đại học*
could you show me the way to …?	
	Ông/bà có thể chi tôi đường tới …?
is it far ?	*Có xa không ?*
is it near ?	*Có gần không ?*
go straight	*đi thẳng*
turn left	*quẹo/rẽ trái*
turn right	*quẹo/rẽ phải*
crossroads	*ngã tư*
T-junction	*ngã ba*
roundabout	*bùng binh*

Taking a trip

I want a ticket to …	
	Tôi muốn một vé đi …
How much is a ticket?	
	Bao nhiêu tiền một vé?
return ticket	*vé khứ hồi*
one-way ticket	*vé một chiều*
I want to go to …	
	Tôi muốn đi đến …
Is there a bus to Hanoi ?	
	Có chuyến xe buýt đi Hà Nội không?
Does this bus go to Sapa?	
	Xe này có đi đến Sapa không ?
train	*xe lửa/ táu hỏa*
car	*xe hới/ôtô*
flight	*chuyến bay*
boat	*thuyền*
ship	*tàu*
ferry	*phà*
When is the next train?	
	Chuyến xe lửa kế tiếp vào lúc nào ?
How long does the trip take ?	
	Hành trình mất bao lâu ?

I want the next train to Huế
Tôi muốn một chuyến tàu sớm nhất đi Huế
I want to go by express train
Tôi muốn một chuyến tàu tốc hành
What time does the train arrive?
Xe lửa đến lục mấy giờ?

What time will the train depart?
Xe lửa sẽ khởi hành lúc mấy giờ?
The train is late
Chuyến xe lua bi tê
The train has been cancelled
Chuyến xe lua bi huy

Shopping

I'd like to buy some clothes
Tôi muốn mua một ít quần áo

shoes	*giày*
sandals	*dép*
socks	*vở*
hat	*nón*
rucksack	*ba lô*
bag	*giỏ xách*
pottery	*đồ gốm*

handicaft
đồ thủ công

paintings *tranh*
How much is it?
Giá bao nhiêu?
It's too expensive
Mắc quá
Can you lower the price?
Có bớt không?

Oh, it's still very expensive
Ồ, vẫn còn mắc lám
Is 10,000 dong OK?
10,000 đồng, được không?
Can I have a look?
Tôi có thể xem được không?
Sorry, I don't like it
Rất tiếc, tôi không thích
Do you have another one?
Ông/bà có cái khác không?
I will take this one
Tôi sẽ mua cái này
They don't/ It doesn't fit me
Nó không vừa với tôi
It's too small
Nó nhỏ quá
Do you have one in a bigger size?
Ông/ bà có cỡ lớn hơn không?

Eating and drinking

Can I have the menu, please? *Xin cho tôi xem thực đơn?*
I'm a vegetarian *Tôi ăn chay*
No chilli, please *Xin đừng cho ớt*
I'd like some rice *Tôi muốn một ít cơm*
MSG *bột ngọt/ mì chính (North)*
chilli *ớt*
spring rolls *chả giò*
noodles *mì; hủ tiếu; bún*
bread *bánh mì*
fish sauce *nước nắm*
soy sauce *nước tương*
meat *thịt*
pork *thịt heo*
beef *thịt bò*
chicken *thịt gà*

duck *thịt vịt*
goat *thịt dê*
fish *cá*
crab *cua*
eel *lươn*
lobster *tôm hùm*
shrimp *tôm*
squid *mực*
egg *trứng*
vegetable *rau cải*
tofu *đậu hũ*
spinach *rau muống*
bamboo shoot *măng*
bean sprouts *giá*
beans *đậu*
cauliflower *bông cải*
green pepper *ớt Đà Lạt*

corn *bắp/ ngô*
steamed *hấp*
fried *chiên/rán*
roasted *quay*
grilled *nướng*
fruits *trái cây*
avocado *trái/quả bơ*
banana *trái/quả chuối*
grapefruit *trái/quả bưởi*
lemon *trái/quả chanh*
longan *trái/quả nhãn*
lychee *trái/quả vải*
mandarin *trái/quả quýt*
orange *trái/quả cam*
papaya *trái/quả đu đủ*
peach *trái/quả đào*
pineapple *trái/quả thơm/dứa*
plum *trái/quả mận/roi*
rambutan *trái/quả chôm chôm*
watermelon *trái/quả dứa hấu*
Do you have traditional food?
    Có món ăn truyền thống không?
Do you have any special dishes?
    Món nào là đặc sản của quán?
It's delicious *Rất ngon*
tomato *cà chua*
carrot *cà rốt*
cucumber *dứa leo*
lettuce *rau sà lách*
onion *hành tây*
potato *khoai tây*
mushroom *nấm*
soup *canh/xúp*
boiled *luộc*
meat *thịt*
sliced grilled beef *bò tung xèo*
beef dipped in vinegar *bò nhúng dấm*
grilled beef wrapped in leaf/pork fat
    bò nướng lá lốt/mỡ chài
diced beef with french fries *bò lúc lắc*
stewed beef *bò kho*
roasted young pork *Heo sữa quay*
fresh spring rolls *gỏi cuốn*
grilled pork noodles *bún thịt nướng*
Trang Bang fresh spring rolls *Bánh
    tráng Trảng Bàng*
pickled pork *dưa đầu heo*
pork/shrimp spring rolls *chả giò thịt/
    tom*
chinese sausage *lạp xưởng*

chicken *gà*
chicken wings fried in fish sauce
    cánh gà chiên nước mắm
chicken salad *gỏi gà/gà xé phay*
coneless chicken feet salad *chân gà
    rút xương*
roasted chicken *gà quay*
grilled chicken *gà nướng*
chicken rice soup *cháo gà*
chicken curry *cà ri gà*

fish *cá*
grilled trout wrapped in banana leaf
    cá lóc nướng lá chuối
grilled trout wrapped in clay *cá lóc
    nướng dất sét*
trout grilled in straw *cá lóc nướng trui*
deep-fried fish *cá tai tượng chiên xù*
fish sour soup *canh chua cá*
steamed fish *cá hấp*
fish hot pot *lẩu cá*
fried catfish with ginger sauce *cá trê
    chiên chấm mắm gừng*
deep-fried anchovy *cá cơm chiên dòn*
crab *cua*
tamarind crab *cua rang me*
salted crab *cua rang muối*
crab steamed with ginger *cua hấp
    gừng*
crab steamed in beer *cua hấp bia*

shellfish *sò*
raw oyster *hào sống*
grilled/steamed shellfish *sò
    nướng/hấp*
shellfish rice soup *cháo sò huyết*
mussel rice *cơm hến*
mussel rice soup *cháo hến*
mussel salad with star fruit *Gỏi hến
    xào khế*
grilled clam *nghêu nướng*

shrimps *tôm*
grilled lobster *tôm càng nướng*
grilled prawn *tôm nướng*
tiger prawns steamed in coconut
    tôm sú hấp nước dừa
shrimps steamed in beer *tôm hấp bia*
lotus stem and shrimp salad
    gỏi tôm ngó sen

seafood hotpot Lẩu hải sản

squid mực
dried squid mixed with grapefruit
  Khô mực trộn bưởi
stirred fried squid Mực xào
deep fried squid mực tươi lăn bột
  chiên

snails ốc
snails steamed with ginger ốc hấp
  gừng
pork stuffed snails ốc nhồi
snails with coconut milk ốc len xào
  dừa

vegetable rau
duck vịt
roasted duck vịt quay
dry duck vịt lạp
duck rice soup cháo vịt
duck with bamboo shoot noodles
  bún măng vịt

frog ếch
frog fried in butter ếch chiên bơ
deep fried frog ếch lăn bột
soup xúp
crab soup xúp cua
fish soup xú bong bóng cá
rice soup with salted duck eggs
  cháo trắng hột vịt muối
crab and asparagus soup xúp măng cua

noodles mì
crispy fried noodles mì xào giòn
chinese duck noodles mì vịt tiềm
won ton soup hoành thánh
Quang Nam noodles Mì Quảng
soup with flat white noodles phở
pork noodles hủ tíu
vermicelli miến
fat round rice noodles bánh canh
fuê beef noodles bún bò Huế

morning glory fried with garlic rau
  muống xào tỏi
spinach fried with garlic cải bó xôi
  xào tỏi
pickled vegetable dưa chua
fried cauliflower bông cải xào
fried pumpkin flower bông bí xào
vegetable soup Canh rau
papaya salad gỏi đu đủ
banana flower salad gỏi bắp chuối

other dishes các món khác
Hué sizzling cake Bánh Khoái
sizzling cake bánh xèo
Cantonese fried rice Cơm chiên
  dương châu
rice in clay pot cơm niêu
grilled pork rolls Nem nướng
pickled pork wrapped in leaf
  nem chua

I'm thirsty Tôi khát nước
Cold water, please Cho tôi xin một
  cốc nước lạnh
no sugar không đường
no ice không đá
black coffee cà phê đen
iced coffee cà phê đá
iced coffee with milk cà phê sữa đá
tea trà/chè (north)
a bottle of beer một chai bia
a can of beer một lon bia
a bottle of mineral water một chai
  nước suối
Is the water safe to drink? Nước uống
  có sạch không?
lemon juice nước chanh
orange juice cam vắt
coconut nước dừa
pineapple shake sinh tố thơm
rice wine rượu đế

Glossary

Amulet protective medallion

Ao dai long flowing silken tunic worn over trousers by Vietnamese school girls and women

Apsara heavenly female figure

Ban village

Ben Xe bus station

Bia hoi freshly brewed beer, 3%, so not too strong, cheap and thirst quenching. Normally drunk squatting on small plastic stools

Bia ôm dimly lit bars with young female hostesses to entertain clients

Binh dân (popular) street restaurants

Bodhi the tree under which the Buddha achieved enlightenment (*Ficus religiosa*)

Bodhisattva a future Buddha. In Mahayana Buddhism, someone who has attained enlightenment, but who postpones nirvana to help others reach it.

Brahma the Creator, one of the gods of the Hindu trinity, usually represented with four faces, and often mounted on a hamsa

Cao Dai composite religion of south Vietnam (see page 474)

Champa rival empire of the Khmers, of Hindu culture, based in present-day Vietnam (see page 409)

Cho market

Chua pagoda, a place of Buddhist worship (see page 60)

Cyclo bicycle rickshaw

Dau Ong Ba ancestor worship

Den non-Buddhist temple

Deva a Hindu-derived male god

Dharma the Buddhist law

Dinh palace or temple for the worship of non Buddhist god, relic or historical figure

Dipterocarp family of trees (*Dipterocarpaceae*) characteristic of Southeast Asia's forests

Doi moi 'renovation', Vietnamese perestroika

Duong street

Funan the oldest Indianized state of Indochina and precursor to Chenla

Ganesh elephant-headed son of Siva

Geomancy the art of divination by lines and figures. Geomancers were responsible for the site and orientation of a palace, tomb or other auspicious building.

Gopura crowned or covered gate, entrance to a religious area

Hamsa sacred goose, Brahma's mount; in Buddhism it represents the flight of the doctrine

Hang cave

Hinayana 'Lesser Vehicle', major Buddhist sect in Southeast Asia, usually termed Theravada Buddhism (see page 470)

Ho lake

Hoi Quan Chinese assembly house or clan house

Honda ôm motorcycle taxi (*ôm*) means 'to cuddle')

Hot toc hair cut

Ikat tie-dyeing method of patterning cloth

Jataka(s) the birth stories of the Buddha; they normally number 547, although an additional three were added in Burma for reasons of symmetry in mural painting and sculpture; the last ten are the most important

Khach san hotel

Lambro or xe lam small, three-wheeled motorized van

Laterite bright red tropical soil/stone commonly used in construction of Cham monuments

Li xi Lucky money given to children in red envelopes at Tet

Linga phallic symbol and one of the forms of Siva. Embedded in a pedastal (*yoni*) shaped to allow drainage of lustral water poured over it, the linga typically has a succession of cross sections: from square at the base through octagonal to round. These symbolize, in order, the trinity of Brahma, Vishnu and Siva

Lintel a load-bearing stone spanning a doorway; often heavily carved

Mahayana 'Greater Vehicle', major Buddhist sect (see page 470)

Mandarin Royal civil servant, emissary of the king

Meru sacred or cosmic mountain at the centre of the world in Hindu-Buddhist cosmology; home of the gods

Montagnard 'hill people', from the French (see page 448)

Moon cakes Cakes eaten at the Mid-Autumn Festival (Moon Festival) made of green bean paste with egg yolk, some with pumpkin seeds or melon seeds in pastry

Naga benevolent mythical water serpent, enemy of Garuda

Nam men (toilet sign)

Nha ga train station

Nha hang restaurant

Nha khach guesthouse

Nirvana release from the cycle of suffering in Buddhist belief; 'enlightenment'

Non lá conical straw hat; non lá bai tho version of the conical hat made in Hué which has a poem woven in

Nû women (toilet sign)

Nuoc mam fish sauce (used for dipping with meals)

Ong Tao God of the kitchen. He ascends to heaven a week before the end of the old year to report to Ong Troi on the behaviour of the family

Ong Troi or **Thuong De** God of Heaven in traditional Vietnamese mythology

paddy/padi unhulled rice or an irrigated field in which rice is grown

Pagoda a Mahayana Buddhist temple

Pali the sacred language of Theravada Buddhism

Parvati consort of Siva

Quan Am Chinese goddess of mercy (see page 61)

Rama incarnation of Vishnu, hero of the Indian epic, the *Ramayana*.

Rattan forest creeper that is woven into baskets or furniture. Sometimes mistaken for bamboo

Rong the Bahnar rong house is instantly recognizable by its tall thatched roof. The height of the roof is meant to indicate the significance of the building and make it visible to all. It is a focal point of the village for meetings of the village elders, weddings and other communal events

Sakyamuni the historic Buddha

Sampan a small wooden boat, traditionally made of three planks of wood

Singha mythical guardian lion

Siva the Destroyer, one of the three gods of the Hindu trinity; the sacred linga was worshipped as a symbol of Siva

Stela/e inscribed stone panel/s

Stucco plaster, often heavily moulded

Stupa dome-like Buddhist monument. Originally a topknot of hair, the building symbolises variously the upper part of the head, a tree's stem and a tower reaching up to heaven

Taoism Chinese religion (see page 471)

Tavatimsa heaven of the 33 gods at the summit of Mount Meru

Tay ba lo (insult) Western backpacker living on a tight budget. Unwashed and badly dressed.

Tet Vietnamese (Chinese) New Year.

Tet Trung Thu Mid-Autumn Festival, lantern festival or mooncake festival

Theravada 'Way of the Elders'; major Buddhist sect also known as Hinayana Buddhism ('Lesser Vehicle') (see page 470)

Uy ban nhan dan People's Committee (ie local government)

Vahana 'vehicle', a mythical beast, upon which a deva or god rides

Viet Cong Vietnamese communist troops who fought the Americans

Viet Minh Vietnamese communist troops who fought the French

Vishnu the Protector, one of the gods of the Hindu trinity, generally with four arms holding a disc, conch shell, ball and club

Xe ôm motorbike taxi

Index → *Entries in bold refer to maps.*

A

accidents 34
accommodation 26
activities 16
air travel
  discount flight agents 21
  getting there 20
ambulance 34
An Binh Island 360
Annam 475
Annam Highlands 476
Apocalypse Now 338
Ap Bac 358
architecture 457
  Hué 460
Army of the Republic
  of Vietnam (ARVN) 418
art 457
  books 483
avian flu 36

B

B-52 memorials 66
Ba Be Lake 133
Ba Be National Park 136
  listings 144
Bac Can 136
  listings 144
Bac Ha 123
  listings 125
Bach Ma National Park
  and Hill Station 198
  listings 201
Ba Chuc ossuary 383
Bac Lieu 373
  listings 376
Bac My An Beach 211
  listings 213
Bac Son 144
Bahnar 449
Bai Chay 154
  listings 158

Bai Tu Long 158
  listings 160
Ba-na villages 251
Ban Co 105
Ban Don 246
  listings 255
banks 37
Bao Lac 133
bars and clubs 31
beer 30
Ben Hai River 195
Ben Tre 358
  listings 364
Betel nut 319
Bich Dong 166
bicycle hire 25
Binh Chau 295
birds 480
birdwatching 16
Black Lady
  Mountain 328
boat tours
  Halong Bay 161
boat travel 23
Bo Cung Pass 141
books 466, 482
border crossings 22
  Cambodia
  Chau Doc 380
  Khanh Binh 383
  Le Thanh 249
  Moc Bai 328
  Tinh Bien 383
  Vinh Xuong 383
  Xa Mát 328
  Xá Xía 383
  China
  Bai Tu Long 158
  Dong Dang 143
  Lao Cai 122
  Laos 175
  Dong Ha 176
  Lao Bao 176
  Nam Can 175
  Savannakhet 176

Bo-Y 252
Buon Jun 246
Buon Ma Thuot 242, 243
  homestays 261
  listings 254
Buon Tur 246
bus travel 23

C

Ca Mau 374
  listings 376
Cambodia
  see border crossing
Cam Ranh Bay 273
Ca Na 276
Can Tho 370, 371
  floating markets 372
  listings 375
Cao-Bac-Lang 136
Cao Bang 137
  listings 144
Cao Dai Great Temple 327
Cao Daism 327, 474
Cao Lanh 363
  listings 366
car hire 24
Castries, General de 109
Cat Ba Island 154, 155
  listings 159
Cat Ba National Park 157
  listings 160
Cat Cat 121
Cau Da 272
Cau Treo 175
Central Vietnam 171-302
Cham 455
Cham art 457
Cham Kingdom 265
Champa 409
Cham Ponagar
  temple complex 266
Cham villages 383
  listings 390

Chau Doc 380, **382**
  listings 389
children 34
  eating out 29
China Beach 210
  listings 213
Cho Ra 133
Christianity 473
Chu Pao Pass 250
climate 16, 477
climbing 17
Coc Bo Cave 140
Cochin China 412, 475
Co Loa Citadel 67
Con Co Island 195
Con Dao 298
  listings 302
Con Dao National Park 300
Confucianism 471
conical hat 464
consulates 35
Continental Hotel,
  Saigon 311
cookery classes 16
  Hoi an 230
crafts 463
Cua Dai Beach 221
  listings 226
Cua Lo 175
Cuc Dua 104
Cu Chi Tunnels 326
Cuc Phuong National
  Park 167
  listings 169
cuisine 28
customs 34
cycling 17
cyclos 25

D

Dalat 232, **234**, **236**
  golf 260
  listings 252
  sights 235
  waterfalls 240
  Xuan Huong Lake 235
Dambri Falls 242

Danang 207, **209**
  Cao Dai Temple 210
  eating 214
  listings 212
  Museum of Cham
    Sculpture 208
  sights 208
Dao 102
Demilitarized Zone (DMZ) 193
Democratic Republic
  of Vietnam (DRV) 413
dengue fever 35
diarrhoea 35
Diem 418
Dien Bien Phu 106, 107, 416
  listings 114
  sights 109
disabled travellers 34
diving 17
  Nha Trang 281
DMZ 193
Doc Lech 270
doi moi 444
dong 37
Dong Dang 143
Dong Duong 224
Dong Ha 176
Dong Hoi 175
Dong Van 133
  listings 134
Dong Van-Meo
  Vac Region 131
Dong Xuan Market 56
Dragon Island 358
Dragon's Jaw Hill, Sapa 119
drama 464
drink 28, 30
drugs 34
Duras, Marguerite 361
duty free 34
dynasties
  Le 405
  Ly 403
  Nguyen 407
  Tran 404

E

economy 443
  books 483
ecotourism 19
Ede 450
electricity 34
elephant rides 262
embassies 35
emergency telephone
  numbers 34
Endangered Primate
  Rescue Center 167
entertainment 31
ethnic Chinese 456
ethnic groups 101, 448
  homestays 261, 262

F

Fan Si Pan 120
fauna 477
festivals 32
  when to go 16
films 486
fire brigade 34
flora 477
food 28
French surrender, 1954 416
Frontier Campaign of
  1947-1950 141
Funan 408

G

gambling 31
Ganesh 459
gay travellers 35
geography 475
Giarai 451
golf 17
  Dalat 260
  Mui Ne 289
  Phan Thiet 289
Greene, Graham 311
greyhound racing 297
Gulf of Tonkin Incident 420

H

Ha Giang 130
  listings 134
Haiphong 146, **148**
  listings 150
Hai Van Pass 197
Halong Bay 152, **154**
Halong City 153
  listings 158
handicraft villages 69
Hanoi 43-95, **46, 52**
  36 Streets 53
  activities 87
  Ambassadors' Pagoda 59
  B-52 memorials 66
  Ba Dinh Square 60
  bars and clubs 81
  cafés 77, 79, 80
  citadel 64
  Cua Quan Chuong 56
  Dai Liet Si 60
  directory 94
  eating 73
  entertainment 82
  festivals 83
  Fine Arts Museum 64
  Hai Ba Trung Temple 67
  Hang Be Market 56
  Hanoi Hilton 58
  health clubs 87
  history 49
  Hoa Lo Prison 58
  Hoan Kiem Lake 51, **52**
  Ho Chi Minh Museum 61
  Ho Chi Minh's house 60
  Ho Chi Minh's
    Mausoleum 59
  Military History
    Museum 64
  Museum of the
    Vietnamese
    Revolution 57
  Museum of Vietnamese
    History 57
  Old City 53
  One Pillar Pagoda 60
  Opera House 56
  Outer Hanoi 65
  Paul Doumer Bridge 65
  Presidential Palace 60
  Quan Am 61
  Quan Thanh Pagoda 65
  Saint Joseph's
    Cathedral 56
  shopping 83
  sights 51
  Sofitel Metropole 57
  Stone Lady Pagoda 56
  street names 54
  Tay Ho Pagoda 65
  Temple of Literature 61, 62
  Tortoise Tower 51
  tourist information 48
  tour operators 87
  Tran Quoc Pagoda 65
  transport 90
  Van Mieu Pagoda 61, 62
  Vietnam Military
    History Museum 64
  Vietnam Museum
    of Ethnology 66
  West Lake 65
Hanuman 459
Ha Tien 386, **387**
  listings 390
health 35
Hien Hao 157
Hien Luong Bridge 175, 195
highland people 448
hill tribes 448
Hindu deities 458
Hinduism 474
history 402
  ancient 402
  books 484
  colonial 412
  pre-colonial 402
  resistance to the
    French 412
HIV 36
Hmong 451
Hmong Kings 132
Hoa 456
Hoa Binh 101
  listings 114

Hoa Hao 384, 475
Hoa Lu 165
  listings 169
Hoang Khai 86
Hoan Kiem Lake 51, **52**
Ho Chi Minh 50, 55, 68,
  140, 174, 320, 413, 434, 443
  Mausoleum 59
  Trail 195
**Ho Chi Minh City 303-350,
  306, 312, 314, 320**
  activities and tours 343
  Apocalypse Now 338
  Archbishop's Palace 315
  bars and clubs 338
  Ben Thanh Market
    (Cho Ben Thanh) 317
  Botanical Gardens
    and Zoo 316
  Chinatown 321
  Cholon 321
  eating 332
  entertainment 339
  Fine Arts Museum 318
  General Post Office 313
  Giac Lam Pagoda 324
  Giac Vien Pagoda 324
  Lam Son Square 311
  Museum of Vietnamese
    History 316
  Notre Dame Cathedral 313
  Opera House 311
  Outer Ho Chi Minh
    City 323
  Pham Ngu Lao 320, **320**
  Phung Son Pagoda 323
  Phung Son Tu Pagoda 319
  Phuoc Hai Tu 324
  Reunification Hall 313
  Rex Hotel 311
  shopping 340
  sleeping 328
  Tomb and Temple of
    Marshal Le Van Duyet 325
  tourist information 308
  tour operators 344
  Tran Hung Dao Temple 325
  transport 345

Vinh Nghiem Pagoda 325
War Remnants
  Museum 315
Xa Loi Pagoda 315
Ho Coc 295
Hoi An 216, **218**
  Assembly Halls 220
  listings 224
  Merchants' houses 220
homestays
  Buon Ma Thuot 261
  Kontum 262
homosexuality 35
Hon Chong 270, 389
  listings 390
honda ôm 25
Hon Gai 154
Hon Mot 269
Hon Mun 269
Hon Rom 286
Hon Tam 269
hospitals 36
hostels 27
hotels 26
Hre 455
Hué 177, **180**, **184**, **186**
  Amphitheatre 193
  architecture 460
  City centre 184
  climate 178
  Elephant Temple 193
  Imperial City 180, **181**
  Imperial tombs 185
  listings 199
  Perfume River 185
  sights 180
  Thien Mu Pagoda 187
  Tomb of Dong Khanh 192
  Tomb of Duc Duc **191**,
    192
  Tomb of Emperor
    Gia Long 187, **187**
  Tomb of Emperor
    Minh Mang **189**, 190
  Tomb of Khai Dinh 192
  Tomb of Thieu Tri 190
  Tomb of Tu Duc 190
  transport 205

Hung Kia 103
Hung Kings' Temples 67, 68
Huong Giang 177

I

immigration 40
Indochina Communist
  Party (ICP) 413
Indochina War
  (1945-1954) 413
Indochina War
  (1954-1975) 416
insurance 36
International Rice
  Research Institute 370
internet 36
invasion of Cambodia 432
Islam 474
Island of the Coconut
  Monk 358

J

Japanese Covered Bridge 217
Japanese 'occupation' 413
Johnson, Lyndon 420

K

kayaking 17
  Halong Bay 162
  Kontum 262
Ke Ga 295
Kenh Ga 168
Kennedy, John F 418
Khai 86
Khe Sanh 195, 425
Kim Lien village 174
Kinh 455
Kissinger, Henry 427
kitesurfing 18
Kontum 249, 250
  homestays 262
  listings 256
Krishna 459

L

lacquerware 463
Lac (White Thai village) 103
Lai Chau 113
  listings 115
Lak Lake 245
Lakshmi 459
Lang 198
  listings 201
Lang Ga (Chicken Village) 241
Lang Son 142
  listings 145
language 36, 466
Lao Bao 176
Lao Cai 122
  listings 125
Laos
  see border crossings
La To 52
Lat village 241
Lau Chai 120
laundries 28
law 38
Le Dynasty 405
Le Loi 405
lesbian travellers 35
Le Thai To 51
Le Thanh 249
Le Thanh Ton 406
literature 466
Loc An 295
Long Hai 294
  listings 296
Long Xuyen 384
  listings 390
Lung Phay Pass 141
Lung Phin 133
Ly Dynasty 403
Ly Thanh Tong 61

M

Mahayana Buddhism 470
Mai Chau 102
  listings 114
malaria 35
Ma Pi Leng Pass 133

Marble Mountains
  (Nui Non Nuoc) 211
Marco Polo 409
markets 29
media 37
medical services 36
Mekong Delta 351-400
  floating markets 372
  geography 476
  history 354
  hydrology 355
  transport 354
Meo Vac 133
  listings 135
Mieu Island 269
Minh Danh 294
minorities 448
Mnong 245, 453
money 37
Mong Cai 158
  listings 160
Monkey Island 157
Montagnards 448
motorbiking 17, 261
  hire 25
  taxi 25
Mount Fan Si Pan 120
Mui Nai 388
Mui Ne 285
  listings 286
Muong 102, 452
Muong Lay 111
  listings 114
music 31
My Khe Beach 210
My Son 222
My Tho 356, 357
  listings 364
My Tho's islands 357

N

Nagas 460
Nam Can 175
Nam Cat Tien National
Park 242
  listings 254
Nam Dinh 168

  listings 170
Nam Khan 175
Nam O 199
Nam Phao 175
Nandi 459
National Liberation Front
  of Vietnam 417
newspapers 37
Ngang Pass 175
Ngoan Muc Pass 276
Ngoc Son Temple 52
Ngo Dinh Diem 416
Nguyen Dynasty 407
Nguyen Trail 406
Nha Trang 265, 267
  directory 284
  diving 281
  fishing 282
  listings 277
  therapies 282
  waterparks 282
Nhi Thanh 143
Ninh Binh 164
  listings 169
Ninh Chu
  listings 279
Ninh Chu Beach 276
Ninh Van Bay 270
Nixon, President Richard 427
Non Lá 464
Non Nuoc Beach 212
  listings 214
North Vietnam 97-170
  Far North 129
  northeast 136
  northwest Vietnam 100
Nui Ba Den 328
Nui Sam 381
  listings 389
Nung 453

O

Oc-Eo 385
Oc Om Boc Festival 372
Ong Ho Island 385
opening hours 38
Open Tour Bus 23

P

Pac Bo 139
Pagoda 461
Paracel Islands 440
Paris Agreement (1972) 427
people 448
People's Liberation Armed
  Forces (PLAF) 417
Perfume Pagoda 69
Perfume River 177, 185
Phan Rang 274
  listings 279
Phan Thiet 285
  golf 289
  listings 286
Phat Diem 166
Phi Hay 113
pho 28
Pho Bang 132
Phoenix Programme 426
Phong Nha Cave 175
Phong Nha-Ke Bang
National Park 175
Phu Quoc Island 395, 396
  diving 400
  listings 397
  Sao Beach 397
  transport 400
Plain of Reeds 363
Play Ku 247, 248
  listings 256
Pleiku
  see Play Ku 247
Po Klong Garai 275
police 25, 34, 38
politics 434
  books 483
population 448
Po Ro Me 275
Porte d'Annam 175
postal services 38
public holidays
  when to go 16
Public holidays 33
Pu Ka village 110
Pu Luong Nature
Reserve 103

Q

Quan Am 61
Quan Ba 131
Quang Ngai 271
  listings 279
Quan Lan Island 158
Quan Vu 52
Quiet American, The 311
Quoc Dan Dang
  (VNQDD) 413
Quy Nhon 270
  listings 279

R

Rach Gia 385
  listings 390
rail travel 22, 23
Rama 459
Red River Delta 476
religion
  Christianity 473
  Confucianism 471
  Islam and Hinduism 474
  Mahayana Buddhism 470
  Taoism 471
religion 20, 470
restaurants 28
Rex Hotel 311
Rhodes, Alexandre de 412
rice wine 30
river travel 23
Rock Pile 195

S

Sa Dec 361
  listings 366
safety 38
Saigon
  see Ho Chi Minh City
Salangane islands 269
Sam Mountain 381
Sam Son 174
Sapa 117, 118, 121
  Dragon's Jaw Hill 119
  listings 124

people 119
sleeping 124
therapies 127
trekking 120
Sa Phin 132
Sarasvati 458
SARS 36
Sedang 455
Sen 174
shopping 33
Sin Chai 121
Sin Ho 113
  listings 115
Siva 459
sleeping 26
snake wines 31
snorkelling 17
Socialist Republic of
  Vietnam (SRV) 431
Soc Trang 372
  listings 376
Son La 104
  listings 114
Son My (My Lai) 271
Son My (My Lai)
  Massacre 273
souvenirs 33
spas 18
Special Air Service (SAS)
  424
sport 16
Spratly Islands 440
Stieng 455
strategic hamlets 418
student travellers 39
Sunbeam Bridge 52

T

Tam Coc 166
Tam Nong Bird
  Sanctuary 363
Tam Thanh Cave 143
Tan Son Nhat Airport 345
Taoism 471
Ta Van 120
taxi 26
Tay 453

Tay Ninh 327
Tay Phuong Pagoda 69
Tay Son Rebellion 272, 407
telephone 39
television 37
Temple of Literature 61
Tet 32
Tet Offensive 425
Thac Ba Lake 129
Thai 454
Tham Coong 105
Thang Long 49
Thanh Hoa 174
Thap Ba Hot Springs 270
Thap Doi
  Cham towers 271
Thay Pagoda 69
theatre 31, 464
Thuan An Beach 195
Thuan Chau 106
Thuy Duong 294
  listings 296
time 39
Tinh Bien 383
Tinh Túc 133
tipping 39
Tonkin 475
tourist information 39
tour operators 39
tours 19
Trai Mat 241
  train travel 22, 23
Tra Kieu 224
Tran Dynasty 404
Tran Hung Dao 52
transport
  air travel 20
  bicycle 25
  buses 23
  cyclo 25
  honda ôm 25
  motorbike 25
  motorcycle taxi 25
  getting there 22
  river boat services 23
  taxis 26
  train 23
  traveller's cheques 37

travelling with children 34
Tra Vinh 360
  listings 365
Treaty of Tientsin 412
trekking 18, 120
  Kontum 262
  Play Ku 262
Tri An Lake 242
Trung Nguyen 32
Trung sisters 66
Truong Son Mountain
  Range 476
Truong Yen 165
Tuan Giao 106
Tuan Tu 276
tuberculosis 35
Tu Duc, Emperor 190, 412
Tu Ton Rose Garden 362
Tuyen Quang Province 129

Vietnamese Communist
  Party (VCP) 434
Vietnam wars 413, **419**
  books 485
  tours 18
Vinh 174
  listings 176
Vinh Long 359
  listings 365
Vinh Moc 195
Vinh Te Canal 381
Vinh Tuy 129
Vinh Xuong 383
visas 40
Vishnu 459
voluntary work 42
Vung Tau 291, **293**
  greyhound racing 297
  listings 295

X

Xa Linh 103
Xa Mát 328
Xà Xía 383
xe ôm 25
Xeo Quit Base 364
Xin Man 129
Xom Mo 102
Xtieng 455
Xuan Thieu Beach 199

Y

Yen Minh 132
  listings 134
Yen Tu Mountains 155
Yersin, Alexandre 233, 269
yin and yang 472
Yok Don National Park 247
  listings 256

U

U Minh Forest 375

V

Van Long Nature
  Reserve 168
  listings 169
Viet Cong 417
Viet Kieu 456
Viet Minh 413

W

war veterans tours 249
water puppetry 31, 316
water puppet theatre 464
Westmoreland, General
  William 422, 426
White Silk Lake 65
windsurfing 18
wine 30
working in Vietnam 42

Advertisers' index

Credits

Footprint credits

Project editors: Felicity Laughton,
Nicola Gibbs, Jo Williams
Layout and production: Davina Rungasamy
Colour section: Pepi Bluck
Maps: Kevin Feeney
Proofreader: Ria Gane

Managing Director: Andy Riddle
Commercial Director: Patrick Dawson
Publisher: Alan Murphy
Publishing Managers: Felicity Laughton,
Nicola Gibbs
Digital Editors: Jo Williams, Jen Haddington
Marketing and PR: Liz Harper
Sales: Diane McEntee
Advertising: Renu Sibal
Finance and administration:
Elizabeth Taylor

Photography credits

Front cover: Mekong Delta: Bill Bachmann
Back cover: Hué, Imperial City: Ludovic
Maisant / hemis.fr
Page 1: Keren Su / Danita Delimont /
awl-images.com
Pages 2-3: Philippe Body / hemis.fr
Page 6: Franck Guiziou / hemis.fr; Claire
Boobbyer; René Mattes / hemis.fr; Ludovic
Maisant / hemis.fr; Bruno Morandi / hemis.fr
Page 7: Philippe Body / hemis.fr; Philippe
Body / hemis.fr; Peter Schickert / Alamy;
Claire Boobbyer
Page 8: Romain Cintract / hemis.fr

Footprint feedback

We try as hard as we can to make each
Footprint guide as up to date as possible
but, of course, things always change. If you
want to let us know about your experiences
– good, bad or ugly – then don't delay, go to
footprinttravelguides.com and send in your
comments.

Publishing information
Footprint Vietnam
6th edition
© Footprint Handbooks Ltd
Janurary 2011

ISBN: 978 1 907263 22 4
CIP DATA: A catalogue record for this book
is available from the British Library

® Footprint Handbooks and the Footprint
mark are a registered trademark of Footprint
Handbooks Ltd

Published by Footprint
6 Riverside Court
Lower Bristol Road
Bath BA2 3DZ, UK
T +44 (0)1225 469141
F +44 (0)1225 469461
footprinttravelguides.com

Printed in India by Nutech
Photolithographers, Delhi.
Pulp from sustainable forests.
Distributed in the USA by Globe Pequot
Press, Guilford, Connecticut

Every effort has been made to ensure that
the facts in this guidebook are accurate.
However, travellers should still obtain advice
from consulates, airlines, etc about travel
and visa requirements before travelling. The
authors and publishers cannot
accept responsibility for any loss, injury or
inconvenience however caused.

asian trails

Journey through lost kingdoms and discover the hidden history of Asia to let Asian Trails be your guide!

CAMBODIA

Asian Trails Ltd. (Phnom Penh Office)

No. 22, Street 294, Sangkat Boeng Keng Kong I

Khan Chamkarmorn, P.O. Box 621, Phnom Penh, Cambodia

Tel: (855 23) 216 555 Fax: (855 23) 216 591

E-mail: res@asiantrails.com.kh

CHINA

Asian Trails China

Rm. 1001, Scitech Tower, No. 22 Jianguomenwai Avenue

Beijing 100004, P.R. China

Tel: (86 10) 6515 9259,& 9279 & 9260 Fax: (86 10) 6515 9293

E-mail: kris.vangoethem@asiantrailschina.com

INDONESIA

P.T. Asian Trails Indonesia

Jl. By Pass Ngurah Rai No. 260 Sanur

Denpasar 80228, Bali, Indonesia

Tel: (62 361) 285 771 Fax: (62 361) 281 515

E-mail: info@asiantrailsbali.com

LAO P.D.R.

Asian Trails Laos (AT Lao Co., Ltd.)

P.O. Box 5422, Unit 10, Ban Khounta Thong

Sikhottabong District, Vientiane, Lao P.D.R.

Tel: (856 21) 263 936 Fax: (856 21) 262 956

E-mail: vte@asiantrails.laopdr.com

MALAYSIA

Asian Trails (M) Sdn. Bhd.

11-2-B Jalan Manau off Jalan Kg. Attap 50460

Kuala Lumpur, Malaysia

Tel: (60 3) 2274 9488 Fax: (60 3) 2274 9588

E-mail: res@asiantrails.com.my

MYANMAR

Asian Trails Tour Ltd.

73 Pyay Road, Dagon Township, Yangon, Myanmar

Tel: (95 1) 211 212, 223 262 Fax: (95 1) 211 670

E-mail: res@asiantrails.com.mm

THAILAND

Asian Trails Ltd.

9th Floor, SG Tower, 161/1 Soi Mahadlek Luang 3, Rajdamri Road

Lumpini, Pathumwan, Bangkok 10330

Tel: (66 2) 626 2000 Fax: (66 2) 651 8111

E-mail: res@asiantrails.org

VIETNAM

Asian Trails Co., Ltd.

5th Floor, 21 Nguyen Trung Ngan Street, District 1

Ho Chi Minh City, Vietnam

Tel: (84 8) 3 910 2871 Fax: (84 8) 3 910 2874

E-mail: vietnam@asiantrails.com.vn

CONTACT

Contact us for our brochure or log into

www.asiantrails.info   www.asiantrails.net   www.asiantrails.com   www.asiantrails.travel